European architecture in the twentieth century

Arnold Whittick

European architecture
in the
twentieth century

Abelard-Schuman

An **Intext** Publisher

New York

Copyright © 1974 by Arnold Whittick

Library of Congress Cataloging in Publication Data
Whittick, Arnold, 1898–
European architecture in the twentieth century

Bibliography:
1. Architecture—Europe—History. 2. Architecture,
Modern—20th century—Europe. I. Title.
NA958.W49 1974   720'.94   74-13637
ISBN 0 200 04017 0

New York, Abelard-Schuman Limited,
257 Park Avenue So.
10010

Published on the same day in Canada by Longman Canada Limited
Printed in Great Britain

Dedication

To my wife,

who was my patient and sympathetic
companion on many journeys to
look at modern European architecture,
and who often, in conversation, helped
to clarify appreciative and critical
appraisements

Acknowledgements

I am deeply grateful for the cooperation and assistance afforded me in the early stages of this history by the late Wilfred Salter, one time Assistant Secretary of the Incorporated Association of Architects and Surveyors and Editor of the Association's Journal: *The Parthenon*. I also thank the Leverhulme Trustees for a Research Award which enabled me to complete the work, and the Librarian and Staff of the Royal Institute of British Architects for facilities and help in research which they have kindly given.

I have in addition a sense of obligation to very many persons who have helped me in various ways. They are so numerous that it would make a long list to mention them all. I am, however, particularly conscious of early help and encouragement given by the late Eric Mendelsohn, Sir Charles Reilly and Johannes Schreiner; and for information, advice and assistance, or for facilities for seeing notable examples of modern architecture: to Dorothea David, an architect in the architectural department of the City of Zürich, to Lotte Jank (Biedenkopf), Gérard Kaufman (Paris), Hanna Schweizer, Walter Segal, Ursula Weiss (Berlin) and Giovanni Coppa Zuccari (Rome). I have also received much help, always courteously and generously given, from the architectural departments of many European cities and I hope the results of such help will be to some extent apparent in this history.

ILLUSTRATION ACKNOWLEDGEMENTS

I gratefully thank the following for photographs and plans, or for assistance in procuring illustrations:

Alvar Aalto, Helsinki; Aarhus University, Denmark; Architectural Press Ltd; Athens Airport (The Manager); Stewart Bale; The Reverend B. W. Barker, Rector of St. Nicholas, Burnage, Manchester; Bauhaus-Archiv, Berlin; G. Blinne, Pastor of the Church of St. Engelbert, Cologne; British Airport Authority; British Broadcasting Corporation; British Iron and Steel Federation; British Railways Board; Burgerspital, Basel; Cambridge University Library; Cement and Concrete Association, London; Commissariat General au Tourisme, Paris; Commission for the New Towns—Crawley, Hemel Hempstead and Welwyn Garden City; Corporation of the City of London; Giovanni Coppa Zuccari, Rome; Czechoslovak Embassy, London; Dalstrom, Stockholm; Danish State Radio, Copenhagen; W. M. Dudok, Hilversum; Fiat Societa per Azioni (Sig. Augusto Constantino), Turin; Fribourg University, Switzerland; Rudolf Frankel; French Embassy, London; Professor E. Maxwell Fry, C.B.E., R.A.; Sir Frederick Gibberd, R.A.; Goteborgs Stadskansli, Sweden; André Granet, Paris; Greater London Council; Royal Greek Embassy, London; Walter Gropius; Professor Hardt-Waltherr Hamer, Berlin; Housing Centre, London; Italian State Railways, Rome; Kjeld Jensen, Police Chief Inspector, Copenhagen; Kodak Ltd, London; Landesbildstelle, Berlin; Landeshauptstadt, Dusseldorf; Julian Leathart; Le Corbusier and Pierre Jeanneret; London Transport Board; Lossen Foto, Heidelberg; Manchester City Library; Malmo Stadstheater, Sweden; Sir Edward Maufe, R.A.; Mrs. Eric Mendelsohn; Municipal Construction Office, Munich; Netherlands Embassy, London; Royal Norwegian Embassy, London; Novositi Press Agency, London; Sven Pedersen, City Architect, Arhus, Denmark; Pitkins Pictorial Ltd; Erwin Rockwell, Planning Officer, London Transport Executive; Roche Products Ltd, Welwyn Garden City; Professor Alfred Roth, Zürich; Royal Festival Hall, London; Royal Horticultural Society, London; Royal Institute of British Architects; Royal Liverpool Philharmonic Society; Barbara Schnelle of Stuttgart University; Sir Giles Scott, Son and Partner; Walter Segal; Society for Cultural Relations with the USSR; South Hospital, Stockholm; Spanish Embassy, London; Sir Basil Spence, O.M.; Stadt Stuttgart Hochbauamt; Swedish Embassy, London; Swedish Tourist Agency; Town and Country Planning Association; C. Cowles-Voysey; Professor Basil Ward; Ursula Weiss, Berlin.

(A considerable number of the photographs were taken by the author.)

Contents

Contents

Preface

THE aims of this history can best be explained by amplifying the well-known definition of good building given by Vitruvius which has had much influence on European thought since the manuscript of his work was discovered in the mid-fifteenth century. After referring to the different types of building, Vitruvius says, 'Haec au tem ita fieri debent, ut habentur ratio firmitatis, utilitatis, venustatis, (1.III.2). These three terms have been variously translated as durability, convenience and beauty (Morgan), as strength, utility and grace (Granger) and firmness, commodity and delight (Wotton). It seems to me that stability, utility and delight accord best with modern English feeling. It is the delight which a building gives that makes it architecture. To appreciate architecture in its full significance it is essential not only to enjoy buildings and the urban environment aesthetically, but to understand the other requisites of good building defined by Vitruvius: of the needs and purposes for which buildings were erected and of constructional developments. R. G. Collingwood said in his *Outlines of a Philosophy of Art* that no event in the so-called history of art can be explained by reference to the principles of art itself. To explain the history of architecture we must study the technique of building construction and the social purposes which buildings are erected to serve'. Purpose and construction provide the subjects for artistic expression and it is necessary to understand these subjects in some degree so as to appreciate the expression.

In the early part of the century, covering the years before and immediately after the First World War, it was possible in studying contemporary architecture to consider together buildings designed for different purposes, the reason being that they were often designed in a similar manner and clothed in the same style, and their function was accordingly not reflected in their external appearance. At that time the starting point of the design was more often than not the elevation—a handsome symmetrical façade in the Renaissance or classical style, irrespective of whether the building was a town hall, bank, school or college, hospital, town or country mansion, library, museum, theatre, departmental store or factory. Or, if the elevation was not the actual starting point, plans were made with such handsome symmetrical elevations in mind. The changes that were taking place in design and construction were apparent only in a few pioneer works.

In the period between the two World Wars, substantial transformations were apparent that were determined by design being more guided by the purpose of the building with full advantage being taken of new methods of construction. The continuation of the general survey of characteristics of all types of building considered together, which had been fairly common in architectural histories, would have made difficult the detailed study of the significant architecture of the period which demands presentation according to types of buildings, because the character of design was determined more by the purpose that the building was to serve. In recording the architecture of the inter-war period it was necessary, therefore, to study carefully the origin and social and economic purposes of the buildings. Thus the architecture of the period from 1920 to 1940 is reviewed according to types of building, and most of these studies are prefaced by a brief history of the particular type from its origin.

In some cases, such as theatres, it is necessary to go as far back as ancient Greece, or in the case of churches, schools and hospitals to the middle ages, but in other types such as power stations, railway stations, airports, cinemas and buildings for broadcasting the origin is recent.

In the review of the new classical revival of the thirties, comprising Part IV, which to some historians marks a break in progress of at least a decade, the more general method appropriate to stylistic architecture is again employed. In the remaining period after the Second World War the study of buildings according to their distinctive purposes and types is resumed, but more broadly as functionalism is a little less insistent. The period that in retrospect seems to emerge as the great one of the century in distinctive functionalist architecture is from about 1920 to 1935. After that the emphasis and excellence is more in city and town planning.

Social and economic purposes and method of construction may determine the character of a building, but it is the artistic ability of the architect which gives it the third Vitruvian condition of delight. Some critics and historians would say that it is this third condition which makes a construction architecture as distinct from building. This is a modern meaning given to architecture which is fairly widely if not generally accepted, for some writers still adhere to the meaning of architecture in its original sense as the work of the architect (αρχιτεκτων) meaning master builder.

In the eighteenth and nineteenth century, however, when philosophers classified the arts for the purpose of philosophic assessment, architecture, with poetry, painting, music and sculpture was classified as one of the fine arts. Thus according to this a building to qualify as architecture must give aesthetic pleasure. That mainly is the sense in which the term architecture is employed in this book, yet at the same time, in the evaluation of a building, the extent to which it fulfils its purpose and the efficiency of its construction are considered almost equally important. A more explanatory title for this history would perhaps have been *The Purposes, Construction and Delights of European Buildings of the Twentieth Century*.

Social and economic needs and constructional efficiency provide subjects for the architect by which he can give environmental pleasure and satisfaction, which will be all the more vital if he treats each subject logically according to its merits. The architect must resist the influences of a tradition which says a church must look like a church, a town hall like a town hall and a factory like a factory. How do we acquire our notions of the appearance of these buildings to which new designs are expected to conform? We acquire them from the traditional forms of these buildings and thus to fixity of concepts which is inhibiting to original design. If a church looks like our concept of a factory yet it is beautiful in the abstract, so much the better for the church. It is after all the satisfactory pattern of coloured shapes that make the pleasing urban environment whatever the types of building. This theme is developed in the last chapter.

Thus in the aesthetic effects of the urban environment, buildings of many different types must necessarily be considered together, but analyses of reasons why they have their particular forms is necessary for full appreciation. The design, form and pattern of a Gothic cathedral, like Chartres, are magnificent, but an understanding of its religious purpose enhances appreciation.

Because of exigencies of space this picture of European architecture in the twentieth century must necessarily be a broad, impressionistic one. I have, however, aimed to comprehend all the manifold movements and developments that are significant, and to consider in building 'why' as well as 'how'. I have tried to avoid being ideologically exclusive. That would give only a partial picture which in the longer perspective of history is apt to be misleading; while ideologies too often get mixed with irrelevances which distort a balanced picture. I have, therefore, endeavoured to gather the fruits of tradition as well as comprehending significant innovations.   ARNOLD WHITTICK

Postscript—most of the buildings described in this history are still standing, but I am aware that this is not the case with all, and where I have known of the demolition of a building I have mentioned it. There may, however, be other cases of demolition of which I am unaware, for it has not been possible with so many examples studied over a period of nearly thirty years to check each one.
Significance for architectural evolution is in the design of a building, and it has its place in the narrative whether it still exists or not. That the outstandingly good buildings of their kind should continue to exist and be maintained in good condition is one of the purposes of European Architectural Heritage Year 1975—A. W.

PART I

Historical Background and

Early Years of the Century

to 1918

Liverpool Cathedral, 1903–73, view looking east through the arch of the nave
Architect: Sir Giles Gilbert Scott

1 Revivalism

AT THE BEGINNING of the twentieth century the revival of the great architectural styles of the past had almost spent itself and was dying. Yet the age of revivals forms one of the principal backgrounds of many modern architectural developments and it is important to understand the essential principles of the kinds of architecture that it was attempted to revive. A revival without development is unlikely to produce a great architecture because the vitality which can only arise from contemporary social and spiritual needs, would not actuate the revival of a style which belonged to a remote and necessarily different mode of life. To revive an art successfully it is necessary to revive the kind of life that produced that art. Some have realized this and have established small communities imitating the life which had been the setting of the art they wished to revive. Such communities, by their remoteness from contemporary life and by their cancellation of much material and social progress, really demonstrate the impossibility of successful revival. The gradual and somewhat conservative development from old forms and styles that we see in much Renaissance work is different.

Before the eighteenth century European architects had reached Greek architecture mainly through Roman architecture and the interpretations of Vitruvius. But towards the end of the eighteenth century artists and scholars began to travel in Greece, Asia Minor, and what were once Greek colonies, while Greek sculptures and architectural fragments and drawings of Greek temples began to be transported to the museums of Europe, the transportation by Lord Elgin of Parthenon fragments to England in the early nineteenth century being a noteworthy example. The classicism of seventeenth- and eighteenth-century literature and the desire for classical perfection in art which had been a passion with Winckelman, and which had passed in a modified form to the influential figure of Goethe, prepared the ground for the enthusiastic reception of the more complete material revelation of Greek art; and these, with the Renaissance preparation, resulted in the Greek revival of the late eighteenth and early nineteenth centuries. It was the strongest and most widespread of European revivals and manifested in every important capital in Europe. The adaptation of Greek architecture

3

to various types of building was done with varying success. There is little distinction between buildings of different capital cities, and it would be possible to join the parts of London, Berlin, and Leningrad in which groups of buildings of the classical revival are situated without any feeling that they are a mixture of buildings from different parts of Europe. In Leningrad some of the classical buildings were designed by foreign architects, principally French and the Scottish architect, Charles Cameron, who had been invited for that purpose.

Throughout this classical revival there is a general tendency to go farther and farther back so as to imitate the original classical architecture of the sixth and fifth centuries B.C. In the initial stages a mixture of Hellenistic influence is apparent, but with greater familiarity with the original Greek we find a closer adherence to the beautiful proportions of the Greek temples. The exterior of the Madeleine in Paris, designed by Pierre-Alexandre Vignon in the early years of the nineteenth century, is a fairly close imitation of the Greek temple, the *cella* being adapted to the needs of a modern church. In Harvey L. Elmes's St. George's Hall, Liverpool, completed in 1839, the inspiration of the Greek temple is obvious, but its purpose of Hall and Law Courts involves more originality in adaptation, and this is done with such sublety and refinement as to make it one of the flowers of the Greek revival. This building has had great influence on much subsequent architecture in Liverpool, many municipal and other buildings in the vicinity being designed to conform with it. In the British Museum, built by Sir Robert Smirke between 1823 and 1847, the Parthenon is largely taken as a model, although the Ionic order is employed instead of the Doric. In the classical revival of Germany and Russia there is a stronger movement towards Greek sixth- and fifth-century work. In Klentze's work in Munich and more particularly in Schinkel's work in Berlin, the classic Doric and Ionic architecture of Athens is followed in such works as the Museum of Antiquities, the New Theatre, and other buildings, all of the first half of the nineteenth century. This striving towards classical purity was very strong in Leningrad, the Doric temple of Poseidon at Paestum, of about 450 B.C. serving as the principal model, the Bourse building being a partial reproduction. So anxious were the architects to reproduce what they imagined to be the original Greek effects that they coloured many of their buildings[1].

Slightly later, partially as a revolt against this supposed cold and scholarly art (although I think it was produced by many artists with deep emotion and enthusiasm as in the case of Ingres), there arose the romantic movement, itself partially a revival of the romanticism of the Middle Ages. Significant figures for architecture are romantic novelists like Mrs Radcliffe, Scott, and Horace Walpole who writes *The Castle of Otranto* with its medieval setting and artificial mysteries, and who builds the quaint Gothic contraptions at his villa on Strawberry Hill between 1753 and 1778, which was for some time a lone herald of the Gothic revival many years before Wyatt's Fonthill Abbey, the second bizarre yet important example of the Gothic revival in England, built in 1796–9. The Romantic movement spread throughout Europe flourishing chiefly in Germany, England, France, and manifesting in literature, music, and painting, hardly touching sculpture, and apparent in architecture as the Gothic revival and partially as a more pregnant romanticism. The Gothic revival developed chiefly in England, in Germany and the Scandinavian countries, in the Low Countries, and to a less extent in France, but it was not, with the exception of England, so widespread as the Greek revival. It may be said of the Greek and Gothic revivals that they sought to imitate as closely as possible their originals. The closer their buildings were to such originals the better their authors were pleased. The Brandenburg Gate is closer to a Greek gateway than is a Roman gateway, and St. George's Hall, although being much nearer in purpose to a Roman basilica than to a Greek temple, is much more like a Greek temple than was a Roman basilica. Roman architecture developed from Greek, but in these works of the modern classical revival close imitation of Greek buildings is attempted.

Originality and design were necessary in adapting these styles to buildings of which there were inadequate prototypes. In the Houses of Parliament (1840–60) for which Sir Charles Barry made the plan on classic lines and Augustus Pugin the Gothic dress, the Parliament Buildings at Budapest (1855–70) by Steindl, and the Law Courts (1874–82) by G. E. Street, the Gothic style was used with less sense of incongruity than for railway stations and insurance offices. With churches there could be the strictest imitation, as in so much of the copybook architecture of Sir Gilbert Scott. The adaptations of Greek temples to Parliament buildings, town halls, museums, and other institutions are legion, and they are generally of greater merit than Gothic revivalist work because they are often of excellent scale and proportions where columns, walls, and openings are well related. The dignity and repose of classical architecture is more often a successful reminiscence than the aspiration of Gothic, even in churches. Greek architecture seemed to be easier to adapt than Gothic.

CONTRAST OF THE GREEK TEMPLE AND GOTHIC CATHEDRAL

It has often been said that a Greek temple and a Gothic cathedral are the greatest creations of architectural genius, and that Greek and Gothic represent absolutely antithetical styles. As this is pertinent to certain later architectural eclecticisms it is important to be fully conscious of what the essential qualities of each are.

The Greek temple has, more than any other building, determined the classical tradition in architecture. It was built to house the image of the god, and the people worshipped in the open with the temple in view. Generally only priests entered. Thus the exterior of the temple, being before the eyes of the people as they worshipped, and being the home of the god, was made as grand and impressive as possible. And when sculptors like Phidias created the gods in gold and ivory they were idealized beyond any particular individual, and were given a majesty and calm that was conceived as

5

godlike. The temple was built in harmony, and the pervading qualities were majesty, grandeur, and repose. The Greeks were great geometricians, and, like some modern mathematicians, they believed that the universe obeys mathematical law, and that its mysteries might be solved by mathematics. In building and architecture geometry was a profound influence. Greek temples were built according to the strictest symmetry, and although many of the architectural forms could be traced to organic origins, they clearly endeavoured to order them on a geometric basis. Thus has been established the classical tradition of architecture, where grandeur of appearance, symmetry, and geometric planning are conspicuous features. As a result of the influence of the architecture of the temple on buildings of more utilitarian purpose, convenience and efficiency are often subordinated to these principles.

A Greek temple, like the Parthenon, or the temple of Poseidon at Paestum, both of the mid-fifth century B.C., was a simple walled building called the *cella* in which was the image of the god, and this was surrounded by a peristyle, with single rows of columns at the sides and double rows at the front and back. The temple was covered with a sloping roof which permitted a pediment at either end generally filled with sculptures. A small temple consisted of the *cella* with columns and pediment at one end with walls of the *cella* built between the side columns or pilasters appearing in the walls. There are numerous stages between these two. It is important to note that in the *cella* the walls are structural and supporting, and that apart from sur-rounding columns, all Greek, Roman, and Renaissance buildings follow this method of the solid structural wall, and that much of the effect of Roman and Renaissance building depends on the impression of weight and mass given by the solid supporting wall.

A Gothic cathedral is the most formal of medieval buildings, and this is due partly to Roman influence in planning, but more, I think, to the symbol of the cross which forms the plan of most Gothic churches. But if we consider the plan of monastic buildings, or of a medieval castle or manor house, we find an irregularity very different from classical symmetry. This irregularity is clearly the result of planning according to convenience. Monastic buildings are generally planned in conformity with a certain layout with the cloisters to the north or south of the nave and the refectory on the further side with the chapter house and dormitory to the east, and the other buildings grouped round. The whole arrangement, though similar in numerous examples, is irregular and is entirely different from formal symmetrical planning of Greek and Roman buildings. It may be argued that the layout of the buildings on the Athenian Acropolis is not formal and symmetrical, but irregular. It was the purpose, however, in placing these buildings to present to those entering the Propylea the most im-pressive view of the temples, and this is done by placing them slightly diagonally to the percipient from the Propylea. Appearance is thus an essential purpose.

6

The transition from Romanesque to Gothic meant a change from walled to framed structure. The structural reasons for the change were to obtain a wider span, and to facilitate the vaulting and roof intersections over rectangular spaces, which is explained in numerous text books[2]. The vaulting was made possible by the use of buttresses to take the outward thrust. The whole became a framed structure, and made possible the large windows familiar in Gothic cathedrals. It will be seen later that there are certain similarities in this framed structure and the modern steel frame.

During the latter part of the nineteenth century there was a growing restlessness among many architects resulting from a dissatisfaction with a mere imitation of past styles. Many architects looked back again to find other styles to revive, some turned again to the Renaissance traditions of the eighteenth century, some tried to devise a totally new style expressive of the age, one manifestation of this being *Art Nouveau*.

Among other styles that architects of the late nineteenth century sought to revive were Byzantine and Romanesque. This was particularly so in Germany and France, where numerous churches were built during this period in these Early Christian styles or a blending of the two. Examples of modern French Byzantine churches are S. Pierre de Montrouge, by Joseph A. E. Vandremer, and the church of Fouviere at Lyons, finished in 1884. The cathedral of Marseilles built by Leon Vandoyer and Henri Espirandieu is a mingling of Romanesque and Byzantine, and many smaller churches, like that of S. Luc at Nîmes, are built in a similar way. Perhaps the finest modern Romanesque Byzantine building in France is the great church of Sacré Cœur in Paris, built in the last years of the century to the designs of Paul Abadie. The old Trocadero, built for the exhibition of 1878 and destroyed to make room for a new one for the exhibition of 1937, was a modern adaptation of Romanesque. Revival of Romanesque is strongly apparent in England, either as a modern adaptation of the style or as a prominent ingredient of eclectic work. A familiar example of the former is Alfred Waterhouse's Natural History Museum at South Kensington, built in 1879. It would seem that in the later stages of the Gothic revival, in the effort to produce something fresh, architects went farther back in time to periods prior to Gothic, a tendency which, we have seen, occurred with the Greek revivalists. Later still there is a movement to revive Egyptian styles.

Paris had been the art centre of Europe in the eighteenth century and it continued so during the nineteenth century, and artists from every country were constantly looking to this centre for guidance. French influence may have prompted the adoption of the Byzantine style for Westminster Cathedral especially as it has certain French Romanesque elements. The decision was taken by Cardinal Vaughan because, it was argued, if built in the Byzantine style the shell could be erected fairly quickly and thus the church could be ready for use in a short period while the interior decoration could be continued in the course of many years, as funds were available. Also, it was argued, the Byzantine style would make possible a wide open nave and choir and would thus be suitable for preaching to a large congregation. There was also a reluctance to build in the Gothic style because of competing with Westminster Abbey, but the stronger objection to Gothic was probably because each part is finished as it is built, the decorations being more an integral part of structure than in Byzantine work, and thus it would be far longer before the church could be used. John F. Bentley, the architect, studied for the work in France, Italy, and Greece, giving especial attention to Italian Byzantine churches and Santa Sophia. The plan has similarities to that of the French Romanesque cathedral at Angoulême, but St. Marks and Santa Sophia are the principal inspirations from which many features are directly borrowed. Many of the marbles used extensively in Santa Sophia are being used in Westminster Cathedral. One somewhat romantic episode is connected with the columns of the nave. When William Brindley discovered the quarry which had supplied the *verde antico* marble columns for Santa Sophia, he found several worked columns lying in the quarry like those at Santa Sophia, and these were used for some of the columns at Westminster.

It was originally the intention to cover the entire interior walls and saucer domes with marble and mosaics, but this has been abandoned because of cost, and the marble facing has been carried to the balustrade above the arcading and a little higher on the piers. The light effect of the pale marbles of the lower part is agreeable, but the dark greyish brown bricks above give a sense of gloom which also suggests mystery. The form of the interior would be better appreciated if it were more generally discernable.

THE REVIVAL OF CLASSICAL AND EARLY RENAISSANCE ARCHITECTURE

The striving for originality among European architects at the end of the nineteenth century and in the early years of the twentieth took many forms. The majority of architects still sought for inspiration in the great architectural styles of the past rather than in the scientific and social developments of contemporary life. The principal movements based on revivalism were a freer treatment of Classical and Gothic architecture, the latter chiefly in ecclesiastical work, a movement that was to have many interesting results later; a return to Renaissance architecture before the period of the Greek revival[3]; and a revival of, or rather an incorporation of features of other, more remote, architectural styles like Egyptian, Assyrian, and Saracenic. Often there was a mixture of many styles which resulted in eclecticism, which was generally most successful when one style dominated.

In the desire for freer treatment of classical architecture, and in the revival of various phases of Renaissance work, there appeared a stronger expression of national characteristics, and it is not difficult to distinguish the work of different countries by distinct qualities. Later German Renaissance work, for example, has a massiveness and heaviness in contrast with more ornate and lighter late French Renaissance work; and the return to early periods of Renaissance was generally influenced by those native traditions with which early Renaissance work was mingled.

The freedom of later classical revivalist work is seen in such buildings as the Palais de Justice at Brussels, by Polaert, completed in 1883, the Exchange in the same city, and the Paris Opera House (1874) by Charles Garnier. These buildings represent various degrees of freedom in the treatment of classical architecture, the first mentioned being perhaps the most Greek in character, while the last has a florid character in much of its ornament reminiscent of Baroque, although it is essentially classical in spirit.

The Grand Palais by Thomas Louret and the Petit Palais by Charles Girault in Paris were built for the exhibition of 1900. The latter is the finer building and it has had considerable influence on twentieth-century Renaissance architecture. The Ionic colonnade appearing on the façade of the building, the entrance with the semicircular entablature abutting the central dome, and the sculptured embellishment are all very happily proportioned and related. Although there are numerous ornamental features they all keep their place and are all subordinated to the main lines of the design. One feels that this building is typically French, and many English buildings of the twentieth century with a distinctively French character owe something to it. This influence is particularly apparent in the work of two firms of architects: Lanchester, Stewart and Rickards, and Mewès and Davis. The former was responsible for Cardiff Town Hall and Law Courts, completed in 1906. The treatment with the horizontally recessed masonry joints, the application of ornament and sculpture, and the light effect accomplished by the use of sunk panels and concavities is strongly reminiscent of work like the Petit Palais. Lanchester and Rickards designed the Central Wesleyan Hall, Westminster (1906–12), in which there is the same treatment of masonry and application of ornament, and the use of a square dome similar in shape to the two square domes of the Petit Palais. The spaciousness of every part of the interior is noteworthy.

Charles Mewès, who died in 1914, was an architect of international scope. He not only did a considerable amount of work in his native France, but also in Germany and England. In his German work he was assisted by A. Bischoff, and in his English work by Arthur J. Davis, who had been trained at the Ecole des Beaux Arts. We have to thank Mewès and Davis for the introduction of French lightness and elegance into London architecture. The most important works are the Ritz Hotel and the *Morning Post* building in the Strand, both erected in 1906, and the Royal Automobile Club building in Pall Mall, completed in 1911. These three buildings are more restrained than most contemporary French work, and ornament is used sparingly and with taste. The Ritz Hotel was the first steel frame building in London, but it retains the massive-wall character of a Renaissance building, for which London County Council requirements may be partly responsible. It is simple in treatment, with a very happily proportioned arcade over the footway. The *Morning Post* building is even more successful. The adaptation to an awkwardly shaped site has been made with consummate skill, and resulted in a building where lightness and refinement are prominent qualities. It is in marked contrast to the heavy and clumsy Gaiety Theatre building on the opposite corner, designed by Norman Shaw. Unfortunately when the *Tatler* and *Sketch* took the building they did much to spoil it when they added two storeys, thus disturbing the fine scale and proportion of the design. The Royal Automobile Club building is again distinguished for French elegance, having a grace of line and detail which helps to make it one of the most attractive club buildings in London, while it has notes of revivalism, symptomatic of the time, in the Egyptian Swimming Pool and Greek Turkish Bath.

There was much official building in London and other British cities during the early years of the twentieth century. Many buildings were erected in Whitehall and appear for the most part as free treatments of classic architecture, with the traditions established by Inigo Jones and Chambers exercising a strong influence. Such work as the War Office (1906), designed by William Young, and the Government Offices in Whitehall (1908), designed by John Brydon, are examples. They are somewhat fat and heavy, and neither has the distinction and excellent proportions of Sir Gilbert Scott's much-abused Foreign Office. Similarly heavy, where masonry is inartistically obtrusive, is the London County Hall, designed by Ralph Knott, begun in 1912 and completed a few years after the First World War. Its pitched tiled roof with tall chimneys characteristic of medieval buildings seem out of harmony with the heavy Renaissance façades. The horizontal implications of the river front are ignored, especially in the recessed semicircular central façade with its colonnade. In the building as originally planned this central feature was placed on the other side, where it would have been better, but Norman Shaw, being one of the assessors, liked it on the river front, and his wishes appear to have prevailed. There is little to justify it. The purpose of the building does not demand it, and, as C. and A. Williams-Ellis (*The Pleasures of Architecture*, London, 1924, p. 221) have aptly remarked, it 'eats into the accommodation as a boy's bite into a sponge cake'. The opportunity of a fine river front was not taken as it might have been.

Renaissance architecture in Germany in the late nineteenth century seems to vary between classical Renaissance and Baroque. The Reichstag building in Berlin by Paul Wallot, erected about 1890, has a classical colonnaded façade with central pedimented portico and rectangular glass dome, all suggestive of French influence. Berlin Cathedral, by Julius Raschdorff, built in 1893, is reminiscent of Italian Baroque. It has a central dome with four corner turrets and a very ornate and 'cut up' effect, the two-storeyed façades being made up of numerous small features which destroy what grandeur a simpler treatment of a building of this size might have achieved. Later German Renaissance work became simpler, due partially to the influence of Ludwig Hoffman, who designed the massive Imperial Law Courts at Leipzig, completed in 1895, and the Town Hall at Berlin, completed in 1912. The latter has something of the massiveness and heaviness that seems to make some later German Renaissance architecture expressive of German character.

The square character and restraint of the Royal Palace at Stockholm, designed by Nicodemus Tessin during the late seventeenth century, seems to have influenced later Swedish Renaissance architecture and encouraged Greek influence. Swedish classical buildings during the twenty years prior to the First World War have this square character. They are designed with more simplicity than contemporary French work. The Royal Opera House at Stockholm, completed in 1898, and the Houses of Parliament, designed by Aron Johansson and completed in 1905, are examples. There is considerable plain wall-surface in the former example, while the dominating features of the latter are the long colonnades decorating the principal façade in which is a square-topped central feature. Another important work of Aron Johansson is the new building of the National Bank of Sweden, Stockholm, completed in 1906. Here the influence of early Florentine palaces is apparent in the rusticated masonry of the ground floor, but again the paramount influence is the Royal Palace, which determines the large rectangular blocks, while the classic revival is responsible for the introduction of Corinthian pilasters and the application of Roman ornament.

Among the legacies of the Paris Exhibition of 1900 must be reckoned that wild riot of ornament and decoration which manifested in the Milan Exhibition of 1906. The buildings of the Paris Exhibition were certainly ornate in character, but the architects of the Milan Exhibition, in their profuse use of ornament, seemed determined to leave the French Exhibition well in the shade. In these Renaissance buildings almost every available space is decorated with enrichments, cornices, pilasters, and human, animal, and vegetable sculpture, often of a symbolic character. I am unaware whether it was intended that any of the buildings should be permanent, but a fire which destroyed many of them decided otherwise.

But such a manifestation was rather the exception than the rule in Mediterranean countries, for later classical revivalist work in these countries is generally less free than in the countries of northern Europe. The most famous work of the kind was the Monument of Vittorio Emmanuele at Rome, by Sacconi, built to commemorate Italian national unity, effected after 1870. The monument is on a grand scale, being over 400 feet long and 200 feet high. It consists of an equestrian statue of the king mounted on a pedestal on a terrace approached by steps at either end. At the back of this is an immense colonnade, each column being 50 feet high between two flanking projecting blocks faced with porticoes and surmounted by bronze groups. This huge monument has an appropriate setting, being the terminal feature of the Corso Umberto, and is thus seen to advantage. It is largely classical in conception but savouring of the grandeur and ostentation of Rome rather than the dignity and austerity of Greece. In marked contrast to the late free classicism of northern European countries is the classical revivalist work in Athens itself, purer and closer to originals, it seems to me, than the earlier work in Berlin, Liverpool, or Leningrad. One explanation is obviously that the power of the Greek originals is more immediate and dominating than it could be elsewhere.

After Greek independence in 1830 modern Athens was built to the north of the Acropolis. Parts of the medieval city were included, but these formed only a small part of the modern city. The plan of the new Athens, the work of the German architect and archaeologist Schaubert, is a symmetrical geometric conception in the classical tradition. Three principal streets form a triangle and at their meeting-points are placed important buildings. The layout of streets between the principal thoroughfares follows the Greek chess-board pattern with the exception of the small part of the medieval town, which has an irregularity which spoiled the classic completeness of Schaubert's scheme. Most of the important buildings erected between 1834 and 1914 were the work of German architects, a circumstance probably due to the fact that German archaeologists were more active in Greece than were those of other nations. Among the earlier buildings were the Academy, the University, and the Royal Palace, all of which were built during the eighteen-thirties. Both the Academy and the University, designed by the elder Hansen, are reproductions of Greek temples adapted for their purpose. The Royal Palace, by Gartner, is more interesting. It has a simple principal elevation with numerous square window-openings in plain walls, and a central feature with a portico of columns and pedimented top. There is little relation between the central feature and the flanking masses, but such shortcomings are somewhat mitigated by its quiet restrained character.

The National Museum, by Lange, completed in 1889, is another reminiscence of Greek temples, but the best of these monumental public buildings designed to revive the temple architecture of ancient Greece is the National Library, which makes a group with the older buildings of the Academy and University. The National Library was built in 1901 by Theophilus Hansen, and appears as a central temple with Doric portico and two smaller flanking temples joined by recessed masses. The flanking masses are decorated with simple pilasters. Like the Academy building the only feature which is not largely a reproduction of the work of the fifth century B.C. is the curved stairway in front of the principal entrance. The commercial buildings and houses of modern Athens, though considerably influenced by the public buildings, are designed with more freedom, and in some cases they are a frank essay in Italian Renaissance. Schliemann's House, for example, is clearly Palladian in character[5].

The public buildings of modern Athens are closer to the ancient originals than any other Greek revival buildings in Europe. The proximity of these originals has been

12

given as one reason, but another reason is that they are realized in the same material, namely, white Pentelican marble, while the Greek revival buildings of Liverpool, Berlin, and Leningrad are realized in coarser limestones and sandstones. Similarity of climate helps the impression. Another reason for their being more accurate reproductions of the proportions and details of Greek temples is possibly that their authors were really more archaeologists than architects. The result is that something of the purity, chasteness, and dignity has been captured. But it is a reminiscence; the buildings have a romantic quality because they are dreams of the past, but they do not belong to the urgent industrial life of modern Europe. The significance of these modern Athenian buildings for later European architecture is that they seem to have been a considerable influence in later Fascist architecture of Italy and National Socialist architecture of Germany.

The return to Renaissance work prior to the Greek revival meant generally a return by many architects to various periods from the inception of the Renaissance in their country to the end of the eighteenth century. The particular period selected was generally a matter of individual taste. As Renaissance was influenced in its developments by the earlier traditions of each country, and by the work of individual architects, this return meant partially a return to native traditions. For example, in England, some architects sought for models in the transition from late Gothic to Renaissance during the sixteenth century, others in the forms that lingered in domestic architecture of the seventeenth century, others in the classical domestic architecture of the eighteenth century, while others followed the work of individual Renaissance architects. It would be safe to assume, in looking at the Belfast City Hall, completed in 1906, that its architect, Sir A. Brumwell Thomas, had considerable enthusiasm for the work of Wren, as this building is stylistically partly an adaptation of St. Paul's Cathedral for the purpose of a City Hall. The dome and the four corner turrets and the principal portico are fairly close copies of these features in St. Paul's.

More interesting is the revival of early Renaissance work in which some features of the Gothic style are retained. The Hotel de Ville in Paris was built in 1871 by Ballu and Deperthes in the early Renaissance style of the former building. Gothic characteristics in this building are seen chiefly in the stone mullions and transoms of the square-headed windows of the first storey. Early Renaissance palaces and large houses are the prototypes before the full influence of classical architecture had developed. It is difficult to assess the influence of the Hotel de Ville, but many subsequent buildings of considerable importance represent a similar revival of early Renaissance. Two prominent examples are the Palace of Peace at The Hague, by the French architect L. M. Cordonnier, completed in 1913, and built in the style of sixteenth-century half-Gothic and half-Renaissance Dutch architecture, and the Victoria and Albert Museum, at South Kensington, designed by Sir Aston Webb and completed in 1908. Although the Victoria and Albert Museum is mainly early Renaissance in style and has a symmetrical plan, with the exception of the adjustments necessitated by a corner site with two street elevations, it has several late Gothic features[6]. As in the Hotel de Ville the rectangular windows with stone mullions and transoms are late Gothic reminiscences, while the radiating arched crowning feature above the central space has Gothic rather than Renaissance prototypes in such spires as that of St. Nicholas, Newcastle, and St. Giles, Edinburgh. The use of red brick with stone dressings at corners and round entrances and windows is a revival of English Renaissance under Dutch influence at the time of William and Mary. In modern Renaissance it was employed by Norman Shaw, and became popular for a time with English architects.

Archaeologists during the nineteenth century greatly extended the field of history, revealing to us the remains of ancient civilizations. Before the nineteenth century very little of the actual remains of Egyptian, Assyrian, Babylonian, and early Greek art was known. Most educated people had a vague impression of ancient Egyptian civilization and art, and an even more vague impression of ancient Assyrian, Babylonian, and pre-classical Greek art and civilization. It was not until the systematic exploration of Egypt begun by Richard Lepsius following the preparatory work done by F. Champollion in 1826, of ancient Babylonia and Assyria by M. Botta and Sir Henry Layard in the eighteen-forties, and the work in Greece begun by Schliemann in about 1870, that the art of Egypt, Assyria, and pre-classical Greece became at all familiar. At the same time archaeological work in other fields progressed. Also the introduction of speedier travel by the advent of railways helped to familiarize the products of ancient cultures in different parts of the world. All this had its effect on architecture, and architects of the early twentieth century, in their restless striving for originality and search for fresh decorative motifs, introduced ornament from the architecture and art of ancient Egypt, Assyria, Persia, and other ancient civilizations. Although mostly confined to the introduction of decorative motifs so that one might say that a building has a slightly Egyptian or Assyrian or Persian character some architects designed buildings completely in the Egyptian style. These archaeological revelations had a most salutory influence on modern sculpture, helping to free it from the tyranny of the classical tradition.

PALACE OF PEACE DESIGN COMPETITION

The best notion of the character of European architectural design, representing at least 95 per cent of work in the ten years preceding the First World War, is, I think, afforded by the designs submitted at the international competition for building the Palace of Peace at the Hague. A small minority were the pioneers and progressive architects, who were striving to make architecture a living thing growing out of contemporary life.

Mr Andrew Carnegie allocated $1\frac{1}{2}$ million dollars to the Dutch Government for a building for an International Court of Arbitration and for a library in connexion therewith, the two to form a Palace of Peace. An international competition for the design of the building was held and certain famous architects were specially invited to compete. In April 1906, 216 designs were submitted. Six prizes were offered and these in order were won by L. M. Cordonnier of Lille, A. Marcel of Paris, F. Wendt of Charlottenburg, Otto Wagner of Vienna, H. Greenley and H. S. Olin of New York, and F. Schwechter of Berlin. The plans of the six premiated designs and the forty other designs chosen for publication by the Society of Architecture at Amsterdam are symmetrical, with the single exception of F. Schwechter's, in which at the rear there is a non-symmetrical note. But here the general similarity of the designs ends. What is remarkable is the great diversity of treatment, plans, and styles, yet very few of the designs viewed in the retrospect of sixty years can be regarded as of great merit. The site being an open one and the planning offering no very difficult problem— merely the alternative of combining the court and library in one block or separating them, all the designs showing one of these alternatives—architectural skill and originality centred chiefly in the style of the building. Generally, expression of purpose was lost in the all-powerful habit of designing in some style of the past. It would not be difficult to tell in looking through the forty-six designs from which countries many of them emanated, as many seem, in a curiously revealing way, to express national characteristics. Cordonnier's project, placed first, was designed in accordance with the traditional local architecture of the sixteenth century, and this circumstance influenced the judges. The design appears now as an ornate revival of the architecture of transition from Gothic to Renaissance with Romanesque elements mixed in. It was modified in the actual building completed in 1913, becoming simpler. A. Marcel's design, placed second, was so close a copy of Girault's Petit Palais that it is a wonder that the judges did not rule it out on the ground of lack of originality. The two German designs, placed third and sixth, were designed in the classical Renaissance style, but with a heavy, massive treatment which is so marked a character of late German Renaissance work.

Two of the most original designs were submitted by Otto Wagner and H. P. Berlage. Both have an eclectic tendency and both abandon the excessive emphasis on the main entrance. Neither is equal to the best of their earlier work. Berlage's design has a flat central dome and a campanile is introduced, the whole betraying Byzantine influence, but what is important is that it shows a tendency towards the use of simpler unornamented masses which characterizes Berlage's Amsterdam Exchange building (see Chapter 5).

Two designs submitted by two architects from Helsingfors show a refeshing simplicity. One by E. Saarinen employs Egyptian decorative features, while the other design, by Jarl Eklund, is a simple treatment of Romanesque. Carl Hocheder, a Munich architect, showed a design with very strong Baroque influence. J. Ping Cadafalch's (Barcelona) design is an adaptation of Spanish Gothic; Smits and Fel's (The Hague) is another simple version of Romanesque, while Valenten Vanerwyck's (Ghent) contribution is designed in the late Flemish Gothic style. It will be seen from these notes that the influence of native traditions on architects is partially responsible for the expression of national characteristics in these designs. The Italian contribution from Guiseppe G. Mancini of Rome is somewhat amusing in this respect. It is the most grandiose design of the collection, and it is an expression in architecture of bombast and pomposity.

The designs submitted by English architects show little originality and are strongly reminiscent of prominent London buildings. Jan F. Groll's design is a mixture of the Natural History Museum and the Imperial Institute, the designer bearing in mind, perhaps, that the architect of the latter building was one of the assessors. Henry T. Hare's design suggests the Wesleyan Hall at Westminster, although it is too early to be a copy, while J. Coates Carter's design is an eclectic work very much influenced by Norman Shaw. Among the best designs submitted were those in the classical style, two being from Eduard Cuypers of Amsterdam and Henri Eustache of Paris. The former is simple and massive, with large windows and a central dome; the latter is a restrained, dignified classic design with a felicitously proportioned central portico of Corinthian columns. It is the most Greek in feeling of all the designs. Many of the other projects submitted show a mixture of various styles—Egyptian, Greek, Assyrian, Romanesque, Byzantine, Saracenic—often extravagant and bizarre and having very little relation to the purpose of the building. Such, roughly, was the state of architectural design as practised by many well-known architects in Europe in the years preceding the First World War.

References and Notes

1. Reproductions of coloured elevations of four classical buildings in Leningrad are given in the *Architectural Review*, vol. lxxi, May 1932, plate III.
2. Good explanations are given in Sir Banister Fletcher's *History of Architecture on the Comparative Method*, seventeenth edition, London, 1961, pp. 368–73.
3. For the history of Renaissance architecture the reader is referred to the many excellent works on the subject, among which may be mentioned *The Architecture of the Renaissance in Italy*, by W. J. Anderson and A. Stratton, 1927; *A History of French Architecture 1494 to 1661*, 2 vols., 1911, *and 1661–1774*, 2 vols., 1921, by Sir Reginald Blomfield; also his *A History of Renaissance Architecture in England*, 1897. There is a good classified account in Sir Banister Fletcher's *History of Architecture*, twelfth edition, 1945, and a good short survey in Nikolaus Pevsner's *An Outline of European Architecture*, a Penguin Book, 1942.
4. C. and A. Williams-Ellis, *The Pleasures of Architecture*, London, 1924, p. 221.
5. An account of modern Athens, with several illustrations, is given by Lionel B. Budden in the *Architectural Review*, 1912, vol. xxxi, p. 315; vol. xxxii, p. 6.
6. Late Gothic applied to secular buildings is often called Tudor in England, but here all Tudor architecture is comprehended as late Gothic.

2 Eclecticism

MENTION HAS BEEN MADE of the restlessness of architects during the late nineteenth century arising from the dissatisfaction with merely imitating past styles. Prompted to search for something that would lead them to create a style more expressive of contemporary life or, at least, to the creation of a more original architecture, some architects tried to achieve that originality by blending historical styles and thus becoming eclectics. This blending was generally most successful when one style dominated, or when the whole building was of restrained character. The Imperial Institute at South Kensington, built in 1887 to the design of T. E. Collcutt, is an example of a mixture of Romanesque, Gothic, Byzantine, and Renaissance motifs, with the first most pronounced, but all unobtrusive because ornament is kept flat and restrained[1]. But where there is not this restraint the result is apt to be bizarre, as in that earlier curious eclectic work, Sir Gilbert Scott's Albert Memorial (1861–4), derived in its main form from a thirteenth-century reliquary, and which is an obtrusive mixture of classical, Gothic, Byzantine, and Baroque styles involving an incongruous mixture of materials. Its setting in Kensington Gardens opposite the Albert Hall is, however, superb.

A typical architect of the last quarter of the nineteenth century was Richard Norman Shaw. His earlier work, which is by far the most important, is of a functional character emerging from Gothic (see Chapter 3), but he moves from this promising start to eclecticism and later still to classicism. Norman Shaw was greatly enamoured of the picturesque, which gave a florid character to many of the eclectic works of his middle period, works like New Zealand Chambers in Leadenhall Street (1872), Albert Hall Mansions (1879), the first Alliance Assurance Building, Pall Mall (1882), where Romanesque, Renaissance, and Gothic motifs are freely mixed. The New Scotland Yard building (1888), regarded by many as his masterpiece, is an original mixture of Gothic and Renaissance elements, dominated by the picturesque effects such as the corner turrets. In many houses built between 1870 and 1890, of which 'Pierrepoint' at Farnham in Surrey (1876) is an example, there is a profuse use of half-timber work as decoration, and he, more than any architect, is responsible for the craze for sham half-timber effects which characterize so much English housing of the present century. Later still, Shaw renounced his earlier romantic tendencies, and became another architect of the classical Renaissance tradition in many of his later country houses, in the second Alliance Assurance building, St. James' Street (1903), and in the Piccadilly Hotel (1905).

Buildings of an eclectic character were erected in most European countries during the last years of the nineteenth century and early years of the twentieth. Many of the town halls built in the vicinity of Paris and in English and German provincial cities were of this kind. Some, like the Hotel-de-Ville in Paris (see Chapter 1), are more accurately described as a revival of early Renaissance where many Gothic elements were mixed with the Renaissance importation, while others are more clearly blendings of distinct styles, with Romanesque often prominent. None of the eclectic buildings so far mentioned are of great architectural value. Although the Scotland Yard building has been much praised, Sir Reginald Blomfield referring to it as 'the finest public building erected in London since Somerset House'[2], it seems to me incongruous and unsuitable in design. This was built as a central police administrative office, and yet Shaw gave it a suggestion of a medieval castle. The corner turrets which help to convey this are prominent features but hardly grow out of the purpose of the building, and are really little better than large stuck-on ornamental features. There is, too, an incongruous effect in the large stone ornamental Renaissance features perched high up at the roof gables, for they have little relation to the general design of the building, and appear merely as inharmonious applied ornament. It is one of the consequences of an insufficiently digested eclecticism.

Eclectic is a term derived from the Greek, originally applied to philosophers who borrowed from many schools of thought. The term has been used extensively in art criticism in modern times to apply to an artist who selects features from many schools and styles and blends them. It is often used in a derogatory sense of an artist who does little more than that, but is generally charitably withheld from an artist who so blends what he selects from various schools and styles that he forms a fresh and original creation. There are some who would still speak of such artists as eclectics, if the various sources of their art can be seen in different schools. Thus Raphael and Augustus John, although both original artists who have made important contributions to the art of painting, are sometimes called eclectics, because elements in their work are traceable to many different sources. Motifs from other artists' work are clearly recognizable, but they form parts of something entirely new. It is thus possible to speak of eclecticism in a disparaging sense where the elements are not blended to make any new and original work, but merely given an impression of piecing together or of a not very well-mixed hash. At the same time it is legitimate to speak of eclecticism in a better sense, where, although motifs have been selected from different sources, their essential character has been absorbed by the artist, and they have been welded together to produce something entirely new and beautiful. It is in this latter sense that I think of Liverpool Cathedral, by Sir Giles Gilbert Scott, as eclectic. Here is an eclecticism of a deeper and more serious kind than any to which reference has so far been made. As it is one of the greatest buildings of the twentieth century it merits some detailed consideration.

Most churches built during the Victorian Age were designed in the revived Gothic style. The work varied according to the preferences of the architects, and it is not difficult to distinguish the work of one architect from another. Of the architects principally responsible for Victorian churches—Pugin, Butterfield, Scott, Pearson, Street, Bodley, Sedding, and a few others—some, like Pearson, seemed to favour one particular phase of Gothic; some, like Pugin and Butterfield, were more interested in Gothic construction than design; while others, like Scott and Bodley, versatile with their copy-books, would pass from one Gothic style to another at the wish of their clients, or according to the known taste of competition assessors. Pearson, who was one of the most original of Victorian architects within the confined limits of revivalism, introduced a new note in using brick for the exterior of churches in the Early English or Decorated style. These brick exteriors often have a breadth, simplicity, and dignity which is impressive, a good example being St. John's Church, Upper Norwood, with its large, plain wall-surfaces. Such examples may have contributed to the use of brick in large, plain surfaces which is a feature of much modern church architecture.

LIVERPOOL CATHEDRAL

Most Victorian church architecture follows Gothic fairly closely, with minor notes of original treatment. Liverpool Anglican Cathedral represents a refreshing and original departure from Victorian custom with a totally new conception.

The See of Liverpool was formed in 1878, and in 1885 powers were obtained to build a cathedral. An eclectic design, by Sir William Emerson, partly Gothic, partly Renaissance, with a dome, was approved. This project was abandoned. The matter was revived in 1900, and after some controversy the site of a disused quarry near an old cemetery on St. James's Mount was chosen. The choice was admirable because, being on ground well above the level of the city, the cathedral would have an elevated and dominating position which would allow it to be seen from miles around, from the countryside, and from ships approaching the river and harbour from the sea.

The selection of Giles G. Scott as the architect in 1903—he was then only 23 years of age—was the result of a competition[1] in which G. F. Bodley and Norman Shaw were assessors. In their recommendation they referred to Scott's design as having 'that power combined with beauty which makes a great and noble building'. The cathedral committee were a little apprehensive about appointing so young a man, inevitably

19

with so little experience in directing building operations, so G. F. Bodley was appointed joint architect with Scott. Bodley died, however, in 1907, and Scott henceforth carried out his own design alone.

The earliest part of the cathedral to be completed was the Lady Chapel, which was consecrated in 1910. It is the part of the cathedral which is the closest to traditional Gothic, having here and there, especially in the roof and windows, the character of work of the Decorated period. This was, I suspect, partly due to Bodley's influence. The reredos, for example, was the joint design of the two architects. The Lady Chapel has, however, much that is original. The proportion of low arcade and high clerestory, double the height of the arcade, is unusual, and gives a massiveness to the lower part. The upper part, like traditional Gothic, is essentially a design in line emphasized by decorative ribbed vaulting, and in this it differs from the later work in the cathedral where linear motifs are more restrained and subordinated to mass effects.

After Bodley's death Scott became more and more dissatisfied with his original design. This had consisted of a cruciform plan with single transepts and twin towers over the transepts. The nave was longer than the choir, and each was broken by a series of cross-bays which were to be lit by tall lancet windows. The Lady Chapel was at the east end (the liturgical east, as the cathedral, owing to exigencies of site, is orientated more nearly south and north, the south forming the liturgical east), with a square chapter house to the north. In 1910 a new plan was adopted, and this is the plan of the cathedral as it is built. This consists of four transepts on either side of a central space above which rises a single central tower. The choir and nave are made of equal length, and the chapter house is altered from a rectangle to an octagon and reduced in size.

The cathedral is built mainly of red sandstone from the Woolton quarries, a few miles away, with a certain amount from the Rainhill and Runcorn quarries for the interior[2]. The foundations are of brick and concrete, and the outer roofs above the stone vaulting of the choir and transepts are of reinforced concrete. The main floor consists of tiling on concrete slabs laid on reinforced concrete beams, some of which are hollow for the circulation of warm air; for in heating the cathedral the method of the Romans of circulating hot air under the floor is employed. Additional heating is supplied by radiators placed under the windows.

It is the largest cathedral in England with a total floor area of 100,000 square feet, which compares with 227,000 of St. Peter's at Rome, 59,700 of St. Paul's, 63,800 of York Minster, 107,000 of Milan, 128,500 of Seville, and 190,000 of New York.

Although designed with Gothic calligraphy, it is a building which departs considerably from traditional Gothic, acquiring a character which links it with the classical tradition.

20

Liverpool Cathedral, 1903–73, general view of exterior to the completion of the first bay of the nave

Architect: Sir Giles Gilbert Scott

Plan of Liverpool Cathedral

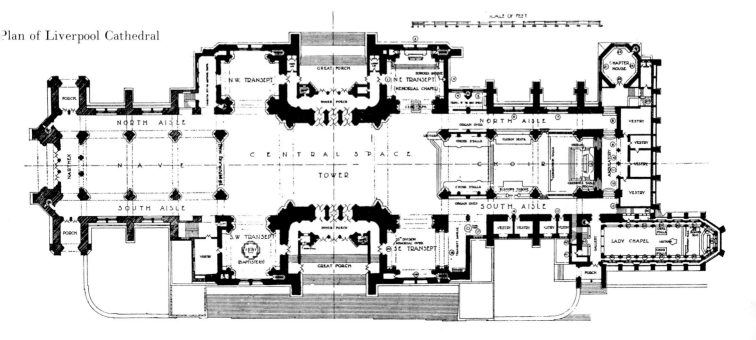

It is as if the spirit of Gothic architecture had extended its hand backward in time to grasp that of classical architecture, and it is therefore inevitable that it has a little of the character of the actual intervening Romanesque work. This is seen particularly in a modification of the Gothic framed structure and the use of a massive wall-structure. Instead of a light stone frame and flying buttresses to take the thrust of the vaulted roof, there are massive, solid, pier-like buttresses, through which the aisles have the effect of being tunnelled; and the rounded pointed windows suggest a movement from Gothic to Romanesque, as if half inclined to become completely semicircular again. This contributes to a structure which has a massiveness and grandeur, a breadth and repose combined with a spirit of aspiration which is unique, and this combination is the result of blending Gothic linear design with classical mass and breadth. The plan is based on classic symmetry with transepts, choir, and nave all equally balanced round the central space, and the massive square central tower, with the four rectangular blocks of transepts buttressing it, is essentially classical in conception.

Massiveness, dignity, power are the dominating qualities of the exterior, but the interior is even more impressive. Here breadth of design is eloquent in the large bare wall-spaces of the lovely pale crimson sandstone patterned with wide white joints, while the piers ascend without a break to the springing of the arch which reaches in the shadows of the vaulted roof to a height of 116 feet in the choir and transepts[3], and 176 feet in the central space. The choir span is 61 feet, thus narrow in proportion to height, a circumstance which enhances the spirit of aspiration, enhanced also by the fading of forms in the shadows of the vaulted roof, as a sense of mystery is thereby created. When standing in the central space and looking towards the choir, one has the impression of architectural magnificence and perfection, an experience that comes not often in life. A note of criticism is prompted only when one looks from the choir to the central space at the relation of the arch of the central space and the arch of the choir. It seems that the former does not curve in harmony with the latter, the span is relatively too wide. If the same proportioned arch had been employed for the opening to the central space I think the effect would have been better.

The cathedral is eclectic in the best sense, and in being so is expressive of the age which produced it, as it represents the meeting and intermingling of two great traditions when the moment of such confluence is possible. In another, different, sense it is expressive of its age. It is full of beautiful details, of lovely, precise, carved ornament in such central features as altars; but these are produced very differently from the ornament of a medieval cathedral, when much was left to the individual freedom and taste of each carver, so that carving in medieval churches is conspicuous for its variety. In Liverpool Cathedral all details are conceived and precisely defined by the architect, and the carver follows closely the mind of the architect. Thus the whole work to the smallest detail is completely the product of one mind. This control by one

Interior of Liverpool Cathedral looking east

mind, this adherence to the precise formulations of the designer, belongs more naturally to a machine age than to free medieval craftsmanship. It is thus in this sense expressive of its time.

What is the essential life and spirit behind this meeting of two traditions, this attempted blending of the breadth and repose of a Greek temple with the aspiring character of a Gothic cathedral? The emphasis of vertical lines, which conduces so much to the spirit of aspiration, is eloquent in the long vertical interior piers running into the pointed arches of the vaulted roof; yet a feeling of repose is blended with that impression by the introduction of large, unbroken, rectangular spaces, and horizontal lines and forms emphasized here and there. The energy and somewhat restless character of many a Gothic cathedral is thus modified. Sir Giles G. Scott himself says[4] that 'in most Gothic cathedrals the emphasis of the vertical is unduly stressed and thereby a great deal of calm and serenity is sacrificed', and there is a 'feeling of restlessness which tends to destroy repose and peace'. And further, 'it comes to a question of balance, like everything in nature, and at Liverpool I have endeavoured to combine the uplifting character imparted by vertical expression with the restful calm undoubtedly given by judicious use of horizontals'. And so 'subsequent alterations that have taken place have all been with a view to reducing the vertical character, and thereby emphasizing the influence of the horizontals'. This tendency of blending the breadth and repose of Greek architecture with the aspiration and energy of Gothic is a characteristic of Sir Giles Scott's later work and of much other modern church-designing, probably due partly to his influence.

The monolithic character of the Greek temple enshrining the god within expresses the spirit of resignation—to fate, to death as final and irrevocable. The mystic *cultus* known as Orphism that Polygnotus seems to have expressed in the Lesche paintings so minutely described by Pausanias; the vague notions of a beautiful land in the West and of Hades, derived from Homer; and the theories of Platonists were but the religious speculations of fanciful minds. In spite of these, the religious feeling of the average educated Greek was that of resignation to the thought that death is the end. It is revealed consistently in the sad farewell scenes on the Greek stelae of the fifth and fourth centuries—a source of information telling of the feelings of the Greek people far more reliable than the fancies of theorists, or the entertaining speculations of philosophers. Did not Pindar say 'desire not a life immortal, but use to the utmost the tools that are in thine hand'? And similar is the sentiment that pervades the famous oration of Pericles, who ruled in Athens when its greatest architectural glories arose. This resignation emanates partly from the Greek worship of reason, and hence a rationalism, a philosophical acceptance of the inevitable which gives to their creations a serenity and repose, tinged here and there with a beautiful melancholy.

A Gothic cathedral energetically struggles to be free from all such resignation. Here is the restless striving towards heaven, the fervent worship of the God in heaven that, to the medieval mind, existed somewhere above in the ethereal blue. Pillars within stretching in long vertical lines to the pointed arches and vaulted roofs, and towers and steeples without soaring upwards to the sky, all express in unison fervent worship and heavenly aspiration. As Goethe says: 'The steeples are not like cupolas, to form a heaven within, but strive towards heaven without.' And what was this present life to the Christian, contemporary with the raising of these cathedrals, but a preparation for the next? His life was a constant worship and glorification of God, a constant aspiration to be worthy of the richer and greater life to come, and he expressed this spirit in his places of worship.

Two more complete contrasts of form and spirit can scarcely be imagined. Yet the Renaissance was in many ways the intermingling of Christianity with Greek culture. Those eager thinkers of the fifteenth century feverishly endeavoured to reconcile forces that appeared almost irreconcilable. A great civilization, often profound, idealistic, and noble in its thought, existed before Christ was known, not as the herald of Christ, but in many important ways distinctly different from the things that Christ taught. And so many, like Pico della Mirandola, embraced the most Christian-tempered of the Greeks, like Plato, as the chief ray of hope in their attempted reconciliations, but ultimately gave up the task in despair. These eager minds are of value today chiefly as throwing light on one of the most interesting periods in the development of thought. The reconciliation that they attempted was destined to lead to something else. Greek religious thought and Christianity have never been reconciled, but they have intermingled and the modern world is the richer for it. The passing years have shown that by taking the best of Christianity and the best of Greek culture we achieve a bigger, fuller life than each can give us separately. The modern world dates from the Renaissance, a movement not yet completed, for that intermingling of the two chief sources of spiritual and intellectual life is constantly going on and fresh contributions are made very year. Much in the older Christian doctrines is now rejected as gross superstition, much of the fervid Christian sentimentalism is dissolved by a reason inherited from the Greeks, much medieval bigoted and philistine morality, which had a late outburst in the Puritans, has been rationalized by the Greek love of beauty; while strains of brutality and harshness in Greek life have been softened by Christian kindliness; and the sentiment of love grows to greater magnitude than hitherto with the advent of Christian belief and thought. It is not too fanciful to carry the notion to architecture and see in Liverpool Cathedral, and buildings in a kindred style, an expression of the blending of these two cultural forces in our lives. In sharing the spirit of such work we are but children of a Renaissance which represents the confluence of Greek culture and Christianity.

One thinks of Bach's organ music as most fittingly heard in a Gothic cathedral with the music soaring upwards with the long vertical piers, and reverberating among the vaulted roofs. Yet however much one feels of the Christian spirit in Bach's music, however much it suggests Fra Angelico's choirs of angels echoing through Gothic churches, his music is essentially classical in form, and like Liverpool Cathedral, it seems to blend the spirit of classical beauty of form with Christian aspiration. In Liverpool Cathedral Bach's music has a setting which is the creation of the same spirit, and to absorb them together, through the medium of the magnificent cathedral organ, is one of the rare experiences of life.

ANTONIO GAUDI AND THE CHURCH OF THE SAGRADA FAMILY

A totally different yet unique, original, bizarre and somewhat extravagant eclectisicm, where the various styles and motifs are integrated in a fantastic unity, is seen in the work of the Catalonian architect Antonio Gaudi (1852–1926). In his student days and early years of practice Gaudi was much influenced and inspired by medieval art and in many of his early designs the Gothic style is followed, with, however, a very personal interpretation. As a result of a visit to Andalusia and Tangier in 1887 he began to mix oriental and Islamic motifs in his Gothic designs, and was later influenced by the *Art Nouveau* movement to which references are made in Chapter 4. As he evolved he went more and more to the direct inspiration of natural forms, so that much of his work is a combination of various styles and motifs drawn directly from nature. These varied qualities are most completely displayed in his principal work: the immense Church of the Sagrada Familia, Barcelona, on which he was engaged from 1883 to his untimely death as the result of a street accident in 1926.

Church of the Sagrada
Familia, Barcelona
1883–1926

Architect: Antonio Gaudi

A design in the Gothic style had been prepared for this church in 1882 by del Villar, and Gaudi was appointed architect a year later. Although he abandoned del Villar's design he was yet influenced by it in the early stages of his design which were largely of a Gothic character. As the work proceeded other elements and motifs were

26

introduced, oriental, Islamic, *Art Nouveau* and the infusion of forms directly derived from the natural world and integrated by his very distinctive and original genius. By the middle of the twentieth century the Sagrada Familia Church, although unfinished came to be widely esteemed as one of the most notable, original and strange architectural creations of the century.

Within an overall rectangular plan the cruciform shape forms the interior with a large apse holding a central altar of the Virgin, while at the main crossing is the chief altar of Christ. According to the numerous plans, models and perspective sketches, the terminations of the nave and transepts were to have groups of four skittle-like pinnacles rising above three pyramidal porches. Only one of these façades was completed, that of the Nativity which shows porches with a profusion of religious figures among vegetation. Rising above these three porches are the three perforated pinnacles which began as Gothic then change to a mixture of styles and motifs: Romanesque, *Art Nouveau* and finally to a strange assortment of geometric shapes inspired by the contemporary cubist movement. Over the central space there was to be a tall spire surrounded by a cluster of lower spires. In the designs for the interior, Gaudi employed columns which spread above the capitals as tree branches to the vaulting which has a mixture of parabolic forms and forest-branch effect. I believe that this forest-like conception of the interior would have pleased Ruskin. Gaudi also employed slanting columns, and the whole conception is a remarkable combination of historic styles, modern contemporary motifs and personal adaptation of natural forms. It is among the unique buildings of the world, and is a monument to a very original architectural genius. Aesthetically it were better, perhaps, if left unfinished, like an unfinished symphony of a great composer[5].

REFERENCES AND NOTES

1. When it was proposed in the mid-fifties to replace the Imperial Institute building with one to meet modern requirements, the necessary expansion protests were made against its destruction. As a compromise the tower was retained and is now surrounded by modern steel and glass buildings designed by Norman and Dawbarn and erected in 1960–65.
2. Particulars of this competition are given in the *Official Handbook of Liverpool Cathedral*, by Vere E. Cotton, 9th edition, 1936, pp. 10–11.
3. An idea of this height may be obtained from comparing it with the two highest English medieval interiors: Westminster Abbey which is 101 feet, and York Minster which is 99 feet. Greater heights are seen in French Gothic Cathedrals. The choir of Bauvais is 157 feet high and the nave of Amiens is 140 feet high.
4. In an article in the *Morning Post* on the day of the consecration of the choir, 19 July 1924.
5. For details of Gaudi's life and work see the biography by George R. Collins in *Masters of World Architecture* series, New York and London, 1960. A bibliography is included.

3 Romanticism, utility, and the search for a living architecture

EARLY IN THE nineteenth century a few noteworthy architects expressed vague dissatisfaction with designing in the styles of past civilizations, and asked why an architecture expressive of contemporary life could not be evolved. About 1830 Karl Friedrich Schinkel came to England and visited Manchester and the growing industries of the north. He felt that the revived Greek architecture, some of the finest examples of which he was the author, was completely out of touch with this growing industrial life, and he wrote in his diary: 'All great ages have left a record of themselves in their style of building. Why should we not try to find a style for ourselves?'[1] Still, Schinkel continued to design fairly closely to Greek models, yet with a sensitive feeling for proportion which proclaimed him an artist of rare distinction. He had made one attempt earlier, in 1820, towards a more expressive architecture, in the design of a departmental store[2], which shows very large windows with pilasters between, making façades somewhat like the gridiron steel-frame façades of the twentieth century. It is a remarkable forecast of things to come.

Henri Labrouste designed the Library of Sainte-Geneviève in Paris (1843–50), and the Bibliothèque Nationale in Paris (1858–68). They both have restrained exteriors of classical design, the former with symmetrical plan, but the latter with a plan which, though influenced by classical formalism, has a certain irregularity determined by considerations of convenience and function. The iron and glass construction of the interiors facilitates the functional developments. Labrouste's conception of architectural practice was not that of his contemporaries: of designing in a style and beginning with a fair appearance and trying to make fulfilment of purpose conform to these, on the contrary it was that of designing for purpose with appearance conforming to such designing. Much earlier, in a letter written to his brother in 1830 regarding instruction of pupils in his *atelier*, he says: 'I tell them that they must derive from the construction itself an ornamentation which is reasoned and expressive. I often repeat to them that the arts have the power of making everything beautiful, but I insist that they understand that in architecture form must always be appropriate to the function

28

for which it is intended.'³ These principles seem to have determined the progress in functional planning made by Labrouste from the Library of Sainte-Geneviève to the Bibliothèque Nationale. As early as 1830, we find in the thought of Schinkel and Labrouste the first seeds of the new architecture that were to grow so exclusively and slowly in England during the last forty years of the nineteenth century, to struggle more vigorously and widely in Germany, Austria, Holland, Belgium, and France in the early years of the twentieth century, and to blossom in the period between the two great wars. Labrouste's pronouncement in 1830 that 'in architecture form must always be appropriate to the function for which it is intended' represented one of the earliest conscious recognitions of the conditions of a living architecture, and an anticipation of modern doctrine.

Schinkel might have seen the basis of a living style, about which he asked, in some of the factories and warehouses of that industrial England which prompted the question. These buildings were designed solely for utility; appearance and style were not considered, and it is improbable that architects designed them. The best are probably the work of engineers, and many were probably designed as the result of consultations between the factory and warehouse owners and the building contractors. We know that Thomas Telford designed several, one being the warehouse at St. Katherine's Docks in London, built in 1824–28. Other early industrial buildings, noteworthy for good, straightforward, and efficient design, are the Francis Hill factory at Malmesbury, built in 1790; Bentley's piano factory in the Stroud Valley, built a little later; and Stanley Mill in the Stroud Valley, built in 1813. All these buildings are well lighted, having large horizontal windows, while cast iron is used for interior columnar supports in many of them. Although strictly utilitarian the plain walls, well-proportioned windows, and general, simple, efficient character make the best examples far more expressive of the life of the time than modern commercial buildings dressed as Greek temples or medieval monasteries.

The railway station offered a new type of building, and, apart from the stylistic hotel buildings that formed the frontages of large termini, it was generally designed on utilitarian principles. The roofs are often interesting as constructions, and also sometimes succeed in being works of art. The concentration on utility, and the consideration afterwards of appearance growing out of function, has resulted in some beautiful examples, like the station at Frankfurt (1868), the Gare du Nord in Paris (1862), and, finest of all, King's Cross Station, designed by Lewis Cubitt in 1852. It is a building growing out of purpose, and logically and beautifully expressing that purpose. Two semicircular arched roofs of glass and iron (originally wood) extending the whole length of the platforms are supported in the centre by columns connected by a series of well-proportioned arches. These arches are repeated on the arrival platform side, beyond which is an arched road for traffic, well placed, but effectively subordinated. Offices, waiting rooms, and restaurants are arranged along the departure platform. Here is the perfect arrangement for a railway terminus, and it provides a splendid basis for the architectural unity of the station. The two circular roofs are felicitously proportioned and related to each other, while the long vistas with the articulation of the arcade arches between afford an aesthetic pleasure akin to that yielded by the nave of a Romanesque cathedral. The exterior façade is simple and austere, and is an excellent example of the exterior expressing the interior shape and purpose.

If factories and warehouses built during the years of the Industrial Revolution had sometimes claim to architectural distinction, the same cannot be said of industrial housing, which was mean, squalid, unhealthy, and miserable in the extreme, too mean to be regarded as utilitarian. Resulting bad health and a high death-rate prompted Government legislation. Improvements were slowly effected, but the early bad industrial housing remained because the supply of houses has never reached the demand. Improved housing in the nineteenth century was very slowly effected, mainly, in the first instances, by the enterprises of companies like Krupps at Essen, and Cadbury's at Bournville. We had, generally, to wait a long time, until after the turn of the century, before low-cost housing on an extensive scale, reached such a quality that it was of a sufficiently good standard of planning and appearance even to be considered as architecture. It is in the houses of the well-to-do in England that some of the most progressive and distinctive architecture of the late nineteenth century is found.

Designing more in accordance with purpose and structure which resulted in these houses and which led to a more vital and living architecture arose to some extent from the Romantic movement. It has been said (Chapter 1) that the Romantic movement arose partially as a revolt against supposed cold and scholarly classical art, but it is something deeper than that. The essence of the romantic feeling is a yearning for that which is remote, and it is often prompted by a dissatisfaction with the present, a distaste for surrounding life, and this is expressed by a desire to get away to something more congenial. Goethe's *Sorrows of Werther*, an early work of the Romantic movement, expresses the restlessness and dissatisfaction of many young men with life as they knew it, and the suicide of Werther is not merely a fiction, but symptomatic of the epidemic of suicides in Germany at the time. Goethe records in his autobiography how he, himself, toyed with the idea of suicide. Charlotte is a symbol of the remote and unobtainable.

Wordsworth, another significant figure of the Romantic movement, expresses so often the flight from the world about him and seeks refuge in the past or in the quiet woods and fields. 'The world is too much with us', he exclaims, and concludes this famous sonnet by asking for 'Glimpses that would make me less forlorn'. And the romantic urge of Shelley, Coleridge, Keats, was stimulated by the growing commercial and industrial life with its ugly living conditions of the workers. W. R. Lethaby remarks 'that it was probably a manifestation of a protective instinct mysteriously aware of what was to happen in the coming age'. 'Wordsworth', he adds, 'seems first to have seen things in the new way.'[4]

This developing industrial life, carrying with it so much that was distasteful to idealistic thought, inevitably stimulated a looking back and an attempt to revive the happier ages of the past, and thus it greatly stimulated the Gothic revival. The finer aspect of this revival was the romanticism that resulted in the domestic architecture in Germany of Ludwig Persius, and that in England of Philip Webb, Norman Shaw, C. F. A. Voysey, and their followers.

Ludwig Persius was a pupil of Schinkel, and in designing houses, many of which are in Potsdam and the vicinity, he followed rather the medieval work than the classic work of his master[5], and made his plans more in accordance with convenience and purpose, while he orientated them not as an abstract geometric layout, but in accordance with the sun and the character of the ground. He related his houses to their garden setting, and comprehended both as a unity, thus being somewhat of a forerunner of the garden city, and of the domestic architecture of Voysey and Frank Lloyd Wright. His houses are still stylistic in appearance, being designed mainly in the Romanesque style, but he rendered the great service of freeing the plan from classical symmetry and formality. He had some following after his death in 1845, and was regarded as the founder of the Romantic school of architecture known as *Landschafts-Architektur*[6]. The school did not develop very extensively.

THE INFLUENCE OF THE PRE-RAPHAELITES

The romantic manifestation in England of Pre-Raphaelitism was associated with the domestic architecture in which design, more in accordance with purpose, and building with a greater sense of the fitness of materials, first arose. William Morris and his friend Edward Burne-Jones had a deep and romantic love for the art and life of the Middle Ages, and they attempted to revive the conditions of work that they felt had made medieval craftsmen happy. The creed of the principal Pre-Raphaelites, Rossetti, Millais, and Holman Hunt, arose from a dissatisfaction with so much of the melodramatic, theatrical, commercial, and insincere painting since the Renaissance, and they desired to paint more in the sincere spirit of earlier painters, with their faithful and minute renderings of natural forms. It was a romantic yearning for the remote.

Though Ruskin, Morris, and Burne-Jones were stimulated in their thought by this romanticism of the Pre-Raphaelites, and of earlier poets like Scott, Wordsworth, Coleridge, Shelley, and Keats, their romantic impulses were intensified by the detestation of the sordid industrial life growing in mid-nineteenth-century England, involving long hours of monotonous machine work in factories for people who lived in foul and sordid conditions. Machinery was also responsible for the ugliness of things of everyday use, such as were exhibited at the Great Exhibition of 1851. The machine, but more particularly its improper use, was blamed for this ugliness, unhappiness, and squalor. And thus there is that yearning for the partial revival of that happier medieval world. 'The social life of the Middle Ages allowed the workman freedom of individual expression, which on the other hand our social life forbids him', says Morris[7]. By this passionate romantic social feeling he was led to the pronouncement that 'Art is Man's Expression of His Joy in Labour'[8]. He condemned mere utilitarianism, however good the work, if it was the product of machinery. The life of the Middle Ages 'did not put into the hands of the workmen', he writes[9], 'any object which was merely utilitarian, still less vulgar; whereas the life of modern times forces on him the production of many things which can be nothing but utilitarian, as, for instance, a steam engine'. Architects later were to see much beauty in the steam engine and other such machinery, a beauty perhaps equal to the best of William Morris's own productions, and to those of medieval craftsmanship which he loved so much. William Morris and his associates were too intent on looking romantically backward into the golden age of the medieval world to think seriously of the aesthetic possibilities of machine production.

Yet looking romantically backward as they did, it was William Morris and his architect, Philip Webb, who, more than Schinkel, more than Persius, more than Labrouste, took the most decided step forward towards an architecture expressive of purpose and of contemporary life, a step which is important more for its influence than for the actual work that was produced.

ENGLISH DOMESTIC ARCHITECTURE OF THE LATE NINETEENTH CENTURY

After William Morris married he wanted a house and he and his architect, Philip Webb, built one at Bexley Heath, now famous throughout the world as the Red House. In looking for furnishings he found none of a sufficiently good standard among contemporary productions, so low was the state of applied art; so, with his associates, he formed a firm under the name of Morris, Marshall, Faulkner and Co to produce the furnishings for the house. This firm continued afterwards, but initially in a somewhat unbusiness-like manner, until it was better organized on business lines by Warington Taylor. It has continued ever since. But furniture and interior decoration, which was the product mainly of good designers and hand craftsmanship, could only be purchased by the well-to-do, a circumstance rather bitterly resented by Morris, when he remarked that he spent his life 'ministering to the swinish luxury of the rich'[10]. The poor, presumably, were to have machine-made articles or go without.

The Red House was the first of many houses by Philip Webb—and they represent the eve of the great achievements of English domestic architecture from about 1860

to the outbreak of the First World War (Webb died in 1915). They were designed
as the result of logical thought about the purpose they were to serve. The Red House
(1860), the house at Palace Green, Kensington (1868), Joldwynds, Surrey (1873),
Clouds, East Knoyle, Wiltshire (1881), Coneyhurst, Ewhurst (1886), Standen, East
Grinstead (1892), Exning, Newmarket (1896), are some of the best-known examples of
his houses, and if the plans of these are studied, it will be noted that they are all
designed primarily with a view to the convenient relationship of parts, while some are
orientated so as to get a fair degree of sunlight for the principal rooms. It must be
admitted, however, that the Red House is unsatisfactory in this last respect as the
principal rooms face north. The L shape was adopted in the Red House and many of
his later houses. The advantage of such a shape is that it allows for rooms to be
arranged in a sequence which is generally convenient as, for example, the sequence of
scullery, kitchen, pantry, dining room, drawing room; and at the same time allow
for maximum window space. Webb did not avoid symmetry because it was a
characteristic of the imported Renaissance architecture he disliked. If by symmetrical
planning the purpose of the house could be equally well achieved he employed it, as
in houses like Clouds and Smeton Manor[11], in the valley of the Swale. Clouds shows
the influence of symmetrical designing more than most of his houses. Lethaby
points out with reference to it, 'symmetry is a guide up to a point but nothing of
importance is sacrificed to it'[12]. Webb never planned symmetrically for the sake of
symmetry, as did Renaissance architects, even if he were requested to do so by a
client. If the client was insistent Webb's reply was that the client should get another
architect. Webb always made it clear to his client that the house was to be built as he
(Webb) thought it should be built. It would be a good thing for architecture if all
architects could show this independence. Too often their attitude is that of Basset, one
of Webb's assistants, who remarked that 'Webb will worry himself to fiddlestrings if
he argues so much with his clients; I would put the drains on the top of the house if
they wanted it'[13]. Another valuable contribution that Webb made to modern
architecture was his expressive and appropriate use of materials. He always studied
local materials and buildings so that his house should belong to its surroundings. Thus,
if the traditional building material of a district is limestone, or sandstone, or brick,
this determined the selection of his building material. Thus Arisaig, near Fort William,
on the west coast of Scotland, is built of the hard local stone, Clouds, in Wiltshire,
is built of local sandstone, while the Red House and other houses in the southeast are
of brick. His London houses, like that at Palace Gardens, are generally built of brick
with stone dressings. He studied all materials used in building and tried to use them
well. As Lethaby remarks, 'he was deeply interested in limes and mortars, the proper
ways of laying roofs, tiles and forming chimneys, of finishing plaster ceilings and
mixing whitewash.'[14]

Although Philip Webb was influenced by Gothic architecture, and this influence is
apparent in his work, his houses are in no sense stylistic. He aimed at carrying on the

33

medieval tradition of good, honest, and efficient building, from the point where it had been interrupted by the importation of Renaissance architecture. 'Architecture to Webb', says Lethaby[15], 'was first of all a common tradition of honest building. The great architectures of the past had been noble customary ways of building, naturally developed by the craftsmen engaged in the actual works.'

It is probable that Webb's work had some influence on the early domestic architecture of Richard Norman Shaw. The extent of that influence is deduced from Shaw's work, as he never acknowledged it. Of the same age (born in 1831), Shaw succeeded Webb as Street's chief draughtsman, and afterwards was Nesfield's partner until 1868. Shaw designed a very large number of houses from 1868 to about 1900, but very few are as good as Webb's. Unlike Webb, Shaw was not content with simple direct building, but introduced 'period' ornamental features, the principal early essays of which were in the Tudor style with half-timbered effects, which he employed as early as 1868 in the house at Leys Wood, Sussex, and which he used in numerous subsequent houses.

Though many of his early plans are determined mainly by convenience, he rarely seems to be free of the influence of traditional symmetrical planning, and later makes it a definite aim. His best houses are those in London, where the Tudor influence is succeeded by that of the brick architecture, high chimneys, and gables of the Dutch-begotten Queen Anne style. What makes them good buildings has nothing to do with stylistic reminiscences, they are good because they have a simple and dignified appearance, and because they are planned with purpose rather than with symmetry as the guide. Some of the best examples are in Queen's Gate. The best, I think, are numbers 180 and 185, built in 1885 and 1890, where simplicity, dignity, and planning for purpose are most apparent. The larger house at 170 is designed symmetrically and is less interesting. One of Shaw's best plans was that for the house he built for Edwin Long, at 42 Netherhall Gardens, and which was destroyed about 1937. Probably one of the reasons it was so good a plan is that Long's requirements were rather exacting. On the ground floor the rooms are arranged in convenient sequence, from scullery, kitchen, servants' sitting room, pantry, servery, and dining room, with a long corridor with porch at the side at one end and stairs at the other end. On the upper floor is a large studio and drawing room placed conveniently in relation to each other. There are numerous details in the plan which testify how well thought out it is. As Sir Reginald Blomfield says, 'the plan was an admirable example of skilful planning to meet special requirements. In its way it was one of the best pieces of domestic architecture that Shaw ever did, and illustrates his originality in planning. Instead of following accepted conventional models, Shaw faced each problem on its merits, with full and very alert consciousness of the possibilities of effect latent in his plans when translated into terms of building'[16]. The curious thing is that Shaw later restricted his freedom to 'face each problem on its merits' by returning to the symmetrical convention, and Blomfield approves this change.

The work of C. F. A. Voysey (born 1857) is the product of the same spirit and belongs to the same movement as that of Webb and the best work of Shaw. His best work is at least equal to the best work of Webb, and some critics would regard it as representing the finest achievement in domestic architecture in Europe for the period, from about 1888 to about 1908. Like the work of Webb, Voysey's houses were not designed to follow any particular style, but were the product of simple, direct, and honest building. Voysey used materials well, his houses have simple exteriors, with a generous and effective use of plain surfaces; none of Shaw's sham half-timber work. He had a liking for stuccoed or whitewashed treatments. He planned his houses strictly according to the purpose they had to serve, and the majority have the convenient chain of rooms, formed as an L or E, and orientated with thought of the sun. Also he wedded his houses satisfactorily to the garden setting, and his planning generally continued with the garden; thus he is a link, unconsciously perhaps, between Ludwig Persius and Frank Lloyd Wright. A particularly good example of his work is The Homestead, Frinton-on-Sea. It is planned as an L, the parlour and dining room being along one arm, running north and south, with the kitchen and scullery in the other arm, running east–west, with the garden designed as part of the plan. Other good examples are Perrycroft, Colwall (1893), a house at Sackleford, in Surrey (1897), The Pastures, North Suffenham, Rutland (1901), and his own home, The Orchard, at Chorleywood (1899). It will be noted in Voysey's houses that the elevations are generally less symmetrical than either Webb's or Shaw's. They are dictated very largely by the plans, and are an expression of the natural arrangement of each house. More than with any houses of their time it is possible to tell internal arrangement by the appearance of the exterior.

Webb, Shaw, and Voysey were the three chief architects of domestic buildings in Europe from about 1860 to 1905. No other European architects built houses in that period at all comparable with theirs. Their influence in Europe has been wide and profound. In England they were followed by a very large number of architects, who, though producing many good works up to 1919, added nothing to their achievements, but merely produced variations on their themes. Among their most successful followers in the field of domestic architecture in England were Baillie Scott, C. R. Ashbee, W. R. Lethaby, P. Morley Horder, Arnold Mitchell, A. N. Prentice, Sir Edwin L. Lutyens, and Ernest Newton. The influence is seen in smaller houses designed for repetition in numbers. Rarely does the work of these architects reach the standard of Webb, Shaw, and Voysey, but being mainly actuated by the same principles of functional design, and simple, direct, and efficient use of materials, it is generally good work. With Baillie Scott's houses there is a somewhat conscious looking back to the small medieval country house, repeating many of its features without sufficient reference to modern purposes. There is a tendency in his houses to revive the hall as the central feature with smaller rooms grouped round. In the plan of a house that he published in *The Studio* of 1900 the hall is the large central room with other rooms grouped round, and the rooms are significantly called refectory, bower, den, instead of dining room, drawing room, and study.

Some architects, like Sir Edwin Lutyens and Ernest Newton, seem to find it difficult to resist the impulse to make symmetrical plans and elevations. In the case of Ernest Newton, though many of the plans are good, they are restricted in freedom by this symmetry, and with Sir Edwin Lutyens's houses, although in many of the plans convenience of arrangement was considered, the elevations are symmetrical, which often means some discord of the two. A significant example is an early work: Mount Blow, Great Shelford, where the symmetrical fenestration does not correspond with the more irregular arrangement of the rooms. This passion for symmetrical elevations means that he sometimes puts odd little windows into rooms, which are not explained from the interior, the reason for their insertion only becoming apparent when the exterior symmetrical elevation is seen.

As previously indicated, English domestic architecture from 1860 to 1905 had a profound influence on many continental architects, especially in Germany, Austria, France, Holland, and Belgium. Hermann Muthesius, the German architect, had spent some time in England from about 1898 to 1903, and he was full of enthusiasm for English domestic architecture—an enthusiasm he imparted to his fellow German architects in several books. *Die englische Baukunst der Gegenwart* was published in Leipzig in 1900, *Dasenglisc he Haus* in Berlin in 1904, and *Kunstgewerbe und Architektur*, in which there is a chapter on *Das englisc he Haus*, in Jena in 1907.

The influence of English domestic architecture on the Continent before Muthesius wrote his books is not easy to assess, but many houses in Germany, Austria, France, and Belgium appear to show its influence. Belgium offers an interesting parallel to the building of the Red House in Henry Van de Velde's house in the Avenue van der Raye, at Uccle, a suburb of Brussels. When Van de Velde married, he built himself a house between 1893 and 1895, about thirty-five years after the Red House, and finding, like Morris, contemporary interior decoration and furnishing of a very low quality in design, he designed them himself. It would appear that building and furnishing his own house, because nothing in contemporary art was of an artistic standard that he required, was the result of Morris's example. Sigfried Giedion does not think that Van de Velde followed Morris's example, but rather that 'identical conditions led to identical reactions'[17]. Van de Velde probably knew about the Red House and its furnishing, and it may have prompted similar action. The conditions in Belgium were not dissimilar from those in England thirty years earlier, for Belgium was one of the earliest of continental countries to become industrialized.

One of the notable German architects, whose domestic work appears to show English influence, is Peter Behrens. Like Van de Velde and many other famous architects he began as a painter, and later turned to designing objects of use of all kinds from buildings to teacups. In 1901 Behrens built himself a house at Darmstadt, and this represents his first building. It is not improbable that the design of this house, with its emphasis on verticals and its curved gables, was influenced by C. R. Mackintosh.

Peter Behren's house at Darmsdadt designed by himself 1901

Behrens followed this with several houses, all somewhat in the English style, up to about 1910; among them a house at Wetter in the Ruhr (1904), the Haus Obenauer at Saarbrücken (1905), and two houses in the Eppenhaus Garden Suburb at Hagen (1908 and 1910)[18]. The last two are conceived on formal and symmetrical principles, but the others, like the best English houses, are determined by convenience and have irregular plans and groupings of the various parts. One of the best, the Haus Obenauer, clearly shows Voysey's influence, and like Voysey's houses it has large, plain, white walls. Compared with English contemporary work, a slightly more adventurous treatment is found in these houses, in the very large windows employed for the principal living rooms, and in some cases, for example the house at Wetter, almost a glass wall, thus bringing light and air into the room to a greater degree than before. This is a significant advance.

In buildings other than houses the development towards a living, expressive, and functional architecture was later in starting. It was probably as the result of the example of domestic architecture that freer planning for public and commercial buildings began; but also, I think, because the crowding of buildings in London and other big cities presented awkward sites for new buildings, and symmetrical plans were often impossible, while the sites were sometimes so awkward that the problem of fitting the parts into a desirable sequence made the employment of classical formalism very difficult. It is interesting to note that some of the best plans from about 1885 to 1914 were evolved in this way. As is so often the case in art, it would seem that the severer the restrictions the more ingenious the design. (One of Norman Shaw's best plans was the outcome of exacting demands.) The Bishopsgate Institute, built by C. H. Townsend in 1892–4, is an example. The site is long and awkward with a small frontage to Bishopsgate between other buildings, and in this area a large hall, lending and reference libraries have been provided on the ground floor in sequence along a corridor, from which stairs ascend to a large reading room on the first floor. The difficulties of the site have been well overcome. In his Whitechapel Art Gallery (1897–9) C. H. Townsend had more freedom, but he has employed symmetry here only where it suits purpose as well as a less formal arrangement. In the elevation, for example, the upper part is symmetrical, but he places the entrance to one side, to allow for an exit to the right. To have had the entrance in the centre would have meant, to the architect, some sacrifice of the efficient fulfilment of purpose.

The Glasgow School of Art, by C. R. Mackintosh, is often claimed as one of the pioneer works of a living, modern architecture, and there is justice in the claim; but to say that it is the first building of the new architecture or the first modern building is an extravagant claim. It is one of many pioneer works produced between 1890 and 1914 which laid the foundations of the new architecture[19]. In the earlier part, built in 1898–9, there is, as in Townsend's work, a combination of the symmetrical and asymmetrical, and the building is designed excellently for the purpose it is to serve, with very large windows, as is required by an art school. There is an economy of ornament, and the structure is not concealed but is rather made the most of and taken as a decorative motif as in the gallery supports of the library. Its value is that, like Webb's houses, it is direct, honest building where purpose guides its design and where structure and materials are frankly revealed and themselves supply the decorative motifs.

The departure from the formal symmetrical plan we have noted in Labrouste's Bibliothèque Nationale, built between 1858 and 1868. Such departures throughout Europe up to the last decade of the nineteenth century were rare exceptions to the general rule. When they did occur it was generally in smaller buildings which had to fit awkward sites in congested areas of cities, and the virtue of the irregular plan arose out of necessity as in the case of the Bishopsgate Institute. But during the nineties, and more in the early twentieth century, partially as a result of the example of the English house and of a weakening of the classical tradition of symmetry, the plan dictated more exclusively by convenience was gradually becoming a more conscious aim. The house at 12 Rue de Turin, in Brussels, built by Victor Horta in 1893, famous for its *Art Nouveau* decorations, shows a remarkable organization of interior space. It is a long, narrow site between other houses, and although the front part of the ground floor is symmetrical, in the remainder this symmetry is abandoned for more convenient planning, while rooms are related at half-storey levels so as to get the maximum accommodation in so limited a space. In his House of the People, at Brussels, built in 1897, Horta has evolved even more flexible planning for an awkward but much more spacious site. This building is also significant as a notable pioneer work in iron and glass construction. The Amsterdam Stock Exchange building erected from 1898 to 1903, by H. P. Berlage, is another building which shows this growing freedom in planning, and examples become commoner every year. A building like the administrative headquarters of the Mannesmann Tube Company, Düsseldorf (1911), by Peter Behrens, represents an interesting advance in functional planning because the size of the rooms is determined by space required for the free and efficient movement of a team of clerks, and this office unit is repeated, and determines the use and size of standardized steel stanchions. The plan results largely from considerations like this. The growing freedom of interior space designing was to be greatly assisted by the increasing use of steel, concrete, and glass.

The influence of Otto Wagner is important in the movement towards a living architecture, especially in his teaching. In 1894, when 53 years of age, he became professor of architecture at a Vienna Academy. So far he had produced buildings in the Renaissance tradition generally with a tendency towards more and more simplification. But his teaching at the Academy, the essence of which is contained in a book entitled *Moderne Architektur*, published in Vienna in 1895, is not based on his earlier practice. He, like Schinkel and Labrouste many years before, felt the need for an architecture that emerged from and expressed contemporary life. He believed in the use of materials that modern industry could provide, and in an honest expression of these materials. He also believed that objects could not be beautiful unless they were well fitted for their purpose. Amongst his later works there is some exemplification of his principles, the block of flats in the Neustiftgasse, Vienna (1902), and the Post Office Savings Bank in Vienna (1904–6) being among the best examples. He rarely departs, however, from classical symmetry in his planning. His teaching raised considerable opposition amongst conservative and academic thought, yet many of his pupils later became important figures, and his teaching contributed to laying the foundation of a great school of modern architecture.

REFERENCES AND NOTES

1. Quoted by Walter Curt Behrendt in *Modern Building*, London, 1937, p. 39.
2. Reproduced in Bruno Taut's *Modern Architecture*, London, 1929, p. 35.
3. Souvenirs d'Henri Labrouste. Notes recueillies et classées par ses enfants (Paris, 1928, privately printed), p. 24, quoted in Sigfried Giedion's *Space, Time and Architecture*, Cambridge, USA, 1941, p. 154.
4. W. R. Lethaby, *Philip Webb and his Work*, London, 1926, p. 128.
5. In addition to the monumental buildings in the Greek style for which Schinkel is mainly known, he designed a villa like a medieval castle for Prince Wilhelm at Potsdam and made several other projects of a like nature.
6. Some reference is made to Persius' work in Walter Curt Behrendt's *Modern Building*, London, 1937, pp. 43, 47.
7. The Revival of Architecture, *Fortnightly Review*, 1888.
8. Art Under Plutocracy. Lecture at Oxford, 14 Nobember 1883.
9. The Revival of Architecture, *Fortnightly Review*, 1888.
10. W. R. Lethaby, *Philip Webb and his Work*, London, 1935, p. 94.
11. This house is described by W. R. Lethaby in his book on *Philip Webb and his Work*, London, 1935, p. 95.
12. W. R. Lethaby, *Philip Webb and his Work*, London, 1935, p. 101.
13. W. R. Lethaby, *Philip Webb and his Work*, London, 1935, p. 117.
14. W. R. Lethaby, *Philip Webb and his Work*, London, 1935, p. 122.
15. W. R. Lethaby, *Philip Webb and his Work*, London, 1935, p. 119.
16. Sir Reginald Blomfield, *Richard Norman Shaw*, London, 1940, p. 44.
17. Sigfried Giedion in his book *Space, Time and Architecture*, Cambridge, USA, 1941, p. 217.
18. These houses are illustrated in the *Architectural Review*, vol. lxxxvi, August 1934, pp. 40 and 42, and September 1934, p. 84.
19. This term is employed in the sense that it is used by Walter Gropius, Eric Mendelsohn, and others of its exponents. It is not an ideal term, but it is a concise designation of what is regarded as a living architecture expressive of man's social, scientific, and industrial progress.

4   *The search for a style—Art Nouveau*

FOR THE LAST twenty years of the nineteenth century Brussels was one of the chief
centres of European art, and was more liberal in its attitude to new movements and
young artists than any other European capital. It welcomed Cézanne, van Gogh,
Seurat, Rodin, and others, and was a centre for the development of ideas and
movements. It was here that *Art Nouveau*[1] was born and Henri Van de Velde and
Victor Horta are usually regarded as its authors[2]. It was part of the general effort to
originate an art which was not dependent on historical styles, and it manifests as an
art of rhythmical lines and appears in many forms of plastic and pictorial art from
book illustration to architecture. Its first conspicuous manifestation in architecture was
in the decorations of the house in the Rue de Turin, Brussels (1892–3), designed by
Victor Horta, mentioned in the last chapter. Here the iron columns and balustrade
and the wall decorations consist of flowing rhythmical lines. In Horta's later work, the
House of the People in Brussels (1896–9), also mentioned in the last chapter, the
decoration is still of a similar character, especially in the balcony railings of the hall,
but it is much more restrained.

There are many speculations on the origin of the style. The decorations of Horta's
House bear closest resemblance to the tendrils of plants, and these might have
provided suggestions, but they do not explain why such decoration is employed.
Giedion[3] thinks it is the linear decoration of iron constructions: 'the unrolled curls and
rosettes that are to be found under the eaves of so many Belgian railway stations.'
But these are of a much more confined, conventional, and static character, and could
hardly prompt the free linear rhythms of *Art Nouveau*. It is possibly another legacy of
medieval and early Renaissance art, and is really a late development of the Pre-
Raphaelite movement. In turning to early Italian painters for inspiration the
Pre-Raphaelites inevitably became aware of the decorative value of linear rhythms
apparent in early Sienese painters like Duccio and Simone Martini, and in later
Florentine painters like Fra Filippo Lippi, in whose pupil Botticelli, linear rhythms
became an important decorative aim, associated, it must be remembered, with the

development in Florentine painting to express movement. In those reliefs of the fifteenth-century sculptor Agostino di Duccio which represent angels playing musical instruments, there is clearly an attempt to express musical rhythms in the lines of the angels' draperies, and these rhythms are as extravagant as any in Renaissance art. Rossetti's early work shows the influence not only of Botticelli but of Fra Filippo Lippi and Benozzo Gozzoli; but there is no doubt that Burne-Jones evolved his linear patterns under the spell of Botticelli. Also the Pre-Raphaelites were greatly influenced by the drawings of William Blake, where line is used almost as rhythmically as in Botticelli's work. The work of Rossetti and Burne-Jones led on to Aubrey Beardsley, while the Pre-Raphaelite influence in many German, Belgian, and Dutch artists like Ferdinand Hodler, Fernand Khnooff, and Jan Toorop, in which the use of line as a major motif in design, may have provided one of the origins of *Art Nouveau*. As an example of the influence of the Pre-Raphaelites on the Continent it is interesting to look at a decoration by Otto Eckmann of a page of the magazine *Pan*[4], which has a head after Rossetti and leaf decoration after Morris. If Eckmann did not know the work of Rossetti and Morris his decorations represent a remarkable artistic parallel.

At this time music was exerting some influence on the sister art of painting, as may be seen in the work of Whistler, where tones and colours were related and pictures were conceived very much under the influence of thought in terms of music. Music also clearly had some influence on the rhythms in Rossetti's and Burne-Jones's pictures—how often are dreamy women depicted playing musical instruments. In a picture like Rossetti's *The Bower Meadow*, it is not only the dance but the all-pervading music which influences the rhythms.

One expression in England which had more the character of an adopted artificial form of decoration imported from Belgium as distinct from its direct evolution from Rossetti, Burne-Jones, and Beardsley, is in the decorations to the Cranston tea rooms at Buchanan Street, Glasgow, in 1897, by C. R. Mackintosh and George Walton. In the three subsequent Cranston tea rooms the linear character of the decoration is not so pronounced. In Mackintosh's other decorative work the liking for fanciful line is apparent, and this influence may have been responsible for Mackintosh's exaggeration of verticals in backs of chairs and in the linear emphasis of structural members in the Glasgow School of Art.

One of the principal contributions of *Art Nouveau* to architecture emerges in the work of Van de Velde. Since the publication of Darwin's *Origin of Species* in 1859, theories of evolution and of the development of organic life were more and more influencing European thought, and it had some influence on thinking architects, among whom were Gottfried Semper, the German architect, and Van de Velde, who expressed his indebtedness to Semper's teaching[5]. Van de Velde tries to associate the linear rhythms of *Art Nouveau* with structure, and he tried to think of rhythmical lines as lines of force. Thus in the furniture and decorations he designed for his house at Uccle, the tables and chairs all have curved supports, and staircase balustrades he made curved instead of straight. A later work, the Theatre, which he designed for the Cologne Exhibition of 1914, shows a similar predilection for curved forms[6]. He was fortified in this by the belief that organic forms are of this kind. Van de Velde expressed in architecture and decoration what van Gogh expressed in painting.

From 1878 to 1886 van Gogh was chiefly in Belgium and he exerted some influence on Belgian art of the nineties. In van Gogh's painting there is apparent an intense apprehension of the life and colour of the natural world, of the growth of trees and flowers and grass, and of the shimmering atmosphere. It is this essential rhythmical life of the organic world that Van de Velde tries to incorporate into his designs of buildings and furnishings. From this there develops the idea of organic unity as a principle of architectural design which has been one of the principal creeds of some of the best modern architecture. Van de Velde's work and theories lead on to the work of Eric Mendelsohn, of whom Van de Velde is reported to have said: 'I have found a follower at last'.[7] There was a parallel line of thought, with certain differences, in America in the theories and work of Louis Sullivan and Frank Lloyd Wright, the latter of whom had considerable influence in Europe, first in the Netherlands, then in Germany and later in other countries.

Art Nouveau spread from Belgium and England to other parts of Europe, to France, Germany, Austria, The Netherlands, Italy and Spain, and it acquired various names in these countries. In Belgium it was often called by the expressive names of coup de touet (whiplash) and paling (eel) styles; in England the modern style; in France it was sometimes called style nouille (noodle style) or style Guimard, after the architect Hector Guimard; in Germany it was called Jugendstil (youth style) from the name of the periodical Jugend; and sometimes by the expressive terms: Lilienstil (lily style) and Wellenstil (wave style). In Austria it was associated with the Sezession group and received that name; in Italy it was known as Stile Floreale or Stile Liberty, because of the designs sold in Liberty's shop in The Strand, London; in Spain it was called Modernismo.

The chief French architectural exponent of *Art Nouveau* was Hector Guimard (1867–1942) who designed, in the early years of the century, an apartment block, called Castel Beranger in Rue La Fontaine, Passy, which has several curved forms and decoration typical of the movement. He also designed several typical houses of which the most notable is the Castel Henriette (1903) with its asymmetrical curves, tree forms and contrasting stone finish. His most dramatic display of *Art Nouveau* decoration is, however, in the well-known and familiar entrances to the Paris Metro. Other French architects that show in their designs strong *Art Nouveau* influence are Xavier Schoellkopf, especially in Yvette Guilbert's house in the Boulevard Berthier,

43

Paris, with its curly ornate façade; and Jules Lavirotte whose building in the Avenue Rapp, Paris, shows a very richly ornamented *Art Nouveau* entrance.

In Germany *Art Nouveau* manifested much less vigorously than in France, and few German architects seem to have been greatly influenced by it. Alfred Messel's Wertheim Store (1896) has sometimes been cited as an example, and if so, it is a very restrained one. Its influence is more strongly apparent in Austria, especially among the artists of the Viennese Sezession, of whom the chief were Gustav Klimt, Josef Hoffmann, Otto Eckmann, Hermann Obrist and Joseph Olbrich, of whom the last mentioned made the most significant contribution to *Art Nouveau* architecture. In 1898 he designed the Sezession exhibition building in Vienna which has a simplified square block of slightly classical character surmounted by an ornate floreated dome, like a trimmed laurel bush, as Maurice Rheims describes it[8]. The principal *Art Nouveau* motif in this building, however, is the tree-like decorations on the side walls.

The Grand Duke Ernst Ludwig of Hesse was a notable patron of the arts at the time of the *Art Nouveau* movement, and wishing to found a colony of artists in Darmstadt he invited several architects to design buildings for the purpose—the Mathildenhohe, and houses for artists. Olbrich, Behrens, Christiansen and Huber were the principal architects who went to Darmstadt. Olbrich designed four houses, one of which is illustrated and shows clearly the influence of *Art Nouveau* in the curved shapes and the decoration on the walls. Behrens designed a house for himself and Olbrich also designed the large house for the Grand Duke Ernst Ludwig, with its impressive *Art Nouveau* entrance porch flanked by two massive and rather overwhelming figures. The group of architects mentioned were responsible for the Mathildenhohe Complex of buildings, the Hochzeitsturm (Wedding Tower) being the design of Olbrich. The curious five-figured pinnacle represents a hand symbolizing the marriage of the Grand Duke Ernst Ludwig and Eleanore von Solms-Lich. It hardly makes a beautiful shape but approximations to it have been repeated since.

Art Nouveau manifested strongly in Italy, particularly in Milan and Turin, much of the work being done by unrecorded architects. Much of it is a mixture of *Art Nouveau* motifs with a highly ornate surface decoration as in Giuseppe Sommarugas' Casa Castiglioni (1901) in the Corso Venezia, Milan. Distinctive and typical *Art Nouveau* treatment where the curves and patterns characteristic of the style are apparent appeared in two of the buildings by Raimondo D'Aronco at the Turin Exhibition of 1902, the Central Rotunda and the Pavilion of Decorative Arts. A distinctively *Art Nouveau* house is at 99 Via Scipione-Ammirato, Florence, designed by Michelazzi (1901) in which the flowing curves over the windows and entrances have something of the character of drapery. Although all the arches are different a pleasing harmony is achieved which makes this one of the most beautiful of *Art Nouveau* houses.

Sezession exhibition building, Vienna, 1898

House at Darmstadt, 1906

Architect: Joseph Olbrich

Mathildenhohe building with the Hochzeitsturm
(Wedding Tower), Darmstadt, 1907

Entrance to the house of the Grand
Duke Ernst Ludwig, Darmstadt, 1902

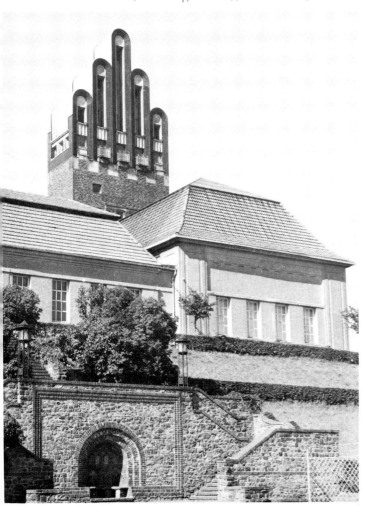

In Spain the most distinctive *Art Nouveau* works in architecture emanate from that strange and original architectural genius Antonio Gaudi. A brief description of his most famous work, the Church of the Sagrada Familia, has already been given in Chapter 2, Eclecticism. The design of this church is the result of many influences and ideas fused by the architect's genius, and *Art Nouveau* was one of many motifs. The period of the most marked manifestation of *Art Nouveau* in Gaudi's work is from about 1902 to 1909 and is seen most conspicuously in the Casa Batillo (1905–1907) and the Casa Mila (1905–1909) both in Barcelona. In both there is an association of *Art Nouveau* rhythms with natural forms seen in such features as the tree-like forms of the mullions of the first floor windows, and the fern-like balcony fronts of the Casa Batillo, and again in the massive trunk-like columns and simulation of foliage of the balcony fronts of the Casa Mila. In both he uses a great variety of materials, stone, brick, ceramic tiles, iron, timber, very expressively, and it is notable that he employs parabolic arches in the attics of both buildings.

There was a tendency in much historical and critical writing between 1930 and 1950 to contend that the influence of *Art Nouveau* died about 1908 and had little subsequent effect on the development of art and architecture. This may have been the case in the 20 year period mentioned, but it was not so before and after that period. *Art Nouveau* had some influence on the German Expressionist school which was probably one of the contributory causes of the Surrealist movement; Art Nouveau also probably contributed to the development and encouragement of abstract painting of the twentieth century, and probably had some effect on the line of thought that led to the theory of organic unity in architecture. It contributed by its example to the formation of the Deutscher Werkbund in 1907, formed largely in protest against following historical styles in the production of objects of everyday use, and with a view to prompting the design of these objects in accordance with the needs of the time. Its founders were willing to use modern machinery for the purpose. This represented a reconciliation of art and the machine, more successful than anything Morris had achieved; but Morris in his maturer thought contended that machinery was to be accepted if it made men's lives easier, and that he was antagonistic to its improper use rather than to the machine itself. And it was Fischer's argument at the first meeting of the Deutscher Werkbund that it was our inability to use machines well that made machine work inferior. The example of the Deutscher Werkbund partially prompted the formation of the Design and Industries Association in 1915 but, more importantly, it led to Gropius's Bauhaus in 1919.

A revival of interest in *Art Nouveau* in all its forms began about 1955, and numerous books were written on the subject and several exhibitions held. In these later appraisals of the work of the movement it was realized that a considerable number of very distinctive works of art were created in the rhythms of *Art Nouveau* and the movement is not without influence on many of the decorative patterns of the sixties.

Three such masterpieces as Mendelsohn's Einstein Observatory at Potsdam, Rudolf Steiner's Goetheanum at Dornach and Le Corbusier's Romchamp Chapel owe something to both *Art Nouveau* and Expressionism.

School of Applied Art,
Weimar, 1906
Architect: Henry Van de Velde

REFERENCES AND NOTES

1. The movement was known by different names in different countries mentioned later in the chapter.
2. The actual originator of the movement is not very apparent. Nikolaus Pevsner, *Pioneers of the Modern Movement*, London, 1936, p. 99 ff., gives first prominence to Horta, although he acknowledges Van de Velde's contributions. Walter Curt Behrendt in his accounts of *Art Nouveau in Modern Building*, London, 1937, does not even mention Horta.
3. Sigfried Giedion, *Space, Time and Architecture*, Harvard University Press, Cambridge, USA, 1941, pp. 224–225.
4. Reproduced in Nikolaus Pevsner's *Pioneers of the Modern Movement*, London, 1936, p. 112.
5. Mainly contained in *Der Stil in den technischen und tektonischen Kunsten*, Munich, 1863.
6. In this theatre Van de Velde eliminated the sharp separation between stage and auditorium that had become customary in theatre design, and conceived the whole as one room with the stage the same width as the auditorium.
7. Eric Mendelsohn himself told me this. These may not be the actual words, but I have reproduced the sense as I remember it.
8. Maurice Rheims, *The Age of Art Nouveau*, Paris, 1965, English translation 1966. This is one of the most complete and profusely illustrated books on *Art Nouveau* in which all the various fields of visual art in which it manifested are included.

47

5   *Towards simplicity*

ONE OF THE STRONGEST and most widespread movements in the search for an architecture that should emerge from and express contemporary life was the somewhat negative movement towards simplicity. The movement was spreading at the end of the nineteenth century and was familiar in most European countries during the early years of the twentieth century. It was an attempt to purify architecture, to remove the accretions of style, to get back to simple and direct building so as to form a fresh starting-point for the architectural expression of the spiritual, social, and economic life of the time. It manifested in most branches of architecture, in ecclesiastical, commercial, administrative, and domestic buildings. In industrial buildings its manifestation was less apparent, because such buildings in the nineteenth century, being more strictly utilitarian, were more generally examples of direct building for purpose without being designed in an historical style, and without stylistic ornament. In the early nineteenth century the really living architecture was found in factories and warehouses. We find, too, that progress in building construction and the more extensive use of new materials often develops sooner in industrial buildings than in other types. To these must be added buildings, like railway stations, where utility generally decisively overrides considerations of appearance.

It was in Holland and Austria that the early stages of the movement towards simplicity were most vigorous and produced the most outstanding results. A little later the movement appeared with excellent examples in Germany and Sweden, and still later it spread decisively over the whole of Europe, although the Mediterranean countries were the slowest to receive the influence.

This movement, however, really originates with the English school of domestic architecture from 1859 onwards, in which we find the return to simple, direct, honest building and the expressive use of materials, and with the work and example of the Dutch Gothic revivalist architect P. J. H. Cuypers, and with Otto Wagner in Vienna. Before Cuypers, who was active between 1850 and 1890, much Dutch architecture was of a very ornamental kind with stucco façades. Cuypers's Gothic was a simple type, but the value of his work lay chiefly in his uncovering the brick behind the stucco and using materials frankly and expressively. Cuypers's work led to a fresh valuation in Holland of the aesthetic claims of constructional materials. In the work of many Dutch architects of the early twentieth century there is a returning delight in brick—the traditional building material of the country—and in the plain brick wall. Dutch buildings between 1898 and 1917, in which this movement towards simplicity is apparent, are the New Exchange, Amsterdam, by H. P. Berlage, previously mentioned, the Headquarters of the Diamond Workers' Trade Union, Amsterdam (1900), also by Berlage; the Hotel American, Amsterdam (1900), by W. Kronnhout, which, though eclectic with a mixture of Romanesque, Gothic, and even Arabic elements, shows a distinct tendency towards broad treatment and general simplicity; the Barracks at Nymegen (1908) by J. Limburg, broad and simple in treatment with a dome suggesting Byzantine influence; the Observation House for children at Amsterdam (1910) by Jan de Meyer, symmetrical, simple, and restrained; and the Federation of Sailors' Building at Den Helder (1914) by P. Kramer, simple, massive, and square, in which there is a nice adjustment of horizontals and verticals. The blocks of flats by M. de Klerk, built during his short career show this movement, each successive block or group becoming simpler than its predecessor. The Housing Blocks, built in 1913 and 1914, and the Post Office Housing Block, built in 1917, both at Amsterdam, are broad and simple in treatment, yet with numerous picturesque elements like odd curved-headed windows, circular projecting features, and decorative notes on the plain surface of the wall. M. de Klerk's post-war work (see Chapter 12) becomes simpler still with a very sparing use of those picturesque features which the average Dutchman finds it difficult to relinquish.

It is, however, the work of Berlage that had the greatest influence in Europe in the early years of the century, due mainly to the Amsterdam Stock Exchange building. Reference has been made to its plan, while it has an interesting iron and glass roof, but it is no less important as a building which is an early example of the sloughing of stylistic and ornamental accretions and of the use of the plain brick wall as an element in design. In the interior, flat, elliptical arches are supported by square, brick pillars, and stone blocks flush with the pillars serve as capitals. This illustrated part of Berlage's creed that 'we should show the naked wall in all its sleek beauty—pillars and columns should have no projecting capitals: the joint should be fused with the flat surface of the wall'[1].

This trend in Dutch architecture is seen in Germany and Sweden. In the latter country there are considerable similarities with Dutch work, especially in the use of plain brick walls, but there are usually traditional Swedish features which distinguish the buildings, such as the Baroque octagonal domed turrets and the onion domes. A good example of this trend towards simplicity and the use of large expanses

Town Hall, Östersund, Sweden, completed 1912   *Architect: I. Wallberg*

City Law Court, Stockholm, completed 1913
                    Architect: Carl Westman

University of Technology, Stockholm, 1914–1922
general view from the entrance to the main court
                    Architect: Eric Lallerstedt

of plain brick wall is the Town Hall of Ostersund, designed by Wallberg, and completed in 1912. It is a symmetrical building with projecting wings and a large central tower-like structure surmounted by an octagonal onion dome, and although there are small decorative features like small arched string-courses, the plain brick walls contribute much to the general effect. Another Swedish building, completed about the the same time (1915), that provides a kindred example is the City Law Courts at Stockholm, by Carl Westman, which was probably partly inspired by the sixteenth-century castle of Vadstena and is symptomatic of the Swedish tendency prevalent at this time towards the perpetuation of traditional national architecture. It is broadly and simply treated with large areas of plain brick wall and with decorative features and stone dressings appearing on a few focal points like the main entrance. Sir Reginald Blomfield thought this building 'the finest piece of modern architecture in Stockholm'[2]. In his description of it he says that 'the tower rises sheer from the front wall of the building without that break forward which an ordinary designer would almost certainly have given it. The buildings terminate at either end in plain gable, there is no particular detail anywhere to arrest the eye, and I believe that it is this concentration on the essential qualities of architecture, the abstinence from irrelevant detail, the noble scale, and the deliberate austerity of the design that makes this building so impressive.' Work of a similar kind continued in Sweden during the following twenty years.

The movement towards simplicity in England had begun with the domestic architecture of Philip Webb and Voysey and some of their followers. The first larger building, other than industrial, that shows a big step in this direction, in which historical styles are sloughed, is the Glasgow School of Art. In the early years of the twentieth century the movement towards simplicity was spreading, although in most building it was tentative with a partial elimination of ornament. Among the buildings conspicuous for greater simplicity are those of H. Percy Adams and the architects associated with him. Adams shows an appreciation of the value of plain walls, whether stone or brick. Two good examples of his work, completed in 1906, are the Royal Victoria Infirmary, Newcastle-upon-Tyne (in conjunction with W. Lister Newcombe), and the King Edward VII Sanatorium, Midhurst, Sussex. There are obvious differences in these buildings, the former has a restrained admixture of classical elements, while the latter is derived somewhat from seventeenth-century English domestic work, but they are both characterized by large, plain brick walls, the former with stone dressings. A slightly later work, which Adams designed in conjunction with Charles Holden in 1911, is the Bristol Royal Infirmary extension, in which a degree of simplicity is achieved that contemporary critics regarded as unpleasantly severe. It is a symmetrical design conceived in the classical spirit, while its plainness and its dependence for effect on the relations of plain masses represent a decided movement towards an architecture freed from historical styles and ornament.

Otto Wagner's contribution to the movement was significant. As he develops from his

51

traditionally Renaissance early work, his designs become simpler with less and less ornament, so that the classical columns with bases and capitals of a portico become simply plain, square shafts, as may be seen in the Stiftung Lupusheilstatte, Mittelbau. As his book *Moderne Architektur* shows, he became interested in the geometrizing of architectural forms, and contended that all such forms should conform to geometric principles. He seemed to think that good proportion and great architecture could only come into being by conformity with geometric law, a creed that has had great influence in some modern European architectural developments. Otto Wagner's own work shows the steady tendency towards greater simplicity, the already mentioned Vienna Post Office Savings Bank and the flats in the Neustiftgasse, Vienna, being the best-known examples. The former, though broad and simple, still has traces of Renaissance influence in the grooved masonry, and in the application of sculpture; the same reminiscence remains with the latter, but here there is a more complete deletion of ornament. These buildings may or may not have been designed in accord with the geometric principles Wagner advocated. They are certainly well proportioned, and the windows are happily spaced on the façades.

Among the numerous architects whom Wagner influenced were many who continued this movement towards simplicity and who were influenced by his geometric theories. When Joseph Hoffmann designed the Purkersdorff Sanatorium, in 1903, he was encouraged by the example of Wagner, for this building has plain stucco walls, unadorned window openings, and a purified appearance, that was not only rare at the time but reached a degree of external simplicity that Wagner even did not achieve. This was Hoffmann's first important building (he was born in 1870), but it is not typical of his work. He had a liking for ornament, and the majority of his buildings display a free and original adaptation of the Renaissance style. The famous Palais Stoclet, in Brussels, built in 1906, has a certain kinship with the Purkersdorff Sanatorium, as it has large expanses of plain wall, but there are numerous ornamental features, and the tower is surmounted by elaborate sculptured ornaments. The design of the Purkersdorff Sanatorium was probably influenced by economic considerations, and by the utilitarian character of the building; nevertheless, it represents a considerable step towards the simple yet effective treatment of façades where artistic quality depends on the relation of squarish masses and on the spacing and proportions of the windows. In his later work, after the First World War, he occasionally returns to this early simplicity, but not with the same exclusiveness.

It is, however, to Adolf Loos, perhaps more than to any architect of the early twentieth century, that we owe the most outstanding advance in the direction of simplicity. The simplicity of his buildings, of the exteriors rather than the interiors, was due to his professed objection to ornament. His well-known passionate declaration in a Viennese café that 'ornament is a crime' is no exaggeration of his attitude, although it is not easy to reconcile this with many of his interiors and furnishings where certain ornamental features appear. These interiors, however, are very English in character, and demonstrate his great enthusiasm for English domestic architecture, principally that of Webb, Voysey, and their followers. It is possible, too, that his campaign against ornament may have been influenced by this English domestic architecture, for the exteriors of Voysey's houses are examples of a fine and tasteful simplicity. Loos[3] also felt that architecture should not be regarded so much as an art, but rather as the craft of building, and if ornament grew legitimately out of some types of building in the past, he failed to see how it could emerge from the modern architecture of steel and concrete where the machine plays an increasing part.

Loos's early work consisted principally of houses, and we find that these were designed with severely plain walls and flat roofs and have generally a cubic appearance. His window openings are not formally and symmetrically placed unless this arrangement is as convenient as any other; convenience rather than symmetry or proportion determines their placing. A good example of one of his houses is that designed for Doctor Scheu, in Vienna in 1902. A certain irregularity can be noted in the placing of the windows, while at one side the house is set back storey by storey.

Loos did not apparently adopt geometric principles of design, like Wagner, but he probably influenced certain later movements in that direction. Contemporary with the early work of Loos was the cubist movement in painting. This probably originated with Cézanne, although Cézanne cannot himself be regarded as a cubist. Cézanne appeared to believe that the essential basis of all natural forms is geometric, for he contended that 'everything in nature is shaped according to the sphere, cone and cylinder'. The influence of Cézanne, especially after his death in 1906, was extensive and profound, and to many painters, in the two decades after his death, his sayings were rather in the nature of oracles. There is no doubt that his emphasis on the solidity of objects in his own paintings, and the influence of the saying quoted, were powerful contributory factors in the cubist movement, which may be said to have begun about the time of Cézanne's death. The movement was away from the picture of natural forms and towards the conversion of these forms to geometric solids, or to abstract designs. The followers of the movement were able to elicit support from the Greek passion for geometry, and the belief held by many Greeks that geometric forms were the essential basis of all natural forms, and that the pattern of the universe was a geometric one. Further, Plato's suggestion in the Philebus that geometric forms have an absolute beauty gave additional support. 'I mean', says Socrates, 'that straight lines and curves and the surfaces or solid forms produced out of these by lathes and rulers and squares . . . that these things are not beautiful relatively, like other things, but always, and naturally and absolutely.'[4] This theory of absolute beauty for geometric forms is certainly a great encouragement to cubists and those who design according to geometric law. But the theory of absolute beauty for anything is untenable.

Cubism and the geometric theories that brought it into being have some influence on modern European architecture. Adolf Loos did not design according to geometric principles, but his simple box-like cubic exteriors were contemporary with cubism in painting, and he provided examples for Le Corbusier, who was clearly influenced both by Loos and cubism, and who seems to believe in the absolute right and beauty of design that conforms to geometric law. In 1915 Le Corbusier made a sketch in which terrace houses are grouped on three sides of a square, designed with flat roof and general square effect, the influence of cubes being apparent, and the result is not unlike a simplified version of English Georgian architecture. This tendency is governed by the conviction that all great architecture and design are based on geometric law. Such a movement is assisted in its initial stages by the general movement towards simplicity which had exercised some influence on most European architecture by 1914, and which, by getting rid of past styles, was certainly an important contribution towards an architecture emerging directly from contemporary life.

REFERENCES AND NOTES

1. Berlage, *Gedanken uber Stil in der Baukunst*, Leipzig, 1905, pp. 52–3, quoted by Sigfried Giedion, *Space, Time and Architecture*, Cambridge, USA, 1941, p. 254.
2. Reginald Blomfield, *Byways: Leaves from an Architect's Note-book*, London 1929, p. 274.
3. His opinions are given in his book, *Ins Leere gesprochen (Spoken into Space)*, a collection of essays.
4. Translated by E. F. Carritt, *Philosophies of Beauty*, Oxford, 1931, p. 30.

6 *The early architecture of reinforced concrete*

THE MAJORITY OF early buildings in reinforced concrete were mainly industrial, like factories, grain silos, warehouses, and railway constructions. Its employment in buildings where architecture is more a conscious purpose was more gradual. Many European industrial buildings were built of reinforced concrete in the first decade of its extensive adoption, that is, from about 1894 to 1904, and the majority of these buildings were constructed by the Hennebique method. Among them may be mentioned grain silos at Brest, Strasbourg, Genoa, and Dunston-on-Tyne; the electric power station at Basel; large factories like the Marconi Factory at Genoa, and many warehouses for railway companies, including British companies. These buildings express in their appearance, somewhat timidly perhaps, the method of construction. Some of the interiors hold promise of new architectural effects resulting from the new construction.

Buildings of a more ceremonial character constructed of reinforced concrete during this first decade have generally a more traditional appearance and reveal their construction less. Among them are the Hotel Gallia at Cannes, the Hotel Imperial at Nice, the New York Fire Insurance Company at Paris, the Court House at Messina, and the Hospital Major at Turin. During this period Hennebique built a reinforced concrete house at Bourg-la-Reine, in which he tried to demonstrate the possibilities of his method of construction. The design includes cantilevering of upper floors, and a generous provision of roof gardens.

A noteworthy early expressive use of reinforced concrete appears with Anatole de Baudot's church of Saint-Jean l'Evangéliste, Montmartre, built in 1894. It is constructed of a reinforced concrete frame with thin walls between. The piers and arches of the interior are part of the frame and contribute largely to the decorative character of the church.

Auguste Perret, with whom his brother G. Perret is associated, was one of the first architects to use this method of construction extensively. He used it expressively, so that it determines very largely the design and appearance of his buildings. His first work is the house at 22 Rue Franklin, Paris, where he used a slender reinforced concrete frame, quite adequate for its purpose, as time has shown, but which made the authorities and others apprehensive that it might collapse. The tall, narrow façade of the building, with long, vertical lines, clearly expresses the construction. Another early work of Perret is the garage at Rue de Ponthieu, built in 1905. Here the reinforced concrete frame again determines the design of the façade, which anticipates numerous later buildings, with its square frame and large areas of glass between; while the interior of the garage shows a ferro-concrete balcony construction with post supports that forms the prototype of much that came later.

Reinforced concrete was employed in the buildings for Tony Garnier's 'Cité Industrielle' which was designed in 1901–4. This 'Cité Industrielle', although remaining but an idea, has had considerable influence on town planning, but its present pertinence is that this exercise in ferro-concrete designing laid the foundation of much of Garnier's future practice. Some of the constructions in this scheme, such as that for the Central Railway Station, incorporate developments which were not to be realized until later. As this plan was not published until 1917[1], it is possible that Garnier made additions and modifications in the interval.

With the second decade of extensive development of reinforced concrete construction, from about 1904 to 1914, we pass from the pioneer stage to established and confident practice. During this period numerous improvements and elaborations were introduced in the frame method, more complex structures were designed, while several new methods were developed, the principal of which was the slab and column construction designed by the Swiss engineer Robert Maillart; parabolic vaulting developed by Freyssinet; and, a little after this period, a method of constructing domes and barrel-vaults first developed by Dischinger and Bauersfeld, known as shell concrete and sometimes referred to as the Zeiss-Dywidag method derived from the names of the firms for whom these engineers worked. The development of the last-mentioned method occurred later in the nineteen-twenties.

Although alternatives to the Hennebique, Coignet, and Considère methods began to appear before 1919, they did not represent any extensive practice, and these three methods of frame construction almost, if not quite exclusively, held the field. A large number of buildings was erected in France, Germany, Holland, Switzerland, and Italy in which these methods were used. Among them was the famous Queen Alexandra Sanatorium at Davos, built in 1907. In this building Pfleghard and Haefeli were the architects, François Hennebique was the engineer, and Robert Maillart the contractor[2]. The principal façade with the sun balconies has the appearance of an all-over pattern of squares, formed by the ferro-concrete frame. It is a type of hospital construction

Architects: Auguste and Gustave Perret

Garage, Rue de Ponthieu, Paris, 1905

Théatre des Champs-Elysées, 1911–14, exterior

Foyer of Théatre des Champs-Elysées

Auditorium of Théatre des Champs-Elysées

that was later followed extensively. Auguste Perret continued to work on the frame principle, and to this period belongs his famous Théatre des Champs-Elysées (1911–14). The exterior of this building expresses less of the new construction than Perret's two earlier works mentioned. The frame structure has clearly influenced the design, but it is encrusted with marble and has a somewhat restrained Renaissance dressing with its decorative sculptured panels. The interior appearance is more decisively influenced by construction, especially in the vestibule with its frame pattern ceiling and column supports; but the beautiful part of the interior is the long, unbroken curve of the balcony front, which gives rhythm and distinctive character to the whole. The frame construction employed is a combination of the Hennebique, Coignet, and Considère methods. The spiral binding of the rods in the square uprights follows Coignet, while the spiral binding of the circular columns follows Considère.

These frame constructions are obviously similar in principle to the post and lintel construction in ancient buildings, brought to architectural perfection in ancient Greece. Numerous medieval buildings and modern houses, built with the timber frame, follow the same principle of construction. In the evolution of the steel frame it emerged from the cast-iron column supporting the iron beam in the floor, and this was repeated on each floor. Linking the whole firmly into a continuous frame, whether of steel stanchions or reinforced concrete beams and piers, gives the added strength of the monolithic frame.

With the method introduced by Robert Maillart employed both in his industrial buildings and bridges, a different principle is involved. Reinforced concrete is used, principally as a slab construction, with columnar supports where necessary. An early example is a bridge built in 1906 over the Upper Rhine, at Tavanasa in the Grisons. A flat concrete slab forms the deck or platform of the bridge which is supported by a vertical slab, the bottom edge of which is shaped as an arch and pierced at the sides. It is an amazingly plain and simple structure. The beautiful line of the arch is accentuated by the piercing which helps to give the feeling of thrust, and thus vigour and life to the design. P. Morton Shand most aptly describes its form as 'suggestive of a pair of skates joined toe to toe with a thin sole running along the top of their blades: a form of surprising lightness and grace completely alien to all preconceived conceptions of that solidity of appearance which used to be deemed the cardinal aesthetic criterion of any fine bridge'[3]. Unfortunately the bridge was destroyed by an avalanche in 1927. This method of slab construction was employed in many of Maillart's bridges built between the wars.

Maillart used the method of slab construction supported by columns in a warehouse at Zürich in 1908. Each floor is a continuous slab without frame construction and is supported by octagonal columns with spreading capitals. These capitals are reinforced by rods, which spread laterally, and by support rings, which in turn support the slab

58

Jahrhunderthalle, Breslau, 1914, interior
Architect: Max Berg

Airship hangars, Orly, 1916, designed by E. Freyssinet

or floor rods. This method is generally known as mushroom slab construction, first so-called in Germany, being a translation of the German term *Pilzdecke*. About the same time a similar method was first employed in America by the engineer C. A. P. Turner, which differs from that of Maillart in that a panel or slab, like the Greek abacus, appears between the capital and the ceiling. The Turner system is much heavier and bulkier than that of Maillart, which has proved to be susceptible of several refinements. Maillart continually experimented with the method and used it for many industrial buildings. In 1910 he made an experimental model structure, and in 1913–14 he used the method in a cardboard factory at Lancey in France, where he had circular columns instead of octagonal. Here the columns are more slender and the curved capitals merge almost imperceptibly into the slab roof. The early work of Maillart was an important influence in subsequent reinforced concrete design.

The reinforced concrete parabolic vaulted buildings, many fine examples of which were to appear between the wars, was first employed by E. Freyssinet in the airship hangars at Orly, which he built for the French Government in 1916. The structure is a kind of long corrugated parabolic arch, with panes of glass let in the narrow strips between the arched members. Here the walls and roof are brought together in a continuous structure. A reinforced concrete construction of 1914, impressive for its dramatic size, is the Jahrhunderthalle at Breslau, designed by Mex Berg. The reinforced concrete dome is about 213 feet in diameter, thus of considerably greater span that any dome then in existence. It was constructed of heavy ribs of concrete with glass panels between. The bulk and weight appears to have much of the bulk associated with masonry domes. A great advance in lightness was made some years later in constructing domes and vaults of shell concrete.

REFERENCES AND NOTES

1. Tony Garnier, *Etude Pour la Construction des Villes*, Paris, 1917.
2. Sigfried Giedion (*Space, Time and Architecture* p. 372) speaks of Maillart as a pupil of Hennebque and refers to Maillart as the engineer and Hennebique the contractor in this building. P. Morton Shand, on the contrary, in his article on Maillart in the *Architectural Review* of September 1940 speaks of Maillart as the contractor and Hennebique the engineer. Shand records that Maillart first set up as a contractor, and went to Russia just before the First World War. After the war, having lost all his money, he returned to Switzerland and set up as an engineer.
3. *Architectural Review*, vol. lxxxviii, September 1940. This is an appreciation written shortly after Maillart's death in 1940. See also *The Journal of the Royal Institute of British Architects*, September 1938, pp. 957–69.

7   Industrial housing estates 1870–1916

THE LARGEST OF housing enterprises in Europe undertaken by industrialists for their
workpeople in the late nineteenth and early twentieth centuries was that of Krupps
at Essen. The various colonies were begun in 1870, and by 1910 the Krupps works
housing colonies accommodated 46,000 people. The oldest colonies, consisting of the
districts called Westend, Nordhof, Baumhof, Schederhof, and Cronenberg were erected
from 1870 to 1875. After 1893 the colonies of Alfredshof, Friedrichshof, Altenhof,
Margarethenhof, Dahlhauser Heide, Emscher Lippe, and Colony Gaarden were
added. Cronenberg, one of the earliest, is an example of formal symmetrical chess-
board planning clearly influenced by traditional classical ideas adapted to tenement
house layout. The buildings consist mainly of three-storey blocks with from about
twenty to forty dwellings in each block. 'Throughout, each staircase gives access to six
dwellings, each comprising a small landing with a separate front door.'[1] The buildings
are constructed of stone and brick. Each tenement block is in the middle of a garden,
and there is a central park for the colony.

Alfredshof, begun in 1894, was at first something of an experiment. All the colonies
before 1893 consisted of tenement blocks. By 1894 the influence of English domestic
architecture, chiefly as the result of the healthy concentration on purpose of the
architects who followed Morris and Webb, was being felt on the Continent. But it was
an architecture mainly of two-storey, one-family houses, and the type as well as design
began to be adopted in some quarters. Thus Alfredshof, largely as the result I think
of English influence, was commenced as cottages. These cottages were for one, two,
three, or four families; each family having its own private entrance and small garden.
Cottages to accommodate 232 families were completed by 1899, when the building
came temporarily to an end. It was recommenced in the colony in 1907, but by that
time, owing to the extension of Krupps's works and the consequent increased demand
for accommodation in the area, it was continued in several-storeyed flat buildings. This
had been the provision from the beginning in Friedrichshof, where the blocks were
arranged round courtyards kept as gardens.

A later colony is that of Dahlhauser Heide, built in the Bochum district for the miners of Hannover and Hannibal. Again practically all the accommodation is in semi-detached cottages. The irregular plan is very different from the formal plan of the earlier colony of Cronenberg. Here there are few straight roads, instead they curve about the site, and one thinks rather of the medieval village than the classical city. This change in planning in Germany results partially from the diffusion of Camillo Sitte's enthusiasm for medieval planning, given in his book *Stadtebau* published in 1889, and partially from English influence where there is a similar diffusion of medieval thought resulting from the Pre-Raphaelites and William Morris. These influences are apparent not only in the changed planning of the communities, but in the domestic architecture. The first tenement blocks of Cronenberg are simple, with little ornament, as becomes their strictly utilitarian purpose, but at the same time they have a certain classic restraint. With the later tenement blocks of Alfredshof medieval influence is apparent in the introduction of picturesque effects, such as the high-pitched roof making a great expanse of tiles, the windows in the roofs, and the ornamental curves over entrances and windows. In some of the colonies traditional Dutch picturesqueness plays a part. In the cottages at Dahlhauser Heide there are the sharply sloping roofs, and decorative devices like shutters, and half-timber work in the gable ends are introduced, and the whole is characteristic of the very strong tendency of the time both in England and Germany of trying to create the medieval village. As domestic architecture, where the purpose has been to house the poorer strata of the population, Krupps's housing at Essen must be regarded as one of the best European examples of the late nineteenth century, and as a social achievement it is more important. Catherine Bauer[2] says of this housing.

'There is little housing in all Europe which is physically better than that of the Krupps. They had three acknowledged purposes: to attract the best workers and keep them efficient, to inspire 'filial loyalty', and to ensure that Essen itself should be a wholesome, attractive, and modern city. As for the last purpose, they succeeded quite remarkably. Their own large-scale construction served to heighten competition, lower speculative land prices, and raise the standards of purely commercial building. Their favourable attitude towards city and regional planning makes the Ruhr district today one of the most advanced and orderly regions in the world in this respect.'

Contemporary with the development of the Krupps's housing colonies in Essen, Bournville and Port Sunlight in England were being planned and built. They provide two further examples of what had been done by Sir Titus Salt at Saltaire. These English industrial housing estates differ, however, in many respects from the colonies at Essen. At Essen the colonies were developed in relation to steel and armament works and coalmines; the housing is thus in an area of heavy industries. What was planned at Essen in the interests of good living conditions for the workpeople was elsewhere mainly a haphazard growth and an indiscriminate mixture of factories and houses, resulting in overcrowding and slums. Germany being later to develop industrially than England had the advantage of profiting by some of the evil consequences of unplanned and haphazard growth of mixed industrial and housing areas.

Saltaire, Bournville, and Port Sunlight arose from the establishment of light industries in the country. These were not developments, like Essen, of essentially industrial areas by reason of access to raw materials; on the contrary they represented a break with the custom of building factories in the central industrial areas, and of building them instead in the country a few miles out. It was part of the general impulse, so strong in England at the time, to get away from the congested and often squalid industrial centres to the fresh air, green fields, woods, and streams of the country. These industrial estates were a valuable contribution to social progress, for in their planning an attempt was made to view social life as a whole, for in addition to providing healthier living conditions and social amenities, places of work are in satisfactory relation to homes. They were contributions towards the fuller social conception of the garden city, fuller because it had the scale and comprehensiveness that Bournville and Port Sunlight necessarily lacked.

The flight of the middle classes from the industrial centres[3] which created the sprawling suburbs was of a totally different character, and constituted a social development unsatisfactory in many ways. As these industrial areas became more congested, smoky, dirty, and squalid, the more well-to-do, finding their surroundings becoming less pleasant, escaped to the country on the outskirts of the town. This happened first in London, which had a population of over a million in 1800, and the process spread to other large cities in England where the defensive wall had long ceased to exist, and horizontal extension by means of suburbs was possible. In the rest of Europe, because the defensive wall was often maintained until the middle of the century, vertical extension by means of tall tenement blocks had been more the custom, and thus suburbs developed later than in England.

The escape of the middle classes to the country and the development of suburbs was not attended by any comprehensive planning where the part was related to the whole, it was mainly haphazard. London presents the greatest example of this growth in Europe. And as cities grew it meant that to get to the country one had to go farther and farther out, so that gradually we find some of the inner suburbs becoming overcrowded like the central areas, except where measures had been taken to prevent crowding, and the pleasanter suburbs are generally on the outskirts. Partial exception must be made in areas like the western parts of London, but even here there has been a gradual movement outward of residential areas, produced less by industry than by expansion of business from the City westward.

To argue that suburbs are the negation of good social planning is not to contend that suburbs viewed as isolated residential areas are not often well planned. Hampstead Garden Suburb is an example of good isolated planning; but suburbs are not good social planning because they are planning for a part and not the whole of life. Hampstead Garden Suburb was originally planned by its founder, Dame Henrietta Barnett, as a place where 'persons of all classes of society and standard of income should be accommodated'; but the proportion of poor people accommodated is almost negligible, and it has become almost exclusively a middle-class suburb, thus resulting to a considerable extent in that social exclusiveness and isolation which is the negation of social wholeness and unity. Architecturally, however, Hampstead Garden Suburb is one of the best things in housing that was accomplished in the decade before the First World War.

Although suburbs were produced mainly by middle-class escapism, they were fostered to some extent by official policy in rehousing. In rebuilding in overcrowded areas local authorities had to accommodate the persons displaced, and in high densities of 200 or 300 to the acre this was possible only by building blocks of flats. Later it was realized that such rehousing might be greatly assisted by reduction of densities and accommodating part of the population elsewhere. In England the Housing of the Working Classes Act of 1890 empowered the London County Council to provide dwellings for the working class either inside or outside the County. From the time of its foundation in 1889, the L.C.C. continued the work of the Metropolitan Board of Works which had begun to clear insanitary areas in 1875. The first of the really comprehensive slum-clearance schemes of the L.C.C. was that of the Boundary Street area of Shoreditch, which was carried out in the eighteen-nineties and completed in 1900. In this scheme 5,719 persons were displaced and 5,524 were rehoused, leaving only 195 to go elsewhere. A more spacious layout was achieved in the rehousing with broader roads radiating to a large central circus, but this, together with the improved and more generous accommodation for almost the same number in the area, was accomplished only by building five-storey blocks of flats. In building these flats economy was necessarily a paramount consideration, and architectural scope was, therefore, limited. The buildings are simple in appearance with restrained Elizabethan stylistic touches here and there, as in some of the gables, and the general effect is not unpleasing. The gardens that appear between some of the blocks enhance the general effect.

This is a typical rehousing scheme in a congested area of London. Although in this particular case nearly the same number were rehoused in the area, and this was so in many other schemes[4], in other cases much less accommodation was provided. In compliance with the powers under part III of the Act of 1890 the Council acquired sites for housing in suburban areas, like White Hart Lane Estate at Tottenham, and Norbury Estate to the north of Croydon, both of which were planned in 1901.

The L.C.C. continued this policy. It contributed to the development of suburbs, and to the process of adding to the urban sprawl which every year continued farther and unbrokenly into the country.

I cite the case of London because it is the biggest and worst example in Europe of suburban growth. What happened there happened also, but to a less extent, in the other big cities of Europe, in Glasgow, Liverpool, Manchester, Birmingham, Paris, Bordeaux, Berlin, Hamburg, Cologne, Vienna, Budapest. It was haphazard and unplanned in relation to the whole, it produced that uneconomic separation of people's homes from their places of work, because the suburb does not really comprehend social life as a whole. A planned relation of homes and work places in the nineteenth century is seen at Saltaire, Guise, Essen, Bournville, and Port Sunlight.

Bournville[5] was an enterprise largely to provide better working and living conditions than were likely to be found very easily in the centre of Birmingham where the original small Cadbury factory was situated. 'Why should not the industrial worker enjoy country air and occupations without being separated from his work?' asks George Cadbury. He adds: 'If the country is a good place to live in why not to work in?' That: 'without being separated from his work' is one of the valuable social contributions that suburban development tended to ignore.

The Cadbury factory was built in 1879 near the Bourne stream, five miles southwest of Birmingham, when a few houses were provided for those who had to be near the factory, but only two of these now remain. The housing estate, called Bournville Village, was begun in 1895, and it has continued to be developed ever since. Originally the houses were occupied by employees of the Cadbury firm, but in 1900 a separate body called the Bournville Village Trust administered the estate, so that it ceased to be housing attached to a particular industrial firm. This was a step in social progress, for it is not conducive to the independence of a citizen that his employer and landlord should be the same person or institution.

In 1907 the estate covered an area of 500 acres, and it has since grown to 1,086 acres. The influence of the medieval village is strong in the planning of Bournville. With the exception of the principal main Bristol road, none of the minor roads are straight or formal, and curved roads and informal effects increase with later sections. There are plenty of open spaces, parks, and recreation grounds in central areas, while many of the houses back on to small recreation grounds or children's playgrounds. Facilities like schools are provided. Housing densities in Bournville are generally between six and twelve to the acre. The early cottages follow the type common in the late nineteenth century, with the kitchen and scullery projecting at the back. They are laid out spaciously, but are not of architectural interest. Some later houses are less stereotyped, and some built about 1907 on the Bournville Tenants Estate show the invigorating influence of Philip Webb, Voysey, and their followers, and are simple in treatment without ostentation, while materials are used expressively. The standard of more recent houses varies in excellence.

Port Sunlight[6] is the result of an enterprise similar to that of Bournville. It is smaller, covering in 1916 an area of 222 acres, on which about 2,000 houses are built. Many of the houses and cottages have some claim to architectural distinction. The factory, which lies to the southeast, was built in 1888, and since then the housing estate has continually developed. The plan is more formal than Bournville, and consists of a centre with straight, spacious avenues at right angles, and in the surrounding areas the housing plots are irregular rectangles and triangles. Backyards, not individual gardens, are provided for the houses, but in the large area at the back of the houses are allotment gardens for communal use, an arrangement which is not so popular as the separate family garden adjoining the house. Medieval tradition has determined the design of most of the cottages and small houses. Picturesque effect has occasionally been the aim with some of the houses, and sham half-timbered work, due doubtless to the example of Norman Shaw, appears frequently. But there are some excellent designs where simplicity and expressive use of materials are apparent.

Some of the early cottages, designed by W. Owen, were awarded the Grand Prix at the Brussels Exhibition of 1910. They are simple, brick houses, with decorative tiling in the gables and part of the first floor. An excellent group of small houses in Greendale Road, designed by Sir Ernest George and Yeates, are somewhat in the manner of Voysey's houses, for they have the same simple façades with large horizontal windows, and large, plain walls with white cement rendering. The interesting group of terrace cottages with a curved front, in Lower Road, designed by Sir Charles Reilly, affords an excellent example of combining a row of terrace houses satisfactorily into an architectural unity. In some houses stone is employed as a dressing for windows and doors, and in the examples at Pool Bank designed by Wilson and Talbot, late-Tudor square-headed mullioned windows are introduced effectively. In the cottages in Pool Bank, designed by Douglas and Minshall, the ground-floor windows are treated in a similar way, and simple buttresses are employed, no doubt to make the late medieval reminiscence complete. In these compactly planned cottages, with simple but well-proportioned exteriors, designed between 1895 and 1914, lies, the chief architectural distinction of Port Sunlight, rather than in the pseudo half-timbered buildings, and the later classical buildings of the Art Gallery and bandstand in the central avenue called the Diamond.

Industrial housing estates like Earswick, near York, and Somerdale, near Bristol, have followed the examples of Bournville and Port Sunlight, and several others have been developed. Bournville and Port Sunlight are important, not only because they set an example to other later enterprises of a similar kind, but because they represented links between the ideas of Owen and Buckingham, and the Garden City organism first completely conceived by Sir Ebenezer Howard, and first realized in Letchworth. Also it is possible that they, with continental examples like Guise and Essen, had some influence on Tony Garnier's celebrated design for an Industrial City.

REFERENCES AND NOTES

1. *Guide to the Workman's Colonies*, Essen, Ruhr, 1911, compiled for The Garden Cities and Town Planning Association. The guide gives in a brief form much useful information about the colonies.
2. Catherine Bauer, *Modern Housing*, London 1935, p. 89.
3. This is dealt with at length in Lewis Mumford's *Culture of Cities*, London, 1938, pp. 210–22.
4. An account of the schemes up to 1912 is given in *Housing of the Working Classes*, London, 1913, published by the L.C.C.
5. A well-illustrated brief account of Bournville is given in *Sixty Years of Planning: The Bournville Experiment*, 1939.
6. A discursive and laudatory account of Port Sunlight is given in T. Raffles Davison, *Port Sunlight: A Record of its Artistic and Pictorial Aspect*, London, 1916. The excellent illustrations of the book constitute its chief value.

8 Howard's garden city and Garnier's industrial city

EBENEZER HOWARD's idea of a garden city was first outlined in his book *To-Morrow: A Peaceful Path to Real Reform*, published in 1898[1]. The purpose of the book, as stated in the introduction, was to suggest a means whereby the continual influx of the population to the overcrowded cities might be arrested. 'It is well nigh universally agreed', he says, 'by men of all parties, not only in England, but all over Europe and America, and our colonies, that it is deeply to be deplored that the people should continue to stream into the already overcrowded cities, and should thus further deplete the country districts.' Howard quotes many famous men who point out the evil of this continued migration into the towns. Sir John Gorst said in 1891 that 'the interest and the safety of the towns themselves were involved in the solution of the problem'; and Dean Farrar remarked that 'if it be true that great cities tend more and more to become the graves of the physique of our race, can we wonder at it when we see the houses so foul, so squalid, so ill-drained, so vitiated by neglect and dirt?'

The causes which draw people into cities, Howard contends, may all be summed up as attractions, and the remedy lies in presenting greater attractions elsewhere. Each city may be regarded as a magnet, and the remedy is to provide a greater magnet. He defines both the town magnet and the country magnet, and then says: 'But neither the town magnet nor the country magnet represents the full plan and purpose of nature. Human society and the beauty of nature are meant to be enjoyed together. The two magnets must be made one.' He says later that 'town and country must be married, and out of this joyous union will spring a new hope, a new life, a new civilization', and he states that it is the purpose of his book 'to show how a first step can be taken in this direction by the construction of a town–country magnet'.

Garden City is the town–country magnet. In the hypothetical example the city is built in the centre of 6,000 acres, occupying about 1,000 acres for a population of 32,000. The balance of 5,000 acres forms a permanent green belt, mainly for agricultural purposes. The city is conceived diagrammatically as a circle, with six boulevards, radiating to the centre, which is occupied by a garden of about five and a half acres. Surrounding the garden are public buildings: the town hall, concert and lecture hall, theatre, library, museum, picture gallery, and hospital. Beyond these is a public park of about 145 acres, which is encircled by a wide glass arcade, which Howard calls the 'Crystal Palace', which can be an attractive resort in wet weather. Part of it is designed for shopping and part as a winter garden. Surrounding this arcade is 'fifth avenue', lined with trees, on the farther side of which are houses. The next circular road is 'fourth avenue', and then 'grand avenue', the total width of which is 420 feet. Schools with their playgrounds, and churches, occupy sites in the centre of 'grand avenue'. The last and outer ring forms the industrial area, with a circle railway near by. The whole is shown clearly in the diagram which first appeared in Howard's book.

The scheme has obvious physical similarities to Buckingham's 'Victoria', but it has considerable social and political differences as Howard is careful to point out[2]. In Buckingham's scheme the whole town is owned and controlled by a company that is responsible for all industrial undertakings, and there are several prohibitions like the exclusion of intoxicants. Howard's scheme, on the contrary, allows for free enterprise and association of all kinds, and imposes no undemocratic restrictions on its inhabitants.

Provision is made for an increase of population above the planned limit of 32,000. 'It will grow', Howard states, 'by establishing another city some little distance beyond its own zone or country so that the new town may have a zone of country of its own.' He continues: 'This principle of growth—this principle of always preserving a belt of country round our cities would be ever kept in mind till, in course of time, we should have a cluster of cities . . . grouped around a central city that each inhabitant of the whole group, though in one sense living in a town of small size, would be in reality living in, and would enjoy all the advantages of, a great and most beautiful city.' He thinks of the central city as slightly larger, with a population of about 58,000.

Howard's book is one of the most important contributions to town planning, conceived primarily in its social aspect, and is the greatest English contribution to town planning of modern times. The idea has been realized not perfectly, but sufficiently to incorporate essentials: firstly in Letchworth, commenced in 1903, secondly in Welwyn, commenced in 1920 and thirdly in the many new towns designated in Great Britain and in other European Countries from 1946 onwards[3].

The garden city idea has often been criticized as not being sufficiently comprehensive, and of not solving the problem of the big city. It is too early to say whether it is the most successful method of avoiding the anti-social haphazard growth of overcrowded cities. To those who say it does not solve the problem of the big city it might be replied that economic and social developments may make the big city an anachronism, and its gradual disappearance and the substitution of garden city clusters may be the most serviceable development for economic and social life of the future. It must be sufficient here to emphasize that the garden city satisfies most social requirements of the full life. The town is sufficiently small for the country to be within easy reach of the inhabitants, yet sufficiently large to support the amenities and cultural facilities of town life such as schools, halls, libraries, theatre, exhibition galleries, community centres, and good shopping centres, amenities that will be more fully provided as social life develops. A town of 10,000 would be too small to support most of the amenities of town life, whereas a town of 30,000 can more adequately do so. Some would say it should be 50,000, others 100,000[4], but these are differences of degree rather than of principle. There are sound arguments for doubling the sizes given by Howard, thus 64,000 and 112,000 for the central city with the pattern remaining essentially the same.

The garden city is designed so that people who work there live there. The green belt can provide fresh food for the town, so that the farmer has a market near at hand. The great merit of the garden city and the garden city cluster is that it is the most successful attempt so far made to plan for social life as a whole in all its many aspects. In fact, the fuller realization of the idea is held by a large number of sociologists as the essential requirement of planning. They are fortified in their conviction by the success of the two first examples, followed by the thirty new towns.

To-Morrow evoked fairly widespread response and hardly more than six months after its publication, in June 1899, the Garden City Association was formed to propagate Howard's ideas. It was felt by the Association that steps should be taken to put the ideas into practice, and that land should be secured and a garden city built. In 1902 the Garden City Pioneer Company was formed, which secured the Letchworth estate. First Garden City, Ltd, was formed in 1903 to promote the development and the pioneer company was dissolved. The work of planning Letchworth, the first garden city, was entrusted to Sir Raymond Unwin and Barry Parker[5].

Application of the theory to an actual site produced something very different from Howard's diagram. The first garden city is built on a site that includes the villages of Letchworth, Willian, and Norton. The total area is about 4,500 acres, of which about 1,500 acres will ultimately be occupied by the town and 3,000 acres by the rural belt. The planners have taken advantage of natural features, with the result that there is a very irregular demarcation between the town and the rural belt. The chief factory area lies to the east of the town on either side of the railway which runs east–northeast from London. The centre of the town is formally planned, with a principal thoroughfare—Broad Walk—running almost north–south, forming the main axis. The remainder is irregularly planned in the tradition of the English medieval village. In or near the centre are the town hall, grammar school, museum, a concert hall, theatre, and an educational settlement; and here also is the principal shopping area.

The educational settlement is mainly for cultural activities for adults, and is a form of community centre. Places of worship and cinemas are adequately provided, but there are no public houses, as the inhabitants have consistently outvoted a substantial minority. There is a generous provision of open spaces, both as parks and for recreation. Most of the roads are lined with well-selected ornamental trees, and many of the footways are separated from the roads by a grass verge. The houses are for various grades of income, from the poorest to the well-to-do, and all have gardens in relation to their size. The general impression of the residential part is of a town set in a garden.

What is the architecture that emerges from this social experiment? Considering the period before 1914, the houses, like those of Port Sunlight and Hampstead Garden Suburb, develop from the medieval tradition through the minds of architects like Norman Shaw, Philip Webb, Voysey, and their associates. They vary in excellence. Many of the best are by the planners Sir Raymond Unwin and Barry Parker, where simple and direct effects are achieved with expressive use of materials as in pairs of houses at Lollershott West and on Letchworth Lane. There are similarly good houses by Bennett and Bidwell on Broadway, by Charles H. Spooner on Pixmore Way, and by Aylwin O. Cave on Spring Road, but there are also several where sham half-timber work is much in evidence. The house called Red Hawthorne, situated near the point where Wilbury Road joins Norton Way, is interesting for its construction. It was built in 1909 of fifteen large pre-fabricated units which compose walls, floors, stairways, and ceilings, made of rubble mixed with half-portion of cement. It was built in three days, and cost £200, of which £50 was spent on transport from Liverpool, where the parts were made. Accommodation consists of a drawing room, dining room, and kitchen on the ground floor, and three bedrooms on the first floor. Its flat roof strikes a very modern note in Letchworth[6].

The architecture of the centre of the town is not distinctive. The buildings of the central square have a spacious layout, and a uniform but not very interesting architectural character, but the streets of the shopping areas, although originally having a certain architectural unity, show the repetition of units of somewhat mediocre design. Since 1914 what unity existed has been in some parts destroyed and these present an inharmonious mixture as in Eastcheap, which is rather to be regretted. The architectural failure of the centre of the town can hardly vitiate the social experiment, but it is regrettable. The architectural unity of the streets of Bath, the repetition of well-proportioned and dignified units, gives so much aesthetic pleasure that one is always deeply grateful for its creation. Letchworth is in a different idiom, but the principle of the satisfactory relation of parts to a whole achieved in some measure by the repetition of well-proportioned units with a variety according to differences of purpose can apply equally. If Letchworth is a brilliant success socially it is hardly that architecturally. It might be argued that it is well suited to its purpose, but beauty does not necessarily emerge from that. It has well-designed houses pleasingly set in gardens and some lovely roads, but it fails where buildings compose the more formal street effects of its central areas.

The garden city movement thus begun had a considerable influence throughout Europe, and garden city associations were formed in most European countries—in France, Germany, Austria, Belgium, Holland, Italy, Poland, Hungary, Spain[7]. Although, after England, France was the first to form such an association in 1904, it was in Germany that the movement was strongest, and many schemes were promoted there which were inspired by the movement. Those which most closely correspond in conception to the true garden city are Hellerau, near Dresden, commenced in 1908, and München-Perlach, but they are much too small for full realization of the idea. Numerous garden suburbs were developed in the early years of the century like Stockfield, near Strasbourg, an enterprise of the municipal authority; and Altona, near Hamburg, designed for a population of 30,000. Also numerous industrial estates on the lines of Bournville were developed, but no garden city of the scale and social comprehensiveness of Letchworth had really been started elsewhere in Europe before 1914.

In the interest shown in the movement, especially by municipal authorities throughout Europe, there was not a sufficiently clear understanding of the difference between a garden city and a garden suburb. A full appreciation of the social value of Howard's conception should prevent confusion with the garden suburb, which, agreeable as it may be as physical planning, is a growth that must be severely restricted if it is not to destroy by its very existence good social planning.

Some of the many garden suburbs in Germany and England commenced in the early years of the century offer good and interesting examples of domestic architecture, both of the slightly larger detached house and of the smaller houses forming units repeated in a unified whole. There are some good examples in Margaretenhohe, a garden suburb for old people near Essen, where features of German medieval domestic architecture are incorporated; and in Hellerau, where the simple units with plain white walls and sharp-pitched roofs repeat satisfactorily. It is perhaps not mere fancy to think of the influence of Voysey and Peter Behrens. But that which is architecturally the finest in the decade before the First World War is Hampstead Garden Suburb. The reason for this is that its architecture is partially a product of the tradition begun by Morris and Webb, which resulted in such excellent domestic work for the period from 1860 to about 1905, when English building in this sphere was a model and inspiration to numerous continental architects as mentioned in Chapter 5. Hampstead Garden Suburb was begun in 1906. Its original 243 acres, since enlarged to 317, were planned by Sir Raymond Unwin and Barry Parker, in consultation with Sir Edwin Lutyens. The central square and immediate surroundings are formal and symmetrical, and remind one of classical and Renaissance planning, while the outer areas are more irregular and emerge from medieval planning. The two churches—St. Jude-on-the-Hill and the Free—the Institute in the Central Square, and the houses facing it and on the approaching roads were designed by Sir Edwin Lutyens. The other houses in the suburb were designed by various architects, among them Sir Raymond Unwin and Geoffrey Lucas, and they were designed chiefly in that medievally inspired tradition so powerful at the time. The visitor to the suburb would probably be impressed by the formal centre surrounded by buildings in which Renaissance tradition is freely interpreted—stone dressings on brick buildings is a favourite theme—but in which symmetry is insistent; and by many of the winding roads of the other parts flanked by houses in which medieval picturesqueness and expressive use of materials is frequently recaptured. Lutyens is eclectic in the church of St. Jude-on-the-Hill in combining the spire and vast expanse of pitched roof with an otherwise Renaissance design, which is completely dominant in the interior.

Almost contemporary with the planning of the first garden city, Tony Garnier was working on his plan for an industrial city. He actually made the plan in outline in 1901, while the details were worked out by 1904, but it was not published until 1917[8]. He made designs for every detail, and made plans and perspective drawings of all the buildings, including a considerable variety of houses. It has many features similar to Howard's garden city. It is planned for a population of 35,000, and includes industry, housing, social and recreational amenities, cultural facilities, and, like Howard's plan, it comprehends social life as a whole. It is also a progressive contribution to architectural design. The plans and drawings represent a great achievement, and it is regrettable that so fine a design has so far existed only in imagination. Perhaps one day it will have a physical existence necessarily modified, although Garnier's work at Lyons incorporates features of it, while it has had some influence on subsequent town planning and architecture.

The imaginary town is planned and situated on an undulating site on the north bank of a river from which the ground rises gently. The residential area is roughly of a long rectangular shape, in the centre of which are the public buildings devoted to culture and recreation. There are assembly halls, museums, library, exhibition galleries, two theatres (one open air), a high school, and a sports ground. To the north higher up on the slopes is the health centre, with hospital, sanatorium, and convalescent homes, separated from the residential area by a strip of open space. To the southeast, nearer the river bank, also separated from the residential area by a strip of open space, is the industrial area connected with a goods station.

Although it is planned for a population of about 35,000 there is provision for extension of both industrial and residential areas, but Garnier does not indicate the limits of the extensions. They would take place, presumably, to the east of the industrial area, while

the residential strip could be extended westwards, and northwards at its eastern
extremity. But it is clear that if the town grew very much the amenities for 35,000
would be inadequate, and the distance of people's homes from the industrial area would
be inconveniently increased. To the suggestion that new amenity centres and new
industrial areas could be added, it must be replied that you are merely adding one
town on to another and creating limitless lineal development. This has its advocates
provided the strips of open space are always preserved so as to ensure close proximity
of built-up areas and open spaces, but it renders difficult the satisfactory proximity of
more extensive country areas which is so good a feature of the garden city.

The architecture of Garnier's Industrial City is inspiringly progressive. The whole city
is built in the new medium of ferro-concrete—factories, public buildings, and houses.
At the same time Garnier was an enthusiastic classicist, and the influence of his early
training and successes never left him. In winning the *Prix de Rome* he satisfied
judges dominated by classical ideas. In the architecture of his Industrial City, and in his
executed work at Lyons, he adapted the dignity, restraint, and proportion of Greek
architecture to modern requirements. The remarkable series of drawings give the
impression of a city not dissimilar in character and atmosphere to the imagined cities
of ancient Greece. This is especially so in the residential area. The houses are arranged
in a series of five or six long plots, the outer ones only are near the roads, the others
being separated by footways lined with trees. They are one- and two-storey houses,
and are mostly detached or semi-detached. Most of the smaller houses have a living
room, kitchen, bathroom, and two or three bedrooms. They are orientated with due
regard to the sun, they all have flat roofs, there is little ornament, and they depend
for architectural effect on the balance of horizontals and verticals and relations of
openings to wall spaces.

REFERENCES AND NOTES

1. A second edition was published in 1902 under the title *Garden Cities of To-morrow*.
   Third edition, edited by F. J. Osborn with an introduction by Lewis Mumford (1946).
2. Ebenezer Howard *Garden Cities of To-morrow*, pp. 110–12.
3. See Frederic J. Osborn and Arnold Whittick, *The New Towns—the Answer to Megalopolis*,
   London, 1963; second edition 1969.
4. In Sir Patrick Abercrombie's *Plan for Greater London*, London, 1944, the maximum size
   of the proposed eight new towns is 60,000.
5. A full account of the genesis and early development of the first garden city is given in
   C. B. Purdom, *The Garden City*, London, 1913.
6. Described in *La Cite Jardin* by Georges Benoit-Levy, Paris, 1911, vol. i, p. 94.
7. An account of this movement in Europe is given by Georges Benoit-Levy in *La Cite
   Jardin*, vol. iii, p. 109 ff. A briefer account is given by E. G. Culpin in *The Garden City
   Movement Up-to-Date*, London, 1913, p. 61 ff.
8. Tony Garnier, *Etude pour la Construction des Villes*, Paris, 1917.

9 *The foundations of a new architecture*

AN ARCHITECTURE that emerges logically from economic and social needs, and from technical development, and which in its forms is expressive of contemporary life, was beginning to be established during the few years before the First World War. We can remember how Schinkel sighed for a living contemporary architecture: 'All great ages have left a record of themselves in their style of building. Why should we not try to find a style for ourselves?' In the few years before the war, Europe, for the first time since the fifteenth century, was beginning to leave a record of itself in building which was the independent outcome of its stage of technical and social evolution, and thus the twentieth century was beginning to evolve an architecture expressive of its own life, dependent on the past only in the sense that experience equips an artist and technician to solve the problems of his own day.

In the preceding chapters the principal developments that led to the new architecture have been traced[1]. Noted first was the aim of Labrouste, and of Morris, Webb, and their followers that 'Architectural form should be appropriate to the function for which it is intended', to quote the words of Labrouste; secondly, the striving for a living style, and such creations as *Art Nouveau* which, though not fundamental, probably had an invigorating effect on thought about the principles of design; thirdly, the movement towards simplicity, which played its part in the search for a style by the rather negative process of eliminating ornamental dressings taken from the past. Additionally there is the fundamental contribution of the work of engineers in their use of new materials of iron and later steel and concrete, and the new methods of building these brought into being with their greater structural possibilities. In Chapters 7 and 8 the influence of social needs was considered. Most of these factors contribute to the creation of a living architecture. It is, however, principally the appropriateness of form to function, the sloughing of the ornament of past styles, and the use of materials with greater structural potentialities that provide the basis of modern building which is essentially of its age. But something more is required of a living architecture. In addition to good efficient structure suited to its purpose, it should be expressive of these qualities[2], it should give a feeling of unity in which the parts organically relate to the whole, and it should be a pleasing combination of forms irrespective of its other qualities. The fulfilment of these conditions is necessary if a full degree of aesthetic appreciation is to be aroused.

As previously mentioned (Chapter 4), Schinkel might have seen the basis of a living style in the factories and warehouses in the north of England that he visited, for it is mainly in industrial buildings that there is the first and most vigorous expression of the new architecture. In such buildings a primary concern is with utility, efficient design for purpose being an industrial asset and a more important consideration than appearance, while the employment of methods and materials with greater structural possibilities, offering greater speed, economy, and efficiency in building are of paramount importance to the industrialist. Thus a large proportion of the early steel-framed and ferro-concrete buildings are of an industrial character, like warehouses and factories. The majority of office and public buildings, erected before 1914, in which new materials and methods of construction are employed, have very much the appearance of stone or brick buildings in a traditional style. In addition to the Ritz Hotel and others already mentioned, the Royal Liver building at Liverpool, completed in 1910, and designed by W. Aubrey Thomas, is an example of a building constructed of a ferro-concrete framework, but is stylistically a mixture of Romanesque, Byzantine, and Renaissance, into which, however, a slightly modern character is infused in the massive façades due to a tentative expression of the structural framework.

English domestic architecture from 1860 to 1905, as represented by the work of Webb, Shaw, Voysey, and their followers, was the most important in Europe and exerted a wide influence. It represented an important contribution to the realization of a living and expressive architecture. After 1905 the progressive development continued mainly in Austria, Germany, and France. Much good work in domestic architecture was done in England between 1905 and 1915 by many architects following Webb, Shaw, and Voysey, mentioned in Chapter 5, examples of which are seen in Hampstead Garden Suburb considered in the last chapter; but they merely continued the good work of the forty previous years: they did not develop or add anything to it. These architects did not study the possible use of new materials like steel and concrete, or new methods of building. And in some of the works, such as the less satisfactory examples of Baillie Scott and Guy Dawber, there is a tendency towards sentimentality in efforts to recapture medieval character and atmosphere.

In Germany, on the contrary, architects take the stage at which the architects of England had arrived by about 1905 from which to develop further and it is mainly in Germany, Austria, and France that progressive development occurs, although isolated examples of progressive work appear in many European countries. Some occur in Britain. Among them are the examples collected by Nikolaus Pevsner. In saying that the main developments from 1905 to 1915 took place in **Germany**, Austria, and France, I do not suggest there were no progressive examples in other European countries. A certain number are found in Italy, Poland, Hungary, and more particularly in the northern European countries, such as Holland, Denmark, Sweden, and Britain. They are the work of isolated individuals rather than work emanating from groups with unified convictions. Some of these isolated examples in Britain are noteworthy. Lion Chambers, Glasgow, designed by Salmon, Son and Gillespie about 1908, although well behind Perrett's work a few years earlier, does partially express its ferro-concrete frame construction, mixed a little with traditional stylistic features. More impressive are some of the examples collected by Nikolaus Pevsner and dealt with in an article in the *Architectural Review* (vol. xci, pp. 109–12, May 1942) with the suggestive title of 'Nine Swallows—No Summer'. He actually cites more than nine, but probably thinks that only nine may really be regarded as pioneer examples of the new architecture. Many other examples, however, could be added to the industrial buildings in ferro-concrete that he mentions (some are mentioned in Chapter 6). A large number of such factories have gridiron façades, due to the pattern of the concrete frame. Pevsner mentions some interesting houses, one being a simple flat-roofed house of brick, built in Stafford in 1908 by Edgar Wood. He also mentions a flat-roofed block of offices, built by J. Henry Sellers, also in 1908. Both these buildings have large plain walls and large simple windows pleasingly spaced.

The most modern buildings erected in London before the First World War were Sir John Burnet's famous Kodak building in Kingsway, built in 1911, and the Stationery Office warehouse, built two years later by Sir R. J. Allison. In the former building the site is somewhat awkward, and there is an attempt to adapt a symmetrical plan to it, but the steel frame of which the building is contructed partially determines the design of the façades. Above the second floor the effect is of large glazed areas and bronze panels between stone-faced uprights, conveying faint reminiscences of Renaissance pilasters. The Stationery Office warehouse is constructed of reinforced concrete and expresses its frame in its gridiron façades.

Peter Behrens, more progressive than his English contemporaries, follows English domestic work up to 1905 and then develops further, as we have noted in Chapter 4. But it is in his industrial buildings that we find the greatest progress and the greatest use of the new methods and materials. Behrens became architect of the A.E.G. (General Electric Company of Berlin), and the buildings he designed for this company represent some of the most impressive examples of the new architecture before 1914, some of which are illustrated. In these industrial buildings of Behrens full use is made of the pioneer work of engineers. This is seen especially in the spanning of big spaces with steel and glass roofs, as in the Turbine factory which he built in 1909 and in other shops where large machinery is employed. The immense Turbine factory in the Huttenstrasse, Berlin is constructed of a steel frame which is strongly apparent in the

A.E.G. Turbine Factory,
Huttonstrasse, Berlin, 1909

Architect: Peter Behrens

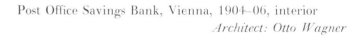

Kodak House, Kingsway, London, 1911

Architects: Sir John Burnet, Tait and Lorne

Post Office Savings Bank, Vienna, 1904–06, interior

Architect: Otto Wagner

Fagus boot-last factory, Alfield-an-der-Leine, 1911

Architects: Walter Gropius and Adolf Meyer

appearance of the building. The top of the end wall denotes the shape of the steel
and glass roof. There is grandeur in the steel uprights with large spaces of glass
between, and broad corner masses. It is industrial architecture at its best. The
Assembly Shop, built 1911–12 is similar in shape to the Turbine factory but not quite
the same sense of grandeur is achieved. The side façades, for example, being broken
up more, have not the impressively long lines and large masses. But generally in most
of Behrens's industrial work of this period the building expresses its steel skeleton and
the general effect is massive and simple, and sometimes with that touch of grandeur
notable in the Turbine factory.

Contemporary with these industrial buildings of Peter Behrens are some interesting
contributions to the new architecture by Hans Poelzig. The work of Poelzig is always
original, and often daring and he seems to regard architecture as an exciting
adventure. In 1911 he built a chemical factory at Luban of which the forms clearly
express its brick structure. The large number of small windows was probably one of the
requirements of the factory, but it is difficult to think how the small circular-headed
windows are functionally satisfactory. They are apparently a decorative device that
appealed to Poelzig, as he introduced them to an even greater extent in a design for a
water mill made in 1910[3]. In this water mill are two blocks connected by a bridge over
a lock, and on the walls facing each other are projecting glass and steel structures,
which represent a more modern note than the remainder. But more important than
either of these is the Office Building at Breslau, completed in 1912. Here the steel-
framed structure is clothed fairly massively, but the frame controls the design, while
glass occupies almost wholly the intervening spaces. And here, for the first time, we
have the horizontal emphasis in the façade, introduced by long unbroken bands at
each floor level. This was to become later a favourite motif, first in German office and
store buildings, then in buildings of all types throughout Europe.

In the developments of the new architecture it is possible to trace two distinct streams,
and two main schools of thought. It is convenient to think of them as medieval and
classical. Architects who belong to the former may not be conscious of medieval
tradition, and the bulk of their work may be industrial and determined largely by
industrial requirements and the pioneer work of engineers. It is rather a habit of
thought. If a typical medieval architect had to design a modern factory he would have
designed it very much as does an unrestricted exponent of the new architecture. He
would consider the most convenient plan, the best way of building to satisfy purpose
most efficiently, and he would certainly have employed the most recent materials and
methods of construction. The point is he would not have been troubled by any beliefs
that building should conform to any laws other than those determined by its purpose
and efficient construction. One may say, broadly, that the progressive architects of
England, Germany, Holland, Sweden, and Denmark are of this school. But the
architect in the classical tradition has so often a sense of the divinity of geometric law,

and a belief that building, if it is to be of architectural value, must conform to geometric law. (Discussed in some detail in Chapter 30.) The question it is important to ask in reflecting on this phase of modern architectural development is: does this belief in the divinity of geometric or mathematical law, which seems to have been a belief of many of the ancient Greeks, as of some modern mathematicians, handicap architects in the full development towards a living architecture? This phase began in Austria with the doctrines of Otto Wagner, and its influence is apparent in the work of Adolf Loos, as previously noted, and in that of Tony Garnier, and later in the work of Le Corbusier and those influenced by him. It would seem, then, that it is in Austria and France that this phase finds its chief expression.

There is a suggestion of this difference between medieval and classical influence in the work of Poelzig and Behrens. The massive proportions and monumental grandeur of many of Behrens's industrial buildings suggest the influence of classical tradition, while his German Embassy at St. Petersburg (Leningrad) is essentially a classical conception; whereas the work of Poelzig has a romantic and less formal quality suggestive of medieval tradition. But it is not so much in grandeur of character that the classical strain is most potent in the new architecture. It is rather, as before insisted, the divinity of mathematical law and geometric forms, the authority of Plato in the *Philebus* when he claims absolute beauty for 'straight lines and curves and the surfaces or solid forms produced out of these by lathes and rulers and squares', which is the most potent influence in the classical strain in the new architecture as distinct from the freer developments which are not circumscribed by such authority. Although Behrens is undoubtedly influenced by effects of classical grandeur, he is in no sense restrained by the aesthetic divinity of geometric form and classical proportion.

USE OF NEW MATERIALS

In their use of the new materials like steel and concrete, and consequently new methods, architects like Wagner and Garnier are restrained by the classical tradition. It is in roofs demanding steel and glass, where the classical tradition can hardly be so insistent, that we find the greatest freedom. Yet with Wagner the schematic welding of such features with classical character is done with consummate artistry. The steel and glass roof of the Post Office Savings Bank in Vienna, built in 1904–6, is of an elliptical shape, but is welded with complete harmony to the restrained square-like character of the remainder of the building. Tony Garnier, in the Cattle Market and Abattoirs at Lyons built in 1913–14, covers the vast market hall, with a steel roof of 262 feet span, with slanting box girders, but he makes the exterior shape flat, with step effect. In the covered street the roof is of flat, boxed steel girders.

Garnier chooses ferro-concrete as his favourite medium because in this, rather than in steel and glass construction, he can express his classical feeling more strongly. It will be remembered that his Industrial City is all conceived in reinforced concrete, and

classical forms dominate the conception of most of the houses and some of the
other buildings, although here and there, as in the railway station, he adventures with
the potentialities of the new medium. In the Cattle Market, in the Hopital de Gragne
Blanche (1911–12), and in the School of Arts, completed in 1917, all at Lyons, the
dependence for effect on the balance of horizontals and verticals, and the relation of
window openings to wall spaces, are all conceived with the classical tradition as the
all-important background. In the School of Arts the magnificent entrance is adorned
with large architectural fragments—parts of a Doric temple and an Egyptian column,
while Ionic and Corinthian capitals appear on pedestals at the foot of the staircase.
Garnier must have been happy designing the Sports Stadium at Lyons, completed in
1910. Although Greece and Rome were obviously much in mind when he designed it,
ferro-concrete is used expressively so that he achieves long, unbroken sweeps, and a
fine Doric austerity. It is thus obvious that ferro-concrete had an appeal for Garnier
because it is a reinforced synthetic stone capable of design in the same spirit as Greek
architecture. But it is when his background of classical architecture becomes dim, and
he ventures with his material, as in the railway station and in the hospital and
sanitorium of the Industrial City, that he makes the most valuable contribution to
architectural and constructional development.

The early work of Auguste Perret, the other great French pioneer in the new
architecture, has been considered in Chapter 6. His house at 22 Rue Franklin, his
garage in Rue de Ponthieu, Paris, and his Champs-Elysées theatre are, in their
architectural forms, expressive of the structure he employs. The first two, although
earlier by several years than the Champs-Elysées theatre, are much freer expressions,
as the theatre is more strongly influenced in conception by classical forms. The design
of the garage in the Rue de Ponthieu, where glass occupies most of the spaces in the
concrete framework, is the most free expression of structure and purpose, but even
here the symmetry and nice relation of horizontals and verticals in the façade suggest
that classical dignity is not forgotten.

The architect who, before 1914, advanced most decisively to building in which full
advantage is taken of technical and industrial developments in design based on the
the best fulfilment of function was Walter Gropius. The cradle of so many of the
great architects of the period between the wars was the *atelier* of Peter Behrens.
Walter Gropius worked there from 1908 to 1910, and among other assistants and
students at various times were Mies van der Rohe, Le Corbusier, who, however, was
there rebelliously only for five months, Steinder, Johannes Schreiner, and many
others. Gropius was impatient to start on his own, and his first work was the Fagus
boot-last factory at Alfred-an-der-Leine, built in 1911 in collaboration with Adolf
Meyer, now famous as one of the milestones in the evolution of modern architecture.
In this factory the potentialities of steel and glass are realized as fully as ever before.

The structure is a steel frame supporting floors, and the walls have become just glass screens fixed to the frame. As if to emphasize the non-structural screen-like character of the glass walls, and their dependence on the frame, there are no structural uprights at the corners, but the glass screens continue uninterruptedly. These transparent walls partially negate the distinction between inner and outer space, and give the workers within the feeling, as far as light is concerned, of working in the broad daylight out of doors, yet protected from rain and cold.

Gropius designed buildings for the Deutsche Werkbund Exhibition at Cologne in 1914, the Administrative Office Building being the most important. This building is symmetrical with a central entrance; the central portion of the front part of the building is faced with brick, but spiral staircases at the wings are enclosed entirely by glass, which continues at the sides and on the first floor for the whole length of the rear of the building. The steel frame holding these glass screens is reduced almost to an efficient minimum of bulk, and never before had a structure given so completely an impression of lightness. The weather-protecting elements separating the interior from the 'open air' have become light and intangible. In the glass towers enclosing spiral staircases we have for the first time what was to become so distinguishing a feature of many later buildings, particularly departmental stores. This building had a flat roof that could be used for dancing, and which was appropriately covered. At the back of the building were a hall of machinery and open garages, also designed by Gropius in collaboration with Meyer. The hall of machinery had a slightly pitched roof, the steel frame curving from the walls, which were largely glass between the stanchions. All these buildings were destroyed during the First World War.

At this Deutsche Werkbund Exhibition were buildings by other architects like Peter Behrens, Josef Hoffmann, Van de Velde, and Bruno Taut, showing the progressive spirit of the new architecture, although not quite so convincingly and decisively as in Gropius's work. One interesting structure from the standpoint of the use of glass was Bruno Taut's glass house, which consisted of a twelve-sided drum on which was a pointed dome, all of glass, enclosing a circular staircase. Taut had already been responsible for a sixteen-sided steel-framed water tower at Posen (1910) and an octagonal steel-framed exhibition building at Leipzig (1913). All are similar in conception, belonging clearly to the same family of growths[4].

Some of the more conspicuous features of the new architecture that appear as the result of technical development can be usefully recapitulated. There is the frame structure, either of steel joists or reinforced concrete, with greatly increased spans, where desired, with non-structural screens between, which can be transparent or opaque, so that it is possible to erect wide-spanned transparent structures beyond the powers of previous ages; cantilevering which renders possible considerable structural projection without support; the reduction of bulk so that the width of walls at the base of a high building need only be a small proportion of the bulk if constructed of stone or brick; the flat roof which gives greater freedom in planning and which renders additions to the structure much simpler[5]; and the element of standardization and mass production made possible by steel because large sections can be made in factories and can be assembled speedily in all weathers.

The strivings of various architects towards a living architecture culminated in the establishment of the new architecture in the few years before 1914. The architects who did most in the later phases of this movement, that is, roughly in the early years of the twentieth century, were Otto Wagner, Adolf Loos, Auguste Perret, Tony Garnier, Henri van de Velde, H. P. Berlage, Heinrich Tessenow, Peter Behrens, Hans Poelzig, Adolf Meyer, and Walter Gropius, to whom may be added Louis Sullivan and Frank Lloyd Wright in the United States of America. The new architecture thus established is a true living architecture because it arises from the needs of the time, because in the best examples the most satisfactory fulfilment of purpose determines design, because technical advances in construction made possible by the use of materials like steel and concrete are utilized according to their capacities, and because architectural expression and beauty emerge from purpose and structure. These are the fundamentals of the new architecture, and it more completely realizes the requirements of a living architecture than any other contemporary work. But it would be a mistake to say that it is the only living architecture that had been achieved in the early years of the twentieth century. There are degrees and the new architecture represents the most complete degree. A building, whatever the nature of its structure, which is merely dressed in past styles, and which is planned in accordance with its stylistic elevations, is the complete negation of a living architecture, but there are many buildings which are between these two extremes. A building may be the product of a traditional style, and it may depend mainly for its character on that style, yet modern structure modifies it to a degree so that it becomes a blending of a past style and expression of modern structure; it is thus, to a degree, living architecture. If also the plan begins with purpose rather than conformity to a stylistic elevation, then it is to a further degree living architecture. There are a large number of buildings in Europe, erected between 1900 and 1914, that belong to these categories, and they were increasing in number every year, beginning mainly as industrial buildings and manifesting later in buildings of all types.

If a building is an original creation because it is a fresh interpretation or adaptation of traditional styles, or if it is an eclectic blending of traditional styles, then it may be a living architecture in a different sense. The supreme example of this is the Anglican Liverpool Cathedral, which is an eclectic blending of classical and medieval forms, and as modern human culture is a blending of Greek and Christian thought and influence, this Cathedral is clearly an expression of living culture. As we shall see later, ecclesiastical architecture, because it has to satisfy such very different requirements from industrial architecture, can live in a very different way. Liverpool Cathedral leads on to many later churches which are very much products of contemporary life, although, as can hardly be expected, when their purpose is borne in mind, they rarely achieve that more exclusive expression of our own life conspicuous in the new architecture.

That leads naturally to the importance of purpose in all building. The purpose of an industrial building is very much the product of our own industrial era, whereas the purpose of a church is the product of a spiritual life covering the period of Christianity. Other buildings lie between these. Whatever we may say about the development of construction in determining the forms of a building, it is, after all, the purpose the building has to serve which is the most important consideration of all. An architect may be technically equipped, he may be an artist, but unless he can plan so that the purpose of the building is well served by his design, he can never be completely successful as an architect. And before he can design so that a building can serve its purpose well he must understand that purpose. If it is a factory he must know the process of manufacture within that factory; if a house he must know family needs, requirements, and habits; if a school he must have some notion of the aims and methods of modern education; if an office block he must know how the work of a modern office is conducted; if a hospital he must have some notion of progress in medical science and the physical requirements of medicine and surgery; if a cinema or theatre he must know their different requirements. He must be a sociologist, a technician, and an artist. Without being all three he can never be a competent architect.

It may be objected that clients can inform the architect of the requirements of a building. But unless he knows how the purpose of various types of building can best be served by design as a result of knowledge of their requirements, he will not very intelligently interpret specific and individual requirements for any type. Insufficiency of such knowledge will reduce his powers as a creator.

The manifold purposes of modern buildings lead necessarily to specialism among architects, and in the period between the wars there was an increasing tendency towards specialism. This has its dangers, and the best architects specialize least. After all, variety gives greater scope for the technician and artist, and the intelligent architect should be able to comprehend all the essential purposes of modern building. In those who contributed chiefly to establishing the new architecture from Labrouste, Morris, and Voysey to Garnier, Behrens, and Gropius there is a social breadth of view which distinguishes them from most contemporary architects. And it is precisely this closer contact between the realities of social life and building that was the chief cause in the liberation of architecture from the tyranny of past styles, and its subsequent vigorous life.

REFERENCES AND NOTES

1. I use the term 'new architecture' as it is the term used by its principal exponents.
2. What constitutes the basis of the aesthetic appreciation of architecture? For the present context it must be necessary to accept art broadly as the expression of life and the creation of beauty. Whatever else it may be, it would be difficult to deny convincingly that art is based on these two fundamentals.
3. Reproduced in Bruno Taut's *Modern Architecture*, London, 1929, p. 61.
4. They are illustrated in Bruno Taut's *Modern Architecture*, London, 1929, pp. 55, 56, 59, and 60.
5. Six important advantages of the flat roof over the 'old penthouse roof with its tiled or slated gables' are given by Walter Gropius in his book *The New Architecture and the Bauhaus*, London, 1936, p. 23.

Administrative Office Building of the Deutsche Werkbund Exhibition, Cologne, 1914
Architects: Walter Gropius and Adolf Meyer

PART II

Tradition, Transition and Change

1919—1941

Library at Viipuri (formerly in Finland now Vyborg in USSR, ceded in 1947) 1933–35

Architect: Alvar Aalto

The building was extensively damaged during the Finnish–Russian War. It was rebuilt in 1961. The shell of the building and the main parts were rebuilt as they were before so as to preserve the essential character of Aalto's design. Much of the furnishing was restored as it was originally, but there have been a few minor changes such as some rearrangement of the book shelves and the introduction of a small stage in the lecture room (see pages 170–172)

10 Housing, urban overcrowding, planned dispersal and expansion in the post-war period 1919-1925

ONE OF THE great needs in Europe in 1919 was for houses. At the outbreak of war in 1914 hardly one country in Europe had satisfied the demand for dwellings consistent with a reasonably good standard of living. Keeping pace with the demand was most difficult in countries where there had been a rapid increase in population, in Germany, Great Britain, Holland, and Belgium; but in some countries where the increase had been less rapid, as in France and Sweden, the problem seemed hardly less acute, because, if the magnitude of the problem was less, the magnitude of effort to solve it seemed to be correspondingly less.

The larger industrial countries, England, Germany, and France, were each confronted at the end of the war with a shortage of at least a million dwellings. The greatest shortage of all was in Russia, but owing to the continued attacks on the Soviet Union, internal strife, and famine, the rectification of this shortage had to be delayed for some years after most other countries had made some advance with their housing. The more urgent task of feeding this vast and increasing population had to be undertaken first. Later the Soviet Government vigorously endeavoured to alleviate this housing shortage.

In the belligerent countries there was a certain amount of housing by Government and Municipal Authorities for war-workers, and some of these schemes are interesting as planning and construction[1], but they were generally on a small scale. Building other than for war needs had practically stopped in belligerent countries, while in the neutral countries it had been greatly reduced. But the neutrals had the advantage of avoiding that break in the operations of their building industries that was inevitable with the belligerents. Thus, recovery for the neutrals was less difficult, and it is therefore not surprising that the results achieved by them in planning and housing in the early post-war years compare favourably with that of the belligerents. The best results from 1919 to 1924 were achieved in Holland.

89

Housing in this post-war period can be separated into schemes of an emergency nature, some of which were of a temporary character, and schemes in conformity with long-term planning. In trying to provide houses quickly it was not always possible to wait until fairly extensive plans for residential areas could be put into operation. In some cases, however, plans had been prepared before the war, and facilities for putting them into operation were less subject to delay than entirely new plans; also many schemes had already been begun and operations had been merely suspended. To meet the large demands many new plans had to be prepared, and suitable land had to be acquired before the houses could be erected. Looking back it may be said that one of the reasons for the failure to build houses at all commensurate with requirements was that plans were prepared too late. For example, the London County Council prepared a large number of plans in 1919 and 1920 for block dwellings in the centre and for cottage estates on the outskirts: large schemes like those at Becontree, Roehampton, and Bellingham, none of which was commenced before late 1920 about two years after the Armistice; while in many estates which had already been begun well before the war, like White Hart Lane Estate, building was not restarted until 1920. If more plans had been prepared during the war and the Government had given facilities for putting these plans into operation immediately the war was over, and had exercised adequate control over the prices of building materials, England might have built the million houses which she wanted in the period of 1919–23 instead of a mere 250,000.

The high cost of materials was perhaps the most important reason for the failure in most countries in Europe to produce houses on a scale commensurate with demands. The difficulties were considerable in the victor countries, Great Britain, France, and Italy, but they were much greater in the defeated nations. In England in 1921 the price of timber was 300 per cent above 1914 prices, sanitary fittings 284 per cent, slates 225 per cent, lime 200 per cent, and these coupled with an increase in labour costs of 170 per cent meant that it cost 250 per cent more to build a house in 1921 than in 1914. In Holland during the years 1919, 1920, and 1921 the increase above pre-war cost for building houses was between 250 and 275 per cent. In 1922 prices began to fall, and in 1924 were about 150 per cent above the pre war level[2]. It was much the same in France, Belgium, and Italy, and the Scandinavian countries. Rigorous government control of the price of building materials was a solution which most governments seemed reluctant to adopt. The rising cost of building materials while wages did not increase to the same extent meant that the gap between the cost of houses and the wages of the majority was becoming greater. Before the war the gap had never been closed; in fact it had been increasing, and after the war it widened to an extent that imperilled the foundations of economic life. Because poorer people could not afford dwellings supplied by private enterprise, housing for the lower-income groups was becoming more and more a public concern and a matter for which governments and municipal authorities were making themselves to an increasing degree responsible. Subsidies had been given in some cases by governments, and by the

90

municipal authorities. After the war, to solve the difficulties created mainly by the high cost of building materials and a general lack of preparedness with planning and housing schemes, municipal authorities took a greater share in the provision of houses for the lower-income groups; while to meet the greatly increased cost of building some governments gave subsidies for houses erected both by municipal authorities and by private enterprise. This policy of subsidies was adopted in Great Britain with the Act of 1919; in Germany and Holland the housing subsidies which had already existed since the beginning of the century, and in France since 1912, were extended, while in Denmark and Sweden special subsidies were granted from 1917 to 1922 to meet the high cost of building. In most countries of Europe in the decade following the war the majority of houses were built with official aid.

The difficulties were especially acute in the defeated nations. Their failure to provide dwellings that were urgently wanted, particularly by the poorer people, was not wholly their responsibility. The uncertainties that existed until the peace treaties had been determined, the solution of the greater problem of feeding the people adequately and of reducing the numbers dying from malnutrition, the extensive alterations in national boundaries and the strife attending these adjustments, made it very difficult to formulate an adequate housing policy in the immediate post-war period. Especially was this the case among the countries in eastern and southeastern Europe, where territorial changes were most extensive. The migrations of population that these alterations of boundaries and the attending strife involved aggravated the difficulties. The shorn countries of Austria and Hungary had large influxes of refugees. In both, want and starvation were acute, and there was little opportunity for ambitious planning and housing schemes in this period of emergency. In Vienna, where conditions were very serious, the Socialist City Council attacked the difficult problem with vigour. High tenement dwellings built close together represented much of the unimaginative housing of working people in the previous fifty years. From 1919 to 1923 every available emergency accommodation had to be utilized. Families were housed in old military huts and barracks, extra storeys were added to existing low buildings, dwellings begun in pre-war days by private enterprise were completed, and a colony of houses was built in the old Schmetz Parade Ground. In this way 3,673 homes were provided by 1923[3]. Planning and housing on an ambitious scale and of a progressive character was to come later, and it is interesting to note that with these initial disadvantages Vienna in the following decade was to be responsible for housing that, of its kind, was second to none.

Germany did not have quite the same almost overwhelming difficulties with which to contend as the small countries of southeastern Europe. Germany was fortunate in having a democratic and progressive government, she still retained over four-fifths of her territory and population, and she was not confronted with quite the same problems of redistribution and adjustments as the countries in the southeast. With the exception of Russia, her population of 65 million people was still the largest in Europe and her area was only slightly less than that of France and Spain. Before the war it had been necessary to maintain a high annual production of dwellings of about 200,000 to meet the demands of her rapidly increasing population, but this production had proved insufficient, and like other countries she still had a housing shortage at the outbreak of war. Her financial difficulties and inflation proved a great obstacle, but when the currency was stabilized in 1924 this difficulty was, in some measure, removed. In 1919 and 1920 the emergency accommodation it was necessary to provide for families with no homes of their own was obtained mainly by converting old barracks and large houses. This was done chiefly by municipalities. In addition to subsidies for housing schemes, towns were greatly assisted by the extension of municipal ownership of land. Much of the best housing in the early period was accomplished by a policy of decentralization from the congested areas of the large cities.

The problem presented by the overcrowding of cities and the urban sprawl into the countryside, experienced in the early nineteenth century, was becoming more and more acute after the First World War. It existed in all the large cities of Europe, in London, Berlin, Paris, Vienna, Manchester, Liverpool, Glasgow, Hamburg, Stockholm, Amsterdam, Milan, and Rome, and in many others in varying degrees. There had been agitation for years for measures to secure an abatement of overcrowding; the movement away from the centre of London had begun with the flight of the middle classes to the suburbs, followed by the slum-clearance schemes and the provision of housing estates on the outskirts by the London County Council. What had happened in London happened also in many other European cities. But there was considerable dissatisfaction among planners with the way it was done. It was argued that the decentralization was so often merely a lateral extension of the city, merely further urban sprawl, so that the country was retreating more and more from those who lived in the centre. The solution, it was argued, was not the suburb but the satellite town, which, like the garden city, should be socially comprehensive. Like that, it should have its own industries, so as to secure a satisfactory relation between a man's home and place of work; it should have adequate shops, educational and recreational facilities, and it should be large enough to support these in fair measure, but above all it should be surrounded by a rural belt. It will have been seen that this idea of the garden city had exercised a wide influence in Europe before the First World War and that many attempts were made to build them. Only Letchworth, however, was a complete example. There was too often no clear distinction in the minds of planners between the garden city and garden suburb.

The conviction was growing among enlightened planners and sociologists that planning should no longer be local in character, with planning schemes terminating at the city or town boundary, but that they should be regional in scope and comprehend the whole urban development in any particular area. Most industrial areas in Europe

92

consist of clusters of physically unseparated and indistinguishable small towns generally with one larger central town. Examples are the small towns grouped round London, Berlin, Paris, Hamburg, Cologne, Brussels, Birmingham, Manchester, the cluster of towns in the Ruhr and in the pottery district of England, and many other similar areas. About 1870 these were much smaller towns, each separated from its neighbouring town by rural areas. But with the increase of industry and population they gradually spread towards each other, and joined, so that the whole of each area became one great industrial, urban mass, with only a few open spaces which, in their location, are no longer indicative of town boundaries. Manchester, which affords a good example of this, is surrounded by sixteen boroughs which, with Manchester, have spread and joined up in one vast conurbation, as Patrick Geddes called it. The necessity of planning these areas as a whole was being more and more realized, so that the extensive urban and industrial sprawl unbroken by open spaces and rural belts could be checked in the interests of health and good living conditions. But planning of this regional character remained for the most part the conviction of an enlightened and progressive few, and it recommended itself only very slowly to governments and municipal authorities; while there was always opposition on the part of small boroughs to sacrifice any of their powers to a regional planning authority. County planning authorities, determined in their jurisdiction by ancient boundaries, have little relation to the realities and needs of planning.

BUILDING A BETTER WORLD

During the First World War there was a general feeling that there should be efforts to build a better world, and this was supported by a degree of propaganda, calculated not without its effect on morale. In the sphere of planning and housing it was merely emphasizing what many planners and sociologists and a few architects had been advocating for years. When the war was over the same theme was continued. Lloyd George, in a speech at Wolverhampton shortly after the Armistice, said, 'We must make Britain a fit country for heroes to live in.' He continued: 'Slums are not fit homes for the men who have won this war or for their children. They are not fit nurseries for the children who are to make up an imperial race, and there must be no patching up. This problem has got to be undertaken in a way never undertaken before, as a great national charge and duty. It is too much to leave it merely to municipalities. . . . The housing of the people must be a national concern.' Yet, if we judge by the first five years, Britain failed and failed miserably in this task. Why?

Among the reasons already indicated were lack of adequate control of the prices of building materials and lack of preparedness with planning schemes. Lloyd George was too late. What has been quoted should have been said and acted on in 1916, and government machinery and plans prepared so that a fair planning and housing programme could have been put into operation immediately the war was over. Everybody agreed that such an aim as Lloyd George indicated was right, and should be

93

resolutely pursued. They probably agreed in every country in Europe. Yet the means whereby it might have been accomplished were rejected because of other interests and because of sentiment. On the one hand there was objection to controls which were essential to the work of reconstruction. People cried out for a return to the so-called freedom of 1914. On the other hand there was considerable nonsensical and sentimental objection to planning. People confused the issue and thought their lives would be planned for them. Sentimental architects like Voysey and Baillie Scott wrote articles objecting to control and planning[4]. The former says: 'Town planning is the outcome of a belief in a fundamental principle which is false. The principle is collectivism. The drilling and controlling of the multitude—the formalism of Prussian militarism.' The thought here was widely shared and it presented one of the great obstacles to regional planning and to the improvement of home environment. Such opposition occurred in many countries. In some of the smaller nations, however, like the Netherlands, Denmark, Sweden, and Norway, the ideas of regional planning and housing as a responsibility of the State had made more progress.

The opposition mentioned did not deter the eloquent and vigorous advocacy of regional planning and of the necessity of comprehensive measures to get rid of slums and to develop residential areas with adequate space, good surroundings, recreational and cultural facilities with the country within easy reach of those who live and work in the town. To give the majority of people such conditions of life could be accomplished only by taking them from the congested centres of the cities and providing accommodation for them elsewhere, by the enlargement of small towns and villages, by new towns, or by further suburbs. Further suburbs, it was objected, would just add to the evils of urban sprawl already indicated, and each suburban addition would not have a corporate life of its own but merely be a small insignificant addition to the existing colossus. These objections were very largely ignored, as also was the solution advocated by many planners and sociologists throughout Europe of regional planning by means of satellite towns. F. J. Osborn told[5] how he, C. B. Purdom, and other followers of Howard had written 'articles in popular papers, lobbied political parties, and toured mayoral parlours in an endeavour to get the Government and the great municipalities to translate our very practical proposals into action'. Early in 1919 the Garden Cities and Town Planning Association presented a memorandum to Dr Addison, President of the Local Government Board, in which it proposed that a committee should be formed to consider 'the development of new industrial centres on the garden city principle' and also that there should be a national town planning commission with regional officers. The official reply was that there was no time to consider such proposals until the housing problem had been dealt with. Official blindness could not see that here were real proposals which could form a substantial basis for better housing and for better home environment.

WELWYN GARDEN CITY

The advocacy of planned dispersal, both of population and industry, to be accomplished by regional planning with a system of satellite towns built on garden city principles, was confronted very largely with an apathetic public. To the majority the ideas savoured of Utopianism, and, therefore, were regarded as not entirely practical. Like all great social ideas that appear new it took time for them to gain acceptance. Still something was done. Referring to the most important post-war step F. J. Osborn recalls that, whilst he and others were engaged in vigorous propaganda, Howard had secured a site for the second garden city of Welwyn, which C. B. Purdom calls the first satellite town[6]. The enthusiasts had wanted several, sufficient to accommodate a fair dispersal of population from overcrowded centres. They had got one.

The land for this new garden city covers an area which was originally 2,378 acres (periodic subsequent additions have increased it to 4,317 acres), lying twenty miles to the north of London and served by the railway from King's Cross. Planned by Louis de Soissons, and commenced in 1920[7], it follows the principles which determined the planning of Letchworth. Originally limited in population to 36,500, the maximum was subsequently increased to 50,000. (It had reached about 45,000 in 1972.) It was designed so that most of the people living there work there and for varied income groups with facilities for a social mixing of these groups. A green belt surrounds the town. The industrial area lies to the east of the main south–north railway and the town centre lies to the west with the residential areas on both sides of the railway.

Some of the site planning for the houses is interesting and shows considerable advance in ingenuity and variety on Letchworth. This is achieved by the employment of the close or cul-de-sac running off from the traffic road. This has numerous advantages. It is more economical because there is not the same length of through-traffic road required for residential areas, the culs-de-sac can be lightly constructed service ways, while they ensure a greater degree of quiet and safety for children than through roads. The architectural effect can often be very pleasing if the houses are well designed. Barry Parker has employed this cul-de-sac planning, often with an octagonal arrangement of houses, with some measure of success at Earswick, and there are a few attractive examples in Hampstead Garden Suburb. Louis de Soissons employed many different types of cul-de-sac, which give considerable variety to the residential areas. Formal geometric patterns determine the planning, and if the houses are to be satisfactorily orientated, plans must be varied according to position. The planning of houses should begin with a consideration of what is most agreeable to the family, and a house in a northern climate should surely be orientated according to the sun. No room should face north, but in these culs-de-sac these considerations are necessarily subservient to siting according to geometric patterns. They may give variety and interest and a certain picturesqueness, but it is questionable if planning here starts at the right point. It would be better to let the grouping of the houses round the cul-de-sac be

95

determined by the sun than by geometric patterns. The grouping of houses for American war-workers at Aluminium City near Pittsburg, built in 1943, offers an illuminating contrast. These houses, designed by Walter Gropius and Marcel Breuer, are sited irregularly according to the sun, and with complete disregard of any formal or geometric layout. They represent the culmination of twenty years' progress in this matter.

The early houses in Welwyn Garden City are mostly the traditional type with a greater degree of simplicity than in most of the houses in Bournville, Port Sunlight, and Letchworth. The plain wall is often used with good effect, one noteworthy example being the houses in Handside Close, designed by Louis de Soissons. There is still, however, in many of the small houses the reminiscence of the medieval cottage with its small windows.

What enthusiasts for large-scale measures, regional planning, garden cities, and satellite towns had recommended was to continue an unrealized ideal, a dream until the Second World War. Instead, piecemeal, small-visioned planning producing the further urban sprawl into the countryside continued by means of new suburbs. The London County Council contributed to this with its cottage estates, some of which had been begun before the First World War, while others were planned in 1920 and developed a little later, as previously noted. The most ambitious of these is Becontree, east of London, covering an area of 2,770 acres, which the London County Council claimed to be the largest municipal housing estate in the world[8]. Five hundred acres are reserved for open spaces, 118 acres of which form the large central Parsloes Park. The estate is planned for 25,039 dwellings, to give accommodation for 112,570 persons, mostly displaced from the overcrowded areas of the County of London. The best that can be said for Becontree is that it provides better accommodation for most of the people who came to live there from the slums. But contrast it with Welwyn Garden City. Welwyn covers approximately the same area. It is to have a maximum population one-third that of Becontree. Being completely surrounded by country it has an identity and corporate life of its own, providing its own amenities, whereas Becontree, instead of being surrounded by country, is joined on to Ilford as another vast suburb with insufficient amenities in its own area. In Welwyn most of the people who work there live there, whereas in Becontree most of the people go elsewhere to work, mostly to London—a none-too-pleasant journey. The people who work in many of the neighbouring factories, such as Ford's, at Dagenham, have found it difficult to get accommodation in Becontree because the persons displaced from London, most of whom go there to work, have priority. All classes of society live in Welwyn; in Becontree one class is segregated together. Lastly, Becontree is built on first-class arable land, thus some of the best food-growing land in the country, yet hardly any of it is used for agriculture. Welwyn is built on arable land less valuable than that of Becontree, yet half of it is used for agriculture in the form of a green belt. Welwyn belongs to that brave new world full of promise and happiness, Becontree to a continuation of that dreary unimaginative world that has been so often the setting of the Industrial Revolution.

Although the authorities in other European countries seemed generally as slow as the authorities in England to realize the value of planning on a regional scale, where the region is determined, not by ancient boundaries, but by modern urban and industrial development, there are some noteworthy and enlightened exceptions. One of the most ambitious and comprehensive of these regional schemes is that of the Ruhr district in Germany, comprising 1,482 square miles in which is a population of four millions and over 300 local authorities. The planning of this vast area is the responsibility of a Federation appointed in 1920, and its function is to determine the main lines of communication, to criticize and assist in the preparation of town plans, to reserve open spaces, and to sanction new housing schemes. A step towards regional planning was made in France with the Town Planning Act of 1919, and in accordance with the Act Paris and the Department of the Seine organized a competition for the planning of the region surrounding Paris. Many of the schemes submitted recommended dispersal by means of satelite towns and garden cities. Holland and Italy provide examples of large areas of reclaimed land, the Zuyder Zee and the Pontine Marshes, which are planned as a whole. The former was begun in 1920, and has been developed in sections covering a total area of about 865 square miles. The first district, Wieringermeir, to be developed covers an area of about 77 square miles and consists of fourteen villages. Housing, agricultural, and industrial areas are planned in satisfactory and convenient relationship. Each village is provided with essential educational and recreational facilities, including a school, a cinema, and places of worship. The planning of the reclaimed Pontine Marshes, covering an area of 300 square miles, was begun several years later.

Most regional plans in Europe were concerned with dispersal and avoidance of further congestion of the big cities, and although few were on the scale recommended by enlightened and progressive planners, yet a start was made with some, while modified schemes on a much smaller scale were in some cases adopted. In Germany the policy of building garden suburbs was extending, and few big German cities are without them. Several were developed shortly after the First World War. Good examples are those planned and built by Peter Behrens in the vicinity of Berlin, Neusaburg (1919), Nowawes near Potsdam (1920), and Forst in the Lausity (1919). But though garden suburbs were being extensively planned, the idea of the complete satellite town planned on garden city principles, like Letchworth or Welwyn, was not adopted as many planners wished. The nearest approaches to the more complete satellite towns were a few industrial housing estates. Hellerau, north of Dresden, and Altona, near Hamburg, continued to be developed after the war. Hellerau, a little over 500 acres in extent, is obviously too small for satisfactory development as a town. It is not merely an outlying suburb, however, for a few industries are established there so that many of the people who live there also work there. Peter Behrens was responsible for several of the estates built there after the war, in 1920. We have already noted that Behrens in his early house designs was greatly influenced by English domestic architecture, and this influence is still apparent in many of the houses in Altona, with their plain brick walls, windows reminiscent of English Tudor, and large expanses of roof with 45 degrees pitch. Dutch influence is probably also a factor. Hilversum in Holland and Zlin in Czechoslovakia are industrial towns which have been considerably developed between the wars. The planning of each has clearly been influenced by garden city principles, and each has a distinct identity and corporate life of its own.

SATELLITE COMMUNITIES

Stockholm provides an interesting example of satellite estate development. The municipal authority had been acquiring land on the outskirts for a decade before the war to be developed as estates of family houses. Several of these estates were being developed in the post-war period. They were spaciously planned, and each estate was in a large measure surrounded by open country. A considerable number of the houses are built of timber and were erected by the tenants or owner-occupiers. These estates are often called garden cities, but they have not the social comprehensiveness of the true garden city as developed in England according to the ideas of Howard. They are suburbs in a sense, but they do not continue the urban sprawl into the country, as they are often separate residential entities surrounded by green belts.

Schemes for satellite town or satellite estate development have been prepared for many Scandinavian cities. In Copenhagen there has been a development of satellite residential districts, mainly at the junctions of main roads[9]. These districts are developed under garden city influence, but they are too small to be regarded as good satellite towns. A scheme for the building of several satellite districts of Trondhjem, in Norway, was prepared by Sverve Pedersen in 1918. The town of Stjordalshalsen, planned by Pedersen in 1920, was built fifteen miles to the east of Trondhjem, which, although small, is conceived with the social comprehensiveness of a garden city.

Extension by means of satellite towns presupposes the desirability of limiting the size of cities. In unchecked urban sprawl of big cities, the delights and benefits of the country which are especially important to children are more difficult of access. Thus, it is argued, in the future towns should be limited in size, and many of the large congested industrial cities should gradually be reduced in population by dispersal. The social and economic advantages of this are being more and more realized, and it is regrettable that governments did not pay more attention to such recommendations in the post-war period of 1919–24. London, the worst example, continued its haphazard urban sprawl and enlarged its population by nearly two millions between the wars. Amsterdam, on the contrary, is an example of planned expansion on a regional scale, not by satellite towns but by continued urban extension, and it is a plan that has been much praised by those who do not wholly favour satellite town and garden city development[10].

Amsterdam had increased rapidly in population since about 1880, when it was 330,063. In 1921 it had risen to 683,136. Since 1866 plans had been considered for the extension of the city, but little of an ordered character had been done until the present century. Accommodation for the increasing population had been provided by closer building in the centre by means of tenement blocks. The consequent congestion gradually resulted in slums, and thus the merchants and well-to-do, who had lived in the centre, often in houses which also formed part of their business premises, finding the city a less and less pleasant place in which to live, moved to the outskirts. Their vacated premises were often occupied by many poorer families. Amsterdam was but one example in this respect of what happened in most of the large cities of Europe.

Amsterdam lies to the south of the confluence of the rivers Y and Amstel. It has been developed mainly on a half-spider-web plan formed largely by intersecting canals, and surrounded by a city wall. This has long been regarded as a classic example of organic planning. Lewis Mumford says of it that, though it is geometrical, it 'is a magnificent adaptation to economic and social opportunities'[11].

The plan of 1866 was prepared for extension all round the city walls. Based on formal classical geometric principles, in which the gridiron and radiating systems and handsome boulevards were conspicuous, it had some degree of unity, fairly satisfactory relation of parts, and included a generous provision of open paces. But the plan was not followed and extension was left mainly to haphazard private development. In 1902 a plan was prepared by H. P. Berlage for the southern extension. Nothing was done, however, until 1915, when Berlage revised his plan, and the extension was commenced shortly afterwards mainly on the lines of this plan, which, however, is of a general character subject to modification by the municipality. It is much freer, less rigid, less geometric than the scheme of 1866. Wide boulevards allowing garden strips and trees are conspicuous, each street is conceived as an entity for Berlage insists that the dwellings in a street should be designed as a whole. He advocates block dwellings as most satisfactorily conducive to this architectural unity. This southern area of Amsterdam is developed on these principles and the block dwellings present some of the most interesting examples of modern Dutch romantic architecture in the work of M. de Klerk, P. L. Kramer, and others.

Wide boulevards, fine unified architectural effects mingled with greenery, symmetrical planning, constitute a fundamentally formal classical conception. The planning starts with an aim at fine appearance. The orientation of the blocks of dwellings is not dictated mainly by family needs or by the sun, but by the geometrical layout of streets.

99

This extension to the south meant that the country was no longer so readily accessible, and a considerable number of parks were provided as compensation. When the city extended only a little beyond the city walls, the need for parks was not felt. It is a question, therefore, whether the extension has been wise. Do parks compensate for the loss of open country on the boundaries of a city limited in size? Would it not have been better to have planned this extension as a satellite town ten miles farther out? The same question arises with the garden villages and communities that are being developed to the north of the city on the farther side of the River Y. Among these communities or garden villages are Buiksloterham, Oostzaan, and Nieuwendam. The influence of the English garden city is apparent, but they cluster far too closely round the city, and in this they share the planning defects of the London County Council cottage estates.

The southern extension of Amsterdam provides one of the best examples in Europe of a school of thought in planning which is opposed to the garden city, satellite town school. It is a school which believes in the planned extension of the big city, with the provision of ample open spaces for physical recreation; and believes in handsome, dignified appearance as a principal aim to be achieved by formal planning, with the street as the unit to be designed architecturally as a whole. Which of these schools of thought is closer to human needs and desires, which considers more directly the welfare of family life, its freedom, and the growth and delight of children? In a residential area, and the greater part of every town is primarily that, there are the fundamental questions in planning, and these human considerations must be the starting point. There can be little doubt that the garden city and satellite town method of extension serves these fundamental human purposes better than suburbs finely planned on formal geometrical lines[12].

Numerous theoretic town-planning schemes were prepared at this time. As in the past, they were prepared with the idea of providing a solution of the social and economic evils like overcrowding and slums, transport congestion, separation of homes and places of work, scarcity of open spaces and inaccessibility of country, that had arisen from haphazard urban development; and they mostly belong to the two schools of thought, the advocates of the garden city and satellite town, and the advocates of planned city extension. Paul Wolf, who was city architect of Dresden, belongs to the former school. He prepared a plan of groups of three garden cities with a maximum population of 100,000. The garden cities occupy the corners of an equilateral triangle, each being surrounded by agricultural land. Three principal avenues run from the central open space of each garden city and meet in the centre of the triangular space where there is an administrative building. An avenue runs between each town and is crossed by a main road which connects the towns laterally. In another scheme for a satellite town Paul Wolf plans it as an elliptical diagram, with administrative, cultural, and recreational buildings in the centre, surrounded by a series of four elliptical belts: (1)

residential area, (2) gardens, (3) houses and gardens, and (4) open country. The industrial area is to the east a little separated from the town.

In 1924 Adolf Rading prepared a plan for a city on the green wedge principle. The central town is compact and closely populated, and four wedges of agricultural land penetrate almost to the centre of the town. Between these wedges beyond the town are residential areas interspersed with pleasure gardens, market gardens, and orchards. This green-wedge principle was to be developed by later planners, and was to become an important feature of the development of many important cities, Moscow being a conspicuous example.

The planning theory that excited the most widespread influence at this time was that of Le Corbusier, which he evolved between 1915 and 1922. From his reflections in *Vers une architecture*, published in 1923[13], it would appear that his idea for his city had its germ in a report of an interview that Auguste Perret had with a reporter of the *Intransigeant*, describing an idea for a city of towers. This seemed an original conception, but there were some extravagant and fantastic features in Perret's scheme which Le Corbusier endeavoured to rationalize. The centre of the city was to consist of a group of towers, each designed on an equilateral cross plan, which was to house the business and administrative offices. Near these are the civic and entertainment buildings. Situated to the west and extending from the central area is a large park, and surrounding the whole is a large residential area. To the east is the industrial area, separated by a green strip. Open country surrounds the city and some little distance away, a distance which is not specified, are garden cities. Two main traffic arteries running north–south and east–west cross in the centre of the group of towers. These traffic arteries are raised on concrete piles above the ground from 12 to 16 feet, and are used for passenger motor traffic. The goods traffic goes below. This idea Le Corbusier had developed as early as 1915 when he visualized a whole town on two floors. The streets for pedestrians and passenger transport are on the upper floor; and goods transport, having access to the ground floors of buildings, and all the main services— water, electricity, gas, sewers, telephone—are arranged on the ground floor. This obviates the necessity of burying all these and also makes them easily accessible. This two-level city scheme was first thought of by Leonardo da Vinci and is the best part of Le Corbusier's plan. Its value is considerable and it has exercised some influence in encouraging multi-level development for the centre of cities.

The general plan of the city has certain points of similarity with Howard's garden city clusters with a central city of 50,000 and surrounding cities of 32,000. But Le Corbusier's central city is much larger, and the garden cities clustering round are more in the nature of residential districts set in the open country. Le Corbusier's plan must obviously involve some limitation of the size of the city, because if it expanded without restriction it would join with the garden cities and much of the virtue of the plan would be lost. Le Corbusier does not indicate the limit. He altered this plan later in *La Ville radieuse*, where the garden cities are abandoned and provision is made for expansion east and west, somewhat on the lines of the lineal city.

REFERENCES AND NOTES

1. In Sir Lawrence Weaver's *Small Houses and Cottages*, London, 1925, there is an account of some of the war housing in Great Britain at Gretna Green and Dormanstown.
2. *Amsterdam: Development of the Town Housing Improvement*, Town Printing Office, Amsterdam, 1924, p. 26.
3. See Elizabeth Denby, *Europe Rehoused*, London, 1937, p. 151.
4. *The Architectural Review*, vol. xlvi, 1919, On Town Planning by C. F. A. Voysey, p. 25; The Charm of National Planning by Baillie Scott, p. 43.
5. F. J. Osborn gives this account in the preface to the second edition of *New Towns after the War*, published in 1942. The first edition was published in 1918 as by New Townsmen, who were F. J. Osborn, W. G. Taylor, and C. B. Purdom, but written by the first-named.
6. An excellent exposition of satellite towns, and a description of Letchworth and Welwyn, are given in C. B. Purdom's *The Building of Satellite Towns*, London, 1925; part 3 is devoted to Welwyn Garden City, the first satellite town.
7. It was taken over by a Development Corporation in 1948.
8. *London Housing*, published by the L.C.C., 1937, p. 154.
9. A plan of this is given in plate I of C. B. Purdom's *The Building of Satellite Towns*.
10. Sigfried Giedion, for example. His description of the Amsterdam plan, given under the heading Amsterdam and the Rebirth of Town Planning, appears in *Space, Time and Architecture*, 1940, pp. 517–58.
11. *Culture of Cities*, London, 1938, plates 16 and 17.
12. There is not space to give my reasons here, but some of them are given in my book *Civic Design and the Home*, London, 1943, where I discuss with men and women in the Forces the sort of dwellings and environment that satisfy family needs.
13. An English translation by Frederick Etchells of the thirteenth French edition was published in 1927.

11   *Variations on classical and Renaissance themes*

DURING THE THIRD DECADE of the century the volume of building of almost every kind gradually increased and by 1930 was greater than it had ever been before. At this time Europe enjoyed a fair degree of political freedom and social and economic development, to be succeeded in the years 1930–3 by economic depression which reduced the volume of building, but it was to increase again for a further six years until the outbreak of the Second World War.

Political freedom and economic development had a marked effect on architecture and building. Economic conditions affect the quantity of building but political conditions affect its character. It is often asserted that art can flourish only in conditions of freedom or enlightened patronage, and the former was present in many countries in Europe during this period, especially in Germany, France, Holland, Denmark, Sweden, Norway, Czechoslovakia, and Switzerland. This reflection has greater significance in the light of the changes that took place in German architecture when it passed from a democracy to a dictatorship in 1933. It is in some measure due to the conditions that existed in the democratic countries that architecture during this period displayed much vigour and original development. There is no more vital period during the century than this.

The architecture of Europe in the middle of the inter-war period (about 1925 to 1934) may be broadly classified as architecture that evolves mainly from traditional styles and methods, in which traditional materials are expressed; and architecture that springs rather from a logical solution of problems arising from the purpose and construction of the building and from the newer materials presented by modern industry. This is not to say that traditional architecture does not involve a logical solution of building problems, but such solutions are reconciled with traditional practice, and the method of design follows traditional principles, with varying degrees of modification, while the method of design in the new architecture is more on an empirical basis. An example will elucidate the distinction.

103

An architect designing in the classical tradition endeavours, as a matter of habit, to make his plan symmetrical. He will often begin with the imposing symmetrical elevation and design his plan accordingly. It will often mean much hard work and constant trial and rejection to achieve a plan at once convenient and symmetrical so that the building functions well. Often the task proves too difficult and the convenience is sacrificed to the symmetry. In designing logically from purpose an architect of the new school is not handicapped by obligation to make his plans or elevations symmetrical: the function of the building is his main guide, and his elevations and the general design of his building spring from that.

Adherence to tradition is a matter of degree. It may be a fairly close following of some powerful tradition like Roman or Gothic; it may be based on traditional methods yet modified by modern construction and a general impulse towards simplicity, or it may take the form of original variations on themes set by traditional architecture. There are numerous important examples in Europe of all these in the period from 1920 to 1935. Similarly, although the designs of the architects of the new school emerge logically from purpose, their work demonstrates that there are very different ways of solving building problems, while there are differences in the aesthetic principles actuating their work. Further, wider social and economic considerations, such as the benefits of standardization and mass production, have had their effects on some phases of modern architecture.

A fairly close following of classical and Renaissance architecture persisted to a degree in all European countries, but most strongly in England and the Mediterranean countries. Whereas it was the prevailing architecture in nearly all European countries before 1914, it was much less so after the war, especially in France, Germany, Scandinavia, and the Low Countries. In England it was still so during the post-war years, from 1920 to 1926, but less so during the following period, from 1927 to 1933. In many of the other European countries where the classical and Renaissance styles were closely followed, they were often modified by an original treatment or by some expression of structure or effects of simplicity. The volume and importance of building mainly in the classical and Renaissance traditions during the twenties being greater in England than elsewhere in Europe, it therefore claims some attention; but there are also some significant examples in Sweden and Italy.

The tradition broadly designated as classical, including its revival the Renaissance, has many phases, but all serve to determine the designs of the followers of this broad tradition. There are the Greek, Roman, and early and late Renaissance styles, and examples may be found that follow principally one of these and examples which are mixtures of two or more. In this tradition the phases of Greek, Roman, and Renaissance architecture, are, to the free classicist, a common stock from which he may draw. Thus we find Greek or Roman the main source, as in some of the work of Sir

Edwin Cooper, Vincent Harris, and Curtis Green. In other work, as in some of Sir Edwin Lutyens's buildings, the astylar façades of early Renaissance palaces in Florence and Rome are followed; or a mixture of Greek, Roman, and early Renaissance, as in the work of Sir Reginald Blomfield; or later Renaissance, as in some of the work of Herbert J. Rowse.

There is some similarity in appearance between much Renaissance architecture of the seventeenth and eighteenth centuries before the Greek revival, and much Renaissance architecture in the twentieth century after the Greek revival. In the latter the influence of Greek architecture is naturally stronger, and the desire for more exact reproduction of classical details with less interpretative freedom is apparent. Also the more exclusively Greek revival was not entirely dead, because many buildings of the period immediately before and after the First World War were designed in the Greek style, as, for example, Sir Edwin Cooper's Marylebone Town Hall and Alexander Klein's large house in the Ballenstedter Strasse in Berlin.

Most large buildings erected in the early post-war period and designed in the classic or Renaissance style were constructed with a steel frame and faced with stone or brick. In this they were essentially different from the Renaissance buildings of the seventeenth and eighteenth centuries, but in the majority of buildings in this style erected between 1919 and 1924 that difference is not very apparent in their appearance. The classical tradition persisted to some extent in most European countries after the war, but most strongly in England. In Holland and the Scandinavian countries other more native traditions were stronger; in Germany and France buildings in this tradition were to a greater extent modified by new methods of construction. In many European countries numerous public buildings like town halls, office blocks, particularly banks and insurance offices, museums, and departmental stores in the third decade of the century, were designed in the classical Renaissance style. Many large buildings that were conceived before the war were carried out after the war according to the original designs with little modification; and many buildings of this traditional kind that were designed soon after the war to be erected as soon as the availability of materials and labour would permit, were designed very much as they would have been before the war. To such architects the war was just a break, it effected no change in their architectural thought.

If one looks at the buildings of famous architects designing in the classical Renaissance style in the decade following the war, one would not be aware that they were built with a steel frame as the essential structural feature. They appear as if built of stone or brick very much like Renaissance architecture of the seventeenth and eighteenth centuries. The steel construction was employed, not as providing character for expression, but because it allowed some reduction of bulk and because of the commercial consideration that the steel frame is a much more rapid method. At the same

105

time it would be impossible to deny certain valuable architectural qualities in such work. Designing ability is displayed in the adaptation of the classic style to the building problem, but, as is almost inevitable with classic symmetrical elevations, one gets the impression that the designs commenced with these elevations, and the plan and interior arrangement of the building had to accord with the elevations. This was often done with considerable ingenuity. In the Police Headquarters at Copenhagen, designed by Hack Kampmann and completed between 1920 and 1924, the triangular site is a little irregular, yet, as will be seen from the illustrations, the plan is as symmetrical and formal as possible, and it is clear that the designer was thinking of the effect of his elevations, particularly of the effect of the colonnade of the circular court. It must be admitted that many of these buildings in the classical Renaissance style have considerable beauty of proportion which gives aesthetic pleasure. In the Wolseley building (now Barclays Bank), Piccadilly, London (1921–22) and the London Life Assurance building in King William Street (1921–23) both by W. Curtis Green the proportions of the coupled columns in the recess formed to receive them on the first, second, and third floors of both buildings are very satisfying; in the Wolseley building the circular arches on the ground floor seem to be almost perfectly proportioned. To realize how finely proportioned is the broad massing of this building, which received the R.I.B.A. Bronze Medal for street architecture in 1922, one should compare it with W. Curtis Green's later Westminster Bank building at the corner of Piccadilly and Albemarle Street, which has little of this grand and massive simplicity, but is cut up into comparatively unsatisfactory related parts. The Police Headquarters at Copenhagen is also noteworthy for excellent proportions and broad and impressive simplicity. Among some architects of this group there was a degree of originality in the treatment of Renaissance. While preserving stone or brick constructional character, Sir Edwin Lutyens often exercised a unique artistic fancy in his treatment of design combined always with an unerring sense of good proportion. In the well-proportioned Britannic House in Finsbury Circus he introduced within the general unity of the design a variety of Renaissance idioms with delightful effect, giving here and there a note of gaiety which is captivating.

Some architects, as distinct from those already mentioned, in their treatment of Renaissance, while using steel-frame construction, allowed the reduction of bulk to influence the appearance of the buildings, and some combined this with a greater degree of simplicity and allowed the plain wall to play a greater part in the design. This is seen in the work of Gunnar Asphund in such an example as the City Library, Stockholm, and in the secular work of Sir Giles G. Scott in examples like Clare College, Cambridge, but more particularly in the office building in Finsbury Square. It would be difficult to say if that lightness of effect in Sir Giles Scott's work of this kind is due more to a recognition that the steel frame means a much lighter building constructionally, and that this should logically have an effect on appearance, or whether it is an effect of the use of plain brick walls and avoidance of features like rusticated

106

Police Headquarters, Copenhagen, 1919–23
Architect: Hack Kampmann

Britannic House, Finsbury Circus, 1922–24
Architect: Sir Edwin Lutyens

Above—view of the circular courtyard, below—air view

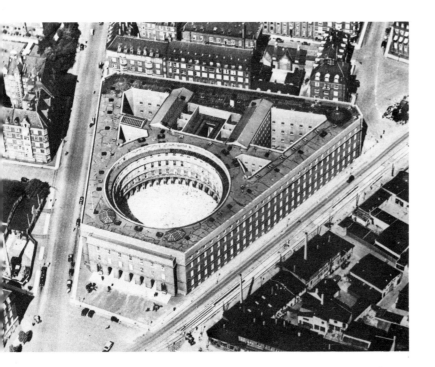

stonework that would give an effect of heaviness. It is probably a combination of the two. Features like window reveals, which in strictly traditional Renaissance work are kept fairly deep to give the necessary massive effect, are in Sir Giles G. Scott's early work kept almost as narrow as the steel frame will permit. In later work of this kind by this architect, such as the Cambridge University Library, the steel frame is clearly expressed in the façades.

TRANSITION FROM TRADITIONAL RENAISSANCE TO EXPRESSION OF MODERN STRUCTURE

In many industrial buildings as early as the eighteen-nineties, the steel or concrete was clearly apparent in the appearance; but in most buildings of a partially ceremonial character which were being designed in the traditional classical Renaissance style, the steel frame only very gradually affects the appearance of the building. Early examples where the steel frame has clearly influenced the design of the façade is Alfred Messel's Wertheim store in Berlin (1896), and Kodak House in Kingsway (1911) (see Chapter 9). It appears by slow degrees in buildings that are conceived more academically and the steel frame gradually asserts itself in the elevations, until in many façades it determines the essential character. The stages are: (1) where it is faintly apparent; (2) where it becomes more assertive; and (3) where, although the building is designed on the classical principles of symmetry and formal arrangement, the decorative character of the façades emanates mainly from the steel frame, or in some cases the reinforced concrete frame, although this was not used to so great an extent for such buildings until later. The transition is accompanied by elimination of ornament and a greater simplicity in the general effect. The movements towards simplicity and expression of construction are contemporary and the negative process of eliminating ornament and thus, preparing a clean sheet for expression, is a condition of the latter. The transition can be studied in numerous examples of buildings erected during the six years from 1919 to 1924. In the first stage pilasters that form a prominent decorative feature of the façade became simpler, the bases and capitals are either more simply treated than in the traditional classical, or some simple ornament or moulding substituted. The spaces between pilasters are often increased, and bronze horizontal bands sometimes appear between the windows in the recesses formed by the pilasters. Examples of this kind are Heals in Tottenham Court Road, designed by Smith and Brewer, the Blackburn Assurance Co building in Liverpool, and Waterloo Station. The simplified treatment in each case is mainly the result of the influence of structure. In a building like Devonshire House in Piccadilly, designed by Sir Charles Reilly and Thomas Hasting, the steel frame is less apparent in the façade pattern, but there is a feeling of it in the comparatively thin walls, conspicuous in the narrow window reveals, and also in the large showroom windows on the ground floor. Belonging to this initial stage of transition is the impressive railway station at Stuttgart, designed by Paul Bonatz and F. E. Scholer, which, though classical in conception, is modified in design by the frame construction.

A second stage is where these decorated uprights have ceased to be pilasters, and where the horizontal stanchions also become apparent, with the result that the gridiron pattern seen often in factories forms a decorative basis for the façade. An excellent example of this is Adelaide House, London Bridge, designed by Sir John Burnet and Partners. The more complete transition is when all Renaissance and classical ornamental features have disappeared and the design, although determined by classical symmetry and proportion, is partially an expression of the method of frame construction. We find this in the large office block in Utrecht, designed by G. W. van Heukelom. It will be seen from the plan and elevation that the conception is symmetrical and formal, but the particular character of the façade, with the long, vertical, straight shafts and the subordinate horizontal members make the complete transition from a façade of classical pilasters to long, straight members that reproduce the forms of the steel frame. Another Dutch building where classical conception determines design, yet where modern structure is expressed, is the Radio Station at Kootwyk, designed by J. M. Luthmas. It is not difficult to see in this a transformed Greek temple, where instead of a comparatively heavy stone construction it has a lightness of aspect, seen especially in the treatment of windows, made possible by steel.

Industrial buildings offer the most modern examples. These, it must be remembered, are distinct from the more functional and progressive type of building where expression of purpose and structure makes it a more living architecture than this academic classical work. The industrial buildings with which we are at present concerned are conceived in this traditional classical spirit where formal and symmetrical plans and elevations are a law never to be broken. They are interesting as examples of this transition from classic decoration of façades to those determined by steel-framed construction. Among the noteworthy examples are the Wallace Scott Tailoring Institute, Cathcart, near Glasgow, designed by Sir John Burnett, Son and Dick; the Gros Grosskraftwerk, Klingerberg, in Berlin, designed by G. and W. Klingerberg and W. Israel; and the massive and impressive Schaltwerk-Hockhaus in Siemensstadt, Berlin, designed by Hans Hertlein. In the last-mentioned the long verticals seem to be added to the façade as if to give the necessary emphasis to the steel frame.

This vertical emphasis by means of long vertical pilasters or shafts in such buildings as the office block at Utrecht and many others which were designed at this time, is probably in many cases only partly prompted by the steel frame. Vertical emphasis, like horizontal emphasis, an early example of which is the office building at Breslau, designed by Hans Poelzig, is partially due to the emphasis of the character of the building. With a long vertical rectangle there is a natural inclination to emphasize its verticality, and the same with the horizontal rectangle. Buildings were becoming simpler and larger; they were being built higher, and the influence of the vertical emphasis of soaring American buildings was being felt in Europe. In London new buildings rose to a height of 100 feet, which often meant a shape vertical in character, and simple decorative effect meant emphasis of this vertical character. In the case of a long block its length was often emphasized by unbroken horizontal bands, as was often the case in Germany at this time, or it was punctuated with vertical bands, which can hardly be said to be vertical emphasis, but a character transferred from the emphasis of vertical shape, or as articulation of the horizontal mass.

The best examples are afforded generally by those that are made distinctive by the individual touch of their designers. Whether we like them or not we can say broadly that the buildings of Sir Edwin Lutyens, Sir Herbert Baker, Sir Reginald Blomfield, and Herbert J. Rowse have a distinction conveyed by the personalities of their architects that is lacking in a large amount of other work in the classical or Renaissance tradition. The work of Sir Reginald Blomfield is saved from being merely copybook work by a distinctive robustness and vigour. Although Blomfield uses the steel frame construction, he is thinking of the effects of stone construction in his classical façades, and evinces a particular affection for these effects because he emphasizes the solidity and heaviness of stone. He frequently used rusticated masonry, examples being the Carlton Club and the United Universities Club, both in Pall Mall. Like so many architects who adhered fairly close to the classical Renaissance tradition, he seemed happiest when engaged on work of a monumental character, and it is no accident that his best work is probably the Menin Gate, which forms the Memorial to the Missing at Ypres. Blomfield himself referred to this and the Lambeth Bridge as his best work. The Menin Gate is reminiscent in character and form of a classical temple. At either side is a peristyle of Roman Doric columns, while at the ends are large circular central arches flanked by small lintel arches. It is felicitously proportioned and is a work in which the architect gave of his best. The Menin Gate has undoubtedly deeply impressed many who have seen it.

Although Sir Edwin Lutyens adhered almost as strongly to classical principles, there is a far greater degree of originality in his work, while his buildings—especially the façades—are distinguished by a rare beauty of proportion. If by architect we mean one who, in considering the purpose of his building, studies the relevant social requirements, plans his buildings accordingly and tries to reconcile his elevations to the plans, and also considers the limitations and potentialities of various methods of construction, then we must hesitate to accord to Sir Edwin Lutyens the appellation of great architect. But he was a great artist in architectural proportion and in evolving a sequence of forms. As a planner he was less satisfactory than many who were his inferiors as artists. Few would regard the buildings of Sir Edwin Cooper, for example, as having the originality or beauty of proportion of those of Sir Edwin Lutyens; indeed, Cooper's building appears so often as mere conscientious adaptations of classical architecture to modern building. Yet Cooper's plans are evidence of a constant endeavour to make them serve the function of the building as well as possible while conforming with symmetrical elevations. But so often in Lutyens's work—and we

110

find it in the earlier country houses and in some of the larger later work—the plan is adjusted to the elevation with some sacrifice in its functional efficiency. There are brilliant exceptions such as the Viceregal Lodge at Delhi, which is certainly one of his best buildings, but which is outside the scope of this survey. Often, however, we find that much of his best work is either where he has been able to concentrate on the elevations and leave to other architects the task of reconciling plans to these (as in the case of the Midland Bank Head Office in Poultry), or in work of a purely monumental character, in which sphere Lutyens has created some of the finest works in the whole history of architecture.

The commemorative architecture of Sir Edwin Lutyens is again characterized by felicity of proportion, while there is often a chasteness and simplicity particularly suited to this form of architectural expression. In 1919 Lutyens stated his theme of the Cenotaph with the dignified and impressive design in Whitehall, and he produced a very large number of variations of this theme in many of the cities and towns of England; but never, I think, did he produce another cenotaph with such fine proportions as that of the national monument. One dramatic use of the theme is in the military cemetery of Etaples, where two cenotaphs rise above a pair of arches flanking a vast platform in the centre of which is the cross of sacrifice, designed by Sir Reginald Blomfield, and the stone of remembrance, also designed by Sir Edwin Lutyens. He was responsible for a large number of memorial fountains, of which that to the R.N.V.R., near the Admiralty, and that to George V, at Windsor, are examples. And of smaller work, some of his memorial crosses are beautiful and original in design. Chiefly noteworthy are his memorials to the missing in France, designed for the Imperial (now Commonwealth) War Graves Commission, and especially his magnificent Somme Memorial at Thiepval. For this memorial Lutyens takes the theme of the monumental arch and treats it as only an architect of genius could.

The Roman monumental arch was revived in France to celebrate the victories of Louis XIV in structures like the *Porte Saint-Denis* and *Porte Saint-Martin*. The *Arc de Triomphe du Carrousel* erected by Napoleon is an imitation of that of Septimus Severus, but in the impressive *Arc de Triomphe de l'Etoile* there is some attempt to give a three-dimensional character by introducing arches at the sides, though it still remains essentially two dimensional. With Lutyens's Somme Memorial Arch the three-dimensional character is completely achieved. Each side has three circular arches (a central arch flanked by much smaller arches), and they appear as pierced blocks built up in a nicely calculated sequence. On the two principal sides the arches are on a larger scale than on the other sides, and this subordination of one to the other gives an agreeable variety. The principal central arch is lofty and supports the central masses which build up in satisfying sequence to the summit. The arch with the massive superstructure seems really to be supporting something, and is very different from the Roman arches that support a sculptured group like a quadriga. And, again, unlike the Roman and late Renaissance arches, there is hardly any sculpture in the Thiepval Memorial; the effect—and it is magnificent and impressive—depends on the sequence of ascending masses, the relation of plain surfaces, and the light and shadow of the blocks pierced by the tall arches. It expresses magnificently a feeling of aspiration, a reaching to higher things, and, situated on a low hill with a view of the Somme battlefields which form the graves of 73,367 unknown and unidentified dead, it seems to me unsurpassed among the great memorials in history[1].

This work has more the true classical spirit than any other of the period. It must be remembered that a Greek temple is made externally magnificent and impressive to inspire reverence and worship. That was its purpose, and that was the purpose of the Thiepval Memorial, and the architect has succeeded, as did the Greek architects. Another impressive memorial arch, although on a smaller scale is that in Victoria Park, Leicester, which is similar in design to his All India Memorial at Delhi. Lutyens's head office building of the Midland Bank (1926–30) occupies a somewhat awkward site from Poultry to Princes Street, with a branch of the National Provincial Bank occupying the corner, but there is a fairly long frontage to Poultry to give Lutyens an opportunity of designing an impressive façade, while there is sufficient frontage to Princes Street to make possible a continuation of the theme. Lutyens has made full use of his opportunity. The Poultry frontage has a central entrance with circular-headed windows on either side of the ground floor. Then for three floors are square-headed windows, and on the fourth floor they are circular-headed again. The windows of the second, third, and fourth floors are enclosed in a tall, circular-headed, recessed space which serves to hold them together. The masonry is rusticated, and it is clear that the astylar façades of early Florentine palaces have been the inspiration. Above the fourth floor the building is designed on a cross-shaped plan, and this upper part resembles the design of a Renaissance church, with nave and choir in the centre of this section of the building parallel with the frontage, and transepts across the building—the end of one coming immediately above the entrance—while the centre of the cross is surmounted by a flat dome. This upper part seems to be a natural sequence to the lower mass. The Princes Street side of the building is treated in a similar way. It would seem that the plan is evolved from these elevations, and they appear as two symmetrical variations on the architectural theme. For original treatment and felicity of proportion this is one of the finest buildings in the Renaissance tradition erected in the twenties.

In the vicinity—that is, grouped round the space in front of the Royal Exchange— a number of other bank buildings were erected about the same time. There is Lloyds Bank, Cornhill, by Sir John Burnet and Partners, the Westminster Bank in Lothbury by Arthur J. Davis, the National Provincial Bank by Sir Edwin Cooper, and the extensions to Soane's Bank of England by Sir Herbert Baker. All of these are designed in the classical Renaissance tradition with a good proportion of the copy-book type,

Radio Station at Kootwyk, The Netherlands, 1920–22
Architect: J. M. Luthman

ffice Block, Utrecht, 1920–22
Architect: G. W. Van Henkelom

India Building,
Liverpool, 1928–29

Architect:
Herbert J. Rowse

Iidland Bank, Poultry,
ondon, 1926–30   *Architect:*
r Edwin Lutyens in association
ith Laurence M. Gotch

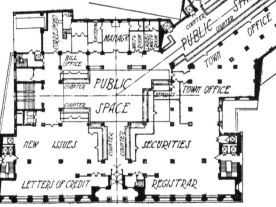

—plan—main front to Poultry

Central Post Office,
Piazza della Vittoria,
Brescia, 1928–32

Architect:
Marcello Piacentini

but there is little originality of treatment or expression of the architects' personalities. The Westminster Bank has something of the lightness and grace of Davis's earlier work, like the *Morning Post* building or the Royal Automobile Club. Sir Herbert Baker's Bank of England is not his happiest work. The interiors are better than the general exterior, where he has failed to maintain the restrained dignity of Soane's wall.

The massive and simple Renaissance of Florentine and Roman palaces, where much ornament or columns or pilasters rarely appear, is more acceptable in a utilitarian building like a bank or office block than the peristyle of a Greek or Roman temple. Lutyens's Midland Bank has more in common with a Florentine palace than with a Greek temple; no columns adorn the façade, but in the other banks in the vicinity columns and porticos are common features.

It is of the more restrained Renaissance palaces, when pilasters were beginning to appear[2], that one thinks in contemplating Herbert J. Rowse's two large buildings in Liverpool, completed in 1929. These buildings are Martins Bank and the India Building. The former, which is a large ten-storey building, has much of the simplicity of an early Renaissance palace and belongs to the period when classical ornament was beginning to decorate façades, accompanied by a lighter treatment and character. Rowse uses the pilasters sparingly and with restraint. Above the fourth storey the blocks of the building are set back in series, and the front of the sixth and seventh storeys is faced with a row of pilasters, above which is an ornate cornice, the whole having a frieze-like effect. Not much can be seen above this from the street. Martins Bank, however, is fairly simple in treatment, and the India Building, although even simpler, is not so pleasing in its general effect.

In Sweden at this time there was little work that could be considered as a slavish adherence to classical or Renaissance tradition, which rather manifested in original and sometimes fanciful treatment. An excellent example is the Concert Hall at Stockholm by Ivar Tengbom which is a fanciful treatment of the classical theme. The entrance portico, although derived from Greek architecture, is very different, for it consists of a row of tall, slender, octagonal columns with Corinthian capitals of a proportion totally different from the classical. The theme is continued in the interior with the tall, slender columns forming a background, with proscenium, to the orchestra and, running round the hall, linking the two side and end galleries with the roof. In the decorative work of the interior the architect was assisted by Carl Milles, Isaac Grünewald, and Erald Dahlskog. The whole building forms a delicate and graceful composition.

As is well known, marble has been used in Italy as an exterior and interior veneer to stone and brick since the Middle Ages. St. Mark's, Venice, built of brick (the chief building material of Northern Italy), is covered inside and out with marbles and mosaics which definitely have the appearance of veneers; but Milan Cathedral, also built of brick, with the roof constructed of blocks of marble, is covered externally with white marble and has the appearance of being built of that material. (How many guide books dramatically state: built entirely of white marble!) Its appearance is, therefore, to an extent, false. Florence Cathedral, built of stone, is also covered externally with marble—white and coloured marbles arranged in panels—though it definitely has the appearance of a veneer. Fergusson has the same quarrel with it that he expresses about Milan, but this is hardly justified.

This use of the marble veneer is one of the most interesting features of modern Italian architecture and it is one successful way of facing a concrete building. Marble retains its colour and a good surface for centuries in the Italian atmosphere, but it could not be used to the same extent in England for it would not long retain its colour and good surface in the English city atmosphere without frequent cleaning.

The buildings of the Piazza della Vittoria at Brescia, built in 1927–32 and designed by Marcello Piacentini, take one back to the Middle Ages yet are linked with the present. The 'Tower of the Revolution' is like a Venetian building of the Renaissance, the National Assurance Institute and the National Treasury of Social Assurance buildings are inspired by the Romanesque style, while the Central Post Office is an essay in the modern 'rational' manner; yet they are all based on classical principles. The idea so to connect the past with the present may be underlying the whole scheme, for the 'Arengario' (pulpit) situated at the north end of the square has panels carved on its face depicting scenes from the history of Brescia. All of these buildings are constructed of reinforced concrete frames with brick walls, but the Post Office, symmetrical in plan, is perhaps alone in expressing the character of its structure. The two buildings of Romanesque inspiration seem to be the most completely satisfying, the arrangement of the circular arches in the arcade and tower of the National Assurance Institute forming a unified whole[3]. We see in this Piazza the beginnings of an architecture which became closely associated with Fascism in Italy— the blend of classical principles and modern starkness.

REFERENCES AND NOTES

1. The Somme Memorial by Lutyens is described and illustrated in *Their Name Liveth*, Imperial War Graves Commission, London, 1954, pp. 15, 16. See also Arnold Whittick, *War Memorials*, London, 1946, p. 35 and figures 35 and 36.
2. The Rucellai Palace in Florence, built in 1451, is generally considered to be the first building in which pilasters were used in the façade.
3. This arcade is faced with Corneto marble, while the upper part is brick. The arcade of the National Treasury of Social Assurance and the 'Tower of the Revolution' are faced with Badia S. Benedetto stone, the upper part of the former with Mazzano (dark) and Botticino (light) marbles, the Post Office and with alternate bands of Ceppo and Mazzano marbles.

115

12 *Romantic and original treatment of traditional styles*

TWENTIETH-CENTURY ARCHITECTS designing fairly closely within the classical or Renaissance tradition find justification in doing a thing in a certain way because it has been done in that way by great cultures and peoples in the past and has received the sanction of generations. Methods of construction and needs change, and new types of building are required, yet to such architects classical principles of design remain as guides, and they are less interested in original and personal expression than in conforming worthily to old and venerated standards and principles which, having served the past well, will serve us too. Artists, on the other hand, who strive for originality are generally forceful individuals who are discontented with merely following what others have done, for they rightly consider that change in life demands a response in expression.

In architecture originality has many sources on which it can feed, but it is generally limited by historical and practical conditions, and, to a partial extent, by prevailing taste. In the restless period of transition from about 1908 to 1924 original architects were still conscious of the deadening influence of the classical and Gothic revivals, but by this time there were many ways in which originality could be successfully stimulated and meet with some degree of acceptance. Especially was this so in non-belligerent countries like Holland and the Scandinavian countries generally where architectural evolution did not suffer the same break or pause as in most of the rest of Europe.

The ways in which originality appeared to be stimulated during this period were by a search for ideas, forms, and decorations in the remote past; by further research into natural forms; by a use of rhythm suggested by other arts like music, of which *Art Nouveau* was a partial manifestation; by the suggestion of dynamicism in the new building material—steel; and by reasoning on contemporary building needs, the purpose of buildings, methods of construction, and the logical emergence of design from these, consistent with aesthetic values.

116

As already implied, the countries in which work of this original and romantic type was found to the greatest extent during this period (1908–24) were Holland and the Scandinavian countries, where building during the war, although greatly reduced, did not cease, and revival after the war was rather a swell of activity than a restarting as with the belligerents. This is one of the reasons why some of the most interesting architecture immediately after the First World War is found in these countries. Another reason is that although small they are among the most socially progressive countries in the world, and this is generally a healthy background for artistic expression.

Reference has been made (Chapter 5) to some of the architecture in Holland and Sweden as indicative of the movement towards simplicity. This is continued with rare distinction in the work of W. M. Dudok in Holland and Eric Lallerstedt in Sweden; but in taking up the story the romantic strains claim first attention. In Holland during the present century a strong romantic affection for the native material brick is manifest. It was P. J. H. Cuypers who, during the latter part of the nineteenth century, brought 'the brick out from behind the plaster facing again', to use the words of J. P. Mieras[1]. In Amsterdam and neighbouring areas, especially Hilversum, this triumphed over all expression of the new materials and methods of construction. Rotterdam and its vicinity, where J. J. P. Oud was the great architectural exponent and influence, offers something of a contrast, for here was building belonging more to the new architecture. But, dissimilar as was the work of M. de Klerk and W. M. Dudok, they both show the same romantic affection for brick as a building and decorative material.

A noteworthy Amsterdam building in which is vividly expressed these romantic tendencies is the Head Office building of Shipping Societies, designed in 1914–16 by J. M. Van der Mey with the assistance of M. de Klerk and P. Kramer. The construction is of reinforced concrete, yet its very elaborate brick clothing with terracotta and concrete ornament has no marked relation to its structure. Much has been written about this building, and many explanations of its supposedly irrational character have been attempted. One is the architects' feeling that as it was impossible to express structure in the exterior brick clothing, one might as well be thoroughly romantic and pictorial and give full play to artistic fancy. On either side of the entrance are the symbolic figures of the Indian and Atlantic Oceans, and on other parts of the building are objects connected with ships, like ropes, cables, cordage, and cork jackets. The signs of the Zodiac are included, while the patterning of tiles in an entrance gable is suggestive of the ripple of the sea. Motifs of this kind form a profuse decoration of the building[2], but it does not appear overloaded with ornament which is all kept within the broad embracing lines of the façades. The general design has a clear vertical emphasis which might be regarded as remotely indicative of the concrete frame beneath.

Such sculptured and ornamental embellishment has often been a conspicuous

117

characteristic of the great architecture of the past, particularly of Greek and Roman temples and of Gothic cathedrals. The architects of this building have done very much the same. Just as the Gothic architects used the subjects and symbols of their religion so these architects have used the subjects and symbols of the sea and ships, and they have made full use of the motifs that the subjects supplied. The value of the building as architectural expression is that instead of copying the works of the classical and Gothic architects, and using the forms and decorations they evolved, Van der Mey and his assistants have taken a subject of today suggested by the purpose of the building. In this way it is living and expressive architecture. But there is failure to achieve anything like the beauty of Greek or Gothic architecture because the sculptured ornament is not so well related to structure and general form.

About the same time (1914–16) as this Shipping Societies' building was being erected, P. Kramer, who had assisted Van der Mey, was working on the building for the Federation of Sailors at Den Helden which offers a mild contrast. Instead of the surface of the façade being fully enriched with mouldings, figures and ornament, the effect is of plain, brick wall surfaces and of masses pleasantly related. Yet there are characteristics which show something of the same spirit. In the top of the tower the decorative features are derived from ships, one detail being treated like a Gothic gargoyle, while in the ornate brickwork of the entrance there is again a patterning which fancy suggests might have been prompted by the sea.

Many young architects immediately before, during, and after the First World War were given opportunities for architectural expression by the enterprising Director of Housing in Amsterdam, Aerie Keppler. During these years an extensive housing scheme was in operation and a very large number of tenement blocks were built by the Public Utility Society. Architects were given some freedom, and there seems to have been a monetary allowance for that extra which could give the buildings some architectural distinction. This is a refreshing exception to the general rule for buildings of this type. Among the architects were M. de Klerk, P. Kramer, G. J. Rutgens, J. F. Staal, and H. Th. Wiydeveld. The first two seem to have been the most fanciful and original. The earlier blocks of M. de Klerk, designed between 1913 and 1918, are more fanciful and exuberant than the later blocks, designed between 1919 and 1923. Most are of four or five storeys and are generally of some length which gives considerable scope for fine architectural treatment. The top floor in the mansard roof in most of the blocks is utilized as storage space, and this explains the treatment of the upper part of the façade, which often has a finish of black tiles and small windows, with crane and pulley above for the haulage of goods.

In one of the earlier blocks of de Klerk[3] the intervals where the entrances, staircases, and lifts appear are marked by a fanciful external treatment consisting of a vertical mass with a parabolic top between chimney shafts. In another, a little later (1917–18),

Left—office building of the Federation of Sailors at Den Helden, The Netherlands, 1914–16

Architect: P. Kramer

Right—Head Office Building of Shipping Societies at Amsterdam, 1914–16

Architect: J. M. Van der Mey

Tenement houses of the Public Utility Society at Amsterdam, 1922–23

Architect: P. Kramer

School at Hilversum, The Netherlands, 1923
Architect: W. M. Dudok

Group of Tenement Blocks, Amsterdam, 1920
Architect: M. de Klerk

Public Baths at Hilversum, 1924   *Architect: W. M. Dudok*

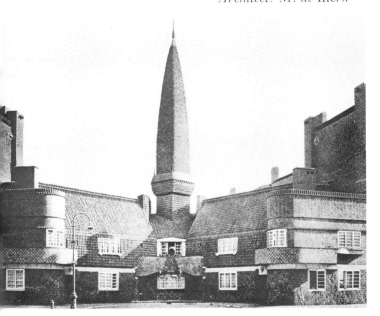

the decorative element consists chiefly of undulations on the tiled surface of the top storey and turrets, and the terminations of the blocks, but here the most fanciful treatment is found in the Post Office, which lies at the end of the two parallel blocks. The principal entrance is in a circular tower, with a waved tiled frieze, while the squarish windows are varied in treatment and entrances are set in accented façades with parabolic tops flattened at the apex. In the varying wall surface of this Post Office the bricks at the base are laid vertically; higher they are laid horizontally, and above this, covering the mansard roof, are black tiles. But the most adventurous and fanciful of all de Klerk's groups of tenement blocks is that designed in 1917, but not actually completed until 1920, in which a space between two five-storey blocks with turreted ends approaching each other, as it were, at a slight angle, is treated by carrying the buildings inwards at the reduced height of two storeys, and placing a delightfully picturesque spire at the point where they meet and forming a little triangular nook in the roadway. This spire serves no utilitarian purpose, it is just significant of the Dutch love of the picturesque.

De Klerk's later work shows a tendency to become simpler and the plain wall surface begins to play a bigger part, yet the ingenious and fanciful designer is still apparent. In the block built in 1921–2 the manner in which the balconies of the three storeys are connected by jam-pot windows gives a dynamic effect of somewhat restless quality to the façade. These tenement blocks by de Klerk represent a considerable achievement for a young architect. It would have been interesting to see how this talent would have developed later, but in 1923 de Klerk died at the early age of 39.

Some of the housing work of Kramer has the same fanciful character, but here again there is a strong tendency to greater simplicity in later work. In the housing block called 'De Dageraad', erected in 1921, decorative motifs are the round turrets over entrances, and in one corner treatment, in which shops appear on the ground floor, a series of rolls gives a somewhat bizarre, yet distinctive picturesque effect of broad, round surfaces and slight undulations, somewhat like the plain dresses of the buxom Dutch women.

Much other Dutch architecture of this time has a similar picturesque and fanciful quality. The work of J. van Laren, of which the shop at Hilversum is typical, is noteworthy in this respect. Some of the architecture in Hamburg at this time manifests a similar romantic quality in which brick is the prominent material, suggesting the influence of contemporary Dutch work. In the Chile House, built by Fritz Hoger in 1923, there is the same romantic feeling, but there are obvious differences. There is even a partially barbaric feeling in the somewhat crude treatment of the decoration on the ground floor derived from Gothic sources, while the decoration of the upper part of the façades forms an all-over pattern rare in Dutch work.

To turn from the work of M. de Klerk and P. Kramer to that of W. M. Dudok, who was engaged from 1917 on a considerable amount of building in Hilversum, is to experience what on a first impression is a marked contrast. The buildings of de Klerk and Kramer are decorated with fanciful forms. These forms are generally ornamental embellishments which have some relation to the internal organization of the building, or to its structure. But none of this fanciful decorative embellishment appears in the contemporary buildings of Dudok. Instead the exterior beauty of his buildings depends on plain walls, on the texture and colour of the brick surface, and on the relations of the plain walls and masses that compose the buildings. The differences are thus obvious enough, but on further reflection the similarities become more apparent. The same romantic affection for the traditional material brick is hardly a similarity in design, but the varieties of surface treatment, the adherence to appearances which are generally structurally possible in brick, although steel and concrete is occasionally used in the construction, and a liking for horizontal emphasis broken here and there by dramatically placed verticals are qualities shared by both. While showing much of the romanticism of de Klerk and Kramer, Dudok was clearly influenced by the work of Berlage and de Bazel, with its greater simplicity and closer relations of form and structure, where the appearance of the building is expressive of its purpose and interior organization.

Hilversum is a small modern town about fifteen miles southeast of Amsterdam. Development began just before the First World War, and it was then that Dudok began designing buildings for the town, for which he was the principal architect. Buildings erected in this early period, and completed in the five years following the war were public baths, two schools, an abattoir, an electric draining mill, and some houses. One of the earliest, the public baths, is symmetrical in design, but this symmetry is rarely followed in later work. In his schools there are no *a priori* considerations of this kind, the most convenient plans are adopted, and the appearance of the building, the elevations and composition of blocks, grow out of the plans. The happiest effect, as with one of the schools, is where large areas of plain surface and long unbroken lines are important elements in the composition. But it is probable that much of the aesthetic effect of these buildings is in the subtle relations and sequence of simple plain blocks, and the effect of a synthetic combination of these into a unified whole. Dudok has the facility of relating these masses with a nicety and in such a way that complete satisfaction is experienced, a facility that has rarely been surpassed among modern architects. These blocks and large, plain surfaces allow for fine broad effects of light and shadow, and this is greatly enhanced by the pleasing colour of the pale red and yellow bricks. In the later work of Dudok in Hilversum the same fine unerring sense of proportion and effective use of large, varied brick surfaces is apparent. His work has had considerable influence on slightly later building in England, and there can be little doubt that many of the brick buildings in which the broad plain wall surface is an important element in the design owes something to Dudok.

121

The most notable architecture of Sweden in the period immediately before, during, and after the First World War was, more clearly than elsewhere, the result of a search in the past for an architecture dignified, impressive, and natively expressive. The inspiration of modern buildings like the Stockholm Law Courts, designed by Carl Westman (1912–15), and the University of Technology, designed by Eric Lallerstedt (1914–22), seems to have been the castles of the Wasa dynasty in the sixteenth century, the period of transition from medieval to Renaissance architecture. The chief of these castles are Gripsholm, Vadstena, Uppsala, and Kalmar[4]. In looking at the last-named, with its large plain walls, small windows, and massive towers terminated with ogival roofs, supporting lanterns, and spires, much of the inspiration of the modern buildings cited is apparent.

Vadstena Castle is in many ways a prototype of Westman's Law Courts. The principal front of the castle with its simple massive tower clearly suggested the treatment to Westman, and one gets the impression that he wished to give his building something of the character of a sixteenth-century Swedish castle. But it has a considerable degree of originality especially in the treatment of the tower, the front face of which is flush with the wall, instead of projecting. The qualities which Sir Reginald Blomfield admired in the building (see Chapter 5) like the abstinence from irrelevant detail, the noble scale, and the deliberate austerity of the design are precisely the qualities that are found in the sixteenth-century Wasa castles, and the austere quality of design is partly the romantic return to the style of these castles, which, it seems, very largely prompted the character of these Law Courts.

A similar romanticism prompted Eric Lallerstedt's University of Technology, which has several features in common with Westmans' Law Courts, especially the treatment of a tower with wall flush with the façade. This is really a small university city, because it consists of a considerable number of buildings grouped round several courts. Although there is some variety in the treatment of the various buildings, the prevailing style—the plain walls and small windows, and somewhat massive effect—is again reminiscent of the old Wasa castles. It is built of red brick, a much-favoured material in Stockholm at this time, due partly to the influence of the architecture of Holland and Hamburg, but also probably to the influence of the medieval brick buildings of Lubeck, which was another object of the romantic gaze of the contemporary Swedish architect. Here and there in the courts of the university are sculptures of a symbolic or legendary character, generally of granite, seen to good advantage against the red brick of the walls.

THE STOCKHOLM CITY HALL

The search of Swedish architects of this time was essentially for an expressive native style. The Law Courts and University of Technology were two results. Similarly, though more fully, the most famous Swedish building of this period, the Stockholm

122

City Hall, was an attempt at a full expression of a people, past and present, in architecture, sculpture, and painting, suffused with all the romance that can be associated with national and local pride. If ever a building was a child of romance it is the Stockholm City Hall. It was commenced in 1912 and completed in 1923 to the designs of Ragnar Ostberg. It is impressively situated on the north bank of Lake Malar on a corner formed by an arm of the estuary. Famous are views of the building from across the water, either from the south bank of Lake Malar or from the island of Riddarholm, to the southeast in the centre of the estuary, and on which lies the old city.

The City Hall is planned round two courts, the large Civic Court and the covered Blue Hall. If the building is approached from the City Hall Bridge, which crosses the mouth of a northern branch of the estuary to the east, one goes through the north entrance into the Civic Court, and walking to the south side sees the sparkling waters of Lake Malar through the triple colonnade. The Blue Hall is entered from the west side of the Civic Court, and this is the route generally of the public. The City Councillors go to the great tower on the southeast corner and ascend through the Arch of the Hundred to the Council Chamber on the first floor.

The building consists of a ground floor, basement, and three upper floors. The first floor is the principal, being devoted to all the more ceremonial functions, the remaining floors being occupied principally by offices. On the first floor, in the space between the Civic Court and Blue Hall, is the Golden Chamber, the principal assembly hall, seating 750 at a banquet, and reached by a staircase from the Blue Hall. A study of the plan will show that the arrangement of the various apartments has been designed with a strong feeling for ceremony combined with a sense of mystery often experienced in Gothic architecture. Consider, for example, the more ceremonial approach to the Golden Chamber from the great tower. One passes through the Arch of the Hundred along the Gallery on the south side, and through the Three Crowns Chamber which forms an ante room to the Golden Chamber. Or consider the approach to the Council Chamber from the Blue Hall. One ascends the staircase and enters the long Council corridor on the north side and enters the Council Parlour, an ante room to the Council Chamber. The use of long corridors is reminiscent of the corridors in the old Swedish castles. The main constructional material is red brick, which determines the generally vivid hue of the building. The bricks, familiar in Sweden, measure approximately $3\frac{3}{4}$ inches by $5\frac{1}{4}$ inches by $8\frac{3}{4}$ inches, a little higher and wider than the brick most commonly used in England.

The great tower at the southeast corner is 354 feet high above water-level to the Three Crowns, and the external measurement at the base is 53 feet 6 inches by 55 feet, with walls about 13 feet thick at their base. The foundation of the tower consists of a concrete platform supported on eight concrete pillars, each 17 feet in diameter, four at the corners and four at the middle of each side. They rest on the solid rock, which is higher at the northwest corner. The tower tapers about 3 feet, and up to a height of 133 feet the wall is built solid, and this part is terminated by the vault of the Arch of the Hundred. Up to this point is a stairway and a lift, and above is a tower passage inside the thickness of the wall. The belfry at the top is constructed of wood, above is the columned circle, and above this is the small ball surmounted by the three crowns.

Many are the sources of the style of this City Hall. It is the result of a discriminating eclecticism combined with the creative genius of its architect. Many of its features recall the palaces of Venice, and the arcade on the southern side is not unlike that of the Ducal Palace at Venice. Motifs taken from Greek, Roman, Byzantine, Romanesque, Gothic, Renaissance styles are all subjects of the architect and combined in the design. In the capitals of the columns of the portico that runs round the Blue Hall is a variety of pictorial ornament. The entrance from the gallery of the Blue Hall in the northeast corner is Baroque in character with Ionic capitals and twisted columns; the north stairway has Roman Doric columns, with Gothic vaulting; the entrance door of the President's room is flanked with Corinthian columns; the cornice of the Blue Hall is derived from medieval castles; and the window openings are of infinite variety, square head, Roman, Byzantine, Gothic, while the terminations of the towers are derived mainly from Byzantine sources. But all this curious mixture, which seems to concentrate the whole history of Swedish architecture in a single building, is fused into an harmonious whole. With all these differences of style there is no sense of incongruity, no sense of discord, and it is perhaps the architect's greatest achievement that he has combined these several diverse styles so successfully in a single building, which is also very much a setting for the symbolic expression and pictorial history of Stockholm by means of sculpture and carving on the exterior, and fresco, mosaic and tapestries inside. It is almost as richly ornamented with symbolic sculpture and carving as a Gothic cathedral.

The several towers have their symbols and are generally called by these names. The great tower derives the name by which it is known from the three crowns which surmount it. Just by on the eastern side is the maiden tower. North and south of the Golden Chamber are the towers surmounted by the sun and moon, while the northeast tower is crowned with Karin's sceptre. Along the cornice beneath the projecting timber on the eastern façade is a series of gilded figures in relief representing the workers of Stockholm in the 800 years of its history. Each century has its particular workers: the fifteenth century is represented by the glass worker, the wood carver, and the warrior, and the nineteenth century by the scientist, engineer, and politician. On the northern façade are several groups of sculpture, and a series carved on the keystones above the windows represents legends and history of the eight centuries of Stockholm life. Of the three rows of capitals in the southern porticoes the inner and outer are richly carved, the inner depicting scenes from the life of youth, its work, sport, and pleasures, while the capitals on the outer row are mainly of historical and religious subjects. The capitals of the columns in the Blue Hall are similarly carved with historical and legendary subjects associated with Stockholm. Among the most interesting of the sculptures are those in the towers. On the Three Crowns tower surmounting the buttresses of the four corners of the belfry are bronze figures of Mary Magdalene, St. Nicholas, St. Claire, and Ulrica Eleanora. At the top of the Moon tower is a group in copper, of a fisher-boy cocking a snook at a bishop, which illustrates one of the old legends of Stockholm. But the most elaborate is the group of St. George and the Dragon on the Maiden tower, fitted with mechanism for movement The contest is watched by the Princess who sits within the Maiden tower. At 12 noon and 6 p.m. the bells play, St. George leads the Princess to his horse, then comes the Page with the dead body of the Dragon, and the procession moves to a gate in the great tower which is opened by a porter.

The paintings, tapestries, and mosaics decorating the interior similarly illustrate the various legends, symbolism, and history connected with the life of Stockholm[6]. To the people of Stockholm it is much more than a utilitarian City Hall; it is an expression in architecture, sculpture, and painting of their history and romance. The City Hall of Stockholm is one of the most famous European buildings erected in the twentieth century; it has been widely and enthusiastically admired, and many who had decried twentieth century architecture have made an exception in the case of this building.

There have been few exceptions to the chorus of approval. That learned architectural historian, Sir Reginald Blomfield, made serious qualifications in his admiration[7], but it must be remembered that Blomfield was always prejudiced in favour of the application of classical principles to design, like symmetry and formal disposition of parts. The Stockholm City Hall follows rather medieval principles of the convenient sequence of rooms, although on the first floor with an eye to ceremonial effect. It is essentially medieval and not classic in its conception. Blomfield is unhappy about the western extension beyond the Moon tower, which he says 'goes on as it likes and ends anyhow'. On the contrary the design seems to be a careful study of the relation of masses. The convenient plan suggested the masses, but their satisfactory sequence is the result of consummate artistic treatment. What is it, after all, which makes this building so impressive, and one of the unforgettable spectacles of Europe?

All that wealth of pictorial history and legend giving richness to the building's texture is kept subservient to the controlling lines, and the silhouette of the building seen from across the water has a satisfying artistic completeness. Beginning with the vertical mass of the tower, the eye moves westward along the long horizontal mass of the southern block abutting the tower, then notes the accent of the Moon tower, and is lastly engaged by the subordinate mass of the western block, a subordination effected

City Hall, Stockholm, completed 1923   *Architect: Ragnar Östberg*

Above—general view, below—arcading, waterside terrace

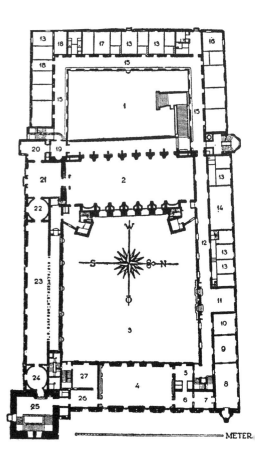

PLAN OF FIRST FLOOR

City Hall, Stockholm—above—the Blue Hall, below—view from south terrace

by a drop in the horizontal line, the subtlety of which can be appreciated on nearer view. The Baroque summit of the Moon tower introduces an attractive note of gaiety which, with many other factors, constitutes the appeal of the building to such varied taste.

SOME SCANDINAVIAN CHURCHES

The romantic adaptation of ideas culled from the remote past, combined with considerable originality, had interesting manifestations in many churches built in the early twenties. A few of the best examples can also be taken as representative. Two of the most original are the Engelbrekt church, designed by L. I. Wahlman and completed in 1914, and the Hogalid church, designed by Ivar Tengbom and built in 1918–23, both in Stockholm. The design and style of both churches have been based partially on German and Swedish Romanesque, but at the same time both are original conceptions. The Engelbrekt church, built on a rocky prominence above its surroundings, with full advantage taken of this situation, is built of brick with Greek cross plan, the central space rising higher than the arms, while a tall, slender tower rises at the corner, formed by the central space and southern arm. This tower is square two-thirds of the way up and then changes to an octagon and to more ornate treatment. The design of the interior is open without aisles and with a clear view of the altar. The choir, nave, and transepts have vaults consisting of a series of high elliptical or parabolic arches rising from the walls, and the bays are a series of circular arches. The whole effect is massive and simple, full effect being given to the unbroken lines of the parabolic arches, which are its most distinguishing and original feature. Sir Reginald Blomfield admired this church greatly and he alluded to it as 'much the most original and in some ways effective modern church that I have seen in any country'[8]. Another church by L. I. Wahlman is the Swedish church at Oslo, built a little later, but this is small and a much less ambitious work, although in features, like the flat elliptical-headed narrow windows and the square tower surmounted by a series of diminishing octagons for the spire (not unlike that of Wren's Church of St. Brides, Fleet Street, London) it clearly betrays the same designer.

The Hogalid church is similarly well situated on a hill on Sodermalm, and full advantage again has been taken of the situation, so that this lofty architectural composition with tall twin-towers at its eastern end dominates the surroundings. It is a well-known landmark, and can be seen from Lake Malar and most parts of the city. Like the Engelbrekt church it is built of red brick and is inspired by Romanesque architecture. The conception of the towers is based on those of Visby Cathedral, on the island of Gotland, and the architect may also have been influenced by some German Romanesque churches. But in this octagonal tower with wide bulbous moulding, changing to square and surmounted by onion terminations, Byzantine influence is as strong as Romanesque. The church has a rectangular basilican plan, and the interior, less exotic in treatment than much of the exterior, has lofty semicircular vaults, with a series of circular arched bays in the wall. The whole is open so that one has a clear view of the altar from all parts.

This church represents an interesting departure from the usual course of Tengbom's work. Most of his preceding and succeeding work was more in the classical tradition, although with originality and personal feeling. One of the most important of his earlier works is the Stockholm Enskilda Bank, completed in 1915. which is essentially a simplified rendering of classical architecture with an emphasis on monumental massiveness.

Swedish and Danish architecture followed the many stylistic developments that spread over Europe—Romanesque, Gothic, Renaissance—but there were often national and local characteristics which became strong distinguishing features. In the medieval architecture of Skane, which forms the south western tip of Sweden, and which was once part of Denmark, many of the buildings exhibit features which mark them from the work of other areas in Sweden and Denmark of the same period. One feature is the prominent stepped gable seen in many buildings, such as the Glimmingehus, a work of the end of the fifteenth century, and Troup Castle, a work of the sixteenth century. It is this prominent feature which has dominated the conception of the exterior design of St. Hans Tveje Church near Odense in Denmark (begun in 1921 but not completed until 1940), but the motif has been applied by the architect, P. V. Jensen Klint, with considerable originality. The plan is rectangular with a deep aisle three bays long to the south. The western end of the church is terminated by a half-octagonal apse, and the eastern end has a low rectangular tower, terminated by a double pitched roof faced with step gables which are emphasized by a fluted decoration on the front façade terminated in the form of a triangular plain wall. The treatment is repeated for the porch on this front, and for the three bays of the aisle on the south side, and it is this motif, suggested by fifteenth- and sixteenth-century buildings of Skane, which determines the style of the exterior. The fluted wall design is an effective decorative emphasis. The interior of the church has Gothic arches for the wall bays, and parabolic arches for the roof vaulting, again a mixture of traditional and original treatment which is notable if not entirely successful.

The tendency towards simplicity which became stronger after the First World War was not without its influence in ecclesiastical art. Although in the gradual breaking from the mechanical and imitative work of the Gothic revival, inspiration was sought from still earlier styles like Romanesque and Byzantine, there was, at the same time, a desire to give a more religious, less worldly atmosphere to interiors. It was logical that the clergy and their architects should turn to the early days of the Church, and to those phases of early Christian architecture in which the religious atmosphere seemed strongest. The simplest and most austere churches in which a sense of space was also apparent, formed the most satisfying examples for study. The results of this study

129

The Engelbrekt Church, Stockholm, 1908–14
Architect: L. I. Wahlman

The Högalid Church, Stockholm, 1918–23
Architect: Ivan Tengbom

St. Paul's Church, Derby Lane, Liverpool, 1922
Architect: Sir Giles Gilbert Scott

War Memorial Chapel, Charterhouse, 1922–26
Architect: Sir Giles Scott

began to appear in many churches built in the period following the war. Also the increasing costs of material and labour demonstrated the economical advantages of austerity and simplicity.

The movement to design more strictly according to suitability for purpose, which was one of the essential contributions to a new architecture, exercised some influence on architects of churches. The question was asked afresh: what is the purpose of a church building, and what form serves that purpose best? The answers varied with the religious denomination, but that which might be given for the Protestant church would be that a church is built to give shelter to a number of people of a parish to worship God; it is, therefore, an assembly hall, with an altar as a focal point, in front of which there is space and facilities for priests to conduct that worship, and to give religious instruction and guidance. Ceremony, music, and decorative art provide aesthetic attributes which felicitously conduce to worship.

Does the traditional cruciform plan, with aisled choir and nave, serve the purpose best? It was the traditional form from the early Middle Ages, beginning generally with Romanesque churches, until the Reformation. When the first Protestant churches were built after the Reformation, such as the Wren city churches, the cruciform plan gave place to the rectangular plan, and the church interior became closer to the secular assembly hall with aisles retained and the triforium becoming a side gallery.

SOME ENGLISH CHURCHES

With the Gothic revival the cross plan returned, but from about 1910 this consideration of designing according to suitability for purpose began to effect changes in church plans, because the reply to the question whether the cruciform plan with arcaded aisles, choir, and nave serves the purpose of the building best could not always be given an unqualified affirmative. For the purpose of ceremony and processions, yes; but for the purpose of seeing the priest conducting the worship near the altar, for the purpose of seeing the preacher, for the purpose of that desirable religious unity of the many worshipping as one, it was clearly not the best plan, particularly for those seated in the aisles, who suffered from the obstructions of the columns in the nave, or those seated in the transepts, who often had several obstructions of different kinds.

The most drastic change to overcome these difficulties was to revert to the rectangular basilican plan, and eliminate arcaded aisles, but there are varying degrees of compromise, one being to have the rectangular plan, yet retain aisles, make them narrower, and use them only as corridors. In many churches built in England from 1910 to 1925 some of these varied solutions can be seen, but it is rather a negative process of deletion; there was then no stating the problems and finding an entirely new solution. That was to come later.

131

Thus in many churches we find the cross plan abandoned, and the rectangular basilican plan adopted either with or without arcaded aisles. At the same time a growing simplicity and austerity are apparent. Brick or stone walls are covered with plaster, and often plain columns with simple bases and capitals are employed with varied success. The complete effects of the tendency are not manifest until later, the church work from 1919 to 1924 being, as already implied, largely transitional. The three churches from Sweden and Denmark just described may come in this category, but they are distinguished by an uncommon degree of originality. More pedestrian work moving in the same direction may be found in many excellent churches of this period, examples being in England. A few of these are simple brick churches, often with no tower or spire, in which large surfaces of plain wall, both externally and internally, are conspicuous characteristics—churches like St. Stephen's, Grimsby, designed by Walter Tapper, St. Saviour's, Acton, by Edward Maufe, and St. Catherine's, Hammersmith, by Robert Atkinson. The last mentioned is notable as being, as far as I know, the first steel-framed church building in England. The steel frame was adopted because it meant speedier construction. It was completed in 1922 in six months at a cost of £16,000, and it is estimated that if the traditional methods of building had been adopted it would have taken double the time and money. The plan is rectangular, it has brick exterior facing in which large plain surfaces contribute much to the effect, the windows have semicircular arches, while the barrel-vaulted interior has a dead white plaster finish, with a black dado. The conception has been inspired by the simpler early Christian churches of Italy[9]. Many later churches in England are constructed and designed in a similar manner.

The dominating ecclesiastical work during this period in England is that of Sir Giles Gilbert Scott, and the tendencies noted are apparent in his work, conditioned always by the characteristics of his strong individual style. Among the churches Sir Giles Scott designed during this period are St. Paul's Church, Liverpool, the Church of Our Lady, Northfleet, Kent, and the War Memorial Chapel at Charterhouse. In these churches there is the change from the traditional cruciform plan to the rectangular plan. The architect to Liverpool Cathedral is most apparent in the church at Northfleet, where Gothic forms with classic restraint, and emphasis on horizontals and verticals are reminiscent of the cathedral. The square opening from the nave to the choir, the triple clerestory windows, enclosed in a square head, are examples of this, while the massive square tower is a foretaste of that for Liverpool Cathedral. St. Paul's Church is very different. The liking for plain wall-surfaces is apparent, but the composition of the exterior is essentially of triangular forms—of pitched roofs and pyramidal spire surmounting the square tower—and of circular arches that enclose the triple windows, and which terminate the recesses of the tower.

The War Memorial Chapel at Charterhouse is more traditional, inspired by the period of transition from Romanesque to Gothic. In the wall structure and the turrets at the ends there is the Romanesque character, but most of the arches are Gothic, though less sharp than Early English. The tall lancet windows are recessed from the interior wall and on the exterior the series of projections with gable tops and buttresses framing the windows are reminiscent of Liverpool Cathedral. Here is eclecticism to a degree, but very much in the spirit of the Romanesque–Gothic period of transition.

Some of the work of German exponents of the new architecture can be rightly classified as romantic but of a different kind, as, for example, some work of Hans Poelzig in conceptions like the remodelled Grosse Schauspielhaus with its concrete stalactites, or Eric Mendelsohn's Observatory at Potsdam. Here is romanticism which does not involve the search among traditional styles. Poelzig may have had in mind the cave with stalactites as a subject for his decorative purposes, thus representing a search, not among architectural but natural forms, while Mendelsohn was clearly thinking of optical instruments as suggestions for the decorative forms of his structure. These are non-traditional experiments in expression, and although romantic in the more adventurous sense they obviously belong to a study of the development of the new architecture, of which they are phases.

REFERENCES AND NOTES

1. J. P. Mieras and F. R. Yerbury, *Dutch Architecture of the 20th Century*, London, 1926, p. vi.
2. In an article entitled The Rococo of To-day in *The Architectural Review* of August 1921, Halsey Ricardo, who mistakenly speaks of this building as an hotel, gives an enthusiastic description of the ornament.
3. See article Modern Dutch Architecture by Howard Robertson on de Klerk's tenement blocks in *The Architectural Review* for August 1922. Also Howard Robertson's article with the same title in *The Architectural Review* for September 1923, which deals also with the work of Kramer and Dudok.
4. See Thomas Paulsson, *Scandinavian Architecture*, London, 1958, pp. 103–122.
5. Sir Reginald Blomfield, *Byways: Leaves from an Architect's Note-book*, London, 1929, p. 274.
6. Further information about the profuse decoration of this building can be obtained from a guide written by the architect, Stockholm, 1926.
7. Sir Reginald Blomfield, *Byways: Leaves from an Architect's Note-book*, London, 1929, pp. 274–9.
8. Sir Reginald Blomfield, *Byways: Leaves from an Architect's Note-book*, London, 1929, p. 271.
9. A description with an illustration of the steel-frame construction is given in *The Architectural Review*, vol. liii, July 1923, p. 209.

13 *New forms and experiments in the early twenties—some industrial, domestic and ecclesiastical buildings*

THE MOST IMPORTANT developments leading to the new architecture discussed in Chapter 9 can be briefly restated as an increasing appropriateness of form to function, the sloughing of ornament derived from past styles, the use of materials with greater structural potentialities provided by modern industry, and the closer study of economic and social needs in relation to building. These developments were not made without the consciousness that building, if it is to be architecture, must afford some degree of aesthetic delight, but it was accompanied, at the same time, by the conviction that beauty can be discovered in hitherto unsuspected places, and that much that was once regarded as merely utilitarian can give aesthetic delight. The creative process resulting from the developments enumerated was prompted by reasoning on contemporary building needs, on the purpose of a building, on methods of construction, and on the logical emergence of design from these consistent with aesthetic value, which might be entirely new and hitherto unsuspected. Many of the principal characteristics of the new architecture were apparent in some of the buildings by Peter Behrens, Walter Gropius, Heinrich Tessenow, Adolf Meyer, Tony Garnier, Auguste Perret, and a few others erected in the years preceding the First World War. The war meant a pause in the evolution, but the movement was renewed with increasing vigour, imparted somewhat by many young newcomers to the scene, among them Le Corbusier, Eric Mendelsohn, Ludwig Mies van der Rohe, and J. J. P. Oud.

Many of the important pioneer developments took place in buildings with a utilitarian and non-ceremonial function. Particularly in the later pre-war stages of the evolution up to 1915 many of the principal developments were in industrial buildings, and the turbine and electrical factories of Behrens, and the Fagus boot-last factory of Gropius and Meyer. Industrial buildings should be prominent in the vanguard of the new movement because with these more than with most other types efficient fulfilment of purpose is a matter of some economical urgency. The progressive manufacturer will hardly allow traditional forms to interfere with the most efficient adaptation of premises for the purpose they have to serve, and any improvements such as the use of materials that could effect more rapid and economical building, and new methods of construction that could assist and render more efficient processes of manufacture were generally welcomed. The argument that retarded the development towards a living architecture in many other types of building, was that this traditional form has served us very well in the past, that the principles of design by which it evolved have been followed with success since the days of Ancient Greece and Rome, and produced some of the finest architecture in the world, and thus we must be very careful before we depart from these well-tried methods. This argument had less weight in the design of industrial buildings intended for processes of manufacture that were new and constantly changing, and for which there existed little tradition. But even though this was generally the case there were many industrialists and their architects who aimed at giving beauty and dignity to their factories by architectural embellishment borrowed from past styles. Both architect and industrialist would consider it bad business to allow such embellishment to interfere too much with the efficiency of the building, but in many cases efficiency suffered a little. Where the utmost light is desirable and a maximum is obtained by a glass façade like that in the Fagus boot-last factory the introduction of classic stone columns or pilasters on the façade would obviously defeat that purpose in some degree. But the industrialist and his architect responsible for this might argue that a factory with a handsome and beautiful appearance is an advertisement for the products manufactured there, and is also of value to the reputation of the firm. This argument is even stronger with some forms of commercial buildings, such as departmental stores. In these, large open spaces with a maximum of light are desirable, therefore a street façade with large glazed areas is the most efficient. To introduce classic pilasters or columns, as in the Selfridge building in Oxford Street, London, is to reduce the light. But a monumental classic façade, it would be argued, gives impressiveness to the building, which is valuable as a magnet for customers, while there is now almost total dependence on artificial lighting.

During the years before and after the First World War, this was probably the thought of the majority of industrialists and architects. Where the industrialist did not give much thought to the appearance of his factory, these embellishments were eschewed and there was exclusive concentration on efficiency. It is work of this kind that was partially conducive to the development of an architecture expressive of the age. It is thus clear why industrial buildings in this early stage made a great contribution to the development of such architecture.

But there is another category of industrialist and architect (probably the industrialist led by a progressive architect) who made the most vital contribution. They are those who believe that the industrial or commercial building should serve its purpose with the utmost efficiency, and should be designed accordingly; they also believe in aesthetic values, but that its beauty should not be acquired by the use of embellishments derived from past architectural styles, but should emerge directly from the purpose and

135

construction of the building. The architects and industrialists who could think like this before 1914 were rare. We have already considered those who could do so—Behrens, Gropius, Meyer, Garnier, Perret, and a few others. This was a logical process of design, but what prevented the majority thinking and acting in this logical way was the inability to see beauty in these industrial and commercial buildings of steel and concrete which were in their appearance a logical expression of purpose and structure. The beauty had to be discovered as the beauty of any startlingly original work has to be discovered. When first created such a work is subjected to abuse for a period, whether it be a musical composition of Stravinsky or Bartok, a Pre-Raphaelite, Impressionist, or Surrealist painting, or a stone carving of Epstein (all of which were of the kind that suffered heavy abuse). Later the antagonism dies, the admirers increase, and often the work takes its place among the beautiful creations for which we are grateful. This is very much the case with the architecture of steel and concrete. When no aesthetic claims were made for it, and it was just a racing stadium or a factory or a bridge serving a utilitarian purpose, when it was, in fact, just building, it met with no antagonism. But when aesthetic claims were made for it, and this type of architecture was employed for buildings in the centres of our cities, which are often partly settings for traditional ceremonies, and for our homes, then the antagonism was strong, precisely because of this inability to see beauty in the new and strange.

The number of notable people in the nineteenth century who, like Ruskin and Morris, could see no beauty in structures of iron or steel was legion. Morris, staying in Paris as near as possible to the Eiffel Tower, as this was the only place in Paris where he could not see it, was symbolic. The average manufacturer desiring to give aesthetic interest to his factory, or shopkeeper desiring to give this to his departmental store, turns to the established architectural traditions; the stark factory or store of unornamented steel, concrete, and glass, depending for beauty on proportion, mass, line, and light and shadow, was aesthetically negative to him. While the appreciation of the new architecture presented difficulties to the majority at this time, the pioneers were enthusiastic for the beauties of the architecture of steel, concrete, and glass, and they were also enthusiastic for the beauties of many machines like the aeroplane and motor car.

LE CORBUSIER'S IDEAS AND MENDELSOHN'S EARLY PROJECTS
This enthusiasm is the spirit of Le Corbusier's book *Vers une Architecture*[1], published in 1923, which aroused widespread interest in Europe and met with no small amount of abuse and derision from older traditionalist architects. One important section of the book is entitled: 'Eyes which do not see', with sub-sections dealing with liners, aeroplanes, and automobiles, in which Le Corbusier seeks to show how, as they develop, they are designed more and more strictly for the purpose they have to fulfil, and how they conform to the same principles of design as the great examples of classic architecture like the Parthenon. Under one illustration of the front-wheel brake of a

Delage motor car, he says: 'Cette précision, cette netteté, d'exécution ne flattent pas qu'un sentiment nouveau, né de la mécanique. Phidias sentait ainsi; l'entablement du Parthénon en témoigne. De même les Egyptiens lorsqu'ils polissaient les Pyramides. C'etait au temps où Euclide et Pythagore dictaient la conduite de leurs contemporains'. (This precision and this neatness of execution do not belong only to a newborn feeling for mechanism. Phidias felt like that; the entablature of the Parthenon is evidence of this. It was the same with the Egyptians when they were finishing off the Pyramids. It was at this time that Euclid and Pythagoras were dictating to their contemporaries.)

Le Corbusier points that design of things of use—aeroplanes, motor cars, buildings— evolves towards a standard and then efforts are made to perfect and beautify that standard. He remarks that 'Phidias, in building the Parthenon, did not work as a constructor, engineer or designer. All these elements already existed. What he did was to perfect the work, and endue it with a noble spirituality.' Le Corbusier thus sees in modern building, becoming more and more machine-like because the essential constructional material—steel—is the same, similar principles of design and the same evolution as in the great architecture of the past. Le Corbusier noting the parallel sees in the new architecture possibilities of beauty of the same high order as in the classic architecture of Greece.

Significant also were the sketch-projects of buildings of steel, concrete, and glass made by many young architects, in which there was obviously considerable aesthetic delight in the forms resulting from the use of these building materials. Among the most noteworthy sketch-projects were those of the young Eric Mendelsohn made from 1914 to 1920. His earliest sketches of buildings like halls, law courts, and religious buildings are classical in character, but after this start Mendelsohn concentrates mainly on industrial buildings. He conceives these in terms of steel and concrete, using those materials according to their character, and letting them largely determine the forms of the building[2]. As Sheldon Cheney says, 'Mendelsohn in these sketches made buildings expressive of the 'feel' of the machine.'[3] Although acutely sensitive to the architectural beauties of the past, especially of Greek and Gothic architecture, Mendelsohn realized that the architecture of today is an architecture of an industrial civilization in which the materials are steel, concrete, glass, while various new materials are being constantly invented, and that the creative imagination of the architect must work in these terms. The very nature of the sketch-projects demonstrates that they were made partially with an aesthetic purpose. (A selection is illustrated.) It will be seen that most of them are industrial buildings conceived in terms of the tensile strength of steel, that linear emphasis is strong, while they were designed with the feeling for the character of the modern industrial machine. Perhaps the aesthetic element is the strongest, for Mendelsohn was an original artist. With the artist there is often the necessity of taking a subject for expression apart from decorative emphasis of a utilitarian structure, and thus we find in many of these sketches a tendency towards the use of forms which are symbolic

General view,
first floor plan and
preliminary sketch

Observatory of the Astro-Physical Institute, Potsdam, 1930 (widely known
as the Einstein Tower)   *Architect: Eric Mendelsohn*

The other illustrations are of sketch projects made by the architect
between 1914 and 1918—warehouse, gas works, temple of
light and optical factory

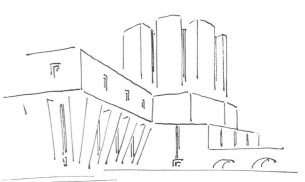

of the purpose of the building, as the verticality of a Gothic church is symbolic of aspiration. Of the sketches illustrated it is clearly apparent in the optical factory and the goods station, and we see it even more marked in the Observatory at Potsdam. Mendelsohn had been trained as an architect, but from 1912 to 1914 he was occupied with stage designing and painting and had been influenced by the German Expressionist movement. These circumstances coupled with other influences like *Art Nouveau* and the work of Van de Velde considerably affected Mendelsohn's approach to architecture. In these three influences we find the emphasis of linear rhythms prominent. German Expressionism, which was one of the movements leading to Surrealism, was largely a reaction against Impressionism and was formed partially under the influence of van Gogh and Edvard Munch, in whose work linear rhythms are used as a vital expressional medium, in the one as expression of the life and growth of natural forms in the landscape, and in the other as an expression largely of human emotion. Linear rhythms are fundamental in *Art Nouveau* and Van de Velde tried to associate rhythmical lines with organic forms and the sense of growth, which was a powerful influence on Mendelsohn and on his ideas of organic unity. The strong feeling for line in Mendelsohn's work, due largely to the influences mentioned, was from the first wedded to the tensile qualities of steel as a structural medium, which is seen in the sketches, and in much of his most important work, but even when this association is not so determining a factor in design, the linear quality is still strong, as in his early Observatory at Potsdam.

Indicative of the general feeling towards the machine-like architecture of Mendelsohn's sketches, is the startling effect they produced when exhibited at Paul Cassirer's Galleries in Berlin in 1919 under the title of Architecture in Steel and Reinforced Concrete. Many architects and critics were puzzled, some derided them as not architecture, while they aroused enthusiasm among others. But the chief difficulty seemed to be to accept this kind of work as architecture. Mendelsohn's earliest important building completed in 1920, the Einstein Tower at Potsdam, was one of these small sketches realized in an actual structure. It was because Findlay-Freundlich had seen Mendelsohn's sketches for Observatories that he recommended him to Einstein and the German Government as the architect for this observatory to be built for further researches into Einstein's theory of relativity. The building was conceived in reinforced concrete, and was begun in this material, but the principal part was built of brick and covered in cement rendering, although the top part was finished in concrete. The building has been criticized on the grounds of its construction; some have said: being conceived in reinforced concrete and built of brick it is a constructional sham. The reason for the brick construction has been variously stated, but Mendelsohn himself stated that it was due to the difficulty at the time of procuring adequate quantities of cement; it was built, however, as originally conceived in the sketch with brick as a substitute material. Linear rhythm is a guiding factor in the design, while in its forms there is clearly symbolism of optical instruments, seen especially in the deep curved window recesses which allow for an interesting play of light and shadow, while there is a sense of the mysterious in the building which pervades subjects like physics and astronomy.

The inability to reconcile direct expression of structure and purpose of a modern steel-framed or concrete factory or departmental store with ideas of beautiful appearance, that is, architecture, was symptomatic of a general divorce of art and modern industry which existed in the nineteenth century. Art was then something applied, like the columns of the Selfridge store, and the real structural form of half the objects produced for the home in the second half of the nineteenth century was obscured by irrelevant ornament grafted on. The realization that the unique beauty of an object arises from its character, and that this must emanate from its purpose and structure and can belong to the products of the machine as well as to the products of hand craftmanship, was very slow in coming. William Morris turned his back on modern industry, but the Deutsches Werkbund, founded in 1907, made the first effort on a big scale toward the effective employment of the machine in which aesthetic values are considered. This grew in strength and led to the formation of similar associations in other countries. In the spring of 1919 Walter Gropius became head of the Weimar School of Arts and Crafts and also of the Weimar Academy of Fine Art, which he very shortly amalgamated into a Hochschule für Gestaltung, or High School for Design, under the name of Das Staatliche Bauhaus Weimar. Simply stated, the Bauhaus was dedicated to the training of artists for the production of beautiful objects of use by the machine.

From 1919 to 1924 Gropius was primarily engaged in organizing training at the Bauhaus, so that during this period he was responsible for only a little building work. One work which should be noted, however, is the reconstruction of the Municipal Theatre at Jena, which Gropius designed in collaboration with Adolf Meyer, and completed in 1923. It is characterized by large plain surfaces, the effect being dependent largely, both in the exterior and interior, on the relations of rectangular masses, the larger masses being solid with a carefully calculated punctuation of voids. Gropius was also engaged on a few projects at this time, the most important of which was for an international academy of philosophical studies (1924). This building was conceived in reinforced concrete, and was designed strictly in accordance with convenience and the logical sequence of parts. The blocks are long and there is considerable horizontal emphasis by means of balconies. Its distinguishing architectural feature is the relation of these blocks, which give the impression of an underlying unity in the scheme[4].

Peter Behrens's Turbine factory in the Huttenstrasse, Berlin, for the A.E.G. (General Electric Company of Berlin), as previously noted makes a tremendous step forward in modern design. In many of Behrens's industrial buildings the classical tradition is strong, and this classical influence gives them a monumental quality. The buildings

140

are partially transitional from the classicism of the old order to the architecture of steel and concrete. Behrens did not break free from this tradition and accept the new idiom so completely as Gropius had done in the Fagus boot-last factory, and this classical influence is quite as strong in the large amount of work by Behrens in the early twenties. Fundamentally it belongs to the new movement, although influenced by Classicism. His earlier work (see Chapter 11) is mainly in the classical tradition, showing tendencies rather of a negative character, like greater simplicity.

Two of the largest buildings by Behrens erected at this time are the I.G. Farbenindustrie Aktiengesellschaft—Chemical Factory and Dye Works—at Hochst-am-Main (1920–4) and the Gutehoffnungshütte—Good Hope building for extracting by-products of coal—at Oberhausen (1921–5). The site of the former building is long, and borders a slightly curving road. The plan is irregular and obviously the aim was to use the site to the best advantage without restrictions that might have been imposed by more formal planning. The building is a steel-framed structure faced with brick, and brick is used for some of the interior facings. It is employed throughout with a decorative intention that shows Behrens's affection for the material. In some of the interiors the decorative effect is of a romantic character, as in the grand hall with flute-like forms in bricks of various colours, no doubt to symbolize dyes. There is a definite monumental quality in the exterior that makes one think of some of the old warehouses built in England a hundred years earlier.

The immense Good Hope Industries' buildings are of steel frame construction faced with brick, and the decorative pattern of the bricks on the walls again demonstrates Behren's liking for this material. Probably because Behrens had a more spacious and open site this building is more formally planned, and symmetrical arrangement has played some part in the design. In one principal block two staircase towers are arranged at regular intervals, and the whole effect is somewhat of rectangular masses building up in classical harmony. In another block, although the planning is of a similar symmetrical kind, there is considerable emphasis on projecting flat roofs, and the effect of the edges is carried on by the introduction of concrete bands, either flush or as string courses, effects not unlike those in some of Frank Lloyd Wright's buildings. The general impression of this building is that the architect, though conscious of industrial needs and of serving these efficiently is yet by thought and training in the classical tradition.

When we consider Behren's non-industrial work of this period, like the Monastery of St. Peter, Salzburg (1924–5), where the type of building has a long history, the Renaissance tradition is dominant and wholly determines the style. But with the block of flats that he built for the Vienna Council in 1924–5 traditional influences recede, although again in the symmetrical massing the classical feeling is still strong. The type of building is important with Behrens. If the particular type has few

141

Chemical Factory and Dye Works at Hochst-am-Main,
Germany, 1920–24   *Architect: Peter Behrens*

General exterior view and interior of entrance hall (right)
which shows decorative use of brick

Hall for Fairs, Breslau, 1924, an example of wide span
timber roof construction   *Architect: Max Berg*

Hat Factory at Luckenwalde, 1921, showing construction
of sheds in reinforced concrete, and (below) general view
                    Architect: Eric Mendelsohn

precedents, as in some industrial buildings, then functionalism becomes correspondingly more prominent; if the type is rich with precedents, then Behrens's design in style and planning conforms in greater degree with what is traditionally accepted. But none of the work of this kind from 1918 and 1924, not even the dye works at Hochst-am-Main, is so fine an expression of purpose and modern structure as the turbine factory. Later, in the tobacco factory at Linz in Austria, Behrens could use steel and glass with a feeling for their structural potentialities and lightness unsurpassed at the time.

Although much industrial building is construction for a special manufacturing process, for a large number of industries there are certain requirements in common, and one of the principal of these is the enclosing of a large space, without or with as few intermediate supports as possible. The open expanse of enclosed space, the large hall, is a characteristic of much industrial building, and one of the problems of progressive design is to devise light, economical, and efficient structures to span these wide spaces. The remarkable engineering feat of the Galerie des Machines of 1889 with its span of 378 feet has not been surpassed, and the spans of halls for factories and exhibition buildings are generally considerably less. Progress has been made, however, in the greater lightness of structure and greater economy of material.

The principle of construction in which ribs of steel or reinforced concrete spring from the floor was followed in many industrial halls built in this period between 1919 and 1924. In the roof of St. Pancras Station of 1868 the arches spring from wall corbels; in the Galerie des Machines of 1878 from iron columns, the upper part of the wall being part of the roof girder which turns to a pitch of 20 degrees. The next stage of resting this girder on the floor was realized in the Galerie des Machines of 1889. The reinforced concrete parabolic arches of the airship hangars at Orly (1916) were a variation on the same theme and a considerable number of further variations were made in the following years principally in Germany and France.

A variant of this rib construction is employed in the hat factory at Luckenwalde, designed by Eric Mendelsohn in 1921. The factory consists of four long sheds and a dye works built parallel. The sheds are built of a series of reinforced concrete arches springing from the floor on the same principle as the Paris Exhibition buildings (see illustration). The dye works represents a special construction devised for efficient use. It consists of two tiers of concrete arches, the upper supported on the lower. This construction was devised to provide a drying loft, and special ventilation produces a stream of air along its whole length, so that a kind of wide chimney is provided. Here is a building designed strictly according to the purpose it has to serve, and how much thought was given to pleasing appearance it is difficult to determine, but there is little doubt that the clear structural lines of the arches in particular are of aesthetic interest Among other industrial and exhibition buildings of the hall type of this period are the Hall at Magdeburg for Agricultural exhibitions and sport built by Bruno Taut and

143

Clothing Workshop,
Paris, 1919

*Architects: Auguste
and Gustave Perret*

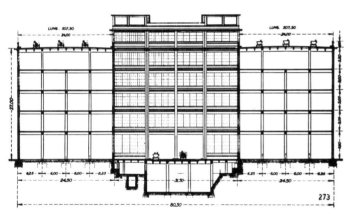

Sectional elevation

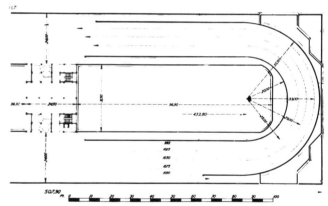

Plan of track

Fiat factory—the car ramp leading to track for testing cars on the roof of the building

Ramp giving access to roof

Fiat automobile factory at Lingotto, near Turin, 1919–22
Architect: Matte Trucco

Aerial view of factory

Johannes Göderitz in 1922, the Hall for Fairs at Breslau built by Max Berg in 1921, a clothing workshop (1919), and a scenic decorators' workshop in Paris (1923) built by Auguste and Gustave Perret. The first-mentioned has segmental arched ribs of reinforced concrete held together by transverse ribs. The interior effect with long apex skylight is impressive. A similar low segmental arch is used in the Hall at Breslau constructed of wood, but here the arches are carried on short columns, and a flat roof is clipped to the arches and held firmly in position by them. The Perret brothers in their two Paris workshops mentioned use the semicircular arch. In the clothing factory it is a reinforced concrete frame structure with balconies round the central space, while the semicircular arches serve to hold the flat roof in position as in the Hall at Breslau. In the decorators' workshop the semicircular ribs determine the internal form of the building. Where the arches are just structural and there is no attempt to let the general form follow them, as in the Paris clothing factory, the aesthetic effect is far less agreeable than where the form follows the arches, as in the Hall at Magdeburg, and the decorators' workshop in Paris. Such interiors have some aesthetic interest and if fairly large, are impressive.

The largest European factory built at this time, and one that provides an example of design controlled by industrial purpose is the Fiat Automobile Factory at Lingotto, near Turin, built in 1919–22. The design is the interpretation by the architect, Matt Trucco, of the requirements of the President of the Fiat Company, G. Agnelli.

Of reinforced concrete frame construction the factory is about one and a quarter miles in length. It is designed for the logical sequence of operations in production, from the entrance of the raw material to the testing of the automobiles. At either end of the building, which is five storeys in height, is a special ramp from the basement to the roof (see vertical sections) on which there is a testing track 78 feet wide and banked at either end to afford scope for high speeds. The façades of the building have the gridiron appearance formed by the concrete frame and the floors. Four light wells are formed in the centre of the building, or to vary the description, the centre of the building between the tracks is open, and three blocks connecting the long side blocks are introduced at regular intervals, each of which rises higher than the track and provides access to it. Here is an example where purpose has determined the design of the building, and it demonstrates why it is that in modern industrial building we have the basis of a true contemporary and living architecture.

HOUSING IN THE EARLY TWENTIES

Housing, in the form of blocks of flats, rows of small houses, and individually designed houses, does not present a very large number of examples in the early twenties that belong to the new architecture, but from 1925 onwards they are more numerous. The most notable between 1919 and 1924 are some blocks of flats at Rotterdam, and rows of houses at the Hook of Holland by J. J. P. Oud, houses in La Cité Moderne at

Brussels by Victor Bourgeois, some blocks of flats in Vienna by Josef Frank, and a few early houses by Le Corbusier, namely that at Vaucresson built in 1922, the house for the painter Ozentant built in the same year, and two houses at Auteuil built in 1923. These will be considered in Part III as they can then be considered in sequence with Le Corbusier's other houses.

J. J. P. Oud became housing director of Rotterdam in 1918, and shortly afterwards built several blocks of flats for workmen. The large block known as 'Tusschendyke' was built in 1920. In its directness, simplicity, and purity, in which all ornamental effects are eschewed, it offers a mild contrast to the romanticism of the Amsterdam flats of de Klerk and Kramer. Yet it does not represent a full utilization of structural possibilities, and the somewhat small vertical windows which occupy the street façade and the upper part of the façades facing the inner court are traditional types. The same can be said of the flats of Josef Frank, built in and around Vienna (Altmannsdorf 1921, Hetyendorf 1922, Traiskirchen 1922, and Kongressplatz). These flats of Oud and Frank and those of Behrens previously mentioned are rather transitional in character, and do not yet represent a full acceptance of the new structural possibilities.

In a letter written in 1923 Eric Mendelsohn makes some interesting and highly personal comments on the contrast between Oud's work at Rotterdam and contemporary work at Amsterdam[5]. He speaks of Oud as functional and coldly objective and Amsterdam as dynamic and visionary, and suggests the value of reconciliation between the two. 'Both are necessary', he says, 'and both must find each other. If Amsterdam goes a step farther towards ratio, and Rotterdam's blood does not freeze, then they may unite. Otherwise, Rotterdam will pursue the way of mere construction with deathly chill in its veins, and Amsterdam will be destroyed by the fire of its own dynamicism. Function, plus dynamics, is the challenge.' It is characteristic of Mendelsohn to place this emphasis on dynamic qualities, and I think his requirements would be partially met in the workers' houses at the Hook of Holland, built by Oud in 1924–5. Here definitely is a dynamic quality, while full advantage of modern construction is taken in the design. The planning of each unit is extremely ingenious, as much as possible being introduced into a too severely restricted space. The houses are built of concrete in long rows, with a balcony on the first floor, the unbroken line of which emphasizes horizontal effect. They are curved and have entire glass screens on the ground floor. Large horizontal windows are used, the spacing of those on the first floor in relation to the plain wall is effective, while the houses compose into a unified whole.

La Cité Moderne in Brussels, built by Victor Bourgeois in 1921–2, composed of rows of one- and two-family, two-storey houses, and three-storey flats, represents a planned development and a conception of house blocks that seems to owe something to Tony Garnier's Cité Industrielle. The houses are built of brick with flat roofs, the windows are fairly large, horizontal rectangles, and diagonal projections are used in several to

147

capture light. Here is a rather tentative note with design of transitional character. Progress with the new architecture in the first few years after the First World War was not very marked—conditions were against that—rather the work of this period consolidated the stage reached before the war. From 1924 to 1932 real advance was made and this was a period of great constructional and architectural achievement.

Did the First World War contribute much to architectural progress? If we consider the movement towards a living architecture that had been growing in the years before the war, it merely served to arrest for a time that movement, and we cannot say that any real advance was made until five years after the end of the war. But for the war the movements would surely have been a continuous development, and it served to retard that development. But there is another aspect. An upheaval like the war prompted a re-examination of values, and less willingness to accept standards of the past that had not served them too well. There was consequently less respect for tradition, and this state of mind probably effected a readier acceptance of new forms more expressive of contemporary life. Also the war produced a general desire for higher social standards, especially for those who had not enjoyed good standards in the past. Higher social standards mean better and more spacious housing accommodation, better health services, more social amenities. All this means more building to satisfy these requirements. This was so in every European country, but the change was probably greatest in Russia, where the Revolution in the interests of the majority was greater than elsewhere. This general desire in Europe for higher social standards had, therefore, a tremendous effect on the volume of building. It was not apparent at once owing to the difficulties of political adjustments and economic reconstruction but it began to manifest from 1924 onwards. It is very doubtful if the volume of building in Europe from 1924 to 1939 would have been so great but for that legacy of the war that required a higher general standard of living.

References and Notes

1. English translation by Frederick Etchells under the title *Towards a New Architecture*, London, 1927.
2. Many of these sketches are illustrated in my book on *Eric Mendelsohn*, London, 1940.
3. *The New World Architecture*, London, 1930, p. 97.
4. The model is reproduced in Sigfried Giedion's *Space, Time and Architecture*, p. 396.
5. See Arnold Whittick, *Eric Mendelsohn*, second edition, London, 1956, p. 65.

14 Tradition, transition, functional design and modern construction—some public buildings, libraries and town halls

THE PROCESS OF SIMPLIFICATION had continued since the beginning of the century, and it reached its culmination in the early thirties. Architecture which is completely denuded of ornament must have good proportion if it is to give aesthetic pleasure, and if it is to be expressive and interesting it is desirable that it shall have definite character. Ornament, after all, has valuable aesthetic and expressive functions if well used, and unless there is something else in its place which serves these functions more will be lost than gained. Used in excess, used without fitting relation to the basic forms of the building, used in an assertive and obtrusive manner, ornament can be distasteful, vulgar, and ugly, but used well ornament serves to emphasize the form and style of a building, it gives variety by breaking up a plain surface, it serves as accent and punctuation, it helps to give effective light and shadow, and it often tells us something about the purpose of the building it adorns.

In many buildings, especially office blocks, there is an almost complete absence of ornament, while the proportion is not particularly good, nor have they any positive or definite character. Take, for example, Bush House, in London, by Helmle, Corbett and Harrison, which was built between 1925 and 1928. It occupies a splendid position in the centre of a segmental site with Aldwych on the north and the Strand on the south. It consists of a central block and four wings, two east and two west. The façades of these wings represent the negative process of simplification. Above the ground floor a large number of plain, square-headed windows in a plain wall are unrelieved by ornament or emphasis of any kind except for a balustrade in front of the set-back at the top. The whole façade is dull and monotonous. The windows are regularly spaced, and their width is only a little less than the space between them, while vertically the relation of voids to solids has a similar sameness. The ground floor is decorated with some very flat pilasters which have little relation to the flat, uninteresting façade above. Contrast the western block in Aldwych with the façade of India House, built by Sir Herbert Baker a little later. This façade has considerable variety and ornamental embellishment, which not only serves to emphasize forms but expresses the purpose of the building, and adds much to its interest. The windows have considerable variety of form, and although they may not all be in perfect harmony there is no very strong discordance, while this variety certainly gives interest. The function of the ornament is to symbolize the purpose of the building.

Over the main entrance is a large window with the Star of India above the keystone. On either side are Indian columns, with elephants forming the bases, while seated tigers are perched on the summits. Some of the windows have balconies, and these have trellised fronts similar to those surrounding Buddhist shrines. All the ornament, both inside and out, is expressive of Indian life and helps to give character and interest to the building. If the building were badly proportioned or the ornament badly applied, this interest would not save it from being an ugly building, but the proportion is generally good, and the ornament is applied in harmony with the general form. It succeeds in being interesting and expressive, which can hardly be said of Bush House. This applies less to the central block of Bush House than to the wings, for it has obviously been the aim to make the north and south entrances the focal points of the whole building. Particularly is this so with the north entrance, which acts as a terminal feature to Kingsway, one of the finest streets in London. Across an immense arch is a lintel, beneath which are two heavy classical columns. On the lintel stand two figures, on either side of an altar, each holding a torch. The whole effect is architecturally ridiculous. If the two massive columns are placed under the lintel with the intention of supporting the figures, then the impression is that they are unnecessarily heavy and that they have not been given enough work to do in proportion to their bulk. This is thinking in the structural terms of stone, but Bush House is a steel-frame building and the lintel is a steel girder encased in stone, and it does not need the columnar supports. It is obvious to anybody conscious of the structure of the building that the columns do not support the lintel. If very beautiful proportion had resulted this structural sham might have been excusable, but it is largely because it is a structural sham and the architects were neither thinking properly in terms of stone nor steel, but were muddled between the two, that the proportion is bad. Also, the lintel placed across the circular arch strikes a very discordant note. The smaller south entrance is much happier in proportion and effect, but it does not save Bush House from being architecturally one of the least satisfactory buildings erected in London between the wars.

There are several important buildings in Europe which have similar dull and monotonous façades without character or expression, which are the result of this negative process of simplification. Simplicity is most effective when there is definite character. Indeed, it may reveal character more than if the building were embellished with ornament.

One important reason for the stripping of ornament and the elimination of forms characteristic of historical styles was the desire to make a fresh start towards a living

150

architecture expressive of contemporary life. The most effective way of doing this is to make a complete break, as did the exponents of the new architecture, and solve problems by logical thought about purpose and structure rather than by adhering to traditional methods of design. But in transitional architecture this is arrived at by slow stages. When the stage of complete stylistic negation is reached, before something positive takes the place of the old, it is architecturally for the time being a retrograde step. You are at the bottom of the hill before the fresh ascent. It were better to preserve some traditional style or character than have such complete negation. A building of the type exemplified by the Art Gallery in the Gotaplatzen, in Gothenburg is exceedingly simple, with an almost complete absence of ornament, but here an arcade derived from Renaissance architecture which forms the principal façade, gives character to the building. This art gallery is a survival of the Gothenburg Exhibition of 1923. Designed by A. L. Romdahl, it occupies a central position in the Gotaplatzen and is flanked by two more recent buildings, the City Theatre, designed by Carl Bergsten and completed in 1934 (seen to the left in the illustration) and the City Concert Hall (seen to the right), designed by Nils Einar Eriksson and completed in 1934, while the famous 'Poseidon' fountain by Carl Milles is in the centre. The design of the Art Gallery influenced the proportions and treatment of the two later buildings, and though simple, with plain wall surfaces, they both preserve affinity with classical architecture by the rows of classical columns in front of the long, wide window running the whole length of the façade, and turning the corner in the case of the City Theatre. Here is transition from classical to the new architecture very clearly expressed.

The monotony of a very large number of plain, vertical, rectangular window openings all alike and evenly spaced on a plain wall, with about the same distance between them horizontally and vertically as their width and height, is frequently seen in tenement blocks throughout Europe built during this period. Fortunately there are several also with distinctive character, some by de Klerk, Kramer, and Gropius. To give more interest and character is not a question of expense, but of design. It is often just as economical to design a tenement block with façades of an interesting character, with forms attractively emphasized, as to design a monotonous characterless façade. An example which gets very near to complete monotony is the large tenement house of Engelshof, in Vienna, designed by Rudolf Perco. Here the whole conception is based on classical symmetry and the rectangular windows are all of the same size with approximately the same distance between them as their width and height. The sameness is relieved a little by some recessions, and slight horizontal emphasis at the top and to connect the windows, also by corner balcony treatment, but the whole effect is typical of the barrack-like monotony which too often is found in large tenement blocks.

Shell Mex House in London, built in 1929 by Messrs Joseph, presents a tremendous façade to the river, and much of it is unrelieved monotony of square-headed windows

151

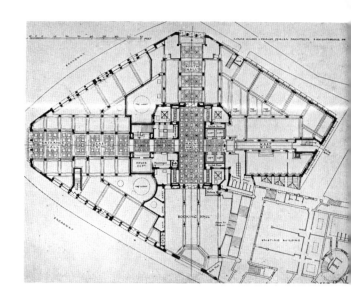

London Passenger Transport Building, St. James's, 1929,
view from Broadway and ground floor plan
Architect: Charles Holden

Götaplatsen, Gothenburg. In the centre is the Art Gallery,
on the left, the City Theatre, and on the right, the
Concert Hall

Architect: Nils Einar Eriksson
Architect of the concert hall: Sven Markelius
Architect of the theatre: A. L. Romdahl

India House, Aldwych, 1929
Architect: Sir Herbert Baker

on a flat wall, although the windows, being considerably larger than the spaces between them, have a much better effect than those of Bush House. Seen as a whole from across the river, or from Hungerford or Waterloo Bridge, the building is given interest by the punctuation of the two circular-headed windows flanking a central one at the top, and the set-backs, or recessions, at the sides and top which give a building-up effect. The climax is the square, fat clock tower, but it is an unsatisfactory climax, because its form does not appear to be in good formal sequence to the masses below. Being approximately one-third of the whole width of the façade, the proportion is not very happy. Lower and broader would have suggested a more pleasing sequence. Brettenham House, along the river to the east, near Waterloo Bridge, is another example of simplification where interest is achieved by a sequence of forms building up to a climax. It was designed by William and Edward Hunt, and completed in 1928. The recessions are pronounced on the narrow river façade, and the blocks are pleasantly related and more effective than in Shell Mex House. The long western elevation is attractively punctuated by tall, circular-headed windows rising the full height of the building, which mark the lifts and stairs opposite the entrances on the eastern elevation.

Many architects, anxious to eliminate stylistic ornament, yet desiring to give an interesting and attractive effect to their elevations, endeavour to do so rather by recessions and the relation of masses, or by variety in the sizes and shapes of the windows—sometimes, of course, by both. Windows well placed and well proportioned on a wall can given a very pleasing impression, but it is generally the result of nice and subtle calculation and strong artistic feeling, while it has to be done in conjunction with the adequate lighting of the building. An architect may not desire to depart from the traditional vertical window, although modern construction would enable him to do so. One finds it in the very plain exterior of the Stockholm City Library, designed by Gunnar Asplund and built between 1924 and 1928. In the two upper storeys of the square block the long and short vertical windows are carefully spaced on the wall with good effect, while the tall windows of the central drum above the Lending Library are also well spaced.

The Civic Centre at Swansea, designed by Sir Percy Thomas and completed in 1932, and the Headquarters of the Royal Institute of British Architects in Portland Place, by Grey Wornum completed in 1934, are British examples of good window spacing on plain walls.

The negative process of eliminating traditional styles and ornament was often accompanied by the more positive process of searching for subjects for expression. The most obvious subjects are revealed in the growing tendency to express structure and to emphasize the general form of the building. They are simple motifs, but they do arise from contemporary conditions and are clearly a small step towards a modern expressive architecture. In work that derives from classical and Renaissance architecture expression is generally wedded to traditional symmetrical planning, traditionally porportioned windows, and other attributes of a similar character.

In a building, like an office block, occupying a regular shaped site, the pattern made by the steel frame and demanded by the requirements of the building often consists of rectangles, with the structural emphasis and greater bulk in the vertical stanchions, although here and there, according to the nature of the structure, increased bulk and load bearing is given to certain horizontal stanchions. A typical example is Vintry House, near Southwark Bridge, which was built in the late twenties. In this steel-framed construction the stone facing from the second to the seventh storey consists of long uprights which cover the vertical stanchions, and this vertical emphasis, and the comparatively thin wall, suggesting a veneer rather than solid masonry, emanates largely from the nature of the structure. There are details and touches of ornament which clearly derive from Renaissance architecture, but they are subdued and the whole building is a compromise between the Renaissance palace and the expression of modern structure. Here is a type of transitional architecture of which there are a large number of examples in Europe built at this time, especially in England. Some of the work of this kind has an individual distinctiveness which is often given by the treatment of material, and by emphasis of particular forms.

VERTICAL EMPHASIS IN THE DESIGNS OF FAÇADES

Probably the main reasons for the vertical emphasis which is noteworthy in the late twenties are the influence of the steel structure, the desire to give character by emphasizing the form of the building, and the influence of the American skyscraper. The last two reasons are really the same, as the vertical emphasis in most skyscrapers is an emphasis of the character and form of the building. With European buildings the increase in height in the centres of cities permitted by by-laws meant that with office blocks presenting a flat façade to the street the form that suggested itself for emphasis was a vertical rectangle. Emphasis of this kind would probably have occurred without the example of American skyscrapers, but they probably gave considerable encouragement to European architects to venture more daringly with this motif.

Although it was the increased height of buildings in closely built city centres that contributed largely to the style, some of the best examples are of buildings which are situated with spacious surroundings. These are more complete three-dimensional compositions, whereas so many buildings in the centres of cities are between other buildings and present just flat façades to the street, or occupy corner sites, and face partly to a narrow, minor street. One of the finest buildings of the type being discussed, which has the advantage of a good situation with spacious surroundings, is the large new library of Cambridge University, which was completed in 1933 and designed by Sir Giles G. Scott. Constructed of a steel frame, which finds some expression in the

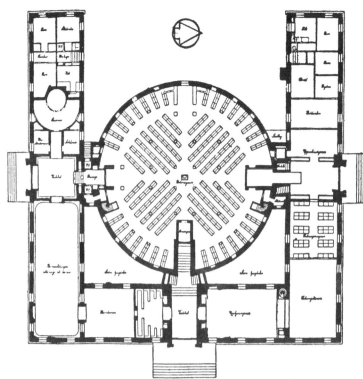

Stockholm City Library, 1924–27   *Architect: A. Gunnar Asplund*

Above—interior of the lending hall, right—plan and exterior.
The west side was added in 1932 thus
completing the square

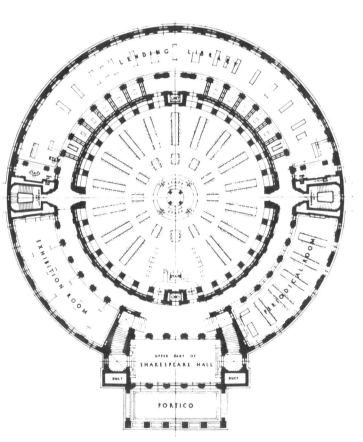

Manchester City Library, 1929–34, plan and exterior

Architect: E. Vincent Harris

appearance, the unbroken long uprights of the shafts between the windows on each wing, and the long upright windows of the tower give a very strong vertical emphasis to the whole.

In Alfred Messel's Wertheim Store in Berlin, built in 1896, one of the first buildings in Europe in which the steel frame is expressed in the façade, there is a vertical emphasis, rather ornately embroidered with decoration of a medieval character. Marked vertical emphasis, combined with sloughing of ornament and increased simplicity, appears more and more, so that by the late twenties numerous interesting buildings were erected in which this attribute was the most arresting feature. Among them may be mentioned the Scherl Publishing House, designed by O. Kohtz; the Book Printing Works at Tempelhof, Berlin, designed by Eugen C. Schmohl; and the Karstadt Store, Berlin, designed by Schafer.

The Scherl Publishing House and the Karstadt Store are both large buildings, designed in the classical tradition. The former has a massive central tower buttressed by two large wings. Along the whole façade are long unbroken shafts between the vertical windows from the first to the fifth storey, with a frieze of windows and two balconied recessions at the top.

The Karstadt Store has two towers symmetrically balanced towards the ends of the long block, and the whole effect is one of rather aggressive and heavy vertical emphasis. Here is an effort to create a distinctive style from verticality, but the whole is overdone and the effect is crude and a little oppressive.

More restrained and agreeable is Schmohl's Book Printing Works at Tempelhof, where the tower in relation to the blocks and the series of windows terminating in circular-headed windows on the top storey, together with long unbroken vertical mouldings running the full height of the building, suggest at a distance, from across the water, an effect somewhat reminiscent of a medieval cathedral.

This vertical motif is found throughout Germany at this time with varying decorative embroidery and emphasis. In northwestern districts, where brick is a favoured material, it wholly determines the external appearance of buildings such as the Stummkonzern Skyscraper at Dusseldorf, designed by Paul Bonatz and completed in 1925, and the *Hanover Advertiser* Offices at Hanover, designed by Fritz Hoger and completed in 1927. There are fewer dramatic examples of this vertical emphasis at this time in other European countries, probably because there was a less decided break with traditional ornament and styles than in Germany and a less vigorous search for new expression. In France, as in England, the expression is more mild and blended with more restrained classical feeling, as we see in the façade of the Salle Pleyel in Paris, and in the interesting Town Hall at Boulogne, designed by Tony Garnier and

Debat Ponsan. In one part of this building the vertical emphasis is very marked; in another, long windows (see p. 185) in the same alignment are linked together in vertical sequence.

In Germany vertical emphasis is found in buildings in the direct line of development from classical and Renaissance architecture, whereas the horizontal emphasis, such as is found in the work of Eric Mendelsohn, the brothers Luckhardt, and Mies van der Rohe, belongs more to the new architecture.

One of the reasons for this difference is the window opening. In the more traditional work, although the steel frame or reinforced concrete frame construction is employed, the windows are of the traditional vertical shape. In the view of the traditionalist it is preferable to light an office room which has, say, an external wall 20 feet long with two or even three vertical windows than with one horizontal window, because the traditional effect is desired. The tradition however was partially determined by the exigencies of stone or brick construction. With a building which is designed, not according to traditional practice, but according to function and the capacities of modern structure, it is the logical process to have a large horizontal window. In the former the unit of repetition has a vertical character, in the latter a horizontal one, and connecting them in a comprehensive form gives the emphasis described.

LONDON PASSENGER TRANSPORT HEAD OFFICE

Several buildings of a simplified classical traditional appearance designed at this time were begun with a close attention to function and convenience at the outset. The architect studied the purpose of the building and the site, and determined the plan accordingly, but in so doing he was inevitably influenced by traditional methods of classical symmetry and balance as a habit of thought. His training determined this. Whether the best plan evolves as a result of this training is always a question. Then, having determined the plan, the whole building is conceived in simplified traditional terms. Two examples of this are provided by two of the finest buildings erected in London during the period from 1924 to 1932. The Head Offices of the London Passenger Transport Board at St. James's, designed by Charles Holden (of Adams, Holden, and Pearson) and built in 1929, and Broadcasting House in Portland Place, designed by G. Val Myer (see also Chapter 29). Both are designed in a classical idiom, and in both the starting-point was satisfactory fulfilment of function and adaptation to a site. It is useful to cite Charles Holden's own explanation of how the design of the London Passenger Transport building began. The offices are built over St. James's Station, which had to be incorporated in the design. 'The site', he says[1], 'was very irregular and not at all the shape shown on the plan of the present building. . . . After trying many plans it occurred to me that it would be a great convenience to an office worker in Victoria Street if he could be allowed to cut across the site to St. James's Park Station instead of having to go round a blind corner, where the station would not be in sight and many people would have difficulty in finding it. A line was drawn along the desirable route of this imaginary passenger, and this line produced an outline shape which was roughly an isosceles triangle, which, bisected, established the central area of the future plan.' 'I do not think', Holden continues, 'that I was ever more excited in my life than when I realised the full possibilities of this cross-shaped plan—good light, no interference with neighbour lights; short corridors; and a compact centre containing all services, complete with lifts and staircase communicating directly with all four wings. The completed building was the direct expression of the form which emerged from the imaginary traveller's path.' The starting-point of this design is more concerned with the convenience of the traveller using St. James's Station than with the function of the block of offices, but thought along these lines suggested a good plan for the offices. It is regular, and the general appearance of the building with its slight vertical emphasis achieved in the façades by the windows being slightly recessed in vertical channels gives the whole a restrained classical effect. Particularly satisfying in the whole composition are the recessions above the seventh storey and the building up of masses in well proportioned sequence to the central tower. The building is adorned with a few sculptures—two over the office entrances called 'Night' and 'Day', by Jacob Epstein and several symbolizing the winds on the spaces forming the frieze of the seventh floor by Eric Gill, Henry Moore, and others. These sculptures are used as decorative points of accent or punctuation. They are carved in the same stone—Portland—with which the building is faced. They are essentially architectural sculptures, and have the effect of growing on the building as an organic part. Especially is this so with the two large and more arresting carvings of 'Night' and 'Day' by Jacob Epstein, which take their place exceedingly well over the two entrances and against the stone background.

As if to emphasize the connexion of the carving of 'Day' with its material and its architectural setting, Epstein has left the legs of the large seated figure almost like rough blocks of stone. The integration of these sculptures with the building is also effected by a similar massiveness and simplicity in the treatment of both. A similar use of sculpture appears at Broadcasting House where the group of Prospero and Ariel, by Eric Gill, appears in a niche over the entrance, but here the integration is not quite so successful, a circumstance in some measure due to the more stylistic and archaic treatment of the carving.

In the general movement towards simplicity the plain wall was more and more apparent as an effective part of design, and this was particularly so with the brick wall. In a material like brick, which allows for an interesting variegated texture or patterning, a large flat wall can be very attractive, more so than is generally the case with concrete or even an ashlar stone wall, although stone walls with uneven surfaces are often very pleasing. The brick, however, must be of an agreeable colour, like fawnish brown. Red brick being more positive in colour is generally less agreeable at

Cambridge University Library, 1931–34,
exterior, reading room and first floor plan

Architect: Sir Giles Gilbert Scott

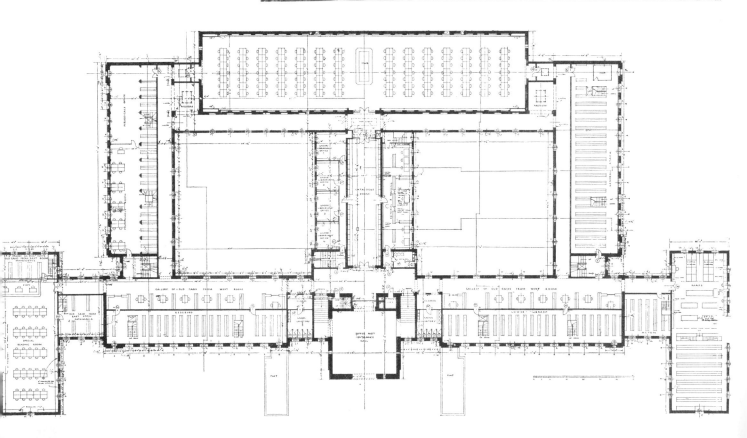

first, because harmony with surroundings, whether town or country, is less readily obtained, and the red brick has to weather for about fifty years before it becomes sufficiently harmonious. A contrast of this kind can be seen at Chesterfield, in Derbyshire. The Town Hall, built during the period under review, is faced with stone and red brick, while the Rural District Offices that lie at the back of the Town Hall are faced with fawnish brown bricks. The red bricks look harsh and discordant, while the fawnish brown bricks are soft in tone and harmonize with their surroundings.

THE PLAIN BRICK WALL

In addition to being part of the general movement towards simplicity the plain brick wall as an element in design in modern architecture emanates from the greater expression of structural materials, a movement which began before buildings were constructed of the steel frame. We find that desire to express the structural materials in the work of Philip Webb. An effective use of the plain brick wall in Victorian architecture is found in the churches of J. L. Pearson, a particularly fine and dramatic use of it being in St. John's Church, Upper Norwood. Pearson's churches probably look better now than when they were first erected, as he used a red brick which is now softened in tone. But the country in which the plain brick wall was used most frequently, having a widespread influence throughout Europe, was Holland. P. J. H. Cuypers in the latter part of the nineteenth century (see Chapter 5) returned to the expressional use of brick, which was seen also in the buildings of de Klerk and Kramer, and W. M. Dudok, who is one of the great European masters in the use of the plain brick wall as an element in architectural design. Similar developments occurred elsewhere in Europe, particularly in north Germany, the Scandinavian countries, and England, sometimes partly as the result of Dutch influence. In no type of building is this plain brick wall used so effectively as in one phase of modern church design.

Dudok continued to build at Hilversum throughout the period between the wars, particularly schools and the beautiful Town Hall which is a fine composition of balanced horizontal and vertical masses and plain surfaces. Among the buildings in Germany where the plain brick wall was effectively used is the Zollhafen Fire Station, by Fritz Schumacher, and the office building and warehouse at Hamburg by Gerson. These are very different buildings, but in both the plain brick wall is a decisive element in the design. In the latter the two side spaces of one façade are just plain walls for the whole eight storeys. The wall curves outwards slightly at the corners and sculptures adorn the lower part of vertical shafts, both of which are effective touches.

In England, apart from churches, some effective uses of the plain brick wall are found in the work of Sir Giles G. Scott. Cambridge University Library has brick facing, and other noteworthy works are the impressive Battersea Power Station and Cropthorne Court, Maida Vale, both of which were commenced in 1929. The nicely calculated recessions in the brick-faced blocks that support the three tall chimneys of the Battersea

Power Station have a very pleasing sequence, while the very large areas of plain brick and the simple decorative treatment like a fluted frieze seem to give this massive structure a pleasing lightness. When the sun shines on this structure and casts shadows across the plain brick surfaces with their slightly variegated texture, the effect is one of considerable beauty.

SOME NOTABLE LIBRARY BUILDINGS

The spread of education during the present century and the big increase in the production of books and periodicals have been accompanied by a great expansion of library services of all kinds, from the great national and university libraries down to small municipal libraries. An inevitable consequence of this has been that in the period between the wars a large number of library buildings of all types were erected in Europe. The largest libraries built, or commenced, during the 'twenties' were all designed on classical principles with formal symmetrical planning and of handsome dignified appearance. This continued until the early thirties when a departure on more irregular functional lines began.

Five typical examples of large library buildings erected during this period, which exemplify in different ways an adherence to classical methods of design, are the Stockholm City Library, the Manchester City Library, the Cambridge University Library, the National Library in Berne, and the Lenin State Library in Moscow. The first important example of a break with this formal symmetrical planning occurs with the Viipuri Library in Finland.

Before the early nineteenth century, libraries were rooms or halls with shelves of books ranged round the walls, often arranged with an eye to their decorative effect, and the reading desks or pews were grouped in the centre. With the increase in the size of collections the problem arose of storing the books, and thus began the scientific planning of libraries. For the large reference library two main sections had to be provided: reading space and storing space and their satisfactory relation, and most designs of libraries show various methods of meeting this requirement. There are numerous accessories, like catalogue space, and in some libraries lecture and exhibition rooms or halls are comprehended in the general scheme.

The British Museum Library in London, the Bibliothèque Nationale and the Bibliothèque Sainte-Geneviève in Paris are important European Libraries of the nineteenth century that represent three methods of planning and the relation of reading space to the book-stacks. The British Museum is the classic of circular libraries, the idea for the design having originated with Sir Anthony Panizzi, the librarian who collaborated with Sydney Smirke, the architect. Panizzi was probably influenced in his ideas by the French architect Benjamin Delessert, who proposed in 1835 a circular reading room, with book-stacks surrounding, for the Bibliothèque Nationale. Older

Swiss National Library, Berne, 1929–31, general
view, front entrance and ground floor plan

Architects:
  A. Oeschger, J. Kaufmann and E. Hostettler

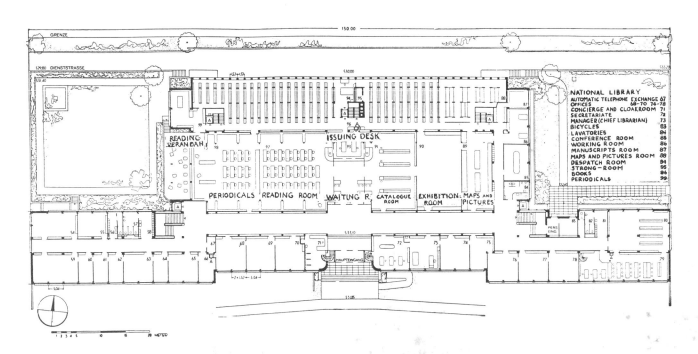

NATIONAL LIBRARY
AUTOMATIC TELEPHONE EXCHANGE 67
OFFICES   68-70 74-78
CONCIERGE AND CLOAKROOM   71
SECRETARIATE   72
MANAGER (CHIEF LIBRARIAN)   73
BICYCLES   83
LAVATORIES   84
CONFERENCE ROOM   85
WORKING ROOM   86
MANUSCRIPTS ROOM   87
MAPS AND PICTURES ROOM   88
DESPATCH ROOM   94
STRONG-ROOM   95
BOOKS   96
PERIODICALS   99

circular libraries are the Radcliffe Library at Oxford, built in 1738, and the earlier Wolfenbuttel Library, built in 1706, but these did not involve any separation of book-store and reading space. In the British Museum Library the librarians and catalogues are in the centre of the reading room from which the reading desks radiate. Book-stacks occupy the spaces round the reading room and are noteworthy for the gridiron floors which let light through to all floors from the glass roof.

The advantage of the circular reading room of the British Museum, with the librarians in the centre easily accessible and in a position of supervision, is obvious, but it is questionable whether the book-stacks are as conveniently related to the reading room and as compactly designed as they might be, as most readers are aware, for they often have to wait a very long time for books.

In the Bibliothèque Nationale the reading room is rectangular, with an apse at one end for the librarian, and at the rear of this is the rectangular book-stack known as the *magasin central*. Here is a closer relation of store space and reading space than at the British Museum. In the Bibliothèque Sainte-Geneviève, which was built a little earlier (1843–50) than the British Museum and Bibliothèque Nationale, the limitation of space rather forced the architect, Henri Labrouste, to the solution of placing the store immediately below the reading room so that there is vertical connexion. These three main types influenced all subsequent designs of large libraries.

The circular type had been adopted for several large libraries between the building of the British Museum reading room and the outbreak of the First World War, one of the most interesting being the Picton Reading Room at Liverpool, designed by Cornelius Sherlock and completed in 1879. A large stack of books is accommodated in the reading room itself, in shelves round the walls and projecting forward in bays. The dimensions are 100 feet diameter and 60 feet to the top of the dome which has an 'eye' light in the centre 24 feet in diameter. Below the reading room is a large hall for meetings and lectures.

CITY LIBRARIES OF STOCKHOLM AND MANCHESTER

The first large library with a circular hall as a central feature built between the wars is the City Library at Stockholm designed by E. Gunnar Asplund. It was commenced in the autumn of 1924 and completed in the autumn of 1927. The central feature is the large cylindrical lending hall, which is enclosed on north, east, and south sides by rectangular blocks containing reading and study rooms and offices. Books are arranged round the walls of the lending hall in three tiers while immediately below is the book-store. When the need arises it is the intention to build a book-stack on the west side and complete the square enclosing the circular reading room. The library is designed so that the three entrances are arranged as close as possible to the centre of the lending hall to give quick and easy access to the counter. From the narrow hall of

163

the principal entrance a narrow stairway cuts into the circular space half-way to the centre, and access from the other two sides is similarly arranged, although the passages are arrested earlier (see plan).

One very attractive feature of this library is the semicircular legend room in the south wing, designed for storytelling and reading to children. The building is constructed of brick faced with stucco both internally and externally. The floors are of concrete of filler-joist construction, and the flat roof over the cylindrical lending hall is of steel frame construction with copper covered panels. This cylinder rises above the level of the surrounding blocks and the hall is lighted by a series of tall vertical windows. They are well spaced, but as it should be the purpose in designing a library to make it as light as possible, these windows might have been larger with advantage.

Externally this is hardly a beautiful building. The cylinder rising in the centre of a square block punctuated by three central entrances and vertical windows is symmetrical and a little stark, and the cylinder does not relate organically to the square mass. Originally it was intended to roof the lending hall with a dome, and this would certainly have had a more agreeable external effect[2]. It is rather for the planning that it is worthy of note.

The tradition of the large circular reading room is followed in the Manchester City Library, designed by E. Vincent Harris, which was begun in 1929 and completed in 1934. This is the largest municipal library in Great Britain, a circumstance which has a certain fitness, as Manchester was the first to open a library under the Public Libraries Act of 1850, while, outside London, it is the centre of the largest urban area[3]. The reading room forms the central feature; it is situated on the first floor and, like the Picton reading room at Liverpool, it follows in principal the interior of the Pantheon. It is 127 feet in diameter and 92 feet high from the floor to the dome, and is lighted from the top by a circular opening 41 feet in diameter. Set a little way from the wall is a colonnade of twenty-eight columns. The desks are arranged radially, and in addition to desk lights there are twelve bronze floor standards from which a soft light is reflected from the surface of the dome. Underneath on the ground floor is the book-stack and from this lifts for books and message tubes connect with the reading room. A circular service counter is in the centre of the reading room, and this encloses an open well to the book-stack. Books reach readers in a few minutes from the store, and it is probably in this respect one of the most efficient libraries in the world.

Surrounding the stack and reading room is a storeyed ring 42 feet wide housing the various other departments. On the first and second floors are the lending, technical, commercial, music, and special reference libraries, study room, and map room. The third floor is devoted to offices and the fourth to the printing and binding departments, and additional storage should this be needed. This storeyed ring is surmounted by a low-pitched roof; it rises above the dome, which is therefore not seen externally. At second and third floor levels a Doric colonnade surrounds the building. The main entrance is through a Corinthian portico into a large rectangular vestibule called the Shakespeare Hall, flanked by flights of steps which turn from landings into the great reading room.

The functional excellence of this library resides mainly in the satisfactory relation between the stacks and the reading room, but the planning of the remainder is open to the criticism that too much has been sacrificed to monumental classical impressiveness. The reading room has certainly an impressive grandeur, but it is difficult to resist the feeling that this with an impressive classical exterior were among the principal aims of the design. It would seem that the other departments were just put round the central reading room, and it is questionable whether they are the best shapes, for they make supervision difficult, while they are not as well lighted as they ought to be. One can think of blocks abutting the central reading room transversely and serving their purpose better, or arranged as a square as in the Stockholm Central Library. Such an arrangement would have secured better supervision in the various rooms and would have given better natural lighting.

A disturbing feature of the exterior is the relation of the square portico to the circular building. There is little organic coherence, and it appears as an unrelated architectural fragment stuck on to the main building. The Pantheon has a pedimented portico similarly related to a circular building, but here it seems to be more an integral part of the whole achieved somewhat by a continuation of decorative motifs from the circular building to the portico.

An elaborate steel framework forms the bones of the construction of the Manchester Library and the network of steel was, for those who saw it being built, not without beauty, but no indication of this is apparent in the appearance of the building which is designed in terms of its facing material of Portland stone. This library building, though it has outstanding merit in one respect—that of the efficient relation of stack to reading room—is generally an example where the influence of the classical tradition has resulted in a building not as well suited to its purpose in all respects as it might have been.

CAMBRIDGE UNIVERSITY LIBRARY
Built about the same time (1931–4), but totally different in conception, is the great University Library at Cambridge, designed by Sir Giles G. Scott. It occupies a splendid open position beyond the Backs, on the same axis as the memorial buildings of Clare College designed by the same architect.

The plan is symmetrical. There is a long front block facing east, three transverse blocks and a rear block, enclosing two internal courts. At the end of the front block are two small projecting wings. Over the central entrance a great square tower rises to a height of 160 feet and the total length is 420 feet. The principal rooms are situated on the first floor. On either side of the entrance hall steps lead to the first floor corridor. Along the corridor of the front wing are exhibition cases, the room at the south end of the corridor is a special reading room and that at the north end is the map room. The south block is the periodical room, while the centre is the catalogue room leading to the general reading room 194 feet long by 40 feet wide, occupying the west block. The book-stacks in seven storeys occupy the north block and the front east block on either side of the tower, which is also a supplementary stack should need arise, and which initially housed periodicals. The nearest stack to the reading room is thus in the north block. The ground floor is occupied by part of the Royal Library and by staff rooms.

Has functional planning been sacrificed to classic symmetry and formal design? Does it fulfil that essential requirement of a satisfactory relation between the stack and the principal reading room such as we find in the Bibliothèque Nationale or the Manchester Library? Instead of making the stack adjacent to the reading room it is spread out along two other sides of the building in accordance with the formal symmetrical layout. Is it an example of strict fulfilment of function being subordinate to the demands of formal planning on classical principles?

The building has considerable beauty both internally and externally, and is a further example of verticals and horizontals dominating the design, with subdued variations of diagonals and round arches. The interior of the reading room is particularly pleasing. It is lighted from both sides by a series of semicircular windows which are repeated the entire length of the walls. The whole decorative character is restrained, and a fresh yet restful atmosphere is created by the cool colour scheme of the silver-grey tables, the blue chairs, and floor, and the oak ceiling patterned with emerald. The colour scheme of the other rooms is varied, while along the corridors there is pale subdued colouring with brown Hornton stone dadoes.

The building is of steel frame construction with the steel book-stacks structurally independent of the walls, one tier supporting the next. It is faced with brick of a pale fawn colour, bright in the light and soft in the shadows, while there are stone dressings in the principal entrance and pediment. The steel frame construction finds some expression in the design with the vertical emphasis of the tall narrow windows, and the long lines of the tower; while the low-pitched roof, the low pediment over the tall round arch of the entrance, and the flat pyramidal summit of the tower are all contained in the broad rectangular masses of the building in an effect of large plain wall-surfaces of a light fawn texture articulated with a decorative patterning mainly of vertical strips. The character of the design derives, it seems, partly from construction, partly from function, and partly from aesthetic intention, resulting in an effect of simple, monumental grandeur.

SWISS NATIONAL LIBRARY

The Swiss National Library at Berne is an example of a very close and convenient relation of the main reading room and the book-stack, and it is not improbable that the Bibliothèque Nationale partly inspired the design. This Swiss National Library was commenced in 1928 and completed in 1931, and was built to the designs of Oeschger, Kaufmann, and Hostettler. It is set in spacious surroundings with a large grammar school of a similar size situated a little to the south, while to the north is a small park and playing fields. It is symmetrical in conception with a long low block flanked by higher blocks forming the principal frontage, which faces approximately south. The higher wings turn northwards and connect with a tall, nine-storey block which forms the book-stack. Immediately in front of this book-stack on the ground floor is the main reading room and periodicals room on one side of the central space with delivery desk, and the catalogue room and exhibition room on the other side. Opening from both the periodicals room and the catalogue room with their glass walls is a reading terrace which looks out on to the garden. At the east end of the book-stack on the ground floor are small map and manuscripts rooms, and along this east side are also conference and writing rooms. Along the front of the building are offices separated from the reference library section by a wide corridor used for exhibitions. The basement is principally for the storage of archives.

The front of the building and the wings are well lighted with large windows which externally form a scheme of horizontal emphasis of alternating bands of fenestration and wall. The tall book-stack built of reinforced concrete has a vertical emphasis with narrow windows. Although in the general layout of this library formal symmetrical principles of design are followed, and it appears an imposing and handsome building, this provides the general framework into which good functional planning and modern treatment of windows giving good lighting are incorporated. It is more successful in functional planning than the Cambridge University Library, but one would hesitate to accord it the same architectural distinction.

LENIN STATE LIBRARY, MOSCOW

The Lenin State Library in Moscow is important by reason of its size, being the largest library in the world, while the building is worthy of study because of the arrangement of a large number of departments which its function necessitates and the manner in which the fundamental requirement of the satisfactory relationship of the main reading space and principal stack is secured. The building has in the main a simplified classical exterior, but the plan does not follow any formal symmetrical principle, but appears to be determined by the most logical sequence consistent with its classical exterior.

The library building was commenced in 1927 and completed in 1938, the architects being V. A. Shchuko and V. G. Gelfrein. It has been built on land adjoining the old

Lenin State Library, Moscow, 1927–38,
exterior view, main hall, ground and
first floor plans

*Architects: Vladimir Alexseevich Shchuko
and Vladimir Georgievich Gelfrein*

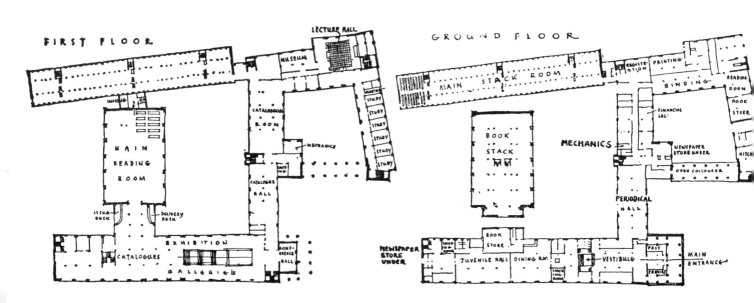

Rumyantser Library which is now used partly for exhibitions. Plans of the library are illustrated. It will be seen that the buildings form two courts with a central building in the larger western court.

A good way of giving an idea of the arrangement of the departments in conjunction with illustrations is by means of an imaginary guide. One enters from a spacious forecourt raised from the street level and situated at the southeast of the building at the corner of Mokkovaya and Komintern Streets. The main entrance is fronted by a portico with tall square columns. In the entrance hall is an information office of a general character, not pertaining to the library alone, and post and telegraph offices and telephone booths. The first floor is the principal floor which is reached from the main entrance by means of a handsome staircase. Spacious exhibition galleries are on either side of the staircase well on this floor. Exhibitions are mainly displays of new books and included are bookstalls of the various publishing houses should the visitor desire to purchase any of the exhibits.

Immediately in front of the visitor when he has ascended the staircase to the first floor is the catalogue hall, while there are further catalogue rooms opening from the exhibition galleries at the east end. Turning right from the main catalogue-hall one enters the main reading hall, which forms the central building of the larger courtyard. This reading hall accommodates 700 readers. On either side of the entrance to it are the issuing and delivery desks. At the rear of the reading hall, and planned transversely with it is the tall book-stack, ten storeys high, designed to hold six million volumes. A further stack is provided underneath the reading hall sufficiently large for another million volumes, while space for a further two million volumes will be provided in the old library.

The close proximity of the reading room to the tall stack at the rear and that underneath makes possible the speedy supply of books to readers, and in this respect this Lenin State Library must be regarded as a good example of library planning. The books from the old library are conveyed by a small electric train through an underground tunnel.

In addition to the main reading hall are other reading halls, and rooms for various purposes on other floors, making altogether accommodation for about 1,400 readers. On the first floor the main departments are a conference hall at the east end of the exhibition galleries, a lecture hall and museum on the north side of the smaller court and a series of study rooms along the east side.

Returning to the ground floor, immediately ahead of the vestibule is a dining room, and beyond is the juvenile reading hall with a book-store of children's books adjoining. Turning to the right from the entrance, along the block that divides the two courtyards, is the periodicals hall. Grouped round the small courtyard on the ground floor, which, incidentally, is entered through an open colonnade, are offices, workrooms for printing and binding, and a further reading room and book-store. In the second and third floors are further reading rooms for special studies, including military and legal rooms and further offices.

The building is of reinforced concrete construction faced with pale grey granite. Although the planning appears to be mainly functional, the architecture is mainly a conception on classical lines. The aim has clearly been to give a feeling of impressiveness and dignity combined with simplicity, and the theme employed to achieve this is of plain square columns which cluster round the forecourt and of vertical shafts between the windows of the long façades. Sculpture by Moukhina, Krandievshaya, and Manizer is introduced in the classical manner. A double sculptured frieze appears at the front corners of the mass above the main entrance on either side of a large central inscription panel, while on the roof, silhouetted against the sky and in line with the vertical shafts between windows on the street façades, are a series of statues—a familiar classical theme. The main interest of the library as a building lies in its planning and the arrangement of the various departments. It follows the best traditional methods, and is a good example of logical and serviceable design.

In designing the exterior the architects had in mind its proximity to the future Palace of the Soviets for which, with B. M. Iofan, they were also architects. The design of the palace consisted of a series of immense fluted drums surmounting each other, getting narrower and taller as they reached the colossal figure of Lenin, the top of whose head would have been about 1,365 feet above the ground, thus exceeding the height of any other building in the world. The structure was to stand on a large, approximately rectangular base with a concave front, the whole base-structure being surrounded by a colonnade of simple square columns, which sets the theme for the character of surrounding buildings, including the State Library. The project for the Palace did not materialize.

AALTO'S VIIPURI LIBRARY

A significant contrast to the five examples of library buildings designed in the twenties, was the library at Viipuri designed by Alvar Aalto. In all the five examples the traditional classical influence of style and planning is very strong, either in the symmetrical planning, as in the first four examples, or in the style of the structure which, if not a copy of a classical style, as the Manchester City Library, is broadly based on classical design and proportion involving, in some cases, simplification of classical features like columns and pilasters.

The designer of the library at Viipuri, on the other hand, is independent of classical architectural influence, and designs his structure on the basis of logical fulfilment of

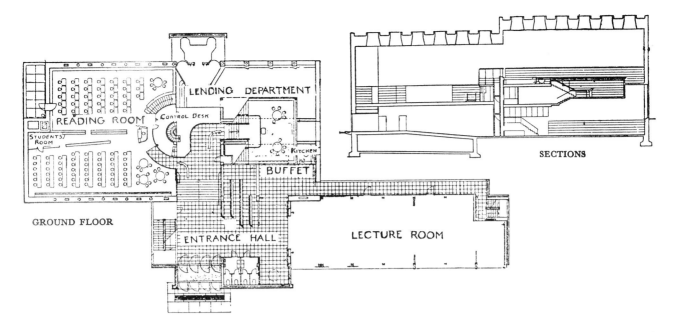

GROUND FLOOR

SECTIONS

Library at Viipuri, 1933–35, plan and exterior view (see note p. 88)

Architect: Alvar Aalto

purpose. The purpose is studied, and the design is determined by that purpose without regard to traditional architectural principles of symmetry or style; and a very original building has resulted. It is the first example in Europe of a library of any size in which there has been a complete break with classical principles of design and appearance. The original design for this library was awarded the first prize in a competition in 1927, but owing to opposition to the design and to economic difficulties the building was not commenced until 1933. This period was utilized by the architect to make many revisions. It was completed in 1935. When the library was built Viipuri was a town of east Finland, but as a result of the Peace Treaty in 1947 it was ceded to the USSR and is now named Vyborg. It suffered extensive war damage and was rebuilt.

The purpose of the building is twofold: to provide library premises for the town, and a headquarters for a local cultural society. The building consists of stack, lending and reference departments, children's library, a large lecture room, offices, and refreshment rooms. The twofold purpose clearly suggested the two long blocks arranged in echelon fashion but closely integrated. In the larger block, facing west, is the library, while the main floor of the smaller block, facing east, is occupied by the lecture room. In the central part of the ground floor on the east side towards the park is the main entrance hall. On entering, to the right is the long lecture room; in front, occupying the larger block, is the library proper, with the reading room on the left and the lending section on the right. Dividing them is the librarian's control desk, raised on a central platform. This platform continues round the three sides of the lending department so that a well is formed in the centre, which is reached by two flights of stairs, each of which is divided in the centre by a handrail. Another short flight between these goes to the entrance floor and to the reading room level.

The reading room is divided in its centre by two tall bookcases, between which is access to a small room for students. The librarian's desk in the centre is connected by tunnel and spiral staircase with the book-stack on the lower ground floor, and the closest relation of reading room, lending department and book-stacks is thus secured. The lecture room is long and narrow, with one long side of large windows opening to the park, and it can be divided into sections by means of movable partitions. The architect aimed at making this lecture room acoustically satisfactory for debates, so that a speaker in any part of the room could be heard without difficulty. For this purpose Aalto provided an undulating pinewood ceiling, and the result is claimed to be acoustically almost perfect.

Although famous as a functional library building, what of its value as architecture— that is, building that affords aesthetic pleasure? Much of the clean simplicity of the interior gives the kind of quiet, restful feeling desirable in a library. The exterior is somewhat like two long boxes held together, one with plain walls, the upper parts windowless, the other with the horizontal windows of the upper floor and the large windows of the lecture room stretching its length. The box-like effect is relieved by different roof levels, and by the projecting entrance on the west side, and the recessed upper southwest corner. The proportions are generally very pleasing.

SOME TOWN HALLS OF THE TWENTIES AND THIRTIES

Buildings designed partly as a setting for ceremonial, partly with a view to expressing the dignity of the institutions for which they are provided, like parliaments and local governments, important professional institutions and banks, have rarely provided the most original and expressive examples of modern architecture. This is not difficult to understand, because with such buildings tradition is very strong. There is an admirable ready-made classic architecture to confer grandeur, dignity, and impressiveness as well as these qualities could be expressed; while, if this means some sacrifice of the most convenient building for modern requirements, the sacrifice is justified because of the symbolic value of tradition and dignity. At least that is probably the more or less conscious thought that prompts the majority of designs of this character.

Among buildings of this type, of which a large number were either built or conceived in Europe during the twenties and early thirties, were city and town halls. These mostly follow traditional types of planning, of symmetrical arrangement of parts with a dressing of classical architecture, sometimes a fairly close copy of Greek, Roman, or Renaissance, sometimes these styles much simplified, while sometimes the Gothic style is chosen. There are a few interesting exceptions to these adherences to tradition and stylistic dressings in town halls asymmetrically planned with dependence on formal massing rather than on ornament for architectural effect.

The town hall usually provides a setting for traditional ceremonial, while it is often an architectural expression of civic dignity, and these factors have acted as a brake on functional developments. This occurred less with churches which are also designed as a setting for traditional ceremonial, and which also should have a degree of dignity. Yet with modern churches, most of which are on new estates, economy has been the mother of invention to an extent not obtaining with town halls, and this prompted in the case of churches a more exclusive attention to logical adaptation to purpose, resulting in some very original designs. There was also a degree of missionary zeal in establishing churches in the new estates of the modern world, and this urged the adoption of an architectural idiom that should be contemporary in spirit. There is less of such spirit actuating the modern town hall building. It must, like the mayor and corporation, maintain the ancient dignity and traditions of the town, and if it often does so somewhat staidly, this is not out of character. But there are significant exceptions. The modern town hall came into existence in the twelfth century at a time when trade was gradually passing from the control of feudal lords and monasteries into the hands of merchant citizens. The town hall was originally in the centre of the town, generally the market place, and consisted of a hall for meetings of citizens, with a belfry to summon them. Indeed the belfry seems in some cases to have been prior to the hall.

173

Thirteenth-century examples remain in Italy, among them the Palazzo Vecchio
in Florence, the Palazzo Pubblico in Siena, and the Palazzo del Municipio in Perugia.
These buildings are three or four storeys high, generally with the hall on the first floor,
with offices and storage rooms in the remaining parts of the building. A conspicuous
feature of all these buildings is the tall belfry. This is likewise a conspicuous feature of
some of the famous Gothic town halls of Belgium, like that at Brussels built early in
the fifteenth century. But the belfry is not an invariable feature of the Belgian Gothic
town halls; in some it is absent, or replaced by a group of turrets, as in the ornate
Town Hall at Louvain, built in the middle of the fifteenth century. The Guildhall,
London, and the small Guildhall at Cirencester are Gothic examples of the fifteenth
century in England, and these are without belfries. The fact that many guild halls
were also town halls was due to the close association of merchant guilds with municipal
government.

In France early town halls were often combined with the market hall which was often
an arcaded hall on the ground floor with assembly hall above and a belfry at the side, a
good remaining example of the twelfth century being that at S. Antonin. A similar
type was widely adopted in England and several remain, such as the half-timber
structure at Ledbury, built in 1633, and that at Abingdon which, though small, is of a
handsome Renaissance design with tall pilasters reaching to a cornice on the second
storey. The later development was the elimination of the arcaded market hall as the
town hall grew larger.

With the great increase in population in Europe in the nineteenth century and the
growth of cities and towns, town halls were provided on a much larger scale with a
greater number of departments.

The Hotel de Ville in Paris, built by Ballu and Deperthes in 1874–84 much on the
lines of the former building, destroyed in 1871, although larger, seems to have had a
considerable influence on town hall design since, not only in France but in other
countries. Impressive in this building is the size and magnificence of the suite of
reception rooms. The building is a large rectangle with two courts in the centre. On
the ground and mezzanine floors are most of the administrative offices and on the
first floor are the principal rooms comprising the large *salle des fetes* with *salle a
manger* adjoining, while on the farther side is the *salle du conseil*, much smaller than
the principal reception rooms.

Other smaller *hotels de ville* built in the following thirty years, like that at Tours
(1896–1904) designed by Victor Laloux, that at Neuilly near Paris (1882) designed by
Dutocq and Simonet, and that at Versailles (1900–4) designed by Le Grand, follow
approximately the same plan as the Hotel de Ville in Paris. In these examples the
plan is symmetrical and rectangular with the administrative offices situated chiefly on

the ground and mezzanine floors. The first floor, on which are the principal rooms, is reached by a handsome staircase approached from the central entrance. The principal rooms are the *salle des fetes*, which is the largest and which corresponds to the English assembly hall, the *salle du conseil*, or council chamber, and the *salle des mariages*, as handsome provision for marriage ceremonies is a common feature of many European town halls. There is sometimes a *salle de reception* adjoining the *salle des fetes* and often a *salle a manger*. Approximation to this pattern is found in many contemporary English town halls.

In several of the larger town halls built in England during the nineteenth century the chief feature is the large hall. Those at Birmingham and Leeds, built about the middle of the nineteenth century in the classic style, are of considerable size and were designed not only for functions of the mayors and councils, but for concerts, musical festivals, and meetings of all kinds, the purpose being the provision of a hall for public gatherings of various kinds under municipal auspices. The Manchester Town Hall, built in 1868, and dressed in the Gothic style, has a smaller hall than those of Birmingham and Leeds, but the administrative offices were much larger; even these, however, proved insufficient, and extensive additions were made in 1937.

The tendency in design since the First World War has been to reduce the scale of the ceremonial and reception rooms, because social functions and lavish entertainment by the mayor and council have diminished, while the administrative offices often greatly increased in proportion. In many of the smaller town halls the assembly hall was part of the mayor's suite and was used almost exclusively for the social functions of the mayor and council, and it was rarely made available for privately sponsored entertainment, like concerts and dancing. This has changed and in providing the assembly hall as part of the municipal buildings one of the reasons is to make available a hall for the town for a variety of purposes, whether officially or privately sponsored, very much in the spirit of the large halls of the bigger cities. The growth of the administrative offices in proportion to the rest of the building is due partly to the increase of population and partly to the greater scope and responsibility of local authorities since the First World War. Such departments as health and housing are much larger, while new departments have been added, like town planning and motor licensing, and this expansion will probably continue. This is changing the balance of the town hall structure.

There emerges in the early twenties a set pattern with the rigid symmetrical plan. The general disposition of this plan is similar to that of the Hotel de Ville, Paris, and consists of a large rectangular block, with two courtyards round which are grouped the various rooms and offices on two or three floors. The council chamber is a central feature placed at the rear on the first floor. The assembly hall is often at the rear approached from the central entrance hall, sometimes through a reception room. Town

175

halls built in the twenties and early thirties that approximate to this general layout, although varying in minor features, are those at Worthing, Walthamstow, Barnsley, High Wycombe, Beckenham, and Southampton. That old traditional feature, the tower, persists. It has lost its function as a belfry to summon citizens to a meeting, but instead it has become a clock-tower with chimes; sometimes it is a water tower, and sometimes it is also used for storage. In the modern town halls of Walthamstow, Barnsley, Swansea, and several others it is a tall square tower, but in many smaller town halls, like those at Peterborough, Worthing, Bridlington, it has dwindled to a turret over the centre of the building.

In the planning of town halls several problems of grouping arise which should, as far as possible, be determined by logic and convenience; but the difficulty is that not everybody agrees on what is the most logical and convenient arrangement. There would probably not always be agreement between members of the town council and officials of a department, and often a compromise has to be reached. The main parts of a town hall might be broadly classified as (a) the ceremonial and social parts, sometimes called the council suite, in which is included the assembly hall, the council chamber, committee rooms, and (b) the administrative or departmental offices. The assembly hall is sometimes classified separately from the council suite[4], but, bearing in mind its traditional function, it should logically be included. In the first is the mayor's room and all sections concerned with receptions and entertainments by the mayor and council. What is the best physical relation of these sections; what is the relation of the council chamber to the mayor's parlour and reception rooms, and what is its relation to the committee rooms? Should the council chamber be regarded as part of the ceremonial section, or be regarded as a kind of board room closely connected with the administrative offices? Also should the committee rooms be centrally situated near the council chamber, or should each committee room be close to the administrative offices?[5] There are arguments for and against these alternative arrangements. There are, however, a few paramount considerations which should influence planning.

One is that as the assembly hall is used both for council functions and privately sponsored functions, it is perhaps desirable that it should be entered from the council suite and be provided with a separate entrance for the public. A good example of this arrangement is the Town Hall at Worthing, designed by C. Cowles-Voysey, where a reception room underneath the council chamber and approached from the main staircase hall is connected with the east side of the assembly hall. The entrance for the public is at the south end. This convenient integration of council suite with assembly hall is achieved on a bigger scale in the Leeds City Hall designed by E. Vincent Harris.

Another consideration of planning is that the council generally meets only once a month and for that reason it is not important that the council chamber should be closely connected with other parts on the ground of convenience. Another consideration

176

City Hall, Swansea, 1930   *Architect: Sir Percy Thomas*

is that committees meet more frequently and constant reference has to be made to documents in the administrative offices. When the architect has devised his most convenient arrangement, it is unlikely that it will be a formal symmetrical plan, yet up to about 1930, in addition to trying to find the best arrangement, he had the difficult task of fitting this into a symmetrical plan—a rectangle with two courtyards and the council chamber on the first floor at the rear. Fortunately, a break away occurred in the earlier thirties, led by Dudok.

The council chamber itself has been the subject of more diversity. There are several different arrangements in town halls built in this period. A popular form is the horseshoe type, as at Southampton and Swansea; other similar forms are the semicircular and sectoral, as at Nottingham and Stretford; another form is the circular, as at Cardiff; another, the oval, as at Leeds, while there is what is called the House of Commons type, as at Beckenham. All seem to be fairly satisfactory with the exception of the last mentioned, which is not the best form to encourage speakers to face and address the chair, while it suggests an arrangement for two opposing parties. For many years at Beckenham, these opposing parties were non-existent, the whole council consisting of Conservatives and Independents[6].

The formal symmetrical plan in addition to increasing the problems of the planner, makes flexibility difficult. This has serious disadvantages. With the extension of local government and the need for more administrative offices it is a great advantage to extend these as required, and provide for such extensions in the design. This is difficult to accomplish in a formal symmetrical plan in which classic balance on either side of a central axis obtains, and a more irregular yet dignified design would be more practicable in this respect.

The town halls built in England during the twenties and thirties show a slow trend from the traditional Renaissance, common in public buildings at the beginning of the century, to a more simplified dressing of the same formal basic symmetrical plan. Among the early examples of the period following the First World War are the town halls of Peterborough designed by E. Berry Webber, and Worthing designed by C. Cowles-Voysey. Both have a grand pedimented portico with classic columns at the entrance, above which are the central turrets. Otherwise the Worthing Town Hall is refreshingly simple, with well-spaced windows. The façade on either side of the portico at Peterborough is marred by shops. Here is a curious contradiction. A massive Corinthian portico to give dignity, and then a row of shops to take it away. I suppose the shops pay for the portico.

The theme of the classic portico is continued in the large new city hall at Leeds, where it graces the front in a spacious setting. This part forms one side of the assembly hall, which is the terminal feature of a building complex extending to the rear and

178

continuing in two fork branches of municipal offices. Flanking this portico are two
Baroque towers and spires, reminiscent of the towers and spires of Gibbs and
Hawksmoor. This façade is at variance with the simpler treatment of the side elevations
of the building, and the whole front has the appearance of a rather ostentatious
dressing, to assert its importance. Barnsley Town Hall, designed by Briggs and Thornely,
is a further example of a town hall in the Renaissance style built during the twenties.

CITY HALL, SWANSEA

The next stage is towards simplification, yet with a preservation of classic formalism
and symmetry. Examples are the town hall at Beckenham and the city halls at
Southampton and Swansea. The last mentioned merits especial attention as a good
example of this phase. Something of an exception to this general trend is the town hall
at Lewisham, dressed in simplified late Gothic or Tudor, but unusual because of a
plan dictated by the curved site which gives the building its special character. The plan
is roughly a rectangular assembly hall to which is attached a semicircular ring of
offices on the first, second, and third floors, and shops on the ground floor.

The city hall at Swansea was designed by Sir Percy E. Thomas in 1930. It is divided
into the separate sections of council suite, administrative offices, and assembly hall
which, with the law courts, forms the civic centre. Grouped round a courtyard, the
buildings are situated in a park near the sea, so that the spacious setting enables the
buildings to be seen to the fullest advantage. The council suite forms the northeast
side of the courtyard and is planned on traditional lines with the council chamber on
the first floor projecting at the rear into the courtyard and above the rates office.
The assembly hall with garage under is on the southeast side and is reached from the
council suite through a refreshment room and is called the Brangwyn Hall by reason
of the large British Empire painted panels by the artist which were originally intended
for the House of Lords War Memorial. On the northwest side are the municipal offices,
which are designed in the practical manner of a comparatively narrow strip with
central corridor and offices on either side, with large well-spaced vertical windows.
The main entrance hall of the council suite forms on the exterior a square block
rising a little above the wings and from this block rises the square tower, 160 feet
high, with a clock on its four sides, with round arches above to transmit the sound of
the chimes. The tower is a central feature of the town, where it can be seen from
most parts, while it is also a mark for ships in the Bristol Channel.

The group of buildings might be regarded as a composition of rectangular blocks
grouped round a courtyard and based on a central axis, yet with a degree of
irregularity. The administrative offices do not exactly balance the assembly hall, as they
are a smaller mass, while the law courts are a lower mass held in the arms of the
two side masses. The whole design is one of recurring themes. A large circular arched
entrance in the centre block is a dominating feature of the council suite façade, in a

long two-storey mass with tall vertical windows well spaced on the masonry walls. This theme is repeated in the frontage of the law courts, while it is varied by the introduction of three arched entrances in the rectangular entrance mass of the assembly hall. The arched opening again appears in the centre of the administrative block, but here without the projecting features and with a more fittingly restrained note. It is the preservation throughout of similar decorative motifs that gives unity to this impressive building. The construction is of solid walls faced with Portland stone on the outer walls, and with brick on the walls facing the courtyard. The buildings with moderate spans have flat concrete roofs while steel stanchions are employed in the case of large spans such as the low-pitched roof of the assembly hall. Steel framing is used in the construction of the tower.

HILVERSUM TOWN HALL

In treatment of elevations it is perhaps not a long way from the Guildhall of Swansea to the town hall of Hilversum, but in the matter of planning the difference is fundamental. The town hall at Hilversum, designed by W. M. Dudok and built in 1928–31, represents a departure from the classical symmetrical method of planning.

The requirements of a Dutch town hall are similar, if not exactly the same, as those of an English town hall. The local councils are called Communes, which vary in size from seven to forty-five elected members. The mayor is a paid official who is appointed by the Crown and who presides over meetings of the communal council. Executive powers are vested in the mayor and from two to six aldermen.

The requirements of a town hall for a town of about the size of Hilversum, that is, from about 50,000 to 100,000 population, are the council chamber, rooms for the mayor and deputy mayors, a reception or citizens' hall, a marriage room or rooms, and administrative offices.

In the Hilversum Town Hall all the rooms are grouped round a square courtyard, mainly in two storeys, but small sections reach higher, while four one-storey arms project in different directions. The main municipal offices are on the ground floor, while the council chamber, reception hall, and marriage halls are on the first floor. The council chamber occupies the south side, with reading room nearby; the reception or citizens' hall occupies the main part of the east side, while the major and minor marriage halls occupy the north side together with the public works administration. The tall square tower with clock, which now also serves the function of a water tower, occupies the southeast corner.

The plan, although arranged round a square courtyard is completely irregular, and is determined by the most convenient and logical arrangement. It is possible that the arrangement was made with an eye to the external architectural composition, but it is

The building is situated among gardens
and this view from the south is across
a rectangular ornamental pool.
The principal entrance on the west side
is separated from the road by wide
lawns and flower beds

The Reception or Citizens Hall

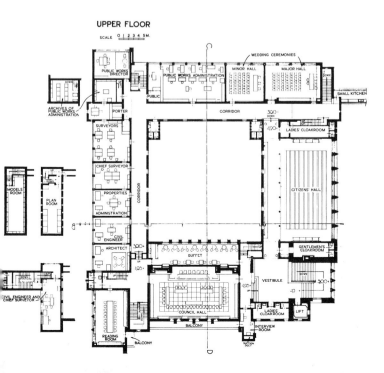

Town Hall, Hilversum, The Netherlands, 1928–31
Architect: W. M. Dudok

equally possible that the logical arrangement provided the subject for the artist without modification, and he made his design on that basis. Often in design the severer the restriction the finer the work of art. It is like the strict sonnet form which has been the vehicle of some of the finest poetic utterances.

The building is situated among gardens. The principal entrance front is on the west side, and this is separated from the road by wide lawns and flower beds. On the south side, that of the council chamber, is a large rectangular pool stretching the length of the building and surrounded by shrubs and plants hanging on the walls. The inner courtyard also contains a pool. This setting among gardens and pools is characteristic of many modern buildings in The Netherlands and often confers an enchanting quality on them.

The walls are of light yellow brick and seen at a distance in the sunlight they appear almost a soft white. The whole building is a very happy design of rectangular masses subtly related to give the same satisfaction as a well-designed cubist picture, but the pleasure here is very much greater because it is a three-dimensional reality enriched by the changing light and shadows and the verdant setting. There is neither dominant horizontal nor dominant vertical massing; one is a kind of counterpart to the other, to achieve a general harmony. To sit in the gardens on the south side on a summer afternoon when the sunlight is moving from the south face is to enjoy one of the architectural felicities of modern building. This is certainly among the finest architectural achievements of the century. In town hall architecture it is the principal event since the completion of Ostberg's masterpiece at Stockholm.

Dudok's Hilversum Town Hall had a marked influence on many subsequent designs of such buildings. Two of the more distinctive which reveal the influence are the town hall at Hornsey, designed by Reginald H. Uren in 1933 and completed in 1935, and the town hall at Cachan on the Seine, designed by J. B. Mathon and J. Cholet, built about the same time.

The Hornsey Town Hall is, like the Hilversum Town Hall, grouped in irregular fashion round a square courtyard with an open garden court on the south. It consists of three floors—basement, ground floor, and first floor. It is well situated, presenting an L-frontage to a stretch of gardens, with a square tower at the corner on the west front, over the principal entrance. Ascending by staircase from the entrance hall to the first floor there is the mayor's parlour immediately in front with the square council chamber (with semicircular seating) to the right on the south side. Committee rooms are on this first floor along the west wing. The town clerk's and members' rooms, inquiry and interviewing offices are grouped in close proximity to the council chamber. Municipal offices are on all three floors on the south side of the building, while the north side is occupied by a large rectangular assembly hall. This has a

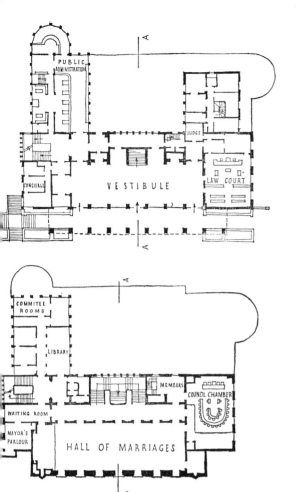

Town Hall, Cachan-sur-Seine, 1934, exterior view and plans—upper ground floor (top) and first floor

Architects: J. B. Mathon and J. Cholet

Town Hall, Boulogne-sur-Seine, 1933–35, exterior view, interior and first floor plan

Architects: Tony Garnier and Debat-Ponsan

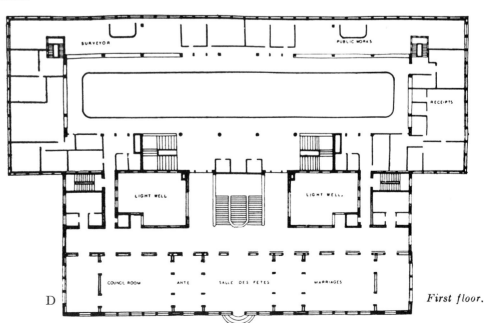

First floor.

separate entrance on the same west side as the main entrance, and it is so arranged as to be easily accessible for the mayor and council, and yet is a unit completely separate from the rest of the town hall. The occasions when the assembly hall is used by the mayor for functions in a borough like Hornsey are not frequent; sometimes little more than the annual mayoral reception and banquet, while the use by the town for a variety of purposes, like concerts, dances, dramatic performances, lectures, and meetings is almost an everyday occurrence. The identity of the assembly hall with the town hall, yet a separate unit, is here achieved in a very satisfactory manner. The whole building is an example where purpose and convenience have determined planning uninhibited by thoughts of symmetry.

The building is constructed of a steel frame with floors and flat roofs of concrete and hollow tiles. The walls are of cavity brick construction, the facing bricks being variegated pale brown $2\frac{1}{4}$ inches thick, with wide horizontal joints in the manner of Dudok's treatment of brick. The surround of the entrance is of Portland stone.

The L-shape of the main aspect, the vertical windows pleasingly patterned on the plain walls, and the focal point of the tower with the gardens spread before it make a very agreeable composition. The effect is restful, suggesting a quiet retreat in the centre of a busy town, calling for more seats than are at present provided. It has not the spacious setting and beauty of Hilversum Town Hall, but the mantle has been worn not unworthily by the English architect, and it is pleasant to remember that the building was awarded the R.I.B.A. bronze medal for 1935.

TWO FRENCH TOWN HALLS

The town hall at Cachan on the Seine is similar in principle of planning to those of Hilversum and Hornsey, and is similar in composition of masses. It has three floors—lower ground floor, upper ground floor, and first floor—with a square tower at one corner. The departments are grouped round a square courtyard, but on one side the building is only one storey high and forms a rear entrance through a double row of brick piers. The building is on a sloping site so that the lower ground floor is below ground on the main entrance side, but is on ground level at the rear courtyard side. The central feature of the upper ground floor is the large rectangular entrance hall, with the law court at one end. The main staircase rises from this entrance hall, and leads to the large hall of marriages and *salle des fetes* on the first floor. This hall occupies nearly the whole length of the building. At one end is the mayor's parlour, with members' rooms nearby, and at the other end is the council chamber, while committee rooms and library occupy the other wing. The mayor often performs the marriage ceremonies, and if not the mayor, the aldermen, which explains the proximity of the mayor's parlour to the marriage hall. Some of the administrative offices occupy the two ground floors, and one wing of the lower ground floor is occupied by the Post and sorting offices.

The building is constructed of reinforced concrete frame and faced with pale yellowish-brown bricks, the horizontal joints being raked out in the Dutch manner. The fenestration of the hall of marriages with its long vertical windows on plain walls is similar to that of the assembly hall at Hornsey, but the treatment of the rest of the exterior shows a more marked horizontal emphasis, with the windows bound together by white stone strips. This horizontal emphasis is strongly marked in the low one-storey block on the east side, with semicircular termination forming the Post Office, a motif which is repeated at the eastern termination of the north wing. In contrast to this horizontal movement is the tower with the strong vertical emphasis of glass and stone strips. The whole composition is more dramatic than the town hall at Hornsey because of the stronger vertical and horizontal movement. In its massing and plan it is a valuable contribution to the architecture of town halls.

As a contrast to the examples considered is the town hall at Boulogne-sur-Seine, designed by Tony Garnier and Debat-Ponsan and built in the early thirties. Here is a town hall, modern and original in planning and structure, yet following the classical principles of symmetry. It consists of two rectangular blocks juxtaposed, one slightly larger than the other. The smaller block on the south houses the ceremonial part, while, the larger block houses the administrative offices. Inserted between them are two square light wells. The principal rooms of the ceremonial block are on the first floor, reached by a central stairway leading from the upper ground floor. In the centre on the south side is the *halle des fetes* and on either side, divided by ante rooms, are the hall of marriages and the council chamber. The administrative offices on the north block are situated along three tiers of galleries arranged round a covered light well.

The building is constructed of a reinforced concrete frame. The exterior treatment of the two blocks is different, the ceremonial block being faced with stone while the office block is left with a concrete finish. The dominating note in the fenestration of the south block is the series of tall vertical windows of the halls on the first floor, the remainder being a somewhat crowded pattern on plain walls. The north block is almost a gridiron pattern of narrow vertical strips between windows, and horizontal bands about table height, designed to give the maximum light. The whole conception is an original treatment on symmetrical principles of planning with modern methods of construction and a functional design of windows in the office block. It is an interesting marriage of classical and modern idioms.

Late in the thirties two town halls were built in Denmark which are significant examples of the change from traditional design to new conceptions. One is the town hall at Aarhus built in 1938–41 to the design of Arne Jacobson and Erik Moller, which was the winning entry in a competition held in 1937. In the original design emphasis was placed on the functional aspect of providing an efficient administrative building; provision for the ceremonial and symbolic character was subordinated to practical needs. Thus the traditional tower was, significantly, not included in the design. This provoked a storm of protest, and there was a demand from the public for a tower which had always been a feature of town hall buildings and which therefore conformed to the popular idea of a town hall. The public clamour was successful and the architects consequently altered their design[7].

As previously mentioned the original function of a town hall tower was, like the church tower, to contain the belfry to summon people to meetings. Unlike the church tower it no longer performs that function, but survives mainly as a traditional form. Having got their tower the people felt that it should continue to perform some semblance of its traditional function, so it serves to celebrate the passing of time. It holds a carillon of 37 bells which play at noon, at 6 p.m. and midnight, when it plays the traditional May song of Aarhus composed by Morren Borup about the year 1500. One large bell marks the hours, and a little more than half way up the trellised tower is a clock. The tower is not necessary, but as it obviously gives pleasure to the people of Aarhus it is desirable. But being an afterthought it is grafted on to an existing design and if it does not wholly integrate it is an arresting feature of the architectural composition.

The building consists of a sequence of three rectangular blocks, two narrow blocks running north–south, joined to the principal wider transverse four-storey block at the northern end, facing a central square of the city. The main entrance leads immediately to the assembly hall which has three tiers of balconies. The council chamber is on the first floor, with a balcony above the main entrance. The council seats are arranged in a circle, with a large map of the town in the centre very effectively woven into the carpet. The long narrow six-storey central office block, with central corridor between offices, links with the main block and a three-storey block at the southern end. Large windows provide adequate daylight in all the offices. The building is of reinforced concrete frame construction with concrete infilling and faced with pale bluish-grey orsgrunn marble from Norway.

The other Danish example is the town hall of Sollerod, a scattered rural area of about 20,000 population north of Copenhagen. The design for this building by Arne Jacobsen and Fleming Lassen was placed first in a competition held in 1939. It was part of a projected group of buildings which included a library and cinema, but these have not yet been built. The town hall, which was built in 1940–42, consists of two long blocks joined so as to incorporate a common staircase. The longer office block is four storeys high, and the other three storeys contain the main entrance hall and council chamber and two committee rooms. An interesting feature of the legislative block is that the fenestration expresses the variety of the internal arrangement. The building is constructed of reinforced concrete and faced with light grey Norwegian marble.
In both these Danish town hall buildings the lingering classicism, the extreme plainness and simplicity, with the repetition of numerous squarish windows, produces a

rather dull and monotonous appearance. Dramatic emphasis and decorative interest are rather lacking.

REFERENCES AND NOTES

1. Lecture on The Aesthetic Aspect of Civil Engineering Design, given to the Institution of Civil Engineers on 26 April 1944, and included in a volume published by the Institution with that title, London, 1945, p. 35.

2. The original designs with a dome were published in *The Builder* for 6 May, 1924. I am not aware of the reasons for the change of design. It is hardly satisfactorily explained by Asplund himself in the article on his building in the *Architects' Journal* for 14 January, 1934.

3. The Manchester conurbation which includes many surrounding boroughs had a population in 1971 of about $2\frac{1}{2}$ millions.

4. C. Cowles-Voysey, the architect of Worthing Town Hall, in an article in Specification for 1934 classifies the accommodation of the town hall under the three sections of (a) Council Suite, in which he includes council chamber, committee rooms, and mayor's parlour, (b) Assembly Hall, and (c) Departmental Offices.

5. These questions are discussed at length by A. Calveley Cotton in his excellent book on town halls, London, 1936.

6. In 1965 Beckenham became part of the Greater London Borough of Bromley and the town hall no longer has council meetings. The council chamber is used as an office.

7. See Esbjorn Hiort, *Contemporary Danish Architecture* (in Danish and English), Copenhagen, 1949.

15 *Ecclesiastical architecture—Early Christian and medieval themes and modern methods*

IN THE COURSE of this history it has been implied that the more a type of building is habitually regarded as mainly utilitarian, the more it is associated with progressive architecture; and the more a type is connected with ceremony of some kind, the more it is associated with traditional architecture. Industrial buildings often are in the van of the new architecture, and it would be natural to look for the other extreme, in which there is the greatest adherence to tradition, in ecclesiastical buildings; for in no type are tradition and ceremony so important. But after the war of 1914–18 the course of architectural history changes. It is rather in public buildings and head offices of banks and insurance companies that the strongest adherence to traditional architecture is found, while there is a surprising number of churches built in Europe after about 1923 which reveal considerable originality in the treatment of traditional themes, some representing a strict and logical interpretation of function so little affected by traditional styles that they logically belong to the new architecture.

From 1923 onwards there was a considerable amount of church building in Europe, particularly in England, Germany, and the Scandinavian countries. One of the principal reasons for this was the development of new residential areas. This took place, as we have seen, largely as extensions of big cities and large towns, not always or mainly because of increased populations, but because of dispersal from congested city centres. What happened in London between the wars happened to a less extent in many of the cities and towns of Europe. With the new residential areas built on the outskirts of cities, came the need for churches in these districts, and this more than any other circumstance was responsible for the large number that were built. And in this church-building one can note a desire to link the Christian religion, with its 2,000 years of traditions, to the social and spiritual needs of modern life. This is apparent in the intention to make the church not only a place of worship for the community, but a social centre as well. Thus we find that many new buildings were planned to comprise, in addition to the church, a hall and rooms for meetings, kitchen, and schoolroom, while the vicarage was often included in the group. Later we find plans for the church and community centre are combined in which there is provision for games and cultural activities. In this movement we get a true revival of the life of the Middle Ages when the parish church was not only a place of worship but the centre of many of the social activities of the town or neighbourhood.

Accompanying this tendency to connect the church and its traditions with the spiritual, cultural, and social needs of modern life is the manifest intention of making this in some degree apparent in the architecture of the churches. The modern movements in architecture in which building is stripped of stylistic ornament, in which the design is more uncompromisingly according to practical purposes and in which new structural materials are employed, appeared to many progressively minded people as the architecture of today and tomorrow, and if the church was to come closer to the life of today, then its buildings should have some flavour of this modern architecture. That is rather the symbolical and expressional aspect. Such a line of thought partially actuated the clergy and architects who were responsible for many churches of modern design. They were also conscious of the functional advantages of adopting some of the methods of the new architecture. Generally the result is a blending of traditional architecture, in which Gothic or Romanesque character is partly present, with the new tendencies.

The economical aspect of church-building of the period is important, and is somewhat similar to the church-building in London after the Great Fire when the people living in or near city parishes greatly needed the restoration of their churches. In religious thought a church is not only a shelter for an altar and worshippers, but a building that by its expressive and beautiful form glorifies God. The process of building should be an act of worship. This is true, but at the same time it is necessary to bear in mind the needs of the people living in the new residential area who are waiting for their church. The amount of money available is limited. A church can be built quickly and economically of plain brick walls and without many of the embellishments and enrichments traditionally associated with church buildings. On the other hand, the church, in the opinion of some, could be built more slowly, with greater elaborations, in a manner more worthy of its lofty purpose. It was the former course that often prevailed. This is one reason, too, why church-building of the period is often more progressive and experimental than in public buildings and head offices of banks. Economical restrictions often make simplicity almost a necessity, while they exercise the ingenuity of the architect to create as impressive an effect as possible with the limited means at his disposal. This necessity for economy really had an invigorating and some would say a purifying effect on ecclesiastical architecture.

As previously discussed the cross plan with aisles may not be the most convenient for the purpose of a modern church in which it is desired that the priest conducting the worship or preaching from the pulpit should be seen from all parts of the church so as to conduce to the feeling of many worshipping as one. Consequently there was a tendency to resort to the rectangular plan[1] with or without aisles. We have also noted that following the Romanesque revival, architects went farther back to some of the simple austere Early Christian churches. Visitors to Florence Cathedral will remember the simple austere interior differing very much from the magnificence, richness, and grandeur of St. Peter's, and guides are fond of quoting a certain Pope who said that in Florence Cathedral one prays, in St. Peter's one thinks. It is this atmosphere suggestive of prayer and devotion, often helped by large plain surfaces and absence of ornament, as if wordly things were cast aside, that appears in some of the modern churches in Europe, and this character as much as Gothic or Romanesque styles is the tradition perpetuated in many recent churches.

Adherence to tradition on the one hand and logical building according to function on the other are matters of degree. Both come together and mingle and the position of a design between these extremes can be indicated by stages. The first conveniently defined stage from the complete adherence to tradition is (a) design which is partially a revival of Gothic or Romanesque or Early Christian, sufficient to give a certain stylistic character, yet modified by considerations of better fulfilment of purpose and study of modern needs, (b) design in which logical fulfilment of function and immediate needs are paramount, in which modern materials and methods of construction are employed where necessary, yet with a character pervading the whole, less by stylistic forms than in features like tall vertical windows in an apse, due to traditional influence, so that the religious character of the interiors of the old churches still lives in the new, and (c) design which is a strict fulfilment of utilitarian purpose with little traditional influence in the determination of character. Many churches, halls, and meeting-places of modern religious sects have buildings of this last kind, but the examples among more orthodox Catholic and Protestant churches are rare. Even where the most modern methods of steel and reinforced concrete construction do much to determine design, and many of the recent structural devices, more associated with factory buildings, are employed, there is still generally the lingering character of traditional church architecture.

SOME AUSTRIAN AND GERMAN CHURCHES

The best examples of the first category are found in England, whereas the best examples of the second and third categories are found in France, Germany, Holland, Switzerland, and Czechoslovakia. Noteworthy examples of the first category other than English are found in the work of the Austrian architect Clemens Holzmeister. His work is mainly traditional, very often of an eclectic character, and sometimes mixed with a strong touch of originality, but not always with very artistic results. He built a large number of churches in Germany and Austria in the twenties. One of the most famous but least satisfactory of his works is the crematorium at Wiener in Vienna. It is a square, symmetrical building with a tower supporting a Gothic dome rising in the

Church at Hamburg, Blenkenese, 1928   *Architect: Clemens Holzmeister*

Women's Church of Peace, Frankfurt-on-Main, 1932   *Architect: Hans Herkomer*

St. Thomas Church, Hanwell, Middlesex, 1933
Architect: Sir Edward Maufe
Right—interior view looking towards the choir

Guildford Cathedral, England, 1933–52

Architect: Sir Edward Maufe

Below—plan, architect's drawing of exterior

Lower right—interior looking towards the choir

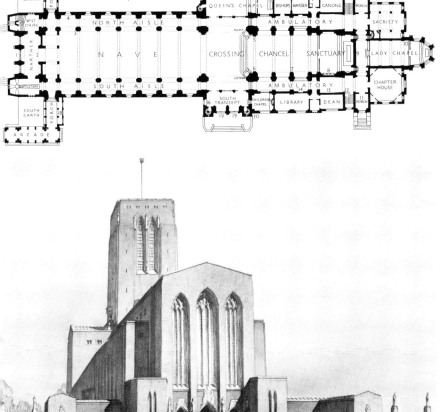

centre over the chapel. One of the principal motifs is the use of the pointed Gothic arch with the springing of the arch at floor level. The exterior of the building looks somewhat like a model fort, although the interior of the chapel has a certain impressiveness.

Among the more original of Holzmeister's churches are the church at Merchingen in the Saar, and the little circular church at Blenkenese in Hamburg. The former is built of stone with a wooden roof, of low pitch on a tau cross plan. The treatment of the exterior is simple, with plain walls, and the church looks very pleasing among the trees. The east façade looks particularly attractive with the large plain wall and a large thin plain cross as a central feature above a simple square entrance.

The circular church at Blankenese is built of brick. In the circular walls are tall round-headed narrow windows pleasingly spaced; and adjoining at the west end is a square tower above the principal entrance. The whole is a composition of well-related, rounded forms, with the one note of contrast in the square tower which saves it from a monotony that it might otherwise have.

Three other interesting German churches built at this time, which are mainly traditional, but with much of modern simplicity, are the Frauenfriedenskirche (Women's Church of Peace) at Frankfurt by Hans Herkomer, the Church of the Holy Cross, also at Frankfurt, by Martin Webber, and the chapel and convent at Tegelort by Felix Hallbach. The first is a group of church, cloisters, and priest's house making a unified composition. The church and cloisters have much the character of simplified Romanesque with plain walls and circular-headed openings, the principal feature of the exterior being three tall narrow niches on the wall of the rectangular tower, which contain three immense figures. The motif of the tall narrow opening is repeated in the cloister arcade. Webber's church is similar in style, with long narrow arches and windows. Construction is of reinforced concrete frame and concrete blocks.

In the chapel and convent at Tegelort, built mainly of brick, a conspicuous motif of Holzmeister's crematorium, of using the Gothic arch with the springing at the base of openings, is employed for the arch separating chancel from nave and for window and door openings. The church has a parabolic roof, while the exterior has a strong vertical emphasis particularly enhanced by the long clean lines of the tower over the sanctuary at the east end.

SOME ENGLISH CHURCHES

English ecclesiastical architecture of the type defined under the first category (a) is well represented by the work of Sir Giles G. Scott, Sir Edward Maufe, Bernard Miller, F. X. Verlarde, and one or two others. Although the ecclesiastical work of Sir Giles G. Scott is basically traditional and mainly Gothic in spirit, he often, as in Liverpool

Cathedral, endeavours to give a classic breadth to his designs, while he constantly tries original variations on his main architectural theme. The conditions imposed in the building of each church are to him opportunities for the creation of an entirely new design, and we can see that although the Romanesque and Gothic traditions remains strong in his churches, they are all markedly different designs, rather as if traditional English language were used for many different and original verse forms giving song rhythms unknown before. How different are the churches of St. Paul at Liverpool, of St. Andrew, Luton, the Church of Our Lady at Northfleet, of St. Francis at Terriers, and many others that could be mentioned. Different as the designs are there is, as well as the persistent traditions, an individual character found chiefly in that distinctive blending of Gothic or Romanesque with classic breadth that makes his work recognizable as one recognizes the individual style of a great artist.

One of the best churches designed by Edward Maufe is that of St. Thomas, Hanwell (1930–2) which in some ways foreshadows his design for Guildford Cathedral. The church of St. Thomas has a rectangular plan with small rooms—chapel, children's corner, and vestries—grouped round the chancel. There is a square tower which rises above the children's corner. The walls are of brick and the exterior is simple with large plain surfaces and tall narrow windows in the nave, and circular window on the east end, with a carving of the crucifixion by Eric Gill which forms the cross on the window. The roof is constructed of reinforced concrete and consists of a lower vault and upper pitched roof, between which are concrete ribs spanning the nave. These ribs spring from the buttresses, while secondary ribs spring from the apexes of the cross-vaults. The buttresses are interesting. In a typical Gothic cathedral of the thirteenth or fourteenth century the roof of the aisle is low and a flying buttress is above taking the thrust of the nave or chancel vault. It was essentially a stone-framed structure in which daring lightness is often apparent. Between the flying buttresses, above the triforium, are the clerestory windows. In Scott's Liverpool Cathedral this frame structure, consisting of vertical and flying buttresses, is made into one solid mass and the roof of the aisle is raised much higher between these great solid buttresses which extend to the arcade of the nave. The aisle is tunnelled through these buttresses. It is a device that was also employed in King's College Chapel, Cambridge, but here it is on a smaller scale than at Liverpool. One advantage of this construction is that it allows for very much larger windows than would be possible with the low-aisle roof, and this advantage is well seen both in King's College and Liverpool Cathedral. The same principle, although differently applied, is found in Ivar Tengbom's Hogalid church. This principle Edward Maufe also adopted effectively in St. Thomas's, Hanwell, where the small aisle arches through the buttresses, and the tall transverse arcade arches make a graceful composition. The interior walls are faced with plaster, there are no mouldings, and the intersecting of plain surfaces and the loftiness emphasized by clean long lines gives an effect of impressive solemnity in a fairly small church.

GUILDFORD CATHEDRAL

The design for Guildford Cathedral by Sir Edward Maufe was the winning entry of 183 in a competition held in 1932. Building commenced in 1936, but was stopped in 1939 shortly after the outbreak of war. Building was not resumed until 1952, and the cathedral was practically completed in 1961. As the building follows the original design of 1932, with only a very few minor changes, it is essentially a conception of the thirties. The design is traditional Gothic very much simplified. The plan consists of the nave, chancel, sanctuary and Lady Chapel in their traditional sequence. The transepts are, however, much abbreviated, the south serving as an entrance porch, and the north as the small Queen's Chapel. The main departure from traditional Gothic is in the treatment of the aisles of the nave, which has some resemblance to Sir Giles Scott's Liverpool Cathedral. Here, instead of low-roofed aisles with triforium and clerestory above and flying buttresses to take the thrust of the main arches as in traditional English Gothic cathedrals, at Liverpool there are solid supporting buttresses through which the aisles are tunnelled. The arches through these buttresses or transverse walls at Guildford, are, however, much higher, and the springing of the vault of the aisles of the nave is at the same elevation as the nave vaulting. The space between the narrow aisle vault and the nave vault permits of narrow clerestory windows. As at Liverpool the height of the aisle vaults permits tall windows, which at Guildford are narrow lancet windows. The cathedral is built of brick, made from clay from the ground on which the cathedral stands, with dressings of Clipsham stone for the exterior. Inside the brick walls are covered with plaster with Doulting stone dressings. The roof is constructed of reinforced concrete and covered with copper. Like Liverpool there is floor heating, hot water pipes embedded in concrete screed beneath the stone and marble floor finishes.

The cathedral is well situated on Stags Hill to the north of Guildford. The plain walls and tall narrow windows conduce to a fat solid monolithic appearance with none of the rich textured effect given by the mouldings, carvings and sculpture of traditional Gothic. In Scott's Liverpool Cathedral the structure is articulated with delicate tracery and carved and moulded articulations, but the bareness of Guildford raises the question whether such massive simplicity is suited to the Gothic style. The interior is more pleasing and although the cathedral is not large, seating some 1,750, the architect has achieved a sense of space and prompted a feeling of exhilaration accomplished partly by the long unbroken lines of the piers and the simple vaulting.

This device of having solid buttresses brought across the aisle with small arches through is used in several other churches built during this period, one interesting example being St. Wilfrid's, Elm Grove, Brighton, designed by H. S. Goodhart-Rendel and completed in 1933. This is also a brick church, and the interior concrete vault, consisting of ribs and panels, has five facets, the lower part of the ribs being embedded in the top of the brick buttresses. This treatment gives an openness to the interior and it has an effect of massive strength which was a little unusual for its time. St. Columba, Anfield, and St. Christopher, Norris Green, Liverpool, are two very different examples of the work of Bernard Miller. Both churches are of brick in which large plain walls are used with good effect, and in both it is the Romanesque tradition which is apparent, yet both have many original features. In the church of St. Columba there is concentration on the altar and sanctuary as the principal part of the church, and this is achieved by stepping the roof up in three stages, from the low roof of the nave, then the intermediate roof, and then the high roof over the sanctuary. This cannot be appreciated from the nave end of the church, but as one moves forward the effect becomes apparent.

The church of St. Christopher has a cruciform plan with a low plain square tower at the crossing. The interior is aisleless with a parabolic roof, with ribs and panels between, a treatment which makes the most of the limited space.

St. Gabriel's, Blackburn, is the best known and most notable of F. X. Verlarde's churches, although not distinguished by the same degree of originality as is found in Miller's work. The exterior and interior appear to have little relation to each other, yet both are effective in different ways. The exterior walls of brick have large plain surfaces with narrow vertical windows, while the square tower and the square façade at the east end are strangely severe and massive for a church. Seeing this end from a distance for the first time, it would not be easy to determine whether it is an industrial building or modern church, but a nearer approach would decide this matter by the details of the openings. The interior is strongly reminiscent of Tengbom's Hogalid church with the same circular vault and the same treatment of aisles and buttresses, but the Hogalid church is loftier, with a more impressive sense of space.

The revival of the austere Early Christian and medieval atmosphere in churches of this period might be regarded as making a virtue of economic necessity. Economical considerations may have contributed to a ready adoption in many cases of an austere style, but it would have come in any case. Not all parishes were compelled to consider economy in a like degree, and if there were more than adequate funds available there was the increasing tendency to devote them to good design, workmanship, and materials than on much decoration. The work of William Morris and Philip Webb was not without its effect on the church. It is a natural consequence of the earnest desire to get closer to the sources of Christian religious thought, and is also part of the sequence of architectural thought to go farther and farther back to fundamentals and origins, from Renaissance to Gothic, from Gothic to Romanesque, from Romanesque to Early Christian. In some of the modern churches under review, the austere and religious early medieval atmosphere such as is found, for example, in some of the monastic buildings of Italy built during the monastic revival, has been recaptured with some degree of success. In some churches it has clearly been a conscious aim, while it is probably felt in varying degrees in one or two of the churches already mentioned. This atmosphere exists in a few of the churches of W. A. Pite, Son, and Fairweather among which may be mentioned St. John's, Beckenham, and the Church of the Holy Cross at Hornchurch. The former has a simple rectangular plan with high arched bays on either side of the nave, the piers of which are pierced with arches, thus forming aisles. The church is built of brick with timber roof. The ceiling has five facets and is divided into panels. The walls are plastered above a brick dado. The large plain wall-surfaces, the general width and simplicity, the subdued colouring, and the feeling of quiet that the whole interior suggests give the impression that here is a place designed for prayer. The Church of the Holy Cross at Hornchurch has a similar character, and the general simplicity and austerity are accentuated by the plain plastered wall-surfaces being continued in the barrel vault. The church has a cruciform plan; it is built of brick and the nave arches are supported on concrete columns.

The distinction between the churches classified under categories (b) and (c) is a very fine one and the main difference exists in the degree of traditional character that remains, and the extent to which logical reasoning about purpose and modern structure determines design. In the former category traditional features are retained in alliance with modern structure, whereas in the latter these traditional features disappear. There are several examples among the buildings for new religious sects. One is the hall built for the Apostolic Community at Siedlung Kiefhoek, Rotterdam, by J. P. Oud in 1929. In Christian Science churches more general architectural styles rather than ecclesiastical forms are followed. New purposes often produce new types of buildings, but they are generally rendered less interesting because of the adherence to traditional styles in current use. A hall built with the purpose of sheltering a congregation of people who, wanting occasionally to read and sing, requires good lighting. A small office adjoining the hall for those who officiate, an altar in the centre, or at one end as a focal point for worship, a reading desk, a raised platform for preaching, and a musical instrument to accompany singing are among requirements varying in importance according to the sect. Steel or reinforced concrete frame structure is employed so as to allow glass walls to give the utmost light. This is a building conforming to barest requirements, and elaborations on the basis of the same logical thinking would be in the direction of improved comfort and accommodation. What becomes of the worship of God and the religious atmosphere the traditionalist may ask? It may be replied that the purpose of building the hall at all is to allow people to congregate to worship God, and the retention of traditional elements of design, merely because they are traditional, will not enable people to worship any better. This is to an extent true, but only to an extent. The suggestion that the building should be beautiful because beauty itself is an act of worship and helps to make the building worthy of its purpose hardly meets the case, because in the elaborations of the hall, beauty can be a purpose and it may result in a building very like a beautiful exhibition hall or factory. It is the character of that beauty which is so important, and that character is closely connected with purpose because it is here of a kind that should suggest the ideas of worship and prayer, and the glorification of the Christian conception of God.

What is the physical character that suggests these ideas? Worship implies the transference of thought from the temporal and finite to the infinite and mysterious, therefore a sense of space and mystery would fittingly characterize a building dedicated to this purpose, and these qualities could be given to a building without dependence on traditional forms. Worship, however, also implies aspiration, a looking upwards from the small self to the Great God, a prostration before the mighty Being who has for long ages been conceived as dwelling in Heaven above. This conception of God and Heaven as above, somewhere beyond the ethereal blue, is responsible for one of the most persistent of all forms in Christian church architecture—that of long vertical lines or masses, curving to an arched summit, in French Gothic architecture.

In many of the modern churches, where traditional forms and ornament seem to have given place to stark simplicity, the vertical line or mass, present generally in long narrow windows, is insistent. Only rarely does the horizontal window so characteristic of modern industrial and commercial architecture appear, and then only subordinately, as in Josef Gočár's church at Prague.

Among the chief tendencies in church design, which emerge in the most modern examples, are the introduction of new structural methods, hitherto only used in factories and exhibition halls, and the desire for more and more simplicity.

CHURCHES OF AUGUSTE AND GUSTAVE PERRET

In France, and later elsewhere, the tendency to plan churches more in accordance with suitability for modern purpose was beginning to be accompanied by the use of new materials and methods of construction and design resulting logically from this. The two most noteworthy early examples in which there is a wholehearted attempt to apply the methods for industrial building to modern churches are the church of Notre Dame de Raincy, near Paris, built in 1922–3, and the church of Ste. Thérèse at Montmagny, built in 1924–5, both by Auguste and Gustave Perret. Both have the rectangular plan with a tower in the centre at the west end and both are constructed of reinforced concrete. In the earlier church at Le Raincy, which is very much the prototype of that at Montmagny, the essential principle of the construction is a roof supported on two double rows of straight, slender columns, the outer rows forming the walls, while between the columns are latticed windows. The roof has a flat segmental vault in the centre, with a series of transverse segmental vaults at the sides, giving the slight reminiscence of bays. Above the plinth, which is about seven feet high, the walls are almost entirely composed of the geometric latticed windows, and this contributes to the

Church of Notre Dame Le Raincy, near Paris, 1922–23, exterior and interior views

Architects: Auguste and Gustave Perret

Church of St. Therese de l'enfant Jesu, at Montmagny, 1924–25, exterior and interior views

Architects: Auguste and Gustave Perret

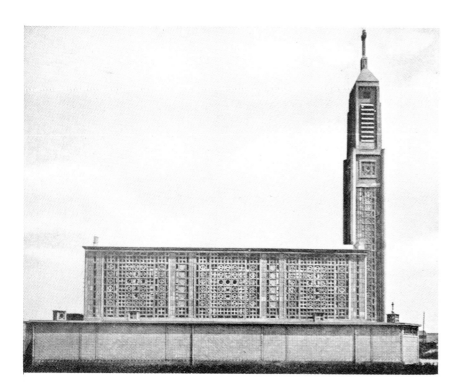

light and open effect of the interior. The tower is in three stages, and its character is very largely determined by the slender rod-like columns. A long window forms a panel in the first stage, a ventilator in the second, with the termination consisting of three vertical concrete rods and decorative fret panels formed to buttress a slender tower.

The motif of the long, plain, slender columns of the interior is thus repeated in the tower. The design, especially the treatment of the columns, has proved very disturbing to many traditionalists. For example, A. Trystan Edwards criticizes the design of the tower[2], which, he says, 'is so strangely composed that it appears to suffer from a mechanical instability'. This impression may be due to judging a reinforced concrete structure according to appearances of stone or brick construction. But what Trystan Edwards particularly criticizes is the lack of vertical punctuation and the lack of terminal features for the long, straight concrete ribs, and he contends that the lack of such punctuation gives rise to the idea that the stages are capable of sliding downwards in telescopic fashion. Associations of this kind, often far more ludicrous, do impose themselves in the contemplation of objects, and this often disturbs aesthetic enjoyment; but it is questionable whether it is valid criticism. Is it essential that a column or vertical rib shall be punctuated with accented terminations? It is true that it is a feature of columns from Ionic to Gothic, but there was no lower punctuation of the Doric columns, while many square Egyptian columns have none, and in much important modern architecture there is no such punctuation. What is far more important is that the column shall be in good proportion to what it supports, a matter which depends on the effect of adequacy of the supporting member. If it appears too weak for efficient support it can hardly be good proportion; if it appears to have unnecessary bulk for what it supports, again the proportion is unsatisfactory. The happy medium is the good proportion, the feeling that it is just right. But it must be related to material. The structural capacities of stone and steel are very different; therefore the delight one has in the good proportion of a structure must necessarily be associated with the feel of the material, the feel of stone which requires a certain bulk for support, the feel of steel, or steel embedded in concrete which requires much less bulk and can be comparatively slender. Traditionalists looking at the tower of the church at Le Raincy are apt to judge it by towers where the walls support and are structural, whereas here they are screens on a framed construction. The vertical ribs criticized by Trystan Edwards are the uprights of the frame, and they are given more prominence than the horizontal members because vertical emphasis was desired. What the architects were clearly anxious to do was to get a pleasing proportional sequence in the three stages of the tower. The same attitude that could not think of Mendelsohn's sketch designs of steel and concrete buildings as architecture finds it difficult to appreciate a church of this kind as architecture. H. P. Cart de Lafontaine, though admitting that this church suggested many possibilities, says that it 'is primarily engineering'[3]. The difficulty, as we have seen, is to judge a work on its own merits; that is, as an expression of purpose and structure and as a composition of forms, without an inhibiting reference to past standards and traditional practice.

As previously indicated the church of Ste. Thérèse at Montmagny follows the same principles of design and construction, although it varies in many details. The same geometric lattice work is used for the windows, indeed, the same moulds were employed as in the church at Le Raincy. The first two stages of the tower are similar, but the terminating stage is much simpler and finishes with a pyramid and cross.

Following similar principles of interior design and construction is the famous church of S. Antonius at Basel in Switzerland, built by Karl Moser in 1924–5. Before designing this church, Moser had probably seen the church at Le Raincy. It is a reinforced concrete frame construction and the roof, like that at Le Raincy, is supported on two double rows of long, slender shafts. In the centre is a barrel vault of ribbed construction forming a pattern of square panels, while the roof between the wall and inner row of shafts is flat with the same ribbed construction. The uprights on the walls are in pairs, which form a flat wall between windows. Two principal entrances are at the sides, and the porches rise to the full height of the walls, with a roof stepped down to the entrances and a series of diminishing shafts on the inside of the porch side walls. The tower is at the other end, and the side is plain (oblong on plan) with a perforated termination. Where, in the churches by Perret, a stylistic motif is the slender, round column or rib, in the Basel church there is a slender, square column or rib, and the whole church is largely rectangular in character—a calculated relation of horizontals and verticals, with a decided emphasis on the latter which is employed very impressively in the two porches. Moser's church has an artistic unity and distinction superior to the earlier French churches, but the originality belongs primarily to the Perret brothers. It would seem that the theme was given to Moser by Auguste and Gustave Perret, and he has produced a beautiful variation of the theme.

Parabolic ribs of reinforced concrete were first used in the airship hangars at Orly, designed by Freyssinet in 1916. This was followed by their use in exhibition halls, like that at Brünn, Czechoslovakia, and the Horticultural Hall in London. The parabolic vault of brick was used in the famous Engelbrecht church in Stockholm, built between 1908 and 1914.

In the church of St. Christopher at Norris Green, previously noted, parabolic ribs of fibrous plaster are held by a steel frame. Two of the earliest examples in which parabolic ribs of reinforced concrete springing from the floor form the essential structure are the church of St. John the Baptist at Molenbeeck, Brussels (1929), designed by M. J. Diongre, and the church of St. Faith, Lee-on-the-Solent (1932), designed by John Seely and Paul Paget. They both show considerable similarity to the exhibition hall at Brünn, with the difference that aisles are introduced, and the ribs become somewhat like deep buttresses towards the base and are pierced by parabolic

200

Church of St. Jean Baptiste, Molenbeck, Brussels, 1929, interior looking towards the altar   *Architect: M. J. Diongre*

St. Nicholas Church, Burnage, Manchester, 1931–32, interior looking towards the altar
Architect: N. F. Cachemaille-Day
of Welch, Cachemaille-Day and Lander

Church of St. Saviour, Eltham, London, 1932, exterior and interior looking towards the altar
Architects: Welsh, Cachemaille-Day and Lander

aisle arches. The principle of construction is the same as that previously noted of which St. Thomas's, Hanwell, is a Gothic example. In the church of St. John the Baptist at Molenbeek the parabolic ribs hold together the walls in three tiers which set back at each stage, terminating in a very slightly pitched roof, and this effect of three tiers determines the exterior form. The much smaller church of St. Faith, Lee-on-the Solent, is in two tiers, with the clerestory curving with the parabolic ribs, and the ceiling slightly pitched, but the exterior does not express the interior design, being merely an ordinary tiled pitched roof with dormers, which are internally the clerestory windows. On the south side of the church is a chapel, porch, and vestries, and the slope of the roof is continued on the central part, flanked by the two entrances. It is difficult to judge the shape and character of the interior by the exterior and there is nothing in this commonplace exterior to lead one to expect the interesting, impressive, and original interior. A small church in which a similar principle of construction was adopted is St. Philip, Osmondthorpe, Leeds, designed by F. R. Charlton and completed in 1932. The ribs, as in the other examples, spring from the floor, but here the parabola is much lower, being almost a semicircle. There are no aisles, and a flat ceiling connects the top of the walls with the parabolic ribs, while the central vault consists of three facets of concrete panels, and externally a pitched tiled roof. In both these examples an interior of modern concrete construction and design is camouflaged externally with brick walls and pitched tiled roofs.

Often the combination of simplicity with devotional character is given architectural interest by original dramatic effects, in the use of light and shadow, in vivid contrasts of colour and of plain and broken surfaces, by impressive verticality or by striking effects of artificial light. We see these tendencies in the churches of Welch, Cachemaille-Day, and Lander, the best known of which built in this period are St. Nicholas, Burnage, near Manchester, and St. Saviour, Eltham. In the former, which was completed in 1931, a particular problem of the plan was to secure the principal entrance at the east end, as this was on the street side. The solution of the problem is interesting. The porch lies on the south side of the apsidal end of the church, and a corridor leads to the baptistry which forms the base of the tower at the apsidal south transept. The high altar is placed just before the curve of the apse and is set against a wall behind which are the vestries, and above, reached by flights of stairs on either side and separated from the chancel by a grille, is the Lady Chapel. On the same level above the corridor leading from the porch is a space for the choir which is open to the chancel except for two octagonal columns. The arrangement can be seen from the illustration. Here is an example where purpose has been considered logically in conjunction with the special problem of an entrance at the east end, with the result that we have an original variation of traditional design. The nave is rectangular, with aisles which have low ceilings. This would have allowed large windows in the nave walls, but instead the architects have preferred a large plain blue-grey plastered wall surface with small clerestory windows, depending for their main lighting on the large rectangular window at the west end. The coloured panelling of the flat wall-board ceiling has a richness in contrast to the pale blue-grey walls.

The church is built of brick, the external facing bricks being of a pleasing soft greyish-yellow hue. Continuous horizontal flutings in the brickwork form a kind of frieze, while vertical flutings and vertical emphasis appear at the porch entrance and the top of the tower and in the shafts of the choir and west end.

The exterior massing accurately expresses the interior organization, for the entrance porch, the balconied choir abutting the chancel, and the low ceilinged aisles are all reflected in the exterior. When this church was completed it was the most original and modern church in England.

St. Saviour's, Eltham, was completed a year later (1932). It is a simpler plan, being rectangular, with a Lady Chapel projecting out a little on the north of the sanctuary, and the vestry on the south. The east end rises a little above the nave, forming a massive tower, and the ceiling above the sanctuary is thereby loftier than that of the nave. The aisles, like those of St. Nicholas, Burnage, have low ceilings, but instead of small clerestory windows, the nave walls have long narrow vertical windows. The church is constructed of brick piers with concrete roof. Inside between the purplish-grey brick piers the walls are faced with pale cream cement. Concrete roof ribs of reddish hue continue the line of the brick piers, and the roof space between is of greyish-green concrete of mottled, slightly scintillating texture obtained by the use of glass in the concrete.

The reredos consists of a series of concrete piers with a figure of Christ carved in concrete in the centre. It accords excellently with the long blue vertical windows above. The exterior facing is of purplish-grey brick. The whole design is characterized by strong vertical emphasis, secured mainly by the long unbroken brick piers and the long vertical slits for windows. Again in this church the interior organization is clearly revealed in the external massing. The interior is open, simple, and broad in treatment and strangely impressive for a church which is not very large, and it must take a similarly high rank among modern churches as that at Burnage. When completed both these churches aroused some antagonism and abuse among the people for whom they were primarily intended, and stones were even thrown at the church at Eltham by outraged people, but the Royal Institute of British Architects awarded it a bronze medal in 1932. Beauty that is new and unfamiliar so often has this effect, and it is more likely to be felt with types of beauty that are associated with old traditions and with the spiritual and ceremonial than with more utilitarian types of building that must change with material progress and changing needs. A modern factory with new methods of construction and more exclusively functional design is welcomed, but if these are applied to churches then there may be abuse and

Church of St. Anthony, Basel, 1924–25, exterior and interior   *Architect: Karl Moser*

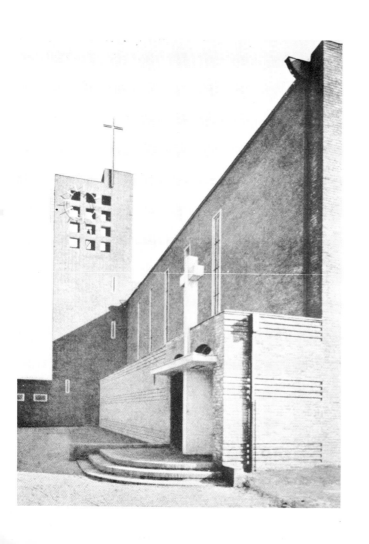

Church at Billstedt (left) and at Wohlsdorf (above), both near Hamburg, and both by the same architects: *C. G. Bensel, J. Kamps and H. Asinck*

antagonism. These difficulties that stand in the way of progressive church design were pointed out by Pierre Vago in writing of Josef Gočár's modern church in Prague. It therefore requires more courage for an architect to design his church logically according to purpose in the modern constructional idioms than if he were designing a factory where he would probably be regarded by progressive clients as not very efficient if he did not.

FURTHER GERMAN AND SOME CZECHOSLOVAK CHURCHES

Two notable churches in Hamburg of this period offer many points of similarity. One is the Protestant Church at Wohlsdorf; the other is the Catholic Church at Billstedt. They are both designed by the same architects—C. G. Bensel, J. Kamps, and H. Amsinck. The reinforced concrete of which the churches are constructed is faced externally with brick. Like the two English churches just described they express the interior by the external massing, and large plain surfaces are important features of the design. In the Catholic Church the aisles, like those in the two English churches, have low ceilings, clearly expressed in the exterior by the low block running at the base of the wall, while the plain plastered nave wall is pierced with tall narrow, vertical windows. The Protestant Church is a rectangular plan without aisles, and a conspicuous decorative feature of both churches is the brick-faced grille of the belfries in the plain square towers. Although there are similarities with the English examples the German churches have greater simplicity, cleaner lines, and broader masses. The Protestant Church at Wohlsdorf being situated on a hill these qualities can be fully appreciated. This simplicity and breadth is carried a little farther in another notable German church—that of St. Matthew, Düsseldorf—and in two interesting Czechoslovak churches in which the use of reinforced concrete has contributed greatly to these qualities.

The Church of St. Matthew, Düsseldorf, was built in 1930–1 to the designs of Wach and Rosskoten. It has a simple rectangular plan with apsidal east end, a gallery on the north side, and a campanile attached at one corner to the main building. The church is faced externally with brick, and internally the walls are finished with plaster, while there is a flat roof with timber joists forming the pattern of the ceiling. Essentially a composition of rectangles with plain surfaces and marked vertical emphasis, it is a simple rectangular block with tall vertical concrete piers the full height of the church at the entrance porch, while the large windows reaching to the roof on the south side, and somewhat smaller in the lower gallery block on the north side, are articulated with plain concrete mullions. The tower is a tall rectangular mass and for the belfry at the top there are long apertures on all four sides with concrete mullions in the centre of each. The composition of the body of the church is one of verticals articulating a horizontal mass, and the plain brick surfaces in relation to concrete piers are used with good effect. The interior is no less effective. The fittings are of wood, simply and impressively designed. For example, the narrow flat wall at the side of the apse is lined with wood to the full height of the church, and this forms a background to the simple pulpit. But what is particularly impressive in the interior is the large thin cross above the small altar, which is placed with careful artistic calculation against the plain wall of the apse with memorable dramatic effect. This dramatic device of placing a large thin cross against a plain wall was frequently employed in German churches of this period with varying success.

The two Czechoslovak churches are both built of concrete, and both clearly express their structure. The church at Prague designed by Josef Gočár and completed in 1929 is a particularly original conception. The main body of the church is built on a plan which tapers slightly towards the apsidal east end, while aisles terminating in two set-backs on either side of the apse have low ceilings. East of the apse is a low mass housing vestries and offices, while at the west end is a long, low porch, and in the centre a tall narrow square tower. The church has the effect of rising high above the low blocks which surround its base. The roof rises in four stages from the entrance at the west end to the roof above the sanctuary at the east end, so that the height of the ceiling above the altar is almost twice that above the entrance. It will be remembered that this device of raising the ceiling in stages towards the sanctuary was adopted by Bernard Miller in his Church of St. Columba at Anfield. There is a balcony at the west end, the underside of which makes a continuous ceiling with that of the aisles. Tall vertical windows occupy the apse, while the aisles are lighted by long horizontal windows. The upper walls at the sides present large plain surfaces, and the whole effect is one of extreme simplicity, with a somewhat novel character emanating a little from the suggestions inherent in the method of construction. Like Perret's concrete churches it is largely a pioneer experiment. It promises rather than achieves a beauty that is new.

Extreme simplicity appears in Jan Visek's church at Brünn, which was the first building of the Czechoslovak National Church. The doctrine of this church is based on the teaching of John Huss. The building is very simply designed so that alterations can be made fairly easily when desired, because it is a feeling of the builders that as their religious practices are subject to alteration, so the building should be. In addition to being a church this building provides for social and cultural activities. It is on two floors. The ground floor consists of a meeting hall, with a stage and vestibule buffet at the west end, and offices and other rooms at the east end. On the first floor is the church, with offices at the east end. The entrance is from the terrace roof of the ground floor vestibule. With the exception of a plain, square tower placed at the south of the sanctuary, the whole plan is symmetrical. The church has two side balconies, over which are a series of vertical windows. Both the interior and exterior are simple to the point of severity with large plain wall surfaces. The simplicity is probably too extreme for most tastes, and some decorative emphasis of form would have given more interest to this building. It is possible that decorative additions may be made later, but it is

Church of Christ the King, Cork (Irish Republic),
exterior and interior with view of altar
Architects: Barry Byrne and J. R. Boyd-Barrett

Evangelical Church of St. Matthew, Dusseldorf,
1932, exterior, and interior with view of altar
Architects: Wach and Rosskotten

to be hoped that these will be part of the architect's conception and an integral part of the design. Another church which might be mentioned as an example of this tendency to extreme simplicity is the Protestant Church at Hedelfingen, Stuttgart, designed by Volkart and Trüdinger. This represents a particularly marked departure from tradition among the older church sects. Indeed the only traditional features are the campanile and the apsidal east end. The body of the church with its plain walls and large horizontal windows might as fittingly be part of a school building.

The designs of most modern churches are controlled in some measure by the material of which they are built, and thus the material and its structural capacity determine to some degree the character of the building. That degree is decided by the designer, who can make the nature of the material mainly responsible for the architectural character, or the material can be subordinated. In modern church design, purpose and traditional forms are generally the chief determining factors in architectural character, but the material and method of construction if fully revealed and not veneered can contribute very largely to this architectural character, as we can see in the modern brick churches, and in the combination of brick and concrete in a church like St. Saviour's, Eltham. Some modern church designs, while controlled by purpose and tradition, are also very largely essays in the application and expression of a modern material to this traditional type of building. Two notable churches of this kind are the Steel Church at Presse, Cologne, designed by Otto Bartning, and the Church of Petri Nicolai at Dortmund, designed by Pinno and Grund.

There is one interesting characteristic of the plans of both which is worth noting. In the modern tendency to abandon the cross plan and to employ the simple rectangular plan, with or without aisles, the intention is to have the church as open as possible, so that the officiating priest at the altar, lectern, or pulpit can be seen in comfort from any part of the church. In these two churches, as in Gočár's church at Prague, instead of the rectangular plan we find that it tapers towards the altar. These would appear to be designed so as to serve the purpose indicated even better and the designers were probably influenced by the modern theatre or cinema plan. In some churches, however, the reverse obtains, and the building broadens towards the sanctuary. An example of this is the Church of Christ the King at Cork in Ireland, designed by Barry Byrne and J. R. Boyd-Barrett; and in some later churches the plan approximates to the diamond shape. These differences are due to conceptions of the relative importance of the sanctuary and congregation. In the two German churches the importance and convenience of the congregation is the chief consideration, but in the Irish church the greatest prominence is given to the altar and sanctuary, with the space for the congregation dwindling towards the west. This church is, however, remarkable in many ways. It is built of concrete with monolithic walls and from a central tower at the west end a series of vertical shafts with slits for windows decrease in height as they spread out to the east end. This effect is continued in the east wall,

208

while the reredos is formed of a series of shafts ascending to the centre from either side, a design which is unusual and impressive.

Otto Bartning's church at Presse, Cologne, completed in 1928, is constructed mainly of a steel frame and glass, the steel stanchions being uncovered. The walls of the main body of the church are thus glass with steel ribs, and plain steel stanchions mark the aisles from the nave, while four stanchions form the reredos, which has a large crucifix in the centre. The roof is pitched, and the exterior of the east end is not unlike, in general outline, the east end of a French Gothic cathedral, like Bourges, if one thinks away the buttresses. The rich stained-glass windows which surround the church seem to correct the austere effect of the steel stanchions; and the Gothic reminiscence is stronger than one would expect. The west end is broader in plan and rises higher than the rest of the church. The central feature is formed by two oblong towers flanking a slender cross. Vertical rows of bells can be seen on either side of the towers, and the framework of the walls of the whole of this western block is filled with opaque material, thus differing from the glass walls of the nave and sanctuary.

The Church of Petri Nicolai at Dortmund is an essay in reinforced concrete construction applied to the problems of modern church design. The construction consists of a series of approximately flat concrete arches (actually there is a slight cant of about two degrees), the uprights of which spring from the floor and spread a little towards the top. There are six of these, at intervals of about 15 feet, and about 45 feet high. The space between the arches is occupied by windows with concrete lattice, except for a dado about 7 feet 6 inches high. This forms the nave which is the main body of the church. The sanctuary at the east end is a block with glass lattice concrete walls, a little narrower than the nave, while there is a vestry below. The organ and choir are at the west end, and here, with an apsidal wall to the south, is the baptistry. A tall campanile is attached to the church at one corner. An opening at the top of the tower on four sides is broken by concrete shafts into three vertical lights. Four groups of four slits perforate the tower at intervals. An interesting feature of the east end is the covered way surrounding the church, which is reached by doors on either side of the sanctuary. This goes under the sanctuary at the eastern extremity so that the end wall is supported on the slender uprights of the covered way.

Instead of using the usual stained glass the windows are painted with religious subjects by Elizabeth Coester. The lighting of the church is by means of strips along the edges of the concrete arches. The illustration is of the interior of the church at night and shows this lighting clearly. The concrete of which the church is built has no surface finish and is intentionally left rough to symbolize the poor for whom the Christian religion cares, Christ's saying: 'Blessed are the poor in spirit: for their's is the kingdom of heaven' being the theme for the symbolism. In contrast to the rough concrete is the rich colouring of the painted windows dedicated to the glory of Christianity. The

Church at Prague, 1929, exterior and interior
with view of altar and pulpit
Architect: Josef Gŏcár

View of interior looking east, showing the
tubular strip lighting in the nave
Below—plan

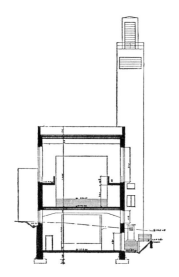

Church at Brunn, Czechoslovakia,
vertical cross section showing
lecture hall below the church
Architect: Jan Visek

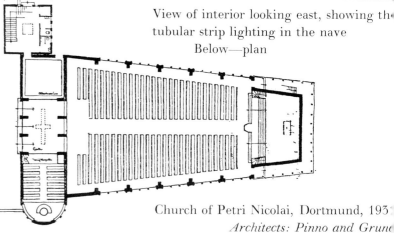

Church of Petri Nicolai, Dortmund, 193
Architects: Pinno and Grun

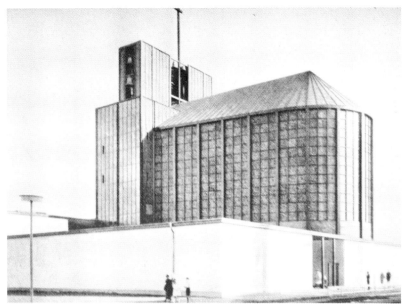

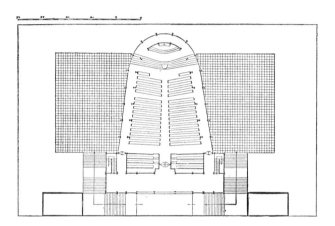

Steel Church at Presse, Cologne, 1931, plan and
exterior and interior views
Architect: Otto Bartning

Church of St. Engelbert, Cologne-Riehl, 1933–34,
exterior and interior views
Architect: Dominikus Bohm

architectural interest of this church is in the application of modern materials and construction, generally more associated, at the time it was built, with industrial architecture than with a type of building governed by ancient traditions.

The last two mentioned churches and those at Raincy and Montinagny by the Perret brothers and that at Basle by Karl Moser are early examples of a tendency in church design in the twenties and thirties, which gathered momentum with the renewal of church building after the Second World War in 1948, to make the interior of the church more functional and open by eliminating transepts and aisles and the barrier between choir and nave, so that every member of the congregation can easily obtain an unobstructed view of the altar, and be brought into closer communion with the service in conformity with the requirements of the modern liturgical movement. This originated at the conference of Malines in 1909 with the proposals of the Benedictine monk, Dom Lambert Beauduin, although they were broadly adumbrated by others in the nineteenth century. A fuller and more general implementation of these liturgical principles was to come later, mainly after the Second World War when the altar was brought forward among the congregation, but this did not materialize to any great extent, and only in exceptional examples, before about 1948. The developments before the war, with a few notable exceptions, were confined mainly to the more open unobstructed interior in conformity with the early church, when the basilicas of Rome, which were halls of justice, formed the prototypes of the early Churches. They were without transepts which constituted a later innovation to conform with the cross plan, but they generally had aisles which mostly disappear in the modern open church.

There are semblances of aisles in the Perret and Moser churches separated from the nave by tall slender columns but giving little obstruction. The two small churches at Hamburg-Blankenese and at Merchingen in the Saar by Clemens Holzmeister are open, but in each case the altar is a little remote. The church of Corpus Christi at Aachen, designed by Rudolf Schwarz and built in 1928–30, is a more significant example of the open interior. The very plain simple rectangular hall is without aisles and the altar mounted on a platform is clearly visible from every seat in the church. This rectangular church with simple belfry tower is in its stark simplicity eloquent of a concentrated austere religious purpose. It prompted many criticisms shortly after it was built, but its eloquent simplicity has won many admirers.

DEVELOPMENTS IN SWISS CHURCHES

Developments towards the one-room open-plan type of church interior are found in many churches in Switzerland during the thirties. The Roman Catholic church of St. Charles, built at the edge of the River Reuss at Lucerne, designed by Fritz Metzger and completed in 1933, has a rectangular plan with slender columns, a flat ceiling and apsidal east end, with the sanctuary open to the nave. On the river façade is a covered balcony which with the square campanile composes very pleasingly.

212

Church of St. Charles, Lucerne, Switzerland, 1932–33, exterior and interior views   *Architect: Fritz Metzger*

Protestant Church at Zürich-Altstetten, Switzerland, 1938–41, exterior and interior views
Architect: Werner Moser

The Protestant church of St. John at Basel, built in 1936, and designed by Ernst F. Burckhadt and Karl Egender, has a rather severe interior without embellishments with a rectangular plan, the sanctuary appearing as a low platform with the choir stalls on the north side, a rather small central communion table, with the pulpit on the south side. The south wall is practically a glass screen. A conspicuous feature of the exterior is the open steel framed campanile fixed to a concrete slab that forms one side.

A third Swiss example is the rectangular Protestant Church at Zurich-Altstetten designed by Werner Moser 1938–41. The sanctuary which is fully open to the nave is raised only two steps. Against the east wall is a slender cross and in front of this is the communion table and pulpit, with the choir and organ on the south side. The sanctuary is lighted on the north side by a tall window and on the south side light shines from a window high above a horizontal screen which extends the whole length of the church. The concentrated light on the sanctuary adds to the dramatic effect. The roof is mono-pitched and slightly curved. The square campanile with lattice windows on two sides is unusually tall which adds to the sense of drama in this very distinctive church building. Peter Hammond[4] said of this church that it is 'the finest Reformed church to be built in Switzerland or in any other country down to 1941, and it will bear comparison with the Roman Catholic churches of Metzger, Baur and Dreyer which, by the late 'thirties, had given Swiss church architecture an unchallenged pre-eminence'.

In this open one-room evolution one significant development was the circular plan. A small circular church by Clemens Holzmeister at Blankenese has already been noted. This has the altar in the traditional place and is on a raised platform in an apsidal recess. A more experimental design is that of the Evangelical Round Church by Otto Bartning at Essen built in 1929–30, where the font is in the centre, with the communion table a little raised nearby. This is a very early example of the central placing of the altar or communion table.

A very beautiful early modern example of a circular church is that of St. Englebert, Roman Catholic Church at Riehl, in the northern part of Cologne, designed by Dominikus Bohm and erected in 1931–32. It has a circular plan for the nave with an entrance porch on the west side, the sanctuary with altar to the east, and a chapel and square campanile on the north side. The building is notable for its roof which consists of eight parabolic vaults, presenting to the exterior eight parabolic façades on the circumference with the roof curving upwards to the central apex. The lighting is by means of small circular windows near the apex of each parabolic wall. In consequence the interior is rather dark giving that sense of mystery which conduces to a religious atmosphere. To me this is one of the most impressive modern church interiors in Europe. A slightly smaller parabolic vaulting encloses the sanctuary which on plan is a rectangular projection from the circle. The altar has thus a little of the remoteness from the congregation of the traditional church, yet one of the purposes of the circular plan in modern churches is to bring the altar more within the congregation that could with this plan partly surround the altar. Interesting, therefore, is the circumstance that Dominikus Bohm's next church, that at Ringenberg, completed in 1935, was the first modern example where the altar is so placed that the congregation is on three sides of it. This is achieved with a transeptual plan with the altar in the centre of the crossing, and the congregation occupying the nave and transepts. From the late twenties until his death in 1955, Dominikus Bohm was one of the most important of church architects in Europe, being the author of several innovations in design with notable results. Among his other churches, all Roman Catholic, completed before the Second World War, was the church at Mainz-Bischoffsheim (1926), the church of the hospital of St. Elizabeth, Cologne (1930–32), which is a spacious rectangular building with an apse, the church of St. Karl-Borromaus, Cologne (1930), and the church at Norderney (1930).

In England there were some experimental developments towards bringing the altar out amidst the congregation, achieved completely in a few small churches. A conspicuous example is the church of the First Martyrs at Bradford, built in 1935, to the design of J. H. Langtry Langton, with a fairly precise briefing by Father John O'Connor. In an octagonal plan circular seating is round a central altar, the first modern example of its kind, as far as I am aware. Although notable for this innovation the church has little architectural distinction. Another church with a central altar is St. Peters, Gorleston-on-Sea, by the famous sculptor, Eric Gill, in 1939. It has a cross plan with altar under the crossing of nave and transepts, and seating is on four sides. Other notable examples of the development towards the physical setting for a more complete participation of everybody in worship is the John Keble Church, Mill Hill, designed by D. F. Martin-Smith (1936) and St. Michael's and All Angels church, Wythenshawe, designed by N. F. Cachemaille-Day (1937). The former has a square plan, and the choir is brought forward to the nave so that the congregation is on three sides of it, although the altar remains a little remote. The church at Wythenshawe also has a square plan, but orientated diagonally with the chancel occupying the east corner and the porch at the opposite corner. The sanctuary corner has tall windows, and the altar itself is brought a little forward. The church is built on a diagonal grid with eight free standing columns which go deep into the ground, a construction necessitated by the character of the site. This is a very original conception which is functionally satisfactory, as every member of the congregation can see the altar clearly, while the choir is brought forward among the congregation[5].

One other significant innovation was apparent in church design during the late thirties. In traditional ecclesiastical buildings the outer world is rather shut out and a deep chiaroscuro is often encouraged as giving a sense of mystery and religious atmosphere, an effect assisted by stained-glass windows for if windows were large the stained glass greatly reduced the admission of light. In contrast to this many architects designed their churches to admit more light, sometimes in a concentrated form directed to the sanctuary, but sometimes to diffuse light in the whole interior. A tendency in Scandinavian churches which began in the late thirties was to have glass walls, not only to admit the maximum light to the interior of the church, but to link the interior with the outside world, and especially the natural world, so as to give a feeling of unity with life and the universe. To achieve this effect a small wood was often planted on the large window-side of the church. Examples of this are the Church of the Advent in Copenhagen, designed by Eric Moller (1938) and the Chapel of the Cemetery at Turku, Finland, designed by Erik Bryggman (1939). In the latter a high window floods the altar, but the nave is in more subdued light because of the upper blank wall, which, however, is supported on columns, but it is between these columns that the trees appear, beyond the glass wall which is hardly apparent. Thus in this interior and in devotion there is achieved this oneness with the natural world.

REFERENCES AND NOTES

1. The rectangular plan is better acoustically than the cruciform. See the essay on Church Acoustics by Hope Bagenal in *Post-War Church Building*, London, 1947, p. 82.
2. A. Trystan Edwards, *Style and Composition in Architecture*, London, 1944, p. 60. This is the second edition of *Architectural Style*, London, 1926.
3. H. R. Cart de la Fontaine, Modern Tendencies in French Architecture in *The Journal of the Royal Institute of British Architects*, 5th December, 1925, p. 71.
4. Peter Hammond, *Liturgy and Architecture*, London, 1960, p. 50.
5. Among the best books on the modern evolution of church design is Peter Hammond's *Liturgy and Architecture*, London, 1960, and *Towards a Church Architecture*, a series of essays on the various aspects of design edited by Hammond, London, 1962.

PART III

Functionalism, Logic and Light

1924–1942

Interior, Exhibition Hall, Klavniko Palace, Brünn, Czechoslovakia, 1928 *Architect: Josef Kalous*

16 The Bauhaus

THE PERIOD BETWEEN the building of the Administrative Office for the Deutsche Werkbund Exhibition at Cologne in 1914 and the Bauhaus at Dessau in 1925 was, architecturally, one of consolidation of the developments so far made, and of tentative experiment, without any very startling advances manifesting in actual building. There were certain interesting developments in construction, mainly in the sphere of reinforced concrete in such work as Freyssinet's airship hangars at Orly (1916), in Mendelsohn's hat factory at Luckenwalde (1922), and in Perret's church at Le Raincy, all of which have been described, while there was progress in an expressive simplicity such as in Oud's housing at Rotterdam. Also Le Corbusier had begun to build the houses for which he was to become so famous, but the most impressive developments of his work were to come a little later, although he was rich in progressive ideas worked out during this period and published in 1924 in *Vers une Architecture*. In the development of the glass screen to take the place of external structural walls, the fenestration of the Fagus shoe-last factory built in 1911 and the staircase towers of the Deutsche Werkbund Cologne building of 1914 had reached a stage which was not carried any farther until the Bauhaus building in 1925. There were many unrealized projects in which experiments were made with the glass screen so that it appears as the most unsubstantial division between inner and outer space, as, for example, Mies van der Rohe's project for a departmental store; while his model for a glass tower (1921) in which thin floors are strung together on slender steel vertical rods and enclosed in glass is a veritable dream of things to come.

More important is the advance made from the Bauhaus onward in the logical building according to purpose so as to satisfy contemporary needs and assist in progress the more efficiently, combined with building that will satisfy aesthetically. The exponents of the theory that fitness for purpose results in beauty, who comprised a minor section of the functionalists, received apparently as little sympathy from Walter Gropius as they did from the traditionalists. He has written that 'catch phrases like "functionalism" (die neue Sachlichkeit) and "fitness for purpose = beauty" have had the effect of deflecting

219

appreciation of the new architecture into external channels or making it purely one-sided'[1]. It may be argued by the exponents of the theory 'fitness for purpose = beauty' that its degree of acceptance depends very much on the comprehension of the dictum. It is not enough to assume that if a building can perform its structural function satisfactorily it results in beauty, because there may be an excess of structure. The structure of Charing Cross Railway Bridge is adequate, but it is not beautiful. The Norman columns of Durham and Gloucester and many other cathedrals give many people the feeling that they are unnecessarily bulky for their structural function. This impression is necessarily dependent on one's association of bulk with the structural capacity of the material. The point is that if the bulk were just right in relation to structural capacity these columns would, to most people, be better proportioned and thus more beautiful.

Consequently the theory of fitness for purpose equalling beauty should mean that the structure fits the purpose like a well-fitting glove, neither too big nor too small, neither too weak nor too strong, but just right[2]. Aesthetic appreciation of this depends, as implied, on knowledge of the structural capacities of material in relation to bulk. Steel is very different from the old materials of stone and brick, and one of the difficulties of many people in appreciating the new architecture is to adjust their perceptions to the structural bulk of steel. Once that necessary familiarity is established aesthetic appreciation is less difficult.

In developing the new structure of steel and concrete it was necessary to calculate the minimum bulk for adequacy, and it is at this point, it could be argued, that one is most likely to design the structure that will give lasting aesthetic satisfaction. As Serge Chermayeff once said, 'a far greater talent is required to create art with the minimum means than with the maximum'[3]. It may be added that art is more likely to be created with the minimum means, and it is the argument of many functionalists that only if an approximation to minimum means is achieved can there be a prospect of complete aesthetic satisfaction. Even if this is achieved it can only contribute partly to the beauty of a building, because in its achievement there can be twenty different designs or conceptions. Gropius separates what he terms 'the practical value of the New Architecture' from the spiritual—'the aesthetic satisfaction of the human soul'.

In the former he includes rationalization—its purifying agency, the emphasis on structural functions and concentration on concise and economical solutions[4]. The distinction is not altogether valid, because if concise and economical solutions result in beauty, which they often do, then a spiritual value is achieved. Gropius connects aesthetic satisfaction with unity and goes on to point out that the new architecture is a matter of new spiritual vision and implies a mastery of space.

This has been demonstrated in many of the great buildings of the past. It is one of the

The Bauhaus, Dessau, 1926. General view showing workshop (left) and students hostel and atelier (right)

Architect: Walter Gropius

Diagram. Key [A] The students' hostel containing 28 studio dormitory rooms. [B] The assembly and dining hall. [C] The workshop wing. [D] The two-storey bridge over the road-way containing the administrative and club rooms and principal's atelier. [E] The school of design

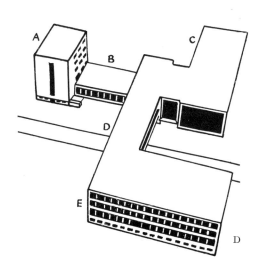

Corner of the workshop

most impressive characteristics of the interior of St. Paul's Cathedral that it stimulates so powerfully the sense of space. But with the glass screen taking the place of the opaque external supporting wall a change in the treatment of space occurs. The division for the percipient between exterior and interior is minimized, and while we are conscious of a solid floor and solid ceiling in a certain space, that space is enlarged by the openness of the glass screen that surrounds the hall or room.

The Bauhaus was moved from Weimar to Dessau on the completion of the new buildings in 1926. Das Staatliche Bauhaus, to give it its full name, was a school of design devoted largely to the mass production of beautiful objects of use. The method of training and the theory prompting it contributed to some important developments in building. Instead of turning his back on the machine, as did William Morris, and concentrating on a few hand-made objects for those who could afford to pay for them, Gropius accepted the machine as a means of widely dispersing well-designed objects. Students were trained in the handling of various materials—stone, wood, metal, clay, glass, etc—in the processes of manufacture, in the principles and application of design, and all cognate subjects, so that they could produce a good design properly suited to its materials and adapted to mass production; the idea being for the artist to create the one beautiful prototype from which thousands could be manufactured by machinery. Training of builders and architects was also included which involved manual work on actual building sites. With this system of producing the well-designed unit from which thousands were manufactured there evolved the system of standardizing units in building and their mass production. If the adequacy of a structural unit can be worked out mathematically so that it is just right, without excess of bulk on the one hand and weakness on the other, and a building is designed on a grid, then the unit can be standardized and multiplied.

Standardization and mass production, in which the standard unit is the creation of a fully qualified technician and artist, not only conduce to a more widespread excellence, but lead directly to more economical building, and in this way building will serve our social needs more fully. It was inevitable that with these ideas Gropius should be one of the pioneers of prefabrication, some of his early prefabricated houses being built in Torten near Dessau in 1927.

The Bauhaus was built by Gropius at Dessau in response to the invitation of the town council. It was the chief building of a group which included some private houses for the teaching staff, a labour exchange, and a housing estate. The Bauhaus is rather like an irregular triscele on plan. It consists of the school of design in one wing, workshops in another, and a students' hostel in the third. As shown in the illustration, the students' hostel is a six-storey building consisting of twenty-eight studio–dormitory rooms designed for private work of the students. Adjoining this building is a low two-storey block which houses an assembly and dining hall. Then beyond this, and turning to the left, is the workshops wing. Turning to the right is a two-storey bridge crossing an intervening roadway. In this bridge are administrative rooms, club rooms, and a private atelier of Professor Gropius. Further on are the various departments of the school of design, a building, like the workshops wing, of four storeys. The Bauhaus is constructed partly of reinforced concrete frame, while in the workshops post and slab construction is employed, the supports being set back to allow a large uninterrupted glass screen. It is interesting to compare this glass screen with that in the Fagus shoe factory. In the latter, although the pillars are similarly set behind the glass, the transparent screen is broken by slender uprights and by opaque bands at floor levels, but in the Bauhaus workshops the transparent screen is unbroken for a considerable extent covering three floors, and, as in the Fagus factory, continuing round corners. This gives that intangible effect which reduces the separation of outer and inner space. It is a stage forward from the Fagus factory and leads the way to numerous large factories in Europe in which the structural members being set back allow for a transparent covering for the whole building. Sigfried Giedion sees in this effect some likeness to certain developments in Picasso's art. 'Two major endeavours of modern architecture, are fulfilled here,' he says, 'not as unconscious outgrowths of advances in engineering, but as the conscious realization of an artist's intent; there is the hovering, vertical grouping of planes which satisfies our feeling for a relational space, and there is the extensive transparency that permits interior and exterior to be seen simultaneously, *en face* and *en profile*, like Picasso's 'L'Arlésienne' of 1911–12: variety of levels of reference, or of points of reference, and simultaneously—the conception of space-time, in short.'[5] Some of Picasso's later portraits show the simultaneous front view and profile[6]. It was a theme with which Picasso continued to experiment, and the connexion with the simultaneity of the perception of inner and outer space made possible by the use of glass is interesting, but it may be questioned if it offers a completely logical parallel. Are they not two different things? There is a clear effort in Picasso's painting to link space and time in a way which can hardly exist in Gropius's treatment of glass in the Bauhaus.

References and Notes

1. *The New Architecture and the Bauhaus*, New York and London, 1936, p. 19.
2. This raises the question of the extent of the safety margin in a structure and what is meant by 'just right'. If the safety factor is so large as to suggest superfluity and waste then it cannot be 'just right', and if it is so small as to prompt apprehension of safety then this also cannot be 'just right'. Security and economy are therefore guides in what is 'just right'.
3. A paper entitled New Materials and New Methods, *The Royal Institute of British Architects Journal*, 23 December 1933, p. 168.
4. *The New Architecture and the Bauhaus*, New York and London, 1936, p. 20.
5. Sigfried Giedion, *Space, Time and Architecture*, Cambridge, USA, 1941, p. 403.
6. Several of Picasso's portraits of this kind painted during the Second World War were exhibited at the Victoria and Albert Museum in January 1946.

17   Industrial buildings and power stations

IN THE BAUHAUS there are many suggestions for lines of development. There is the glass-screen treatment of workshops, there are the horizontal glass and opaque bands of the school of design, and there is the students' hostel with its smaller windows and solid walls. The first two are for work; the other is for domestic needs. One reason why work—design and making—is not done in the open is that protection from the weather is necessary, but if the same openness and lighting can be obtained as in the open air then it is a great advantage. This applies most completely to factories, and perhaps to a slightly less degree to departmental stores and to the major parts of office buildings, schools, and hospitals, remembering that other parts demand some change of treatment according to purpose. In parts of these a degree of privacy is required, a privacy which is not obtained by a translucent material which lets in the light such as frosted glass or glass bricks, but only by a completely opaque wall. With domestic buildings, both flats and family houses, privacy is a prime need, and in densely built-up areas this can only be secured by opaque walls. It is a question of a nice balance between windows which let in as much light as possible, and opaque walls which preserve privacy, but because of the demands of privacy we are never likely to see blocks of flats just enclosed by glass screens as in many factories, with the division of inner and outer space reduced to a minimum. With country houses and some of the larger town houses, where privacy can be secured by trees, an openness for some parts of the houses has been a major development, such as a living room with a glass screen opening to a terrace and glass-walled bedrooms above opening on to balconies.

In factories adequate light is a primary function. Much depends on the manufacturing processes of different industries. It may be of advantage in some cases to have complete glass walls, but in cases where the arrangement of benches round walls proves to be the most convenient planning, then there would be no point in having a glass screen below bench height, and the arrangement of horizontal opaque bands is clearly desirable. Some parts of each factory, such as offices and welfare sections, where a degree of privacy is desirable, do not require windows as large as in the parts of the

224

building where the manufacturing processes are conducted. There is the objection that
the all-glass screen makes the factory too warm in summer and too cold in winter,
requiring extra heating, and that windows of a medium size are in this respect
satisfactory, although they reduce light. Unpleasantness from heat can generally be
minimized by good ventilation and it is conducive to healthy conditions that the air
within the factory should be constantly in motion. It is healthier to work in a
temperature of 21°C (69°F) with the air in constant motion than in a temperature of
15°C (59°F) with the air almost still. Double or even treble glazing reduces heat loss
and effects economy in heating but it means extra capital cost in the building. In many
manufacturing processes air conditioning is an advantage and this requires effective
wall insulation.

Heat and cold can be controlled far more satisfactorily than light. In most industrial
operations as much light as possible is required, the ideal conditions being the light
outdoors under a bright grey sky. The fact that in the centre of the average living
room with a large window the percentage of such light is less than two, demonstrates
the difficulty of admitting sufficient light and the value of as large a glazed area as is
possible. Artificial light at its best is a poor substitute, and it has to be so very powerful
to approximate to anything like the value of daylight, which workers prefer. Therefore,
in making the admission of maximum daylight a primary function in designing
buildings, architects were concentrating on one of the fundamental utilitarian
purposes.

One of the outstanding examples of the use of glass in which the mushroom slab[1]
construction is employed is the Van Nelle Factory at Rotterdam, built in 1927–30,
and designed by J. A. Brinkmann and L. C. van der Vlugt. The group of buildings
comprises tobacco, tea, and coffee factories, offices, warehouses, garages, canteens, and
other minor buildings. The main factory blocks are eight storeys high, marked by
alternate horizontal bands of fenestration and solid wall which can be clearly seen in
the view of the building. The same treatment with narrow horizontal bands at the
floor levels in the glass screen is used for the small three-storey office block but here
an ordinary reinforced concrete frame construction is employed. Treatment varies with
different parts of the buildings according to purpose. Wider opaque horizontal bands
alternate with narrow glass bands, while the façade of one block is curved, which gives
it a particular interest in relation to the square blocks and helps to give the ensemble
a certain life and movement. In this group of buildings there is considerable variety
combined with a satisfying overall unity. This is largely due to the consistency of
treatment allowing glass and the feeling of light together with horizontal emphasis, to
dominate the whole, rather than to a satisfying relation of masses. If these masses had
been in stone the same result would not have been achieved, but glass and the feeling
of light give it an unsubstantial airy quality which is entrancing. The actual form can
be appreciated better at night when the whole interior is ablaze with light, for then the

225

The Van Nelle Factory at Rotterdam, 1930. The group includes tobacco, tea and coffee
factories   *Architects: J. A. Brinkman and L. C. Van der Vlugt*

Boot's Chemical Factory at Beeston, Nottinghamshire, 1931–32. General view   *Architect: Sir Owen Williams*

particular relation of solids to voids can be felt more clearly. Few modern European buildings have been more widely admired by modern architects than this.

In the chemical factory of Boots at Beeston in Nottinghamshire the mushroom slab construction in combination with the glass screen is on a more complete, vast, and uncompromising scale than in any other building in Europe. It was designed by Sir Owen Williams, and was completed in 1932. The whole covers a large area, the mushroom columns support the concrete floors, and the edges of these floors form the only break in the glass screen which encloses the whole building. On the first storey the glass screen is carried the whole length and breadth of the building, and above this storey the five blocks rise another two storeys higher. The upper roofs are of glass bricks. The light and airy effect of the interior can thus be imagined. The glass screen has not quite the unsubstantial airy quality of that in the Bauhaus workshops, because it is interrupted by the floor slab edge, whereas in the Bauhaus even the floor edge is set back behind the screen.

Does this building, which marks an important stage in factory design, afford any great degree of aesthetic pleasure? Some views of parts of the exterior and interior certainly appear beautiful in some aspects, but can the whole be regarded as a work that gives a high degree of aesthetic pleasure? It lacks the interest and variety of the Van Nelle factory and the Bauhaus. The long unbroken end façade seems to demand something to which it can relate satisfactorily, while the side view, with the five blocks rising above the second storey, appears somewhat monotonous. In the case of the Bauhaus and the Van Nelle factory the variety is afforded by the difference of purpose of the various parts, and the same opportunity may not have been presented in the Boots's factory. But in spite of this mild criticism, it remains one of the outstandingly progressive building achievements of the period between the wars.

The Van Nelle and the Boots's factories represent the farthest advance in factory design of the period from 1924 to 1933 of logical building according to purpose in which the admission of light is a primary function. There are, however, several other good examples in Europe of similar developments, but it must suffice to mention a few of the best.

Two other examples of the work of Sir Owen Williams, designed in the early thirties, are a warehouse of Lilley and Skinner (1933), and laboratory of a cement factory at Thurrock in Essex (1932). In the former the mushroom column and slab construction is employed, there are long horizontal bands between windows, and the device of taking windows round the corners is employed. The laboratory at Thurrock is a simple rectangular building. The benches run round the walls with a shelf above, and the walls are opaque to this level and glass above, with slender concrete mullions. Powerful electric lamps are fixed to the mullions with the purpose of providing an equivalent to

227

Boot's Chemical Factory at Beeston, Nottinghamshire, 1931–32. Interior of the packing hall *Architect: Sir Owen Williams*

The Luma Lamp Factory of the Co-operative Society in Sweden, near Stockholm, 1930 *Architect: Eskil Sundahl*

Tobacco Factory of the Austrian State Tobacco Reqie at Linz, 1935
Architect: Peter Behrens and Alexander Popp
Right—exterior detail, the tower adjoining the entrance for vehicles. Sculpture by Wilhelm Frass.
Below, left—layout plan. *Key* [A] Cigarette manufacture. [B], [C] and [D] Tobacco stores. [E] Tobacco preparation and packing.
[F] Entrance and visitors' hall. [G] Administration building.
[H] Retail stores. [I] Welfare buildings. [K] Finance buildings and workshops. [L] Boiler house and machine shop
Below—the main facade of the factory with long bands of steel-framed casements and plain bands of brickwork finished in white rough-cast stucco.

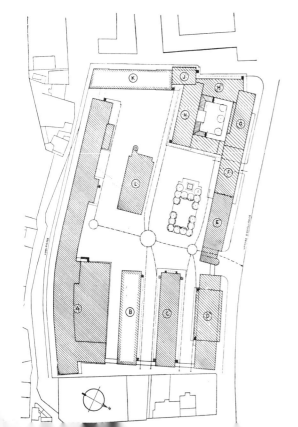

daylight. The roof is opaque, and as the intention was to get maximum light the question occurs why glass panels or glass bricks were not used for the roof. The benches and some of the furniture of this laboratory are of reinforced concrete suitably faced.

Among other noteworthy industrial buildings of this period in England is Viyella House, Nottingham, designed by F. A. Broadhead, built about 1931 as an extension of an earlier factory built in 1919. In addition to the factory are warehouse, showrooms, and offices. It is a four-storey building of reinforced concrete constructed by the mushroom column method. The walls are of wide horizontal glass screens, without intermediate supports, divided by narrow strips at floor level. This is broken in the long street façade by an elaborate decorative central entrance with vertical pilasters reaching to the third storey. It was clearly the purpose to make this entrance imposing because of the commercial and publicity value of making a building look as important as possible. Architecturally it is formal classical design imposed on a modern factory building, very much as grand and massive classical architecture is used for bank buildings, in order to give an impression of importance and stability. The entrance would have been better if it had been more modest, and more in keeping with the general design of the building. Apart from the entrance the building has a lightness and airy quality in which the division of outer and inner space is reduced almost to a minimum, reminding one of some of the early projects of Mies Van der Rohe.

A tendency in much factory design is to have the offices, and perhaps showrooms, in a block facing the road with the main factory at the back. This is a standard design for numerous factories built in trading estates during the thirties. Often the front part is of a symmetrical classical character totally different from the factory at the back, which may be a storeyed building of steel or concrete, or a sprawling one-floor building with a saw-tooth roof. When this method of planning is adopted there is often little unity between one part and another, and the effect is often incongruous. There are numerous examples of this kind along the Great West Road. Often the symmetrical façade is given 'character' by the incorporation of stylistic features from the past. The modern building of today is at the back. It should not be difficult, as the examples in this chapter should demonstrate, to design an effective façade to the road, which need not be a flat façade nor parallel to the road, but which should be, both in use and aesthetically, an integral part of the whole building. Some of the factory buildings of Wallis, Gilbert and Partners, such as the Hoover Factory at Perrivale, which faces Western Avenue, succeed in presenting an imposing façade to the road while appearing to be an integral part of the main factory building.

CENTRAL EUROPE AND SCANDINAVIA

One of the factory areas which developed most rapidly in Europe during this period was that of the Bata shoe industry at Zlin in Czechoslovakia. This town of Zlin, which in 1930 had a population of about 30,000 and was planned for an ultimate population of

229

100,000, is an enterprise of the Bata family. The whole layout was planned by F. L. Cahurn and includes, in addition to factories and offices, a town centre with shopping and recreational facilities, and flats and houses for the workpeople. About 90 per cent of those living in the town are either employed in the Bata industry or are their dependants. Many of the dwellings of the workpeople are small detached houses on the outskirts or on the slopes of hills near woods. They do not line roads but are in large groups orientated according to the sun.

The whole central area is planned on a grid 20 feet by 20 feet. This permits the standardization of building components and makes for speed and economy in construction. Most of the factories have gridiron façades, with the uprights at 20-foot centres, variously filled with glass and opaque materials, often in horizontal bands, but rarely prominent enough to counteract the gridiron effect which is so persistent throughout the town as to afford a very monotonous impression. All the buildings are square blocks and one sighs for a curve here and there and a little more variety. Here is an example where standardization and the obtrusiveness of grid planning has not had happy results; few of the buildings have much architectural interest. The employment here and there of the mushroom column and slab construction in which structural members are behind a glass screen and the introduction of a few curved forms would have given welcome variety.

Some of the noteworthy building of this kind in Europe during this period is found among the Cooperative factories and warehouses such as those in Sweden and the head office of the Cooperative Societies of Holland at Handelskamer designed by H. F. Mertens, which is an interesting reinforced concrete construction with upper storeys cantilevered out beyond the lowest storey, and with long bands of glass. Other noteworthy examples are the Hachette Warehouse in Paris, the Public Garage in Venice, and the Tobacco Factory at Linz in Austria.

The buildings for the Cooperative Union in Sweden were designed by Eskil Sundahl or designed under his surveillance. One whole group of industrial buildings together with workmen's dwellings occupy the small island of Kvarnholm off Stockholm. These comprise the various factories and warehouses concerned with the supply of commodities for the various Cooperative shops. A particularly interesting building is the Luma Electric Light Bulb Factory situated near Hammarbyleder on the shore of Lake Maler. Gardens slope down from the factory towards the lake. It is a large building of five storeys, and consists of three wings projecting towards the lake and connected with a long transverse block. The right wing (looking from the lake) projects a little farther than the others and is surmounted by a glass room in which thousands of bulbs are tested. This gives brilliant illumination, and is a landmark at night for the whole of Stockholm. The building is constructed of a reinforced concrete frame with large horizontal windows between the uprights, and narrow horizontal bands in the wings. In the other façade alternate floors have no windows, the rooms here being used for testing purposes.

At Avestad, near the Dale River, is a large factory built to the design of Vihelm Reinhardt for the Swedish Aluminium Co, for the production of aluminium bars, ingots, and plates. It was necessarily controlled in its planning by the processes of manufacture, yet the exterior presents a symmetrical arrangement of two massive black towers connected by long two-storey blocks with large horizontal windows, the exterior walls being sprayed with aluminium paint producing a light hue in contrast to the black towers. The building is constructed of a steel frame. It is noteworthy as being an example of speed and economy in factory building consistent with a degree of architectural merit. It is about 460 feet long by about 40 feet wide, with one wing about 82 feet long, and yet this large building took only six weeks to erect. The speed and economy was possible because of the adoption of a grid, and the use of a large number of standardized units of the same size, on the principle of the Crystal Palace structure.

The Hachette Warehouse in Paris was designed by Jean Demaret. It is a seven-storeyed building occupying a corner site at an angle of about 100° and is constructed by the mushroom column and slab method. The façade consists of long unbroken horizontal glass screens alternating with narrow opaque bands from floor to approximately table or bench level height. The bands make an unbroken curve round the corner, and an especially interesting feature is that the third, fourth, and fifth floors project beyond the lower floors for a little distance from the long façade and round the short façade. This means that these floors are cantilevered a little farther out from the supports, the value of the feature being that more space is thereby obtained, while it serves to give some architectural variety. The whole building represents a straightforward employment of modern methods of construction in which bands of glass admit almost the maximum of light, while the long horizontal emphasis and the variation given by the upper floor projections produce an appearance expressive of its function and which please with a certain dynamic quality. The uncompromising and unchecked horizontality suggests movement and life, the antithesis of repose.

In its light structural effect the huge Public Garage at Venice is reminiscent of the early projects of Mies van der Rohe. When the road connecting Venice with the mainland was built, this garage was erected. The design was a combined production of the Venetian Municipality and the Azienda Generale Italiana Petrole. It is a six-storey building with long wide glass bands continuing unbroken round all corners for almost the whole circuit of the building, with its length of 650 feet and a considerable breadth, and arrested only by the square blocks at two corners which enclose the spiral ramps, apparent from the segmented façade and long vertical windows. The building is constructed mainly of reinforced concrete framework, with supports set

231

back from the external screens, thus allowing the unbroken bands of glass. Here is a huge building constructed with the utmost economy of material means, with light interiors and a simple and pleasing general effect.

Commenced in 1931 and completed in 1935, the large tobacco factory at Linz was designed by Peter Behrens and Alexander Popp for the Austrian State Tobacco Regie. It is one of the largest, and certainly one of the most impressive, factories in Europe. It replaces an old factory on the same site. The plot is a long rectangle with buildings on three sides, and on the fourth and east side three blocks for the tobacco stores abut endwise connected by a bridge with roadways between. Two buildings of the group are retained from the old factory (blocks marked B and K on the plan). In the open space in the centre of the group of buildings are the boiler machine shop and power station in a building with large glass screens and slender framework. Also in the centre is a recreation area with trees.

The first part of this factory to be built was the section devoted to the manufacture of cigarettes comprising the long narrow six-storeyed curved block on the south side facing the Ludlgasse. The construction is a steel frame with uprights spaced at approximately four-metre intervals. The steel frame is set a little back from the long slightly convex façade and this allows for uninterrupted glass bands the whole length of the building alternating with bands of brickwork faced with rendering. The wide projecting eaves give emphasis to this long horizontality. The slight curve accentuates the rhythm and gives it a powerful dynamic quality. Many façades had been built before with a similar treatment of long horizontal bands of glass, but only Mendelsohn's Schocken store at Chemnitz, built in 1928 (see Chapter 18) has a comparably dramatic effect, and may have inspired the façade of the Linz factory. The actual length of the Linz factory surpasses anything previously built and the question does arise whether the movement might have not been a little more pleasing if it had been arrested at an earlier point. Be that as it may this façade remains one of the most dramatically impressive in modern architecture. The north façade of this long block is punctuated with two vertical projecting masses which house staircases, and these break the horizontal treatment which is otherwise maintained. The motif thus set is continued in almost all the other blocks, and one result is a general effect of lightness. At the entrance on the south side, between the gates and in the centre of a bridge made by the buildings, is a semi-circular projection which is designed mainly as a decorative feature. The projection is mainly of glass with a band of symbolic sculpture, one feature, it would appear, belonging to the new architecture, the other feature one that might take its place naturally on a building in the classical tradition: yet there is no sense of disharmony; indeed, there is a pleasing sense of unity. The sculpture seems to be in a crystal setting and acquires thereby a definite dramatic emphasis[2].

An architecturally distinctive factory in England that has been admired and studied by

Roche Products Factory, Welwyn Garden City, 1939
Architect: O. R. Salvisberg (extension by *L. A. Culliford and Partners* in 1956)

Battersea Power Station. Construction was in two sections: the west section with two chimneys was commenced in 1929 and completed in 1933; the east section was commenced in 1944 and completed in 1946 when two further chimneys were added
Architect: Sir Giles Gilbert Scott

architects and students ever since it was erected in 1936–7 is that for Roche Products at Welwyn Garden City, designed by Professor O. R. Salvisberg in association with C. Stanley Brown. Instead of a formal block of offices backed by a series of sheds that served as a factory as was rather common in England during the thirties, all parts of this Roche Products factory: the administrative section, offices, laboratories and workshops, are designed as an architectural unity in a pleasant setting surrounded by extensive lawns. The generous site permitted later extensions which were carried out after the Second World War. The plan of the building is controlled by logical interpretation of purpose without concessions to traditional formal symmetry; yet although the design is strictly functional the spirit of classical serenity pervades the design as in most of Salvisberg's work. There is a pleasing balance of verticals and horizontals which gives an impression of repose.

POWER STATIONS

Among the largest industrial structures are electricity generating stations, gas works, collieries, grain elevators, warehouses and various kinds of storage structures, and the various structures and stations involved in transportation. (The last mentioned are considered in Chapter 46.) Until the early twentieth century structures connected with fuel and power were not thought of as architecture, and gas works and the increasingly large power stations were from the visual standpoint generally regarded as necessary evils. However, because electricity power stations were such conspicuous structures in the urban scene some attention began to be paid in the twenties to making them as visually attractive as possible, and some visually pleasing power stations were erected in the twenties and early thirties at Klingenberg in Germany, at Budapest (Virgil Bierbauer, architect), at Vasteras in Sweden (Erik Hahr, architect), at Rotterdam (the Municipal architects), and at Zurich (J. Salvisberg, architect). The public interest in the appearance of power stations was partly because of their increasing size and greater urban obtrusiveness. The circumstances attending the building of Battersea Power Station illustrate the public interest in the appearance of such structures. When it was proposed to build a large electricity power station on the south bank of the River Thames, immediately east of Chelsea Bridge and Battersea Park and opposite Chelsea Embankment and Grosvenor Road on the north side of the river, there was a public outcry against a large power station being built in this prominent position in the London scene. The Electricity Authority in reply to the storm of protest said that this site near the river was the most suitable in every way, that it was not possible to find an equally satisfactory site elsewhere, but as a concession to the objection the services of a reputable architect would be secured to design a shell and stacks that it was hoped would be of pleasing appearance. Sir Giles Scott was commissioned to design the building. The result is a massive well proportioned brick structure, with narrow vertical windows and decorative motifs of short verticals and a sequence of articulated rectangular forms as bases to the tall chimneys (see Chapter 14). Shortly after it was erected, the *London Evening Standard* asked its readers to vote for what they considered the most beautiful modern building in London, and this Battersea Power Station received the greatest number of votes. It still appears to most people as an impressive and visually satisfactory building.

Being a visual success it inevitably exerted an influence on the building of subsequent power stations during the thirties, and there consequently arose the criticism that power stations were being built like cathedrals, and that the exteriors of these impressive buildings did not express either the function of the power station or its internal arrangement. They are frankly decorative brick boxes. It was argued that a power station does not require such a heavy cladding, that light screens with large windows are adequate, and that, indeed, it is necessary to cover only some of the plant, while the other plant can be left exposed. From the standpoint of the urban environment there is, of course, no objection to this partial covering of power station plant provided that the general visual effect is agreeable. It would be better to have a power station looking like a cathedral, if this implication carries a building of impressive yet pleasing appearance, than a power station in which half the machinery is covered and half exposed resulting in uncoordinated parts, even though the function is expressed in the design. Where visual considerations are important, machinery is generally put in a box often carefully designed like the bonnet of a car. These developments belong mainly to the period after the Second World War when a large number of electricity generating stations were built and many experimental designs materialized.

Reference has been so far to steam power stations, with coal and oil as the two principal fuels. Hydro-electric development sets a slightly different set of problems and involves a greater variety of structures, while it has less effect on the urban scene as the structures are generally sited in mountainous districts well away from towns. Hydro-electric development involves the construction of dams to impound water, of tunnels and pipes to convey the water, sometimes a considerable distance, and the construction of the power stations. Such constructional work, principally the dam and the power station is often in rather beautiful country and consideration must be given, therefore, to harmonizing the structures with the surrounding country so as not to spoil its beauty. The risk of spoiling beautiful country has often been one of the main objections to such schemes, but it must be admitted that hydro-electric development in Europe has hardly ever spoiled the beauty of the landscape, and in some cases, as in Scotland, has actually enhanced it[3].

REFERENCES AND NOTES

1. The earlier developments of mushroom slab construction are described in Chapter 6.
2. This factory is described and illustrated in *Die Neubauten und Betriebseinrichtungen der Tabakfabrik in Linz*, Salzburg, 1936.
3. See *Power From Water* by T. A. L. Paton and J. Guthrie Brown, Leonard Hill, London, 1960, especially Chapter XXII Amenities.

18   Departmental stores

THE REQUIREMENTS OF DESIGN presented by the departmental store and the large multi-floor shop, although different in many respects from those of the factory building, are yet similar in the important matter of being well lighted. The departmental store, in which are displayed goods on several floors, and which necessitates free and easy movement of customers, requires to be one very large principal room or sequence of large rooms on each floor partially divided by partitions, with adjacent offices. It is essential that each room should be as well lighted as possible, and although there is one school of thought which suggests complete dependence on artificial light, many progressive designers would rather find the solution of the problem in the admittance of the maximum daylight. For most people there is no adequate substitute for daylight, while there is a considerable exhilarating feeling, even in a departmental store, for workers and customers alike to see the bright spring sunlight after the dark days of winter. With extensive floor areas complete dependence on daylight, however large the windows, is not always possible and artificial light has to be maintained constantly in the rear areas. This could be obviated by the introduction of a light well, which would contribute to admitting light from both sides, and minimize the amount of artificial light, but this means a sacrifice of space which in the centre of a large city can ill be spared. An important social question is whether anybody should be condemned to work always in artificial light if it could possibly be avoided, and building regulations should be formulated accordingly.

In many departmental stores, however, even when large windows have been provided, amounting almost to glass walls, they are frequently not utilized and partitions and furniture are sometimes placed so that they partly obscure the windows and make artificial lighting more extensive than it need be. In big drapery stores both assistants and customers often find this a nuisance, and have to take dress materials some distance to the rare places of natural lighting for an accurate judgement of colour. A later development is the windowless wall and complete dependence on artificial light which in the opinion of many people is rather an inhuman development.

236

The departmental store is a modern type of building, with no old traditional prototypes. The first of any size in Europe was the Magasin au Bon Marché in Paris, built in 1876; but there was an interesting anticipation of the modern departmental store in Schinkel's project of 1820 (see Chapter 3). After the Bon Marché store several were built, one of the most progressive in its construction and expression being Messel's Wertheim store in Berlin, built in 1896. The main tendency in departmental store design in the next twenty years was the simplication of the classical façade and gradual enlargement of the windows. A famous and typical example of a departmental store of this period is the 'Samaritaine' store in Paris, built in 1905 to the designs of Franz Jourdain and Henri Sauvage. In this windows occupy almost the whole space between the widely spaced upright piers, that is up to the sixth floor, where set-backs and ornamental effects break this simplicity. This type of design deriving from the classical façade is modified towards greater simplicity and lightness of stone or other facing, and greater expanse of glass. A typical late example is the store of Kendal Milne and Co, at Manchester, designed by J. Beaumont and Sons. A store like that at the Hague, designed by Paul Kramer in 1926, is in this direct line of evolution. The steel frame and reinforced concrete frame are used simply and directly with increasing spans to obtain these larger areas of glass. But it was not until the full potentialities of steel and concrete construction were applied to a logical interpretation of purpose, as distinct from treatment guided by traditional design, that a more completely appropriate form for the departmental store was evolved.

These developments, as in factory buildings, made possible the cantilevering of floors beyond the structural supports, so that the outer wall could be merely a glass screen unbroken by the main structural members.

In many factory designs, such as the Boots's factory, a glass screen encloses the building broken only by the thin line of the floor slab. But where working-benches are placed against the outer walls there is no point in having the glass screen below the level of the bench; it is far better to have an opaque band. In the departmental store the treatment of the external walls depends very much on the interior arrangement, particularly on the placing of the counters and the fittings at their rear and on the placings of showcases and larger objects for sale like furniture. If counters are placed near the external wall, with fittings against the wall, then the window should obviously begin above the fittings. The question is how high should the fittings be taken so as to keep the admission of light as near as possible to a maximum. If the room is 12 feet high and the counter is 2 feet 9 inches high, fittings about 4 feet high would give a window nearly 8 feet high. If an approach to the maximum amount of light is to be secured the fittings should certainly not be higher. This arrangement thus determines the functional façade of long horizontal glass bands alternating with opaque bands.

237

The alternative arrangement of placing the counters away from the external wall, leaving the adjacent space as a corridor for customers, would permit the whole wall to be glass and thus admit more light. It was no doubt an arrangement of this kind which prompted Ludwig Mies van der Rohe to make his designs for Adam's shop in the Leipziger Strasse in Berlin and for the departmental store at Stuttgart. These two projects show the structural supports set well back from the façades which are practically complete glass screens, broken only by the thickness of the floors. They remained only projects and it is doubtful whether they would have been built like this, for in no departmental store yet built, as far as I am aware, has such an arrangement been employed. The arrangement of counters backing on to the walls with fittings behind seems generally to be preferred, and where it is not employed there does not seem to be great value in having a source of light much below 3 feet from the floor. Thus, even in the most progressive designs the opaque band to a certain height above the floor is employed.

In the design with substantial vertical shafts the glass is from floor to ceiling between these shafts, but such designs emanate less from interior organization than from classical tradition in the treatment of the façade. It will be found that the vertical shafts take a good deal of light that would be valuable.

Although the admission of light for every floor is important, it is particularly so with the ground floor on which there is the additional purpose of securing as large transparent areas as possible for the display of goods, and it is of advantage if the expanse of glass is not interrupted by structural supports. Thus we find generally in the progressive examples of the nineteen-twenties that while the structural members appear in the upper façade various devices are employed to remove them from the ground floor windows. Later we find examples of the whole façade thrust well forward from the structural supports.

MENDELSOHN'S DESIGNS

The outstanding achievements in this field of architectural design during the period from 1924 to 1933 before the National Socialist Government in Germany are the large shop and departmental store buildings designed by Eric Mendelsohn. The first of these is the Herpich Fur Store in the Leipziger Strasse, built in 1924. This was followed by the Schocken stores at Nürnberg, Stuttgart, and Chemnitz built in 1925, 1926, and 1928 respectively, and the Petersdorff store at Breslau built in 1927. In the Herpich store the structural supports are set back very slightly from the frontage which consists in the upper floors of wide bands of glass with bronze frames separated by wide bronze window sills and bands of cream limestone, the two upper floors being set back. The shop window on the ground floor is a wide expanse of glass broken only by the slender metal frames, the widely spaced structural columns appearing just behind the glass front. Underneath the bronze window-sills are troughs for concealed

238

lighting, which at night reflects on to the bands of limestone, and on the ground
floor illuminates the firm's name. By the use of concealed lighting, which is also used
in the show-cases, the spectator from the street is not dazzled. A claim for this building
is that it was the first to be displayed at night by calculated effects of lighting.

The principle of construction adopted is a steel frame set a little back from the façade
which is thus a screen attached to cantilevered supports. The same principle was
followed for the ground floor and in the upper floors, but in the latter broader bronze
uprights cover the structural supports than in the ground floor, where these are
negligible.

The Schocken store at Stuttgart was one of Mendelsohn's most famous buildings, and
has been widely imitated. Unfortunately in 1955 it was demolished because of an
urban renewal and town planning scheme. Altogether this was a very original and
unusual design at the time. Built in 1926, the steel frame construction was employed,
and the ground floor on the principal front was thrust forward from this frame so
as to secure an unbroken glass screen. The name 'Schocken' appeared in large
letters above the projecting ground floor. The store occupied an island site with the
principal façade of five storeys to the north. The building had a light well towards the
south, and there was a considerable area of floor space between this and the principal
front of the building. Horizontal glass windows ran nearly the whole length of the
principal façade broken by the structural uprights, which were not sufficient to disturb
this horizontal emphasis. Between the windows were alternating bands of brick and
golden travertine. This horizontal movement was arrested at the west end by a
cantilevered semicircular glass tower, enclosing a spiral staircase, a feature which
Mendelsohn often employed to arrest a long horizontal movement. Although circular
glass staircase towers were used symmetrically at either end of the Cologne exhibition
building, designed by Gropius and Meyer in 1914, their use by Mendelsohn is entirely
different. In the Schocken store at Stuttgart the glass tower, enclosed in steel rings, is
cantilevered out and the aesthetic purpose is partly to arrest movement, like a passage
of music being arrested by a vibrating chord. Mendelsohn generally conceived his
buildings three-dimensionally by rough perspective sketches, and in this store he
balances this glass tower with the staircase tower in the middle of the eastern façade
which rises above the rest of the building and presents a high circular front to the
centre of the building. The balance is clearly seen in the drawing looking down on the
building, but the effect was lost from the street. It will be seen from the illustration that
the horizontal bands continued unbroken round the corner and along the eastern façade,
to be stopped by this second staircase tower, which had a flat façade to the street.

The Petersdorff store at Breslau built in 1927 represents considerable progress in
construction. The façade of the upper floors is thrust forward 11 feet from the structural
upright and is thus a screen consisting of long bands of glass, with slender bronze

frames, alternating with bands of golden travertine edged with the bronze window sills and cornices for the upper floors, and a complete glass front for the ground floor which is set back from the upper wall. Occupying a corner site, the long bands turn in a semi-circular finish which is cantilevered out beyond the ground floor. This is an interesting variation of the glass tower motif.

The Schocken store at Chemnitz[1], built in 1928, is simpler, more direct, and more impressive than any so far considered, and in the opinion of many it is the most beautiful departmental store building in Europe. It occupies a site with a curved front in the Bruckenstrasse at a point where two minor streets join it, and it is this curved front which provided Mendelsohn with his opportunity. The floor plan is roughly the sector of a circle with a radius of about 150 feet, and the circumference forming the frontage about 250 feet. It is a nine-storey building with the three upper storeys set back. The construction is a reinforced concrete frame, with the façade thrust well forward on the cantilever principle from the structural uprights. Thus for nearly the whole length of the façade there are the horizontal window bands, framed in oak, and alternating with bands of golden travertine of almost the same width. In the three upper recessed storeys the structural uprights appear, while the flat roof projects outwards and emphasizes the great curved lines of the building. The two ends are recessed, forming large flat glass vertical panels with grill effect, facing the staircase and lifts. The practical purpose of admitting the maximum light through the screen is achieved, while at the same time the magnificent sweep of these long horizontal bands curving on the convex front has an exhilarating effect. The horizontal movement is sustained for a satisfying moment, and is finely arrested at either end by the vertical glass panels of the staircases. The light rich hue of the golden travertine contrasting with the variegated darks and lights of the windows helps the impressive effect by day, while at night the bright yellow bands of the windows contrasting with the dark opaque bands give a stronger dramatic, if less subtle, effect.

Many of the progressive designs for store buildings in Europe followed the work of Mendelsohn, for from 1927 to 1933 Mendelsohn's influence in departmental store design was probably greater than that of any other architect.

Interesting for the lightness of its steel frame and the cantilevering outwards of the upper floors, so as to get an uninterrupted glass screen for the ground floor, is the small Backner departmental store at Moravska Ostrava in Czechoslovakia, designed by Johannes Schreiner in 1931. Schreiner had assisted Mendelsohn in the departmental stores described, and thus had considerable experience of this type of design. The point about the Backner store is that it is an early example of the upper floors being cantilevered out from the ground floor. The lightness of the steel frame seems to have influenced the light treatment of the façades with the long horizontal windows divided

Herpich Fur Store, Berlin, 1924

Schocken Store, Stuttgart, 1926

*Architect of all buildings on
this page: Eric Mendelsohn*

Sketch showing layout of building
on an island site, and ground floor
plan at the Stuttgart Store.
(This building was demolished to
make room for a road widening
scheme.)

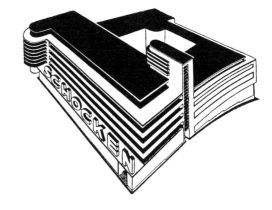

Petersdorff Store, Breslau, 1927

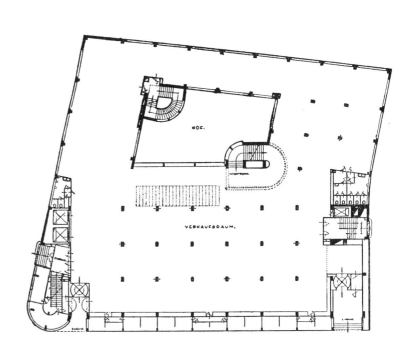

by slender uprights. The spaces between the frame are filled with brick and the walls are faced with stone-coloured ceramic tiles.

Among the other noteworthy store buildings in Germany, in addition to those by Mendelsohn, are the Breuninger store at Stuttgart, designed by Eisenlohr and Pfenning in 1929, and the Telshow Haus Berlin, designed by Alfons Anker and Wassili and Hans Luckhardt in 1928. Both show the use of horizontal bands as in Mendelsohn's work, and both are constructed with the upper floors cantilevered out a little beyond the ground floor. Telshow Haus has a curved front which adds to its effect.

About this time (1929–30) rose the impressive 'De Byenkorf' departmental store on a prominent corner site at Rotterdam. Designed by W. M. Dudok it had many of the characteristics of this architect's work as seen in his buildings of the twenties and early thirties, especially in the composition of masses. It was a six-storey building and both of the principal façades were mainly of glass. The longer façade had three narrow brick-faced bands, marking the second, third, and fourth storeys, and these extended beyond the glass façade and formed balconies on to the large brick vertical mass at the corner. Thus, as in many of the school designs, the horizontal movement was arrested by the vertical mass. In the other façade the glass theme was followed a little differently. Here the floor divisions were even narrower, while the movement terminated in a tall narrow tower surmounted by a beacon light for advertisement purposes. The whole was a felicitous composition in which the main elements were horizontal emphasis balanced by vertical masses, conceived in glass and yellow brick walls in the corner masses and as a frieze of the long façade.

What made it efficient as a departmental store was the large admission of light which the glass walls permitted. Unfortunately one half (the part away from the corner) was destroyed during the heavy raid on Rotterdam in 1940, and the remainder was demolished in conformity with the town planning schemes for Rotterdam.

The International Fair Building at Prague, erected in 1928 to the designs of Josef Fuchs and Oldrich Tyll, is a very large building occupying an island site. In its centre is a large hall surrounded by galleries, which open on to the long glass windows that run completely round the building. Above the first floor the front is cantilevered out except for the staircase and lift towers. Thus the structural supports are set behind the screen. This can clearly be seen in the illustration. The large glass areas, and the absence in the upper floors of any bulky uprights, give this large building an astonishingly light effect. Similar in its general effect is the large office building in Oslo, 'Odd Fellow Garden', designed in 1931 by Gudolf Blakstad and Herman Munthe-Koas. Two store buildings in Oslo which appear to show the influence of Mendelsohn are the twin buildings called 'Storm Bullgarden' and the building called, 'Dobloug Garden',

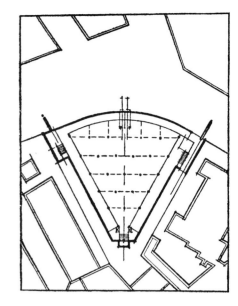

Schocken Store, Chemnitz, 1928,
(now Karlmarxstadt). Night view
and site plan
Architect: Eric Mendelsohn

'De Bijenkorf' Department Store at Rotterdam, 1929–30
Architect: W. M. Dudok

Peter Jones Departmental Store, Sloane Square, London,
1935–36 *Architects: J. A. Slater, A. H. Moberly and
William Crabtree with Sir Charles Reilly as consultant*

International Fair building, Prague, 1928
Architects: Josef Fuchs and Oldrich Tyll

The Dobloug Garden Store, Oslo, 1930
Architect: Ove Bang

both built about 1930. The latter with its curved front is strongly reminiscent of the Schocken store at Chemnitz, with its nine storeys, its long alternating glass and opaque bands, its three recessed upper storeys, and its recessed terminations at either end. But it lacks the dramatic emphasis (such as is given in the cantilevered roof), the fine proportion, and the artistic subtleties of the Schocken store.

Built a few years later, 1935–36, is the Peter Jones departmental store, in London, of which William Crabtree in association with J. A. Slater and A. H. Moberly were the architects with Sir Charles Reilly as consultant. It occupies an island site on the west side of Sloane Square. It is a steel frame construction similar in principle to the construction of Mendelsohn's Columbushaus built four years earlier (see next chapter). The main structural members are set back which permits a four storey light screen façade above the first floor supported on a cantilevered beam. This façade has horizontal window bands alternating with bands of greyish green, while slender mullions fairly closely spaced extend the four storeys. The shop windows on the ground floor are almost uninterrupted glass areas. The sixth floor is set well back with an overhanging roof.

The screen façade generously curved at the corners gives the building a very light appearance, yet in this commanding position it has an imposing and majestic effect which makes it an architectural asset to a square not distinguished by any other notable building.

REFERENCES AND NOTES

1. The name of the city has been changed from Chemnitz to Karlmarxstadt. It is, of course, in East Germany.

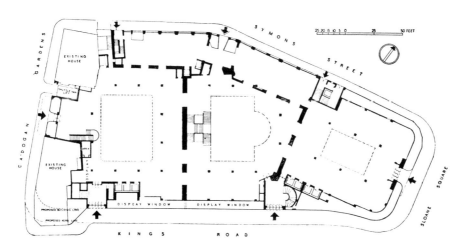

Ground floor plan
Peter Jones store
London

19   Office buildings

OFFICE BUILDINGS OFFER problems akin to those of departmental stores, but with
certain important differences dictated by differences of purpose. It is necessary to state
this obvious fact because there cannot really be any satisfactory interchange of use
from one to the other in a building of any size as has sometimes been done in the past.
Whereas in the departmental store there is the principle of one large room on each
floor, in the office building if this is adopted for some of the floors there must be
scope for partitioning in the event of adaptations for use while in many office
buildings each floor is divided by walls into comparatively small compartments.
Where in the former, light would penetrate some distance from large windows, with
perhaps only the rear portions of the floor requiring artificial light, in the office block
all the small compartments require their source of light. Thus if the block has a fairly
large area and is between other buildings in a street, the light well is essential. That
this light well has so often not been adequate for its purpose means that the rooms on
the lower floors facing on to the well must depend on artificial light.

Often too, a wide expanse of floor between two outer walls has been divided into
four rows of offices, meaning that the inner rooms depend on artificial light. Attempts
have often been made to overcome this difficulty by having glass partitions either
transparent or translucent between the rooms, but sufficient light rarely penetrates
from the windows through the partitions (often double, to allow for a corridor
between) to the inner rooms. This arrangement also has other disadvantages. It has
poor sound insulation, while even with translucent glass, the possibility of some
degree of privacy, which is often desirable in an office, is greatly diminished. Examples
of four rows of rooms with the two inner rows depending partially or wholly on
artificial light in the daytime is now rare but where it occurs it can only be regarded
as bad design, in which the building is not well suited for the purpose it has to serve.
The large open plan which some managements introduce is rarely popular with the
staff and it is doubtful whether it conduces to concentration and efficiency.
The contention with regard to departmental stores must be repeated in the case of

offices—that workers should not be condemned to work always in artificial light, and that buildings should be designed so as to provide adequate daylight for all the offices. This is often difficult in the central high-density areas of large cities, but it provides an argument among many others for adequate standards of space and for a measure of dispersal from congested centres to make these standards possible. The skyscraper is only a partial solution, while by increasing density it creates transport problems.

The designing of an office block is conditioned very largely by the site, its size, and whether the specific purpose is known, that is, whether it is designed to accommodate a particular company or public body, or whether it is built as office premises to be let in sections to various tenants. It is far more satisfactory to design an office block where the specific purpose is known, because the steel or concrete frame can be designed in relation to the desired compartments, and the building can be designed almost perfectly to suit requirements. In the case of a speculative building, to be let to various tenants, it sometimes happens that the required sizes of rooms do not accord with the design of the building, and sometimes partitions between offices abut the centres of windows, or that a room is inadequately lighted by only a small portion of a window. The solution to this problem, however, is the adoption of long unbroken horizontal glass bands, so that, no matter where the partition is placed, the rooms can be assured of adequate light. Some office blocks have been designed to enable partitions to be fitted at any number of alternative points. It is also important in premises to be let to tenants that the distance from one outer wall to the other is not too great. In a site with considerable depth from the street this means the introduction of a light well. Otherwise it means four rows of rooms with the two inner depending almost wholly on artificial light, whereas two rows of rooms each with windows and a central corridor should be the invariable rule with blocks of any size.

Office buildings can be roughly divided into four categories according to the site: an island site, one on which three sides are open, a corner site, and that between two or three other buildings. Offices for public bodies and municipal offices combined with the County or Town Hall often belong to the first category. This combination has sometimes inhibited progressive design, because the dignity of the County or Town Hall has often meant an adherence to classical tradition, to which the design of the offices on the upper floors must conform. In the offices of large independent institutions, or big commercial enterprises there is occasionally progressive design arising from the logical fulfilment of purpose.

One of the most impressive and efficient of office buildings in Europe built between the World Wars is the General Pensions Institute in Prague, designed by Josef Havlíček and Karel Honzík. The design of these architects, subsequently somewhat modified, won the first prize in a competition in 1929, and the building was erected in 1931–3. It has a cruciform plan with additional blocks at either end. In its plan it thus has some

The General Pensions Institute, Prague, Czechoslovakia, 1931–33. Plan of building. View of main block (north-south axis) and one of the flanking blocks (east-west). Reinforced concrete frame construction　　　　　*Architects: Josef Havlíček and Karel Honzík*

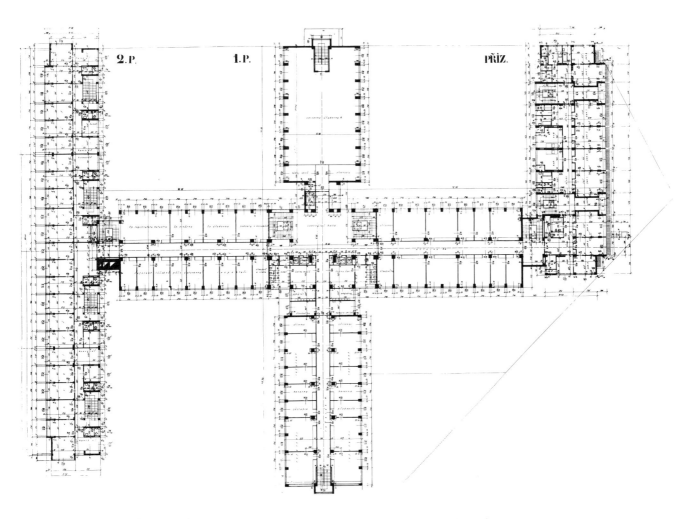

resemblance to the London Passenger Transport Building in London, but the latter, with its large recessed masses culminating in a central tower, is a building in which monumental dignity has been a definite aim; it is essentially in the classical tradition, whereas in the Pensions Building logical fulfilment of purpose has been the principal guide, with little consideration of traditional appearance. The Prague building also has the advantage of a more spacious setting.

The main part of the building forming the cross, on plan consists of one fourteen-floor block orientated in a north–south direction, and a nine-floor block crossing it at right angles in an east–west direction. At the north and south ends are blocks running east–west; that at the north end consists of a row of shops facing on the street, with two rentable office floors above, and that at the south end consists of a block of three-storey flats for the office staff. The building is constructed of a reinforced concrete frame, which is designed on a grid of 11 feet 2 inches by 19 feet to correspond with the office units. The horizontal windows are separated vertically only by the concrete uprights, and are divided by long horizontal bands. The building is faced with ceramic slabs of a yellowish hue and a special sprinkling plant is installed on the edge of the roof for the purpose of cleaning the walls and glass surfaces. These ceramic tiles have a matt surface, which means that they weather pleasingly. A highly glazed surface, apart from reflecting light, hardly weathers, and thus rarely harmonizes with its surroundings. The Prague Pensions Building depends on air conditioning plant for ventilation and for heating. Although the extremes of heat and cold are considerable in Prague, the temperature is kept fairly constant, so that it is not only considerably higher than that outside on a cold winter's day, but considerably lower on a hot summer's day.

Efficient functioning is the aim in the design of the building and its architecture arises from this. The monumental character of the London Passenger Transport Building has been cited as a contrast. The Prague building is larger, yet it has a lightness of effect achieved by the windows stretching between the comparatively slender frame of the building, which is totally different from the heavy, massive transport building. It is the difference between the last stages of the old classical architecture and a new architecture in which the materials and methods of modern science and industry are fully utilized[1].

Two office buildings designed by Eric Mendelsohn are among the most noteworthy European examples, and merit the closest study. Both built in Berlin, one being the offices of the Metal Workers' Union (subsequently of the German Labour Front) erected in 1928, and the other the famous Columbushaus erected in 1931. The building of the Metal Workers' Union occupies the triangular space made by the fork of two streets. The plan approximates to the sector of a circle, but is cut near the centre by the curved front forming the central block of six storeys. The two wings, each of five storeys which radiate, appear to clasp this central mass like pincers. With the curved rear block of two storeys designed to house the printing works of the official journal of the Union, they all surround a central courtyard, which thus acts as a light-well for the offices on the upper floors. The building is constructed of a reinforced concrete frame and faced with cream rendering. Long horizontal windows with bronze frames alternate with these cream bands on the wings, and the horizontal movement is continued in the principal front. I understand that this principal front, being a vertical mass, was originally designed with strong vertical emphasis by means of pilaster-like shafts over the concrete frame uprights, but this was abandoned for the present arrangement. The purpose of this change was due to the greater light being admitted by the adopted design. It is interesting to consider which design would have been the more aesthetically pleasing. The strong vertical emphasis contrasting with the long horizontals of the wings would have been more dramatic and would have been an interesting but very different variation of the theme, seen in the Schocken Store at Stuttgart, of the musical chord arresting the horizontal movement. But as design should arise from the fulfilment of purpose, that adopted is the more satisfactory from such a standpoint. What is lost in dramatic contrast is perhaps more than compensated for by a greater degree of harmony. The question also arises whether there is sufficient aesthetic justification for the first treatment. The chief consideration is that this is an exceedingly well-designed block of offices, with well-lighted rooms, with a general feeling of structural lightness, and with a decorative ensemble that appears to emerge from purpose and structure.

The Columbushaus, which occupied a corner site in the Potsdamer Platz, was a twelve-storey building with one frontage of 210 feet and the other of 110 feet. It was slightly convex on the longer front, which greatly helped its effect. It was designed for shops on the ground floor, restaurants on the lower ground floor and first floor, for offices on seven floors, and restaurant with garden at the top. The depth from the long frontage was 100 feet on the ground and first floors and 80 feet above, the projection of the former being at the rear. This made it sufficiently narrow to admit adequate light for each floor. Lifts and staircases were near the centre, with additional staircases at either end. The staircase at the end of the shorter frontage was expressed on the façade by a vertical grille.

The steel-frame construction of the building merits special study. A heavy stanchion which ran round the building was cantilevered out 5 feet 3 inches at second floor level. This stanchion took the main weight of the steel framework above, and permitted the heavier framework to be kept back from the front, while the weight was transferred to the heavy stanchions below. The garden restaurant on the top floor was sheltered by a roof cantilevered 20 feet.

The slender uprights of the windows were spaced at 6 feet intervals and were designed so as to accommodate a partition which made possible the utmost flexibility in the division of offices. The long glass bands alternating with bands of polished golden travertine continued unbroken along both fronts of the building, arrested only at one end by the vertical staircase grille. The movement was emphasized by the cantilevered roof.

The design appeared to be graced with that simplicity that is akin to the chasteness of early Greek Art, and this gave it a note of harmony with Schinkel's little Greek temples situated on either side of the Leipzig Strasse where it joined the Potsdamer Platz. The situation of the Columbushaus on a corner site open to the Potsdamer Platz, where it could be seen from many viewpoints, helped to reveal the architectural merits of the building. Although conveying a feeling of structural lightness it yet had, by reason of its considerable height and long, unbroken horizontal lines, an aspect of grandeur which made it memorable[2]. Mendelsohn had the rare distinction of being the architect of a departmental store at Chemnitz and an office block in Berlin which it would be difficult to surpass or even equal among the buildings of their kind in Europe built between the wars[3]. Alas, the place where Columbushaus once stood is now a desolate scene near the tragic Berlin Wall.

Several other office buildings of a similar character with alternating horizontal window and opaque bands were built at this time. If not possessing quite the same distinction as the examples analysed, they are yet designed with that progressive spirit in which expressive use is made of steel, glass, and concrete. Among noteworthy examples are the Shell Building in Berlin, designed by Professor Fahrenkamp, a few of the Government Department buildings in Moscow, such as that of the Commissariat for Light Industry, designed by Le Corbusier (see p. 255), with its horizontal emphasis and vertical strips, and that of the Commissariat of Agriculture, designed by A. V. Shehoussev, with its semicircular tower reminiscent of Mendelsohn's Stuttgart store. Another noteworthy example is the large office building in Oslo called 'Odd Fellow Garden', designed by Gudolf Blakstad and Herman Munthe-Kaas, and built in 1931. This occupies a site open on three sides, and the glass bands, patterned with very light vertical stanchions and alternating with light opaque bands, continue without a break completely round the building. The transparent appearance that this treatment lends to the corners gives an effect of structural lightness to the whole building.

Similar in purpose to the Columbushaus is Professor O. R. Salvisberg's Bleicherhof office building erected in Zürich eight years later (1939–40), which is occupied by a departmental store on the ground and first floors and by offices on the three upper floors. Like the Mendelsohn building it has a slight convex façade, but it has not the same dynamic quality, being rather a combination of new idioms and classical restraint, a quality that characterizes most of Salvisberg's design. The ground floor windows are set well back from an arcading and covered way. Inside there are two very dramatic elliptical spiral staircases reminiscent of some of the late Renaissance staircases.

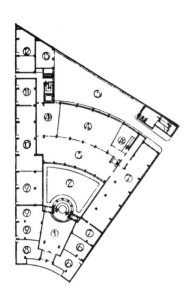

Administration building of the Metal Workers Union, Berlin, 1929
Plan of ground floor of building

Columbushaus, Berlin, 1931
General view from the Potsdamer Platz
Plan of the third to seventh floors

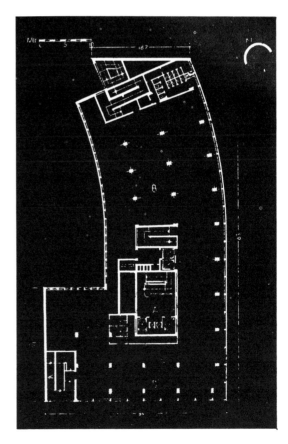

Architect of both buildings: Eric Mendelsohn

Externally the building has a simplicity and quiet classical dignity which make it a very attractive item of street architecture.

SOME ENGLISH EXAMPLES

In England during this period there are very few examples of office buildings of really progressive design. Crawfords' office in Holborn, designed by Herbert Welch and Frederick Etchells in 1927, was regarded, when it was built, as the most modern office block in London, which is an indication of how far behind in modern architectural design London was compared with much that could be seen elsewhere in central and northern Europe. Looked at after nearly half a century, Crawfords' building has little of that light structural effect that is associated with the expensive use of steel and glass. Although there are continuous horizontal opaque bands, the window bands are divided almost into squares by rather massive metal-faced uprights, and this gives a heavy effect.

The only office building in England of this period which seems to rank with the most advanced European examples is Universal House, the building of Beck and Pollitzer at the south end of Southwark Bridge. It was designed by Joseph Emberton in 1931, when the first part, consisting of five storeys with three above the bridge, was built. The narrow thoroughfare of Bankside, which runs along the south side of the Thames, turns a little away from the bank in a diagonal before it passes under Southwark Bridge. It is at this corner that Universal House is built, part of it being supported on stanchions above the slightly curved diagonal road.

The building is constructed of a steel frame with the principal heavy members set back from the façades. This allows for glass bands to run uninterruptedly along the two sides of the building, with narrow opaque bands between. At one end the building projects a little, and the external corners are slightly rounded. The windows, with light metal frames, are taken from table height to the ceiling, so that the opaque bands are considerably narrower. The aim was to get the maximum light, because the purpose for which the building was intended and designed made this of paramount importance. Although only three storeys were completed in 1931, it was designed as a nine-storey block above the bridge with the same treatment throughout. The two top storeys would be set back, and it is ultimately intended to extend the building westwards to connect with Beck and Pollitzer's other premises. The bands between the windows are faced with pale green vitriolite which has a polished surface. The effect of this adds to the general light effect and helps to make the whole building vividly expressive of modern structure, very much in contrast to the heavy drab character of the buildings that surround it.

REFLECTING, GLAZED OR WEATHERING SURFACES IN BUILDINGS

An interesting aesthetic question arises from the use of the polished vitriolite facing.

The weathering of this polished surface is so slight as to have little effect on its general appearance. It will, in fact, if kept clean, retain that bright polished green appearance in thirty years' time, whereas if it had had a stone or brick facing it would have weathered and blended with its surroundings as it could never do with this facing of bright polished green. Some people contend that it is aesthetically desirable that a building after some years should, by weathering, fit harmoniously into its surroundings. It may be argued, on the other hand, that if all buildings were of the same character, that is, consisting of a façade of polished vitriolite, glazed brick, polished granite, glass, or marble, generally with large windows, then a brighter general appearance would be secured and it would merely be a question of form and colour harmony of one building with another. This argument is valid if a whole area is to be rebuilt, or it is a totally new building area. The former is the case with the south bank of the Thames where Universal House is situated; but when it is an area where there are several older buildings that are not likely to be rebuilt for many years, such as public, ecclesiastical, and office buildings, then there is always the risk of a feeling of discord. But if the effect of the building, such as Universal House, is bright and agreeable, the discord is not likely to be serious, and, indeed, may introduce a bright note of contrast which many people may find invigorating. It would be undesirable not to progress in architectural design and experiment with new aesthetic effects because of a possible discord with existing buildings, although such a problem in the hands of a good designer need not often arise. It is questionable whether a building in aggressive rather than mild contrast to its surroundings can be aesthetically acceptable. When the contrast is mild it can add interest and be stimulating, as in the case of the modern buildings so far discussed, but even so it is a question whether facing with a matt surface which weathers, such as the warm buff-coloured slabs of powdered Botticino marble and white Portland stone used for the facing of the Dorchester Hotel, is not preferable, as this facing is weathering very pleasingly. Where, however, in an area of stone or brick buildings large new buildings are faced with polished black granite or polished black glass, the contrast may be so violent as to be environmentally disturbing. Among office buildings there are the *Daily Express* buildings in London and Manchester, which offend many people in this way.

The question may be asked also: is such a building of pleasing appearance in itself without relation to its surroundings? The *Daily Express* office, designed by Ellis and Clarke in association with Sir Owen Williams, is constructed of a reinforced concrete frame and faced with sheets of polished black glass held in position by silver-coloured strips of Burmabright metal. It occupies a corner site, and horizontal window bands continue round both façades from the second to the sixth storey, above which are two recessed storeys faced completely with black glass. The horizontal movement is interrupted on the principal façades by two vertical black glass bands carried to the sixth storey and arranged symmetrically on both sides of the entrance. In architecture, surface texture should conduce to the effect of form, and certainly be subordinate to it.

'Odd Fellow Garden' office building, Oslo, 1931
Architects: Gudolf Blakstad and Herman Munthe-Koas

Offices of the Commissariat of Agriculture, Moscow, 1933
Architect: A. V. Sheho Shehousser

Universal House, Southwark Bridge, London, 1931
(now demolished), with view across the River Thames
Architect: Joseph Emberton

Daily Express office building, Fleet Street,
London, 1930–32
*Architects: Ellis & Clarke in association with
Owen Williams*

Exchange Building, Rotterdam, 1938–39
Architect: J. P. Staat

Palais du Centrosoyus, Ministry of Light
Industries, 1929–33 *Architect: Le Corbusier*

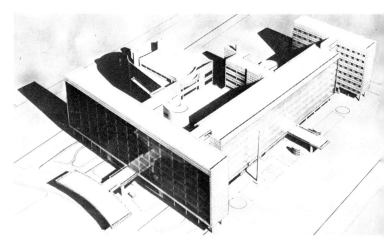

This is best accomplished by subdued colours and textures, like stone and softer-toned brick. But any highly reflecting surface, like polished granite or polished black glass, breaks up the surface into strong lights and shadows, and this disturbs the appreciation of the main form of the building. And never weathering, it will always be like this; it will always jump from its surroundings. Even if the black surface were not polished it is questionable whether it would be an agreeable colour or tone. Light colours are generally more pleasing and exhilarating in the landscape than dark colours[4]. To have many dark colours in one's daily surroundings is apt to be depressing; and to have a city of black buildings, even relieved by fairly large expanses of window, would be a depressing experience. It is difficult to resist the conclusion that for the purpose of advertisement it was aimed to make the *Daily Express* building stand out in strong contrast with its surroundings, and the result is that it can only be regarded as an example of assertiveness in building, and, is rather an unneighbourly building. The Manchester *Daily Express* building is a repetition of a similar effect.

An immense office block in which large glass areas are juxtaposed with stone with good effect is the Centrosoyus building in Moscow (Offices of the Ministry of Light Industries) for 3,500 office workers, designed by Le Corbusier in 1929 and completed after some delays in 1935. A long eight-storey office block is flanked by two transverse wings, the whole raised on columns above the ground floor—the favourite Le Corbusier 'pilotis' device. Horizontal window bands alternate with bands of rose-coloured tuff stone, and the flanking blocks present tall end walls of stone to the street. Provision in the building is made for the recreation of the large staff, and at the rear of the offices a restaurant and large theatre, lecture halls, clubrooms and other leisure facilities are included.

A distinctive and original building that should perhaps be included in the category of office building, although it is also partly of the hall type, is the Exchange building in Rotterdam, on a corner site in Coolsingel, built in 1939–40 and designed by J. P. Staal. It is of reinforced concrete frame construction with the exception of the large exchange hall which has a steel frame and segmental roof, 157 feet span of welded two-hinged trusses, at 39 feet intervals, with the spaces filled with pre-cast concrete slabs holding glass lights. In the centre of this large hall (it is about 250 feet long) is a circular glass pavilion for telephone and telegraph offices. The external appearance is one of lightness and elegance with tall slender square columns supporting, like stilts, the superstructure over a spacious entrance with a broad flight of steps. At the side is a very slender tall bell tower linked with the main building by a glass enclosed stairway. Although the centre of Rotterdam was rebuilt after the destruction in the Second World War, and many notable buildings were erected, this Exchange holds its own as one of the most distinctive.

References and Notes

1. This building is fully described and illustrated in Alfred Roth's *The New Architecture*, Zürich, 1940.
2. The Columbushaus unfortunately no longer exists. Although it survived the Second World War, it was blown up in the process of building the Berlin wall.
3. More detailed accounts of Mendelsohn's buildings are given in Arnold Whittick, *Eric Mendelsohn*, London, 1956.
4. I remember Sir Giles Gilbert Scott saying at a conference on the Bankside Power Station that we should have light-toned materials, like light brick, as facings for our buildings as the effect is much more agreeable than dark materials.

Bleicherhof, an office building and departmental store, Zürich, 1939–40

Architect: Professor O. R. Salvisberg

256

20 *Schools and universities*

THE MOVEMENT TOWARDS the more functional design of school buildings manifested itself a little later and was consequently not so widely apparent during the period under review as in the case of the building types so far discussed. Up to about 1925 the majority of schools in Europe, with very few exceptions, were built acccording to rigid, stereotyped, traditional principles of design which were hardly best suited to the purpose they had to serve.

In the Middle Ages schools and colleges were built, like monastic and domestic buildings, with considerable thought given to convenient arrangement of parts; hence a certain irregularity in their disposition, although the tendency was to group buildings round courtyards, as we can see at Eton and Winchester. Later, with the Renaissance, the buildings were arranged on a more symmetrical plan, with one or two or even three square courts with central entrance, and this formal planning of courtyards or quadrangles became the dominant traditional method of planning for larger schools like the English public schools.

With the spread of education to poorer people in the nineteenth century, smaller schools were built to serve the centres of population. In England many of these were church schools, which were built in an ecclesiastical style and consisted of a few classrooms built round a hall badly lighted by Gothic windows. This type influenced the design of most schools before the establishment of the School Boards in 1870. The old British School at Croydon[1] was a typical example of a small school built in the early nineteenth century. It was of one storey and consisted of a large assembly hall adjoined by two classrooms at one side and a classroom at the end. In these early schools classes were held in the large halls, in addition to the classrooms, often in congested conditions.

With the rapid growth of population in the second half of the nineteenth century, and the advent of compulsory education, the accommodation of schools for young children had to be greatly increased, and this meant a great deal of school building.

257

These elementary schools became larger: they rarely remained at one storey, but were built of two and sometimes three storeys. Classrooms were generally grouped round a hall, as in the older types of plan; but at the beginning of the present century, when greater attention was being paid to the health of children, a more open plan was adopted and the quadrangle type of plan became common, thus both elementary and secondary schools following the type of plans employed for centuries in the great public schools.

Maltby School in the West Riding of Yorkshire, built in 1912, and Middle Crofts School in Derbyshire, built in 1926, are cited by Sir Felix Clay in his book on *Modern School Buildings* as good examples, and they may be regarded as typical of many built shortly before and after the First World War. The former consists of buildings grouped round a square court or quadrangle, the offices and assembly hall on the side of the principal entrance, and classrooms on three sides, with the corridors on the inside. The orientation is such that classrooms on one side face north–northwest and on the opposite side they face south–southeast. The school at Middle Crofts is mixed; the assembly hall is in the centre between two equal quadrangles, with the corridor on the inner side and the classrooms on the outer. The classrooms on one long side face approximately north and those on the other long side face south.

These are typical of the common practice to plan with the corridors on the inner side and the classrooms on the outer side. Sometimes the court is open on one side, or sometimes, in congested urban areas, there is merely a single two-, three-, or even four-storey rectangular block, and this is often the case with smaller schools.

In most of these school buildings, whether the early type of classrooms grouped round a hall, or the quadrangle type, or the storeyed block, a principal aim was a formal symmetrical appearance. Also, the buildings were rarely related in scale to the children who were to occupy them, while many were very solid and incongruously palatial.

One of the most important trends, following the First World War, represented only by a small minority of school buildings, was away from the formal symmetrical type of design towards more convenient, irregular, and flexible plans; in other words, the starting point of design was less the good-looking symmetrical building and more a building that should serve its purpose well and conduce to the health of its occupants. If a design that best fulfils the purpose of a building is symmetrical, then there is every reason why it should be so, but with a school this is rarely the case. With the old traditional type the designs were symmetrical for the sake of symmetry, and this was more important than orientation that would admit the morning sun into classrooms. Also, in the modern conception of a school with changing demand, it is desirable that the design of the building should permit the utmost flexibility, to allow changes and additions. The very nature of a symmetrical conception prohibits this flexibility[2]. Yet the majority of schools in Europe built between the two World Wars were with a formal symmetrical plan, even when there was consciousness of the changed aims in school building.

The general principles actuating the planning of schools hold good whether the school is an elementary or primary school or some form of secondary school. The various requirements are classrooms, assembly hall, dining room, gymnasium, library, art room, science rooms, playground and playing fields, and accessories like offices and staff rooms. In the case of a boarding school there would be the addition of dormitories, of adequate accommodation for meals, and of common rooms. Two fundamental requirements in planning are that the parts should be conveniently related, and that the parts where the scholars spend most of their time, that is, in the classrooms, should be well sited, so that the maximum sunlight, at least for schools in the more northerly part of Europe, should be admitted. (See Chapter 41—Schools 1945–60.)

Compactness is often considered desirable if the parts are to be conveniently related. This would seem to be at variance with the tendency towards the one-storey school as being the most satisfactory. With the tendency to have more and smaller primary schools it would not be difficult, but it would be difficult to obtain compactness in a one-storey secondary school of any size. The arguments in favour of the one-storey school are that it gives greater freedom of planning consistent with good orientation, because top lights can be employed for all the classrooms. Although compactness might be difficult there is the compensation of easy and well-controlled circulation that is possible with the one-storey school building. The decision, however, whether a school should be one, two, or three storeys depends very much on the size of the site in relation to requirements, for where space is limited it is often necessary to have a two- or three-storey building[3]. Yet where there is no lack of space modern schools designed in a progressive spirit have been built three or four storeys high, two examples being the well-known school at Seebach, in Switzerland, designed by Dr Ronald Rohn, and the Stockholm Secondary School for Girls designed by N. Ahrbom and H. Zimdahl.

The design of a school should secure easy and direct communication from all the classrooms to the assembly hall and to other parts, like the art and science rooms used by the scholars. The assembly hall need not be in a central position provided that it is easily accessible. Of fundamental importance is that classrooms should have the maximum sunlight, especially in autumn, winter and spring, because these represent the major part of the school year. It is desirable for classrooms to face approximately south, because this ensures the maximum sunlight for the school day, which is usually from about 09 hours to 16 hours. The corridor should thus be on the north side, and serve as a protection from the cold winds. One development is to have glass walls for the classrooms opening on to a terrace, so that classes could be held in the open in fine weather. This indicates another advantage of the one-storey school, as the provision of balconies to serve the same purpose for upper storeys would prove more costly, while such balconies would overshadow the classrooms below, unless the classrooms on the upper storeys were set back successively.

Making the satisfactory orientation of classrooms a condition of the design, a typical plan has evolved where the long classroom block, either one, two, or three storeys, faces approximately south, and blocks containing assembly hall, gymnasium, science rooms, and offices are placed at right angles on the north side. Sometimes these are connected at their north ends and one or two quadrangles are formed, but more often the intervening spaces are left open. There are numerous variations, however, such as a series of classroom blocks branching approximately either east or west from a connecting stem that runs north–south. But these are developments that occurred later. Modern methods of frame construction permitting large windows or glass walls have been increasingly used. (See Chapter 41—Schools 1945–60.)

The period following the First World War was one of gradual change in the conception and design of school buildings, very gradual at first, and becoming more marked in the late thirties. One of the first important contributions came with the schools designed by W. M. Dudok at Hilversum in Holland during the twenties.

The type of plan he adopted consists of a row of classrooms facing approximately south–southeast, opening from a corridor on the north side. At one end of the corridor are the entrance hall and staircase to the first floor—for they are mostly two storeys—which is a repetition of the ground floor. A wing at one end contains a gymnasium and at the other end rooms for the teaching staff. Views of two famous examples are illustrated. A slightly different arrangement, but following the same broad principles, is the Snelluislaan School at Hilversum designed by Dudok in 1931. This plan is L-shaped with the entrance and staircase at the corner enclosed by a semicircular glass front. Along one wing of the ground floor are classrooms facing west–southwest, with the corridor on the inner side. Along the other wing are staff rooms with the corridor on the outer side. At the end of this corridor is the gymnasium hall. The classroom wing is repeated on the first floor, but in the other wing are special rooms for crafts, needlework, drawing, and natural science, with the corridor on the inner side, and terminating with the last named room. The classroom windows on the west side appear externally as long, unbroken bands of fenestration, with the broad, circular glass enclosure of the staircase at one end. Large windows appear on the north side to give light to the crafts, art, and science rooms.

Most of Dudok's schools at Hilversum have a very attractive appearance in a good setting. Being long, narrow blocks of two storeys the compositions consist of horizontal massing with a contrasting vertical motif at the entrance which is often a glass stairway

260

Elementary School, Hilversum, 1926 *Architect: W. M. Dudok*

Elementary School, Hilversum, 1931 *Architect: W. M. Dudok*

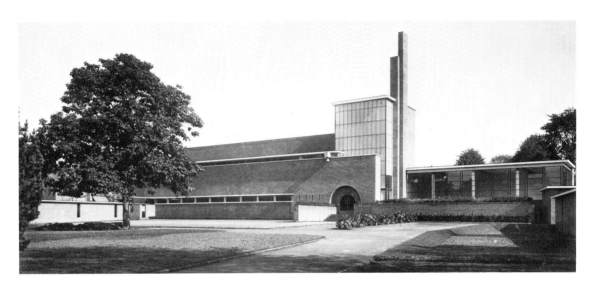

Coeducational School, Villejuif, near Paris, 1931 *Architect: André Surcat*

enclosure. In the elementary school illustrated this motif of design is clearly apparent. This and the Snelluislaan School with the circular staircase and glass enclosure are but two variations of the primary theme. These schools are built of brick which is attractively treated, the horizontal joints of the brickwork being wide and deep, in harmony with the lines of the building, while the vertical joints are almost obliterated.

The more distinctively progressive note in which modern materials of steel and concrete together with large glass areas are used in the construction of school buildings is first seen in the early thirties in a school at Villejuif, east of Paris, in an example in Stockholm, and in the famous open-air school in Amsterdam.

The school at Villejuif, east of Paris, designed by André Lurcat and built in 1931, is somewhat different in plan from that cited as the typical development. It is a combined school for boys and girls, with a kindergarten, and is noteworthy for its original planning. The classrooms are in a long, three-storey block facing south on to a playground. To the west is the kindergarten, and three covered ways run south from the main block, thus forming two quadrangles, one small for the infants, and a larger one for boys and girls, which is divided in the centre. A covered playground runs round the whole quadrangle and is partly underneath the main block, on the ground floor of which is the dining room. The whole structure is of reinforced concrete built with the lightest possible effect, and the windows of the classrooms are almost complete glass walls. It is a school built logically according to the purpose it has to serve, with a skilful use of materials.

The Stockholm Secondary School for Girls, designed by N. Ahrbom and H. Zimdahl, is one of the best examples of schools built in the early nineteen-thirties, and is a simple though large example of typical development. The design was awarded first prize in a competition in 1932 and the school was completed in 1935. It is for 700 pupils and consists of a lower and upper school. One long, four-storey block contains the classrooms of the upper school, and they face southeast, with a corridor in the other—northwest—side. The classrooms of the lower school are separated from the rest and are contained in a special block which is in front of the main building. The lower school block is supported on piles and is open underneath on the ground floor, thus forming a portico for use in bad weather. The portion of the main block behind this contains the art, handicraft, and science rooms, facing north, while at the eastern end of the main block is the gymnasium. Underneath the gymnasium there are dressing rooms, shower baths, medical consulting rooms, and rooms for meetings of school societies. The assembly hall is placed transversely on the northwest side of the main block on an axis with the main staircase, as can be seen on the plan. Its general shape denotes its purpose. The building is constructed mainly of reinforced concrete, with steel frame construction for the roofs of the hall and gymnasium. The concrete walls have an outer insulating section of aerated concrete blocks 4 inches thick.

262

The school stands in an extensive open space surrounded by parks. It cannot therefore be a question of space that prompted the architects to make the school four storeys. Greater compactness and closer and more convenient relation of the various parts is the most probable explanation. To provide the same accommodation in a one-storey building would have meant a considerable spread, and a much greater separation of some of the classrooms from the assembly hall, science and art rooms.

The whole building is an effective logical solution of a problem. The pupils get maximum sunlight in classrooms, there is compactness, and the various parts are well related. In appearance it has that structural lightness which arises from the economical use of steel and concrete.

The two schools which have been taken as examples of progressive tendencies in design of the early thirties show classrooms in rows on the long south façades with very large windows stretching from wall to wall of each classroom. The other walls on the corridor side have smaller windows, while end walls are mainly opaque. The school at Amsterdam for young children designed by J. Duiker in 1930 is an example of a four-storey concrete-frame construction which is enclosed in a glass screen on the same principle as parts of the Bauhaus and Boots's factory. The main part is a square block with one quarter, on the south side, open, and forming terraces on the three upper floors. In the centre of the block is the staircase. Two classrooms enclosed in glass on each of the upper floors occupy the east and west corners. On the ground floor one classroom occupies the west corner while a gymnasium extends beyond the square to the southeast. The heating is by means of ceiling panels, of which there are different opinions. In this design is an appreciation of the value of introducing as much light as possible. After all, if adequate heating can be secured in winter, then the school which is enclosed in a glass screen has the advantage of having light as near as possible to that out of doors. Space necessitated the four-storey structure, and the design must be regarded as a masterly solution of providing the best conditions of light and air in a limited space.

DEVELOPMENTS IN THE THIRTIES

The few examples cited represent the beginning of the more functional building of schools. Slow progress continued to be made, and in the thirties the examples became more numerous, from which a few of the more logically progressive can be selected. Two are open-air schools which may owe something to the Amsterdam example, one in France and the other in Denmark. The open-air school in Suresnes, near the Bois de Boulogne, west of Paris, was built in 1935–36 to the designs of E. Beaudouin and M. Lods. Unlike Duiker's school at Amsterdam the architects had the advantage of an extensive site on the southern slope of Mt Valerien.

This is a primary school for about 350 delicate children and the accommodation is

Stockholm Secondary School for girls, completed 1935.
General view *Architects: N. Ahrbom and H. Zimdahl*

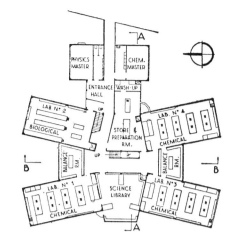

Science building of Marlborough
College, 1931–52. Plan of ground floor
and section

Architects:
W. G. Newton and Partners

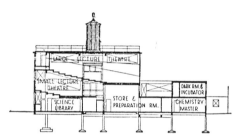

Plan showing assembly hall placed transversely to the main
block and gymnasium at extreme east main block

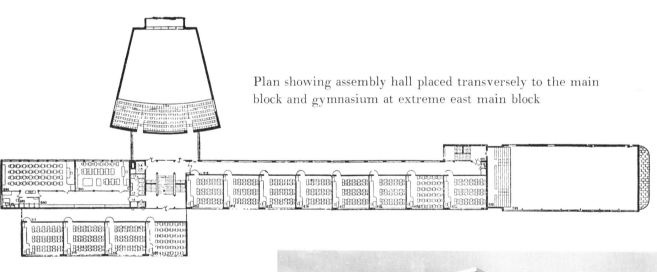

Open-air school at Amsterdam, 1932
Architect: J. Duiker

spaciously arranged on what may be roughly described as a diamond plan. The classrooms are a series of eight boxes with almost glass walls on three sides linked diagonally in sequence to a pergola with overhead way giving access to the roofs of the classrooms. This forms two sides of the diamond. On the other two sides beyond a central garden are a recreation hall and kindergarten in the centre, flanked by the wings for girls and boys on either side which include dining rooms, washing and dressing rooms. The boys and girls attend classes together, but for most other activities they are in separate wings. Access to the roofs is by means of ramps as these are safer than stairs, and one interesting feature is a spiral ramp that encircles a large globe. The whole setting of the school is a woodland park which makes the ensemble very attractive.

The open-air school in Denmark is part of the large 'Sund' school for well over a thousand children, in a southeast suburb of Copenhagen, built in 1938 to the design of Professor Kaj Gottiob. The layout is of a rectangular grouping of classroom wings of three storeys round an elliptical multi-purpose central hall which is perhaps the most interesting feature of the main building. The roof of this elliptical hall is raised a little above the surrounding roofs to allow a lantern light round the circumference. Two galleries run round the hall, the ceiling is decorated with a large compass, and the floor is patterned with diagrams and devices. A stage or platform can be erected at one end. Surrounding the main block are the gymnasia, play areas and garden. The section that forms the open-air school is across a small road to the east and is for about 150 young children who suffer poor health, and it is instituted to give them a chance to recover normal health by staying about a year. The buildings are arranged round a courtyard, with a row of octagonal classrooms on the south side with glass walls for three sides of the octagon on the sun side. Above the classrooms is a long rest room with partly glass roof to admit the maximum sunlight. This room is reached by a glass-walled ramp. On the east and north side of the courtyard are rooms for various kinds of medical treatment with a gymnasium and the usual accessories.

Some of the best designed schools in Europe during the thirties are in Switzerland. They are examples of the general tendency away from courtyard planning to a more extensive spread of the buildings on the site, together with a reduction of height towards the one storey school. Three merit especial attention. One is the combined primary and secondary Kappeli School in a northern surburb of Zürich, built in 1936–37, and designed by A. and H. Oeschger. It is a large mixed school for about 800 on a site surrounded by trees on three sides. The long classroom wing on three floors— semibasement, ground and first floors is orientated northeast–southwest, with one row of classrooms on the southeast side, and the corridor on the northwest side. The basement floor is only 3 feet below ground, which permits of the same size windows as in the upper floors. At the southwest end of the classroom wing is the assembly hall which is used also as a cultural and social centre. A wing runs transversely northwest containing gymnasia and related activities. Beyond a play area to the west is a

265

Kindergarten and to the south there are spacious areas for sport and games. The construction is of reinforced concrete, with interior brick lining, and brick partitions. Spacious layout surrounded by extensive verdant areas distinguish this school.

The Kornhausbrucke primary school also in a northern suburb of Zürich is a smaller school, designed by the Zürich City Architect A. H. Steiner and erected in 1941–42. Here the buildings comprising the school are grouped round a square playground and sports field, with the principal three-storey block for classrooms and teachers room on the northwest side—thus facing southeast to the partly enclosed space. There is a gymnasium on the southwest side and a small pavilion on the northeast side. Construction is mainly of reinforced concrete frame with brick infilling and brick partitions.

The third Swiss school, the Bruderliolz primary medium sized school on the southern side of Basel, built in 1938–9, to the design of Hermann Baur, is notable as being one of the earliest modern one-storey schools in Europe. It is very attractively situated on the eastern slope of a hill with the Daniel Fechter park on the upper west side. To obtain a level site the ground at the upper end was excavated to a depth of eight feet, and a retaining wall built, along which runs a covered way linking the three one-storey classroom blocks orientated east–west with the classrooms on the south side and opening to a paved area and to the playgrounds which separate the blocks. The roof of the classrooms and corridors is almost flat with a slight pitch of two degrees, the former being a little higher than the latter to permit cross ventilation. Although the large windows are provided with sun-blinds these are not always adequate in summer to keep the classrooms from getting unpleasantly warm, but the trees planted a short distance away give some shade and contribute to lowering temperature. The advantage of classrooms facing southeast, rather than south or southwest, is that in the middle latitudes of Europe summer days are warmest at about 14 or 15 hours, by which time the sun has gone off rooms facing southeast that have had the advantage of the morning sun. The school is a pioneer effort towards the one-storey school set in a garden.

Among other early one-storey schools are some in England: the Richmond School in Yorkshire, built in 1939–40, to the design of D. Clarke Hall and the four Cambridgeshire village colleges built in 1930–9. The small school at Richmond for older girls is built on a generous site on the outskirts of the town. The classroom wing orientated approximately north–south (north–northeast to south–southwest to be precise), with large windows facing east and west. They are linked by a corridor with short access corridors to each classroom block and small rectangular gardens are thus formed between the corridor and classrooms. A partly enclosed courtyard is formed on the west side of the classroom wing, with gymnasium at the north end and assembly hall and domestic science room at the southern end, where also is the library

School at the Sound, Copenhagen, 1937–38
Exterior and interior views of the central hall
the main building   *Architect: Kaj Gotkob*

Kornhausbrüke School, Zürich, 1941–42
      Architect: A. H. Steiner, City Architect, Zürich

Kappeli School, Zürich, 1936–37
      Architects: A. and H. Oeschger

Impington Village College, Cambridgeshire, 1939
Architects: Walter Gropius and E. Maxwell Fry

built on the first floor over the teacher's room, the only upper floor in the school.

The construction is of reinforced concrete frame, mainly to take the large windows, and stone, used for the wall of the corridor on the classroom side and for the end walls of classrooms, assembly hall, gymnasium and for parts of side walls. The external finish of the concrete is whitewash which provides a mild contrast to the yellow-grey sandstone walls. Sited to the northwest is a hockey field, while open country surrounds the school.

The first four Cambridgeshire village colleges built in the thirties to serve the needs of rural communities, partly as primary and secondary schools and partly as cultural and recreational centres, were initiated by Henry Morris then County Education Officer. The most famous architecturally of these colleges is that at Impington, designed by Walter Gropius and Maxwell Fry and built in 1938–9. The building is spaciously planned and consists of two long parallel wings orientated northeast–southwest, linked by a long transverse entrance hall which contains the administration office and teachers room. The southeast wing is mainly the school, and consists of a row of classrooms designed for various purposes with a science laboratory at the northeast end. All these classrooms have almost glass walls, opening to a garden on the southeast side, with a covered way on the other side. The northwest wing is mainly for recreational and adult cultural purposes and consists of a workshop at one end and a lecture room and library at the other end, with games rooms, while a fan-shaped assembly hall with stage project from this wing near the main hall where there is another entrance for adults. Only two rooms are on the first floor, one for art and the other for domestic science. The building is generously spread, surrounded by gardens and playing fields. This is a notable example of functional planning for well thought-out needs, confirmed by the experience of those who have used and enjoyed this school and community centre.

The additions frequently made to existing schools for specialized purposes are sometimes ingeniously, progressively and functionally designed. One such is the addition of the science building at Marlborough College, designed by W. G. Newton and Partners, and built in 1931–2. It is a symmetrically planned structure which appears to be admirably suited to the purpose it has to serve. It consists of a central portion from which four rectangular laboratories radiate. The central portion consists of a lecture theatre on the second floor, a smaller lecture theatre on the first floor, and the science library and store on the ground floor. Horizontal windows stretch almost the whole length of the three external walls of each laboratory, and the sills are just a little above bench height. They are all very conveniently related to the lecture room and library. The design is based on a unit of 21 feet 6 inches: the width of each laboratory, while the length is two of these units. This was adopted partly to simplify form-work, as by this method it could be re-used to a considerable extent. This is a compact and efficient building which demonstrates how, in some cases, with comparatively simple requirements symmetrical planning can be a logical solution to a problem.

UNIVERSITY BUILDINGS

The two largest and most ambitious building projects for universities in Europe between the two World Wars were those for the universities of Rome and London, which are described in Part IV, Chapters 31 and 35, concerned with classical monumentality, of which they are conspicuous examples. As the buildings of the University of Rome were by several architects they display some variety of design, but, with the exception of the Institute of Botany and Pharmaceutical Chemistry building designed by Giuseppe Capponi, they all have the grand classical monumental character determined by the superintending architect, Marcello Piacentini.

There is not, with one or two exceptions, a great deal of note among other university buildings erected in Europe between 1919 and 1939. They are for the most part rather of a traditional Renaissance character. The great period of university architecture in the present century is after the Second World War, from 1948 to 1972, with the foundation in Europe of many new universities and the expansion of many existing universities accompanied by a good deal of rethinking on the most functional buildings for their purposes. (See Chapter 42 where the traditions of university building are discussed.) The architecture of two other universities of the thirties merit attention, however, that of Fribourg in Switzerland, and Aarhus in Denmark.

Although the University of Fribourg was founded in 1889, the principal building that is now used was erected in 1938–41, to the designs of F. Dumas and D. Honegger. The classical traditional has clearly influenced its planning which includes a tree-lined avenue to the main entrance along the central axis, with two long narrow classroom wings orientated northeast–southwest parallel with the axis. Over the main entrance the first floor projects with a curved front forming a massive canopy supported on plain columns. Beyond the ceremonial entrance hall and on the central axis is the semi-circular assembly hall with large windows, coffered ceiling and reeded concrete columns. At the southwest end of the southeast wing is a multi-purpose hall for theatre, concerts and meetings. Although influenced by classical formalism in its planning and style it yet expresses the reinforced concrete frame construction of which it is built, suggesting the influence of Auguste Perret, while the canopied main entrance formed by a bulky first floor mass on slender supports—suggesting the drama of structure—link it with the mid-twentieth century.

The university buildings at Aarhus, in Denmark, are totally different and are a long way from the formal classical tradition. This second university of Denmark was founded in 1932 and many of its buildings were erected from 1935 to 1947. The architects, Kay Fisker, C. F. Møller and Povl Stegmann, were appointed as the result

Fribourg University building, Switzerland, 1938–41 *Architects: Denis Honegger and Fernand Dumas*

General view and view of the main entrance

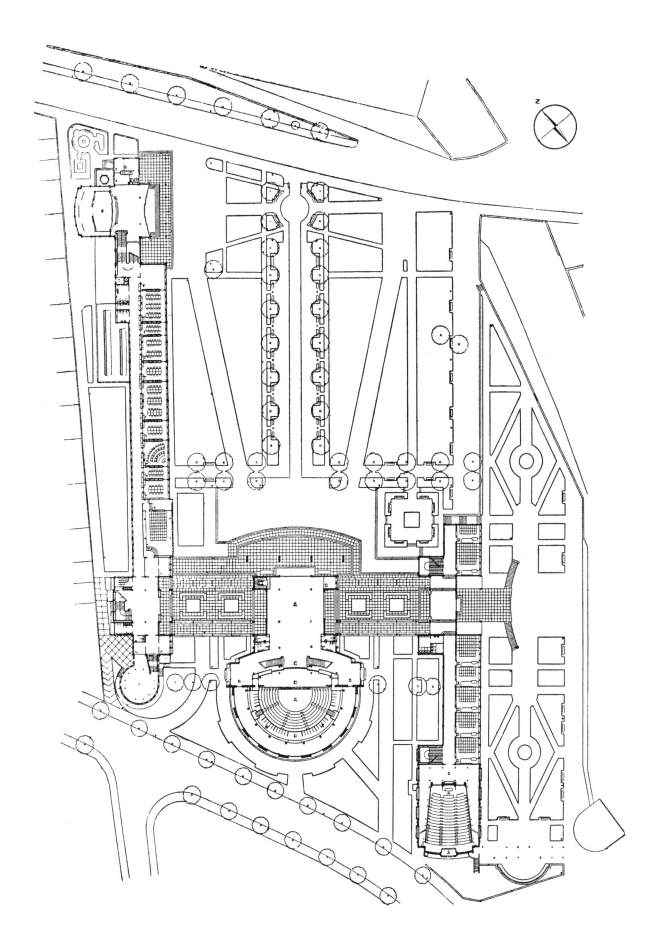

Fribourg University: plan of principal building, 1938–41

of an open competition in 1931. In 1937 the last mentioned retired from the work and later Fisker retired, leaving Møller after 1943 to complete the first group of buildings. Other buildings continued to be added after 1947.

A typical view from Aarhus University

The university is situated in undulating, partly wooded, country. Through the site from north to south is a ravine with a stream which was dammed to form two lakes. The buildings of the University are grouped round these lakes and valley, and full advantage has been taken of the landscape which has been enhanced by tree planting, especially oaks, in harmony with the layout of the buildings. Instead of formal symmetrical grouping on traditional lines, the buildings give the impression of being scattered over the extensive site like farm rather than university buildings. An

272

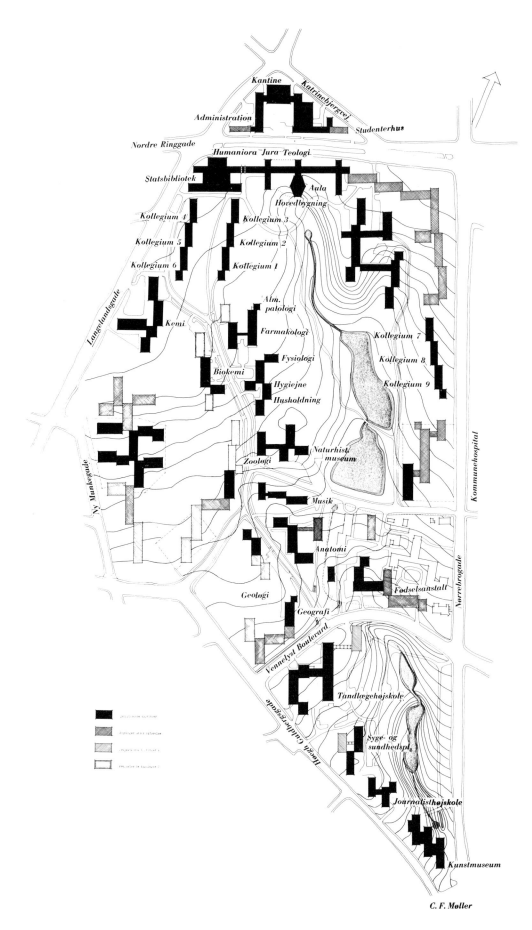

University of Aarhus, Denmark, 1935–47, layout plan
Architects: Kay Fisker, C. F. Møller and Povl Stegmann

University of Aarhus, Denmark, 1935–47

Exterior View

View along corridor

Entrance Hall

Assembly Hall

examination of the plan demonstrates, however, that the grouping is carefully and functionally calculated. At the northern end on high ground is the main building, consisting of a long narrow block east–west which contains the administrative offices, rooms of the teaching staff, and projecting southwards towards the valley, the elongated hexagonal assembly hall, which has a large south window and large plain walls on either side. Inside, this hall has a lofty majestic appearance. Although externally the walls are plain, inside tall concrete shafts continue in the sloping ceiling, and between them are decorative acoustic clay tiles. To the west of the valley are grouped the student colleges, the buildings of the institute of biochemistry and physiology, and the natural history museum, and to the east the institute of chemistry, physics and anatomy, with professors' houses towards the outskirts. Most of the buildings are groups of narrow rectangular blocks joined in various ways, independently designed for their special purposes, with walls of greyish yellow brick, and pitched roofs of about 40 degrees, not perhaps the most artistic slope. The main block other than the assembly hall is three and four storeys high, and the courtyards formed by the wings projecting from the main spine are in two cases enclosed by attractive arcading. The student colleges are four storeys and the east side is patterned with small balconies. Later buildings erected in the fifties conform in character to the earlier, and the whole complex of buildings along the tree sprinkled valley and around the lakes, has a delightful unity and harmony with the landscape. It is rather a rural than an urban scene.

References and Notes

1. Rebuilt shortly after the First World War.
2. C. G. Stillman and R. Castle Cleary in their book on *The Modern School*, London, 1949, frequently refer to the disadvantages of the symmetrical plan. The chances of a logical disposition of units, they contend, 'turning out symmetrically is extremely remote. . . . It is quite difficult enough to design an efficient school without adding a further difficulty in attempting to make the plan symmetrical. In the past, this additional restriction has been frequently imposed because so many of our schools have been built as expressions of civic pride. It has been the almost unvarying tradition that the monumentality and formality associated with civic design could only be expressed symmetrically, although the essential character of a school is far from monumental and formal' (pp. 29–30).
3. In his book on *The New School*, Zürich, 1950, Alfred Roth states the arguments for the one-storey school very persuasively, pp. 36–42. This is one of the best books on schools in Europe built between 1930 and 1950 and covers examples in Denmark, England, France Holland, Italy, Sweden, Switzerland and USA.

21   *Hospitals and health centres*

THE MODERN HOSPITAL develops from, and is an elaboration of, the medieval hospital or alms-house. Like the school it was originally part of the monastic group of buildings and follows the same grouping, with the buildings round a courtyard. One famous medieval example in France, which is still in use, the hospital at Beaune, built in 1443, has timber galleries for open-air treatment opening from the wards. This tendency to build round courtyards persisted with hospital design as with school design to the mid-twentieth century. In view of the appreciation of the value of sunlight one important development is to open the courtyard to the south, but in traditional examples there is the persistence of symmetrical planning whether it is the most suitable for the purpose or not.

Modern medical and surgical treatment and nursing, if they are to function with the utmost efficiency, demand in the hospital a satisfactory relation of parts, ease of circulation, and simplicity of design. For the large general hospital it is debatable whether the vertical or the horizontal building can be the more serviceable. The type is often determined by location. If a large hospital is to be built in the centre of a city, then the vertical type has of necessity to be adopted, and there are examples in Europe of from six- to twelve-storey hospitals, while in the USA, where the vertical type has been extensively developed, there are numerous examples of from ten to twenty storeys. The Hospital Beaujon at Clichy, Paris, designed by Jean Walter in 1937, is a large hospital with 1,100 beds, is twelve storeys high, the highest hospital that I know in Europe.

In Europe the majority of new hospitals built between the wars have been erected on sites away from the congested centres. In many cases, however, the extent of the site is often insufficient for a one- or two-storeyed building to serve the requirements of the hospital, and a many-storeyed building is often a necessity. But when a hospital is large the advantages of having a multi-storeyed building are a greater compactness and closer relation of sections than would be possible with a large hospital all on one floor. The one-floor building is generally more appropriate to the smaller, cottage type of hospital.

A general hospital is one of the most difficult and complex of all buildings to design. Functionalism is the keyword, but in hospital building it is not easy to define, because it is affected by so many factors. The interests of various people—medical and surgical staff, patients and visitors—have to be reconciled with conditions that will afford the best facilities for treatment, ensure the comfort and recovery of patients and also enable the hospital as a whole to operate with full efficiency.

To design a hospital that will satisfy all these requirements is no easy matter, and if architects have sometimes failed it is partly because of the complexity of the task. At the same time it might be said that architects generally could have done better. They have not always concentrated sufficiently on the functional side of the hospital.

Following a competition for the design of the General Hospital, Kuala Lumpur, Malaya, Professor Maxwell Fry, one of the assessors, said in an article on hospital design in *The Builder*, that the competitors (there were 71) seemed more interested in architecture *per se* than in the combination of a practical solution with an architectural interpretation, which is to say that there was a variety of solutions based on purely architectural associations.

With large general hospitals, throughout Europe and America, the tendency has persisted to make them massive, formal and impressive, rather like great Renaissance palaces. The question arises whether this grand palatial character, with its symmetrical massing is consistent with functional design. Where a classical imposing exterior is strongly in the mind of the architect, functionalism has to be reconciled, and in the reconciliation it is clear that in many cases the all important functional aspect of the hospital has been sacrificed.

In hospital design it is a question of making the various parts function satisfactorily, both in themselves and in relation to the other parts, so that they make an efficient unity; it is not a matter of fitting the parts into a preconceived shape, cramming some, with too much space for others, a process which is very rarely satisfactory[1], though traditional.

All the large hospitals built in England between the wars were influenced in design by ideas of classical monumentality and were planned on formal symmetrical lines. An example is the large hospital centre at Birmingham which was the subject of a competition in 1930 won by H. V. Lanchester and T. A. Lodge. Work commenced a few years later and the building was about two-thirds completed at the outbreak of war in 1939, and work continued towards completion in the post-war years.

The hospital for 840 patients (including 100 private) occupies a commanding open site near Birmingham University. It is symmetrically planned on a north–south axis and consists of three main buildings, the nurses home at the north end, the hospital building in the centre consisting of administration block, surgical and medical wings west and east, with the usual accessories, and the medical school at the southern end (see plan). The surgical and medical wings are planned similarly, consisting of seven-storey blocks each forming a square courtyard open to the south and each flanking a larger central courtyard. The wings that extend north–south hold the larger open wards for sixteen beds, while there are a few four and two bed wards. This incorporation of the large open ward is a further following of tradition, and even in the thirties there was a body of medical opinion in Europe opposed to the large open ward as being conducive to hospital infection and of various discomforts to the patient. Small square sun balconies terminate the long wards on the south, while a long bed balcony extends the length of the south side of the transverse connecting block with four and two bed wards. The construction is mainly of steel frame with brick facings.

Built a little earlier although still influenced by traditional monumentality and symmetry, yet combining this with a degree of progressive design, is the Royal Masonic Hospital, at Ravenscourt Park, west of London. Designed by Sir John Burnet, Tait, and Lorne, it was commenced in 1930 and completed in 1932. It occupies a site of about four acres. Traditional formal symmetrical planning is followed in the general layout and interior planning.

The main ward block encloses three sides of a square courtyard open to the south. On the central axis, which forms the communicating spine, running north from the centre of the ward block are symmetrically situated the annexe block and the electrical and surgical block. To the east of the ward block is the administration building. The construction is of a steel frame with brick walls and partitions are of hollow terracotta blocks. The foundations, floors, and roofs are of concrete, the last mentioned being flat to allow their use as open-air spaces when required. At the terminations of the east and west ward blocks are semicircular sun balconies 30 feet in diameter for the ground, first, and second floors, then a set-back with a square terrace opening from the children's ward on the third floor, and on the fourth floor a further set-back to form a balcony for the staff.

Does this symmetrical arrangement give the maximum sunlight to a maximum number of wards at the right time? There is an almost exact identity of wards on either side of the central axis. The small wards (for one, two, three, or four patients) in the east wing receive the morning sun only. The corresponding wards in the west wing have the afternoon sun but no morning sun. The larger wards on the south side of the north block would have more sun, but in the winter the long shadows of the east and west wings would reduce the sunlight considerably. It would have been possible to design the ward blocks so that all the wards faced south or south–southeast, with every ward opening on to a balcony. In planning a hospital it is of the utmost importance that sunlight, especially in the winter, should be considered, but in the traditional symmetrical arrangement of these blocks has this been sufficiently considered?

In view of the different authoritative schools of thought on the subject it is not wise to be too insistent on this point. One opinion is that with good lighting and ventilation, and good heating well controlled, it is not very important that wards should face approximately south, and that sometimes in the anxiety to orientate the ward blocks in this manner architects have sacrificed more than is gained. In a paper on Recent Trends in Hospital Design, by J. Murray Easton and S. E. T. Cusdin, read at the Architects Conference at Dublin in June 1947 (printed in the *Royal Institute of British Architects Journal*, July 1947) this point is discussed. They say: 'that wards should face due south, or perhaps a little east or a little west of south, has tended to become axiomatic. Jean Walter, in his book *Renaissance de l'Architecture Medicale*, has derided this theory. He claims that with good light and modern methods of heating and ventilation it does not matter which way the wards face. We think there is a certain amount of truth in this contention.'

'Many hospitals', they continue, 'have been rendered inconvenient by the insistence on having all wards facing south and all operating theatres facing north, but we cannot believe that in a climate like ours it is reasonable to discard the opportunity, when it exists, of getting sunshine into wards. But other factors such as general convenience, good views, etc, should be given equal consideration with that of south aspect; and an open horizon, be it north, south, east, or west, is preferable to one which is seriously obstructed by intervening buildings.'

As implied in this passage, not to give paramount attention to wards facing approximately south is contrary to the general tendency as exemplified by what are regarded as the most modern hospital designs. Much depends, however, on the type of hospital. If it is a general hospital, planning in relation to sunlight may be desirable, but in the case of a tuberculosis sanatorium, where patients must be protected from the direct rays of the sun, planning for fresh air and avoidance of exposure to the sun are fundamental.

In general hospitals, where the site is open and fairly extensive, it would seem that the brightening effect of sunlight, especially in the winter, cannot be easily over-estimated, and the disadvantages of facing the maximum number of wards approximately south would have to be considerable to outweigh the advantages. It is the tonic and cheering effect on patients which is so important, and it would seem that Jean Walter does not give due weight to this. Easton and Cusdin, elsewhere in their

279

Birmingham General Hospital, 1936–40 *Architects: Lanckester and Lodge*
General view showing layout

Typical floor plan

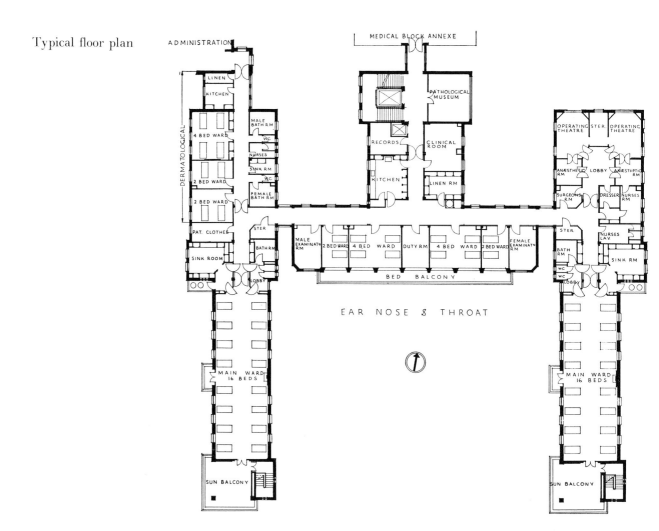

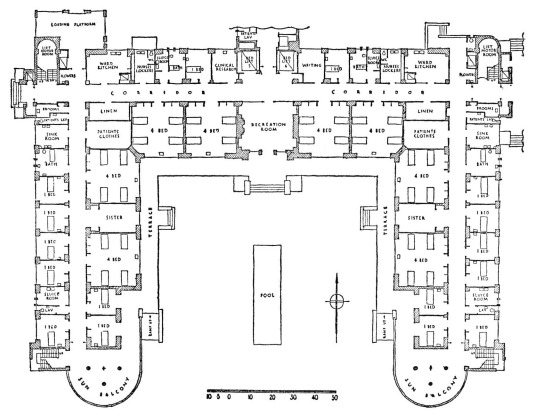

Ground floor plan

Royal Masonic Hospital, Ravenscourt Park,
London, 1930–32

Architects: Sir John Burnet, Tait and Lorne

Front view and entrance

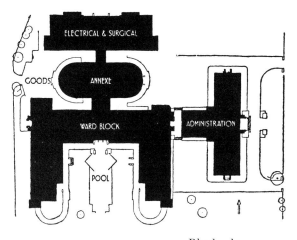

Block plan

paper, refer to Jean Walter's approach to problems of hospital design as functional and mechanistic rather than humanist, and his views on orientation would appear to be of this character. In the most comprehensive view of functional planning, human considerations, like the tonic effect of sunlight in winter, cannot reasonably be omitted.

To return to the Royal Masonic Hospital: in considering the general plan, it is a question whether a more convenient relationship of parts, such as the distance between the operating theatres and some of the wards, and the circulation would not have been better if formal symmetrical planning had not been followed; a criticism which can, however, apply to nearly all of the older large hospital buildings in this country. The influence of tradition often restrains an architect from designing entirely and logically according to purpose. At the time it was built the Royal Masonic Hospital probably marked the greatest advance in hospital design in England, and is significant as an example of transition from classical Renaissance to more functional design, seen rather in features like the receding balconies than in the planning.

The general appearance of the hospital is very pleasing. The large horizontal windows of the ward block are well related to the brick walls, and the horizontal character is emphasized by the lines being carried from one window to the other by a slight recess. This horizontal movement is continued in the semicircular terminations, but is arrested here and there by a vertical mass such as that of the central entrance and the glass corner features enclosing the staircases. Much of the architectural effect is dependent on a nicely calculated relation of horizontals and verticals, and of windows to the plain brick wall surfaces with their agreeable variegated textures.

A few years later than the Royal Masonic hospital and similarly of a transitional character is the Westminster Hospital built in 1936–9 to the designs of Adams, Holden and Pearson. The rectangular site was formerly occupied by the burial ground of St. John's Church. The buildings consist of the hospital proper, the nurses home and medical school, the two last mentioned being built first. The nurses home occupies the southern part of the site, and includes a large handsome common room in the centre of the first floor which opens to a terrace overlooking St. John's gardens, on the north side.

The hospital provides for 443 patients (including 43 private) with an out-patients department. It is an eight-storey building with the main spine block north–south with three projecting blocks both east and west, at the ends and centre thus forming two bays on either side. A north–south road tunnels through and most of the entrances are from this road, an ingenious device prompted by the limitations of space. The west side faces St. John's gardens and in the central wing on the seventh floor, west side, is the simple and impressive chapel which from St. John's Gardens appears as a central monumental feature. The tendency to smaller ward rooms is apparent. These are on

General view from Westminster Gardens

Westminster Hospital, London, 1935–38
Architects: Adams, Holden and Pearson

Floor plan of Westminster Hospital

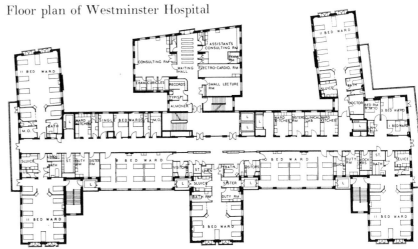

Tuberculosis Sanatorium, Paimio, Finland,
completed 1932 *Architect: Alvar Aalto*

Ground floor layout, plan of Sanatorium
and section through one
of the wings showing
the rows of
cantilevered solariums

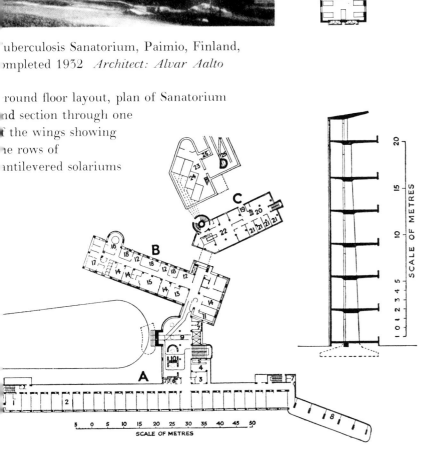

SCALE OF METRES

KEY TO PLAN

A. 1. NURSES' QUARTERS; 2. PATIENTS' ROOMS; 3. DIVISIONAL
DAY ROOMS WITH GLASS WALLS; 4. WASHING ROOM AND
UTENSILS, GENERAL CLEANING AND DISINFECTION; 5.
LAUNDRY; 6. SPUTUM ANALYSIS ROOM IN TWO DIVISIONS;
7. W.C.'S, URINALS, BIDETS, FOOTBATHS, ETC.; 8. 'LYING
HALLS' FOR THE MORE SERIOUS CASES; 9. THE ENTRANCE
HALL; 10. SHOE CHANGING ROOM

B. 11. PORTER, POST OFFICE, WIRELESS, TELEPHONE EX-
CHANGE, ETC.; 12. WAITING NICHES FOR PATIENTS IN
CORRIDORS; 13. ADMINISTRATION ROOMS AND DOCTORS'
CONSULTING-ROOMS; 14. DOCTORS' ROOMS; 15. X-RAY;
16. OPERATING THEATRE; 17. THERAPY; 18. LABORA-
TORIES, DENTISTS' AND APOTHECARIES' ROOMS

C. 19. ENTRANCE FOR PROVISIONS AND FOR KITCHEN AND
BAKERY; 20. SORTING ROOM FOR PROVISIONS; 21. COLD
STORAGE; 22. BAKERY

D. 23. POWER HOUSE; 24. BOILERS; 25. TUNNEL FOR TRUCKS;
26. SHOWER

the first to the sixth floors. The four end wing ward rooms have eleven beds each, the central block two ten-bed wards and one five-bed; but even at the time they were built these ward rooms were considered too large by much medical opinion.

The hospital is of steel frame construction with brick facing, red on the first storey, and multi-coloured Sussex stocks in the upper storeys, which have weathered to a soft purple hue. The windows are tall vertical shapes at the end of the wings, but approximately square in the bays. The open space between the hospital and nurses home forms one of the pleasantest small gardens in London. It originally had a shelter in the centre, but this has been replaced by a fountain which is encircled by plane trees. The headstones from the old churchyard, some of which commemorate well-known people, now line the walls facing the garden.

TUBERCULOSIS SANATORIA
Scandinavia has for long enjoyed the reputation of building some of the finest hospitals in the world, and it has been suggested that some of the hospitals built there since 1930 are in advance of anything built in England. Two of the most famous in the world were built during the thirties; the Tuberculosis Sanatorium at Paimio in Finland (1930–2), designed by Alvar Aalto, and the Sodersjukhuset (south hospital), Stockholm (1933–43), designed by Hjalmar Cederstrom.

In the Sanatorium at Paimio the blocks are grouped irregularly along a central communicating spine being determined in their layout by the requirements of light and air. The long ward block for 290 patients, seven storeys high, has a long row of two-patient rooms facing south–southeast (A on ground plan), opening on to balconies and a corridor on the north–northwest side. These rooms get the sun from early morning until the late afternoon, which is beneficial provided the patient avoids the direct rays. At the eastern end of the block, tilted, with its façade due south, is the solarium, with verandas on balconies on each floor for open-air treatment. The next block to the north along the communicating spine is that containing the operating theatres, dining hall combined with recreation room, library, reading and writing rooms for patients, and administration offices and doctors' quarters. This rectangular block has a long façade due south, so that it is at a slight angle from the ward block and parallel with the solarium. At the western end is a summer terrace with pergola. Continuing north along the corridor we reach another rectangular block, which is constructed with the long façades facing southeast and northwest. It contains kitchen, balcony, and quarters for the nursing staff, storerooms for provisions and laundry. A square block (D) to the northwest of this contains a power house, the bunkers of which are connected through a tunnel with railway sidings. Other blocks are located at some distance from the main group. To the west there is a row of houses for the doctors (E), to the north are houses for employees (F), and to the northeast is a garage (G). There are extensive gardens all round the hospital, laid out a little formally to the south for the use of patients.

The construction is of reinforced concrete frame, faced externally with brick and internally with cork insulating board. The balconies of the ward block and the deep balconies of the solarium are cantilevered, while the walls are built on cantilevered floors.

It is clear that this building is the result of considerable thought about the purpose and requirements of a tuberculosis sanatorium and designed accordingly in terms of modern scientific construction and equipment. The architect was unhampered by restricting thoughts of traditional methods of design; instead, he was fearlessly logical in building according to purpose. The tall, long, narrow, pale blocks with the horizontal emphasis of balconies on the southern façades and the narrow windows on the northern have a certain grandeur. Incidentally, here in the open country seems to be the justification for the many-storeyed tuberculosis sanatorium, as the narrow block reaches upwards, open to the sunlight and bright, clean air at every possible point. It seems to stretch upwards into the fresh air and be more suitable for its purpose than a single-storey block. P. Morton Shand, in an excellent appreciative article on this sanatorium in the *Architectural Review* for September 1933, concludes by saying that 'even if Paimio were not the most revolutionary hospital building erected within the last decade, it would still be of immense significance on account of the structural methods adopted, and the multiplicity of new ideas, details and fitments it incorporates'. It is often regarded as the most progressive and outstanding hospital building erected in Europe between the wars, and is deservedly famous.

One of the main purposes, especially in tuberculosis sanatoria, is more light and air, and the general tendency is to have a long ward block with the long façade on the ward side towards the south, generally a little to the southeast, with the wards opening on to verandas and balconies on to which the beds may be moved. One interesting development is to set back the upper storeys in step formation so that the balconies and terraces are open to the sky. Examples are the famous sanatorium at Guébriant, in France, designed by Pol Abraham and Henry de Meme, and the hospital at Waiblingen, Württemberg, designed by Richard Docker. This was to be developed still further in Wetter's Hospital Louis Pasteur at Colmar in Alsace, where the storeys are not only set back on the south side of the long ward block, but on the north side they successively overhang. The construction is assisted by the series of wings projecting north. This hospital was built, however, several years later.

In thinking of these hospitals it is interesting to glance back about twenty years to what was then the most modern sanatorium in Europe: I mean the Queen Alexandra Sanatorium at Davos, in Switzerland, designed by Pfleghard, Haefeli, and Maillert in 1907. This building is constructed of a reinforced concrete frame; it spreads long façades to the south, with sun balconies on its seven floors, but they are all directly above one another with the exception of the third floor, which has a projecting terrace

285

above the framed canopies of the first three floors. The progress from this to the examples twenty years later is not great perhaps—it exists mainly in the set-back formation of the balconies.

An interesting two-storey sanatorium which is worthy of study is the 'Zonnestraal' at Hilversum, built in 1928 to the designs of B. Bijvoet and J. Duiker. It is constructed of reinforced concrete frame with glass walls between the wards and terraces and balconies to the south, and a generous use of glass in the general treatment. It has not the effect of a building with windows, but rather of a concrete frame and concrete floors and roof with glass walls between—set back where balconies and verandas are required towards the south, and bands of concrete sparingly introduced where required, chiefly on the north façades. The similarity of this design and construction to many factories built by the same constructional methods with the same generous use of glazed areas, must be apparent at once. But features like balconies and verandas, the variations of glass and opaque walls according to orientation, and the transverse grouping of blocks along a spine denote the hospital building.

Returning to Finland, a large children's hospital was built in Helsinki during the thirties, notable for its original design by Erkki Linnasalmi and Uno Ullberg. Lengthy and careful preparation preceded its building, for designing a children's hospital is particularly complex. The needs of different age groups have to be considered, children are more prone to infectious diseases, and fresh air is especially important. Incorporated with this hospital is a medical school.

The plan adopted was that of several wings of three and four storeys radiating like the spokes of a wheel from a circular service and communication block, which terminates in the large principal four-storey ward block with open terraces on the south side, the terrace on each floor being a little recessed from that below so as to get the maximum sunlight on each floor. The three radiating wings are special purpose blocks. The main entrances are on the concave side of the service block, one on the ground floor and one on the first floor reached by a ramp. Although functional efficiency in which design logically responds to needs has been the determining factor, the hospital yet succeeds in being architecturally effective. The construction is of concrete frame with brick walls.

One of the largest and most famous hospitals in Europe is the Södersjukhuset, Stockholm, which was planned in the early thirties and built mainly between 1935 and 1945, although several additions were made later. It was designed by Hjalmar Cederström to take 1,193 beds for in-patients, and with capacity for about 1,000 out-patients a day. The later additions are an after-treatment section, and a children's hospital, so that the whole health centre consists of 16 to 19 different clinics with a total of 1,600 beds. The hospital is planned on the double block system—that is, two long, parallel blocks running east–west, that on the south side with five projecting wings is the nine-storey ward block, with the rooms facing south, and that on the north side is the lower five-storey examination and treatment block for both in- and out-patients. The two are joined by four communicating blocks with sixteen communicating routes.

The size of the separate rooms for patients in the ward block was the result of much research. Rooms with 10 to 20 patients were regarded as relics of a very unsatisfactory era in hospital treatment. Infection, it was contended, could more easily be combatted with few than many patients in a room, while there are other advantages such as quiet and privacy in small rooms[2]. Thus in this South Stockholm hospital many wards consist of five rooms with four patients, four rooms with two patients and four isolation rooms with one patient, and other wards have slight variations of this, but no room has more than four patients. The hospital is of monolithic concrete construction, and many of the walls incorporate light-weight insulating concrete.

A hospital that has several similarities to this Stockholm hospital and built about the same time (1938–44) is the Bürgerspital (now called Kantonsspital) in Basel, with 660 beds. Designed by collaborating architects: E. and P. Vischer; Hermann Baur; Brauning, Lev, and Durig, it is planned on the double block system like the South Stockholm hospital with two long parallel blocks running east–west, the tall eight-storey ward block, with wards facing south, and the three-storey treatment block which contains operating theatres, lecture rooms, laboratories and administration offices. The wards for about 50 patients each are divided into rooms with six and two beds. An interesting feature of the treatment block is the palatial central entrance on the north side, flanked on the second floor by two large semi-circular auditoria, which on the exterior project a little from the main line of the façade and roof and provide a novel feature. An isolation block a little way from the general hospital was added in 1946.

These two hospitals in Sweden and Switzerland have long been regarded as the most progressive contribution in Europe to the design of general hospitals at the time they were built, and it is doubtful whether for many years after the war they had been surpassed for functional efficiency. Andre Schimmerling writing in *L'Architecture d'Aujourd'hui* for November 1947, said that in Europe modern tendencies in hospital design have found in these two buildings their best expression, and he emphasized that problems of circulation are well solved by the transverse connections between the two blocks.

More progress in hospital planning was made in the fifties and sixties, which is necessarily largely of an experimental character. One very important lesson emerges from the designs of both these Swedish and Swiss hospitals: the patient is given full consideration. After all, in hospital design in the architect–client relationship it is the

287

Sodersjukhuset (South Hospital),
Stockholm, 1932–46

Architect: Hjalmar Cederström

General view and plan

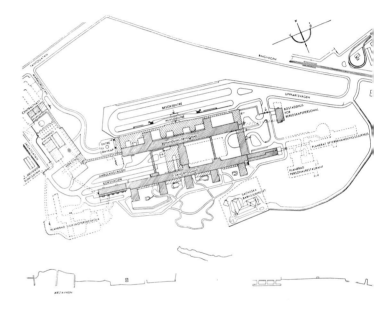

Burgerspital (Citizens Hospital, now called
Kantonsspital), Basel, 1938–44

General view and plan

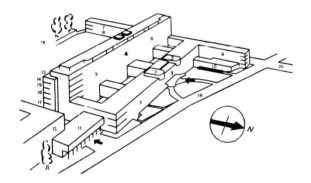

Architects: E. and P. Vischer, Hermann Baur;
Braüning, Lev and Dürig

patient who is the major client, advised by medical, surgical and nursing staff, but the client in the sphere of hospital design has not always an organized voice and is not always heard as he should be. As Hjalmar Cederström, the architect of the South Stockholm hospital said: 'the hospital grew up entirely from within, the function around the sick person in the hospital bed was the point of departure'[3], and, it might be added, that the wishes of the sick person as far as they can be ascertained and as far as practicable, should be consulted before, during, and after treatment, and that 'conditioning of the consumer', prevalent with the mass monopolies, both state and private, of the sixties and seventies, should have no place in hospitals.

The planning of wards, as subsequent developments show, is a subject for almost endless variations and experiments as so many requirements are involved, and is typical of the complexity of hospital planning generally. It is a subject on which there is wide disagreement among experts[4]. One of the principal requirements is the easy and efficient supervision of the patients by the nursing staff. In the old fashioned long open ward with twenty or more beds arranged on either side, the nursing station with the usual ancillaries was at one end, and was not satisfactorily placed. One modern tendency is to move the nursing station to the centre of the ward with patients rooms or cubicles all round, with the ward any shape—square, rectangular, circular. The disadvantage of this is that the room windows face in all directions of the compass, except in the case where the nursing station is only half surrounded, as in the semicircular ward where it is along the diameter with the rooms in the circle east–southwest.

Although these great Swedish and Swiss hospitals are acclaimed as functionally efficient especially in their layouts, they are still rather symmetrical palatial buildings, and the question arises, are the parts and functions still poured somewhat into a mould. In looking at Aalto's Sanatorium at Paimio and Linnasalmi and Ullberg's hospital at Helsinki, the functional efficiency is carried to the architecture.

HEALTH CENTRES

Where the purpose of hospitals is to cure the sick the purpose of health centres is to maintain the health of the community, which should also have the effect of lessening the load on hospitals. Buildings began to be erected for the specific purpose of health centres between the two World Wars and a few have some degree of architectural distinction. They began in the early years of the century as maternity and infant welfare centres, and then broadened to some extent to include general health and welfare. The early centres were usually in church halls, multi-purpose halls, and any premises that were available. Only in the twenties were plans prepared for buildings specifically designed for the purpose.

Two pioneer efforts which were also architecturally distinctive in England were the Pioneer Health Centre at Peckham and the Finsbury Health Centre. The former, designed by Sir Owen Williams in 1934, was an experiment by two doctors, G. Scott Williamson and Innes H. Pearce to assist families of the district in the preservation of good health. Opportunities were provided at the centre for various physical, social and cultural activities, and members could, if necessary, be kept under observation and be given medical advice. The onset of illnesses could be observed from the earliest stages, and although it was not a function of the centre to treat disease, this being done by members' own doctors and by hospitals, early observation of symptoms helped diagnosis and effective treatment. The main function of this centre was to keep people well. The building is set well back from the road among trees. It is a rectangular three-storey structure of reinforced concrete with concrete floors supported on mushroom columns of cruciform section, with glass screens for external walls, similar in construction to Owen Williams' Boots' Factory. The various parts of the building are grouped round a central swimming bath which is covered by a steeply pitched glass roof. On the ground floor is a gymnasium and lecture room at either end, and a long children's play space at one side opening to the southwest and divided from the garden by arcading. On the first floor are two spacious lounges, with cafeteria and kitchen adjoining one, and on the second floor are the medical rooms, library, study and rest rooms. The whole conception was to provide a setting for the healthy, profitable and enjoyable use of leisure—a community centre with the addition of a health service. It soon became famous as a pioneer social and health enterprise, and in architectural circles as one of the notable buildings of the new architecture in which the newest methods of construction were employed, so that its purpose is fulfilled efficiently. It is also aesthetically attractive, especially the centre part of the southwest façade which has a series of six circular bay windows on the two upper storeys above the arcade columns of the children's play space, making an effective architectural composition[5]. Unfortunately, owing to lack of support the centre closed in March 1950. Shortly afterwards the London County Council acquired it, and opened it mainly as a health centre rather to the exclusion of its social and cultural activities.

The Finsbury Health Centre built in 1938 to the design of the Tecton Group was a municipal enterprise to combine all the health services of the borough into one building. These services were previously scattered throughout the borough and consisted of maternity, child welfare and dental services, public health administration offices, laboratory, mortuary, and disinfecting station. The new building to house these services is a little like a butterfly on a north–south axis, with the central cross piece and the approximately rectangular wings. It is a two storey building with basement, the last mentioned housing the mortuary, heating plant, cleansing and disinfecting sections and garages. The design of the centre part is fairly rigid with a spacious entrance hall, with façade of long panels of glass bricks in a concrete surround and terrace above, and on the first floor is a fan shaped lecture theatre which projects above the flat roof and beyond the north façade, forming the large head of the butterfly. This lecture theatre determines the shape of the electric treatment section on the ground floor.

Pioneer Health Centre, Peckham,
London, 1936

General view and ground-floor plan

Architect: Sir Owen Williams

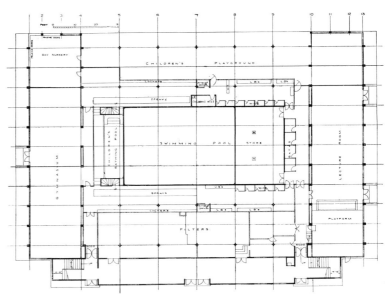

Finsbury Health Centre, 1938
General view from above

Architects: The Tecton Group

The wings which accommodate the tuberculous, dental, maternity and child clinics and various offices are so constructed as to permit flexibility of use by movable partitions, with concrete frame construction and horizontal window and opaque glass bands on the long walls with a square teak grid. The whole conception is a valuable contribution to the design of this new type of building, which also succeeds in being architecturally effective with pleasing relations of masses and textures[6].

Several health centres for children were built in Italy during the thirties, the purpose being to give delicate children the opportunity of restoration to normal health by a stay at such a centre for a short period during the holidays. Some are sun treatment centres and one particularly notable example is that at Legnano, 17 miles west of Milan. It was designed by a group of architects, G. L. Banfi, L. Belgioioso, E. Peressutti, and E. N. Rogers, and built in 1938.

It occupies a generous site in the midst of woodland country. The principal building consists of two main rectangular blocks, the lower one on the north side is for the office reception and cloakrooms, the large taller block on the south side is occupied mainly by restaurant and kitchen, the two being linked by two pergolas. The long restaurant wall to the south is wholly of glass, the supporting concrete columns being set back. In front of this wall, but separate, is the solarium on the first floor and the glass wall of the restaurant opens to the terrace underneath. The space between the restaurant wall and the solarium is designed for the warm air to rise and disperse. The construction is of brick walls on a stone plinth with a projection which holds a trough for plants. The solarium is of timber construction with brick end walls. A staircase ascends to the solarium, with stone faced landing which is used as an instructor's box for open-air exercises[7].

References and Notes

1. See Hugh Gainsborough and John Gainsborough, *Principles of Hospital Design*, London, 1964, especially the first chapter. A forward looking book by a doctor and an architect.
2. See Hjalmar Cederström, *Guide book to Sodersjukhuset Stockholm*, Stockholm, 1946.
3. Hjalmar Cederström, *Guide book to Sodersjukhuset Stockholm*, Stockholm, 1946, p. 16.
4. As an example of the divergence of views among experts on the desirable sizes of wards or rooms see the report of the discussion on Modern Hospital Architecture that took place at the Architectural Association in 1950 (*Architectural Association Journal*, vol. lxvi, No. 748, 1951, pp. 118–130) in which many eminent doctors and architects took part: Dr Rene Sand, R. Llewelyn Davies, Professor H. W. C. Vines, J. Murray Easton, Dr C. T. Maitland, Lionel G. Pearson, Sir Ernest Rock Carling, and a few others.
5. See fully illustrated article in *The Architectural Review*, May 1935, pp. 203–216.
6. See fully illustrated article in *The Architectural Review*, January 1939, pp. 5–15.
7. See description in Alfred Roth, *The New Architecture*, Zürich, 1947, pp. 131–138.

22   *Apartment blocks and flats*

THE SHORTAGE OF DWELLINGS to house the population according to a reasonable
standard had existed in most countries of Europe in 1913. It was greatly aggravated by
the limitations, amounting in some cases to cessation, of house building during the First
World War, by the difficulties attendant on post-war revival, and by the increase in
population. In the first few years after the war little progress had been made, so that
by 1924 the housing shortage was very acute. This was particularly the case with the
big cities with their slums and problems of congestion. The most urgent task was the
rebuilding of the congested and slum areas, and rehousing the population according to
reasonable standards.

In rebuilding congested areas, with their high densities of population, it was found
that if the accommodation for each family was to be greatly improved and the
redevelopment was to be on fairly spacious lines, then tall blocks of flats had to be
built, and even this meant a degree of overspill. There was a reluctance in many cities
to build blocks of flats very high, especially if they were without lifts, as was generally
the case; and the lower and the more spaciously planned were the blocks of flats, the
greater the overspill. Every city had, therefore, its problem of dispersal from the
congested centre. As previously noted (Chapter 7) planned dispersal both of industry
and population to satellite towns built on Garden City principles was proposed in
England in 1919 by the Garden Cities and Town Planning Association. No general plan
on these lines was adopted; the most that the advocates of this policy secured was the
planning and building of the satellite town of Welwyn Garden City. The enterprise
and advocacy of the enthusiasts who recommended this policy and who were
responsible for the garden cities of Letchworth and Welwyn has at last borne fruit in a
National Policy of decentralization by means of new towns in the country[1].

In England dispersal between the wars took place mainly by means of new estates
on the outskirts of the big cities and towns. The new dwellings in the centre, of which
numerous examples can be seen in London, Manchester, Liverpool, and Birmingham,

took the form of blocks of flats usually three to five storeys high, while most of the dwellings on the outskirts were two-storeyed houses with gardens, the majority being terrace or semi-detached houses. These estates of small houses represented generally greatly improved standards of accommodation, although insufficient attention was paid to questions of orientation. The influence of formal and symmetrical planning was still strong, and the custom of designing the layout of roads and planning houses on either side of the roadways still for the most part obtained. Likewise, in the layout of the redeveloped estates in the central districts, departures from formal symmetrical planning for the sake of sunlight were still rare in the nineteen-twenties.

The general rule in England between the wars of building blocks of flats in the redeveloped central congested areas and family houses with gardens on the outskirts was in contrast to what occurred in most other countries in Europe. In Paris and Berlin there was rebuilding in central congested areas, and in each provision was made for overspill. In the case of Paris several new estates were built in the surrounding areas under the auspices of the Department of the Seine, a housing authority formed in 1912 to deal with the area round Paris. Such large estates as Chatenay Malabry, Plessis-Robinson to the south, Cité de la Muette, Drancy, and Cité de Suresnes to the north are examples. In Berlin similar estates known as Siedlungen were built on the outskirts, like Spandau-Haselhorst and Siemensstadt. The estates on the outskirts of Paris and Berlin consisted mostly of apartment houses (flats), and this is the case with the majority of cities in Germany and France, although there are important modifications and exceptions like the estate on the outskirts of Merseburg, which consists of about half small-family two-storey houses and half three-storey blocks of flats. In Belgium and Sweden there was a greater tendency to follow the English custom of building family houses on the outskirts.

The custom in the majority of European cities of building blocks of flats in the new estates on the outskirts rather than family houses as in England is due very largely to habit of thought, certainly not from the choice of the families living in them, because there is overwhelming evidence to show that nine out of ten of these families would prefer two-storey houses with individual gardens. The habit of thought is the outcome of the traditional way of living. The traditional way in Paris, Berlin, and other European cities is in apartment blocks, whereas in England it is rather in the cottage or the small house. (I am for the present alluding to the majority, generally the lower-income groups, including the less well-to-do of the middle classes.) The reason for this difference is probably as much military as anything else. On the Continent the preservation of defensive city walls up to the middle of the nineteenth century forced a considerable degree of vertical extension within the walls, whereas the discarding of such defensive walls in England three centuries earlier encouraged horizontal extension in the form of cottage development.

Block designed by *Fred Forbat*

at buildings in the Siemensstadt Estate,
ear Berlin, 1929–30, designed by a group of
chitects under the general supervision
Walter Gropius

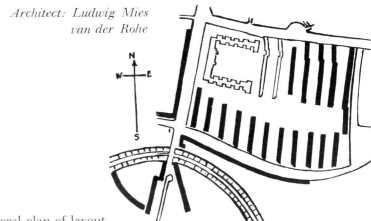

Block of flats
at Weissenhof, Stuttgart,
1929

*Architect: Ludwig Mies
van der Rohe*

General plan of layout

Block designed by
Hans Scharoun

Block designed by
Walter Gropius

The estates, built between the wars, surrounding Paris and Berlin are generally better situated than those of London, because they do not continue the urban sprawl so unbrokenly as in the case of London. There is more open space between them and the central areas, but they cannot be regarded as complete successes in planning because they are not comprehensive units, as in the case of Letchworth and Welwyn. In France, in building satellite towns, or garden cities as they were officially described by the Department of the Seine, it may have been the intention to build them on the lines of Ebenezer Howard's ideas as partially manifested in the two English examples mentioned, but if this were so the principles were certainly not adequately grasped, as they are mainly dormitory areas. The neighbourhoods are generally too small to make self-contained towns in which most of the population can live and work without the frequent necessity of going outside, and they are much too near Paris. The largest of these neighbourhoods is Plessis-Robinson, which includes schools, markets, churches, theatre, cinemas, and many of the amenities usually required; but most of the population have to go outside to work, and among the trials of the inhabitants is the problem of transport to and from the centre[2]. The estates on the outskirts of Berlin, which were more consistently of blocks of flats of from four to six storeys, were smaller than in the case of the Parisian 'garden cities', and they were a little nearer the centre. They were included in the actual area of Berlin with the extension of the boundary in 1935. Being closer they were more in the nature of suburbs in spacious settings than were the estates round Paris, and transport to work was less of a problem. But neither development, from the standpoint of good urban planning, is ideal. If socially and economically comprehensive satellite towns had been built at least twenty miles out, with populations of between fifty and eighty thousand, more in conformity with the principles of Ebenezer Howard or Tony Garnier, the results would have been more socially satisfactory.

In most cases the flats built in the outlying estates both in Paris and Berlin are superior to those built in the redevelopment areas in the centre. The former represent some of the most progressive flat-building in Europe. The new apartment blocks in the central areas built for the lower-income groups are far less satisfactory, particularly in Paris, as, for example, those built on the old fortifications. These are seven and eight storeys high (lifts are provided) and contain very small flats with small rooms, and the density of population is from 350 to 500 per acre.

In the nineteenth century and early years of the twentieth the majority of apartment blocks were built round closed courts, very much in the fashion of office blocks built round light-wells, so that in the rooms on the lower floors facing on to these courts the daylighting is inadequate. Most building of this kind was then in the hands of private speculators, and the tendency was to crowd as many flats as possible to the acre. We can see the results in the congested building of this type in London, Berlin, Paris, and other cities, and it is not confined to the flats of the less well-to-do. The first

296

developments towards large courts resulted from legislation covering planning and density. This was followed by opening the court at one end, and then by variations such as opening the court at the corners. The majority of blocks of flats built by the London County Council between the wars was of this type[3]. The principal part of the China Walk Estate in Lambeth (1928–34) is built round a rectangular garden court open to Kennington Road, and the flats of the East Hill Estate are built round central courts (1925–9). The principal part of the estate consists of two squares formed by blocks of flats of five storeys, each with inner and outer blocks. The centre buildings in the Delaporte Square are round a closed court, while the larger rectangle of the north square is broken. Other examples of similar methods of site planning are seen in the Ossulston, Clapham Park, and Honor Oak Estates, and the immense private development of Dolphin Square, London with its ten-storey blocks, enclosing a spacious lawn, designed by Gordon Jeeves. In later examples there is a tendency to lengthen the rectangles, with the long sides running approximately north–south with the rooms facing east and west. If the buildings are only one flat wide, as they are in most of these L.C.C. flats, then this arrangement for the long side blocks is satisfactory, but the end transverse blocks face north and south, and unless the flats are designed so that living rooms face south, then it is hardly satisfactory. Bedrooms should also get some sun, and it is pleasant for the kitchen to have the early morning sun, but this would sometimes be difficult in the case of the end blocks. Their elimination, as was done in Germany, is the best method.

The methods of site planning in the London examples mentioned were also common at this time in some of the great estates in other countries. At Plessis-Robinson, near Paris, apartment blocks are built round long courtyards broken by a roadway in the centre. A famous example in Vienna is the Karl Marx Hof, completed in 1930 and designed by the chief city architect, Karl Ehn. The area of this scheme is long and narrow, orientated north–south, and the flats are built round spacious central gardens with only a few connecting blocks running east–west. The building is four and five storeys, and the gardens and the whole layout give an impression of spaciousness. There are only twenty-nine dwellings to the acre, which is about half the density of many flat buildings in central areas of Berlin, Paris, and London. But the type of flat planning in the Karl Marx Hof is less satisfactory than the general layout. The flats are back to back, with four on each landing, so that about half in the long north–south rows face east and half face west. Those living in the former must sometimes sigh for the afternoon sun, and those in the latter for the morning sun. Also it prevents cross ventilation.

The first departure on a big scale from formal symmetrical planning and from the custom of building round a courtyard occurs in Germany. From opening the court at one end, generally to the south, the next step is to open it at both ends so that the result is parallel strips running approximately north–south. With the blocks single-flat width it means that they get both morning and afternoon sun. Important examples of this are the Dammerstock Siedlung at Karlsruhe and the Spandau-Haselhorst and Siemensstadt Siedlung near Berlin, while an interesting example combined with two-storey family houses is the previously mentioned estate near Merseburg, planned by Alexander Klein. In this layout, which occupies a triangular site, the three-storey blocks of flats which lie to the east of the estate are oriented north–south. For purposes of good lighting they are more widely spaced than the rows of houses, and we find in most of the blocks of flats planned in Germany in this way on the land outside the cities that fair space is allowed between the strips so as to afford satisfactory daylighting and sunlight. The best example is the Siemensstadt Estate, built in 1929–30 to designs by a group of architects including Walter Gropius, Hans Scharoun, and Fred Forbat. The strips run north–south with the exception of one long strip which runs approximately east–west, in which case the flats are designed accordingly, although they are less satisfactory because of such orientation. The blocks are widely spaced according to the relation of the height of four and five storeys to the angle of light, so that each flat has the maximum of sunlight[4]. In the Cité de la Muette at Drancy (1930–4), designed by Beaudouin and Lods, there are strips of three- and four-storey blocks for families, running northeast–southwest in pairs, with tall, fifteen-storey towers in the centre at the northeastern end containing four small flats on each floor for single persons or couples. The orientation of the three- and four-storey flats is excellent, but it is difficult to appreciate the point of the towers with a flat on each side, where the aspect is likely to be unsatisfactory for the two flats facing northwest and northeast.

CLASSIFICATION OF FLAT TYPES

Many methods of the grouping of flats have been evolved and it is convenient to classify them according to the type of access. A fairly good classification is: (1) corridor access; (2) gallery access; and (3) direct access, with access to one, two, three, four, or five flats on each landing. This is the broad classification followed by F. R. S. Yorke and Frederick Gibberd in their book on *The Modern Flat*[5]. They subdivide the last item into direct single, direct in pairs, and direct grouped. This subdivision is important because there is often considerable difference in planning between the fairly common direct access in pairs and direct grouped. H. Kamenka in his book on flats makes the classification of: (1) the corridor plan, in which he includes gallery access; (2) the individual plan, which comprises direct access to one or two flats to a landing; and (3) the group plan, where the access at each landing is to three or more flats[6]. It is convenient here to take the four classifications of: (1) corridor access; (2) gallery access; (3) direct access to one or two; and (4) direct access to three or more. (This classification is referred to again in Chapter 40 when apartment house design in the period from 1947 to 1970 is discussed, and various types of tower block plan are added to the classification.)

(1) The corridor type as a means of access was very common in England in early flat buildings, but it is attended with many disadvantages and for that reason probably it

has been much less common elsewhere in Europe. In the older types the corridor is generally central between two rows of flats, and thus the building is planned very much as an office block or hotel. One of the disadvantages is that orientation cannot be satisfactory for all the flats arranged on either side of a corridor. Another is that there cannot be satisfactory cross ventilation for the flats, another that it is wasteful of space, and another that there is only one entrance to the flat, which has to serve both as a main and service entrance. From the standpoint of orientation it is better when there is only one row of flats and the corridor is on one side, but when this is the case it more often becomes the gallery access type.

In the most progressive work of this period we do not generally find the corridor access employed except for the smaller type of flat in central areas for single persons, couples, and business people. Kinship with the hotel is apparent. Examples are the Mount Royal Flats in Oxford Street, designed by Sir John Burnet, Tait, and Lorne (1930–4); the Kollektivhus, in Stockholm, designed by Sven Markelius; the Werkbundssiedlung in Breslau, designed by Hans Scharoun (1929); and the Swiss Pavilion in Paris, designed by Le Corbusier and P. Jeanneret (1930–2). The first consists mainly of one-room flats with bathroom and kitchen attached, with the central corridor between two rows. The block of flats in Stockholm consists of one- and two-room flats with restaurant on ground floor, food lifts, and provision on the ground floor for children, who can be cared for while both parents are away at work. The short corridor serves several flats on each floor on either side and at the ends. It might be regarded by some as an approximation to the group plan, or direct access to a group. Hans Scharoun's flats at Breslau are for single persons and couples, and each flat has a living room and bedroom arranged very ingeniously. From the corridor on the first floor one descends to the living room of one flat and ascends to that of another, and again descends and ascends to the bedrooms, which are thus arranged below and above the corridor. A terrace partly covered is on the roof for the benefit of the residents. It is of reinforced concrete construction and has a very pleasing appearance, with the long, horizontal bands of windows of the two wings and the large plain masses of wall.

The Swiss Pavilion in the University City in Paris consists of one-room flats or bedsitting rooms on one side of the corridor facing southwest. The five-storey rectangular block of steel frame construction is perched on concrete stilts which occupy the ground floor, and is cantilevered out. The windows are large to the southwest and small on the northeast corridor side. Projecting from this main block on the northeast side on the ground floor are the hall, reading rooms, and offices enclosed by a concave façade, an effect continued on a reduced scale for the upper storey to house the stairs, lift, and lavatories. The ashlar treatment of the concrete slabs on the large, flat, curved surface combined with the design of the main block hoisted up on stilts gives to the whole an arresting dramatic character.

(2) The gallery access type with the open corridor on one side of a row of flats permits cross ventilation, and if the staircases are at long intervals it is a cheap form of construction. But its disadvantages are considerable and it is probably the worst form of apartment block (flat) planning. In flats privacy is a main requirement, while it is desirable to admit as much light as possible; thus it is a question of adjustment between these two requirements. If living rooms or bedrooms face on to the gallery it is difficult to obtain the degree of privacy that most families would desire, because other tenants would be passing along the gallery at all times of the day and probably late at night. For children going to bed early it is certainly undesirable. For family flats of any size which contain a living room and two or three bedrooms, it is hardly possible to avoid having one of the rooms at least facing on to the gallery. The galleries also overshadow the flats below and thus considerably reduce light. Yet this is the type very largely adopted by the then London County Council, doubtless because of its low cost.

The best examples of this type are where smaller two-room flats are involved, and three fairly good examples from Germany, Switzerland, and Holland are the Dammerstock Siedlung at Karlsruhe, designed by Walter Gropius in 1929, some flats designed by the Italian architect Alberto Sartoris at Vevey in 1930, and the Bergpolder Flats at Rotterdam designed by Brinkmann and Van der Vlugt in 1933. The Dammerstock Siedlung, designed by Gropius, consists of small flats with a living room and bedroom separated from the access gallery by the kitchen and bathroom. A small balcony opens from the living room on the other side. The flats at Vevey for office workers also have the kitchen and bathroom against the access gallery, with the living rooms and bedrooms on the farther side opening on to private balconies.

The Bergpolder Flats at Rotterdam have a living room with two bedrooms, one of which faces on to the access gallery: difficult to avoid if the plan were to be compact. The living room opens on to a balcony which, though continuous, is divided for the private use of each flat.

This block of flats is structurally and architecturally worthy of note. It is ten storeys with basement, which houses the central heating and hot water plant. It is of steel-frame construction with reinforced concrete construction in the basement. The block is orientated north–south so that the flats face east and west, the living rooms facing west. The flats are enclosed between two long horizontal balconies with wide opaque bands on the east access side and glass-fronted balconies on the west side. Slender steel uprights run the whole height of the building at the flat intervals. The staircase and lift at the north end are enclosed in a glass screen, with the exception of the opaque wall at the left, which is faced, like the other walls, with steel sheeting on pumice blocks. At the base of the staircase tower is a short row of one-storey shops. The whole block is a vivid expression of the lightness of modern steel and glass construction.

(3) The direct access to one or two flats per floor is a method of planning which has
been shown to have numerous advantages, and it is probably the best arrangement
which has so far been developed. It affords opportunities for varied planning, and if
the blocks are in strips orientated north–south, so that the windows face east and west,
a maximum of sunlight is obtained, cross ventilation is ensured, while the greatest
degree of privacy is secured by this arrangement.

One flat per landing is not common in large apartment blocks: it is generally to be
found in smaller blocks in central areas on narrow sites between two other buildings,
in luxury flats, and in large houses converted into flats. Access to two flats per landing
is, however, fairly common, and the best examples during the period under survey
are those in long, straight blocks orientated north–south. Examples are the flats at
Weissenhof, Stuttgart (1927), designed by Mies van der Rohe; the estate at
Siemensstadt (1930), designed by a group of architects under the general direction of
Walter Gropius; flats at Pankrac, Prague (1930), designed by Honzík and Havlíček;
and those at Kosice (1931), also in Czechoslovakia, designed by Josef Polasek; the
three-storey flats at Drancy (1930–4), designed by Beaudouin and Lods; and those at
Geneva (1932) and at La Porte Molitor (1923–3), designed by Le Corbusier and P.
Jeanneret.

The flats by Mies van der Rohe, at Stuttgart, formed part of the famous housing
exhibition of 1927 in that city (see Chapter 23). This block of flats is a long strip of
three storeys with a basement and storage rooms, communal laundries and gardens
forming a fourth or roof floor. There are four staircases which serve eight flats of
different sizes, from two to four rooms, on each floor. The block is constructed with a
light steel frame and standardized wall sections and windows, the latter being large
and making continuous horizontal fenestration except for the uprights at partition
intervals. Part of the roof is cantilevered over the garden portion. The slender sections,
large windows, and cantilevered roof give an effect of lightness and airiness which one
has learned to associate with the work of this architect.

The Siemensstadt estate provides the finest and most varied examples of this type of
planning. As previously mentioned, the blocks are mainly orientated north–south, and
are four or five storeys high. They consist for the most part of flats with a living room
and two or three bedrooms, kitchen, and bathroom. The two blocks designed by
Walter Gropius vary slightly. One block has the staircase marked on the west front
with long, vertical glass strips, while balconies open from the living rooms on the
same side. The living rooms of the adjoining flats coming together, one balcony divided
in the centre by a partition serves both. The other block has a similar arrangement of
balconies on the west front, but the staircases are on the east side. Another, designed
by Fred Forbat, has a similar plan, but the balconies on the west side are continuous,
separated by brick partitions extending nearly the height of the building, and both

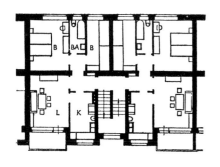 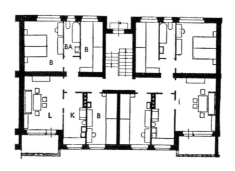

Examples of various types
of flat planning at the
Siemensstadt Estate,
Berlin, 1929–30

Two types by *Walter Gropius*

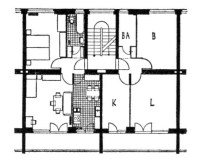 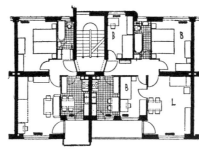 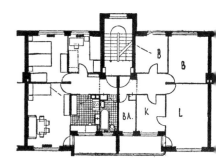

Three types by *Fred Forbat*

Three types by *Hans Scharoun*

Swiss Pavilion,
University City, Paris

Architects:
Le Corbusier
and P. Jeanneret

living rooms and kitchens open on to the balconies. A further variation by Fred Forbat has small recessed balconies similar to those of Gropius, but instead of being in front of the living room they are in front of the kitchen and bathrooms, and they connect with the living room at the ends. In this case the balconies are opposite the staircase on the east side. One block planned in this way is for flats all approximately the same size, with living room, two bedrooms, kitchen, and bathroom, and another block planned on a similar principle has one small flat with one bedroom on one side of the staircase, and one larger flat with three bedrooms on the other side. The former has a small, square balcony accessible from the living room and kitchen, the other has a longer balcony similarly accessible. One of the disadvantages of these otherwise excellent flats is that the balconies of the pairs of flats adjoin and are separated only by a partition. In the Siemensstadt flats, designed by Hans Scharoun, this is avoided, and in all the variations each flat has a balcony clearly separated from that adjoining. In one the small balconies open from living rooms on either side of the staircase, in another block the balcony is in front of the living room, recessed between the staircases and a bedroom, and in another block the small balconies project outwards like a sector shaded on the curved side.

The variations on the theme of two flats per landing in the Siemensstadt flats provide a school of study in this method of planning[7]. Construction is of load-bearing brick walls with reinforced concrete lintels which makes possible the recessed balconies and large windows, and concrete floors.

The general exteriors of these apartment blocks denote fairly clearly their interior arrangement. In many designed by Gropius, Forbat, and Scharoun the staircase, marked by the vertical glass screen, or projecting vertical mass, coming at the interval of every two flats is clearly apparent; while the differently proportioned windows often indicate the rooms, so that to the discerning eye it would be simple to deduce the interior arrangement from the appearance of the exterior.

As can be judged from the general layout plan the strips are widely spaced, with stretches of grass and trees between, tall trees with light delicate foliage, which do not obscure much light, silver birches being generally favoured. The long blocks with pale, plain walls and large windows with a general horizontal character emphasized by the balconies, set in these spacious surroundings and seen in relation to the trees and expanses of grass give a very pleasing general effect which has won the hearts of many visitors, among them young architects from other countries.

The flats at Pankrac, Prague, designed by Havlíček and Honzík in 1930, and those at Kosice, designed by Josef Polasek in 1931, are similar in planning to the Siemensstadt flats of Gropius and Forbat. Both have recessed balconies of neighbouring flats adjoining, and both have an external effect not dissimilar. Those at Kosice are built on three sides of a square with a garden in the centre. The construction is with brick load-bearing walls, with reinforced concrete lintels for balconies and windows. The flats at Pankrac are constructed with a reinforced concrete frame, with walls and partitions of hollow blocks, and double-glazed windows. The long horizontal windows and slender uprights between, and the plain walls contribute to an effect of lightness which in character is similar to the architects' famous Institute of Pensions Building in Prague.

The horizontal blocks at Drancy, three storeys high, varying to four storeys at the ends farthest from the fifteen-storey towers, provide another example of two flats per landing. The flats are of the family type with living room and two bedrooms. It will be remembered that these blocks are orientated northeast and southwest, and are arranged in pairs, terminating at one end in the fifteen-storey tower. In planning the flats, the kitchen, w.c., and laundry with a small balcony, and one bedroom are placed on the inside, and the living room and one bedroom on the outside. The balcony–kitchen–laundry group in each flat is separated from the neighbouring flat on one side by the staircase. By this arrangement the living room and one bedroom on one side faces southeast, and in the block on the other side of the central garden it faces northwest, with the group of balcony–kitchen–laundry and one bedroom facing the reverse way in each case. The only conceivable reason for this unsatisfactory arrangement is that the architects were anxious to have a symmetrical appearance. The staircases with balconies project at regular intervals and opposite each other, like massive buttresses. On the outer, living room side, there is a very dull façade of square windows in which good spacing has been the aim if not the achievement. The construction of these flats is on the Mopin system, with light steel frames and pre-cast aerated concrete panels. Two flats per landing is the method followed in many flats built for working people at this time in France, including those at Plessis-Robinson, to which reference has already been made. Some of these flats, including those at Drancy, provide early examples of the Garchey system of refuse disposal.

Two apartment blocks by Le Corbusier and P. Jeanneret come within this classification —one in Geneva (1932) for professional persons like doctors, writers, and painters, and the other called Parc des Princes at La Porte Molitor (1933). The former is an eight-storey block with four apartments on each floor served by two staircases. In the lower ground floor are garages and heating plant. Those at La Porte Molitor are four-roomed flats for the well-to-do, two to each landing, in a seven-storey building, with a large top-floor studio flat for Le Corbusier himself. The walls of these buildings are almost completely glass. That at Geneva is constructed of a light steel frame with the double glazed windows covering almost the whole of the façades. The bands of the large balcony fronts give the building a horizontal emphasis. The apartment block at La Porte Molitor is between two other buildings. The front is mainly of large glass windows and glass blocks in a slender framework, the whole being supported on reinforced concrete floors held by five reinforced concrete columns. The flats are served

Block of flats (apartment-house)
at Prague-Pankrac, 1932

Front elevation and plans

Architects: J. Havlíček and K. Honzík

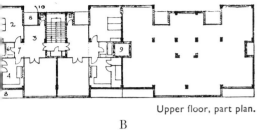

Upper floor, part plan.

B

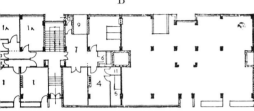

round floor, part plan.

Salvation Army, City of Refuge, 1930–33
early example of air-conditioning

Architect: Le Corbusier

Bergpolder apartment house (block of flats)
Rotterdam, 1933 View from north-west

Architects:
J. A. Brinkmann and L. C. Van der Vlugt

Apartment houses, Doldertal, Zürich, 1935–36

Architects: Alfred and Emil Roth and Marcel Breuer

by staircase and lift which open on to a corridor on each landing, with the flat entrance at either end. A light-well is arranged within the building to give additional light to each flat.

(4) To plan three or more flats per landing and to obtain all the advantages accompanying the two-flat plan requires considerable ingenuity. In four flats per landing, which is the commonest number above two, the flats are generally arranged back to back, so that if the block is orientated north–south one flat faces east and one west, with windows north and south for end flats. Apart from this unsatisfactory arrangement there is no cross ventilation. Examples of this type are some flats in Budapest, designed by Josef Fisher (1930–3), and flats at Casa Rosellon, Barcelona, designed by J. Luis Sert (1929). Where there is plenty of space better planning can be achieved, as in the flats for office workers at Breslau, designed by Adolf Rading (1929). Here the central staircase separates two square blocks, so that they have external walls on three sides. This allows for cross ventilation. The windows on the walls facing inwards must necessarily be small for the sake of privacy. In the fifteen-storey towers at Drancy, four flats are grouped round the staircase and lift. Two of the flats have one room with kitchen and accessories, and two have two rooms with kitchen and accessories. Each flat occupies a corner of the square, and this has two aspects. One of these flats faces northeast and northwest, which is very much less favoured than that facing southeast and southwest. A development of the group of flats per landing which took place later is the cross plan found a good deal in the USA, but that obviously has numerous disadvantages of orientation, while windows facing on to those of another flat on a wall at right angles reduces privacy considerably.

Ingenious planning with five small flats per landing is seen in a small apartment block in Budapest designed and built by Olgyay and Olgyay in Budapest in 1938. It is a four storey block with three central one-room flats and two side two-room flats (each with kitchen and bathroom) so arranged that all flats have principal windows to the south garden—faced with balconies (see plan). The balconies are boxed to give maximum privacy. Garages for all flats are in the basement reached from the street by a ramp. There is an internal stairway from the garages to the flats. On the flat roof is a common sunroom and garden terrace. Although symmetrical the planning is functional and ingenious.

Judging from the best examples in Europe during this period it appears that the most satisfactory type of plan from almost every conceivable point of view is the long block in which the flats are arranged in a row facing approximately east and west, and with a staircase, and lift in the case of tall blocks, serving two flats per floor. This type, forming some of the new estates in the outlying areas of cities, has been associated with flat buildings that are architecturally the most agreeable. If one had to select the finest, architecturally, of the period between the wars it would be difficult to find any to surpass the Siemensstadt Group.

The architectural excellence of this Siemensstadt Group has prompted many young British architects to wish to emulate this achievement and has encouraged propaganda for flats in preference to the traditional two-storey, semi-detached or terrace houses that are commonly built on new estates in the outlying areas of cities and towns in England. It could not be convincingly asserted that flats in five-storey blocks provided better and more convenient accommodation than two-storey houses with a garden attached. Flats may be convenient for bachelors, spinsters, newly married or old couples, but nobody can contend, who has thought of the matter in all its aspects, that flats offer such satisfactory accommodation for family life. The only argument that can have weight is the aesthetic one, and it was the aesthetic aspect which captivated young architects of this period and a little later. How much finer, they argue, to have flats like those of Gropius at Siemensstadt, with spacious lawns spreading on either side and silver birches patterned against the long, pale walls; how much better to have this majestic ensemble than the rows and rows of horrible little suburban villas that have grown in the outskirts of London. Thinking on these lines, F. R. S. Yorke and Frederick Gibberd have placed two photographs together on page 15 of their book *The Modern Flat*. One photograph is of rows of semi-detached houses in a new estate. They pepper the landscape unpleasantly. The estate is typical of many. The other is of a project for a modern block of flats of reinforced concrete construction. It is a nine-storey block on stilts set in spacious surroundings, with formal gardens at one end, an extensive lawn with a group of trees in the foreground, while in the distance is a lake bordered by shrubs and trees. The setting is idyllic, modelled somewhat on the compositions of Poussin and Claude. And the authors say: 'We are giving up this', referring to a country landscape, 'for this', referring to the suburban estate, 'rather than for this', referring to the magnificent block of flats set in the idyllic landscape. It would be possible to find a group of houses as pleasing architecturally as these flats and set in as lovely surroundings. The point is that the authors take a bad example of an estate of small semi-detached houses and compare it with what to them was an almost ideal block of flats set in ideal surroundings. The comparison is not a fair one but it is indicative of the trend of thought common among many young architects in Europe after having the invigorating experience of seeing some of the best German flat buildings in good surroundings.

A few outstanding examples of apartment blocks of various kinds built during the thirties that have become justifiably famous should be noted. Among these are the two small apartment blocks on the eastern slopes of a valley at Doldertal near Zurich, built in 1935–36 for Sigfried Giedion the famous critic and historian of art and architecture and for many years secretary of the Congres Internationaux d'Architecture Moderne. The architects were Alfred and Emil Roth, and Marcel Breuer.

The Doldertal valley is well wooded, with a stream and a general slope towards the

307

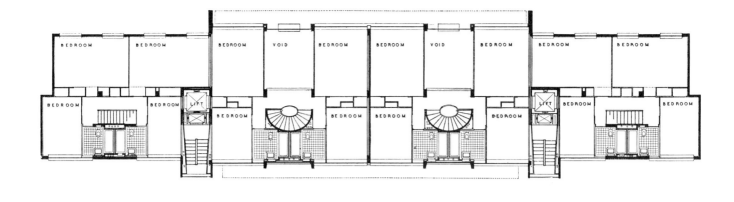

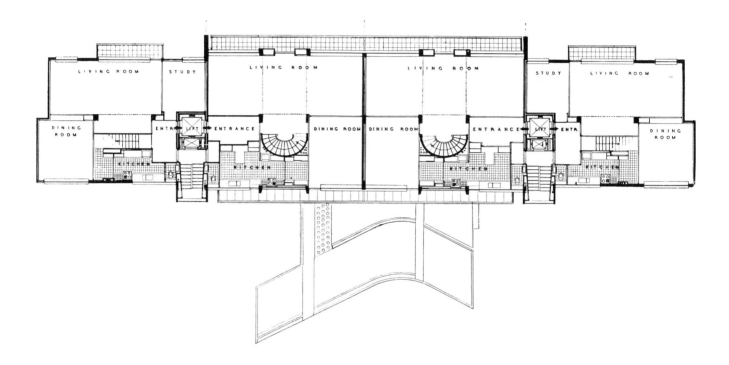

Highpoint flats, Highgate, 1936–38
Above—second, fourth and sixth floor plans; first, third, and fifth floor plans. (Of second block.)
Below, left—entrance porch of second block with caryatid; right—general view of exterior as
it appeared in 1973   *Architects: Tecton*

Front view and plans

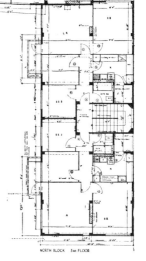

Kensal House, block of flats, Ladbroke Grove, London, 1938–39

Architects: Robert Atkinson, E. Maxwell Fry, C. H. James and G. Grey Wornum

Circular covered walk in front of nursery school attached to block of flats; below—sketch

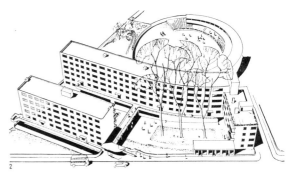

south and is one of the many beautiful spots in the environs of Zürich. The apartment blocks are identical and each is planned like a fat **L** with the external angle due south, thus with the two outer façades and the principal rooms facing southeast and southwest with views over the wooded valley. The site is fairly steep, the ground floor is open at the southwest end with columns as a peristyle to the garages, and is below ground at the northeast end, utilized for laundry and storage. The staircase occupies the northwest wing, with the heating plant below ground. The first floor has a large family flat with three bedrooms, library and large living room, from which a terrace facing southwest opens. Also on this floor is a one room flat with entrance on the northeast side where it is level with the ground. The second floor is similar but with one large family flat with four bedrooms and a music room. The top floor has two studios large and small, and each has living room, bathroom and kitchenette. The construction is steel frame, with cellular brick walls and reinforced concrete floors, the walls and floors being structurally independent. The external finish is of white cement mixed with a natural stone aggregate, while on the studio floor the walls are faced with sheets of asbestos cement to give variety. Horizontal windows and bands of the balcony fronts relating to the verticals of the columns results in very pleasingly proportioned blocks, and the whole effect is enhanced by the woodland landscape of which surprise glimpses can be obtained between the balconies and in all directions from the windows. This is a very happy blending of modern architecture and the landscape[8].

About the same time (1935) a block of flats, called Highpoint, was built at Highgate, a suburb north of London, which aroused much admiration in progressive architectural circles as one of the best works in London of the new architecture. It was designed by the Tecton Group[9]. The block is situated near the summit of Highgate Hill with views mainly to the south. It is eight storeys and on plan consists of two equilateral crosses joined together. On the seven upper floors one flat occupies each of the four arms with the lift and staircase in the centre of the cross—thus four flats per landing. Flats are two and three bedroom types, both with large living rooms.

On the ground floor is a series of bedrooms for maids with a tea room and large hall thus affording more independent living conditions for maids than is usual. Also on the ground floor is the porter's flat and a winter garden. The block is of concrete slab construction and the tall façades are patterned with long horizontal windows and balcony fronts. High on the hill set among trees and shrubs it is a majestic spectacle and it was an inspiring vision for many young architects of the time. Yet its effect on the people of Highgate illustrates one of the major obstacles to progressive architecture with which architects in the thirties in England had to contend. Instead of acclaiming this as an impressive example of modern architecture, as it is now widely accepted, the people of Highgate were so outraged at this monstrosity, as they typified it, that they took steps to prevent the repetition of this kind of building. A Highgate

Preservation Society was formed for this very purpose. Thus, when the clients wished
to build an extension of this block two years later, the client and architects met with
considerable obstruction from the local authority on various grounds based to some
extent on town planning legislation, but to a considerable extent on what the local
authority believed to be the feelings of Highgate residents. Many schemes were
proposed. The first was a repetition of the existing block, but was rejected, and the
scheme ultimately adopted was a seven-storey slab block running south from the
existing building, with gardens to the west, including a swimming pool and squash
courts, reached by an access road along the south of the site, where there is also a series
of garages arranged in eschelon fashion.

The apartments in Highpoint two, as it is called, are large family luxury flats and the
design is original and ingenious. There are six large central apartments and six small
end flats all occupying two floors each, sometimes called duplex flats. Thus each floor
has a row of four flats reached by two staircases and lifts between the central and end
flats, with entrances on the first, third and fifth floors. These two-storey apartments
each have a large living room with long balcony facing towards the garden and the
west, with dining room and kitchen on the other side. On the upper floor, reached by
an internal staircase there are four bedrooms and two bathrooms. The centre part of
the large living rooms of the centre flats rises to the full height of both floors and has
a central window 16 ft high by 10 ft wide. The purpose of these spacious living rooms
is for large family gatherings and receptions. In the end flats the living rooms are
smaller and there is the addition of a study. The penthouse set back on the roof makes
an eighth storey. The entrance hall on the ground floor is flanked by two ramps
leading to the lifts and stairs. In both wings there is a series of maids' rooms thus
following the principle adopted in Highpoint one, while at the rear is a series of
garages and porters accommodation.

The construction of the two end wings of Highpoint two is of concrete wall slabs,
with central reinforced columns and beams supporting the floors. The central part is of
reinforced concrete frame construction, the lift shafts and stairs being constructed
independently.

The general appearance of Highpoint two is slightly less austere than Highpoint one,
achieved by some variety of facing textures, and by the rather fanciful and very
attractive treatment of the entrance. A large canopy with a concave front to conform
with the curve of the drive projects over it, and flanking the approach are two
supporting caryatids, copies of those of the Erectheum on the Acropolis at Athens. These
give a note of fancifulness to the entrance which is welcome after the rather stark
functionalism of earlier essays in the new architecture[10].

An unusual block of flats also in Highgate, built in the late thirties, is that known as
Cholmeley Lodge, designed by Guy Morgan. The distinctive and unusual feature of

this six-storey block is that it is a series of three curves—three quarter circles—on plan with the inside curves facing south and looking over Waterlow Park. There are two- and three-bedrooms flats, and each has a lounge and dining room, separate and combined, and one or two bedrooms on the south side with kitchens and bathrooms, and one of the bedrooms on the north side. All the upper floor flats have balconies towards the south and there are two flats per landing. The radius for the inside curves is 30 feet, the minimum for straight casement windows and straight fittings. The planning is ingenious and the architectural ensemble with the brick faced balconies, is effective. The main economic advantage appears to be that more flats of a given size are included than if it had been a simple straight slab block[11].

The three blocks of flats at Highgate are notable examples of building by private enterprise for the more well-to-do. There were at the same time a few notable Municipal and subsidized flats built in the late thirties of which I give two examples. The Quarry Hill Flats at Leeds, built in 1939, for the municipality in 1939 to the design of R. A. H. Livett, is one of the largest apartment blocks in Europe. It comprises 938 flats and is a seven-storey curved block with internal access to the flats by means of stairs and lifts. A particularly interesting feature of these flats was the introduction for the first time in England of the Evier-Vidoir or Garchy system of refuse disposal by means of an aperture in the sink, a system[12] used earlier in several blocks of flats in France including those at Drancy la Muette, a suburb of Paris, previously mentioned.

One of the most notable schemes for flats for the lower income groups is Kensal House built in 1938, as part of the Kensington Borough Council's slum clearance. The scheme was initiated by the Gas, Light and Coke Company as an experiment in a mass automatic fuel service, and was planned by a group of well-known architects, Robert Atkinson, E. Maxwell Fry, C. H. James, and G. Grey Wornum, with Elizabeth Denby as housing consultant. The site is part of a disused gas works near the railway. Two blocks, each five storeys, run north–south. The long west block is slightly curved and at its north end running at right angles eastward is a short four-storey wing. The buildings enclose a garden with tall trees, and a bridge runs from the street near the short block to a footway in front of the long block. Beyond this is a circular nursery school built on the site of a former gas holder.

Of the 68 flats provided, 54 have three bedrooms and 14 two bedrooms. They are very well planned with the three bedrooms on the east side and the living–dining room, kitchen and bathroom on the west side. There is internal access with two flats per landing, while balconies are provided on the west side. Here were first rate flats at very low rents (in 1938 the flats were 11s 6d a week and 9s 6d a week inclusive of rates), while as buildings they are a distinctive contribution to the modern architecture of London.

In the late thirties the general tendency in Europe was away from the large blocks built round courtyards like Dolphin Square in London, and those built in 1930–3, on the site of ancient fortifications in Paris by L'Immobiliere Construction de Paris, and towards the slab type like those of Siemensstadt Siedlung, Berlin, or the tower type which was a later innovation. At Drancy la Muette near Paris the two are combined with three- and four-storey slab blocks and fifteen-storey tower blocks which, as far as I am aware, were the highest built at that time (1933) in Europe. These formed the basic units of innumerable schemes built since, including the extensive Roehampton development after the Second World War. The tower block, or 'Punkthuse' (point house), as it was called, was developed considerably in Sweden as in such examples as the Guldheden settlement near Gothenburg and the Danviks Cliff settlement near Stockholm. Many of these flats with four to a landing meant an unsatisfactory orientation for two of the flats and many variations in planning were tried by architects to overcome this disadvantage[13]. (See Chapter 40.)

REFERENCES AND NOTES

1. See Frederic J. Osborn and Arnold Whittick, *The New Towns—the Answer to Megalopolis*, London, 1963 and 1969.
2. See Elizabeth Denby, *Europe Re-housed*, London 1938, p. 243.
3. See *London Housing*, LCC, 1937.
4. These calculations were made by Walter Gropius, who was chief architect in the Siemensstadt scheme. Some interesting diagrams, showing how the calculations are made, are given on pages 72 and 73 of Walter Gropius's *The New Architecture and the Bauhaus*, London and New York, 1936.
5. F. R. S. Yorke and F. Gibberd, *The Modern Flat*, London, 1937, pp. 22–28.
6. H. Kamenka, *Flats*, London, 1947, pp. 60–66.
7. These Siemensstadt flats are extremely well illustrated with plans in *The Modern Flat*, by F. R. S. Yorke and Frederick Gibberd, London, 1937, pp. 52–63.
8. A well-illustrated description of the Doldertal apartment blocks is given in Alfred Roth's *The New Architecture*, Zürich, 1947, pp. 47–60.
9. The Tecton Group of architects consisted of Berthold Lubetkin, its founder, Anthony Chitty, Lindsey Drake, Michael Dugdale, Val Harding and Denys Lasdun.
10. A discussion of the difficulties in building Highpoint two and an analysis of the design is given in *The Architectural Review*, October 1938, pp. 161–176.
11. An illustrated description is given in *The Architectural Review*, 1938, pp. 250–254.
12. The Garchy system of refuse disposal is described in Elizabeth Denby's *Europe Re-housed*, London, 1938, pp. 238–241. See also Arnold Whittick, *The Small House: Today and Tomorrow*, second edition, London, 1957, pp. 95–97.
13. See Thomas Paulsson, *Scandinavian Architecture*, London, 1958, pp. 222–227.

23   Houses   1924–1932

THE CHIEF DEVELOPMENTS in planning and construction and the main contributions to progressive architecture are found mainly among the more exclusively utilitarian buildings, while in those partly or mainly of a ceremonial character traditional architecture lingers longer and more prominently. Thus among the most advanced examples are industrial buildings, and town halls and head offices of Banks and Insurance Companies, where impressiveness and ceremonial character are important, are far more traditional in character. Churches, on the other hand, designed so largely for ceremony, reveal, as we have noted, in this period between the wars, less adherence to tradition and considerable originality of treatment. But this has been partially the outcome of new economic and social conditions and new liturgical thinking.

With flats and houses the development in design is not so widely and consistently progressive as in industrial buildings, but in some branches and in some countries it is as marked as in any department of architectural design. We have seen that in flat buildings in Germany from 1925 to 1932 the progress was considerable. Progress in house design was even more marked in Germany and France, indeed if one thinks of the developments in house design in these two countries from 1924 to 1933 it is as remarkable as in any field of architectural design. I refer to the individually designed house, not to the small unit of repetition in collective housing. In the latter field, except for some interesting work by Le Corbusier, J. J. P. Oud, and Walter Gropius, developments were not such as to call for much appreciative comment. The many experiments in house construction which were made in the five years following the First World War resulted in several houses built by new methods, but they were not developed as they might have been and by about 1925 there was a general return to traditional methods of house building. Nor were there, with but few exceptions, important innovations in the planning unit. The old standard plans were varied a little, but were not fundamentally altered. In England, the chief country of urban cottage development, the pattern of parlour and non-parlour type remained very much the same. For example, from 1880 to 1914 a very common type comprised kitchen

314

with scullery, one or two living rooms, and two, but more generally three, bedrooms.
The kitchen and scullery generally projected from the back of the house, thus obscuring
light. After the war the tendency was to eliminate this back projection, and incorporate
the kitchen in the rectangular plan. This served the double purpose of securing more
light for the rear of the house, and building more economically, an important
consideration in view of the increased cost of building. Another tendency, born partially
of the necessity to economize in space and partially of reducing the amount of walking
for the housewife, was to combine the kitchen and scullery in one. With this
combination the kitchen did not become larger, indeed it became smaller, and meals
in the kitchen, which had been common were less easy to accommodate, and the
family was, by this design, more often forced into the dining room or living room to
take meals. At the same time the larder became smaller, because, it was argued, more
frequent deliveries of provisions in urban areas made it unnecessary to store so much.
The substitution of the gas or electric cooker for the solid fuel cooker made a more
flexible equipment of the kitchen possible. Many of these developments were great
improvements, but whether all were is open to doubt. For example, the combination
of kitchen and scullery has many disadvantages, and there were signs in the nineteen-
thirties of a return to the separation, although the scullery had acquired the new
name of utility room[1]. Most of these urban houses, if not all, built since the First
World War had bathrooms which, in this respect, marks considerable progress over
the houses built in the latter years of the nineteenth century.

Although architecturally there is little of note in the small housing unit that was
designed for repetition as terrace, semi-detached, or detached units, between the two
World Wars, that little claims a brief attention. Examples of compact planning for
terrace housing are provided by Le Corbusier's houses built at Pessac near Bordeaux in
1925, by many of the housing schemes of J. J. P. Oud, such as the terrace housing in
the Hook of Holland, built in 1924–5 (see Chapter 13), and the terrace houses at
Amsterdam and Stuttgart, both built in 1927, the last mentioned in collaboration with
Mart Stam, the terrace housing at Romerstadt, a suburb of Frankfurt-on-Main, built
by Ernst May and C. H. Rudloff in 1926, and the prefabricated row housing built by
Walter Gropius at Torten near Dessau. All these houses have a very simple appearance,
with plain walls, and, with the exception of those at Frankfurt, large windows. In
those by Walter Gropius the fenestration expresses the interior function, the long
horizontal windows for the rooms, and the long vertical windows for the staircases.
To most people this modern minimum housing looks a little stark and bare, but it
becomes much more pleasing when seen in relation to lawns, trees, and shrubs, and
when flowers and climbing plants provide a decorative element.

An interesting group of detached units is that of the workmen's dwellings of the
Bata Shoe Factory at Zlin, in Czechoslovakia. In this development the houses are not
sited on either side of the street, but are grouped with the living rooms and bedrooms,

which open on to a balcony, facing towards the south. Each house is surrounded by a garden and access is by paths and service ways. The houses have flat roofs. That they look like so many boxes dumped in a lovely valley is a legitimate architectural criticism, but this does not invalidate their social value and their excellence as planning, while trees variously break the monotonous effects. Here, at any rate, is the right starting point for the architecture of small dwelling units designed for repetition. The orientation is good, and families enjoy a privacy and independence that the completely detached house can give in a greater measure than any other type of dwelling.

That individually designed houses show remarkable progress in planning and design at this time in contrast to that of the unit in collective housing is not surprising. They have been largely separate activities, although in an ideal social state they perhaps should not be, and it is a sign of social progress that they are becoming less so. The contrast was even more marked in England from 1860 to 1914, when such good developments were made in the individually designed house in the hands of Webb, Norman Shaw, Voysey, Ashbee, Lethaby, Newton, Lutyens, and others. These excellent houses were contemporary with the dreary mass housing of the industrial cities. But this better individually designed house exercised an influence on the smaller units designed for repetition, and we see this in some of the houses at Hampstead Garden Suburb, Letchworth, and Welwyn, and other areas in which competent architects were responsible for the designs. Similarly, the influence of the developments of house design in the hands of a few eminent French and German architects began to have its effect on the small unit designed for repetition in the late thirties, and more conspicuously in the period since the Second World War.

Hermann Muthesius, the German architect, had spent some time in England studying domestic architecture from 1898 to 1903, and returned to Germany full of enthusiasm for the work of architects like Webb, Voysey, Mackintosh, and others. He wrote several books in which this enthusiasm is manifest and exercised considerable influence on young German architects at the time. The English influence in Peter Behrens's work is strong in his houses built from 1901 to 1910. In some of these houses there was apparent even more marked development than in contemporary English work, in such features as the introduction of larger windows; in one case, that of the house at Wetter in the Ruhr, built in 1904, amounting almost to a glass wall. In the later houses of Peter Behrens, like the famous house in the Taunus mountains, built in 1931, he became almost as advanced in design and construction as the most progressive exponents. We see in the work of Peter Behrens over a period of thirty years, the stages in the evolution of house design and construction in the early twentieth century.

Important contributions are made by several architects, among the most prominent being Le Corbusier, André Lurçat, Raymond Fischer, and Mallet-Stévens in France; Peter Behrens, Walter Gropius, Mies van der Rohe, Bruno Taut, and Hans Scharoun

316

in Germany; Victor Bourgeois in Belgium; J. J. P. Oud in Holland; and Havlíček and Honzík in Czechoslovakia[2]. The contributions of British architects were to come a little later, and belong to the thirties.

LE CORBUSIER'S EARLY HOUSES

If an architect were selected whose contribution to house-design and construction is the most noteworthy in the period between the wars that architect would most justifiably be Le Corbusier. There are houses by others which are finer than anything Corbusier has done, as, for example, the House Tugendhat at Brunn in Czechoslovakia, designed by Mies van der Rohe, yet when Le Corbusier's work is taken as a whole, when its amount, variety, originality, and beauty are considered it must be regarded as second to none.

Le Corbusier began practice as an architect at 35 rue de Sèvres, Paris, in 1921 at the age of 34. He had then produced a considerable number of projects of a wide variety of buildings but so far only one building had been built from his designs, a house in his birthplace of La Chaux-de-Fonds, Switzerland, erected in 1905. He had done a good deal of writing expounding his architectural theories, and he founded the journal *L'Esprit Nouveau* with Charles Dermée and Amédée Ozenfant in 1920.

During the twenties his work consisted primarily of designing private houses, and it was for the originality, ingenuity and progressive spirit of his domestic architecture in advance of anything elsewhere in Europe that he became world famous. Of the twenty-six buildings that were erected to his designs between 1922 and 1932, eighteen were private houses. He was one of the chief architectural innovators of the century.

Early houses by Le Corbusier[3] are the houses built at Vaucresson in 1922, the one in Paris for Ozenfant, the painter, in the same year, and two at Auteuil in 1923. The external proportions of these houses are very carefully deliberated, and their façades, like those of almost all of Le Corbusier's houses, are designed, he claims, according to classical geometric principles. The house at Vaucresson is a smaller, simple example in which many of the distinctive characteristics of Le Corbusier's later houses are seen in embryo. The plan is a simple rectangle with a projection at one end for the staircase. There are three floors, the living room being on the first floor with a garage on the ground floor. Here we find the open plan employed, because the first floor is in principle one large room with the dining room a recess of the large living room, and the kitchen a small subordinate room adjoining the dining recess (see plan). A movable partition separates dining and living spaces if required. The house is built of concrete, large horizontal windows are used on the sun-side, and long vertical windows make a neck between the house and the staircase projection.

The house for Ozenfant is conditioned by the provision of a large studio which occupies

317

the upper part of the small house, while the houses at Auteuil are two attached houses of three storeys and a roof garden and a picture gallery at one end, all combined in a pleasing unity, which is effected to a considerable extent by the continuous horizontal fenestration of the first floor.

In 1924 Le Corbusier built two houses at Boulogne-sur-Seine, in 1925 a small house for his parents on the shores of the Lake of Geneva, while in 1926 he designed the middle house of a row of three at Boulogne-sur-Seine, the flanking houses being designed by Mallet-Stévens and Raymond Fischer. These are interesting examples of the work of these three architects. Each house was built separately, although they are joined, one wall being built against the other. They are each four storeys, each has approximately the same sized square shape, and each is built of reinforced concrete. It is in the house by Le Corbusier that the possibilities of the structural medium are exploited to their fullest, and his is the most original design. Much of the space on the ground-floor level is open, and the upper floors are supported on three concrete piers between the two party walls. On the ground floor is a small parlour with semicircular front and garage, both set well back, while to the left the space is open to the rear of the house. On the first floor are two bedrooms, boudoir, and bathroom, on the second floor are the living room with dining room opening from it and a kitchen, while on the third floor is the upper part of the living room, a library, and terrace garden, at the front of which are very slender supports to the flat roof. The three slender concrete piers which run from the foundations to the flat roof, between two walls, with concrete platforms for the floors, are the essential structure, and give absolute freedom of planning within this limited space.

In the house by Mallet-Stévens the staircase occupies the left front which is expressed in the exterior by a projecting tower-like form with a vertical window. On the ground floor is the garage, kitchen, and two servant's bedrooms; on the first floor is a large living room, with library at one end and dining room opening from the living room; and on the third floor are bedrooms, bathroom, and the upper part of one end of the living room with a gallery overlooking it. The third floor is a roof garden with a canopy over one part projecting from the staircase tower. Meals are served from the kitchen by means of a service lift. It will be noted from the plans that the partitions have a supporting function, and come one above the other, the structure and design being consequently comparatively traditional and rigid.

A similar character pervades the house designed by Raymond Fischer. The garage is on the ground floor, and the first floor has a large living room, dining room which opens on to a terrace and which is served from the kitchen below, and another small room. The second floor has two bedrooms and a bathroom, with the upper part of the living room with gallery over, somewhat in the manner of Mallet-Stévens's house. The third floor has one small room and the rest is a terrace partly roofed over. Again,

318

Plans of houses

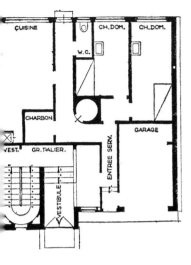

Three attached houses at Boulogne-sur-Seine, France, 1926

Left house, *Architect: R. Mallet Stévens*
Centre house, *Architect: Le Corbusier*
Right house, *Architect: Raymond Fischer*

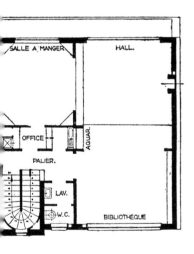

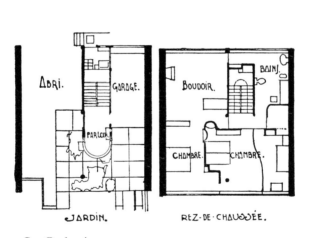

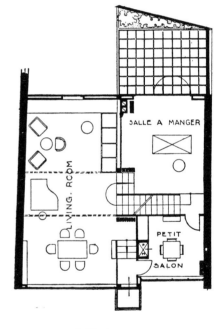

R. Mallet Stévens—ground,
first and second floors

Le Corbusier—
ground, first, second and third floors

Raymond Fischer—
ground and first floors

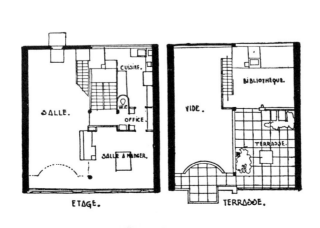

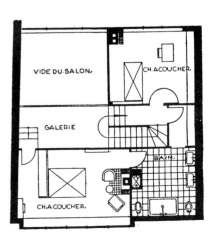

these partitions have a supporting function and come over each other on the various floors.

Note that in Le Corbusier's house the living quarters on the second and third floors are untraditionally above the sleeping quarters on the first floor. It means that one lives at the top, which is open to the terrace and the sunlight and air, and descends half way to sleep.

Although these houses are similar in appearance, yet structurally, and as a design, the house of Le Corbusier offers a contrast to those of Mallet-Stévens and Raymond Fischer, because the structure hangs on three concrete poles between two outer walls, thus giving opportunity for the utmost freedom in planning the floors, an opportunity of which Le Corbusier has taken full advantage; while the other two houses are designed on the more traditional lines of supporting partitions carried up from one floor to another. They have long horizontal windows and cantilevered balconies and roofs, which are modern motifs in which the structural possibilities of reinforced concrete are utilized, giving the impression that they are designed in the same idiom, but there is that very fundamental difference which I have noted, which makes Le Corbusier's design fully of the new world in which all the advantages of the structural medium are utilized, while the other two with all the semblance of the new are still very much traditional in conception and belong as much to the old world as to the new.

In 1926 Le Corbusier designed what is perhaps his most famous work in domestic architecture, the villa at Garches, near Paris. It was completed in the following year. Structurally it follows the same principle as the house at Boulogne-sur-Seine, just described, although it is much larger. The plan is rectangular, and approximates to the golden section, as do the principal elevations. The structure is supported mainly on sixteen central slender reinforced concrete columns, the side walls hanging on long cantilevered supports. The freedom in planning given by this method of construction is fully utilized in the design. The front faces north and the fenestration is designed in conformity with this, the walls being alternating strips of concrete and glass with narrow glass bands on the north side and wide on the south side. The ground floor is occupied by the hall, garage, workshop, and servants' quarters. The first floor has a large, open living room in the centre, with library in the northeast corner, dining room in the southeast corner, kitchen to the northeast, while a garden court with terrace extension is in the southwest corner. There are two staircases, one rising from the hall to the library, and the other from a passage near the garage to the side of the kitchen. The second floor contains the bedrooms, dressing rooms, and bathrooms, and here is another terrace open to the west and enclosed on the three other sides. The top floor consists of a terrace garden on the south side with servants' bedrooms and guests' bedrooms on the north side. These top bedrooms have windows looking on to the terrace, while the north wall is blank. In the centre of the terrace is an elliptical

House at Garches, near Paris,
1927 *Architect: Le Corbusier*

Garden elevation

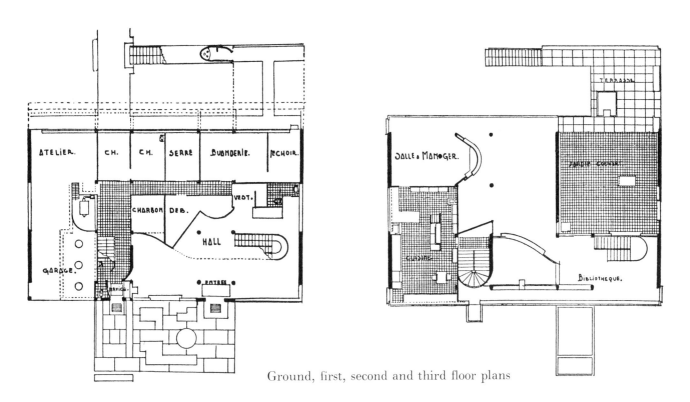

Ground, first, second and third floor plans

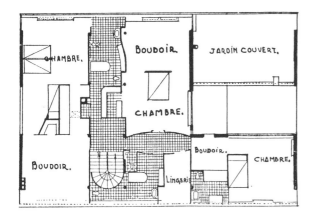

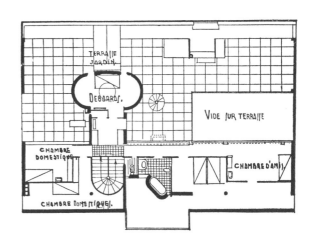

turret with spiral staircase access, called *debarras*, which literally translated means, very significantly, disencumbrance, although for practical purposes it means lumber room, yet architecturally it suggests aerial disencumbrance from the rest of the house. As the illustrations will demonstrate better than any description, the house is a masterly design of much ingenuity in which convenience, health, and joy in sunlight, fresh air, and natural surroundings are considered to the utmost. It is justly one of the triumphs of modern domestic architecture. Although enclosed in a simple rectangle the floor plans are complex, resulting from an imaginative study of human needs and joys. It is a long way from the simple and logical sequence of rooms found in the plans of Webb or Voysey, but it is none the less the result of logical thinking, which has become more complicated because a greater variety of human needs are the determinants. And this logical thought is independent of traditional solutions which really belong to other periods.

The proportions of the elevations are determined by geometric principles, but does the house give aesthetic pleasure without consideration of any *a priori* principles? The elevations offer a contrast determined by the orientation and the result is that the south front is very pleasing, with the broad window bands, the staircase to the terrace and the open square above. It is worthy of note how the introduction of one small yet prominent diagonal gives interest to a design mainly of horizontals and verticals. The north front is much less pleasing with its narrow windows and larger expanses of plain wall. It is agreeable up to the top window band, but the broad mass above does not appear well proportioned or well related to the rest, while the canopy over the entrance is not very happy. But in spite of these notes of criticism the work remains a masterpiece.

WALTER GROPIUS AND PETER BEHRENS

A little earlier, in 1925–6, Walter Gropius built his own house and a pair of attached houses for teachers at Dessau. Pleasantly situated among trees they are built of slag concrete blocks with rendering on the external faces. The walls are supporting elements, and openings have reinforced concrete lintels.

Walter Gropius's own house is orientated with the front north, but the principal living part is to the south. On the ground floor the kitchen and bathroom are on the north side on either side of the entrance, two bedrooms are on the east side, and on the south side is a large living room and dining room, separated by a movable screen, and these open on to a terrace. The first-floor plan is a reversed L-shape, with a terrace to the east and south on to which two bedrooms open. Part of the terrace on the ground floor is covered with a store room opening from a bedroom.

The two attached houses have L and reversed L plans joined, with the long middle mass orientated east–west, the eastern projection being to the north and the western to the south, with ground-floor terraces for both to the east and south. A cantilevered balcony projects from the first floor above each terrace. Each house has approximately the same accommodation with living room, dining room, kitchen, and servants' room on the ground floor, and studio and three bedrooms, two of which are very small, and bathroom on the first floor. The living room and studio are of a good size, but the remaining rooms are somewhat cramped, and a little more space, a matter of two feet both ways, would have improved the accommodation.

These houses have simple exteriors and consist of a pattern of rectangular windows on plain walls. The general mass being horizontal there is a restrained emphasis of this by means of terrace walls, balconies, and slightly projecting eaves. The effect is one of classical breadth and repose. The setting among trees is particularly felicitous, because the branches and foliage provide a pleasing decorative element in the ensemble and accord perfectly with the simple exteriors of the houses. The view of the two attached houses from the east is particularly happy.

Although the developments in domestic architecture described in this chapter were fairly well known among a certain number of architects in England, yet English architects made no contribution to these developments until the last year of the decade, the first important example being the house called High and Over at Amersham in Buckinghamshire, designed by Amyas Connell in 1929. There was one house built in England in 1926, however, which was part of the main stream of such developments in Germany: the house called New Ways at Northampton, designed by Peter Behrens for W. J. Bassett-Lowke. It is significant that an Englishman at this time wanting a house in the modern idiom should go to a famous German architect as one who is likely to give him the design required.

The house is, in many ways, an eclectic design, planned on classical principles, with a romantic medieval character in its decorative embellishments, while in its simplicity, orientation, and large windows on the sun-side it has much of the modern progressive spirit of the twenties. The walls are built of brick, with cement rendering sack finished, while it has a flat concrete roof. The walls and partitions serve a supporting function, and the partitions divide the house similarly on both floors. The house faces north with the garden front to the south, and it will be seen from the two views that the north façade has two small ground floor windows and a central vertical staircase window with large areas of blank wall on either side. The south side has large horizontal windows with loggia and balcony in the centre. The plan is symmetrical, not unlike those of several English houses of the eighteenth century. From the entrance one ascends two steps to the inner hall which admits to the study in the northwest corner, to the large drawing room to the southwest, to the dining room in the centre of the south side, while the east side is occupied by the kitchen, pantry, and maid's room. The dining room and drawing room open on to the central loggia. In a central position on the

General exterior view

Villa Savoye at Poissy, 1929–31
Architect: Le Corbusier

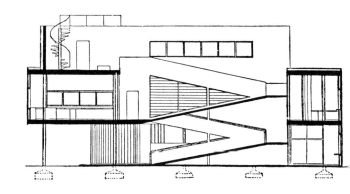

Cross section showing ramps from floor to floor, first floor plan and ground floor plan

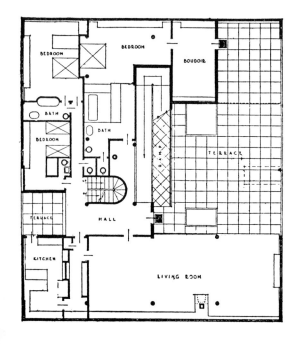

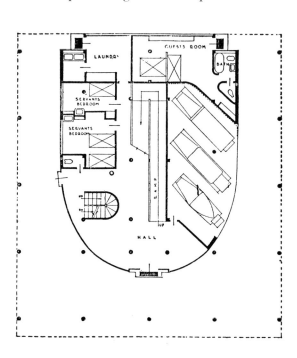

General view of the Weissenhof housing estate, Stuttgart, 1927. Building on the left is the apartment house by Mies van der Rohe. The two houses in the middle distance on either side of the three are by Bruno Taut (left) and Hans Poelzig (right). The two houses in the foreground are by Walter Gropius

Plan of the Weissenhof housing estate

KEY 1–4   *Mies van der Rohe*
    5–9   *J. J. P. Oud*
    10   *Victor Bourgeois*
    11 + 12 *Adolf G. Schneck*
    13–15   *Le Corbusier and Pierre Jeanneret*
    16 + 17 *Walter Gropius*
    18   *Ludwig Hilberseimer*
    19   *Bruno Taut*
    20   *Hans Poelzig*
    21 + 22 *Richard Docker*
    23 + 24 *Max Taut*
    25   *Adolf Rading*
    26 + 27 *Josef Frank*
    28–30   *Mart Stam*
    31 + 32 *Peter Behrens*
    33   *Hans Scharoun*

Note: Houses 16–20, 22–25 and 31, 32 are no longer as originally designed House 21 was demolished and has not been rebuilt

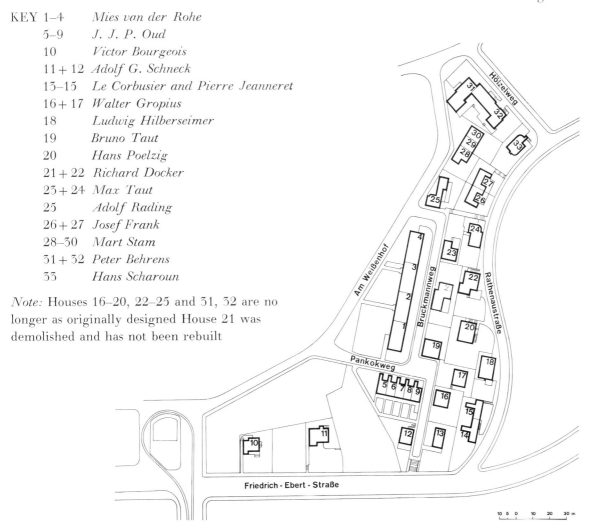

first floor above the dining room is a 'den', intended by the owner, I believe, for the personal use of his wife. It is flanked by two equal sized bedrooms, both adjoined by bathrooms. All three rooms open onto the balcony. Two smaller bedrooms are on the north side.

The architectural distinction of the house depends, as in much of Behrens's work, on the excellence of proportion, on the nicely calculated relation of horizontals and verticals, and of decorated and plain surfaces. The door and windows of the front façade are very pleasingly placed on the large, plain walls, and similarly effective, formal relations can be seen in the interior. A good example is provided by the hall, stairway, and landing. Here the effect is dependent on plain walls with restrained central features. There is a square clock above the entrance, a piscina and fountain enclosed in rectangular forms occupying one wall, and small, vertical, Egyptian murals as centre pieces on other walls. Often the decorative motifs have a medieval reminiscence, like the pattern of some of the window bars, the projecting triangular staircase window and the verticals above it and round the eaves. The house is a blending of tradition with the progressive spirit characteristic of much of Behrens's work. Sometimes he designs completely in the new spirit, sometimes almost purely in the classical spirit, and sometimes his work has a distinctly medieval character, while much is a combination of these elements often with very pleasing aesthetic results, and this house must be acknowledged as one of them.

THE STUTTGART EXHIBITION—1927

In the summer of 1925 a proposal of the Württemberg section of the Deutsche Werkbund to have a housing exhibition at Stuttgart was adopted, and Ludwig Mies van der Rohe was chosen to supervise the work. In the summer of 1926 the Town Council of Stuttgart accepted the suggestion and approved the plans. An Exhibition Committee was chosen and in March 1927 work was started on the site. The project offered scope for the design of some twenty to thirty dwellings, and Mies van der Rohe invited those European architects to design houses whom he thought would make the most valuable contributions to the design and construction of the modern house. Most accepted the invitation. Thus, in addition to Mies van der Rohe, who designed a block of flats which was described in Chapter 22, the following architects were responsible for the houses that formed this exhibition. The German architects: Peter Behrens, Walter Gropius, Hans Poelzig, Bruno Taut, Hans Scharoun, Adolf G. Schneck, Ludwig Hilberseimer, R. Döcker, Adolf Rading, and Max Taut; the Austrian architect, Josef Frank, the French architect, Le Corbusier; and the Dutch architects, J. J. P. Oud and Mart Stam. Although Mies van der Rohe was the general supervisor, all the architects had complete freedom, the only stipulation being that the roofs had to be flat—perhaps an unnecessary provision as it was unlikely that any of these architects would have used pitched roofs.

From the standpoint of architectural design this Stuttgart Exhibition was one of the most important housing events in the period between the wars. The houses represent a considerable variety of designs of much originality and ingenuity. The site is on a hill in Weissenhof, a suburb of Stuttgart, and all the houses still remain, having survived the bombing[4].

The houses are modest in size and are partially essays in providing the minimum accommodation consistent with a good standard of living according to the conceptions of these architects. The contributions of Ludwig Hilberseimer, Adolf Rading, Adolf G. Schneck, Le Corbusier, Walter Gropius, and Hans Poelzig merit some study.

The houses by Ludwig Hilberseimer and Adolf Rading are examples of traditional influence combined with a tentative modern treatment. The house of the former is a two-storey rectangular block with somewhat small traditional windows on plain walls, which, with the partitions, have a supporting function. The principal accommodation is on the upper floor, with living room, dining recess, and kitchen at one end opening on to a terrace, and sleeping quarters at the other end, all rooms opening from a central hall. The ground floor, which occupies only a part of the area, provides further sleeping accommodation, a maids' room, laundry, and storerooms. The use of the remaining part of the area is left to the occupant. This house does not represent any important contribution to planning or construction; at the time it would have been regarded as good steady pedestrian work, except perhaps in England, where anything with plain walls and a flat roof was regarded as startlingly modern unless it was a factory building.

The house by Adolf Rading is more interesting with more thought given to the admission of sunlight. The plan is an L-shape with a short upper stem, and is mainly on one floor with a long side to the south. The open living and dining section is joined by the kitchen, and opens on to a terrace. At the east end are the bedrooms. The upper floor, which is above the living section, consists only of laundry, maids' room, and sun terrace. The living section can be divided by means of sliding and folding partitions running on tracks in the floor and ceiling. The construction is a steel frame with slab walls.

The house designed by Adolf G. Schneck is a three-storey structure of reinforced concrete frame with walls of pumice blocks divided lengthwise into two sections by a load-bearing partition. The living accommodation is on the first floor and consists of living room and dining room on one side of the central wall, and kitchen, utility room, and hall on the other side. The second floor consists of a large bedroom, two smaller bedrooms, and a bathroom which opens to a terrace. On the ground floor are the laundry and store rooms and space for a garage. The purpose of the main central load-bearing partitition is that it makes possible the utmost flexibility of arrangement in each of the

Group of three houses by
Le Corbusier on the
Weissenhof housing estate
(Nos. 13, 14 and 15 on plan
see page 325)

(Nos. 13, 14 and 15 on plan
—*see page* 325)

House at Rupenhorn, Berlin, 1929,
designed by *Eric Mendelsohn*
for himself

Plans

Key to ground floor plan
[A] cloakroom, [B] hall,
[C] music room, [D] dining room,
[E] pantry, [F] kitchen, [G] west
terrace [H] east terrace

Key to first floor plan
[A] study, [B] and [C] bathrooms,
[D] guest room, [E] daughter's
room, [F] bathroom,
[G] wife's room

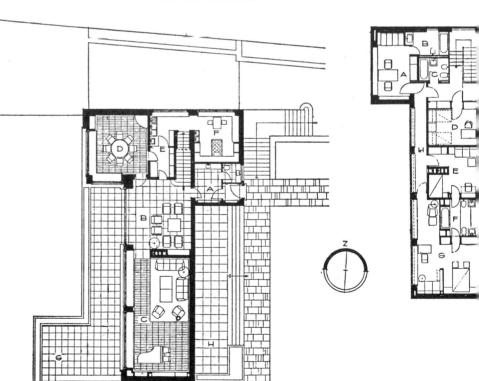

two sections, as the minor transverse partitions, not being load-bearing, permit different divisions on the three floors. This arrangement does not, however, give the same flexibility as Le Corbusier's houses, where the only fixed structural elements are a few vertical columns, the position of everything else between being determined solely by convenience.

Le Corbusier was responsible for three houses, one single and two attached. They are among his most interesting designs and among the most noteworthy at this Stuttgart Exhibition. They represent a more venturesome and experimental approach to the problem of house design and construction than is seen in most of the other houses. Constructionally they are further variations of the method employed in Le Corbusier's houses previously noted and consist for the most part of reinforced concrete or steel posts on which the houses are suspended. In the single house, which is a four-storey structure, these posts are circular on the ground floor, changing to square on the upper floors to take beams and wall blocks of hollow pumice concrete, the ground-floor walls being of reinforced concrete. The house has a rectangular plan orientated with one end to the south, on which side there are large windows which have double glazing and slide horizontally, the other façades being mainly blank walls with a few smaller openings. The main living accommodation is on the first floor, which consists of one large room with living and dining sections separated by a partition from the kitchen and maids' room on the north side. The second floor has the parents' bedroom and dressing room, both on the north side with windows to the west and north, the south end being the upper part of the living room. The third floor has the child's and guests' bedrooms at the north end with a terrace forming the southern half. The ground floor, as in so many of Le Corbusier's houses, is set back from the posts on one side, and consists of entrance hall, heating plant, scullery, and storerooms. It will be seen from the plans that the structure is a double row of five posts flush with the upper wall on the east side from which the ground floor is set back, while the west side is cantilevered out about four feet, the space being occupied by the staircase.

The two attached houses are three storeys high, and consist of a long rectangular block running north–south suspended on a double row of equally spaced square steel posts of double channel section, one house occupying five spaces, the other four. On the east side the wall is cantilevered out a little, and this allows continuous fenestration on the first floor. On the west side each house has a narrow rectangular projection which accommodates the staircase and one room on each floor. Again the ground floor is set back from the row of columns on the east side and at both ends. It accommodates storerooms, laundry, and maids' room. The living and sleeping quarters are on the first floor. At one end is the kitchen and bathroom, and then, in two strips, are the sleeping and living sections, with breakfast room in the wing; certainly an original arrangement, the success of which can only be tested by experience. The living section would be separated from the sleeping sections by partitions, but it is difficult to see the advantage of this strip arrangement as opposed to having the living section at one end and the sleeping the other, with the kitchen and bathroom arranged accordingly. The second floor is mainly a covered terrace and roof garden, with the west wing used as a library. As family houses they are questionable, but as school or hostel buildings they might be admirable. This group, by Le Corbusier, has a very pleasing appearance, and it is clear that considerable thought has been given to the proportions of the rectangular forms and their relations to each other that compose the exteriors. Not the least attractive aspect is the expression of structure in the appearance and the way in which the bones of the construction contribute to the general effect.

With the exception of Peter Behrens's collection of dwellings in a block, not one of his most notable achievements, the other houses at Weissenhof are less ambitious, being generally smaller and nearer the minimum.

The two houses by Walter Gropius are chiefly interesting as an essay in standardization. They are steel framed structures designed on a grid 3 feet 6 inches, with asbestos cement sheets as external facing on slabs of cork with suitable external facing. The plan is square, with rooms grouped round a central hall, dining–living room stretching across one side and kitchen, pantry, and store occupying the remainder, while the upper floor has four bedrooms and a bathroom in one house, and a terrace in lieu of a bedroom in the other house. It seems a simple plan, but a little examination will show that it is very efficient with much accommodation obtained in little space. The main purpose of these houses, however, was to provide a possible model for a unit that could be mass-produced and erected quickly by the use of standardized sections and dry assembly methods.

Similar aims clearly actuated Hans Poelzig in the design of his house, which is of timber frame construction, with timber sheets fixed externally and internally to the frame with a cavity between the sheets. The parts can be standardized and the house can also be erected speedily, having a dry method of assembly. The plan is a square divided into four parts, hall, kitchen, dining room opening on to a veranda, and living room on the ground floor, and bedrooms on the first floor with a roof terrace at one side.

Bruno Taut designed a two-storey house for a family of six, consisting of living room, kitchen, utility room, and one bedroom on the ground floor, and three bedrooms and bathroom on the first floor. The large living room can be divided, by means of folding partitions, into three parts for eating, washing, and leisure. This house was also intended to be a model for mass production and was constructed of standardized sections.

The historical value of the Stuttgart housing exhibition is that it demonstrates, in a concentrated form, the stages reached in the development of house design and construction in 1927 by the most progressive architectural thought in Europe. All these houses were clearly experimental. One or two, though ingenious and original, hardly appear to be the best solutions of the problems presented by housing needs, or as offering scope for further practical developments. The majority, however, are good experimental houses and point a way to further useful development.

1927–32

The principal developments in house design manifested in the examples so far cited are a gradual change from rooms enclosed by rigid partitions and grouped round a hall to a more open plan, in which the living quarters are conceived as one large room, sometimes divided as required by movable partitions; and the change from load-bearing walls and partitions, with similar divisions on each floor, to a frame structure which permits the utmost flexibility and variation in the planning of each floor. These developments are most marked in the designs of Le Corbusier, and up to 1927 no other architect in the field of domestic architecture had been so progressively original. From 1928 Le Corbusier continued to develop on similar lines, but it is inevitable that his work, becoming more familiar, no longer strikes contemporary thought with quite the same dramatic force as in earlier years. His methods were gradually being adopted by other architects and his influence was growing; it was even penetrating that stronghold of tradition, England, where it is apparent in actual work during the thirties.

The developments noted may in some cases have taken place independently of Le Corbusier's influence, and similar results may have been achieved by independent, logical thinking; but if this were so, encouragement for such thinking was probably afforded by the examples of Le Corbusier's houses. For instance, we have noted in the houses erected in 1926 at Boulogne-sur-Seine the contrast between the work of Raymond Fischer and Mallet-Stévens on the one hand, and of Le Corbusier on the other; how the former, though modern in appearance, were largely traditional in planning. Raymond Fischer continued these traditional methods in other houses, as, for example, in the Villa at Marne with its pleasing classical façade not unlike the houses of Adolf Loos. But in a later work, such as the small house in the Cité Lorraine, Paris, and in the house at Vaucresson near Paris, he adopts the method of using concrete piers between the outer walls on the same principle as in Le Corbusier's house at Boulogne-sur-Seine, and secures a similar variation of divisions for each floor.

Le Corbusier was now building an increasing number of houses, among them a house in Paris (Maison Plainex) in 1927, a house in Carthage in 1928, the Villa D'Avray 1928–9, which consisted of some interesting additions to an old mansion[5]. The most noteworthy house, however, built by Le Corbusier since the houses at Stuttgart, is the Villa Savoye at Poissy which was originally designed in 1928, but was not completed until 1931. The principle of construction and planning is similar to that of the Villa at Garches, although the design is altogether different. There is a grid of regularly spaced reinforced concrete piers with some variation in the centre determined by exigencies of design. The chief living accommodation is on the first floor, which is roughly square in plan, with living room and adjoining kitchen, and garden terraces occupying two adjacent sides, and the bedrooms grouped in the opposite corner. In the centre is a ramp rising from the ground floor and continuing to the second floor, while a staircase is situated a little apart near the hall which opens both to living room and kitchen, and connects with the bedrooms. The most attractive feature of the first floor is the spacious living room, 35 feet long, opening for two-thirds of its length to an extensive terrace, which is really another large room without a roof, but with walls and fenestration as in the living room. The ground floor covers a much smaller area, being set back on three sides from the supporting piers. It is curved at one end and consists of hall at this end, servants' room, laundry, and guests' room on the square end, servants' bedrooms on one side and a garage on the other side accommodating three cars diagonally, which has the advantage of affording greater facility for the inspection and examination of cars than if they were arranged squarely. The second floor is mainly a garden and terrace with turrets designed for sunbathing. The walls are of brick and breeze blocks, with ramp walls of reinforced concrete. The roof, with its garden, is constructed of hollow tiles on which is a cement screed covered with bituminous mortar and gravel for the garden parts and concrete tiles for the terrace. The windows have double glazing and slide horizontally, similar to those in the single house by Le Corbusier at Stuttgart.

Opinions differ regarding the appearance of this house. The legs are very conspicuous, and seen at a little distance it gives the impression of a long narrow box carried on legs with some circular forms on the top at one end. The notion of a coffin on trestles is not remote. There is not the same evidence in this design that its proportions were influenced by geometric rules; it seems more exclusively the product of logically thought out purpose. It is not so pleasing in appearance as Le Corbusier's villa at Garches, or his houses at Stuttgart.

FURTHER GERMAN HOUSES

To the west of Berlin, where the Grunewald forest adjoins the eastern shore of the Havel lake, the ground slopes for some distance to the water's edge, and above this slope a road is cut and in 1929 a few modern residences were built along it. The brothers Luckhardt and Alfons Anker designed three houses for this site, and Eric Mendelsohn built his own house there in the same year. Of the three houses by the brothers Luckhardt and Anker the first to be built is of particularly interesting design and construction. There are three floors and a roof garden, partly covered, with a store room. The house is constructed of a steel frame with cavity walls of concrete slabs on the outer side and cork sheeting on the inner, the external face being cement rendered on a wire mesh.

Full use is made of the steel-frame structure in securing the utmost flexibility in the planning of each floor. The stairway is on the east side. On the ground floor are kitchen, laundry, servants' quarters, with a garage under the first-floor terrace. The second floor contains four bedrooms, dressing room, and bathroom. The most distinctive feature of the design, however, is the large living room on the first floor, opening on to a terrace by means of six bays (one being on the south wall). Alternate bays have glass panels, that move horizontally on rollers in front of the other bays which have fixed glass. Radiators are placed between the bays. The terrace is shaped somewhat like the half of a tennis racket, broadening as it swings to the south. In the design of the house full advantage is taken of the lovely views, while it provides full opportunity for the enjoyment of the sun from the early afternoon until the late evening.

The house built by Eric Mendelsohn occupies a similar site. I have described it in my book on Eric Mendelsohn[6], and I think I cannot do better than quote and paraphrase that description.

'The site is a long narrow strip running east and west from the roadway down the slope, gradually widening towards the lake. A stretch of level ground of about 180 feet is occupied by the front garden and the house, and then the descent begins. It is thickly covered with trees: fir, oak, acacia, alder, silver birch, and willow, and with flowering shrubs which in this position seem to continue their rich summer blossoms into the autumn. Where the descent is steepest the path changes to travertine steps. Ascending from the lake towards the house, silver birches spread their delicate patterns against the plain pale walls of the house and against the sky, demonstrating how beautiful is the combination of trees with the large plain masses of modern building.'

The house is constructed of solid brick walls rendered externally, with steel framework for the openings and for the roof, which is covered with copper sheeting.

'The shape of the house is long and narrow, consisting mainly of a series of rooms in succession, with rooms projecting from the main rectangular block on either side at the north end. Built on three floors, the basement (which means only a slight depth, with windows above the ground level) consists of the servants' quarters, store rooms, gymnasium, and most of the machinery connected with various devices in the equipment of the house. At the north end are the garage and service court. On the ground floor (see plan) are the living quarters, which consist mainly of dining room and kitchen at the north end, and the hall and music room extending the whole length of the remainder. These rooms open on to a terrace with an extensive view, the trees of the garden forming the foreground, and beyond these the lake and the blue, distant shore. Between the hall and terrace is a glass wall which sinks into the basement by means of machinery below. The large windows of the music room and dining room

333

sink into the sills on the same principle. The east wall of the hall and music room is windowless and provides, on the exterior, a background to the terrace designed for theatrical performances and dances. The upper floor consists of the bedrooms, bathrooms and workroom, with a breakfast terrace at the north end abutting on the east side. The bedrooms and the guest rooms all face east, with the corridor on the west side.

Throughout the interior there is economy of space by the process of recessing as much as possible in the wall. Thus in the music room, a cabinet for music and one for stringed instruments, and, in the hall, telephone, wireless, gramophone, and records are all built in behind folding and sliding doors; in the bedrooms, wardrobes, cupboards and bookshelves are recessed, and in the daughter's room the worktable folds down from the wall. The radiators are situated beneath the window-sills and are partially boxed in. There is a good deal, therefore, in this house, much of its fundamental mechanism and important accessories, which are concealed from the eyes, like the organism beneath the skin, and not, it is worth noting, paraded as in some buildings.'

It will be seen from the plans that each floor is planned independently without reference to the partitions of the other floors, a freedom which is due to the strong floor construction of steel joists supported on the solid brick walls. This is an interesting point, because, although not a frame structure and totally different from Le Corbusier's methods of hanging the house on concrete poles within the external walls, the method gives the same flexibility. Constructionally, Mendelsohn's house is a composite work of frame and load-bearing walls.

The long low masses of the house wed it very happily to its surroundings. The design appears to be actuated by classical feeling, with its plain, broad, rectangular masses, and it gives an impression of serenity and repose. In designing the house like this Mendelsohn was no doubt influenced by the desire to make part of it a Greek-like setting for dances, but apart from this it may be regarded as a work in the classical vein, different from the more dynamic character of his large store buildings. This difference emanates from the purposes of the two buildings. Mendelsohn quite clearly thinks of a house as a place that should be associated with feelings of rest, peace and repose, and the form of the building should express this, whereas a departmental store is associated with constant movement and commercial activity, and this also Mendelsohn expresses in his store buildings[7].

These houses by the brothers Luckhardt, by Anker, and by Mendelsohn are fortunately situated, as the lovely views spread to the west and southwest and the afternoon sun can be enjoyed in the living rooms and on the terraces. But not always is there that happy union of sun and view, sometimes they are in opposite directions, and the problem on such a site is: which should be the determining factor in the design? This problem confronted Hans Schumacher when he built a house on the bank of the Rhine at Rosenkirchen in 1929, and it was the view that determined the siting. To obtain the view across the Rhine the house is orientated so that the large living room, opening on to a terrace on the first floor, faces northeast, while there is a roof garden above, reached by steps from the first-floor terrace. A glass wall connects the living room with the terrace. It is difficult to think that a living room and terrace should be orientated in this way, even for the sake of a view.

Hans Schumacher was more fortunate in the house that he designed two years later at Cologne west of the Rhine, in the flood area. The house is built on ground raised above the road on the river side. The living and sleeping quarters are mainly on the first floor, with rooms, laundry, and garage on the ground floor. The first floor projects on all sides, which thus provides a veranda all round on the ground floor, and secures a larger area for the first floor. The shape is a long rectangle with the living rooms and bedrooms facing south, and opening to a balcony. To obtain the view over the Rhine a terrace projects eastward to the road, and thus this desirable facility is combined with satisfactory orientation. Both these houses by Schumacher are constructed with a reinforced concrete frame, and the room divisions on each floor are planned independently.

There is apparent in the design of the Cologne house a marine or ship-like character, which the designer probably introduced because of its situation. This character is noticeable in the continuous horizontal fenestration, the long narrow shape, the setback of the top floor, and the curved treatment of the terrace and one of the corners of the top floor. The influence of the design of large modern ships on houses and other buildings has often been observed, and the attractive appearance of modern liners has probably encouraged architects in a logical tendency towards horizontal emphasis. This house of Schumacher's at Cologne is, I think, an example, but the superficial likeness between much modern domestic architecture and the appearance of modern liners is due to their both being the results of logical thinking on somewhat parallel lines, with emphasis of the resulting linear effects.

TWO PETER BEHRENS HOUSES

In Peter Behrens we behold an architect who from the first years of the century until the beginning of the fourth decade continually endeavoured to keep abreast of the most recent developments in architectural design. In his early houses he was in the vanguard of the modern movement, and if he does not retain quite this position in the late twenties it is because, with all his adventurous spirit, he is at heart a classicist, and could never really shake off the influence of the classical tradition. He gets as near to being completely free—not that this is necessarily desirable—in the long horizontally emphasized façade of the tobacco factory at Linz, but the other parts of this factory show here and there this classical influence. In his most modern houses, designed at

335

the end of the third decade, he adopts the large living–dining-room principle, the orientation according to the sun, the freer planning as far as structure permits, but he does not adopt fully the framed structure and the freedom of planning that it gives as do Le Corbusier and Mies van der Rohe.

In his two most interesting houses of this period, the country house at Schlachtensee, near Berlin, built in 1929, and the famous large luxury house in the Taunus Mountains, near Frankfurt, built in 1932, a cognizance of the most progressive developments is revealed in their planning, yet in both solid structural walls are employed, which handicaps a full advantage being taken of planning developments; while in their massive appearance and carefully calculated relations of windows to wall space they are expressive of classical feeling.

The house at Schlachtensee, near Berlin, is a three-storey structure built of concrete with flat roof. The garages, store rooms, and laundry occupy the ground floor, the living quarters, the first floor, and the bedrooms the second. The main part of the house is square in plan with a wing extending to the east, which is occupied by servants' quarters on the first floor and a roof terrace on the second. The divisions of the first floor are followed in those of the second floor. The living room and dining room, separated by a movable partition, lie on the south side. The window openings, which are vertical in shape, are not large, although there is some difference in size between those facing south and those facing north, some of the latter being small openings in large expanses of plain wall.

The house in the Taunus Mountains is probably one of the largest and most luxurious houses built in Europe in this modern manner. Ideally situated on the southern slope of a hill, with a wood to the north and open to the south, it has a long, irregular plan with one long side to the south. It is constructed of brick, faced with slabs of white limestone. There is a great difference between the planning of the two principal floors, but the plans demonstrate that the divisions of the first floor are dependent on the structural walls and partitions of the ground floor. Many additional light partitions on the first floor are necessarily supported by the floor structure, but this does not affect the structural principle. Between the large living room on the ground floor and the dining room there is a wide opening closed by sliding doors. The living room is reached from the hall on the north side, which leads to the pantry and kitchen at the dining room end and visitors' rooms at the other end. On the south side the living room opens to an extensive terrace, while the dining room is separated from the terrace by a veranda. Extending to the west are the servants' quarters, with store rooms and garage at the extreme end. The first floor is mainly occupied by bedrooms, but above the servants' quarters on the ground floor is a sizable terrace, and another at the east end. The windows on the south side are not particularly large, and the plain wall covers a much greater area. The architectural effect is of windows on large, plain wall

336

surfaces, with a strong horizontal emphasis achieved by the accentuation of lintels, sills, terraces, and balconies with their metal rails. This horizontal emphasis, assisted by the flat roof, conduces to a very pleasing harmony with the landscape surroundings, the lines of the hills being repeated, more formally, in the lines of the house. Yet in its massive character, in the relations of windows to large carefully proportioned areas of plain wall, it is still of that tradition where building is aesthetically conceived in terms of stone or brick, and it still betrays something of classical feeling.

HOUSE BY MIES VAN DER ROHE

To turn from this house to the Tugendhat house at Brünn, in Czechoslovakia, designed by Ludwig Mies van der Rohe in 1930 is to experience a contrast. The open and free planning made possible by framed construction, the lightness of steel construction combined with large expanses of glass, are here manifest to the full, and in no European house built between the wars does one get so completely the feeling of spaciousness and lightness, and that minimization of the division between external and internal space as in this house of Mies van der Rohe.

Like Behrens's house just described, this house at Brünn is situated on the southern slope of a hill, and at the point where the house is built the slope is steep. It is a three-storey structure including a low basement for storage, laundry, and heating plant. The house is buttressed against the hill, and the street on the north side is at first-floor level. Here on the west side are the garage and chauffeur's rooms. On the first floor are the bedrooms and nurseries, which open on the south side to an extensive terrace. One descends from the hall to the living room, pantry, and kitchen on the ground floor. The various parts of the actual living quarters are all combined in one large room. There is the living room proper, with the dining space at the west end partially partitioned off by a semicircular wooden screen, one part of which shuts off the pantry. On the north side is the study, the only separation from the living room being a short, pale onyx screen. This living area is thus almost one large room sectionalized. It is as open as anything to be found in any of the houses built between the wars. The wall to the south is entirely of large glass panels, which can be let down into the basement by electrical machinery, so that the whole side can be opened when desired. A recess for roller blinds is provided above the window should the sun become too strong. At the east end of this room is a conservatory, while at the west, dining room end, there is access to the terrace and the steps leading to the garden. Exhilarating as this open treament for the living quarters is, there are naturally some doubts about its desirability. One of these doubts affects the relation of the study to the living room. A study is generally the place for study—for reading and writing—and a condition of its efficiency is that it shall be quiet. When this is open to the living room, where people may be talking, or where the radio might be on, is not this essential condition of a study destroyed? In this desire for the open living quarters have not the architect and his client here gone a little too far?

337

The open planning and the wide space of the living quarters have been made possible by the framed structure. Steel uprights are at intervals cross-shaped faced with chrome bronze and make a square pattern on plan. The walls are generally brick rendered, but the staircase wall is of translucent glass which lights the corridor, stairway, and hall.

The lightness of the structure is apparent in the general appearance of the house. The horizontal emphasis is strong and the dominating note of the south elevation is a broad band of glass between the two pale bands of rendered brickwork. The light, widely spaced steel uprights are the only verticals in the broad glass wall.

At the west end part of the first floor projects over the ground-floor terrace and is supported by two steel columns, with a part cantilevered. Details like this all contribute to the general effect of lightness, and confirm an impression widely held that here is a supreme example of a full utilization of a modern technique of design and construction. No house built since has gone farther in this direction. There remains the question, however, whether a retraction in some features of the planning, such as the study open to the living room, is not desirable, but no retraction is surely desirable in the brilliant use to which the materials of building have been put.

SOME CZECHOSLOVAK HOUSES

Many of the most noteworthy houses built in Czechoslovakia at this time, like the house just described, are built on the slopes of hills, full use generally being made of this in the design. The lowest floor, which houses the heating plant, fuel, and laundry, is on a level with the lower ground, but becomes a partial basement at the other side where the ground floor is level with the higher ground. The particular slope of the ground presents an interesting problem in each case. In a house designed by J. K. Říha in 1930, built near the top of a hill overlooking Prague, the site descends approximately in an easterly direction. The long sides of the rectangular house face north and south, and the lower ground floor, containing store rooms and heating plant, is level with the ground at the east end, while the ground floor at the west end is level with the higher ground which provides the main outlet from the living–dining room through a curved terrace.

In the house at Prague, designed by Adolf Bens in 1931, the ground slopes to the south, and the house presents its main front in that direction, with lower ground floor for storage and heating plant on a level with the ground. Hall and study are on the ground floor, the living–dining room occupying the whole south front on the first floor, with bedrooms on the second floor.

In the well-known house at Smichov, Prague, designed by Josef Havlíček and Karel Honzík in 1930, the ground slopes down towards the northwest, and the living room on the ground floor faces southeast and southwest, with the dining section at the west

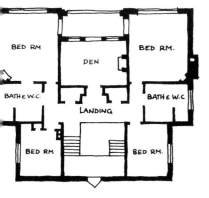

Plans of house at Northampton, 1926

Architect: Peter Behrens

House Tugendhat at Brunn, Czechoslovakia, 1930   View from garden

Architect: Ludwig Mies van der Rohe

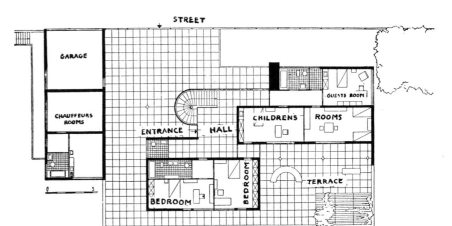

Plan of upper floor on street level

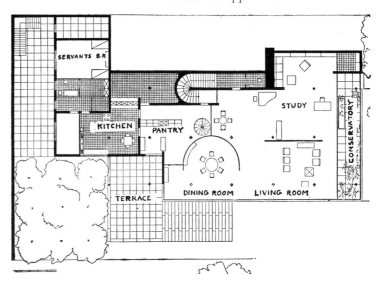

Plan of lower floor on garden level

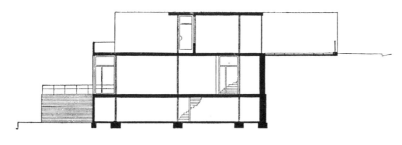

Section

corner approached by an external spiral staircase. These houses, together with a few other examples built on sloping sites, like that at Podol, Prague, designed by Karel Honzík, all follow the same principle of having the lowest floor level with the lower ground at one side and becoming a partial basement on the other side where the ground rises. The ground floor is on a level with the higher ground at the other side, and generally contains the living–dining room and kitchen, the bedrooms are on the first floor, and in many cases there is a second floor occupying part of the area only, with the remainder serving as a terrace, as in all the houses mentioned. This terrace is partially covered in the houses by Havlíček and Honzík by a roof with very slender supports, and in the house by Říha it is cantilevered out. In slightly larger houses, such as that by Adolf Bens, there are variations of the arrangement described although there seems to be conformity to a similar principle.

All these houses are built with a reinforced concrete frame with walls of hollow bricks, either concrete or clay, which are brought flush with the uprights of the frame, while the external surface is rendered. Advantage is taken of this method of construction by planning each floor freely without being restricted by the partitions of lower floors. The windows are large on the sunny sides and smaller on the north sides, and are often taken round corners. The long horizontal windows with but slender metal frames, the plain walls, the slender steel supports for terrace roofs, and cantilevering give a general effect of lightness. This is perhaps more conspicuous in the modern houses built in Czechoslovakia in the period 1928 to 1933 than elsewhere in Europe. Some houses built at this time in Czechoslovakia seem to be used as a means for experimenting with the constructional medium. The adventurous engineer is at work. Not that the functional convenience of the house has been sacrificed, but it is clear that the same result could sometimes have been achieved by means that are less constructionally spectacular. A case in point is the sun porch of a house at Prague, designed by Ladislav Zak[8] in 1932. This square structure is cantilevered out a considerable distance without corner supports. A cantilevered observation platform is also put on the roof. Interesting as this structure is in demonstrating what can be done with cantilevering in the small house, the same results could have been achieved without, and with equal economy of means. This, however, is not very important; what is more so is the appearance, which has the effect of something rather incongruous grafted on. This sun porch, jutting out from the first floor a distance almost equal to the width of the house, is hardly beautiful. Here is exhibitionism in a new constructional medium.

Several houses designed on similar principles were built in Holland in the late twenties and early thirties, one of the most noteworthy being the Sonneveld House at Rotterdam, designed by J. A. Brinkmann and C. van der Vlugt in 1932. This is a three-storey house with a basement, and it has the open planning which a steel-frame construction permits.

340

Here the principal living quarters are on the first floor with living room and library extending as one room, the whole length of the long west side divided as desired by a movable partition. The dining recess opens from the living room and is connected with the pantry and kitchen. The ground floor is occupied by a large hall, study, and servants' quarters; the basement is for storage and the heating plant; and the second floor has the sleeping quarters. The flat roof is used as an open-air room. On the east and west sides the windows are large, the former extending on the first floor between narrow, opaque, horizontal bands to form a terrace on the southeast corner. The projecting rectangular block on the east side houses the kitchen on the first floor, with garage below, and a blank wall protects it from the south. The whole effect is one of lightness and simplicity, with a strong horizontal emphasis. This house may be taken as typical of several other houses by the same architects.

By 1930 houses built according to the principles of functionalism, with a frame structure allowing freedom of planning and built generally with large windows on the sun sides, plain walls, and flat roof, were being erected in increasing numbers in Germany, France, Holland, Belgium, and Czechoslovakia, although they were still exceptions rather than the rule. They were still rare in England and Scandinavia, although after 1930 such houses began to appear, inspired very largely by French and German work, but often designed with considerable originality.

The majority of houses we have considered since 1924 have the rectangular plan with slight variations, and many further good examples could be cited. There are, however, several interesting designs in the late 'twenties and early 'thirties in which the plan is more irregular, where the rooms are planned in sequence according to purpose and without consideration of fitting them into an overall rectangle. We have noted that in the work of Philip Webb, Norman Shaw, and Voysey in the late nineteenth century a favoured plan was the L-shape, because in this way a good, convenient sequence of rooms—kitchen, pantry, dining room, living room—could be obtained with a satisfactory orientation. We find this L-shaped plan still followed when space permitted. An interesting use is made of it in a house at Zürich, designed for himself by the architect Otto Salvisberg in 1930. Here the inside of the L faces southeast and southwest. The principal living quarters are on the first floor, with living room and dining room in the southwest wing on the inner southeast side, the kitchen on the northwest side, the hall at the corner, and a study and studio in the southeast wing. The ground floor consists of a veranda under the living room. This is an original variation of the L-shaped theme.

Houses like this and houses with irregular plans determined mainly by the convenient sequence of rooms are possible only if there are no severe limitations of site. Also, any natural advantages of site necessarily assist the design of the house. We find an example of this very irregular plan, so designed to take full advantage of the views over the

341

open country from as many of the rooms as possible, in the house at Dahlewitz (Germany), designed for himself by Bruno Taut in 1928. Here the main part of the two-storey house is in the form of the quarter of a circle, with the point of the circle due west. In this inner part is the living–dining room, on the northeast side is the kitchen, and in the southwest corner is the library. A wing runs off east at the northeast corner and this contains the larder, laundry, and garage at the extreme end. On the first floor in the area above the living room is a terrace, and cantilevered over this terrace is the flat roof with glass panels.

The free and advantageous conditions of site mentioned influenced some of the early designs in the modern idiom characterized by irregularity of plan that we find in England. The first example, which is famous, is the house called High and Over at Amersham in Buckinghamshire, designed by Amyas Connell in 1929 but it is more convenient to consider this in the next chapter as the first of a sequence of houses by this architect and of the architects with whom he was associated.

REFERENCES AND NOTES

1. I discuss the question of the relation of kitchen and utility room at some length in my book *The Small House: Today and Tomorrow*, London, 1947, second edition, 1957.

2. This list is not comprehensive; there are many who designed good and original houses who are not included, but it is necessary to make a selection.

3. Le Corbusier's Houses are all described and fully illustrated in *Le Corbusier et Pierre Jeanneret*, Œuvre Complète, four volumes, 1910–29, 1929–34, 1934–8, and 1938–46, Zürich.

4. My information is partially derived from a special number of *Die Form* for September 1927, which deals entirely with this Exhibition. Raymond McGrath in his book on *Twentieth Century Houses* mentions Victor Bourgeois, the Belgian architect, as having designed one of the houses, and indicates the position on a diagram. See *Victor Bourgeois Architectures 1922–52*, Brussels, 1952. My impressions are partly derived from a visit I made to Weissenhof in 1951.

5. Descriptions accompanied by plans and photographs of these houses can be seen in *Le Corbusier et Pierre Jeanneret*, Œuvre Complète, vol. i, 1910–29, Zürich.

6. Arnold Whittick, *Eric Mendelsohn*, first edition, 1940, second edition, 1956, London.

7. After the Second World War Mendelsohn's house was the office of the British Control Commission in Berlin.

8. Illustrated in F. R. S. Yorke, *The Modern House*, London, 1934, pp. 128–131.

24 Houses 1932–1942

MANY PROGRESSIVELY DESIGNED modern houses were built in France, Germany,
Holland, Switzerland, Austria and Czechoslovakia up to the early thirties, and then,
for political reasons indicated in Chapter 32, such work greatly diminished in
Germany and the Nazi dominated countries where it had flourished, and the impetus
and the achievements passed to Scandinavia and particularly England which for a
brief period from 1932 to 1940 had once again the finest domestic architecture in
Europe[1], repeating the preeminence that it had previously enjoyed in this field
in the days of Webb, Shaw and Voysey.

FRANCE

After the house at Poissy and during the thirties until the outbreak of war Le
Corbusier's practice diminished owing partly to the reaction in France against modern
architecture and to the wave of neo-classicism, although he was busy on many
ambitious town-planning schemes. His most important buildings of the thirties were
the Swiss Pavilion at the University City in Paris (1930–32) and the Ministry of
Education buildings at Rio de Janeiro which he designed in collaboration with Oscar
Niemeyer and Lucio Costa, but Le Corbusier's was the guiding spirit.

After his outstanding works in domestic architecture during the twenties it is a
regrettable contrast that only two houses were built to his designs during the thirties,
if we exclude the Poissy house designed in 1929 and completed in 1931. These were a
small weekend house near Paris, and a house by the mouth of the Gironde near
Mathes in southwest France, both built in 1935. The latter contains a few innovations.
It is a two-storey, long, rectangular block with basement, orientated north–south with
rooms on the ground floor open to a veranda, and on the first floor to a balcony,
both on the east side. The structure consists of thick stone external walls with one cross
wall and an internal timber framework. The stone walls only partly enclose the house,
and do not extend on the side of the veranda and balconies, nor on the west side
at the south end which is occupied on the first floor by a covered terrace. Cross

343

ventilation is secured by small windows in the stone walls opposite the extensive fenestration on the side of the veranda and balconies. A notable feature is the roof covered with corrugated asbestos which slopes inwards towards a gutter with internal down pipes, thus heralding the butterfly roof. The effective appearance of the house depends largely on the contrast of the heavy rusticated stone walls with the light timber framework and fenestration seen amidst the pine trees that surround the house.

Among the architects of distinctive houses who suffered from the reactionary tendencies in France was André Lurcat who spent most of the period in Russia. But before he left France he designed the justly famous Villa Hefferlin at Ville D'Avray which was completed in 1932. It is an L-shaped two-storey house with roof garden. The L partly encloses a square garden on the north side towards the road. On the south, garden side the living room and dining room open on to a terrace by means of sliding glass doors and the principal bedrooms open to a balcony above. The house is of reinforced concrete frame construction with infilling of cellular bricks for the external walls, with a finish of cement rendering. The roof garden is surrounded by parapet walls, with a lintel and sun-slab on one side, and the first floor balcony is reached by an external stairway. The long garden elevation makes a rectangular mass accentuated by the lines of the balcony and the flat roof giving a marked horizontal emphasis, resulting in a very satisfying composition of the wall and window masses.

One of the most ingenious houses built in Paris in the early thirties was constructed under an existing apartment block, where the occupants of the second and third floors wished to remain. These upper floors were supported on steel columns, the lower part was removed, and an open planned doctor's house constructed of steel, glass and glass blocks was erected in its place to the designs of Chareau and Byroet. The interior is largely open planned, both vertically and horizontally. The doctor's surgery, waiting room and reception are on the ground floor. A large living room with generous height occupies the first floor, and opening from it are the dining room and kitchen, while on the other side is the study. Above are the bedrooms with a balcony overhanging the living room. When this house was built it prompted a great deal of interest in architectural circles and was the subject of many articles in English architectural journals.

GERMANY

In Germany domestic architecture in the progressive spirit of the twenties almost disappeared with the ascendancy of Hitler, the only examples being a few in the early thirties before the full devastating blast of the new Government had been experienced. Hans Scharoun, as mentioned in the previous chapter, was one of the few noted German architects who remained during the Nazi regime. He designed a house for the Weissenhof estate at Stuttgart in 1927, and collaborated with Walter Gropius in the Siemensstadt estate of flat dwellings near Berlin built in 1929, and he had built several other blocks of flats and private houses, but during the thirties, being an architect of the modern experimental school, he suffered enforced inactivity and built only a few private houses. (Later, after the Second World War he became the architect of many original and famous buildings.) The most interesting and best known of the few private houses of the early thirties that he designed was for Herr Schminke an industrialist at Löbau in Saxony in 1933. It is erected on a sloping site so that the principal living floor is level with the ground on one side, and is continued as a spacious balcony on the other, with part open underneath and part a cellar. Another spacious balcony projects from the first floor, and the two are linked externally with each other and with the lower ground level by staircases, while a flat roof projects in unison with the balconies. Large windows and glass screens open from the living rooms to the balconies and the whole conception is an endeavour to merge the dwelling with the landscape. Illumination at night is by indirect and direct lighting partly through perforated ceilings, and when the heavy curtains are drawn across the entire windows there is something of a tent-like effect. The main floor apart from small subsidiary sections is based on the open plan and is essentially one room with parts for dining, music and relaxation. It is a steel frame structure following in principle the houses by Le Corbusier.

Similar in kind is the house at Wiesbaden built for Herr Harnischmacher by Marcel Breuer in 1933, the year the latter left Germany. The conception shows the strong influence of Le Corbusier, the construction is largely a system of concrete poles and steel stanchions on which the house hangs. It is a three-floor building with stores on the ground floor, living room, dining room opening on to a Winter Garden and terrace on the first floor, and bedrooms on the second. The walls are of reconstructed pumice stone blocks with whitish-grey rendering.

Interesting as an example of the use made of an existing feature in determining the character of a design is a house at Saint Martin-les-Metz built for a French client by the German architect Otto Zollinger in 1935. It was erected in the grounds of an old house that once belonged to Marshal Bazaine, the French defender of Metz in the Franco-Prussian War. On the site was an ornamental circular pool which controlled the design of the house. The main garden façade is the arc on the northwest side of the circular pool, a third of its circumference, and thus forming the line of the main living space, on the open-plan sequence of drawing room in the centre with dining room and smoking room on either side, all facing the pool with large windows that glide open to the full length of the circular façade. At the rear are the hall, kitchen and servants' hall. Above the main living area of the ground floor is an extensive terrace on to which, from a central position, the first-floor breakfast room opens, and on either side and in the rear are the bedrooms, with another balcony on the northwest side. The house is built of reinforced concrete with fibrous slabs used in part of the wall construction to obtain both thermal and sound insulation. A summer house on the axis

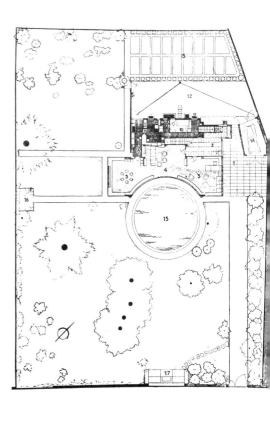

House at St.Martin-les-Metz, 1935

Architect: Otto Zollinger

General view and ground floor plan

Schminke House, Labau, Saxony, 1933

Architect: Hans Scharoun

House at Goldbach, Zürich, 1932–34

Architect: Max Einst Haefell

of the pool and the house is seen at a little distance with its wall decorated with a colourful pattern of leaping deer.

It will be appreciated that in this design an essential purpose has been to make the interior as open as possible to the surroundings by means of the sliding glass walls and the extensive terrace and rear balcony. The somewhat symmetrical character was, of course, determined by the circular pool.

Zollinger designed many houses, but this is perhaps the most original. An earlier example built near Zürich in 1933 is more conventional in treatment and it would seem that a definite existing feature like the pool at Metz provided a stimulus to unusual design.

AUSTRIA

In the early years of the century Austria had been one of the pioneer countries of modern architecture. Much reduced in size after the First World War it yet continued to make important contributions to the new architecture of Europe in the twenties, and this continued well into the thirties, but the increasing tension of life in Austria and the surrender to Hitler in 1938 was not conducive to creative work.

Among the houses built in the early thirties was one by Lois Welzenbacher in the beautiful wooded country near Linz. It is on the southern slope of a hill, against a background of trees, and commands an extensive view over the Donau Valley. A two-storey block contains the large living room on the ground floor with the bedrooms on the first floor. The principal bedroom occupies a semicircular projection with a balcony beyond the ground floor, and provides a covered circular area into which the glass screen doors of the living room open. A curved wing, on the ground floor only, extends eastward, and contains the dining room divided from the living room by a movable partition, and then in sequence the kitchen, servants' room and guest room. The construction is of reinforced concrete and tubular steel frame with brick infilling for the walls faced externally with a white rendering. Again the house is designed to be open as much as possible to its beautiful surroundings, while provision has been made for thermal insulation during the winter. It is an ingenious design inspired by its romantic situation.

Some of the best designs for houses on a modest scale to be seen in Austria of this period are in the group of seventy sponsored by the Internationale Werkbundsiedlung and built in a suburb of Vienna in 1931–33. This was an enterprise by the Österreichisches Werkbund similar to that of the Württemberg section of the Deutsche Werkbund at Weissenhof, Stuttgart, in 1927. Similarly in the Vienna Werkbundsiedlung architects from many countries were invited to prepare designs. Among the Viennese architects were Adolf Loos, Josef Hoffmann and Clemens

347

Holzmeister, and those from other countries included Richard Neutra who had gone from Austria to the USA, André Lurcat of Paris, H. Häring of Berlin, and G. Rietveld of Utrecht.

Although many of the houses are ingeniously planned a classic simplicity characterizes the appearance of many of them which shows the strong influence of Adolf Loos, who was responsible for six of the houses, two pairs of two-storey semi-detached dwellings, and two in a terrace strip. These are typically Loos designs with carefully related window patterning on plain walls, enchanced in the four semi-detached houses by delicately designed first-floor balconies. Showing the influence of Loos are the pairs of houses by the Viennese architects Wagner-Freynsheim, Ernst Plischke and the detached house by A. Bronner and H. A. Vetter, an influence marked by the carefully related patterning of windows on plain walls. Josef Frank, another Viennese architect, adopts a similar simplicity of external treatment. Dining room and kitchen and bedrooms are on the ground floor, with a large living room on the first floor which opens on to a terrace about the same size. In the row of four three-storey houses by Gerrit Rietveld large windows are employed, and a balcony runs along the south side of the second floor with glass doors opening on to it. The house by Neutra is a single-storey structure with basement and flat roof which provides a large open-air room reached by an external stairway.

A somewhat sombre group is the four three-storey houses by André Lurcat which present to the road on the north side small windowed façades with a series of almost blank semicircular staircase towers, but the garden façade on the south side with the roof terrace is more pleasing. When I visited this group of seventy houses in June 1965, trees and shrubs had grown to a considerable extent in the attractive gardens, which partly obscured many of the houses. The effect of the foliage against the plain walls and large windows was very pleasing. Unfortunately on the south side of the group some additional houses had been built since the Second World War which were of crude design and in marked contrast to the felicities of the Werkbund group. I remarked to the Austrian architect who was with me that it was difficult to understand how with the fine example of these houses later architects (or perhaps only builders) could perpetrate such crudities. He agreed, and said rather sadly that the good period in Viennese architecture ended in the early thirties.

There were a few houses of distinction built a little later, during the mid-thirties in Austria—a house by C. S. Prach in the Leopold-Steiner–Gasse built in 1935, and some by Walter Loos (one in Kaasgrabengasse, 1934, and one in Dionysius–Andrassy–Strasse, 1936), all of which show the strong influence of Adolf Loos. As the thirties wore on good work of this kind became less, and with the Nazi threat many architects left the country, Ernst Plischke went to New Zealand and Josef Frank to Sweden.

CZECHOSLOVAKIA

Czechoslovakia was later in being submerbed by the Nazi tyranny, not until the spring of 1939, but it had lived for some years under the constant threat of this occurring, and most of the good architectural work belongs to the early rather than the late thirties. Several interesting progressively designed houses had been built by Josef Havlíček and Karel Honzík in the late twenties. Among the most interesting belonging to the early thirties was a house at Prague designed by Adolf Bens in 1932 and another also in Prague designed by Ladislav Zak in the following year. The former is built on the side of a hill with three storeys and a basement. Three of the four floors are buried on the north side into the hill. The basement has storage facilities and heating equipment, the ground floor approached by a flight of steps on the main entrance side contains the large hall, study, cloakrooms, a small kitchen and housekeeper's room. The first and principal floor has a large living room separated from dining room by a movable partition, and this links with service facilities and kitchen. The second floor holds the bedrooms, with three opening on to a terrace on the south side. The living room has a very large window to the south, almost a glass wall, and opens to a side balcony. The structure is of reinforced concrete frame, with concrete floors and flat roof, the plain walls are finished with cement rendering with a white marble aggregate, the windows have double glazing while due attention has been paid to thermal insulation.

The house by Ladislav Zak is notable for the large projecting cantilevered balcony on the first floor at the west end which forms a sun terrace, and a canopy for the ground floor. The terrace is designed for sunbathing and provision is made for it to be curtained round or enclosed by blinds. A stairway ascends from the balcony to an observation platform above the flat roof, because the house overlooks the Prague aerodrome and the owner was an aeronautical engineer. The house is of reinforced concrete construction with long horizontal bands of double glazed fenestration. The large living room and bedrooms above face south, the house is well insulated and protected on the north side, and is an excellent illustration of a building designed to ensure full enjoyment of the summer months with adequate protection in the winter.

ITALY

Progressive architecture in Italy during the thirties was not entirely submerged by the official neo-classicism, and groups of architects continued to work experimentally with new methods and expression if not with a complete sense of freedom. One was a cooperative group of seven architects known as Gruppo 7 centred on Milan and founded in 1927, of whom the most gifted was Giuseppe Terragni, who designed during his short life (1904–42) several notable buildings including apartment blocks and family houses. Of the latter the most interesting are the two that he designed in 1936, the Villa Bianca at Seveso near Milan, and the Villa Bianchi at Rebbio near Como. They both show the influence of Le Corbusier in their conceptions and introduction of various features. The Villa Bianca at Seveso is a long rectangular block with long horizontal windows on plain walls. It has lower and upper ground floors, the latter a little above ground with the front entrance reached by steps, and the rear entrance by a ramp, a motif which may have been suggested by a similar device in Le Corbusier's Villa Savoye at Poissy. The flat roof is surrounded by square columns and a lintel supporting two long slabs which act as sun shades and which are pleasingly related in mass to the main block of the house. The building is designed with considerable feeling for effective proportion. The Villa Bianchi at Rebbio again shows Le Corbusier's influence. Much of the ground floor area is open and the major part of the house, consisting of the first and second floors, is supported on stilts, with an external staircase access reminiscent of Le Corbusier's Villa de Monzie at Garches. An original motif is the square framing on one elevation of the whole of the upper façade. The roof is not designed for use, but the rooms on both floors open to balconies on three sides towards the sun. Another member of Gruppo 7, Luigi Figini, built an interesting house in 1935 in the 'Villaggio dei Giornalistis' near Milan, which is completely open on the ground floor, the structure being supported on a small forest of stilts, again the influence of Le Corbusier. The long rectangular mass of the house with horizontal emphasis makes a good composition.

Terragni later collaborated with Pietro Lingeri in building apartment blocks in Milan. Lingeri is interesting as being associated with Sant'Elia in the Futurist movement. Later he founded the Italian Rationalist movement. He designed a few houses in the idiom of which the Villa Leoni built on a hilly site by Lake Como in 1939 is the most notable. It is a fairly large house with four floors, and a mono pitched-roof, then an innovation. The various sections on the ground floor are conveniently related with a long living room flanked on either side by a hall and dining room, all open to a terrace to the south overlooking Lake Como. In style it is somewhat Greek in feeling with square columns supporting the extensive porch, a pattern repeated in the framing of the large windows. The roof overhangs on the south side as a sun shade for the second floor and serves to give horizontal emphasis to the south façade. There is still a certain classical heaviness which gives a monumental quality to the villa.

An example of a house ingeniously designed on a rocky site with a view is a villa at Capri designed by Raffaello Fagnoni in 1934. With its semicircular termination built up from the rock it reminds one of the termination of one of the wings of Mendelsohn's hospital on Mount Scopus in Israel. The structure is mainly on one floor with the living room occupying the semicircular end. In a corner of the extensive flat roof is the study with extensive views over the sea. The house seems to fulfil its function very well, yet its architectural character is essentially classical with pilasters on the circular façade and columns and lintel rising above the roof. Both in Lingeri's and Fagnoni's work there is the aim to be functional with modern methods yet the prevailing neo-classicism influences architectural character.

Somewhat similar, yet without classical motifs and more completely modern in feeling
is the small villa on a slope near Lake Maggiore designed by Luigi Vietti in 1933.
It has a square elevation to the road but on the lake and garden side where the ground
steeply slopes it has a semicircular façade with three floors. The large living room on
the first floor has a semicircular glass wall opening to a balcony and protected by the
balcony above into which the bedrooms open. This semicircular treatment of façades
with glass walls in villas on the shores of lakes and by the sea meant very light
interiors and a minimization of the division between inner and outer space which
represents a very important trend in domestic architecture of the thirties.

SWITZERLAND

Architecture in Switzerland had been much influenced by modern German and French
work of the twenties and had made its own notable contributions, which it continued
to do during the thirties. Among the notable examples of domestic architecture is a
large house at Zürich designed by Professor O. Salvisberg and built in 1933, two
houses by Max Ernst Haefeli at Goldbach near Zürich built in 1932–4 and a house at
Binningen designed by Otto Senn in 1935. The house by Salvisberg is a four-storey
structure built on the side of a hill sloping down from the road. The plan is L-shaped on
the two principal floors, one wing is cantilevered outwards over the garden towards the
southwest, which on the first floor contains the dining room, a long living room and
then, turning the corner beyond the hall, the study, studio and the garage on street
level at the end. Above on the second floor of the southwest wing are the sleeping
quarters, with a terrace at one end. The ground floor has the servants' quarters and a
large garden with pool placed at the inner corner of the L with a veranda supported
on slender columns running along one wing under the floor above. In the lower
ground floor are the stores, laundry and heating equipment. In the outer corner of
the L on the north angle is a circular staircase from the lower ground floor to the
bedroom floor. The construction is of reinforced concrete with loadbearing walls
supported on concrete piles and the external finish is in white cement rendering. The
long horizontal windows serve to emphasize the character of the two long wings of the
L, and this is mingled with a very pleasing rectangular massing and a degree of
classical restraint.

The two houses by Haefeli at Goldbach are ingenious and original conceptions, with
all the advantages of a magnificent site on the edge of a wood 300 feet up on the
eastern slopes of Zürich lake. The two houses were for different clients, one being built
about eighteen months after the other, and they represent two interesting variations
on a theme. Each house has an L-plan, the inner angle of both facing south. The one
on the northern side, built first, is a three-storey building with garage, stores, laundry
and heating plant on the ground floor, living room and dining room on the first floor
and sleeping quarters on the top floor. The five bedrooms of the family face south
(there are two for maids on the other side) and open to two large terraces, one at the

east end on the south side the other at the west end linked by a narrow balcony.

The other house is also three storeys, but the lowest floor for storage, laundry and heating plant occupies only half the area of the other floors. The dining room and living room are on the first floor and the sleeping quarters on the second floor with the bedrooms opening to a balcony on the west side linked by a narrow one in the south side, one forming a roof for a veranda below. Separating the bedrooms from the corridor on the north side is a row of bathrooms, which are ventilated by clerestory windows above the corridor which has a low ceiling for the purpose. The house is mainly concrete slab and post construction.

The gardens of the houses are planted with a wide variety of ornamental trees and shrubs, the grouping being particularly thick between the houses to act as a screen. The most notable feature of both these houses is the generous provision of balconies and terraces with rooms with large windows on the south opening on to them so as to obtain that oneness of inner and outer space which is so pleasant in summer. As Professor Alfred Roth says in his valuable description and analysis of these houses: 'the intimate harmony that has been achieved between the spatial qualities of the architecture and the natural surroundings makes these houses of particular aesthetic interest ... The interiors of the houses and the gardens have been designed in relation to each other so that one expands into the other.'[2] When I saw these houses in the early summer of 1966 the trees and shrubs had grown so thickly round them that they appeared very secluded. Space was kept open chiefly on the west side towards the lake.

The house at Binningen, near Basel, designed for an artist by Otto Senn in 1935, is situated on the northern slope of a hill with views to the north towards Basel and the Black Forest. It consists of four floors with living quarters on the upper ground floor, sleeping quarters on the first floor, a studio on the flat roof and storage and laundry on the lower ground floor. As it is buttressed against the hill the entrance to the lower ground floor is on the north side, but that of the upper ground floor is on the south where it is level with the ground, but a storey above on the north side. The living and dining rooms open to a covered corner terrace, and the three bedrooms all open to a covered balcony on the east side. Extensive views can be enjoyed from the flat roof to which the studio opens (occupying about a third of the area). The construction is a combination of steel frame and brick supporting walls with a lime stucco finish. The design is straightforward, practical and functional with everything fitting neatly in a rectangular box, pleasantly articulated. It appears best from the north side, where the three columns forming the porch and supporting the floors above are effective.

THE NETHERLANDS

In the domestic field the talent of Dutch architects expressed itself in mass housing, in tall apartment blocks and in rows of terrace houses and in estates, but less in the individually designed house. Some houses of originality and distinction were, however, built during the twenties such as Rietveld's famous Schroeder House erected at Utrecht in 1924 and some by the partners J. A. Brinkman and L. C. van der Vlught who had become famous for the impressive Van Nelle factory in Rotterdam. They built three houses in Rotterdam in the early thirties which merit attention: van der Leeow's house in 1930, Sonneveld's house 1933, and Dr Boeve's house 1934. The first mentioned is a light framed structure with large areas of fenestration and balconies on the south façade enclosed between almost blank end walls; except that a glass-covered balcony turns the corner on the east side.

That for Sonneveld is a fairly large three-storey house with basement. It has steel frame construction with external brick walls. The principal living quarters are on the first floor and provide an interesting example of open planning. Opening from the large living room is the library, divided only by a collapsible rubber screen, dining room and terrace, from which descends an external spiral staircase at the southeast corner of the house. A circular internal staircase links the floors at the north end of the house up to the roof where it finishes with a straight run. The ground floor, which has the servants' quarters and a study, is recessed on the west side and southeast corners with column supports for the upper storeys which contributes to the architectural effect. Aesthetic values are often related to expression of structure. A horizontal emphasis is given by the bands marking the storeys which continue a little round the south corner enclosing the first floor terrace and second floor balcony. It is an ingeniously designed and beautiful house. That for Dr Boeve is similarly a long rectangular block of four floors with the same construction. The principal living quarters are on the ground floor, but it is not an open plan, a circumstance probably determined by the Doctor's offices being on the same floor as the living quarters of the family. The top floor is partly occupied by a gymnasium and servants' quarters and partly by a roof terrace on the south side enclosed by a glass balustrade. The motif of the circular stairways is again employed. It forms a projection at the north end on the two first floors and the stairway rises from the hall and descends to the basement. Another circular stairway rises from the first floor landing on the west side, to the second floor and roof terrace. In both these houses the heating, larder and storage are in the basement.

SCANDINAVIA

The two hundred years old central European tradition of the population in cities and towns living mainly in apartment blocks has been followed in Scandinavia. In the country there were, of course, mansions and villas for the well-to-do and cottages for agricultural workers. With the increase of population and the spread of cities some of the wealthier residential areas in the suburbs contained groups of detached private houses, some of them individually designed, and although this form of development is necessarily on a comparatively small scale it has, with the spread of wealth, increased in Scandinavia. As pointed out previously, the individually designed house is something of a research laboratory for mass housing, it is a good subject for an architect, and in Scandinavia some of the smaller houses designed for individual requirements occasionally formed models or prototypes, suitably modified, for groups of similar houses.

Climate necessarily controls the type of dwelling. In Norway, Sweden and Finland the winters are long with very short days from November to February and the tendency for the middle classes has been to live in apartment houses in the cities and towns, while possessing a small timber house in the country on the outskirts where they can enjoy the summer during weekends and in the long evenings of daylight. A characteristic of interiors in the houses of northern Europe, which is particularly marked in Scandinavia, is to bring the garden partly inside the house so that it can be enjoyed throughout the year, and often one finds a conservatory extension or section of the living room, full of a variety of plants, and provision is often made for this in a design.

Thus since the twenties of this century the individually designed family house for what might be called the professional and managerial strata of society has become an interesting feature of Scandinavian domestic architecture. Most are traditional in character, but from the early thirties an increasing number are modern and are significant examples of the new architecture.

In Denmark several were built to the designs of such noted architects as Frits Schlegel, Mogens Lassen and Arne Jacobsen. A well-known house by the first named was built at Vedbaek north of Copenhagen in 1937. It is a one-storey reinforced concrete construction, with flat roof, and walls partly faced with red brick. It has an L-shaped plan with a large living room at the corner, with dining room and kitchen adjoining on one side and bedrooms and bathroom occupying the wings. A garage is a little away from the house linked with it by a pergola which connects with a veranda that also forms an open vestibule. An interesting feature is that the ceiling of the living room is higher by some three feet than the other rooms, which gives an agreeable feeling of spaciousness, and also gives attractive variety to the external appearance. Houses by Mogens Lassen are somewhat similar, often with an approximation to the L-plan with a large living room as a dominating feature, and the other rooms comparatively small in size. One built in 1940 in Ordrup north of Copenhagen was constructed of light concrete blocks. The small entrance hall is at the corner of the L, the living room and dining recess occupying one wing and the sleeping quarters the other. The heating stove is brought out towards the centre of the living–dining room. A timber country house not far away in the 'Bel Colle' park at Rungsted designed by Ole Hagen at about the same time is also interesting in the arrangement of the rooms. There is the large central living room with dining room and kitchen on one side and sleeping quarters on the other, all grouped roughly within a rectangle, although a puzzling feature of this house is the small flights of steps from hall to living room and from living room to dining room. In older houses steps often marked the change from the part with the suspended floor to that with the solid floor, or were built for the sake of variety, but the different levels were a great inconvenience. In this house at Rungsted it seems to have been due to the sloping ground, but it is hardly sufficient justification.

The new architecture in Sweden decisively begins with the 1930 exhibition at Stockholm. In the housing section models of flats, terrace houses and villas were exhibited, and during the succeeding ten years some interesting houses were built in the suburbs and on the outskirts of cities by such noted architects as Sven Markelius, Sigurd Lewerentz and the English architect Ralph Erskine who lives and practises in Sweden. The work of the two first named though progressive in spirit and showing the influence of Le Corbusier is yet firmly rooted in tradition. Most of their houses are of timber construction mounted on stone or concrete plinths, which is a traditional method in Scandinavia, but there is, as in Danish housing, considerable change towards the less rigid and more functional and convenient arrangement of rooms grouped round a comparatively large living room. Markelius built several houses in Stockholm and its vicinity; probably the most interesting and progressive was the one that he designed at Kevinge for himself in 1940, but which was not built owing to war restrictions until 1944. It is a one-storey building with basement with an L-shaped plan inwards towards the south and east, well integrated with its sloping woodland site. A large living room with dining annex occupies the corner, adjoined on the north, outer side by the kitchen. A library and study occupy one wing, and sleeping quarters the other. The construction is of wood panels of insulated sandwich design mounted on the concrete walls of the basement. There is a low pitched roof of asbestos cement tiles. In the integration with the garden which has lawn, pavings, shrubs and a bathing pool the aim has been to make possible the utmost enjoyment of the open air in the long summer days.

A novel and unusual house is the one-storey structure set among trees at Storvik, Hammarby, near Stockholm, designed by Ralph Erskine. The rooms are grouped in a rectangular space round a central winter garden which has a skylight above, towards which the long roof slopes. The construction is of timber framework and boarding raised above the ground on a concrete podium. Among the features of the exterior are two tall chimneys that rise to double the height of the long, low house. Another example of a garden within the house is provided by a house at Vastberga, near Stockholm, designed by Backstrom and Reinius. A large square living room terminates on the south and garden side with a sloping glass wall and this end is devoted to a subtropical garden of trees, shrubs and flowers, including a pool, which can be enjoyed throughout the year. The living room is surrounded at the other end by small rooms, and being high there is a staircase from it to the sleeping quarters on the first floor.

355

House at Munksnäs, near Helsinki, designed by *Alvar Aalto* for himself, 1935

Exterior view and plan

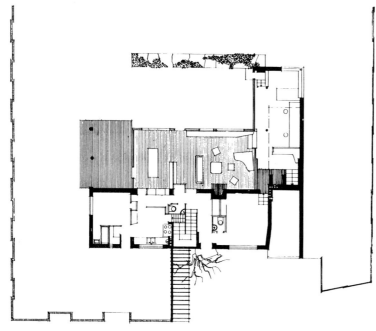

The flattish roof has wide overhanging eaves, it is covered with copper and slopes gently to a central drain.

A few examples of domestic architecture in Norway during this period show a progressive modern spirit, one particularly worthy of note being a house for a doctor in Oslo designed by Herman Munthe-Kass. It is a long rectangular building, one end abutting a steep slope so that at this end the house is on two floors and the remainder on three. The hall and staircase are in the centre with rooms on either side. The large living room with study annex opening to a terrace is on the second floor and on the other side of the landing are bedrooms. The dining room with kitchen adjoining is on the first floor, with a bedsitting room across the landing, an unusual separation of living and dining room, no doubt dictated by individual requirements. The walls of the two lower floors are of reinforced concrete and the top floor of timber cavity construction, with a waterproofed timber roof with a slight fall. There are few and small windows on the north side, but those of the living room on the south and west sides are large. Seen among the trees it makes an interesting pattern with the light concrete walls and the darker timber walls above.

Among the interesting houses built in Finland during the thirties two are outstanding, both erected to the designs of Alvar Aalto; one he built for himself in 1935 and the other for Mairea Gullichson in 1938. The former is at Munksnäs, near Helsinki, and is situated on the well-wooded slope of a hill. It is a two-storey house planned to accommodate the architect's working premises on one side with the living quarters on the other side, divided by the entrance hall on the ground floor and an extensive terrace on the first floor. The large living room on the south and garden side has a dining annex which opens to a covered dining terrace, and these all open to a paved courtyard, separated from the garden by a low wall. The extensive terrace on the first floor is a notable feature, on to which the bedroom landing opens on one side and the architects' working rooms on the other. The house is constructed with steel frame and brick infilling, the floors are concrete and the external facing is cement rendering, timber, and in parts a combination of timber and concrete. There are large blank walls with few openings on the north side, but the south elevation makes a beautiful composition of timber and cement walls, large windows and recessed areas.

The Villa Mairea is a large two-storey house in a pine forest at Noormarkku. It is roughly an L-shaped plan with the entrance hall near the outer corner, and a large living room, music room and winter garden occupying one wing, and dining room, kitchen and servants' quarters occupying the other. Continuing on the line of this wing is a terrace which links with the sauna and pool. On the first floor are the sleeping quarters with a spacious landing and terrace to the east, while a row of bedrooms on the same side have four projecting windows slightly tilted towards the south, so that the series has an echelon effect. As in Aalto's own house the external

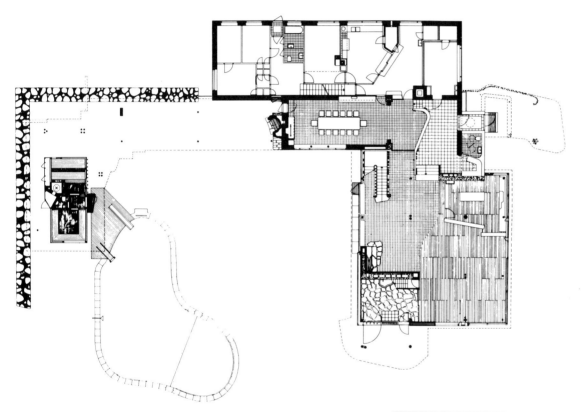

Villa Mairea built in a pine forest at Noormarkku,
Finland, 1938. Two views and plan

Architect: Alvar Aalto

finishes are pale cement rendering and timber in the form of vertical boarding. The functional arrangement of the rooms makes a very pleasing external composition, somewhat like a modern sculpture of a geometric character.

ENGLAND

Although there were very few examples in England of the new architecture by the early years of the thirties, its influence from Germany, France and Holland was beginning to permeate more widely and was greatly accelerated by the migration to England of a number of architects from abroad, among them some of the most famous architects in Germany. In no branch of architecture was the result of this influence more complete and far reaching than in the individually designed house and thus it happened that for the first time since the early years of the century (when Muthesius returned to Germany with enthusiasm for the English house) there were probably more original and notable modern houses built in England than anywhere else in Europe. It was probably another golden age in English domestic architecture although it has required the perspective of history for this to be realized. The circumstance that these houses were in a new idiom, that they were pioneer efforts, and were the results of deeply thought convictions contributed much to their success. There was inevitably much opposition among the conservative adherents of tradition, but these houses were nearly all built for private clients who must have possessed a progressive attitude similar to that of their architects. It is an example where pioneer work was done by the private client and his architect, and these houses were very much the research laboratories from which mass housing for local authorities and others was to benefit.

The architects mainly responsible were the three partners Amyas Connell, Basil Ward, and Colin Lucas, of whom the two first were from New Zealand; the architects who came from Germany and who entered into partnership with English architects, the principal of whom were Eric Mendelsohn, Walter Gropius and Marcel Breuer; the first entering into partnership with Serge Chermayeff (who was born in England of Russian parents), Gropius with Maxwell Fry and Breuer with F. R. S. Yorke; then the Tecton Group founded by the Russian architect Berthold Lubetkin, who was joined by Anthony Chitty, Lindsay Drake, Michael Dugdale, Val Harding and Denys Lasdun; and a few other architects including Oliver Hill, Raymond McGrath and Godfrey Samuel.

THE HOUSES OF CONNELL, WARD AND LUCAS

Amyas Connell and Basil Ward after receiving some architectural training in New Zealand came to England and continued their studies. Connell's first commission was in 1929 for building a house at Amersham for the Greek and Roman archaeologist Professor Bernard Ashmole. This house called 'High and Over' is pleasantly situated on high ground and is built with three wings three storeys high radiating from a central octagonal hall, the ceiling of which extends to the height of two floors. On plan it is somewhat like three equidistant fat spokes of a wheel with the hall as the axle, the direction of the spokes being approximately north, southeast and southwest. On the ground floor, the north wing has the dining room and kitchen, the southwest wing the living room, and the southeast wing the library. The first floor has the sleeping quarters, and on the second floor the centre and one wing are day and night nurseries, while the other wings are covered roof terraces. Large windows are approximately towards the south and small windows towards the north. It is constructed of reinforced concrete which today looks a little heavy, but the pale masses of the house look well amidst the dark cypresses that surround it. The design is original and unusual and is one of the early notable achievements in the new architecture in England. Equally ingenious and notable is Connell's house 'New Farm' at Grayswood near Haslemere in Surrey designed in 1932. It is a two-storey structure with a roof terrace, on a very irregular plan which could best be described as an approximation to a fan with the circumference to the south, and the dining room, study and living room on the circumference, the last jutting out beyond the others. The hall is in the centre and kitchen on the dining room side, and servants' quarters at the back. The room divisions are similar on the first floor with the three main bedrooms on the circumference. The construction is of reinforced concrete, the windows form long horizontal bands, and the staircase enclosed in glass walls ascends to give access to the roof terrace, thus rising well above the rest of the house. The house looks an irregular, yet very attractive, grouping of varied masses very like a sculpture by a constructivist.

Basil Ward became a partner with Connell in 1930. His first venture with domestic buildings was a group of four speculative houses on the 'High and Over' estate at Amersham in 1934. They were all to the same design, of two-storey with a roof terrace and constructed of reinforced concrete.

The third partner, Colin Lucas, joined the 'firm' in 1933. He had already built three small houses, one at Burghclere in Hampshire in 1927, one at Bourne End, Buckinghamshire in 1930 and one at Chelwood Gate in Sussex. All are small examples of functional planning on a small scale, but his more notable work was to come a little later. Although working as partners Connell, Ward and Lucas designed as individual architects for smaller work like private houses to suit individual requirements and collaborated in large works. Thus in the range of very distinctive separate family houses produced by the partnership each one was the responsibility of one of the partners. Perhaps the most important as contributions to domestic architecture of the period, in addition to the two by Connell already described, were another house by Connell at Brentry Hill, Bristol, built in 1935, a house at Moor Park, Rickmansworth, Hertfordshire by Basil Ward, built in 1937, and houses at Woodmancote, Sussex, at Virginia Water and at Hampstead by Colin Lucas, built in 1936, 1937 and 1938. All these houses are of reinforced concrete construction with load-bearing walls with occasional supplementary post and beam construction, thus differing from the modern houses in other countries that have been described. The house at Brentry Hill by Connell repeats the motif of the tall staircase window which rises above the flat roof to which the stairs give access. This small house has a rather conventional arrangement of rooms on either side of a passage-like hall and landing, but there is a very interesting curved sculpturesque concrete covered entrance.

The house at Woodmancote is a small, square, two-storey structure, with a roof terrace partly covered. The living room, which faces south, has a triangular projection with large windows and thus catches the sun for most of the day. It has a dining recess opening to a terrace. A conspicuous feature of the exterior is a tall circular chimney for the living room fire on the wall where it adjoins the one-storey structure of the garage. This chimney rises well above the flat roof; it is very like a factory chimney and could hardly be justified on functional grounds while aesthetically it strikes a harsh discordant note.

Basil Ward's house at Moor Park is one of the best of the group. It is approximately a long rectangle orientated roughly northeast–southwest, with the principal living quarters on the first floor, and the bedrooms on the second floor facing southeast. There are long wide bands of fenestration the whole length of the house, while there is a semicircular projection mainly of glass for the dining room at one end, while the living room opens to a covered terrace. The roof terrace is partly protected by a large concrete slab circular at one end, repeating the motif of the dining room bay. The extensive fenestration and the horizontal emphasis give the house a structurally light appearance similar to some of the earlier continental houses.

Colin Lucas's house called 'Wentworth' at Virginia Water is a rectangular structure with continuous fenestration on the long sides, broad and generous on the south and narrower on the north, which also has the long vertical staircase wnidow. The dining room and kitchen are on the ground floor on the south and north sides respectively. The large living room occupies the centre of the south side and five bedrooms occupy the first floor. The second floor is mainly a roof terrace partly protected by a long horizontal slab but accommodates two further bedrooms. The general effect is of a light glass and concrete structure which looks particularly pleasing among the tall conifers that surround it—a contrast of vertical and horizontals.

The most famous of the houses by the group and in many ways the most notable is the one in Hampstead built to the designs of Colin Lucas. It occupies a sloping site at the corner of Frognal and Frognal Way and is a three-storey rectangular structure orientated north–south, so that the long street façade faces west and the garden façade east. The ground floor is occupied by a garage with a wide entrance underneath the

House at Moor Park, Rickmansworth, Hertfordshire, 1937

Architect: Basil Ward

House at Virginia Water, Surrey, 1937
Front and rear views

Architect: Colin Lucas

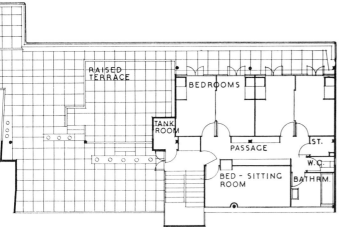

House at Frognal, Hampstead, 1938
Front view, plan of second floor, and garden view

Architect: Colin Lucas

superstructure. At the side is the entrance to the hall adjoined by a playroom and both surrounded by the extensive lower terrace. The first and principal floor has a long living room on the east side, opening to a terrace, adjoined at one side by a bedroom which links with dressing room and bathroom on the other side. Occupying about half the second floor are further bedrooms, with a covered terrace for the rest of the floor. The arrangement was for the parents to have their sleeping quarters near the living room, and the children theirs on the next floor, bedrooms which could be utilized as study rooms as well. A distinctive feature of the house is its construction. The previous houses of the group were constructed mainly with load bearing concrete walls, but this house is constructed in the manner of Le Corbusier's houses with a framework of concrete columns on which the structure hangs. Most of these columns run the whole height of the house, the exceptions being four outer ones that stop at the second floor roof terrace. They form an attractive arcading on the ground floor terrace. An external staircase runs from the garden to the first floor terrace, a diagonal motif reminiscent of Le Corbusier's house at Garches. The garden elevation with its recessions, continuous fenestration and horizontal emphasis is very effective, much more so than the more sombre west façade where flat wall surfaces are more conspicuous. The concrete has been finished in a dull dark red, not perhaps the most attractive hue.

THE GERMAN–ENGLISH PARTNERSHIPS

The Mendelsohn–Chermayeff partnership yielded two interesting houses, one at Chalfont St. Giles, Buckinghamshire, built in 1934 and the other in Church Street, Chelsea. The former is spaciously planned, and from a square structure a long wing projects southwest, occupied on the ground floor by a long living room and hall opening to a terrace enclosed by a wall which extends at the end to form a favourite Mendelsohnian semicircular feature. The stairway from the hall to the sleeping quarter on the first floor makes a quarter circle which defines the elevation on the northwest side, while the long wing extends over that below to cover part of the terrace. Advantage is taken of the sloping ground at the northeast end to provide a lower ground floor for heating plant, storage and a garage. Although there is horizontal emphasis of the rectangular mass by means of the long fenestration these are for the most part framed in plain white walls so that in the massing there is a degree of classical restraint achieved by a balance of verticals and horizontals.

The house in Church Street, Chelsea, was built about the same time as the neighbouring house designed by Walter Gropius and Maxwell Fry. They are on the east side of the street, and opposite on the west side is a row of Georgian houses built in the second half of the eighteenth century. The Mendelsohn and Chermayeff house occupies the south site and presents a long façade to the street, on which side are the kitchen, hall, cloakroom and stairs, providing a barrier for the east, garden side where are the living and sleeping quarters: thus obtaining a fair degree of seclusion. The dining room, library and drawing room, which has a characteristic semicircular termination, occupy one end, and a sunken squash court and garage the other. The circular projection of the living room is mainly glass, and forms a balcony for the principal bedroom above, while it is echoed by the enclosing troughed wall. Again, large areas of plain wall are enclosed in long horizontals partly balanced by verticals which give a sense of repose to the building, and secures harmony with the Georgian houses opposite.

A long wall on the street façade links it with the house on the north side by Gropius and Fry, which is placed end on to the street, with the garden façade facing south. On the ground floor are the sequence of kitchen, dining and living rooms opening to the garden terrace, while the garage and entrance from the street are alongside the kitchen. On the first floor is a generous supply of balconies to which day nursery, study and bedroom open. The second floor covers a small part of the area with maids' rooms and a balcony, the remainder being the flat roof. It will be seen that in this house as much as possible on the south side is open to terraces and balconies, much more so than the comparatively restrained house next door. The two houses however make a harmonious and distinctive architectural ensemble on the east side of Church Street. That they accord so well in general proportions and massing with the Georgian houses opposite should win the hearts of the traditionalists. They are both built of brick with external finish of cement rendering which has kinship with Georgian stucco.

The Mendelsohn–Chermayeff partnership was dissolved at the end of 1936, after which Mendelsohn concentrated mainly on his work in Palestine, while Chermayeff continued for a few more years to practise in England. Among the buildings that he designed was an ambitious and beautiful house for himself at Halland in Sussex. A two-storey rectangular timber-framed structure, on concrete foundations, it is faced externally with cedar boarding left to weather naturally on three sides but painted cream on the long south garden façade. The basic plan of the house is the division of the services— kitchens, bathrooms, stairway—on the north side, and the living rooms and bedrooms on the south side by means of a long cupboard insulating spine running the whole length of the house. The plan on the south side is divided into six bays, the living room in the centre extending to about three and a half bays, with the study—one bay—at the west end, and the dining room one and a half bays at the east end. Part of the dividing walls are sliding screens so that all the three rooms can be thrown open as one space, while room height sliding windows open all the rooms to the terrace. On the east side the terrace projects an arm to the south which terminates in a trellis and nearby is a sculpture of a recumbent stone figure by Henry Moore. Bedrooms and nurseries on the first floor occupy the six bays of the south side which is set back a few feet for a balcony to which the rooms open. Garage, laundry and storage comprise a one-storey block at the east end, and a short verandah in this block links with the long entrance veranda on the north side.

House at Chalfont St. Giles, Buckinghamshire, 1934
View and plans

Architects: Eric Mendelsohn and Serge Chermayeff

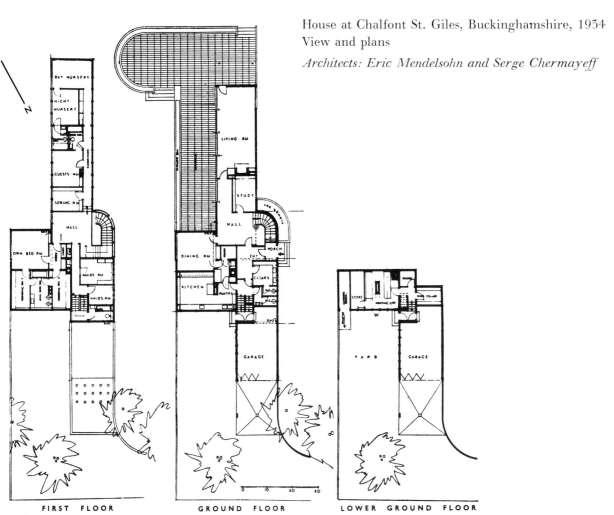

FIRST FLOOR   GROUND FLOOR   LOWER GROUND FLOOR

Two houses 64 and 66 Church Street, Chelsea
Architects of nearer house, *Eric Mendelsohn
and Serge Chermayeff*

Architects of further house, *Walter Gropius
and Maxwell Fry*

Plans of first and ground floor and garden view
Mendelsohn and Chermayeff house

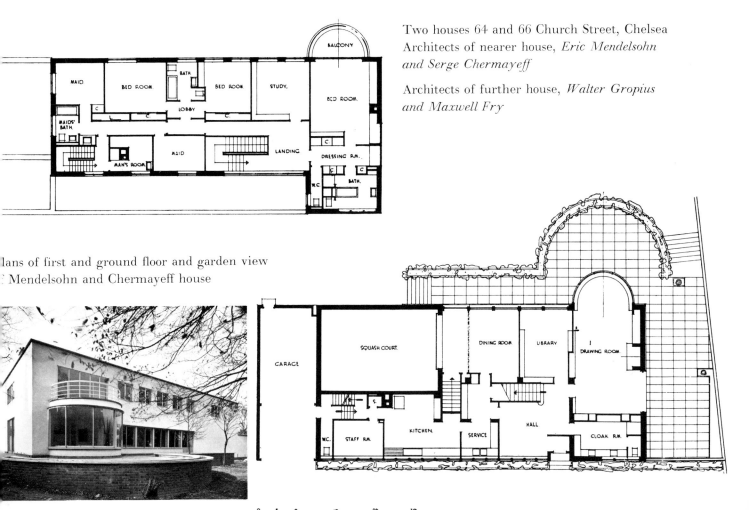

If there is one criticism of so excellent a house it is of the two levels on the ground floor. There are three steps down in the middle of the study, introduced because the owner working at his desk on the higher level can more easily see the view. This also means three steps down from the hall to the living room. The many advantages of having everything on the one floor level are so great that the justification for the steps in this case is a poor one. Still, although it may owe something to Mendelsohn's house at the Rupenhorn, built nearly ten years earlier in 1929, it is among the most notable private houses erected in Europe in the late thirties.

The partnership of Walter Gropius and Maxwell Fry terminated when the former went to America at the beginning of 1937. At this time Maxwell Fry was independently engaged in designing several private houses, among which should be mentioned a house in Frognal Way, Hampstead, built in 1936, a house in Kingston built in 1937 and one at Chipperfield, Hertfordshire built in the same year.

The house at Hampstead occupies a site that falls to the south, with an extensive view over London from the upper floors. This influenced the design. Constructed of reinforced concrete with white rendered finish, it is set well back from the road and is reached by steps and a ramp to the garage on the ground floor which also has the heating plant. On the first floor the large living room with the adjoining dining room, both with large windows, open to the terrace on the south side that extends the whole length of the house, protected by screen walls at both ends. Here the extensive views over London can be obtained. The living room also has a window on the garden side where this floor is at ground level. On the second floor the extensive view can be further enjoyed from a row of three bedrooms. Seen from the road, this white mass relieved by the horizontal emphasis of the areas of generous fenestration, with its setting of trees, is among the beautiful modern houses of London. There is none that I like better.

Somewhat on the same theme, but with a great deal more surrounding space is the house Maxwell Fry built on a site at the corner of Warren Rise and Neville Avenue at Kingston-on-Thames. Again this is a site sloping down to the south and the architect has used it to advantage. The ground floor plan is an **L**-shape with the large living room, study and dining room on the long south side opening to a terrace, well above the level of the garden, with which it connects by a broad flight of steps flanked by a sun room that projects at the west end and to which the living room opens. The line of this elevation is continued by a long wall beyond which is a kitchen garden and swimming pool. The approach to the entrance along the north side is protected by a long cantilevered canopy. The north wing is occupied by the kitchen and servants' quarters. The first floor has the sleeping quarters with two small balconies at either end and the second floor is a roof garden screened on the north side. It is equipped for meals and there is a food lift to it. The garage is in a separate square structure on the

Sun house, Frognal Way, Hampstead, 1936. Front view and plan
Architect: Maxwell Fry

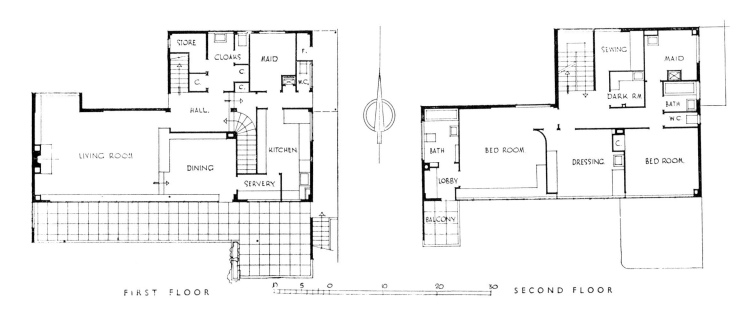

STORE

CLOAKS

MAID

F.

C.

C.

W.C.

C.

HALL.

KITCHEN.

LIVING ROOM

DINING

SERVERY

FIRST FLOOR

5   0   10   20   30

SEWING

MAID

DARK RM

BATH

W.C

BATH

BED ROOM

DRESSING.

BED ROOM.

C.

LOBBY

BALCONY

SECOND FLOOR

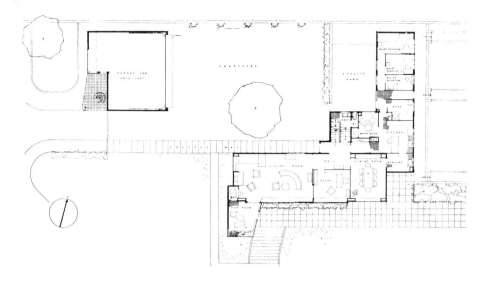

House at Angmering-on-Sea,
Sussex, 1936

*Architects: F. R. S. Yorke
and Marcel Breuer*

House at Kingston, Surrey, 1937

Architect: Maxwell Fry

General view and ground floor plan

northwest side, with flat above approached by a spiral staircase in the corner recess of the building.

The house is designed to facilitate the transition to open-air living, the sequence of rooms is well planned while as an architectural composition it looks well from all viewpoints, but especially from the south with its long pale horizontal masses harmonizing felicitously with the landscape.

The other previously mentioned house by Maxwell Fry, at Chipperfield, in which a studio was an important feature, was built a little earlier, in 1935, for an artist. It is a smaller house but again has a large living room with dining annex facing a terrace on the south side. The large studio is on the first floor with double access by internal and external stairs. The house is constructed of brick cavity walls with the exception of the studio which has a teak framework, and external oak weather boarding.

Marcel Breuer came to England in 1934 and left to join Walter Gropius in America in 1937. During his three years in England he was in partnership with F. R. S. Yorke and they were together responsible for several houses, among them those at Angmering-on-Sea, Hatfield, Lee-on-Solent, Eton and Iver, all built in the years 1935–7.

The house at Angmering is a two-storey, L-planned house, with the first floor as the principal one so as to enjoy the view overlooking the sea. The ground floor occupies only one wing and comprises hall, kitchen, garage and heating equipment. On the first floor are the living and dining rooms opening to a curved terrace on the south side supported by a single column, while a long bedroom wing on the east side stretches south supported on stilts with the garden lawn continuing underneath. All the six bedrooms face east with a corridor on the west side. The design obviously owes something to Le Corbusier, and is one of the early examples in England of an extensive open ground floor area with the first floor supported on a series of columns. It is built mainly of cavity brick walls, but the supporting columns are reinforced concrete on which a reinforced concrete floor slab rests, while a continuous concrete beam runs round the walls at window height. The walls are finished in white and it looks very modern near the sea front in distinctive contrast to a row of traditional detached houses.

The houses at Hatfield and Lee-on-Solent are similar to each other in design, the distinguishing feature of both being the treatment of the living room. Each house is a two-storey structure and the living room with dining recess forms an L-shape folded round the kitchen. There is a large window facing south, the west side with dining recess is one storey in height, but the remainder in the middle of the house extends the two-storey height, with a rather prominent chimney breast in the centre of the

371

house emphasizing the height. A clerestory west window makes the interior very light. On the right of the chimney breast stairs ascend to the first-floor landing which overlooks the living room. This two-storey height giving a sense of spaciousness, although used by Le Corbusier, was new in modern English design. Both houses are built of reinforced concrete load bearing walls five inches thick, finished externally with pale pink paint. In addition to the influence of Le Corbusier, one is conscious of the influence of Adolf Loos especially in the treatment of the exterior, which appears as a carefully calculated composition of square plain boxes.

The small house at Iver has a similar L-shaped living room with dining recess folded round the kitchen, with central flue, and is notable for the extensive terrace on the first floor framed with a concrete beam and supporting slender columns which could be utilized for screening. Simple yet decorative steps ascend to the flat roof. The shadows of these steps incidentally make a very interesting pattern on the plain cream walls.

The two houses at Eton for two College masters are of identical design, more conventional yet with excellent functional plans, with a long living room on the south side of the ground floor flanked by dining room and study, and a series of bedrooms above on the same side.

The Russian architect Berthold Lubetkin, after being trained in Moscow, and continuing his studies in Paris during the twenties where he also worked with Auguste Perret, came to London in 1930 and shortly afterwards formed a firm of architects under the name of Tecton with the five young English architects: Anthony Chitty, Lindsay Drake, Michael Dugdale, Val Harding and Denys Lasdun. The firm became famous for the High Point flats at Highgate, for the Finsbury Health Centre and for buildings at the Zoo, and it also designed a few houses, all of which were progressively modern in spirit. With these individually designed houses the name of the particular architect chiefly responsible is given, thus Chitty and Tecton, and so on.

Perhaps the most notable houses produced by the group were two by Val Harding and one by Denys Lasdun. In 1935 the former built a house at Sydenham in which among other things is a very ingenious solution of several problems imposed by the site and the clients' conditions. The client originally wished to have his house on a site in the Dulwich estate, but the trustees would not give permission for a design of so advanced a character, so a site was found at nearby Sydenham Hill.

As built it consists of two parts: the main part, which is a three-storey framed concrete construction, and a one-storey service wing tapering on plan, at right angles to the house. Linking the two are the kitchen and pantry. The house is orientated with the long sides facing roughly east and west. The living room is at the south end with a long east window which turns the corner for a short distance on the south wall. Next is the hall with its circular staircase and then the dining room. The first floor has a series of bedrooms facing east and opening to the balcony over the service wing. The third floor has a study in the centre, reached by the circular stairway, and the remainder of this floor is a roof terrace. The architectural effect of the exterior on the west side owes something to the row of columns which supports the overhanging first floor structure thus forming a loggia. One feature of the design hardly justifies itself, and rather upsets unity, and that is the circular staircase, which probably derives from this motif being much used by architects in Germany and France and elsewhere during the twenties, but there was generally more justification for its use than in this house. It would have been more in harmony with the design, and certainly safer, to have had a square staircase with three flights and two landings to the first floor, while the semicircular brick enclosure seen externally is rather an ugly feature. But apart from this defect the house is a notable design.

Another house by Val Harding built a little later is in a clearing of a small wood at Farnham Common, Buckinghamshire. The plan is an L-shape partly enclosing a terrace and lawn. The long arm extends eastwards facing south in which are the dining room and nursery, while the living room occupies the short arm at the west end, all opening by means of sliding glass panelled doors on to the covered terrace. The entrance is at the west side, with the garage a little way linked by a flat roof which thus provides a porch or carport. The line of the bedrooms on the first floor all face south, and a balcony runs along the whole length with a terrace over the living room screened on the west (street side) by a trellis the top of which continues the line of the roof parapet. At the corner of the terrace is a spiral stairway which connects with the garden. The whole design is a further example of the easy opening of the interior to the garden and to the fresh air and sunlight, achieved on both floors. One feels that the lawn and terrace in the corner of the L is an important summer room raised a little from the surrounding garden.

Many of the houses described are in the country or on the outskirts of London, designed in a fairly spacious setting where the architect and his client can spread themselves. Building a good house on a comparatively small site in a more central residential area with a fairly high density is more difficult, for the requirements in a restricted area set problems. Yet these often provide a stimulus to ingenuity, and such is the case with the house in New Road, Paddington, designed by Denys Lasdun for an artist and built in 1937. It is a site between existing houses in the Georgian style and the squarish massing of the new house accords well with its neighbourhood. It is a four-storey structure with basement for heating plant and storage. The front of the house faces south. The ground floor is mainly a flat for the servants and has two bedrooms, servants' hall, bathroom, kitchen and servery, with entrance hall in the centre and garage to the right. The first floor has a large living room the whole width of the house, on the south side, with a window for its entire length with sliding panes. A dining recess makes an **L** of the total areas, and the remainder of the floor is occupied by a study. On the second floor are the sleeping quarters, while the entire third floor is occupied by the studio, which has a north light and a sloping roof. The studio has a curved wall on the south side and opens to a south balcony. Both the studio and the living room have a fair span of about 30 feet in both directions and thus a reinforced concrete frame construction was employed with a filling of brick cavity walls.

One of the distinguishing features of this house is the front elevation which strikes a new and unusual note in this part of London. It is a large vertical rectangular mass with a formal symmetrical pattern. The whole of the front ground floor wall is recessed a few feet and there is a single supporting column in the centre in front of the entrance which is flanked with glass bricks. For the first and second floors are two horizontal bands of fenestration and this middle part of the elevation is faced with matt brown tiles. In the centre of the upper part is a rectangular aperture for the studio balcony, the roof of which is a series of open beams. The wall here is painted white with the concrete frame. The side walls of the house are brick. There is some kinship between the treatment of this façade and the geometric abstracts of Piet Mondrian and Ben Nicholson.

This movement of progressive modern domestic architecture spread and several other architects made their distinctive contributions, among them Godfrey Samuel who worked for a time in partnership with Val Harding, Christopher Nicholson, Oliver Hill and Raymond McGrath. It will not be possible more than to glance at some of the houses designed by these architects.

In 1935 Godfrey Samuel designed a house at Bromley on a site that falls to the north on the road side. The house is designed on a **T** plan with the long down stroke facing north and south. Advantage of the slope is taken by placing the garage and heating plant on the lower ground floor, while the ground floor is reached by double entrance steps on either side of the garage. The large living room is flanked by the study and hall from which a central circular staircase rises, and on the west side projecting southwards is the dining room. All these principal living rooms face south to the terrace and garden, the dining room has sliding doors which makes the transition to open-air meals simple, but it may be wondered why sliding doors were not also installed for the living room instead of large windows above a dado. A series of bedrooms on the first floor open to a long balcony on the south, which also forms a protective canopy to part of the terrace below. This is also the case on the north side where a narrow loggia with slender columns extends east of the main entrance. The house is constructed of reinforced concrete with load-bearing walls four inches thick. It makes a pleasing horizontal mass of pale cream amidst trees, punctuated with generous ground floor

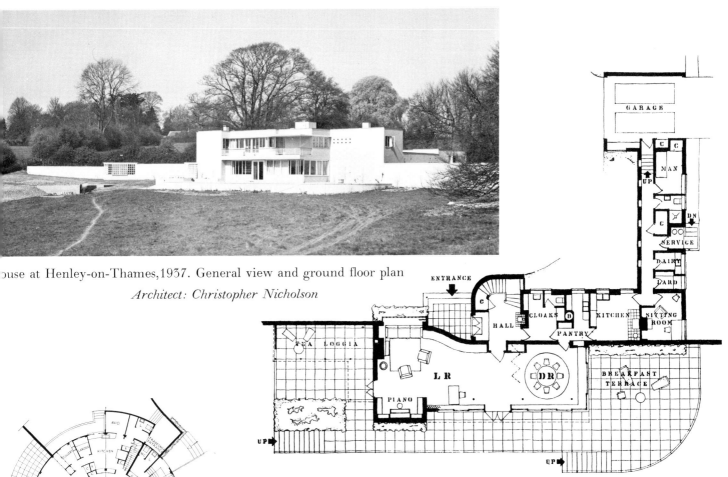

House at Henley-on-Thames, 1937. General view and ground floor plan

Architect: Christopher Nicholson

GARAGE

MAN

SERVICE

DAIRY

YARD

ENTRANCE

HALL   CLOAKS   KITCHEN   SITTING ROOM

PANTRY

TEA LOGGIA

L R

PIANO

D R

BREAKFAST TERRACE

UP

UP

GROUND FLOOR PLAN

House in Surrey, 1937
General view and ground,
first and second floor plans

Architect:
Raymond McGrath

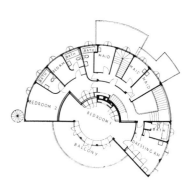

BEDROOM 2

BEDROOM 1

BALCONY

DRESSING RM

MAID

BATH   BATH   MAID

FIRST FLOOR PLAN

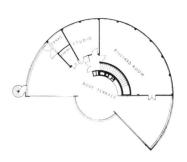

STUDIO

BILLIARD ROOM

ROOF TERRACE

SECOND FLOOR PLAN

fenestration on the south side, with a series of vertical bedroom windows on the first floor. On the north façade the windows are few and small, the principal one being the first floor horizontal strip, which relates well to the extensive mass of plain wall.

The very attractive house designed by Christopher Nicholson for Dr Warren Crowe at Fawley Green, Henley-on-Thames, built in 1936, is situated on sloping ground that falls to the south, from which extensive views over the Thames valley are obtained. It is a long two-storey structure east–west with a narrow one-storey service arm running north at the east end. It has an open plan with a large living room and dining recess, the long side to the south and French windows opening to a very large terrace defined by a low wall and raised from the surrounding garden. The principal bedrooms open on the south to a balcony, which projects from the main structure and gives a strip protection to the terrace below. The house is designed to permit the maximum outdoor living, the dining room opens to a spacious breakfast terrace on the east side, and the living room opens to an equally spacious tea loggia on the west side, while part of the balcony above is a sleeping porch. One interesting requirement of the design is that in spite of the sloping site the whole ground floor must be on one level—a sensible requirement not always followed in modern houses, as we have seen. The construction is a steel frame with 11 inch cavity walls. The exterior has a pale hue and the masses make an excellent composition in the raised terrace faintly reminiscent of massive river craft. The house looks particularly pleasing from the south against the background of trees. There was some difficulty in getting the design approved by the local authority, by whom it was referred to a panel of architects who passed it provided the house was screened by a line of trees[3].

Oliver Hill designed several interesting houses during the thirties, many in beautiful situations, among them a house called Joldwynds at Holmbury St. Mary in Surrey for Wilfred Greene K.C. the famous barrister, one at Wentworth, one at Poole in Dorset, and one at Hampstead, all built between 1933 and 1938. They are fairly large houses all finished externally in pale colouring, and designed with rooms opening to spacious terraces thus providing the utmost facilities for pleasant outdoor living. In most of these houses the architect seems particularly fond of curved shapes. The house at Holmbury St. Mary (the earliest, built in 1933) has a curved wing, a circular termination to the loggia that projects southwards from the dining room, a semicircular staircase, and circular forms in the terrace; the house at Wentworth has a completely circular staircase largely enclosed in glass, and an attractive elliptical sunroom at the west end of the long living room, which gives a curved wall to the guest room above, and these curves are echoed in the line of the chauffeur's bungalow; while the house at Poole has a partly circular treatment of the hall, stairs and garden walls, in the tennis racket shape of the sunroom on the roof terrace. The houses show the influence of Le Corbusier, but they are a little heavy in effect. This is an impression felt particularly with the house at Holmbury St. Mary, parts of which are faintly reminiscent

376

of a Norman castle, an impression rather helped by the cylindrical forms. Incidentally this house on high ground near Dorking has extensive views to the South Downs and on clear days through the Shoreham gap to the sea.

The last of these notable examples of English domestic architecture of the thirties is one in which the circle rather than the rectangle forms the basis of the design; I refer to the house designed by Raymond McGrath in Surrey on a site where old Georgian houses formerly stood as the focal point of about 25 acres of a pleasingly landscaped park. The ground falls gently away to the south, southeast and southwest, and fine views can be obtained in many directions. This circumstance much influenced the very unusual plan. The old coach house has been retained and the new house has been built in front of it.

The central feature of the plan is a circular living room, and folded round this to the extent of nearly five eighths of a circle on the north side is the remainder of the house, with the dining room on the west side and the study on the east side, with the kitchen and hall between. On the first floor the centre circle is the principal bedroom opening to a balcony, with other bedrooms and bathrooms occupying the remainder. The centre of the top floor is a roof terrace backed on the north side by a billiard room and studio. The living room presents its circular glass façade to the terrace and to the sun from the southeast to the southwest, and from this terrace and from the balcony above is an extensive panorama of Surrey and Sussex, with a pleasant foreground landscape remodelled somewhat by Christopher Tunnard when the house was built. A feature of this landscape is a garden temple to the west. In this direction the dining room opens to the winter garden with its three pools, one at the far end being circular among plants and shrubs. The construction of the house is of reinforced concrete ring beams supported on a series of posts, with concrete floor slabs spanning the space between the beams. The walls are finished externally with a pale grey silica paint. The house has a somewhat curious appearance seen against the background of trees on the low hill crest. From the south it looks as though a huge slice has been cut from a cake, and two big plums put back in the centre, an effect which is not unpleasant except perhaps that of the second floor terrace. Articulations like the spiral staircase at the west corner that ascends to the second floor terrace, and the metal balcony balustrade, give pleasing decorative touches on nearer view. The house is a remarkably interesting experiment and it would be instructive to know from the occupants if it proved to be a generally convenient plan.

On the whole the English houses reviewed in this chapter seem to be functionally satisfactory and aesthetically pleasing. There may be occasional small defects. Sometimes the kitchen and dining room are a little too far removed and could with advantage have been brought closer, as for example in the house by Christopher Nicholson, and those by Oliver Hill, while it is a question whether it is satisfactory to have kitchen and dining room on separate floors even though there is a service lift. These houses were designed when servants could be more easily obtained than in the 1970's, when an arrangement other than the closest proximity of dining room and kitchen is likely to be a disadvantage. Another defect occasionally seen is the two-level floor which can rarely be justified on functional grounds in a house. Also the fondness of architects for the circular stairway is questionable. It may be an interesting architectural feature, but it is not as safe as the straight stairway with generous landings. The occupants may not bother about this when they are young, but they will when they are old.

These, however, are minor defects in a very impressive number of outstandingly good houses. They have been rich in suggestion for smaller mass housing since the Second World War and merit continual study. They constitute the finest record of domestic architecture by any European country during the thirties, and seen as a whole form one of the finest English architectural achievements of the century[4].

REFERENCES AND NOTES

1. I refer chiefly to the house individually designed by an architect. This had some influence on the standard of design in housing estates; at the same time much mass housing in England during the thirties was poor in design and construction.
2. Alfred Roth, *The New Architecture*, Zürich, 1947, p. 39.
3. See *The Architectural Review*, 1937, p. 305.
4. Many of the houses built in Europe during the thirties were described and illustrated in many of the more important architectural journals among the principal of which are *The Architectural Review*, London; *Architectural Design*, London; *L'Architecture d'Aujourd'hui* Paris; *Domus*, Milan; *Werk*, Zürich; *Byggmastaren*, Stockholm; *Bauen und Wohnen*, West Germany.

25 Buildings of the hall type—planetaria, market and sports halls

ONE OF THE MOST exhilarating tasks that is given to the architect and engineer is the enclosing of large spaces. In the past the architect has had the greatest opportunities of this kind in religious buildings where worship takes place within the building—as distinct from the Greek temple, where it takes place without—and it was one of the principal purposes of the design of larger churches to convey a sense of vastness and mystery so as to inspire religious feeling. This was done by the lofty vaulted roof of the Gothic cathedral and the barrel vault and dome of the Renaissance cathedral. The baths of Rome, ministering to the luxury of the rich, often had large halls of considerable magnificence, and, later, banqueting and assembly halls were often designed with spacious grandeur; but up to the nineteenth century it was essentially the religious building which was the subject of this important architectural undertaking.

The commercial, industrial, and recreational developments of modern life, and the populousness of modern cities have prompted larger and larger buildings of the hall type like exhibition buildings, markets, libraries, and railway stations conspicuous in the nineteenth century. The *Galeries des Machines* of successive Paris Exhibitions got larger and larger, from those of 1855 and 1867 with their spans of 157 feet and 115 feet to that of 1889 with its span of 378 feet, while several railway stations had been built with very large spans—that of St. Pancras, London with its 240 feet being the largest.

In the twentieth century the types of building in which large uninterrupted space is desired have increased, and may be roughly listed as religious buildings of all kinds, assembly and concert halls, theatres, cinemas, exhibition and market halls, railway stations, sports and games halls, swimming-bath halls, the halls of large industrial buildings, film studios, airport buildings, and sometimes the rooms of warehouses and departmental stores.

One of the purposes in the construction of many types of hall building is to enclose the space without intermediate roof or ceiling supports or as few as possible. It can be appreciated that this is essential in sports and games halls like covered tennis courts, ice-hockey rinks, swimming baths, and is desirable in market and exhibition halls. In departmental stores, factories, and warehouses the necessity of having large uninterrupted space is less, because the showcases and counters in stores, and the machinery and benches in factories can often be conveniently arranged in relation to the supports; but even in these cases it gives greater freedom in the arrangement of fittings if there are no columnar supports for which to allow.

The *Galerie des Machines* of the Paris Exhibition of 1889, with its span of 378 feet, still is I believe unsurpassed in Europe among steel constructions. The most noteworthy steel roofs erected in the late twenties and early thirties of the twentieth century were perhaps those in Germany. One is that of the Leipzig Fair Hall. This building, which was erected in 1928, is remarkable not only for its size but for the speed with which it was erected. The floor space is 453 feet long by 318 feet wide without intermediate supports, and the whole building was erected in seven weeks in the cold months of January and February. The roof is flat, the large horizontal transverse girders spanning 318 feet, being enclosed by exterior and interior glass lights, the latter forming triangular troughs.

Another interesting steel roof of a different type is that of the Festive Hall at Frankfurt designed by Frederick Thiersch in 1927. It consists principally of an elliptical dome which has a span of about 220 feet on its major axis. The dome consists of twenty elliptically curved steel trusses that spring from the second balcony level and are held at the summit by an elliptical girder. The spaces between the steel ribs in the upper part of the dome are filled with glass. The whole effect is one of spaciousness combined with a certain feeling of gaiety, but it is questionable whether details like the perforations of the steel trusses could not have been more happily designed in shapes more harmonious with the general rhythm.

Among the most beautiful forms of construction for large halls that were developed farther in the third decade of the century was the parabolic rib construction, generally of reinforced concrete. We have noted that the Engelbrekt Church at Stockholm (1908–14) designed by L. J. Wahlman has parabolic vaulting of brick, and that reinforced concrete parabolic ribs formed the essential structure of Freyssinet's airship hangars at Orly (1916). This system of construction was adopted in Freyssinet's Market Hall at Rheims (1922), in the hall of the Gothenberg Exhibition in 1923, and very effectively and dramatically in the Royal Horticultural Hall, London, designed by J. Murray Easton and Howard Robertson in 1923, and in the Klavniko Palace of the Brünn Exhibition, Czechoslovakia, designed by Josef Kalous in 1928. In the last two mentioned, neither has the true parabolic shape of the Orly hangars and the Market Hall at Rheims, and are merely approximations to it. In both, the arches are vertical for some distance at the springing, but they are very different in other respects. In the Horticultural Hall the series of approximately parabolic arches hold together a step structure on either side, the vertical sections forming four tiers of windows of heights diminishing towards the top, while the roof at the summit is lighted by an elliptical window in the east bay. Behind the springing of the arches on either side are aisles with flat roofs. The interior is impressive and impels the visitor to look up, take a breath, and enjoy the sense of space.

It is important for the exhibitions of the Royal Horticultural Society that there should be a good control of temperature within the building, and an interesting method of heating was employed. Hot water pipes were embedded in the concrete soffits of the stepped roof so that the large area of low-temperature surface heat is radiated to the floor and reflected back. This is one of the earliest examples of ceiling-panel heating on a big scale.

In the exhibition hall at Brünn a glass roof curves with the parabolic arches, and is connected to a long soffit which joins the high wall with very large windows. At one part the hall is intersected by transepts, and four ribs meet in the centre over the crossing. It is interesting to compare the designs of these two halls in London and Brünn as two expressions in the same medium of a similar purpose.

Less beautiful, but a contemporary development, are the semicircular and segmental reinforced concrete ribbed constructions for halls, of which early examples noted were the Hall at Magdeburg (1922) by Bruno Taut, a clothing workshop in Paris (1919), and a studio in Paris (1923), both by Auguste and Gustave Perret. Halls of this type continued to be built and were especially favoured for sports stadiums and swimming baths, although they are not generally remarkable for any great span. One of the most pleasing examples is the covered tennis courts at Stockholm designed by Ture Wennerholm. The infilling on one side follows the shape of the ribs, but on the other side the ribs are free in front of the balcony recess, below the windows which form top lights on either side.

SHELL CONCRETE ROOFS

The most outstanding developments in the construction of roofs for hall buildings from 1923 are in shell concrete. Previously, big spans had been obtained by steel construction, and to a less extent by ribbed concrete construction. One of the difficulties of covering large spans with concrete roofs was the weight of the concrete; but by the use of shell concrete, which, like the egg shell, is light and strong, this difficulty has been overcome.

Prominent among the pioneers of shell concrete are Carl Zeiss, Deschinger, and Bauersfeld, who made many of the early experiments in different forms. The method evolved by these pioneers is known as Zeiss Dywidag Chisarc and Shell D[1].

Royal Horticultural Hall, London, 1923

Architects: J. Murray Easton and Howard Robertson

Covered Tennis Courts, Stockholm

Architect: Ture Wennerholm

Planetarium at Hanover erected on the roof of the
building of the *Hanover Advertiser*, 1929

Architect: Fritz Hoger

Leipzig Market Hall, 1928. Exterior and interior views

Architects: Deschinger and Ritter

The earliest systems of reinforced concrete construction, the Hennebique, Coignet, and Considère, were post and beam or frame constructions. In these systems the principal loads were taken by the posts and beams, the walls and floor being non-supporting screens. Another system developed later by Robert Maillart was a slab construction with columnar supports, evolved principally as the slab and mushroom construction. Although the column, with its reinforced, spreading capital, is the chief supporting structure, the overall horizontal slab performs very much the structural function of the beams in the Hennebique system. The arched structure is stronger than a flat beam, and directly the Romans used the semicircular arch instead of the lintel of the Greeks they were able to make much wider arches and larger halls, one of the most remarkable examples being the Pantheon, with its concrete dome with a diameter of $142\frac{1}{2}$ feet. It will be appreciated, therefore, that if the slab of concrete is arched in one or more directions it is much stronger than if it is flat. On this principle shell concrete was developed, making possible considerable spans with concrete only 2 or 3 inches in thickness. The method was first used in the domes of planetariums and later for barrel vaulting and polygonal domes[2]. The first of the planetariums in which this thin, hemispherical shell was used was that at Jena, built in 1923. The dome, which has a diameter of 81 feet 9 inches, consists of concrete $2\frac{3}{8}$ inches thick reinforced with steel network.

A little later a considerable number of planetaria were built of shell concrete. In 1926 two were erected at Berlin, two at Hanover, and others at Düsseldorf, Dresden, Leipzig, Nürnberg, and Mannheim. A large one was built at Jena with a diameter of 131 feet, although the thickness of the shell concrete remained $2\frac{3}{8}$ inches. In 1928 a shell concrete dome was used for a planetarium at Meskau, in Russia, and in 1929 for one at Milan, and another German example at Hamburg. A planetarium in course of construction at Berlin is shown in the illustrations. They show the steel network which also supports the shuttering, and the dome being concreted in concentric rings. One of the planetaria at Hanover is erected on the roof of a newspaper building, designed by Fritz Hoger. This dome has a diameter of 69 feet with a shell $2\frac{3}{8}$ inches thick. The exterior of the dome is covered with copper sheets and ribbing radiating from the top, which may have been prompted by a desire to make it in harmony with the long vertical strips that decorate the façade of the building. All these planetarium domes are true hemispheres, although outer domes in some cases rise higher for the purpose of effect.

The next stage was the use of flatter domes for factories. The earliest example of a flat dome of shell concrete is for a factory at Jena, built in 1928, which has a diameter of 131 feet with a rise of 26 feet, approximately one-fifth of the span. The thickness of the shell is $2\frac{3}{8}$ inches. A little later in the same year an even flatter dome was built at the electricity works at Frankfurt. In this case the span is 85 feet with a rise of only 11 feet and a shell $1\frac{9}{16}$ inches thick. This dome is supported on a girder, which is circular internally and octagonal externally, resting on eight columns.

In the early thirties a slightly larger dome of a similar kind was built for the Market Hall at Algeciras, in Spain. It has a span of 156 feet and was thus the first ribless dome to exceed the span of the Pantheon dome. Like the Pantheon it has a centre light with a diameter of 33 feet. The thickness of the shell is $3\frac{1}{2}$ inches. This dome has a support similar to that of the Frankfurt Electricity Works, in that an octagonal tie encloses the ring of the dome and rests on eight columns[3].

Half-spherical domes of shell concrete were used for bandstands and several began to appear in German watering places in the late twenties, two examples being those at Bad Homberg and Bad Schwalbach. These are not unattractive in appearance, certainly a great improvement on the ornamental iron bandstands all too familiar in England. But the acoustical properties of these half domes of concrete are very doubtful. Henry S. Kamphoefur, a professor of architecture at Oklahoma University, who made a special study of the acoustics of bandstands and open-air stages, considered[4] that the ellipsoid and spherical forms have been found to be unsatisfactory. He stated that the sound is reflected all round from the stage to certain points in the audience. They are not only costly to build, but have much less value as a reflector than a simple vertical rear wall behind the orchestra. This, with an enclosed roof rather than side walls, appears to be the most satisfactory form from the musical standpoint, which is after all the main requirement.

If Kamphoefur's contentions are right it would seem that these bandstand shells are not the most suitable forms for their purpose, and one wonders if the urge of novelty or of modernity was not more a determining factor in this instance than suitability for purpose.

A spectacular development of shell concrete is its use in octagonal ribbed domes, the first large examples of which are the two[5] covering the Leipzig Market Hall designed by Deschinger and Ritter, and erected in 1928. Each dome has a span of 248 feet with a roof light 92 feet in diameter, and rests on latticed arches. The thickness of the shell is only $3\frac{9}{16}$ inches. The span is greater than that of any previous dome and compares with $142\frac{1}{2}$ feet of the Pantheon dome, $138\frac{1}{2}$ feet of Florence Cathedral dome, $137\frac{1}{2}$ feet of St. Peter's dome, and 213 feet of the Jahrhunderthalle dome at Breslau. The weight is little more than one-fifth of St. Peter's dome, and one-third of the Breslau dome.

A little later, in 1929, a similar octagonal dome of shell concrete was built for the market hall at Basel, with a span of 197 feet and a shell thickness of $3\frac{1}{8}$ inches. The dome rests on eight corner columns, but there are no supporting arches as in the Leipzig domes.

The interior effect of these large octagonal domes is impressive, and a sense of space is stimulated by the wide unobstructed area covered and the height to the top of the domes. This sense of space would naturally have been greater if the domes had been higher, but the purpose in constructing these roofs to cover a large area for market needs was to make them as low structurally as possible, and it is probable that with further development even flatter and wider domes will be built[6]. These utilitarian considerations are bound to be paramount with buildings like factories and market halls, but with buildings of a more ceremonial character, like religious edifices, stimulation of the sense of space would necessarily be an important consideration in regulating the height of the dome. Still, strictly utilitarian as are the domes of the market halls of Leipzig and Basel they yet add to the sum of architectural experience by enclosing space in such a way as to give a feeling of exhilaration and a sense of vastness. The lighting from the octagonal top lights and by long horizontal windows below the domes, which puts the surface of the shells in soft gradating shadow, adds to this sense of vastness, while the pattern of the radiating ribs in the lights of the Leipzig domes is particularly attractive.

If the interiors of these halls are impressive, the same cannot be said of the exteriors. For a dome to be effective from the outside it must be perched high up, preferably on a drum, and give the sense of climax to the building; and this effect, perhaps more than anything else, is the glory of St. Paul's. When a dome is flat and low on the ground it never looks well. To look well from the exterior it should at least be a hemisphere and mounted well above the ground in proportion to its size. These are the reasons why the dome of the reading room of the British Museum, so impressive from inside, is altogether without architectural effect externally. The planetaria, like that at Jena, with domes which are near the ground and approximately hemispheres externally, are not pleasing, but when they are perched higher and are elongated outside, as in the case of the planetarium on the newspaper building at Hanover, they acquire more architectural distinction. Externally the great domes of the market halls of Leipzig and Basel have little more architectural interest than the exterior of the British Museum dome. The Leipzig Market Hall appears as a long, low, rectangular building, with the third storey set back, and surmounted by two flat octagonal domes, with little rhythmical cohesion between the two, as can be clearly seen from the air view. The view from the ground modifies a little this somewhat abrupt transition from the square mass to the domes, but one is still conscious of it. In the case of the dome at Basel this junction is somewhat obscured by taller surrounding buildings, but it is even closer to the ground than the Leipzig domes and suffers in effect thereby.

The use of shell concrete for barrel vaulting constituted another major line of development. It is a form which has been the subject of much research because it offers great prospects of development for covering large areas without intermediate supports. Barrel vaulting is one of the prominent features of Roman, Romanesque, and

385

Renaissance architecture, and it made possible the covering of larger spaces than in post and lintel construction. It can be appreciated that if barrel vaulting could be used in series without supports at the intersections much larger areas could be covered than by the flat roof, very much on the principle that corrugated iron has a stiffness greater than flat iron of the same thickness. This was accomplished in shell concrete largely by stiffening the arch at the springings with stronger reinforcing rods. It was also felt that the semicircular vault has a greater height than is necessary, and as in the case of the development of shell concrete domes to flatter shapes, experiments were made to reduce the height of the barrel. Elliptical vaults were tried, but these produced complications in construction. It was then found that if the vault is made in the form of a flat arc with edge beams, this solved the problem most satisfactorily. The arc is lightly reinforced with a network of small-diameter rods, while the edge beams are heavily reinforced with larger-diameter rods. A lateral stiffening beam is placed at the ends of a short vault or at intervals in a wider and longer vault. Thus, vaulting can be broadly divided into two kinds—longitudinal barrels and cross or transverse barrels, generally used in series. The longitudinal barrels are a development from the parabolic and semicircular concrete roofs considered earlier in this chapter, particularly examples like the airship hangars at Orly and the market hall at Rheims, the stiffening beams being in the form of the parabolic ribs. Large longitudinal vaults of shell concrete became fairly common during the thirties, the more spectacular development in the twenties being the series of transverse barrel vaults for market halls.

The first example of a transverse barrel roof on a large scale is that of the market hall at Frankfurt-on-Main, which has an unobstructed floor area 721 feet by 164 feet, with a height of 75 feet. There are fifteen elliptical barrels in three groups of five, each barrel being 121 feet long with a span of 46 feet and a shell $2\frac{3}{4}$ inches thick. The difference between the width of the hall and the length of barrel is due to the concrete buttresses, which are inclined inwards to take the edge beams of the barrels, and which form bays with glass walls and soffits. It is important to note that the barrels are elliptical a form which is superseded by the arc in most later examples.

The second important use of transverse barrels on a large scale is in the market hall at Budapest, of which A. de Münnich was the architect. This was built in 1930–1 and has an unobstructed floor space of 787 feet by $157\frac{1}{2}$ feet. The roof consists of eighteen arc shaped vaults which are much flatter than the elliptical vaults of the Frankfurt Market Hall. Each vault is 40 feet wide and the shell is $2\frac{3}{8}$ inches thick. In the front of the building, extending its whole length, is a cantilevered shell construction projecting 20 feet.

Another somewhat spectacular example of shell concrete barrel vaulting is the customs shed and warehouse at Hamburg, erected in 1929–30. The covered area is 1,090 feet by 164 feet, but in this case there is one row of columnar supports in the centre, above

Post Office Garage, Nürnberg, 1929
with cantilevered shell-roof construction

Market Hall, Budapest, 1931
Architect: A. de Münnich

Dome at Berlin Planetarium in course of construction, 1929
View showing men at work on the steel network
which supports the movable forms, and provides the main
reinforcement of the concrete shell

Interior of Market Hall, Frankfurt-on-Main. General view and detail

which is a bow-sprung type of stiffening for the barrel vaults. The barrels are 30 feet wide with a shell $2\frac{3}{16}$ inches thick[7].

Many further developments were made with forms of barrel vaulting, among the principal being the asymmetrical vault and the cantilevered vault. Both forms evolved in response to the needs of certain types of building. The asymmetrical vault had advantages for the aeroplane hangar, where a high door opening is required at one side, and for factories where a north light is required, in which case it became a variation of the saw-tooth roof. In factory roofs of this kind curved concrete ribs are often employed at intervals instead of the stiffening beam.

An early example of the cantilevered shell in roof construction occurs in the post-office garage at Nürnberg, built in 1929. The type of construction employed here consists of twin cantilevered shells with triangular glass between, thus providing good lighting. The floor area is 472 feet by 144 feet, covered by twelve twin cantilevered shells. Each central beam has two intermediate supports. The width of each space is 40 feet, of which 10 feet is glazing, thus the twin cantilevered shell is about 30 feet wide. This system of twin cantilevered shells was used for the platform roofs of Munich East Station in 1920. Roofs of this kind, both single and twin, became comparatively common in the thirties, a few appearing in England, one being the platform roofs at Morden Station.

An interesting form of shell construction occurs in part of a cement factory at Beocin in Yugoslavia, built in 1933. This hall consists of five bays with two apsidal ends. Each bay is approximately 85 feet, the width of the hall, by 40 feet. Instead of these bays being roofed by barrel vaults like those of the Frankfurt and Budapest Market Halls, they are spanned by rectangular domes. The rise of the dome from the sides of the hall is about 26 feet, and from the intersection with the neighbouring dome about $9\frac{1}{2}$ feet. The thickness of the shell is about 2 inches. This type of construction is thus more directly a development from the ribless shell of a planetarium.

In addition to those mentioned a considerable number of halls were built for markets, swimming baths, and tennis courts in Europe at this time, with forms of construction which are mainly developments or modifications of systems that were well known before the First World War. Some of these halls are of considerable size, though none reach the spectacular proportions of the Leipzig Fair Hall with its steel roof span of 318 feet, or the larger structures of shell concrete.

Some of these sports halls are of architectural interest, two which are particularly worthy of note being the swimming bath at Haarlem, built in 1932 to the design of J. N. van Loghem, and the 'Apollo' covered tennis courts and exhibition hall at Amsterdam, built in 1933 to the design of A. Bocker[8]. The former is constructed with a combined steel and reinforced concrete frame and a steel-truss roof with a span of about 80 feet. The latter is designed to serve two purposes—for exhibitions, meetings, and concerts in summer, and for tennis in winter. Adjoining the hall are a restaurant and offices. The building is constructed with a steel frame left entirely exposed, with brick filling for the walls. The roof of the main hall is constructed of six plate girders with a span of 115 feet, the hall being 292 feet long.

The largest hall built in England about this time is the Empire Swimming Pool at Wembley, designed by Sir Owen Williams. The size of the covered space is 341 feet by $236\frac{1}{2}$ feet. Construction is of reinforced concrete frame, on a horizontal grid of 2 feet 9 inches and a vertical unit of 3 feet, thus allowing for the use of standardized units, which contributed to the speed of construction for it was commenced in October 1933 and completed in the following May. The pitched roof is constructed of a series of three hinged arches in reinforced concrete which are held by vertical concrete shafts linked to the concrete gallery and projecting outwards above ground and extending above the plane of the roof. These very largely dominate the side walls of the building.

The architectural merit of this building is doubtful. The interior is more agreeable than the exterior, where the massive side shafts, the four square corner columns with summit boxes, and the low, pitched roof all seem to be a combination of unrelated features. The main preoccupation seems to have been with the construction, which is noteworthy, but it is difficult to resist the feeling that it was built in the belief that if the construction is good, beauty will look after itself. If this is correct the building would appear to be a demonstration against the argument that if a building fulfils its purpose well and is efficiently constructed it automatically results in beauty. The validity of this argument is that efficient construction must have a superlative character, and in the comparatively early stages of reinforced concrete construction we are hardly in a position to be aware of the superlative in such construction.

REFERENCES AND NOTES

1. This method of construction was not employed in England until the early thirties. The licensees for the method in England are 'Chisarc and Shell D' of Liverpool.
2. There is much technical literature on the subject, most of the earlier articles and papers being German. Among the English works may be mentioned *Shell Concrete Construction* by H. G. Cousins, Reinforced Concrete Association, 1948; *The Development and Use of Barrel Vault Shell Construction* by C. V. Blumfield, The Institution of Civil Engineers, 1948; and Shell Concrete Construction by Dr K. Hajnol-Konyi, in the *Architects' Year Book*, ii, 1941.
3. This span for ribless domes has been exceeded by numerous subsequent examples. The largest that I know are those erected by the Navy of the USA to house barrage balloons. These have spans of 246 feet.

4. In an article entitled The Acoustics of Music Halls, *Pencil Points*, September 1945.
5. Most writers refer to three domes covering the Leipzig Market Hall. Three were designed and are shown on the drawing, but only two were erected.
6. Although not of shell concrete, the largest flat dome at the time it was built was the Dome of Discovery at the South Bank Exhibition of the 1951 Festival of Britain. This dome was 365 feet in diameter with a rise of 48 feet. It was constructed of cross-lattice girders covered externally with aluminium and supported on steel, pin-pointed struts. It was demolished shortly after the exhibition.
7. In some later examples the edge beams are dispensed with and adequate stiffening is provided at the intersection of the barrels.
8. Both these buildings are described in detail and copiously illustrated in *The New Architecture*, by Alfred Roth, first edition, 1940; second edition, 1945; third edition, 1947, pp. 151–164.

Interior of Engelbrekt Church, Stockholm, 1908–14. An early and dramatic example of parabolic vaulting, which influenced later designs

Architect: L. I. Wahlman

26 Theatres

IN THE BUILDINGS of the hall type so far considered—exhibition, market, and sports halls—the admission of maximum daylight and the covering of large spaces without intermediate supports are important aims. With theatres, cinemas, and concert halls the aim, as far as the first requirement is concerned, is totally different, because the necessary lighting control is such that lighting is mainly artificial and walls are windowless, with the possible exception of a few concert halls. As with other halls, the area of the theatre or cinema without intermediate supports is of great advantage, while the need for galleries introduces other problems of construction. Only in this matter of covering a floor space of considerable extent without intermediate supports does the design of theatres, cinemas, and concert halls resemble the other types of hall building considered; in all other respects the purpose and design are totally different.

A few theatres and concert halls showing notable developments and changes in design and construction were built in Europe during the twenties and early thirties, but in the category of buildings devoted to pleasure easily the greatest volume of work was for cinemas. From 1924 onwards new cinemas were opened in Europe at a rate of over a thousand a year, and no other type of building designed for pleasure shows anything like the developments and changes that occur in the cinema. One has only to consider the type of building used for a cinema in 1910 with a typical cinema of 1930 to realize what great developments took place. In fact, before the First World War the cinema had little existence as a separate building designed for a specific purpose, different from all other types. This did not really occur until the early twenties. It will be convenient to consider, first, the developments in theatre design that took place during the period; secondly, the cinema, which evolved initially from the theatre or meeting hall; and thirdly, the concert hall, which demands many conditions different from either of the foregoing.

The majority of theatres built in the nineteenth and early twentieth centuries had the horseshoe plan, with several galleries and the framed-picture stage. This was the

391

traditional design since the Italian Renaissance theatre of the sixteenth century, and was adopted alike for small Court playhouses—of which the Theatre Royal at Bristol, built in 1766, is the oldest surviving example in England—and for large opera houses, of which every capital provides an example. The only difference apart from size was that the opera house generally retained boxes all round the lower galleries until a later period, the purpose of this accommodation being social rather than for the enjoyment of the opera.

Most theatres built in the late nineteenth century were, both internally and externally, lavishly decorated with ornament and sculptures derived from classic sources. Three factors which had a considerable influence on the design of theatres began to operate at the turn of the century. Firstly the movement towards simplicity and elimination of ornament; secondly the effort being made by some designers to build theatres which could afford a better view of the stage from every part of the house than was possible with balconies that curved with the horseshoe plan; and thirdly the introduction of steel-frame and reinforced concrete construction, that permitted larger spans and eliminated columnar obstructions. The movement towards simplicity had its effect on the appearance of new theatres, and the use of large steel girders, which could span considerable widths, and cantilever construction meant that the columnar supports of galleries could be eliminated, thus removing these obstructions to a view of the stage. This led to the reconstruction of several theatres, two London examples being Drury Lane and the Savoy Theatre, and it made possible the entire remodelling of the interiors. The Savoy from being one of the typical nineteenth-century theatres became one of the most modern and attractive theatres of the period between the wars. The horseshoe plan with curved balconies meant that for a proportion of seats a good view of the stage was not possible from the side seats of the balconies and gradual changes were made to overcome this disadvantage. One development was to straighten the balconies, and we find this in several of Oskar Kaufmann's theatres, such as the Town Theatre at Bremerhaven (1911) and the People's Theatre at Berlin (1914). In Kaufmann's designs for smaller theatres, in which the length of the auditorium is about the same or little more than the width, the plan resembles a scallop shell, as in the theatre in the Kurfürstendamm (1923), the Komodie Theatre, Berlin (1923), and the Kroll Opera House, Berlin (1924).

A simpler plan evolving at the same time is the fan shape, which first appears in the Wagner Festival Theatre at Bayreuth, built in 1876 to the design of Bruckwald and Semper. Another early example of this fan shape is in the Prince Regent Theatre at Munich, built by Max Littmann in 1901. This was the plan adopted in the Shakespeare Memorial Theatre, designed by Elizabeth Scott, Chesterton, and Sheppard (1930), and in the Cambridge Theatre, London, designed by Wimperis, Simpson, and Guthrie (1929). Among French theatres in which simplicity of treatment is particularly effective combined with some beauty of line and a high degree of comfort, are those designed by Charles Siclis, of which the Théatre Pigalle in Paris, built in 1929, is the most famous, while the Théatre St. Georges in Paris, built in 1929, is a noteworthy small example. The Théatre Pigalle was built for the Baron Henri de Rothschild and seats about 1,100. The plan is still the horseshoe shape, with boxes connecting the three tiers of galleries with the stage. The long sweep of the fluted semicircular balcony fronts is impressive. It was one of the aims to incorporate in this theatre all modern technical devices. Much ingenuity is apparent in the devices for changing scenes and stage effects, including four mobile platforms, while a great variety of lighting effects was introduced. Attention was also given to the design of seating so as to give maximum comfort[1]. The principal façade of the theatre is designed with a view to lighting effects at night: the illumination of letters advertising the theatre and play, and the illumination of the exterior, which is accomplished by circular perforations holding the lights in the underside of the entrance canopy. Lighting by this means is a favourite device of the architect. In the foyer is a large grille of nickel tubes which is illuminated from above by polychrome lights, which gives a bright scintillating effect. The Théatre St. Georges is smaller and simpler, seating about 600, and adjoins an office building. The plan is rectangular, with one semicircular balcony which connects with the proscenium frame, there being no tier boxes. A series of boxes is arranged along the side walls of the auditorium, as in the Théatre Pigalle, but as the walls are straight in the Théatre St. Georges, a good view of the stage from these boxes would seem doubtful. The walls are plain, and the plain balcony front is relieved only by simple lighting fittings at wide intervals.

Rudolf Frankel, the German architect, is responsible for two theatres where simplicity of treatment is combined with dramatic effect. One is the large Schumann Theatre, seating about 3,000, at Frankfurt-on-Main, built in 1931–2, and the other is the small Musical Comedy at Bucharest, built in 1933–4. The former was previously a circus building and was converted into a theatre, and this circumstance is responsible for its design, in which there is a distinct reminiscence of the ancient Greek theatre. It is circular in plan with its one balcony forming a horseshoe front. The back of the balcony recedes deeply in the centre as a rectangular addition to the circular plan. The stage, which is not very deep, has an arc-shaped apron, and this can be extended still farther by raising the orchestra floor. A flat dome gives concealed lighting. The theatre at Bucharest, which has a seating capacity of 700, is, in plan, a rather square version of the fan. It has one balcony, no boxes, and the simplest proscenium frame. It is saved from the severity of the Jena Theatre of Gropius by the use of curves—the curved balcony frame with two projecting wings, and the side walls, covered with orange velvet, which curve towards the proscenium.

Of similar character to this theatre at Bucharest are the Corso Theatre at Zürich, reconstructed in 1934 by Ernest F. Burckhardt, and the Nykoping-Falster Theatre, Denmark, built in 1934 by Taye Ruh. The former, which seats 1,300, has a long

393

rectangular plan; the balcony front is almost straight with projecting wings forming a series of open boxes, somewhat like the ground-floor boxes of the Théatre St. Georges in Paris. The walls have a fluted texture, so designed for acoustic reasons. The Nykoping-Falster Theatre in Denmark has a similar plan to Frankel's Bucharest theatre. The balcony front is lightly curved, and the walls are plain, the whole being saved from severity by the use of curved forms. Attractive colour and lighting schemes in these theatres also serve to modify effects of severity and give a feeling of intimacy. For example, in the Danish theatre the walls are yellow, the curtain cobalt blue, and the chairs are upholstered in red velvet.

In England an example of a modern theatre which has an effective and dramatic simplicity is the Cambridge Theatre, London, designed in 1930 by Wimperis, Simpson, and Guthrie, with interior decoration by Serge Chermayeff. This theatre seats about 1,200. The plan is an approximation to the fan shape, with curved sides. There are two balconies with slightly curved fronts, and one projecting box on either side. The ceiling curves downwards to the elliptical proscenium arch, while at the rear, above the balconies, it is deeply channelled, apparently so designed for acoustic purposes. In spite of this the acoustics in my experience are not good[2], far less satisfactory than in many older London theatres. Another defect in this theatre is that the rake of the auditorium floor is not adequate. Those sitting in the back rows of the stalls do not get a good view of the stage when the theatre is full. A steeper rake with a gradient of at least 1 in 6 would have resulted in a more functional theatre. If one cannot get a good view of the stage because of the obstructions of people in front then one cannot hear so well, because they act as sound absorbents and break the direct paths of sound. Inadequate floor rakes is a common fault in theatre design. Plain surfaces resulting from the greater simplicity of treatment of modern hall interiors are not so satisfactory acoustically as the broken surfaces of the more ornamental interior. A plain, hard surface reflects the sound, and reverberations may be too long. It is necessary, therefore, either to have sound-absorbent materials, like velvet, as in the Schumann Theatre, or specially prepared plaster on certain parts of the walls, or to break up the surface so that more sound is absorbed and less reflected. Various kinds of fluting, as used in some of the theatres mentioned, constituted one of the favourite and most effective devices. One of the most elaborate decorative devices in concrete employed for acoustical purposes is the decorative stalactite of the Grosse Schauspielhaus designed by Hans Poelzig in 1919 although the romantic effect was a determining factor. Acoustical requirements would appear to be a *raison d'etre* for decorative treatment of surfaces.

THE SHAKESPEARE MEMORIAL THEATRE

A notable building that combines originality with traditional character is the Shakespeare Memorial Theatre designed by Elizabeth Scott, Chesterton, and Shepherd. The design was awarded first prize in a competition held in 1928, the building being completed about four years later. The masses that compose the building are a true expression of its purpose and interior organization. Viewed at some distance from the front, from the bridge across the river to the east, a square block rises at the back above the rest of the building. This encloses the high stage grid. The auditorium is fan shaped with a curved foyer, with masses on either side for the circular staircase and offices. The whole is roughly symmetrical with some irregularity in the grouping of the side blocks[3].

The theatre was originally designed with stone facings, but the assessors suggested in their report that 'brick for the external facings would be warmer and more harmonious with the general aspect of the town, and would at the same time be more economical'. The suggestion was adopted, and the character of the design was thereby altered considerably, for it is in the use of brick that an early Tudor feeling is so largely conveyed. For large buildings brick was the most favoured building material in early Tudor times, and probably in no other period of English architecture has it been used with such fine effect, Hampton Court being one of the most vivid examples. The brick for the external facings of the Shakespeare Memorial Theatre is of a reddish hue, selected to harmonize with those used in the district, varied with panels of greyish-blue brick, which is softer in tone. The red brick which predominates appeared a little harsh when it was erected, but it is already mellowing and softening with time. The walls of the entrance foyer and of the circular staircase hall are lined with mauve-grey brick, with darker bricks projecting slightly from alternate courses at the angles and reveals. The floor, faced with Ancaster, Blue Hornton, and Ashburton marbles, harmonizes in colour with the brick walls; the Swedish green marble of the door surrounds offers a mild and agreeable contrast, but the stainless steel which is introduced here and in the paybox offers a sharper contrast. The part of the interior which has the most strongly romantic flavour is the circular hall at the end of the foyer. A fountain is in the centre and the staircase against the wall winds up to the dress circle foyer, the soft shadows suffusing the mild tones of the brickwork and marble, creating an atmosphere in harmony with imagined settings of many of Shakespeare's plays. But the romantic feeling created by the exterior, the entrance foyer, and the fountain hall is hardly sustained by the auditorium and proscenium. Here romantic associations with the past disappear, instead good modern design has been the aim. The walls are lined with wood to a little above door height, and the walls above this are painted plaster. Wood and plaster are similarly used for the proscenium, but all is cut up—there are no dominant masses or lines. It would seem that one of the purposes of this interior was to display, like an interior decorator's showroom, as many woods as possible, for in the wall lining, proscenium, and door panelling, various kinds of mahogany, Queensland maple, ebony, Indian laurel, Andaman Padauk, Australian silky oak, and Indian silver-grey are used. This is symptomatic of an increasing tendency in interior decoration from 1925 to 1939, to use as many woods as possible, mostly as veneers, to demonstrate, it would seem, the rich variety of woods available. In this particular case it was the intention to use woods from all parts of the Empire as an expression of the widespread veneration for Shakespeare, thus their use has some symbolical significance.

In the late thirties a two-storey structure was built on to the river façade by Scott, Chesterton, and Breakwell, consisting of café on the ground floor and restaurant on the first floor both opening on to terraces. The glass walls and horizontal lines of this addition make it an appropriate riverside structure suitable for and expressive of its purpose, but it looks grafted on to the main theatre building. The effect before the addition was more harmonious, and I like to remember the original river façade[4].

The architects could have made the theatre like a medieval castle or classic temple; but in designing a building which says clearly what it is, where the shapes emerging from its purpose determine its exterior massing, and associating this with the past by the use for the exterior of a typical building material of Shakespeare's time, they have secured a very happy wedding of modern character with traditional building.

In considering this question of exterior massing arising logically from its interior design another question must be asked. Is that massing agreeable in the abstract apart from the purpose of the building, just as a picture should be pleasing in design apart from its subject? The building has to be seen in relation to its surroundings; its masses, lines, and colours must compose well. Can the Shakespeare Memorial Theatre be regarded as a satisfactory composition of masses from the purely aesthetic standpoint? The front and middle part, the foyer and auditorium, make an harmonious and agreeable ensemble, but is the large plain mass of the stage at the back satisfactory in itself, or in its relation to the rest of the building? That this is the expression of the internal arrangement, of function, is surely not enough. The forms and their arrangement must be pleasing. Some decorative schematic connexion with the whole by means of a sequence of subordinate masses leading up from the auditorium might have resulted in a more agreeable composition. But, it might be replied, this is not expressing the interior, this is added decoration. But stark revelation of function does not inevitably produce architecture—which is, after all, building that affords pleasurable contemplation—it is the subject with which the architect should produce an aesthetically agreeable design. In the Workers' Club building at Moscow, designed by Melnikov during the same period, there is logical expression in the external forms of the internal design, and the use of modern methods of construction makes of this something of an oddity. The three projecting box-like features cantilevered out from the main building are the amphitheatres or galleries above an auditorium all radiating to a stage. Here are exterior forms expressing the interior, but few regard the building as beautiful, and would consequently hesitate to think of this as architecture.

If the architect adds non-functional forms to give him a desirable artistic result then he is surely justified, provided those forms grow out of and are suggested by the subject

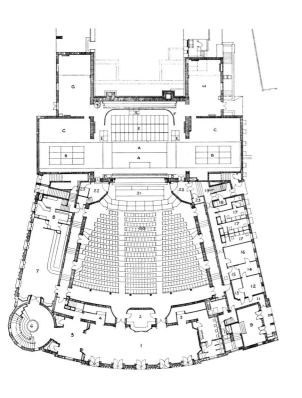

Shakespeare Memorial Theatre, Stratford-on-Avon
Architects: Elizabeth Scott, Chesterton and Shepherd

bove—the building with the later additions of riverside restaurant and café. Left—plan

elow—view of the building from the river as originally designed and completed

and are not foreign importations. When the architects of Siena and Lucca Cathedrals carried the west front well above the roof of the main building and thus in the upper parts forming mere screens, and when Wren added a screen wall for the upper storey of St. Paul's they were contrary to the internal forms but they gave dignity to the exterior and made them more impressive. Although these sham walls have been adversely criticized, their justification by others is on the grounds of external artistic effect which a more accurate expression of the interior would not have given. But again, it may be argued, you may have an exterior which has no relation to the interior or to the purpose or structure of the building, yet if it is beautiful is it thereby justified? The external dome of St. Paul's is of different contour from the internal dome, and has no relation in shape to the brick cone which is its supporting structure, but who would say it is not justified by its beauty?

Here we come to an important distinction between classical and Renaissance architecture on the one hand and strictly functional architecture of the twentieth century on the other, but however one may feel the healthy invigorating influence of the latter one cannot ignore the fact that architecture is building that is pleasing to contemplate irrespective of a knowledge of its purpose, in addition to being an expression of life. These two attributes are in the last resort inseparable, which involves the question whether therefore an architect in designing his exterior can depart too much from purpose and structure. The history of architecture seems to testify that if he does, building ceases to have a living quality, a vitality, which is an important element of beauty, and instead has the deadness of a fancy dress. Just balance would appear to be the secret. To know when to hold back and when to let go, says Havelock Ellis, is very much the art of life. Perhaps Wren let himself go too much in the screen wall—a tall parapet rather than a false upper storey would have been more in keeping with the essential form of the building; while the architects of the Shakespeare Memorial Theatre held back a little too much in the treatment of the rear block. An important point is that something was needed by Wren above the external wall of the aisle, and something was needed in the Shakespeare Memorial Theatre to connect the mass of the high stage grid with the rest of the building by a sequence of subordinate forms.

TRADITIONAL THEATRE DESIGN SINCE ANCIENT GREECE

What may prove to be one important development in theatre design tentatively appears in the third and fourth decades of the century, although signs of it can be seen earlier. Most modern theatres to 1920 were designed on the Renaissance model, in which the auditorium is completely separated from the stage and the play is performed in a picture framed by the proscenium arch. In the opinion of many producers and actors and pioneers of the modern theatre, particularly those who prefer the conventional rather than the illusory method of presentation, this is attended with many disadvantages. It is contended that this separation of audience and players destroys that desirable intimacy between the two, and that it presents difficulties to the actors. In the modern theatre the actors often have to get their voices across the forestage and orchestra before they reach the first row of the audience, and this has probably been partially responsible for the exaggerated, declamatory style of acting which was common in England up to about 1925. A few efforts have been made, principally by the conventional and symbolist school of thought, to overcome these disadvantages by bringing the stage and auditorium—the players and audience—closer together. Max Littmann, in his Munich Arts Theatre built in 1908, and Van de Velde, in his theatre at the Cologne Exhibition of 1914, eliminated the sharp separation between stage and auditorium, and conceived the whole as one room, with the stage the same width as the auditorium. The disadvantage of this separation of stage and auditorium did not exist with the Greek and Roman theatres nor with the Elizabethan stage, and it is the hope of many playwrights, producers, and actors, especially those who prefer the conventional or symbolist methods of presentation as opposed to the illusory or realistic, that theatre design may develop so that the intimacy possible in these theatres may be revived. To appreciate the full significance of this development it is helpful to trace in broad outline the evolution of the theatre form in Europe since the days of Ancient Greece.

The Greek drama and theatre originated from the dithyrambic hymns sung at the festivals held in honour of Dionysus. These hymns were sung to the accompaniment of the flute and dancing, which took place in a circular space round the altar of the god. A dialogue in song may have taken place between the leader of the chorus and the remainder, and here we have the germ of the drama. The theatre was, in its initial stages, largely determined by these rites at the festival of Dionysus. The circular space occupied by the chorus, termed the orchestra, became the central feature. Round this tiers of seats were arranged in the form of a segment of a circle greater than a semicircle.

It is probable that in the earliest Greek theatre, there was no raised stage, but a structure called the skene, providing rooms for actors, was built at the back of the orchestra. Later, a platform called the proscenium was erected in front of the skene and was flanked by two wings built out from the skene. The earliest theatres were probably of wood, but in the fourth century B.C. they were built of stone generally into the sides of hills or on the slopes of the Acropolis, or cut out of the rock. The two earliest remaining Greek theatres are the theatre of Dionysus, on the slopes of the Acropolis at Athens, and the theatre at Epidaurus. The former was completed in 330 B.C. but was begun, and probably used, many years earlier. The latter was completed in 350 B.C. and is the best preserved of all Greek theatres. In this theatre the orchestra is circular, and it had a stage which was supported by a wall 12 feet high, but this may have been a later addition. In the theatre of Dionysus at Athens, the orchestra is cut off at the stage side and becomes semicircular. This stage may also have been a later addition, but the semicircular orchestra became the adopted form. The Athenian theatre appears to have been the prototype of subsequent Greek theatres, some of which remain, among the best being those at Delphi, Egesta, Syracuse, Taormina, Argos, and Ephesus. All these Greek theatres were large, that at Athens providing seating for about 27,500 spectators.

The part played by the chorus is fundamental in a Greek drama, and being placed in the orchestra surrounded by and to a degree identified with the audience in its narrations and replies to the actors, it can be appreciated how close a connexion is thus maintained between actors and audience. Imagine, for example, the performance of a play like the *Agamemnon* of Aeschylus in the theatre of Dionysus at Athens. The screen which was used for scenery in front of the wall at the back of the platform would probably be painted to represent the Palace of Agamemnon. The actors, each with cothurnus and mask, would appear from doors in the back and wings of the platform, while the chorus would occupy the orchestra. The Watchman appears and tells how he has kept watch on Agamemnon's roof for the blazing beacon that is to be the sign of the fall of Troy, then during his speech he sees the beacon and tells of his forebodings at the return of Agamemnon. The chorus then marches in procession into the orchestra, and sings a choral hymn which tells the events that precede and lead to the incidents of the drama. Clytemnestra then enters and is addressed by the chorus and a dialogue ensues. This is followed by another choral hymn in honour of Zeus. Later Cassandra in her dialogue with the chorus tells how she, from her place outside the palace, perceives in its interior preparations for the murder of Agamemnon. Knowing the real and professed cause, and knowing that she is destined for a similar fate, she bodly prepares for death. In walking off the stage she conveys the impression that she is entering the palace. After the chorus has spoken, the truth of Cassandra's forebodings is realized, for Agamemnon cries out from within the palace that he is slain. The scene opens from behind and Clytemnestra is revealed standing over the dead bodies of Agamemnon and Cassandra.

A platform on wheels, called the ekkyklema, appears to have been employed for a tableau of murdered victims of this kind. The audience hears later the circumstances of the death of Agamemnon from the lips of Clytemnestra and bitter dialogue follows. All this takes place with the chorus more than half encircled by the audience, and it can be imagined that this physical circumstance gives an intimacy between chorus and audience unknown to the modern traditional theatre, while devices were employed to give the actors on the platform a more than life-size magnitude.

The Roman theatre when it was built as a permanent stone structure in the middle of the first century B.C. followed the main character of the Greek with, however, many modifications. The earliest was built by Pompey in 55 B.C. The only one that remains in Rome is that of Marcellus, completed in 13 B.C. The best preserved of Roman theatres is that at Orange, in the south of France, from which it has been possible to make a fairly complete reconstruction. Judging from this and other remains the seats and orchestra formed a semicircle, the skene became a three-storey building, and between the projecting wings was a platform about 5 feet high. The stage was roofed over between the wings. These stage buildings extended the complete diameter of the auditorium. A covered colonnade ran round the top tier of the theatre, the roof of which was approximately on the same level as the stage roof. A back curtain was generally lowered in front of the architectural background at the commencement of the play. The orchestra was now occupied by spectators, the space being generally reserved for senators, the action of the play, in accordance with Roman drama, taking place entirely on the stage.

Much of the principal action in the Greek theatre had taken place between the chorus in the orchestra and the actors on the stage; the complete transference of the action to the stage in the Roman theatre meant the first development towards the separation of players and audience, and the first steps towards the modern theatre.

The medieval theatre was little influenced by the Roman, and its most interesting and valuable culmination was the Elizabethan theatre. It was essentially a platform, generally open on three sides, and this platform may have been in a cathedral with a draped background for the performance of passion or mystery plays, or on the cathedral steps, or in the market place. Later, movable platforms were the equipment of troupes of players, and if these were not available wagons sufficed. The platforms were set up in bear pits and inn yards. It was the latter which led to the famous Elizabethan theatre which bears the pattern of such origin. The first to be opened was that built by James Burbage in 1576 which was called simply 'The Theatre', but the most famous is the 'Great Globe', built in 1599 and for ever associated with Shakespeare. The typical Elizabethan theatre was an open courtyard of a circular or regular polygonal form, which may have been eight or sixteen sided[5], surrounded by three-tiered galleries, and with a canopied platform thrust half-way into the centre from one side. The main action took place on this platform, but there was a back stage which was brought into use when required. The audience on the ground generally stood and crowded round the platform on three sides, while the more well-to-do spectators in the gallery encircled three sides of the platform. It will be seen that the relation of audience to players is not dissimilar to that between audience and chorus in the Greek theatre, and a similar intimacy is possible.

The English actor Bernard Miles comments on this question in relating a wartime experience. He remarks that 'Shakespeare's Globe Theatre held just over two thousand people, packed into a space not much bigger than Wyndham's Theatre or The Apollo, each of which holds only about nine hundred', and 'to perform in such a theatre must have been comparable to the experience I had in the Orkneys in 1943, playing on a

401

rough platform slung between the destroyers *Orwell* and *Opportune*, with five hundred sailors surrounding the stage and hanging on to every available projection of the two ships. Actors who have had such an experience must realize how much is wasted in the picture-frame theatre of that close union between actor and audience which is the life and soul of the stage.'[6] He remarks further that the Elizabethan stage 'permitted the play to move swiftly, kept the actors in closest contact with their audience, and allowed the words to work their own magic without heavy-fisted attempts at realistic setting. In fact it was perfectly adapted to the poetic drama which was produced in it, and which cannot very profitably be studied except in relation to it; and it was a very sad day when it disappeared.'

THE ORIGIN OF THE PROSCENIUM STAGE

The beginning of the picture stage, which is the basis of the modern traditional theatre, occurred in Italy in the sixteenth century. The Olympic Theatre at Vicenza, designed by Palladio and built in 1580, is designed on the Roman model, but entirely roofed over. The auditorium and orchestra form a half-ellipse. The highly ornamented three-storeyed Roman skene forms the background of the stage, but in this case a large central opening flanked by two smaller openings provide long vistas for the spectators by means of scenery painted in perspective.

The next major development is seen in the Farnese Theatre at Parma, designed by Aleotti and completed in 1619. This is generally regarded as the prototype of the traditional modern theatre. The evolution in design seems to be the bringing forward of the architectural wall, the enlargement of the central arched opening of the Vicenza theatre, so that it becomes the proscenium arch and the play now takes place in the space beyond the arch. By this development the drama is conceived as a picture play and the influence of the art of painting on this conception is very strong. This has remained the standard conception of the theatre with but few modifications ever since.

During the Puritan rule in England the theatre was prohibited and this resulted in a serious break in the English tradition, for when it was revived early in the reign of Charles II, the theatre was no longer designed on the Elizabethan model, but on the new Italian model, with the Farnese Theatre at Parma as the prototype. Inigo Jones, who was originally a scenic designer for the Court masques in the reign of James I, and who introduced the full Italian Renaissance style into English architecture, was a contributory influence. His Court masques had more the character of the Italian than the Elizabethan theatre, and the tendency to look always to Italian models in the arts rather than to English tradition killed the physical character of the Elizabethan theatre.

The first theatre of the Restoration was that of Drury Lane, and it remained the principal theatre in London for many years. It was destroyed by fire in 1672, and a new one was built to the designs of Wren and opened in 1674. It followed the new Italian prototype with the picture stage and proscenium frame, but Wren apparently aimed at as close a contact of players and audience as the type would permit, but in later modifications of the structure, however, the distance was increased by about ten feet. Speaking of the Restoration theatre, Bernard Miles says:

'The great Elizabethan theatre was chopped off short, and there began that long and melancholy retreat of the actor farther and farther upstage, until, with the introduction of lamps behind the picture frame itself, he was finally cut off from the audience altogether, and a playhouse became a combination of two separate rooms, one containing the audience and the other containing the actors, instead of a single structure containing both.'[7]

As has been emphasized, one of the main disadvantages of this separation of the theatre into two separate rooms, and the play taking place in a picture frame with the actors always behind the picture frame, is the remoteness of actors and audience and the impossibility of obtaining that intimacy which many actors, producers, and dramatists consider desirable. Also it makes three-dimensional effects more dificult, such as would be possible if the audience were grouped on three sides of the players. The arguments in favour of the picture stage are advanced mainly from the standpoint of the illusory or naturalistic[8] method of presentation, so that what takes place on the stage is completely of another world entirely remote from the audience. Wagner in stating the requirements for the Bayreuth opera house, aimed at increasing this remote other worldness and contributed to this by increasing the size of the orchestra and sinking it in front of the stage.

THE REACTION AGAINST THE PICTURE STAGE

The reaction against the picture-stage tradition with the division of the theatre into two separate rooms began in the early years of the present century. It was partly prompted by a desire to recover the intimacy between players and audience that had existed in the Greek and Elizabethan theatres, and partly by the movement towards a conventional, symbolical method of presentation instead of the illusory and naturalistic method. The reaction is greatly supported by the reflection that the two greatest periods of drama in history, the Ancient Greek and Elizabethan, were periods when the drama was conceived more for the open, three-dimensional stage and not the enclosed picture stage.

Goethe was an early pioneer in bringing the stage more into the midst of the audience, and in his plans for the new theatre at Weimar, made in collaboration with the architect, Clemens Coudray, this was one of the aims. But the plans were altered and the theatre was never built entirely as Goethe wished[9].

403

The degree of intimacy possible with the picture-stage varies with the design of the theatre. The greatest possible intimacy for this type of theatre is perhaps reached in one like the Theatre Royal at Bristol, while the Memorial Theatre at Stratford-on-Avon, as originally built, and many other modern theatres are failures in this respect. Bernard Miles says that 'recent architects have presented the actor with the problem of bridging a 20–30 foot gap before his voice and face and personality can begin to register. The Shakespeare Memorial Theatre at Stratford-on-Avon is an excellent example of a modern building put up without reference to the actors' means of expression, and succeeds in violating all the known principles of communication between performers and audience.'[10] A similar view is held by many others. Norman Marshall, a theatrical producer, thinks of it as a failure, and asserts that 'the fundamental weakness in the design of the Memorial Theatre is the gulf between stage and auditorium. This would be a serious enough defect in any theatre, but it is doubly so in a theatre built for the plays of Shakespeare which were written for a platform stage with no proscenium arch and no barrier of any sort between actor and audience.'[11] These defects have largely been rectified by the extensive alterations of 1950–1, in which a forestage that could be adapted for various plays was incorporated. By the use of the forestage the remoteness between actors and audience was eliminated. There is now, in my experience of seeing plays there, no feeling of the proscenium picture frame separating the two, and no curtain is used. When it is lowered once in a performance in conformity with fire regulations it is half-way down the stage.

We have noted that in the Arts Theatre at Munich, built in 1908, and the Cologne Exhibition Theatre of 1914 the aim was to design them so as to bring the stage and auditorium together as one room. Mordecai Gavelik in his book on *New Theatres for Old*[12] remarks that for Fritz Erlen, the stage and scenic designer, and Max Littmann, the architect of the Munich Arts Theatre, 'the architectural union of playing and seating areas became a major item in a bill of reform. The arena of a dramatic performance is not only the stage; it is the stage plus the auditorium. The picture stage is nothing but a relic of Italian opera. The gilded proscenium frame must vanish. In its place we must put the platform stage known to Shakespeare and Molière, re-establishing that intimacy, that unity of player and spectator, which alone can give freshness to the drama. A bridge must be flung across the mystic gulf of Wagner.'

Many attempts were made in the years before the First World War to add a forestage or apron stage so as to bring the players out more among the audience. One interesting experiment was Harley Granville-Barker's use of the apron stage for his presentations of *Twelfth Night* and *Winter's Tale* at the Savoy Theatre in London in 1912. The difficulty of achieving success by adding a forestage in an existing theatre is that if it was not originally designed to accommodate such an addition many of the audience have a poor view of the forestage. The auditorium of the old Savoy Theatre was not deep enough and the gallery was too high for such an experiment to meet with success.

People in the back rows of the gallery could hardly see the forestage, and those occupying side seats of the theatre had a far better view of the apron than of the stage proper.

The first modern example in which the stage is brought right out into the middle of the auditorium in the manner of the Greek orchestra is the Grosse Schauspielhaus, designed by Hans Poelzig in 1919 as a reconstruction of a Schumann circus building. It was so designed with a view to forming an appropriate setting for Max Reinhardt's spectacular productions, in which he could use the whole of the theatre. In the Grosse Schauspielhaus various arrangements of steps leading up from the central orchestra space to the stage are employed, designed according to the production. In a production like *The Miracle* the whole interior should be like a cathedral, with the action taking place in the centre. Thus many of Reinhardt's productions took place in circus buildings, among them being the Grosse Schauspielhaus before its conversion in 1919. The fact, therefore, that it was a circus building made its conversion into a design closer to the Greek theatre than to the modern traditional picture stage theatre an easier development. The same can be said of the Schumann Theatre at Frankfurt-on-Main, designed by Rudolf Frankel in 1931, although here it is more of a compromise with the traditional theatre, and takes the form of a large forestage, which can be extended by raising the floor of the orchestra.

A small theatre in England which is designed so that the stage and auditorium are one, and the stage comes well out beyond the proscenium, is the Festival Theatre at Cambridge. This Theatre was remodelled from the old Barnwell Theatre by Edward Maufe for Terence Gray in 1926. The stage is the same width as the auditorium and spreads well beyond what would be the proscenium in a traditional theatre, terminating in several flights of steps. Norman Marshall, speaking of his experience as a producer in this theatre, remarks that it

'gave one an extraordinary sense of elbow room. The several levels provided by the stage, the forestage, and the steps, gave opportunities for innumerable new combinations of movement and grouping impossible in an ordinary theatre where the actors would be marking one another. It was easy to get the actors on and off the stage without the elaborate and unnatural manoeuvres necessary on a picture-frame stage, as at the Festival; in addition to the usual entrances there were two on the forestage, two more opening on to the steps from where in an ordinary theatre the stage boxes would be, and two more entrances down the gangways of the stalls on to the forestage steps.'[13]

The A.D.C. Theatre at Cambridge, designed by Harold Tomlinson and W. P. Dyson, and completed in 1934, is similar in many ways to the Festival Theatre, which probably influenced the design. In the A.D.C. Theatre there is an orchestra pit which

Malmo State Theatre, 1939–43

   Architects: Erick Lallerstedt, and Sigurd Lewerenty and David Hellden

Malmo State Theatre, interior of auditorium

Schumann Theatre, Frankfurt-on-Main, 1931–32

   Architect: Rudolf Frankel

Left, View of auditorium looking towards stage and below, plan of theatre

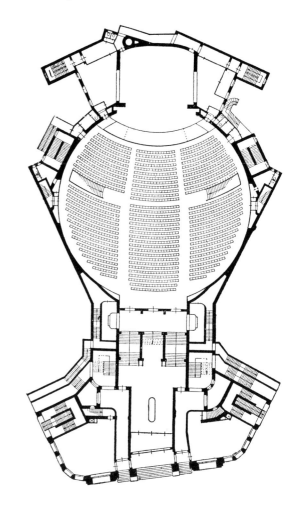

Grosse Schauspeilhaus, Berlin, 1919 *Architect: Hans Poelzig*

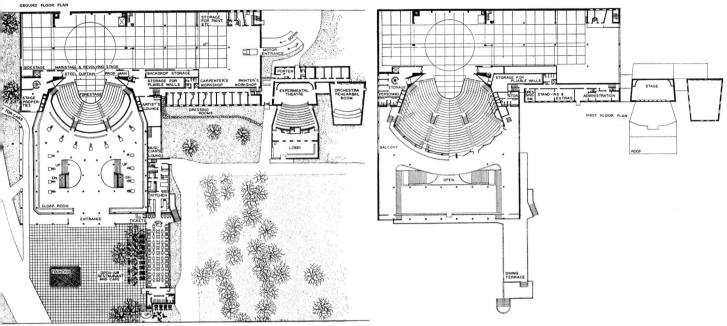

GROUND FLOOR PLAN

Malmo State Theatre,
ground floor plan

Malmo State Theatre,
first floor plan

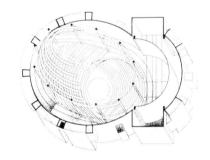

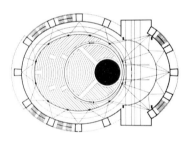

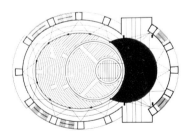

Project for total theatre, 1927,
by *Walter Gropius*

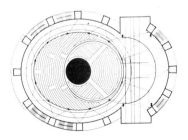

is designed to be covered with a stepped apron stage when required. There are doors at either end of this apron stage, and steps also make possible entrance by the actors from the auditorium. When the apron stage is in use there is a sense of oneness with the auditorium.

An interesting development in the treatment of the stage in relation to the auditorium is seen in the temporary theatre designed by Auguste Perret for the Paris Exhibition of Decorative Art in 1925. Instead of the usual proscenium frame the platform has two diagonal wings projecting forward, and two columns rise approximately at the points of intersection supporting lintels which follow the line of the platform. The orchestra occupies a central space shaped with side diagonals abutting at right-angles the diagonals of the platform. This arrangement gives a closer contact between audience and actors, because the action of the play can take place on the tripartite platform which partly encloses the front spectators, which is the reverse of Greek and Elizabethan theatres where the spectators partly surround the actors[14]. This theatre was an interesting example of reinforced concrete frame construction.

A theatre to combine types designed just before the Second World War in 1939 is that at Malmo in Sweden, of which Erick Lallerstedt, Sigurd Lewerenty and David Hellden were the architects. Building commenced at the beginning of 1941, but as conditions were somewhat precarious because of the war it was not completed until 1943, while the addition of many embellishments were made from time to time. On plan the theatre is a broad fan shape. It has a raked floor with a fairly steep gradient of 1 in 6. Significant features in the design are a movable apron stage and different sizes of theatre made possible by movable partitions. The stage is spacious, with a revolving platform, and beyond the wide proscenium a large apron stage can be moved into position in two sections by means of lifts. Thus the space immediately in front of the proscenium can be used either for front seating, with the traditional performance behind the picture frame of the proscenium, or the whole of the large apron stage can be used for theatrical performances, partly or wholly in the round with the audience forming a half circle round the players; or this apron stage can be used, in the case of musical concerts, by a large orchestra of 80, and when so used wooden screens can be drawn across the proscenium opening to reflect sound. If desired, only the rear part of the apron stage need be used for a partly extended main stage or for a smaller orchestra, as might be needed for operatic performances. The theatre is not only designed for the utmost flexibility for dramatic and musical performances, but the flexibility is extended in accommodating audiences of various sizes. It is fitted with screens so that it can be made in four different sizes. The normal size of the theatre is for about 1,200 when the full apron stage is being used, or for 1,300 when this space is used for additional audience. The size can be reduced to about 800 by a way screen drawn across the theatre on tracks in the ceiling[15]. It can be further reduced by partitions running lengthwise with the auditorium and cutting off the side seats. The theatre can be enlarged by the addition of 500, making a total of 1,700 or 1,800 by the manipulation of the rear wall, which consists of a series of concertina doors and partitions which are collapsible and can be drawn aside and include in the theatre the curved balcony section of the first floor foyer.

The spacious foyers on both the ground and first floors linked by handsome flanking white marble stairways, provide ample room for promenading during intervals, while giving scope for the display of sculpture and paintings, both the permanent collection and temporary exhibitions. Near this theatre–concert hall and part of the same group is a small intimate experimental theatre to seat about 200, an orchestra rehearsal room, and spacious workshops adjoining the stage.

Externally the building is very much in the mid-twentieth century idiom with the main façade a series of large squares and rectangles with the stanchions faced with white marble, framing large areas of glass which serve to make the vestibule and the front floor foyer very light. In the long summer evenings at Malmo this is a valuable asset. A spacious white marble forecourt spreads in front of the theatre, with a beautiful bronze fountain with figures from famous plays. A visit to this theatre is an exhilarating experience.

Theatre design in the mid-twentieth century (1940–70) is still much of an experimental character. It depends partially on whether the illusory or naturalistic presentation is preferred to the conventional or symbolic. In the opinion of many the solution of the problem is a design which makes possible the adaptation for both like the Malmo Theatre. It should thus be designed so that the picture-stage play can be performed, or a play conceived as being performed mainly on a forestage, or on a central space like the Greek orchestra. This would mean, as at Malmo, mechanism for raising the floor of the auditorium to become a part of the forestage, and the easy removal of auditorium seats when required. The Schumann Theatre at Frankfurt-on-Main goes some way in this direction because of the raising of the orchestral floor to add to the permanent forestage. The removal of some of the front central seats and turning the side seats would also make possible the Greek orchestra, as in the case of the Grosse Schauspielhaus. Among designs for theatres that have materialized in which this flexibility is a principal aim, so that the building can be used equally well for a great variety of productions demanding different settings, are Kiesler's plans for an oval theatre and Weininger's for a spherical theatre, but the best known is Walter Gropius's project for a Totaltheater which he designed in collaboration with Erwen Piscator, the Berlin theatrical producer. In this design three forms are combined, the circus with the central arena, the Greek theatre with its semicircular shape, and the picture stage. A model[16] was made of the design. It is so arranged that the tiers of seats can be revolved in sections so that the change from one form to another can be effected quickly. Attempts at designing theatres approximating to this were made in the fifties and sixties and are discussed in Chapter 43.

References and Notes

1. A description of the equipment of this theatre is given by P. Morton Shand in his book *Modern Theatres and Cinemas*, London, 1930, pp. 6–7.

2. The broad principles of good hall acoustics are fairly simple although an exact mathematical application may be a little complex. The simple principle is that reflecting wall, floor and ceiling surfaces should be near the source of sound, and that absorbent surfaces should be at the further end away from the source of sound to prevent echo.

3. Reference is made to the suitability of the design of the Shakespeare Memorial Theatre for its purpose in this chapter.

4. Extensions, including additional dressing rooms, were made to the designs of Brian O'Rourke in 1951.

5. According to G. Topham Forrests' reconstruction the Globe was sixteen sided.

6. Bernard Miles's *The British Theatre*, London, 1948, p. 10. Among actors, preferences for the open stage, bringing them into closer contact with the audience, or for the picture-frame stage differ greatly. While several prefer the former, preference for the latter continues to be expressed. At the Royal Society of Arts Cantor lecture on The Actor, given in March 1952 by Sir Ralph Richardson, I asked which type of stage he preferred, say, acting in a Shakespeare play, and though he said that different actors had different feelings in the matter, he preferred the picture-frame stage. Sir Ralph remarked, however, that there was a movement towards the use of the apron stage.

7. Bernard Miles, *The British Theatre*, London, p. 13.

8. I prefer the term 'naturalistic' to 'realistic' as being more accurate in my understanding of the term. 'Realistic' in art always implies that selection which is typical of reality, and belongs to conventional as much as to illusory technique, whereas 'naturalistic' means natural representation.

9. J. P. Eckermann's *Conversations with Goethe*. The many references to the building of a new theatre at Weimar occur mainly during the conversations in 1825.

10. Bernard Miles, *The British Theatre*, London, p. 36.

11. Norman Marshall, *The Other Theatre*, London, 1947, p. 176.

12. Mordecai Gavelik, *New Theatres for Old*, USA, 1940, London, 1947.

13. Norman Marshall, *The Other Theatre*, London, 1947, p. 55.

14. The same device of a tripartite platform was used by Josef Urban in his project for the Reinhardt Theatre in New York.

15. Hope Bagenal in a paper on General Purpose Halls given at the Building Research Congress in London in 1951 says that these 'curtains' for reducing the size of the theatre are not used in practice owing to a complication in track design. When I visited the theatre in 1954 they appeared to be in working condition.

16. Described in P. Morton Shand's *Modern Theatre and Cinemas*, London, 1930, p. 5.

410

27 Cinemas

THE CINEMA AS WE KNOW IT today began in 1895, when the first public exhibitions of motion pictures were held in New York and in Paris. Exhibitions in the first few years of the cinema were of short films, often of incidents of everyday life, like the *Arrival of a Train at a Station* or a *Bathing Beach*, and were generally exhibited in a café or as a side-show of a fair. Then subjects were chosen from current happenings of dramatic interest, one successful experiment of this type being Meliè's series of films of the Dreyfus case (1898). As films became longer and attracted more interest, exhibitions were given in small halls. Sometimes a film would prove so popular that new halls would be opened to show it. Maurice Bardeche and Robert Brasillach in their *History of the Film* record that in the early years of the century two new halls had to be opened to cope with the demand for the film *Bedtime for the Bride*[1].

Most early cinemas in Europe were converted halls. The rise of the cinema coincided with the decline of the Music Hall; thus many early cinema buildings were the ornate theatres hitherto used for Music Hall. Cinemas built as such, or existing halls converted, were in existence in 1908. In design these early cinemas generally followed the lines of small meeting or concert halls with rectangular auditorium and platform. One of the best of the early German cinemas was the Cines picture house in Nollendorfplatz in Berlin, designed by Oskar Kaufmann and built in 1910.

BEGINNINGS OF FUNCTIONAL DESIGN FOR THE CINEMA

There is evidence in several German cinemas built between 1910 and 1914 that architects were thinking of the cinema as a building with a purpose distinctly different from the theatre and concert hall and as requiring a different design. It is pertinent, therefore, to consider this different purpose and the design that can best satisfy it. Spectators in the traditional theatre look through the proscenium arch into a large box where the performance takes place. It is a three-dimensional performance. The action takes place on the floor of the platform which it is important for the spectators to see, so that the floor of the auditorium is sloped partly for that purpose and partly

411

to enable the spectators to see over the heads of those in front of them. That the actors should be heard is very important so that in the design of the theatre much attention is given to acoustics. Most actors like that degree of intimacy in a theatre which enables them to be heard easily without unduly raising their voices. It is of advantage not to be too far away from the stage; some consider from the fifth to the tenth row of the stalls the best seats, other prefer those in the centre of the first few rows of the dress circle.

With the cinema the performance is by means of a photographic representation on a two-dimensional screen, the third dimension being illusory. The picture area was originally much smaller than that enclosed by the proscenium arch in the theatre, although later it became larger. Because of this the design called for a more complete convergence of the building on the focal point than was necessary to the same degree in the theatre. The picture can be placed at any height above the platform or auditorium for the convenience of seeing.

One of the reasons for sloping the floor of the auditorium in the case of the theatre, that of seeing over the heads in front, remains in the case of the cinema, but the other reasons no longer obtain. Yet it is an advantage for spectators to be as near as possible in horizontal and vertical planes at right-angles to the picture plane and this is an additional reason for sloping the floor of the auditorium so as to bring the rear spectators as near as possible into the horizontal plane. It is a disadvantage for the spectator to be near the screen, the best seats being either midway or at the rear in a medium sized cinema. That is why the pricing of seats in the cinema is reversed when compared with theatre prices, the cheapest seats being in the front and the more expensive seats in the rear. But even in the front seats one wants a reasonable view of the picture, not too blurred or distorted, and cinema proprietors and designers, wanting to avoid these seats being either unoccupied or eliminated, had to throw the screen back from the front rows, and at the same time create an illusion of utmost depth. In early cinemas, especially in England, this problem was not successfully solved so that the front seats were only occupied on sufferance when the rest of the theatre was full, and when, having resolved to 'go to the pictures', the front spectators would rather have the blurred and distorted picture than not see it at all. The various solutions of this problem represented one of the most important technical developments in the cinema. Up to 1929, when talkie films began, the question of acoustics was of less importance in cinema design, yet it was considered in most cases, as music hall turns were often sandwiched between films. This, therefore, provided a further reason for a sloping floor.

It is possible that many early designers interested in the future of the cinema realized these differences of purpose in the cinema and theatre, but there were obviously difficulties of a commercial character. Naturally not every cinema proprietor and potential cinema proprietor could feel in 1908 that the cinema had come to stay, so that in case it turned out to be an evanescent thing, they would naturally like to be free to change the use of the building to the theatre, music hall, or concert hall. Thus it would be undesirable that it should be so designed that a change to these other purposes should be anything but simple, so that the design must not be too much a departure from the traditional theatre. The stage with a fair depth and fair-sized proscenium arch must be provided. And most cinema proprietors ever since have desired this freedom of conversion, a freedom which many have argued has prevented the evolution towards the cinema design which perfectly fulfils its purpose. German cinemas succeeded best.

SOME GERMAN AND SWEDISH EXAMPLES

Many of the early German cinemas built between 1910 and 1924 demonstrate that their designers realized the essential differences between the purpose of the cinema and that of the theatre, and that they were allowed some freedom to work accordingly. One of the first examples of a cinema which was designed, it would seem, mainly as a cinema and less as an adaptation of the traditional theatre is the Union Cinema in Dresden, built in 1911 to the design of Martin Pietzsch. The plan is like an elongated horseshoe with a columnar balcony curving round to the proscenium, but with seats thinning out towards the slips and all arranged with a fair view of the screen. The stage is set well back from the front seats, being separated by the orchestra space. Above this orchestra space is the wide proscenium arch with sides that slope towards the screen and ornamented with vertical strip pattern. This treatment is designed clearly to give an illusion of greater depth[2].

Other noteworthy early German cinemas, all designed specifically for that purpose, with small stage and demonstrating the attempt to give satisfactory vision to the front seats are Emil Schandt's U. T. Tauentgrenstrasse, Berlin, E. Simons's Union-Palast, Kurfürstendamm, Berlin, Hugo Pal's Marmorhaus, Berlin, all built in 1912, and E. M. Lesser's Bavaria-Haus, Berlin, built in 1914. The influence of either the traditional theatre or concert hall is apparent in all the designs, while the exteriors show conventional conformity with the neighbouring street architecture or the prevalent traditional style, but in the treatment of the pictures on a screen in relation to an audience, they are designs which endeavour to serve this purpose well. Oskar Kaufmann's Cines is one early cinema which shows in its exterior, with its blank walls, that the building is for a purpose where daylight has to be shut out, with the exception of the small operational room at the top of the building where light is admitted by three circular windows.

After the First World War luxury building was slower in restarting than the more urgent types of building like houses, schools, and factories, so that it was some years before cinema building began again on a big scale. In most countries it was not until about 1923 that work of any magnitude was in progress, and then the building of cinemas gradually increased in volume so that by about 1929 well over a thousand were being built each year in Europe.

The main differences that can be noted in the typical cinema built in the twenties and the traditional theatre is that the former has generally less depth of stage and usually there is only one balcony instead of two or three as in the traditional theatre. One sees in this an evolution partly from the theatre and partly from the meeting or concert hall. When later, with the era of the 'super-cinema' they became much larger, with seating capacities up to three or four thousand, then two and sometimes three balconies were introduced, and apart from the stage they came nearer in design to the modern opera house.

Perhaps the most notable cinema built in the first few years after the war was the Skandia Cinema in Stockholm designed by E. Gunnar Asplund in 1922. This cinema is rectangular in shape with a balcony at the back and long side balconies. The design is classical in character with emphasis on verticals and horizontals and rectangular masses, while ornament is introduced on the balcony front and on the dado and frieze of the corridors which is a free and individual adaptation of classical decoration made with much taste and refinement. This cinema has been the subject of many eulogies from architectural critics. Christian Barman says that it has become a place of architectural pilgrimage, that it is perfect of its kind and entirely satisfactory as a work of art. Yet he adds that 'ineffectual sighting arrangements and unsprung seats are unable to diminish the popularity of this exquisite interior'[3]. The 'ineffectual sighting arrangements' constitute a criticism and would necessarily prevent its being a perfect cinema. As a decorative ensemble it may be wholly delightful to contemplate, but visitors go rather to see the films than actually to contemplate the building. The spectators are for the major part of their visit in semi-darkness, they are but dimly aware of their architectural surroundings, and a little more strongly conscious perhaps in the intervals when the lights go up.

The architects who were responsible for some of the most noteworthy of the first group of cinemas to be built in Germany after the war up to about 1927 were Fritz Wilms, the architect for the Ufa Company, Hans Poelzig, and Friedrich Lipp. The significant early works of Fritz Wilms are the Ufa Cinema in the Turmstrasse, built in 1924, the Piccadilly, Charlottenburg, built in 1925, and the Mercedes-Palast, Utrechter-Strasse, Berlin, built in 1926. They are all treated with the traditional richness of the theatre, the influence of the new Baroque treatment of Oskar Kaufmann being apparent, particularly in the pleasing interior of the Piccadilly. The most noteworthy of the early cinemas of Poelzig is the Capitol, Berlin, built in 1925. A fairly large cinema, being built for about 1,300, it has a squarish auditorium with broad splays converging towards the orchestra which has a curved front to separate the front row

414

from the stage and screen. Particularly effective is the lighting and interior decorative effect. The ceiling is like a large flat octagonal dome with fluted texture, with four short and four long sides. It slants up from a cornice to another cornice high up when the slant is slightly flattened to culminate in a lantern light. The main lighting is from two chief sources concealed in the lower cornice and direct from the central lantern.

The two most interesting of Friedrich Lipp's early cinemas are the Atrium Cinema in Berlin, built in 1927, and the Capitol Cinema in Breslau, built about the same time. They are both large, and in both the large proscenium opening is designed as a series of receding concavities, like immense flutes. The interiors of both are richly ornamented and the decorative effects are a little heavy.

The exteriors of these cinemas are mainly on classical lines, several being of a monumental charcter. In Wilms's Ufa Cinema the façade is dominated by a series of pilasters two storeys high supporting an entablature, and in Lipp's Atrium Cinema the long curved façade is decorated with pilasters for two upper storeys, above which are a series of three receding masses. Wilms's Piccadilly Cinema has a massive square façade with a large square patterned window in the centre, so designed to light the entrance and to radiate light at night. The entrance to Poelzig's Capitol is in the centre of a row of shops, and is designed in accordance with these. An interesting decorative use is made of lettering for the name of the cinema and the title of the film, and this is illuminated at night.

A NOTABLE ENGLISH EXAMPLE

A cinema of some architectural distinction, built in London in the early twenties, is the Kensington, designed by J. R. Leathart and W. F. Granger. At the time it was completed it was one of the largest cinemas in London, seating about 2,400. Unlike many cinemas built at this time, it was designed as a unified whole, the exterior and interior both being integral parts of one architectural theme. It is classical in conception and the distinction of the design rests very largely on the pleasing relation of verticals and horizontals with the ornamental details all made subservient to this character. The slightly segmented, coffered ceiling seen from the auditorium emphasizes the classical character, while the curve is so slight that seen from the auditorium it in no way disturbs the harmony of the general scheme of verticals and horizontals. The unity of the exterior and interior can be seen in the general effect of each and is noticeable in such features as the similarity of the rectangular proscenium frame, and the rectangular arch over the main entrance, which repeats in proportion the rectangular mass of the front façade, seen to good advantage, as the cinema is set well back on the pavement with projecting buildings flanking it.

In the mid-twenties the cinema was becoming so popular that difficulties were experienced in most districts of accommodating its increasing public. New cinemas were being provided as quickly as possible, while they became larger, so that from about 1926 the super-cinema began to be built. This need presented problems in construction which were most satisfactorily answered by the steel frame. After about 1925 the majority of cinemas in Europe were built by this method. Some cinemas in France, Germany, and Central Europe were built of reinforced concrete, but these were exceptions to the rule. In England I am unaware of one exception among the larger cinemas. The advantages of the steel-frame construction were that it made possible a greater speed of erection than any other method then in use on a big scale, and that wide spaces could be spanned and cantilevering be employed for balcony construction. The difficulty with reinforced concrete *in situ* construction is that it is slower in actual erection and takes a long time to dry out. If the decoration is applied before it is thoroughly dry, when the interior is heated the concrete sweats and spoils the interior finishes. At this time pre-cast concrete was too much in its infancy to be used, but it was employed for later cinemas.

As speed was essential in building cinemas in answer to the constantly increasing demand, it was desirable that every device should be adopted to contribute to this. One method that was adopted in the building of the Kensington Cinema was to build the auditorium and its roof at the earliest possible moment, and construct the balcony independently. This allows for a fair amount of constructional and decorative work to proceed at once.

THE ERA OF THE SUPER-CINEMA

Although the cinema increased considerably in size in most countries in Europe, it was in England (apart from America) that we find the super-cinema reaching the greatest dimensions. Among the early examples of the super-cinema are the Regent at Sheffield (1926), the Regent, Bournemouth (1927), the Regent, Stamford Hill (1928), the Odeon, Edgware (1929), the Empire, Leicester Square (1929), the New Victoria (1929), the Davis Theatre, Croydon (1930), and the Gaumont Palace, Lewisham (1932). These cinemas are interesting for their construction and impressive for their size, but they are not generally of great architectural distinction. They have seating capacities of from three to five thousand.

The two principal structural problems are presented by the roof and the balcony. The low-pitched steel roof truss was adopted in most cases, the roof of the cinema at Stamford Hill being an example. Many of these larger cinemas had domed ceilings constructed of steel ribs which are suspended from the roof trusses, the cinemas at Bournemouth and Edgware being examples. The spans of these larger cinemas are considerable, those at the New Victoria and the Davis Theatre, Croydon, being about 110 feet, while that of the New Empire at Leicester Square is about 120 feet. Large balconies with considerable seating capacity (that at the New Empire, Leicester

416

Square, seats 1,700) meant steel construction on a spectacular scale. The method employed is generally by means of a large main girder which supports the raking, and under girders which cantilever out to take the first few rows of seats. The balcony void behind the main girder is usually occupied by a foyer or restaurant. There are several variations of this construction. In the Kensington Cinema the main girder is segmental in plan to follow the line of the balcony front, as by this method, although costly, the maximum seating accommodation can be obtained. This necessitated heavily plated connexions between the transverse girders to obviate the twisting of the main members. In the larger balconies wing girders are generally employed, as in the New Empire, Leicester Square. Main girders are either a plate girder as at Stamford Hill and as the two large balcony girders in the New Victoria Cinema, or framed as in the New Empire, Leicester Square, and in the Davis Theatre, Croydon. These are of impressive dimensions, the main girder of the New Empire being 120 feet long by 18 feet deep and weighing 97 tons, and that of the Davis Theatre being 110 feet long by 17 feet deep and weighing 50 tons. The frame construction of both these girders is so designed that passages lead through them from the balcony to the foyer. It will be apparent from the construction of these immense balconies involving the extensive use of cantilevering, that they are partially a development of the iron and steel bridge construction of the nineteenth century, especially of the cantilever bridge.

The tendency to build larger cinemas both in England and on the Continent continued until about 1931 when a halt seemed to be called and there appeared a reversal of the trend. The economic crisis at this time reduced building for entertainment, but when the volume of cinema building again resumed its former proportions, as it did about 1934, the tendency was to build them of a more modest size. The size is necessarily determined by the district the cinema has to serve, and the cinema for a small town or small outlying suburb would never have been so large as the cinemas in the bigger cities and suburbs. But in the bigger urban areas cinemas were becoming more modest in size during the early thirties, and it was preferred to build two smaller cinemas than one very big one. When the period of the super-cinema was reaching its zenith the question had been repeatedly asked whether cinemas were not getting too large, whether in this vastness a certain desirable intimacy was not being lost, and whether a smaller building was not more conducive to the feeling of comfort and cosiness which many people, subconsciously perhaps, like in a cinema. Thus the question: 'What is the best size for a cinema?' was often considered and discussed by cinema proprietors and architects, especially in Germany, and it was felt by many German architects that in most respects the desirable maximum seating capacity is in the region of 2,500.

This question of size is bound up with the general question of the interior character of the cinema, and the interior decoration which is most suited to it. From 1924 there were many curious tendencies of a romantic kind in the decoration of cinemas, most of which seemed calculated to give a sense of remoteness from the everyday world.

Interiors were made to look like Italian gardens, or Venetian canal scenes or Spanish patios or medieval cathedrals, anything romantic and remote from ordinary, everyday life. This kind of decoration is seen a little in Italian cinemas, but mostly in English cinemas, and very rarely in German. An early example of the garden effect occurs in the Reale Cinema in Milan, built in 1924 to the designs of Ottavio Cabiati and Ambrogio Gadola, where foliage, flowers, and creepers hang from the side balconies. The Italian villa and garden interiors became common in England in the late twenties. An example of the cathedral interior is the Granada at Woolwich, while the interior of the New Victoria Cinema is meant to suggest a fairy palace under the sea. In the Gaumont Palace at Salisbury, the theme of interior decoration was set by 'Ye Halle of John Halle', a late fifteenth-century structure which forms the entrance vestibule to the theatre.

The 'atmospheric' interiors, as they were called, suggesting Italian gardens and villas in the twilight, or Venetian canals, met with a varied reception among the cinema public. Some, perhaps the less cultured and intelligent, thought they were lovely; others—and perhaps they were the majority—were indifferent, the main requisites in their opinion being the film, a good viewpoint, and comfort; while others—perhaps the more cultured and discriminating—were amused and showed a tendency to ridicule these absurd decorations as they called them. As in the long run the opinion of the third group tells, it began to influence cinema proprietors, who wondered whether it was not all a waste of sugar icing.

Yet the atmosphere and character of a cinema is important. The film is the most important it is true, but most people would hesitate to see a film they very much wanted to see if it were being shown in a bleak cold hall with uncomfortable seats. The reaction might be: 'I will wait until the film comes to so-and-so cinema', which in their mind is comfortable and agreeable.

What, then, is the best kind of interior? There is not a long experience to guide one in attempting an answer, because it it not a building with a long tradition, while that building from which it is mainly derived, the theatre of the stage drama, is essentially different in purpose in many important respects. The answer can best be obtained from those who are serious students of the film, who have habitually visited cinemas, and the interpretation by the artist and technician of the preferences regarding the type of interior in which films should be shown. I venture to cite my own personal preferences because I was a constant visitor to the cinema for forty years, and because I believe these preferences are shared by many cinema enthusiasts with whom I have discussed the subject, and also by a few prominent cinema architects.

There were three cinemas near to where I lived for thirty years all of which I visited frequently. Two, one small and one fairly large, were built in the late twenties, while one of medium size was built in 1938–9. The small cinema, which has an old-fashioned square character with panelled walls, I did not like. I think it was really too small, while the effect was a little hard. The large cinema I liked better, but it was, I felt, too large. The cinema of medium size, built last, I liked best and was the most agreeable cinema which I habitually visited. It was comfortable; one could see well from all the seats, and the general effect was simple, warm, and cosy, while at the same time giving the impression of being large enough to serve a neighbourhood of twenty to thirty thousand. It gave the feeling in intimacy found in a moderate-sized theatre. Part of this is due, I think, to the curved forms of the interior. For example, the walls curve towards the proscenium and have a kind of enfolding character. (The small and medium sized cinemas have since been demolished.)

Of the cinemas outside my own district which I generally visited, I did not like the very large super-cinema or the very small cinema, neither did I like the long interior. The New Victoria, the New Empire, Leicester Square, the Davis Theatre, Croydon (since demolished), and other such super-cinemas were all too large for me and these I generally avoided if I could see the films somewhere else. I think one reason is that they are a little forbidding and not in character with that intimate feeling that I found most people liked in a cinema. The Kensington and the New Gallery I found much more agreeable. In Germany the most agreeable cinema I remember is the Universum Cinema in Kurfürstendamm, designed by Eric Mendelsohn in 1928. This again is a cinema of medium size with a generous use of curved forms. Poelzig's Babylon Cinema impressed me as too long, and that certainly was my feeling about Wilms's Mercedes-Palast Cinema, which has no balcony and is an example of the tendency in the late twenties and early thirties in Germany to build cinemas without balconies.

This is a rough indication of my personal reactions. I would add that one is always pleased by decorative features that give aesthetic pleasure when the lights go up, but these are more appreciated if they are discovered than if they are in any way obtrusive.

I have been encouraged to state my own preferences in the matter of the decorative character of the cinema interior because they seem to accord with the tendencies in design since the late twenties in Germany, France, and Central Europe, and after about 1932 in England. Certain requirements of a general character might thus be formulated from the indications of the designs themselves. It might be said that a cinema should be small enough to conduce to a feeling of intimacy, yet sufficiently large to perform its function of showing films to the best advantage, and that this suggests a cinema with a seating capacity of not very much less than 1,250 and not more than 2,250; that it should be comfortable and that the feeling of intimacy and comfort should be helped by the decorative character, which should consist of broad curved forms, and plain, yet warm and agreeably textured surfaces, with perhaps decorative or dramatic notes of interest at a few focal points, and that the colouring

419

should be warm and soft. The stately and formal or the grand and magnificent interior does not seem to accord with the informal easy-going unceremonious pleasure of the cinema. It requires instead the intimate and cosy character for people who want to relax and perhaps dream in semi-darkness for three hours. Yet, as some of the German, French, and later English examples show, this was often achieved with some degree of architectural distinction.

The tendency can be summed up as a movement towards the cinema of moderate size with simple curved forms, and soft warm colouring and a few decorative notes of dramatic interest as being functionally the most satisfactory, prompted partly by a reaction against the crude and grandiose super-cinema.

SOME DISTINCTIVELY DESIGNED CINEMAS IN GERMANY
AND CENTRAL EUROPE

It is worth while to cite a few examples of cinemas built in the period from 1927 to 1933 which have some architectural distinction and which are exceptions to the over-decorated super-cinema. They are for the most part simple in treatment, depending for aesthetic effect on a discriminating emphasis of line and mass, colour, and textural surfaces. They largely formed the prototypes for the majority of good cinemas in the period from 1934 to 1939.

Two pleasing interiors by Hans Poelzig, in which simplicity is the keynote, are the Deli Cinema at Breslau, built in 1927, and the Babylon Cinema at Berlin, built in 1928. Both are of modest size, seating 1,187 and 1,239, and both are constructed of reinforced concrete, which is a material Poelzig liked and used expressively. The interiors have large plain wall surfaces. The balcony front of the Deli Cinema continues to the side wings and swings down dramatically to the stage and enfolds the auditorium. The ceiling curves down towards the proscenium and is studded with small lights. I have said that the Babylon Cinema was, to my taste, too long, but it has a clean simplicity, without severity, which is attractive. Severity is avoided by the use of curved forms such as the curve of the wall into the ceiling where the lights are situated, and the curved balcony front with wings that effect a junction of the balcony with the side walls.

One of the most famous cinemas built during this period, and one that has been justly admired for its beauty of line, is the Universum Cinema, in the Kurfürstendamm, Berlin, built in 1928, to the design of Eric Mendelsohn. This cinema is part of a large building scheme consisting of buildings arranged round a cul-de-sac running off the Kurfürstendamm. In addition to the cinema which is at one corner, there is a café-restaurant on the opposite corner, while at one side of the cul-de-sac are tall blocks of flats, and at the end is a bachelor hotel.

420

Universum Cinema, Berlin, 1928

Architect: Eric Mendelsohn

View of auditorium and ground floor plan

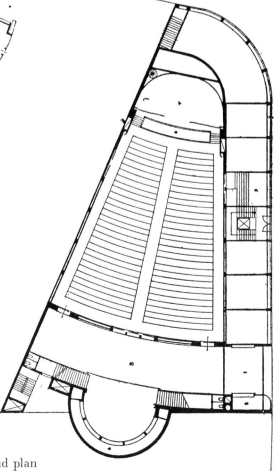

Scala Cinema, Bucharest, 1933 *Architect: Rudolf Frankel*

View of auditorium looking towards stage and plan

The Universum Cinema (subsequently called Luxor Palast) has seating for 1,800. The plan is like an elongated horseshoe which is conducive to a satisfactory arrangement of seats, and makes possible a good and undistorted view of the screen for every spectator. There is a stage of some depth thus allowing the screen to be set well back from the front seats. The interior is finely dramatic. One form of decorative emphasis which the shape and purpose of the cinema suggest is the convergence of all lines and masses towards the stage and screen to conform with the direction in which the audience is looking. This motif finds complete and satisfying expression in the interior of the Universum Cinema. The grand horseshoe curve of the balcony front continues beyond the balcony to the stage; and above the part where the band leaves the balcony are horizontal strips giving the same emphasis, while decorative strips on the ceiling move in the same direction. The sweep of the balcony is echoed by the upper floor of the foyer entrance. What is also noteworthy in this cinema is the unity of the whole interior and exterior. The curved masses and horizontal emphasis of the interior are reflected in the general curved mass and horizontal emphasis of the exterior, the whole design being an organic unity. A comparison of the elevational drawing illustrated with the view of the auditorium will demonstrate this convincingly. This is perhaps the first cinema in the new idiom which shows the complete organic unity of the whole. The Kensington Cinema has a similar unity of interior and exterior but this is classical and more static in design, the lines, masses, and decorative emphasis of the Universum Cinema are a new dynamic conception growing out of the purpose of the building.

The Lichtburg cinema in Berlin, built in 1929 to the designs of Rudolf Frankel, was, I believe, the first cinema in Germany built after the introduction of 'talkies', and was designed with these in mind and with especial attention to acoustics. The cinema occupies a corner site and is part of a larger scheme which includes a row of shops on the ground floor and offices above, which continue in a narrow strip along the street. The corner occupied by the cinema appears externally as a semicircular tower, the ground floor of which is occupied by a circular entrance hall, and the two upper floors by oval dance halls. The cinema is surrounded on three sides by a corridor, a design which greatly assists in shutting out external noise. The façade of the row of shops is marked by long horizontal bands of plain wall and window, to be arrested by the tower of the cinema with vertical emphasis. This tower was designed partially with a view to lighting effects, as its name 'Castle of Light' implies; and its situation on a prominent corner on fairly high ground makes possible the full advantage of display lighting.

The cinema seats about 2,000, it has a squarish, fan-shaped plan, and a stage of sufficient depth for concerts and music-hall, although hardly adequate for the theatre proper. If, however, the orchestra were covered over to form an apron stage this might prove adequate for the performance of plays. The desirable distance from the front seats to the screen is secured by the orchestra and the depth of stage, while the directing line for the eyes is assisted by the convex forms on either side of the proscenium. The cinema is another example of simple treatment where decorative ensemble depends on the effect of line and mass, on large, plain, textured surfaces, on the curved line of the balcony front, on the curve of the ceiling towards the proscenium, and on the radiating lighting troughs of the ceiling.

Another interesting cinema, designed by Rudolf Frankel a few years later, is the Scala Cinema at Bucharest built in 1933. Like the Lichtburg Cinema it is part of a scheme which includes shops and offices, and it has many points of similarity in the treatment. The shops on the ground floor with offices above, form an enclosing and sound-insulating strip on one side of the cinema, and the façade is designed with long, horizontal bands of plain wall and fenestration to terminate over the cinema entrance with a square tower effect with gridiron façade. The plan of the cinema is again the fan-shape. It is built of a reinforced concrete frame with brick filling, and a brick cyclorama forms the back of the stage with the purpose of reflecting sound. Particularly interesting in this cinema is the stepped, terraced treatment of the ceiling, with concealed lighting at the steps. This treatment appears to have been suggested by the camera-shutter form. Again, the interior is one of plain surfaces with the decorative effect depending on textured surfaces and long lines. The colour scheme is interesting. The walls on either side of the proscenium flanking the orchestra are of Macassar ebony, the auditorium walls are covered with bright bronze velour with bronze beading, the ceiling is cream, and the floor carpet and seats are terracotta, with the woodwork of the latter black.

It would be possible to cite many cinemas in Germany and Central Europe built between 1927 and 1933 which are examples of a general movement towards simplicity of treatment and effect, yet which, at the same time achieve a feeling of cosiness and intimacy. The degree in which these qualities are achieved depends very largely on the shapes of the plain surfaces and on their texture. Where the forms are straight, and the surfaces are somewhat cold and minutely textured then the effect is apt to be severe. In a cinema like the Universum at Stuttgart, built of reinforced concrete, to the designs of Albert Eitel, Paul Schmohl, and Georg Stachelin in 1930, the extreme simplicity of the plain surfaces might have been a little severe but for the composition of curved forms. In an interior like that of the Flamman Cinema at Stockholm, designed by Unr Ahren and built about 1929, it is doubtful if in the simplicity of treatment and the expression of reinforced concrete, of which it is built, severity is avoided. The very plain, slightly curved balcony front and the six absolutely plain concrete columns which support the high building above the cinema, and the plain walls relieved only by the rows of lights is an example of simplicity which risks severity especially with the blue colouring of the walls. For a building with the purpose of the cinema the claims of comfort and intimacy are very important.

As already indicated the moderate sized cinema with a simple yet intimate interior which was beginning to be the rule between 1926 and 1930 in Germany and Central Europe was later appearing in England. Up to 1931 was still the period of the bizarre and garish super-cinema, but about 1933 the more modest sized, simpler cinema began to appear[4]. Among the noteworthy early examples of this kind are the Regal, Wimbledon, built in 1933 by Robert Cromie, the Plaza, Sutton, built in 1934 by the same architect, and the Palace Cinema at Chatham, built by Arthur W. Kenyon in 1934. The two cinemas by Robert Cromie have seating capacities near 2,000, that at Wimbledon being a little under and that at Sutton being a little over. In both an effective decorative use is made of the organ sound grille on either side of the orchestra. In the Palace Cinema at Chatham the treatment just in front of the proscenium is interesting. The orchestra space is occupied by a grille, the broad splayed sides are dramatically fluted, while a row of lights appear above the proscenium set in a grille. In all these three English cinemas, the decorative effect depends mainly on colour, texture, curved forms, grilles, and flutings, emerging, it will be appreciated, more directly from function than the imported 'romantic' decoration of the super-cinema.

It has not often been the case in cinema design that we find a complete unity of interior and exterior. This occurs with Mendelsohn's Universum Cinema and with Leathart and Granger's Kensington Cinema, but these are rather the exceptions than the rule. This diversity of interior and exterior is due mainly to the restricted exterior appearance—often sited closely between other buildings with but a small street frontage—and the need for conformity with immediate surroundings. The organic unity of the complete building both interior and exterior is perhaps more possible on an island site where the cinema enjoys some degree of isolation, or where many aspects of the exterior can be seen, and certainly the best external designs occur when these advantages are enjoyed. Mendelsohn's Universum Cinema has these advantages of siting and they are also enjoyed by some of the cinemas in the smaller provincial towns and cities of England where space is not restricted. One that is quite effective is the Gaumont Cinema at Taunton, designed by William T. Benslyn, and built in 1932. It is a composition of large, plain masses in local sand-faced bricks varying from dark to light brown. The front is of square shape with the almost standard character of a row of entrance doors on the ground floor with a window above framed by a plain wall. The window reveals the first-floor foyer, café, or restaurant which is usual in most cinemas. In this example at Taunton there is a frieze of small square windows for the operators' rooms. On the right side of the entrance the wall curves round to the long side façade, and at the farther end is the higher mass at the stage end, and it is the view from this side that is the most pleasing and expressive.

Another cinema built about the same time and enjoying a position where most of the exterior can be seen, is the Odeon at Weston-super-Mare, designed by T. Cecil Howitt. This is a composition of square masses in a series of recessions on a corner site with the entrance with its canopy curving diagonally on plan across them and binding them together at the base. The walls are faced with faience tiles of varying shades of fawn and cream. Other examples of cinemas in good open setting built about the same time are the Regal Cinema, Newcastle-upon-Tyne, designed by Edwin M. Lawson; the Odeon, Worthing, designed by Whinney, Son, and Austin Hall, and the Odeon, Kingstanding, designed by Harry W. Weedon. The last-mentioned is the most striking. A rectangular mass of biscuit terracotta appears against a wide frame of grey brick, and in the centre is a circular entrance above which are three vertical fins which have neon lighting at night. It could not be anything other than a theatre, cinema, or concert-hall. Sometimes when space is restricted a cinema is sited with its length against the street and with entrance at one end, and this gives scope for interesting and original treatment. One type is a fairly plain façade with horizontal emphasis arrested by a vertical mass over the entrance. A noteworthy example in London is the New Victoria where, in the narrow site between streets, the long façade is repeated on both sides. By the small windows and plain surfaces the character of the building is expressed. Where a fair prominence and space is given to the front of a cinema there is scope for some expression. One of the commonest forms of cinema entrance is the massive, square, classical type of which the Piccadilly Cinema, Berlin, designed by Fritz Wilms, and the Kensington Cinema are early examples. There are many later of a similar if not quite as effective character, the Regal Cinemas at Wimbledon and West Norwood and the Plaza Cinema at Sutton being examples. In these cinemas the entrance hall is on the ground floor with a foyer, restaurant, or café above, and this is reflected in the façade, the windows of the first-floor foyer or café being framed in large plain walls. Too often with cinema entrances the front appears as a dressing of stone, terracotta, or brick with some decorative embellishment, while the rest of the building, of which disconcerting glimpses are often obtained, is built of plain brick with pitched roof with no attempt at architectural effect, the reason being that this is behind and not conspicuous. The effect is somewhat like the classical office block in front of the factory on a trading estate[5].

REFERENCES AND NOTES

1. Maurice Bardeche and Robert Brasillach, *History of the Film*, Paris, 1935. English translation, 1938.
2. This and a few other early German cinemas are illustrated in *Theater und Lichtspielhauser* by Paul Zucker, Berlin, 1926.
3. Quoted by P. Morton Shand in his *Modern Theatres and Cinemas*, London, 1930, p. 24.
4. I am obviously speaking of cinemas in large urban areas. In small towns where cinemas would serve only a restricted population they were accordingly limited in size.
5. In this chapter on cinemas several are referred to in the present tense. With the decline of the cinema several may have been demolished or put to other uses.

28 Concert halls, multi-purpose halls, club buildings and community centres

HALLS OR LARGE ROOMS designed primarily for musical concerts have never been common, and in the modern world are a comparatively recent type of building dating no farther back than the middle of the eighteenth century. For an appreciation of the few good examples built in Europe in the twenties and early thirties it is helpful to be aware of the traditions in this type of building.

The ancient Greeks built halls, called odeums, designed primarily for musical performances. One of the oldest, which appears to have formed the pattern for later buildings of the kind, was that built in Athens by Pericles, about 445 B.C. It seems to have been a small square building roofed in for acoustical purposes. Remains of other odeums have been discovered in Greek cities of the mainland, Sicily, and Asia Minor. They appear to have varied in size from accommodation for 200 to a few thousands, like the example at Patras mentioned by Pausanias. A similar type of music hall or theatre was employed in Roman times. Several were built in the capital. The Roman odeum of which remains are most complete is that of Herodes Atticus, at Athens, which was built into the southwestern slopes of the Acropolis in A.D. 160 and which accommodated from 6,000 to 8,000 persons. The discovery of beams of cedar wood on the site suggests that these are the remains of the roof.

Religion and the spirit of worship have always been among the chief incentives and sources of inspiration for music. It was so in ancient Greece and this devotional music contributed to the origin of the drama. In the Middle Ages, the chief patron of music was the church, the church building was where the chief music was heard, and this continued until the late Renaissance. This church music developed from the chanting of psalms and prayers, and the church building formed part of the musical instrument, because its reverberations, often of several seconds duration, contributed to the musical rhythms and harmonies. This led to the polyphonic music of the fifteenth century. Whether churches were designed with a view to excellence of musical tone is an interesting speculation. Some leading figures of the church—St. Ambrose, Gregory the

426

Great, Martin Luther—put great value on music, and some churches are much better acoustically than others which is probably partly accidental and partly the result of design. Early church music was mainly choral and long reverberations suit such music better than instrumental music. It is an advantage when musical instruments are introduced that the reverberation should be less, a condition found in the Thomaskirche at Leipzig, where Bach conducted music for twenty-seven years.

EARLY EUROPEAN CONCERT HALLS

Secular music which began to develop more extensively in the late sixteenth and early seventeenth centuries took two principal forms, opera and chamber music. The early developments of the former were largely an outcome of the Italian Renaissance, and the cradles of most of the early operas were Florence and Venice, the first public opera house being opened in the latter city in 1637. Chamber music was performed in the large houses of cultured persons, and this continued until the First World War in 1914. Public rooms for the performance of chamber music began to be opened in the early eighteenth century. Several old coffee-houses had rooms for concerts, and it was in one of these coffee-houses in Leipzig that the great musical tradition of that city began. In 1713 Hickford's Room in James Street, Haymarket, London, was opened as a public concert room, and in 1739 Hickford opened what he called the 'new Great Room' for concerts at 41 Brewer Street, Golden Square. But although these rooms were used primarily for musical concerts, they were not designed primarily as music rooms with especial attention to musical tone. What is claimed to be the oldest public concert hall in Europe is the Holywell Music Room at Oxford, built in 1748[1] especially for the performance of Handel's oratorios. It has a seating capacity of 300 and is today regarded as acoustically satisfactory.

Leipzig has for nearly 200 years been one of the principal music centres in Europe, and one important contributory factor was the fine series of concert halls built there which have been regarded acoustically as a model for buildings of this kind. The old Gewandhaus, built to the designs of J. C. F. Dauthe in 1780, inside the old Cloth Hall, was the first and this became famous for its beauty of tone. It was pulled down in 1894 and was closely imitated by the Small Hall of the new Gewandhaus. The old hall seated about 500, it was rectangular with curved ends and had a flat ceiling, while the walls were covered with wood panelling.

In 1842 the Conservation Concert Hall was erected near the old Gewandhaus. This is not regarded as so good acoustically, as it has a segmental ceiling which tends to concentrate sound. It follows the old Gewandhaus in its walls of wood panelling which gives brightness of tone. In 1887 the great hall of the new Gewandhaus was built by Gropius and Schmieden and the design was influenced by the old hall, although it is very much larger with seats for 1,560. It is a long rectangle with curved corners, while the wood panelled walls curve up to a flat ceiling. The hall has received tributes from

427

famous musicians from all parts of the world for the beauty of its musical tone, and it is regarded by many as the finest concert hall in the world. Hope Bagenal and Alex Wood say of it[2]:

'There is no exaggeration in its reputed excellence for orchestral music. Every architect who has to build a concert hall ought to hear music within it in order to gain a sure standard of comparison. Tone is both 'full' and 'bright' and at the same time notes are distinct; instruments have 'power' and preserve their distinctive character; the pianissimo playing of 'cellos and double basses is something unrealized in England[3], accompanying is easy; treble and bass parts are at equal strength; there are no bad seats in the hall. The only criticism to be made is that brass is slightly too loud. To hear indeed the highly trained Leipzig Orchestra in the Ninth Symphony, each phrase exactly presenting itself to the ear for the fraction of a second before it is resolved in the great onward rush of the scherzo, to feel the control of sheer loudness maintained by the conductor, is a musical experience of considerable interest to the student of acoustics.'

The earliest concert hall in England large enough for a full orchestra was the Free Trade Hall in Manchester, built in 1856 to the designs of Edward Walters. Although built as a multiple purpose hall, the architect designed it largely with a view to satisfactory musical performances and the design was clearly influenced by that of the old Gewandhaus. It had a cove which connects the walls with the flat ceiling and it was semicircular at one end. The seating capacity was 2,280. It led the way to the Queen's Hall in London, built by Knightley in 1890, which had a broadly similar plan and was of similar size with seating for 2,026. Interesting features of this design were the curved splays at the orchestra end of the hall, which were introduced for the diffusion of reflected sound.

Other halls in England built primarily or partly for concerts are the great oval Albert Hall, in London, built in 1868 to the design of Fowke and Scott, which is very unsatisfactory acoustically because of the great excess of the reflected over the direct sound paths, the smaller Æolian and Wigmore Halls which are excellent for chamber music and solo recitals, and the large Colston Hall at Bristol. Hope Bagenal and Alex Wood made an acoustical analysis of the examples mentioned, and they give a list of eleven concert halls which are acknowledged as excellent for musical tone[4]. These are the vestibule of Balls Park House, Hertfordshire; Holywell Music Room, Oxford; the old Gewandhaus and the new large Gewandhaus, Leipzig; the Conservatorium, Leipzig; Beethoven Saal, Berlin; the Free Trade Hall, Manchester; the Colston Hall, Bristol; the Queen's Hall and the Æolian Hall, London; and the David Memorial Hall, Uppingham School[5]. Conspicuous features of these halls are that they are all based on the rectangular shape, they all have flat ceilings, with the exception of Balls Park House, and the Conservatorium, Leipzig, while most of them have a generous area of wood panelling on the walls which contributes much to the resonance of tone. Bagenal and Wood add other fine buildings of a different character, important for their high standard of tone; these are two churches, the Thomaskirche, Leipzig, to which reference has already been made, and St. Margaret's, Westminster; two opera houses, Covent Garden, London, and the Wagner Theatre, Bayreuth; and the Examination Hall at Cambridge. It will be noted that of this total of sixteen, one—the Bayreuth Opera House—has a fan-shaped plan. All the others have parallel side walls.

These are some of the important halls in which a fundamental purpose of design was good musical tone, and these constitute very largely the tradition that existed for the architect in the period between the wars. Progress has been made in the period in the study of acoustics, thanks to the researches of people like W. C. Sabine, P. E. Sabine, F. R. Watson, V. O. Knudsen in America; and Hope Bagenal, Alex Wood, and J. E. R. Constable in England, and the results of these researches necessarily affect design.

If a hall designed primarily for orchestral or other musical concerts is to fulfil its function well it must be conceived partly as a musical instrument, like the box of a violin or the sound board of a piano. The acoustical requirements of music are different from the acoustical requirements of speech, and therefore there must be differences in the design of concert halls on the one hand, and lecture halls and council chambers on the other, as there should be some difference in the design of an opera house and a theatre for spoken plays. But a very large number of halls, especially those in small towns, are necessarily multiple-purpose halls, for none of which purposes can they be quite perfect unless designed primarily for one.

The differences of requirement of music and speech are in the length of reverberation. Music is more effective with a longer reverberation than speech, and this affects the shape of the hall. Different forms of music require different reverberations for full effectiveness, thus choral music requires longer reverberation than instrumental music and that is why the former is often so effective in a church where the reverberation is generally long.

ACOUSTIC REQUIREMENTS

In a hall designed for music or speech every member of the audience should be in the direct path of sound, and this is most likely to be the case when the stage or platform is clearly visible to the whole audience. But even when this is so the direct sound path may be weak for some of the audience, as, for example, those sitting near the platform, as sound rises, or for those sitting at the back of the hall under the gallery. The direct sound path has thus to be reinforced by reflected sound from walls and ceiling, and reflectors are introduced for this purpose. The fan-shaped hall, which seemed at one time to be supplanting the horseshoe plan, may be one of the best shapes for seeing, but it is debatable whether it has acoustical advantages over the rectangular shape. By widening the back of the auditorium in the fan shape more seats are gained in the width, and for the same accommodation it is not necessary to have the same depth of balcony as in the rectangular or horseshoe plan. It is argued by those who advocate the fan shape that this helps to avoid the pockets of weak sound under the balconies. The disadvantages for hearing of the front seats beneath the stage or platform are overcome for the seats a little farther back by a fairly sharp rise in the floor. In the Festival Theatre at Bayreuth, the first of the fan-shaped theatres, this was overcome for the front seats which are on the same level as the stage, the orchestra being sunk.

One disadvantage of the fan shape is the difficulty in a large hall of obtaining reverberation without echo for the front seats near the orchestra, for the rear concave wall reflects the sound back to this area. To reduce the echo absorbent surfaces would have to be introduced, but as it is not possible to obtain absorbents which are more than 70 or 80 per cent effective there cannot be complete elimination of echo. The best concert halls of the past mostly have a long rectangular plan usually with a generous area of wood-panelling which gives resonance and the desired reverberation[6].

In an endeavour to overcome the defects of the fan-shaped plan Hope Bagenal in an experimental design introduced panels and ribs into the walls, convex surfaces in the proscenium walls and straight stepped rear wall. He speaks of the fan shape as 'a modern type defective as it stands and waiting for the next step in experimental design'[7]. Whether as Hope Bagenal says 'a very necessary functionalism calls for the maintenance of the fan-shaped auditorium but with a splitting up of surfaces, and locating of diffuses' is open to question. It is a subject of controversy among architects, many of whom advocate the rectangular shape[8]. Frederick Gibberd adopted the fan shape for his design for the Oxford School of Dramatic Studies, but gave stepped treatment to the walls, which, as Hope Bagenal, says, breaks the side walls thus randomizing the reflections[9].

In addition to the desirability of reinforcing direct with reflected sound it is important in designing a large hall to avoid any great excess of reflected, over direct sound paths, such as occurs in the Albert Hall. Lofty, domed, or vaulted ceilings, common in large churches, are well known for this. Concave surfaces concentrate sound, whereas convex surfaces diffuse sound. Both perform these functions in different parts of a hall. Then there is the question of the positioning of reflectors and absorbent surfaces. Reflectors are desirable near the source of sound, in the splays in front of the proscenium arch, in the part of the ceiling more immediately above the source of sound where special reflecting canopies are often placed, and at points where the direct sound may be weak. Absorbent surfaces are important for breaking up the diffusion. For example, large, plain surfaces of a material like plaster with low sound absorption, do not produce so satisfactory a decay of reverberation as a surface broken, or decorated, or texturally porous. With the broken, more porous surface the decay is more minutely graduated.

A concert hall worthy of note, built in England during the twenties, is the White Rock Pavilion at Hastings, designed by Charles Cowles-Voysey and Hugh T. Morgan and completed in 1926. Restrictions were imposed on the design by the limitations of the site which was not sufficiently deep from the street to allow a spacious layout, and the plan gives the impression of a somewhat cramped arrangement of entrance and foyer, while the front façade is flush with the domestic buildings leaving the usual width of footway. If the building could have been set back a little it would have gained in dignity, and there would have been that desirable space for the congregation of visitors which occurs outside a hall of this kind. The restriction also meant that the hall is unusually broad in relation to depth; while the smaller hall that had to be provided in accordance with requirements, has been placed in the basement surrounded by concrete walls as a protection against flooding.

Restrictions for the designer sometimes act as a stimulus, and the more difficult the problem the more ingenious the solution. Certainly with these restrictions one of the best concert halls in England has been produced. Although designed mainly with a view to efficiency for orchestral concerts and musical recitals it is also used for drama, music hall, and dances, and could be described as a multi-purpose hall, although these other uses appear to have been an afterthought which is often the case when a hall has to pay.

A low platform with splayed sides and segmental ceiling provides the space for the orchestra. The walls have wood panelling introduced to give the desired reverberation.

The broad auditorium is surrounded on three sides by a balcony of uniform depth, sufficiently shallow, to avoid acoustic shadow underneath the balcony. The hall has a flattish, segmental ceiling with a large skylight which is the principal source of daylight. At night a curtain is drawn over this skylight which acts as a reflector to the electric lighting. An arched treatment at the back and sides of the balcony, continued as rectangular columns and pilasters below, provides the main decorative effect of the walls, which are otherwise plain with a rough plaster texture.

The shape of the hall and the wall surfaces, especially the wood panelling round the platform, are calculated to give good musical tone. The architects were advised by Hope Bagenal in designing for acoustical efficiency and the hall has the reputation of being excellent in this respect. Every member of the audience is in the direct path of musical sound and the sight lines are good. Unfortunately the hall has not been improved as a musical instrument by its use for drama and music hall. When originally designed there was just the platform for the orchestra, but its use for drama meant the introduction of a proscenium arch, and heavy curtains. But economics and variety of demand necessarily determines a multi-purpose use.

The general effect of the interior is restrained without being severe. At the time it was built it was simpler in treatment than any other building of the kind in the country. The exterior is designed on symmetrical classical principles with a note of gaiety that is suitable for its purpose of entertainment in a seaside resort. This gaiety is introduced by such features as the circular plaques in the walls, the pinnacles at the top of the red pantiles surmounting the wings, and the light-cream cement rendering. The exterior also expresses its interior arrangement. The bow-shaped central façade, recessed on the first floor for a balcony which is used for refreshments in the summer, denotes the foyer, while the square flanking masses house a square tea room in one and a smoking room in the other.

Perhaps the most famous concert hall built in Europe during the twenties (1925–7) is the Salle Pleyel in Paris, designed by André Granet. Unlike the famous concert halls of the past, the plan is a trumpet or long-fan shape. Very careful attention was given to the shape with a view to good musical tone, and the architect was advised by the acoustical expert, Gustave Lyon; but whether it is entirely successful has been questioned by some critics. The platform fits in as part of the hall without any break, and the ceiling curves from the back of the platform in one continuous line, while the two balconies have tilted undersides to avoid acoustic shadow. The walls and ceiling are severely plain, and the abutment of the balconies against the walls has an uncompromising abruptness. There is no attempt at rhythmical connexion and the effect is a little harsh. Below the main hall on the ground floor are two smaller halls, the larger being the Salle Chopin, which indicates its purpose. The street façade of this building which forms the main entrance is a simple and dignified elevation with a row of tall vertical windows as the central feature. The main hall on the first floor is reached by staircases on either side of a spacious hall opening from the vestibule.

Three notable concert halls were built in Sweden during this period. Reference has already been made to one in an earlier chapter on traditional buildings that show variations on classical themes. This was the Concert Hall at Stockholm, built in 1926 and designed by Ivar Tengbom. This hall follows the traditional rectangular shape with balconies surrounding the auditorium on three sides while the space for the orchestra is designed to give the feeling that it is in the same room as the audience without any effect of separation as in some earlier concert halls and in traditional theatres. The change from this traditional concert hall to that at Hälsingborg, designed by Sven Markelius and built in 1931–3, is considerable, because the latter has all the aspects of the new architectural idiom. The hall is rectangular, with a flat ceiling, and the floor rises gently from the orchestra in the front part of the hall and then steeply at the rear. There is no balcony. Two corridors form aisled seats near the walls, and above these corridors, running nearly the whole length of the hall, are two strips of lineal lighting suspended a short distance from the ceiling. The sloping floor is designed to be removed in sections and the hall can be used for banquets and dances. Over the platform for the orchestra is a sound reflector. In theory the hall should be excellent for musical tone, and has the reputation of being generally satisfactory.

The entrance is through an elliptical vestibule which connects with a corridor leading to the foyer, this entrance group being sited at right angles to the concert hall. The exterior expresses the interior design, with blank walls and a series of vertical concrete constructional shafts for the concert hall, and a large window above the entrance, and continuous windows round the elliptical form of the vestibule to give the maximum of daylight, and also at night to radiate light and to attract.

The Concert Hall at Gothenburg

Built a little later, in 1932–4, is the Concert Hall at Gothenburg designed by Nils Einar Eriksson as part of a scheme to which reference was made in Chapter 12. The interior walls of this concert hall curve on plan in a series of steps towards the orchestra, and in the steps are long vertical slots for indirect lighting. As in the Hälsingborg Concert Hall the floor slopes up gently from the orchestra, and then a little more sharply at the rear. The ceiling is very slightly segmental transversely, and is almost a segment longitudinally. An organ projects above the orchestra and the underside of the organ gallery acts as a reflector. The walls and ceiling are lined with plywood, to give the necessary resonance.

The hall is on the first floor, the ground floor beneath being occupied by cloakrooms. At the orchestra end of the hall on the ground floor is a small hall with a rehearsal room above. A cantilevered balcony in the spacious foyer on the first floor gives access to the high rear seats. The foyer is reached by staircases from the vestibule below.

The exterior is designed partially to conform with the City Theatre opposite, but at the same time it succeeds in expressing the interior design. The upper part of the front is almost wholly a large window with a series of column-like mullions, a treatment which corresponds with the narrower horizontal window opposite. Below is a plain wall and the cantilevered canopy of the entrance. The side walls are plain, patterned with slits and small square windows. The whole building makes a rectangular block for the copper-roofed concert hall rising as a curved-topped mass from its centre.

A concert hall of this period which is regarded as good acoustically by many musicians is the Palais des Beaux-Arts in Brussels, that was built to the designs of Victor Horta in 1925–9. This hall, which seats 2,150, is egg-shaped on plan, with an almost flat floor and two tiers of side and end balconies and curved ceiling with a succession of sunk panels. The rear of the platform is stepped with the organ occupying the end wall. From the balconies are columnar supports for projecting entablatures which give the impression of supporting the ceiling, but which, like the elaborate ornament in older halls, serves the acoustic function of breaking up the sound and reducing reverberation to the desired length, which is calculated at 1.42 seconds[10] when the hall is fully occupied. Although designed primarily as a concert hall and used mainly as such, it is also used as a cinema, occasionally as a theatre, and for conferences.

A new hall which is interesting as inviting comparison with an older hall within the same building complex is that in the Kongress building at Zürich, built in 1937–9 to the designs of Max E. Haefeli, Werner M. Moser and Rudolf Steiger. In 1895 a concert hall, designed by the Austrian architects Fellmer and Helmer, was built to seat 1,546, with flat floor, balcony at the sides and end, flat ceiling with generous coves, and organ at the rear of the orchestra platform. As becomes the date of its erection it is richly ornamented which conduces to its good acoustics, as it ranks among the best in Europe. Its reverberation time is 1.6 seconds when full. A small hall for chamber music adjoins it.

In 1936 it was decided to erect a congress building in which the existing hall would be incorporated, and this was completed in 1939. It included meeting rooms and restaurants on the ground floor opening on to gardens which face the lake (although unfortunately divided from it by a road now busy with traffic). On the first floor is the old hall and a new hall has been incorporated of about the same size, separated from the old by a spacious and handsome foyer. The new hall has a flat floor with balcony at the end and sides, with a flattish segmental ceiling. This hall with its simple plain treatment is a contrast to the richly ornamented earlier hall, and it is much less satisfactory acoustically. The most distinctive features of the whole building are the very spacious and attractive foyer with the large tall windows making the interior very bright, and the fenestration of the restaurants facing the gardens, which in summer provide open-air extensions of the restaurants.

Concert Hall, Stockholm, 1926
Architect: Ivar Tengbom

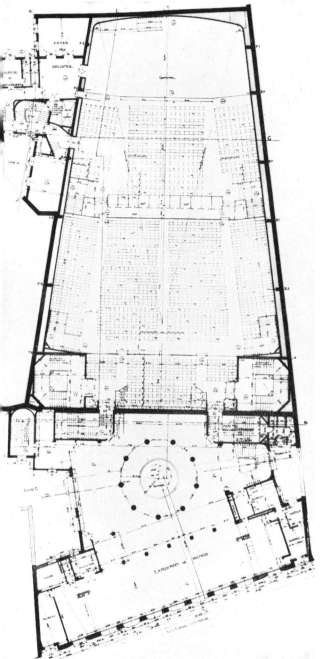

Architect: Sven Markelius

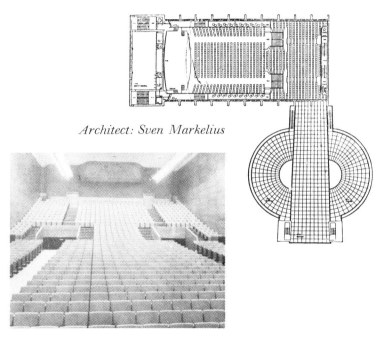

Concert Hall, Halsingborg, Sweden 1931–33. Interior and plan

Salle Pleyel, Paris, 1925–27
Plan and section

Architect: André Granet

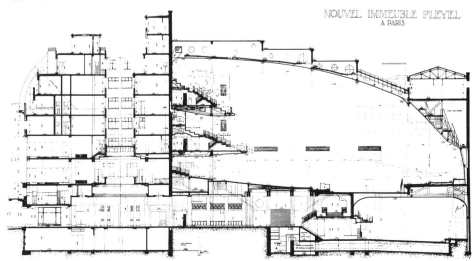

NOUVEL IMMEUBLE PLEYEL
A PARIS

Late in the thirties another notable concert hall was built in England—the Royal Philharmonic Hall, Liverpool, to replace that destroyed by fire in 1933. It was designed by Herbert J. Rowse to seat 1,700, with accommodation on the platform for an orchestra of 100, backed by tiers for a choir of 185. The large balcony with a steeply raked floor does not project over the auditorium but comes above the row of slightly elevated boxes against the rear wall. The walls and ceiling of the auditorium and the ceiling of the platform are a series of broad channels introduced for lighting and for acoustical purposes. On the whole this is one of the finest of concert halls. It is good acoustically, the sight lines are good, the seating is very comfortable while the avoidance of a seating area under a balcony in a large hall is an acoustic advantage. The area under the balcony and above the entrance hall is utilized on the first floor as a handsome Greek-like foyer, large enough for banquets and dances, with walls faced with Roman stone with decorative motifs and a terrazzo floor. The construction is mainly of steel framework within solid brick walls and reinforced concrete roof. The exterior has a simple, classical dignified appearance with vertical emphasis, broad simple masses of light sand-coloured brick wall with the distinguishing feature of two flanking tower-like projections on either side of the entrance.

MULTI-PURPOSE HALLS AND ENTERTAINMENT BUILDINGS

Many buildings for recreation cater in the one structure for several different kinds of entertainment such as drama, music, dancing, exhibitions and games of various kinds, with restaurant and cafe also included. Such buildings are erected, not so much in large cities that can easily support single and special purpose entertainment buildings, but in smaller cities and towns, where the population may not be adequate to support separate buildings for the various entertainment purposes, and particularly towns which are holiday resorts. To cater for the entertainment of visitors to seaside towns, promenade piers began to be erected in the late nineteenth century in several English resorts. They were built with open supporting framework so as to afford a minimum resistance to the sea. A hall that could be used for concerts, the theatre and later the cinema, was generally erected on the pier with sometimes other small pavilions for various amusements. Very few of the structures on these piers are of architectural merit and it seems that seaside entertainment buildings that possess any degree of architectural distinction are generally on shore. Perhaps the most notable erected between the wars in England was the De La Warr Pavilion at Bexhill-on-Sea, built in 1934–5 to the designs of Eric Mendelsohn and Serge Chermayeff who won the competition award. It consists of a long low building by the sea with a spacious entrance hall in the centre terminating on the façade towards the sea, with a semicircular glass projection enclosing a spiral staircase—a typical Mendelsohn feature. A long thin arm stretches to the east, with restaurant on the ground floor and library and lounge on the first floor. The walls here are essentially glass screens divided by concrete mullions, those on the ground floor opening to an extensive terrace. The broader wing to the west has blank walls enclosing a multi-purpose hall—theatre, concert hall, ballroom. An even distribution

436

Kongress Building, Zürich, 1937–39, foyer and exterior view
Architects: Max E. Haefeli, Werner M. Moser and Rudolf Steiger

Royal Philharmonic Hall,
Liverpool, 1934–35

Architect: Herbert J. Rowse

Front view, rear elevation,
auditorium and foyer

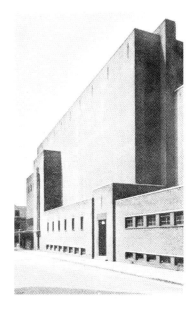

General view

Ground floor plan (facing pag

De la Warr Pavilion, Bexhill-on-Sea, 1935
Architects: Eric Mendelsohn and Serge Chermayeff

South staircase and terrace facing the sea

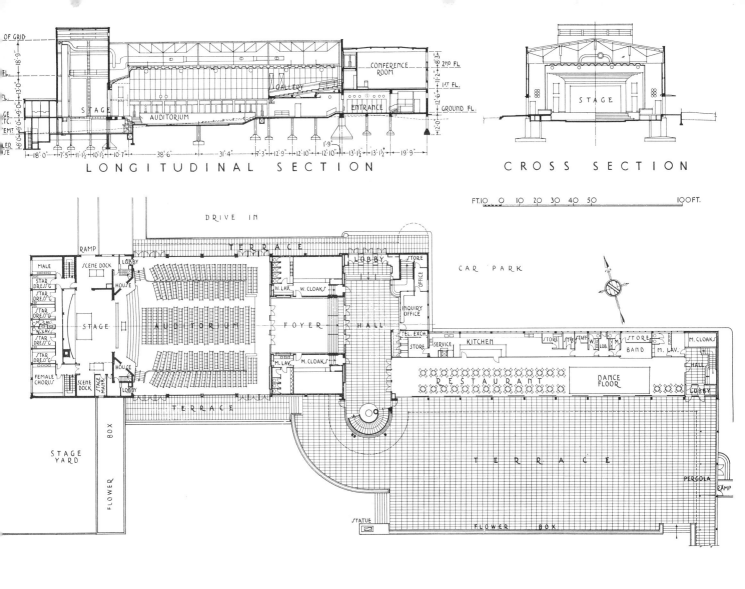

LONGITUDINAL SECTION

OF GRID

CONFERENCE ROOM

GALLERY

STAGE

AUDITORIUM

ENTRANCE

2ND FL
1ST FL
GROUND FL

18'0" 7'5" 11'6" 10'10½" 10'7" 38'6" 31'4" 7'3" 12'9" 12'10" 12'10" 13'1½" 13'1½" 19'9"

CROSS SECTION

STAGE

FT.10 0 10 20 30 40 50   100 FT.

DRIVE IN

TERRACE

CAR PARK

RAMP

MALE

SCENE DOCK

LOBBY

STAR DRESS'G
STAR DRESS'G
STAR DRESS'G
W. LAV.
STAR DRESS'G
STAR DRESS'G

STAGE

AUDITORIUM

FOYER   HALL

W. LAV. W. CLOAKS

M. LAV. M. CLOAKS

LOBBY

STORE
OFFICE

INQUIRY OFFICE

EL. EXCH.

STORE

SERVICE KITCHEN

STORE STAFF W. STORE BAND M. CLOAKS

RESTAURANT

DANCE FLOOR

LOBBY

HALL

FEMALE CHORUS

SCENE DOCK

STAGE MGR

LOBBY

TERRACE

STAGE YARD

FLOWER BOX

TERRACE

PERGOLA
RAMP

STATUE

FLOWER BOX

Maison du People at Clichy, 1938–39   *Architects: Eugene Beaudovin and Marcel Lods*

Plan of building arranged as a market hall

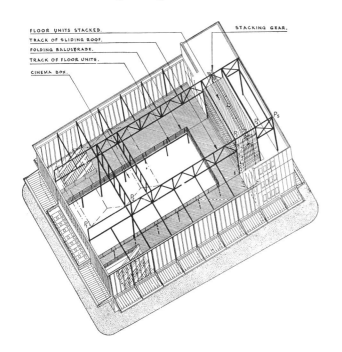

FLOOR UNITS STACKED.
TRACK OF SLIDING ROOF.
FOLDING BALUSTRADE.
TRACK OF FLOOR UNITS.
CINEMA BOX.

STACKING GEAR.

Plan of building arranged for cinema

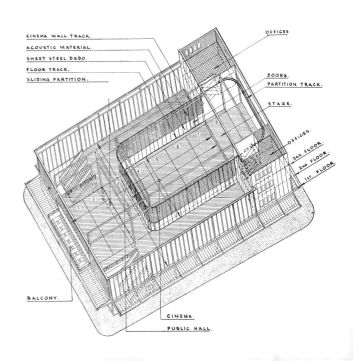

CINEMA WALL TRACK.
ACOUSTIC MATERIAL.
SHEET STEEL DADO.
FLOOR TRACK.
SLIDING PARTITION.

OFFICES

DOORS
PARTITION TRACK.

STAGE.

OFFICES
3RD. FLOOR.
2ND FLOOR.
1ST. FLOOR.

BALCONY.

CINEMA

PUBLIC HALL.

of sound was the aim in the design of this hall, obtained by a sound board over the forestage, and a special reflectant ceiling, involving a patterning of large saucer-shaped recesses. The construction of the building is of welded steel framework.

The main impression of the exterior is of a long low building with glass panelled wall extending eastward, a blank wall extending westwards, with the central hall between. Its character of long horizontality articulated in the centre with a semicircular glass projection is to some extent determined by its position by the sea. Only partly completed, it was originally conceived with a circular swimming pool between the pavilion and the sea on the axis of the main hall, and reached by a pergola at the east end. Continuing the axis line a short pier for bathers juts out to sea. A curved wall westward completes the enclosure of the terrace and extensive lawn. At the west end a short flight of steps descends from the lawn and flanking this a pedestal was to hold a figure of Persephone by Frank Dobson. She was designed gazing out to sea in the direction of Beachy Head to symbolize the awakening in the Spring to the joys of earth.

Other seaside recreational buildings of a similar modern character in which steel and concrete and large areas of glass were the principal media were occasionally erected in Europe during the thirties. A particularly notable example again in England, and built a little earlier than the De La Warr Pavilion, was the Royal Corinthian Yacht Club building at Burnham-on-Crouch, designed by Joseph Emberton in 1930.

The building is situated on the north bank of the river Crouch. It is a steel-frame structure of three floors, with brick cavity walls faced with cement, erected on a concrete platform supported on concrete piles with their foundations in the river. The first two floors are occupied by clubrooms and the third floor by bedrooms, each floor opening on to a terrace. At the east end is the staircase block with an additional floor forming a turret with a balcony, which serves as the starting box. Almost the whole of the south wall is of glass, while the end walls and the north walls, towards the cold winds, have only narrow slits for windows. The value of large glass walls to the south in this situation, although apparent in the summer, may cause apprehensions about maintaining a good interior temperature in the winter, but they sometimes assist in doing this because Burnham-on-Crouch has a high record of sunshine, and the winter sun shining on the glass, contributes to maintaining the temperature.

The glass façade and the horizontal emphasis of the white terraces makes this building harmonious with its setting and suggest that here is a marine architecture which, while having something of the character of a modern liner, yet has the static quality that roots it to the earth. It has the brightness and lucidity which goes well with the clear, bright atmosphere of its location. Although simple and direct in design it succeeds where a more elaborate and stylistic design would have failed.

440

In several other buildings erected at the water's edge in various parts of Europe at this time the horizontal implications of the situation determine to some extent the design. Several of the lakeside buildings in Switzerland are attractive examples, while Norway provides a notable example in the Sundoya Restaurant on Lake Tyrifjorden, about 20 miles from Oslo, designed by Bjercke and Eliassen in 1934. Built on an island of the lake linked by a road to both shores, it is a three-storey building with a definite horizontal ship-like character. On the ground floor a long restaurant opens to a terrace on the south side, with a lounge and entrance hall enfolding a spiral staircase on the east side. Guest rooms are above.

Club buildings to serve small areas and community centres began to be erected in increasing numbers during the thirties. The genesis of the modern community centre can be traced to the founding of social and university settlements in the late nineteenth century. In the thirties community centres arose in the neighbourhoods of towns and suburbs as places where residents could meet for social purposes and where voluntary societies and local clubs could pursue their activities, while they were often linked with health centres. In the early days of community centres, the premises were sometimes in school buildings, but were more often of a makeshift character in a church hall or old house, or something similar. Buildings designed specifically as community centres were rare before the Second World War. Those that were provided were often designed as part of a school like Impington Village College (Chapter 20) or part of a Health Centre like that at Peckham.

A development somewhat similar to the community centre in England is that of the workers' clubs and palaces of culture in Russia. These were first housed in the early twenties in the palaces and large houses of the Russian Royal Family and aristocracy, but later special buildings were erected, designed according to the particular requirements of each club. But the building of community and health centres in England and workers' clubs in Russia, although having tentative beginnings in the thirties, did not become specific architectural exercises until about 1950 when they became fairly common.

A need in small cities and towns, as previously implied, is the building and hall that can be used for a wide variety of purposes. Multi-purpose halls are most efficient if they can be functionally adapted for different purposes by mechanical devices, similar to the changes and conversions in the total theatre by Walter Gropius (see Chapter 26). Many ideas of this kind had been forthcoming before the Second World War, but few materialized. One that is notable for prompting further developments on similar lines is the Maison du People at Clichy, designed and built in 1938–9 by Eugene Beaudovin and Marcel Lods. This building comprises a market hall, a public meeting hall, also used for concerts and theatre, a cinema and offices. The market hall is used in the daytime and is converted to the other uses in the evenings. The conversion is ingenious, made possible by the steel frame and panel construction. The market hall consists of a ground floor occupying the whole site, surrounded by a gallery on three sides. When the the building is converted to a public hall for meetings, concerts or cinema, the balustrade of the gallery is folded down, and the open well is closed by sections of floor, which are stacked in a space above the hall stage, and moved into position to form the floor by a motorized operation. When used as a cinema the central part of the first floor is generally enclosed by partitions[11].

The exterior of the hall is effective with a pattern of vertical strips of enamelled steel with glass windows backed with translucent fluted plastic, thus giving a soft light to the interior.

References and Notes

1. See J. H. Mee, *The Oldest Music Room in Europe*, London, 1911.
2. Hope Bagenal and Alex Wood, *Planning for Good Acoustics*, London, 1931, p. 90. This is one of the best accounts in English of halls of various kinds studied from the standpoint of their acoustical value.
3. This was written in 1931. It is a little doubtful if it would still have been written after the completion of the Festival Hall in London in 1951.
4. Hope Bagenal and Alex Wood, *Planning for Good Acoustics*, London, 1931.
5. Of these the Queen's Hall was destroyed by bombs in 1940, the Colston Hall referred to is the second which was altered in 1936 when the seating capacity was increased. This did not improve the acoustics. In 1945 the hall was destroyed by fire. It was rebuilt in 1950–1.
6. It is outside the scope of this work to consider scientifically the problems of acoustics. If the reader wishes to study the subject further the book by Bagenal and Wood, previously cited, is a detailed study of the subject. See also Hope Bagenal's later work *Practical Acoustics and Planning Against Noise*, London, 1941. The report on Sound Insulation and Acoustics by the Acoustics Committee on the P.S.I.R., Post-War Building Study No. 14, gives a brief survey. Another useful book in which the principal concert halls of the world are studied from the standpoint of good acoustics is Leo L. Beranek's *Music, Acoustics and Architecture*, New York and London, 1962.
7. Hope Bagenal, *Practical Acoustics and Planning Against Noise*, London, 1941, pp. 81–84 and 113.
8. The Festival Concert Hall in London built in 1949–51 is rectangular on plan with splayed sides for the orchestra.
9. Paper on General Purpose Halls given at the Building Research Congress 1951.
10. See Leo L. Beranek, *Music, Acoustics and Architecture*, New York and London, 1962, pp. 556–557.
11. For a detailed description of this hall see article in *The Journal of the Royal Institute of British Architects*, August 1946, pp. 448–455.

29 Buildings for broadcasting 1922–1940

A NEW PURPOSE for building arose in the twenties with the beginning of broadcasting, and several buildings of functional and architectural interest were erected in Europe for this purpose between the two world wars.

Broadcasting began in the USA in 1920 and in Europe in 1922. Great Britain was a little ahead of other European countries and, was followed closely by the Scandinavian countries, Germany and The Netherlands. France and the Mediterranean countries were a little later in following.

In Great Britain there was a little broadcasting by a few industrial firms and by amateurs from early 1922, but the systematic broadcasting with a service for the public did not begin until the establishment of the British Broadcasting Company Ltd, in October, 1922. The Company initially established eight stations in the most densely populated areas—London, Birmingham, Manchester, Newcastle, Cardiff, Glasgow, Aberdeen and Bournemouth—between November 1922, when systematic broadcasting actually began, and October 1923. The headquarters were at Magnet House, Kingsway, London.

In the early days of broadcasting in Europe there was some uncertainty as to its future, and thus existing premises were generally adapted for studios and offices, and it was not until the late twenties that sufficient confidence in the future prompted the erection of special buildings for the purpose, and many of the earliest buildings were transmitting stations. Few of these had architectural distinction, perhaps the most notable of the earlier examples is the short-wave station at Kootwyk in Holland designed by W. J. Luthmas. Several regional transmitting stations were built in Great Britain during the late twenties. The London Regional Station at Brookman's Park near Potters Bar was built in 1929, with the first twin-wave transmitter in the world. In spite of a necessary primary concern with function the building is formal, massive and symmetrical with a Greek-like reminiscence. It provided the model for several subsequent transmitter buildings.

The first premises of the BBC in Kingsway proved inadequate from the outset, and a search was made for new premises. As a result the empty west wing of the building of the Institution of Electrical Engineers at the corner of the Embankment and Savoy Hill was acquired and the BBC moved there in March 1923. To make the new premises suitable much conversion and some extensions had to be made. For example, the first studio was built on the top floor and came into use in May 1923. It was small, heavily draped and acoustically rather dead, and was used for a variety of purposes: talks, drama, and for orchestral and choral music for which it did not provide the best conditions. Another studio much larger (45 ft by 30 ft) was provided in the building in the autumn of the same year, and this also was used for a variety of purposes from reading the news to a military band. It was soon obvious that for efficient broadcasting and with further developments more ample accommodation would be necessary, but one of the difficulties was to get widespread acceptance of broadcasting as a potentially important communicating, entertainment, educational and cultural medium, for in the mid-twenties only a very small proportion of the public in European countries listened to broadcasts, probably not more than 20 per cent. An event that gave a tremendous fillip to broadcasting in Britain was the General Strike in May 1926, for when other means of communication, like newspapers, almost ceased to function the BBC carried an all-day service of news and general information, which not only told what was happening during the course of the strike, but had a moral effect in combating a feeling of isolation. At the end of 1926, The British Broadcasting Company Ltd, ceased to exist and was succeeded by the British Broadcasting Corporation[1]. From 1923 to 1927 the number of wireless licences in Great Britain had risen from about 200,000 to about 2,000,000, but still only a fairly small minority of households.

In the early days of Broadcasting, Great Britain was followed closely by Denmark and Sweden. Actually by 1930 the number of licences per thousand population in Denmark and Sweden was ahead of Great Britain. (Denmark 119 per thousand, Sweden 79 and Great Britain 76.) Other countries where broadcasting was becoming popular were Austria and Germany. As previously mentioned it was far less popular in the Mediterranean countries. Climate may have some influence. After the establishment of the Corporation and the rapid growth of broadcasting in the late twenties, it was essential to acquire much more adequate premises. By this time several of the various studios required were scattered about London and the vicinity.

The new headquarters building of the BBC was commenced in 1929 and completed and in use in 1932. It is situated in Langham Place at the north end of Regent Street and near the old Queen's Hall in the very centre of London, which no doubt was a

Broadcasting House, London, 1929–32   *Architect: G. Val Myer*

Exterior view of main entrance elevation, Langham Place. Interior of concert hall

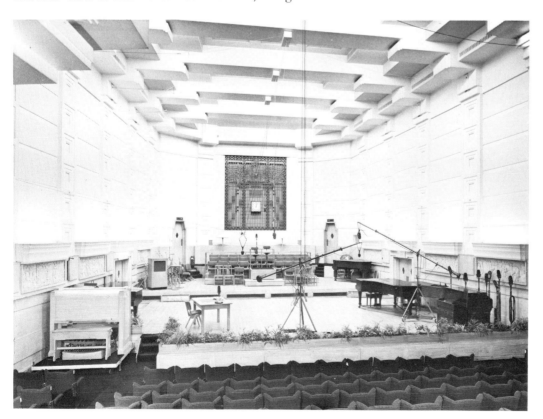

determining factor, but the site is hardly large enough to allow for future expansions, which, as events have shown, have been much needed. The site has been criticized on these grounds, as, for example, by Professor C. H. Reilly, writing of the architecture of the new building in the BBC Year Book for 1933. How the directors, he says, 'came, to choose such a site it is a little difficult . . . to understand. One would have thought that they would have made every effort to have obtained a free open site instead of a restricted one, a site where their building could have expanded upwards and outwards as best suited its peculiar character'. This is a valid point. It is far more important for a broadcasting headquarters building which is to contain offices and studios to be sited on land large enough to permit expansion, than that the position should be central. As it is the studio accommodation has become inadequate, and studios are distributed in various parts of London, at Maida Vale (3 studios) in the Camden Theatre, the Aeolian Hall and many other places. In several other capitals in Europe this mistake has been avoided.

The building to which a brief reference was made in Chapter 14 was designed by G. Val Myer. The purpose of the building—a new purpose with no prototypes—was to house the various studios for broadcasting with the related control room and accommodation for technical equipment, and to provide the various administrative offices as efficiently as possible. It was necessary to make the studios acoustically satisfactory for their various purposes and to insulate them from external noise. The problem of providing the required twenty-two studios was made more difficult because of the limited space, and it was impossible to arrange them in a horizontal grouping while providing the necessary sound insulation. Difficult problems often beget ingenious solutions and that provided by Val Myer in this building is an example. Instead of a horizontal grouping—all on one floor—the studios are grouped partly vertically in a tower served by lifts, in the centre of the building with thick brick walls round them for insulation, and artificially ventilated, while the administrative offices are placed round the outer part of the building with adequate natural lighting and ventilation.

Two studios for Vaudeville and Dance Bands, separated by waiting and storerooms, are in the basement, and the large concert hall of 120,900 cubic feet vertically spans three floors—lower ground, ground, and first floor. This is separated from the studios immediately above on the third floor by insulating offices and storerooms. On the third floor were the studios for talks, religious services and children's hour. On the fourth two news rooms, then another acoustic separation from the studios above by means of offices and music library on the fifth floor. The sixth and seventh floors have ten studios for speech, musical comedy, gramophone and effects. Lastly on the top floor is the large studio for military bands, which is the only studio to have natural lighting. On this floor also is a small studio for debates, and the control room. The most notable room in the suite of offices is the semicircular Council Chamber.

Externally the most effective part of the building is the semicircular south façade with the main entrance with Eric Gill's carved statue of Prospero above the recession of the fifth and sixth floors flanking the central shaft surmounted by the clock, all with a patterning of vertical windows on plain walls. It is not only a pleasing building itself, but relates well to its surroundings, especially to the two-tiered circular colonnades of Nash's church of All Souls, while it forms, with the church, an interesting visual terminal feature for Regent Street and Langham Place.

One of the most important factors in designing studios for broadcasting is satisfactory acoustics, which have requirements somewhat different from traditional concert hall and theatre acoustics. In the case of the large concert hall at Broadcasting House, it was finished in the rough for the experts to test its acoustic qualities and then its finishing materials were determined after consultation[2].

About the same time as Broadcasting House was being built in London, a large building with the same purpose was being erected in Berlin. This was on a much more spacious site than the London building and permitted sound insulation by means of courtyards. The site is roughly an equilateral triangle, with a five- and six-storey continuous office block forming the periphery, and the concert hall and studios forming the central block, flanked by open courtyards, and joined to the outer blocks centrally at the base of the triangle and at its apex. Although in the forefront of European broadcasting, yet about a year later than Great Britain, Germany was able to profit by British experience. In one important matter the British system, however, was not followed. Instead of one organization with its headquarters and main facilities in the capital city, as in Great Britain, in Germany several companies were formed with centres in the large cities all over Germany—Berlin, Hamburg, Frankfurt, Munich, Leipzig and other cities. Each company and centre made its own programme, but later fusion and cooperation developed under the umbrella of the Reichs-Rundfunk-Gesellschaft. In Great Britain, of course, regional centres gradually organized their own programmes necessitating buildings with studios for the purpose.

From the architectural and planning standpoints among the notable headquarters and studio buildings for broadcasting are those at Hilversum, near Amsterdam, and Broadcasting House in Copenhagen. In the former, built to the designs of Merkelbach and Karsten, the site was such as to allow room for expansion. The first part, consisting mainly of concert hall, studios, control rooms and cafe was completed in 1936. With the expansion of broadcasting, additions were made in 1938–40, and further additions after the war in 1947–9. The theatre and concert hall are fan shaped with balcony, and adjoining this on the west side and contained within a general curve are a series of studios for music and talks, mostly on the first floor, together with control rooms and stores. Sound insulation of four of the studios is effected by separation by two stairways. Additions made in 1938–40 consisted of a large restaurant on the first floor

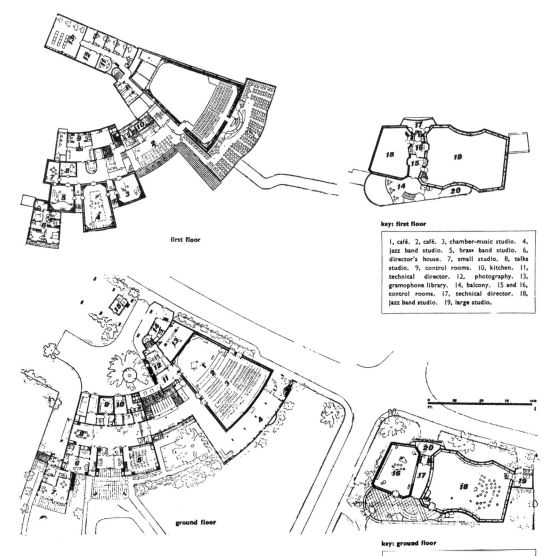

first floor

ground floor

Broadcasting Studios at Hilversum, 1938–40

Architects: Merkelbach and Karsten

Plan and exterior view

raised on pilotis at the end of the concert hall and presenting an attractive curved façade to the south. Also raised on pilotis at the stage end of the hall is the addition of a series of first floor rooms including a gramophone library. The later additional studios provided after the Second World War are in a separate building, across the minor road on the south side and reached by a tunnel. The construction is of reinforced concrete frame and the whole attractive group is planned and built with flexibility and consciousness of expanding needs.

The Copenhagen Radio House was designed and built mainly between 1936 and 1940, and although used from 1941 onwards was not finally completed until after the withdrawal of the German forces in 1945. The architect was Vilhelm Lauritzen, the chief engineers responsible for technical matters were Kay Christiansen and Fr. Heegaard, with Chr. Nokkentued and Vilhelm Jordan responsible for the acoustics. The site is an extensive one with scope for additions. The essential character of the plan is the grouping of the principal large studios round a central lounge. In front of this to the south are the administrative blocks facing Rosenorns Alle, and to the east is the large concert hall. The administrative blocks are designed on a 50 square feet grid, so that all office dimensions are multiples of this while window mullions are at 3 feet intervals against which office partitions can be placed. The administrative blocks are long and narrow with central corridors and offices on either side; the east and longer block is four storeys, and the western block five, the latter being well set back. Near where they adjoin is the main entrance leading to a handsome entrance hall with floor and walls lined with marble from Greenland, and large windows occupied with decorative plants facing the street. Beyond the hall is the cloakroom, to the right of this is the staircase leading to the office, but straight ahead is a short stairway down to the artists lounge, central to the large studios.

There were eighteen studios when the building was originally completed in 1945. A few small studios for news, talks, interviews and discussions are in the western administrative block; and the large studios to the right and left of the long central lounge are mainly for music, designed to hold audiences as well as performers. The largest for theatre and various forms of entertainment holds an audience of 250. The next studio (3) is for choirs and small orchestras which has adjustable panels for acoustic purposes. Studio 4 is designed for smaller groups and soloists. On the left hand side are four studios of different sizes for a variety of purposes, soloists, plays, jazz bands and discussions, while one is for sound effects. The main administrative blocks are built of reinforced concrete frame, but the studios are built of brick, and for sound insulation purposes each studio is a separate structure on a separate foundation.

The concert hall (studio 1) to the east, which is the pride of Radio House, has a fan-shaped plan, with platform with two terraces for orchestra of a hundred backed by an organ. There are 1,200 seats for the audience divided equally into 400 each on the ground floor and in the two balconies. The volume is 42,000 cubic feet. The roof is curved shell concrete 4.8 inches thick, with a concrete undulating ceiling below 2.4 inches thick, covered with strips of beechwood on laths. The walls like the other studios are of brick lined internally with laminated wood for acoustic purposes, the degree of sound absorption being determined both by perforation of the sheets and filling the space between the brick walls and wood lining with materials of different density. In some of the studios the wood panels are clipped on and can be removed to vary the reverberation. Although linked both with the studio group and the administrative building the concert hall has a handsome separate entrance from Julius Thomsens Gade with a spacious foyer. Externally the whole building is faced with pale yellow unglazed tiles. Although the group of buildings on this corner site is composed of diverse elements as determined by their purpose, they combine well into a satisfactory ensemble. It is essentially a building in the modern functionalist idiom, whereas Broadcasting House in London, in spite of its modern purpose, belongs a little to the old world of traditional Renaissance architecture. Also on the site of Radio House in Copenhagen there is scope for expansion which was felt to be needed in 1950. The Copenhagen Radio House is possibly the best building for Broadcasting erected in Europe before 1945.

The acoustics of sound broadcasting in the period between the wars was very much in its infancy. The main problems occurred with the broadcasting of orchestral, choral and other music where a room or hall of a certain size was necessary, large enough for an audience, because this appears to have a psychological effect on performers. Also a large number of concerts are broadcast from concert halls and opera houses designed acoustically for giving the best results to the audience in the hall. There are, however, certain differences of requirements in such halls and studios designed for broadcasting, although as in the case of the concert hall in Radio House at Copenhagen the obvious intention was to satisfy both.

When speech is broadcast from a large room with reflecting surfaces the listener in his room at home gets both the direct and reverberating sound, and unless a long reverberation is a desirable effect, as may be the case of a ghostly character in a play, this is a disadvantage and with rapid speaking there is a blurring of speech. The listener also gets the reverberation in his own room at home. For talks, news and discussions, direct sound is all that is needed, and thus these are broadcast with advantage from small rooms with little or no reverberation. With the large concert studio the matter is far from simple, especially as good reception both in the hall and at home is a matter of opinion. The subjective conditions of music acoustics prevents it being an exact science, while different music requires different reverberation. For me a reverberation of 1.5 seconds is excellent for a Mozart symphony, but too short for a Handel choral work, where I feel it could be 3 seconds with advantage. In piano music, too, the differences are apparent. In Mozart sonatas where the dance is apparent

Copenhagen Radio House, 1936–45

Architect: Vilhelm Lauritzen

Interior of concert hall, general exterior view and plan

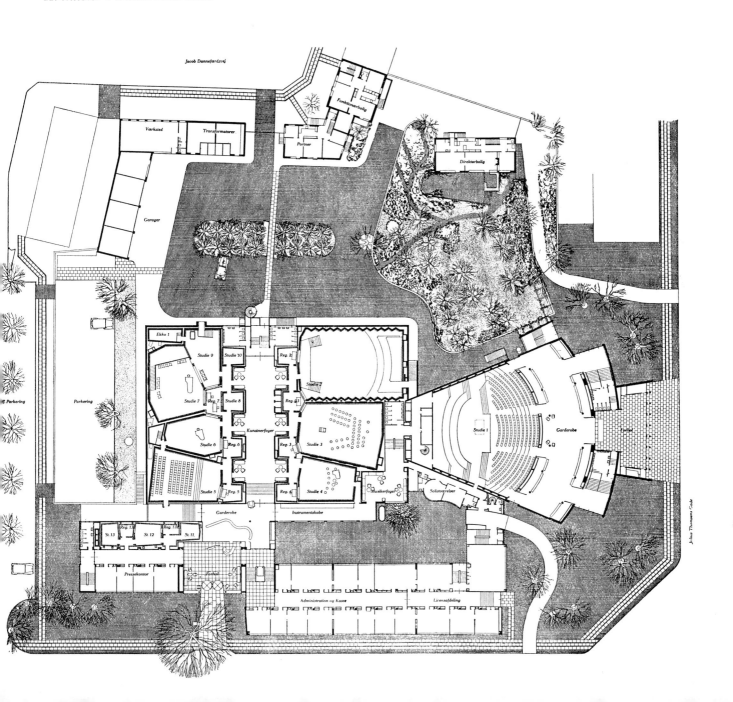

a short reverberation of 1.5 seconds emphasizing the staccato effect is desirable, but in the impressionistic piano music of Debussy something a little longer is required.

In the large concert hall it is generally the practice to have the reflecting surfaces near the source of sound, with the absorbent surfaces away at the back of the hall to prevent echo, and various vibrant or perforated panels between. The purpose is to throw the sound out to the audience, and the aim is that in all positions the same sounds are received, an ideal impossible of achievement, because there are inevitably some parts of the hall better than others for hearing. To be very near the orchestra is not to hear it as one, while there are generally a few acoustic shadows in a hall. In broadcasting from such a hall it is necessarily the aim to place the microphone in the one position that gets the best and most unified reception, and this is the purpose in the smaller musical studio. In the early days of broadcasting it was sometimes the practice to have two or more microphones, especially if there were several soloists in a choral work, but this practice was abandoned as not giving the best reception.

The aim in the music studio is to get the same sound in all parts of the studio, which means the right degrees of diffusion and absorption. This gives flexibility in the placing of microphones. A good condition would apparently be to reduce reverberation to a minimum and have, as in speech, only direct sound. This would be possible with a soloist, but would be impossible with an orchestra of say 40 even if they were closely packed. Also with the studio almost dead the orchestra and individual players would hardly hear themselves, which has a bad psychological effect. Some reverberation, about 1 to 1.5 seconds, is necessary and unity of sound can best be achieved by diffusion.

T. Somerville, an acoustic expert of the BBC, pointed out in referring to the design of concert halls where the purpose has been to reflect the sound forward from the orchestra towards an audience, 'that if done efficiently the diffuse conditions necessary for good acoustics cannot be obtained'. He contends that, 'under conditions of complete diffusion, the production of a sound at any point in an enclosure results in an even distribution throughout the enclosure'. He goes on to point out that 'as no orchestra can ever approach a point source dimensionally, the only way to obtain an even distribution of sound energy and to be sure that every instrument can be heard at every other point in the enclosure is to make sure that scattering is very efficient.'[3]

A good deal of experiment was conducted in the thirties with methods of diffusion. One was the installation of cylindrical diffusers for walls and ceiling. When the concert studio in Geneva was built with a volume of 130,000 cubic feet it had flat walls and the diffusion was regarded as unsatisfactory, and engineers had difficulty in finding good microphone positions. Wooden half-cylinders were introduced in 1947 along the walls and this greatly improved the diffusion[4]. The difficulty here, however, is that diffusion is only on one horizontal plane, and in order to get it on a vertical plane as well, horizontal cylinders must be introduced and this was done in a music studio in Berne in 1950. It is possible that the best means of getting satisfactory diffusion is by scattering, that is by having irregularities with alternate reflecting and absorbent surfaces. It is a subject in which experimentation is probably endless, but it is of importance to the architect called upon to design studios of broadcasting and concert halls.

The acoustics of broadcasting studios may have some influence on the future design of the concert hall for direct listening. Formerly the aim in concert hall design was to reflect the sound from the orchestra to the audience, but the more even diffusion of the studio for broadcasting has clear advantages also for the concert hall apart from the considerations of broadcasting.[5]

REFERENCES AND NOTES

1. Much of the information regarding the early days of broadcasting in Great Britain is taken from the *BBC Year Books 1930–1933*.
2. See notes on the Building by the architect G. Val Myer in the *BBC Year Book 1932*, pp. 57–62.
3. T. Somerville, *Acoustics in Broadcasting*, Building Research Congress, London, 1951.
4. See W. Furrer, *Modern Continental Practice in the Acoustical Design of Broadcasting Studies*, Building Research Congress, London, 1951.
5. It is not possible to consider more than very briefly the subject of the acoustics of broadcasting studios and concert halls, even if I were qualified to do so. There are several useful books and papers on the subject among which may be mentioned:
F. L. Ward, Helmholz Resonators as Acoustic Treatment at the New Swansea Studios, *BBC Quarterly*, Autumn 1952.
G. L. S. Gifford, Membrane Sound Absorbers and Their Application to Broadcasting Studios, *BBC Quarterly*, Winter 1952–3.
P. H. Parkin and H. R. Humphreys, *Acoustics, Noise and Buildings*, London, 1963.
Leo L. Beranek, *Music, Acoustics and Architecture*, New York and London, 1962.
Sandy Brown, Acoustic Design of Broadcasting Studios, *BBC*, London, 1964.
D. K. Jones and H. D. Harwood, *Recent Research on Studio and Sound Problems*, BBC, London, 1967.

PART IV

Political Determinism and

Classical Monumentality

1930–1940

Headquarters Building of the Royal Institute of British Architects, London, 1932–34

Architect: G. Grey Wornum

30 *The power of the Greek, Roman and Renaissance traditions*

THROUGHOUT EUROPE IN THE late twenties and early thirties there was a resurgence of nationalism that gradually grew in strength and became a contributory cause of the Second World War of 1939 to 1945. It began with Fascism and the rule of Mussolini in Italy during the twenties, it manifested in Germany with National Socialism and the rule of Hitler in the early thirties, it manifested on ideological grounds in Russia, and to a less extent as a kind of defensive repercussion in France and Britain, and the smaller European countries.

This wave of nationalism and intensification of pride in country had a tremendous influence on architecture, and the thirties present a very pronounced example of political power determining the character of contemporary architecture. It was displayed principally in buildings of a monumental quality, in government, public and civic buildings, sports arenas, university buildings and headquarters of large institutions and business firms, rather than in buildings of a more strictly utilitarian character. The intention was to symbolize in the principal buildings of the time the grandeur and achievement of the state. Such buildings were erected at Nürnberg for the purpose of celebrating the achievements of German National Socialism; or in the exhibition in Rome projected for 1942 by Mussolini to show to the world the achievements of Fascism and the Italian State, an exhibition with an intended legacy of a handsomely planned area south of the city with permanent monumental buildings, several of which were erected before the war ended the scheme. On a smaller scale civic dignity found expression in the monumental town halls that were built all over Europe at this time.

To express the achievements and greatness of a state in buildings the architects of Italy, Germany and Russia working in conformity with their briefs aimed at a monumental architecture of grandeur and dignity, that should, at the same time, be expressive of the age. The buildings must be monuments of these great ages in Italy and Germany. To Mussolini and Hitler and their architects Marcello Piacentini and Albert Speer and others, the requisite monumental architecture was not to be found

457

in the new movements where design begins with utilitarian purpose and is realized by modern industrial methods with the modern materials of steel, concrete and glass. To them such architecture seemed inadequate. How then was such an architecture to be achieved? It must be monumental, that is, it must act as a reminder of achievement, but at the same time the reminder must be couched in the most dignified terms. Such an architecture was most obviously to be found in the great classical buildings of Greece, Rome and the Renaissance that exhibited the qualities of permanence, solidity and dignity in a more marked degree than any other. For these qualities one turns to such sources rather than to, say, Gothic that with lofty vaults in stone framed structures and large windows suggests lightness and an evanescent mysticism rather than permanence and weight. In a later age architects may have seen this monumental quality in the grandeur and impressiveness of large scale structures, but this was perhaps too progressive and imaginative for the forces that at that time guided the fate of European countries. Such imaginative conceptions belonged, however, to the work of the truly modern architects like Le Corbusier and the Germans who left their native land.

The question arises: can this classical monumental architecture be expressive of its age as its authors desired? The meaning of monumental is to remind, and to remind of the age in which the buildings were erected they should be expressive of that age. But if the characters of classical dignity and grandeur are borrowed for the purpose it is in the nature of false monumentality, and that must be the criticism of the classic monumentality in architecture that accompanied the wave of European nationalism during the thirties. True monumentality, that is architecture which commemorates by being expressive of its age, is found rather in buildings which are structures arising with the conditions of the age, preferably with a certain grandeur and magnificence, and not buildings in which character is borrowed from a past age whether it be ancient Greece, Rome or the Renaissance. Thus the truly monumental architecture of the Victorian age is seen in the great railway termini, great bridges like the Forth bridge and magnificent hall buildings like the Crystal Palace.

In the classical monumentality that obtained in the thirties there were, however, degrees. Many architects, even Piacentini and Speer, tried to give the revived classicism some modern feeling. Many did so mainly by simplification which often resulted in severity and dullness. Others endeavoured to reconcile the revived classicism with designing strictly according to utilitarian purpose, while others found in various Greek, Roman and Renaissance principles of design formulae for dignity and monumentality which they applied to modern buildings. Others were influenced, even hypnotized, by classical mathematical principles of proportion.

All this means that classical principles of design were still very much active as an undercurrent in architectural practice, and the desire for classical monumentality prompted a renewed study of these principles. One such study, illuminating because it was off the beaten track, was that of the progressively minded Le Corbusier who renewed with vigour in the thirties and during the Second World War the study of the principles of proportion that he had begun earlier[1]. The results of his earlier studies can be seen in *Vers une Architecture*. One result of his later studies is his two volume work on *The Modulor*, the first volume carrying the subtitle 'a harmonious measure to the human scale universally applicable to architecture and mathematics' and the second 'let the user speak next'[2]. Some exemplification of his theories is apparent in his work. Other architects of the avant garde in whose work classical principles of design are apparent are Mies van der Rohe, Walter Gropius and Giuseppe Pagano.

In the functional architecture of the twenties in Germany, central Europe and France design emanated largely from purpose and efficient construction, and from the decorative expression of these by various means, but with architecture based partly on classical principles there are additional determining factors of design, planning and proportion, variously venerated by architects which are prompted mainly by aesthetic and esoteric motives. They result in a kind of authority in design itself, based on organic form, geometry, mathematics, musical scale associated with cosmic theories, apart from the use and construction of a building, all of which variously served in the practice of classical monumentality.

These principles have evolved in modern times with a variety of origins and traditions giving rise to various yet related systems of design. For the sake of clarity a rough classification should be made to cover their manifestations in modern European architecture.

There is (1) the stylistic perpetuation of Greek, Roman or Renaissance architecture which may include also a system of designing in one of the other classifications; (2) proportion based on the human figure and a system of measurements derived therefrom; (3) proportion based on repetition of geometric figures by a system of ratios and on the musical scale; (4) proportion based on incommensurables like the golden section φ and the $\sqrt{2}$ rectangle θ.

(1) In the stylistic perpetuation of Greek, Roman and Renaissance architecture forms and ornament were copied, and this means that the forms of ancient buildings were adapted to various buildings. It was a process begun by Alberti and Palladio and other Renaissance architects and followed by architects of the western world ever since. It meant taking a portico of a Greek temple, or Roman triumphal arch, and placing it on the west wall of a Christian church, or in the centre of the wall of a Palace, or College building or modern bank. In the case of Alberti and Palladio these adaptations were done with considerable ingenuity, and to precise mathematical principles of proportion[3].

Buildings in the classical style were also planned symmetrically and the proportions of the parts were mathematically related. With the general forms, the ornaments, the carvings of capitals, the flutes of columns, the mouldings of base and entablature were also adapted, and in much architecture of the twentieth century the ornament was often given a different and original character, as in some of the Scandinavian adaptations, or ornament was eliminated, but the essential classical forms remained. The stylistic perpetuation was so strong in some European countries, chiefly Italy, Germany and Russia, during the thirties, that as already noted it amounted to a new classical revival.

(2) The system of architectural proportion emanating from the human figure has a considerable literature from Vitruvius to Le Corbusier. Before Vitruvius the Greek sculptor Polycleitus (fifth century B.C.) defined mathematically the ideal proportions of the human figure and this had considerable influence on later Greek sculpture. Such proportions were applied to the design of temples. Vitruvius, who based his theories partly on the precepts of Greek architects of the Hellenistic period (Hermogenes, Arcesius and Pythius), theories which he was presumably able to verify by a study of the actual buildings, says that a temple must have a proportion worked out according to the members of a well-shaped man[4]. Vitruvius goes on to suggest that measures were derived by the Greeks from the members of the body—the finger, palm, foot and cubit[5]. He also shows how certain basic geometric figures are derived from the human figure. 'In the human body,' he says, 'the central point is naturally the navel. For if a man be placed flat on his back, with his hands and feet extended, and pair of compasses centred at his navel, the fingers and toes of his two hands and feet will touch the circumference of a circle described therefrom. And just as the human body yields a circular outline, so too a square figure may be found from it. For if we measure the distance from the soles of the feet to the top of the head, and then apply that measure to the outstretched arms, the breadth will be found to be the same as the height as in the case of plane surfaces which are perfectly square.'[6] This had considerable influence on Renaissance architects. The enthusiasm for the circle and square as a basis for plans and proportions seen in the theories and buildings of Bramante, Alberti, Palladio, Serlio and others owes a good deal to Vitruvius whose treatise was almost an architectural bible for three hundred years[7]. The preoccupation for many years in the fifteenth century with the centrally planned church based on the circle and the square, owes much to Vitruvius, while mathematical manifestations discovered by the Greeks from Thales and Pythagoras to Euclid and Archimedes gave a magic to numbers and suggested a divine association for architectural design based on mathematics. Rudolf Wittkower epitomizes the spirit of classical design in the Italian Renaissance when he says 'the conviction that architecture is a science, and that each part of a building, inside as well as outside, has to be integrated into one and the same system of mathematical ratios, may be called the basic axiom of Renaissance architects. We have already seen that the architect is by no means free to apply to a building a system of ratios of his own choosing, that the ratios have to comply with conceptions

of a higher order and that a building should mirror the proportions of the human body; a demand which became universally accepted on Vitruvius' authority. As man is the image of God and the proportions of his body are produced by divine will, so the proportions in architecture have to embrace and express the cosmic order.'[8] And that cosmic order is revealed in the discoveries of Greek mathematicians.

Such thinking and architectural practice persists in the middle of the twentieth century. Many architects feel that mathematics based on the proportions of the human figure, on natural phenomena and the movement of cosmic bodies should form the basis of architectural design. To cite Le Corbusier as an example is to cite an architect whose influence was probably greater than that of any other in the mid-twentieth century. He writes in the first volume of *The Modulor* in support of the derivation of a system of measure from the proportions of the human body, and takes as a standard a man with arm upraised, 2.20 metres (7 feet, 9 inches). This is related to the height between floor and ceiling which Le Corbusier had noted in a wide variety of houses in various countries[9]. 'Take,' he says, 'a man-with-arm-upraised, 2.20 m in height; put him inside two squares, 1.10 by 1.10 metres each, superimposed on each other; put a third square astride these first two squares. This third square should give you a solution. The place of the right angle should help you to decide where to put this third square. With this grid for use on the building site, designed to fit the man placed within it, I am sure you will obtain a series of measures reconciling human stature (man-with-arm-upraised) and mathematics....'[10] These were instructions to Hanning, one of his young collaborators, given in 1943. After describing a few calculations he announces that the GRID was born—although as later reflections show not without uncertainties. As there is some confusion of thought among writers on the subject[11], it should be emphasized that the grid has the double function of securing good proportions considered aesthetically, and of lending itself to infinite combinations of mass production, taking in the elements of prefabricated buildings, and joining them without difficulty[12].

The standard of proportion evolved by Le Corbusier is associated with the golden section, and with the musical scale, and he has endeavoured to make it as far reaching and comprehensive in its origins and applications as possible, while there is a hint of the association of a mathematical order with the divine. Mathematics he says 'holds both the absolute and the infinite, the understandable and the forever elusive. It has walls before which one may pace up and down without result; sometimes there is a door; one opens it—enters—one is in another realm, the realm of the gods, the room which holds the key to the great systems. These doors are the doors of the miracles. Having gone through one, man is no longer the operative force, but rather it is his contact with the universe'.

(3) Architectural proportion is defined by P. H. Scholfield in his book on *The Theory*

461

of Proportion in Architecture as 'the creation of visible order by the repetition of similar shapes'[13]. The definition covers perhaps most examples of proportion in buildings but it is a question whether it is sufficiently comprehensive for not all proportion depends on repetition. It is possible in a limited way to have good proportion without the element of repetition. One could say of a doorway, or a stele, or panel that is a simple rectangle with, say, a pedimented top that it is of good proportion although there is no element of repetition. The same could be said of a column. A rectangle based, say, on the golden section would be to most people a well-proportioned rectangle, because in the relation of the two sides there is an element of design since there is an element of choice, but one would not speak of a well-proportioned square, circle, or other regular geometric figure.

For other than the simplest architectural designs the element of repetition is an important factor. The methods of repetition admit of considerable choice and have been the subject of much discussion. They can be broadly classified as rational and irrational or commensurable and incommensurable. The former is based on simple ratio of two magnitudes capable of a common divisibility[14] and of geometric progression. Renaissance architects based much of their design on commensurable proportions with, it was claimed, the authority of Vitruvius. The magic of numbers in the system of commensurables was considerably fortified by the translation of the divisions of the musical scale into spatial measurements and it is a factor to which Le Corbusier refers in *The Modulor*[15]. Pythagoras discovered, and it is generally regarded as his major achievement, that musical intervals depended on the ratios of the lengths of string of the same tension. Thus the octave is in the ratio of 2 : 1, the fifth 3 : 2 and the fourth 4 : 3. There is some correspondence here to the proportion 12 : 9 :: 8 : 6 the perfect proportion of the Greeks which, as legend has it, Pythagoras introduced from Babylon. The ratios of the musical octave fifth and fourth would be 12 : 6, 8 and 9.

Among the most famous examples of design based on commensurable magnitudes and influenced by the Pythagorean discovery of musical ratios spatially translated are the proportions worked out by Francesco Giorgi for the church of S. Francesco della Vigna at Venice which Wittkower has described in some detail[16]. The basic numbers for these proportions are 1, 2, 3, 9 and 27, based on the conjectural theories of Pythagoras who combined mathematics with religious mysticism. 1 is man, 2 is woman. Man plus woman is 3 from which life is generated. The first extension is 3 squared, 9, and the final extension is the cube 27, and the proportions of the church were based on these numbers. Similar arithmetical ratios governed the designs of numerous architects of the Renaissance, particularly Alberti and Palladio and their numerous followers throughout Europe. They still exercise a considerable influence because there is still a considerable body of architects in most countries who think of architectural proportion as a matter of sequence of arithmetically related shapes.

462

(4) Yet the systems of proportion which seemed to have had the greatest influence in the mid-twentieth century are those based on incommensurable magnitudes, the principal of which are the golden section φ and the square root of two rectangle. The former is defined in the two propositions of *Euclid* (2.XI and 6.XXX). It can also be defined as the division of a straight line into two parts so that the relation of the shorter to the longer is as the longer to the whole. If the line measures 1 the relation is approximately 0.381965 to 0.618035, or 19 to 31, but not exactly.

The golden section which has had so much influence on many modern architects in the classical tradition, among them such different architects as Sir Edwin Lutyens and Le Corbusier, has a doubtful origin. The first extant definition of it occurs in Plato's *Timaeus*, written a hundred years before *Euclid*. Timaeus is explaining to Socrates a theory of the cosmos, and he says that 'It is not possible that two things alone should be conjoined without a third; for there must needs be some intermediary bond to connect the two. And the fairest of bonds is that which most perfectly unites into one both itself and the things which it binds together; and to effect this in the fairest manner is the natural property of proportion. For whenever the middle term of any three numbers, cubic or square, is such that as the first term is to it, so is it to the last term—and again, conversely, as the last term is to the middle, so is the middle to the first,—then the middle term becomes in turn the first and last, while the first and last become in turn middle terms, and the necessary consequence will be that all the terms are interchangeable, and being interchangeable they all form a unity.'[17]

Plato approached mathematics from the standpoint of a philosopher and metaphysician and he rather used it for his philosophic purpose. He derived most of his knowledge of mathematics from Pythagoras whom he appreciated as a great mathematician. Pythagoras was also a religious mystic who saw the universe as having been created on mathematical principles, as modern scientists like Sir James Jeans and Sir Arthur Eddington were inclined to do. Plato was partially a follower of Pythagoras and it is possible that the ratios given in *Timaeus* as interchangeable and thus forming a unity, were derived from Pythagoras, who gave the proposition a mystic significance which it has also acquired in modern times. Much of *Euclid* is the formulation and repetition of the work of former mathematicians, and it can be conjectured from the evidence of Plato that the two propositions defining the golden section were formulations of one by Pythagoras. The ratio appears to have been known during the Renaissance in Italy following the translation of *Euclid* from the Arabic into Latin in 1354 by Campanus. Luca Pacioli, a friend of Leonardo da Vinci, was much preoccupied with the ratio and wrote a little book on the subject which he called Divine Proportion, but it does not seem to have influenced the designs of Renaissance architects to any marked extent.

Interest in it was revived about the time of the Greek revival in the early nineteenth century and it has been a powerful influence since, due partly to the suggestion of divine significance, although most architects who have used it would probably say that they are guided mainly by aesthetic considerations. I believe, too, that many architects who consider that proportion is mainly a matter of individual feeling would, if they found that the windows they had designed were very near to the golden section rectangle, alter them to conform to that magic proportion. I remember Walter Segal, an architect of the modern school, remarking to me that if the windows he had designed turned out to be near the golden section rectangle he would alter them to make them exactly so.

The square root of two rectangle, expressed θ, is an incommensurable that has also considerable influence in modern architectural design, and if it has not the mystic significance of the golden section it has properties which make it unique and venerable. Vitruvius suggests it as one proportion for the atrium of a house, 'by using the width to describe a square figure with equal sides, drawing a diagonal line in this square, and giving the atrium the length of this diagonal line' (VI. III.3.). Being an irrational proportion it did not find favour with architects of the Renaissance, but in the modern revival of incommensurables it has been used a good deal in design by architects working in the classical tradition. A notable example is Sir Edwin Lutyens who apparently changed from using the golden section to the $\sqrt{2}$ rectangle[18].

In discussing this change P. H. Scholfield[19] says that 'the transition from the φ rectangle to the $\sqrt{2}$ rectangle might appear to be a retrogressive step to those who see no virtue in any system of proportion not based on the golden section. But although $\sqrt{2}$ and the associated number θ have certain limitations compared to φ, they also have great advantages, provided that the limitations can be overcome. They have a far richer geometrical background, being related to the radial symmetry of the square, the octagon, and various star octagons, to the proportions of expanding systems of squares and circles and of star octagons, and to systems of repeat symmetry based on the square.' Scholfield adds later that 'it is just possible that Sir Edwin Lutyens' change from φ to $\sqrt{2}$ will turn out to have been, not retrogressive, but an experiment of the greatest value.'

Not least of the attractions to the designer of $\sqrt{2}$ rectangle is that it is the only rectangle which, when equally divided, results in rectangles of the same shape or proportion with the result that by using this rectangle all parts of a design can be continually divided and be of the same shape as the whole.

Architects are inevitably conscious in some degree of the principles of classical design that have been briefly enumerated, and many have been influenced by these principles in their work. In so far as the principles have governed design apart from the purpose and construction of a building, so have the architects been governed by the classical tradition. It is all a matter of degree from stylistic adaptation to principles of proportion. The value for modern architecture of the principles contained in ancient architecture and in the classical tradition is to apply them to present day problems in complete consistency with designing according to purpose and with modern techniques and construction. Herein is the border line between traditional classical architecture of varying degrees in which classical design—Greek, Roman or Renaissance—is a determining factor, and modern architecture where purpose and construction and their expression are the determining factors and classical design is brought in as a much respected adviser, but in no sense as a determinant.

In the following six chapters the architecture of the thirties where the classical tradition has been a determining factor is reviewed. It shows varying degrees of classical character and manifestation from the stylistic imitation to the stark and severe, simulating as modern architecture. Although manifesting throughout Europe in very different political climates, this varying classical architecture whether in Italy, Germany, Russia, France, England and the other European countries results to a considerable extent from political, economic and social assertiveness and a consequent desire for monumental expression. There are examples where it has been thought that Greek, or Roman or Renaissance character is appropriate to a modern purpose without assertive monumentality. But more often in the thirties classical monumentality was symbolical of political power, and of municipal and institutional importance. For that reason, as previously observed, it is chiefly found in buildings where some architectural expression beyond material function is desirable, expression of grandeur and dignity and suggestion of solidity and durability in buildings of state, town halls, large museums, and art galleries, sports arenas and the headquarters of important firms and professional bodies. It is a significant historical example where architecture, more than in most periods, was influenced and partly controlled by political power and ideologies. But in using a Greek, Roman or Renaissance character for this monumentality it is neither expressive nor significant of its age and results in a pseudo rather than true monumentality. Such architecture of the period, however, has varying debts to tradition and in some cases the borrowed classical idiom is treated with originality with often interesting and notable results.

REFERENCES AND NOTES

1. See Le Corbusier, *Vers une Architecture*, Paris 1923. English translation, London, 1927.
2. Le Corbusier, *The Modulor, vol. I*, Paris, 1948, *vol. II*, Paris, 1955. English translation, London, 1954 and 1958.
3. Several examples are given by Rudolf Wittkower in his *Architectural Principles in the Age of Humanism*, London, 1952.

4. *Vitruvius*, III.I.I.

5. *Vitruvius*, III.I.V.

6. *Vitruvius*, III.I.III. M. H. Morgan's translation, Harvard, 1914.

7. Geoffrey Scott in his *Architecture of Humanism*, London, 1914, says of Vitruvius that 'Europe, for three hundred years, bowed to him as to a god.' See p. 195.

8. Rudolf Wittkower, *Architectural Principles in the Age of Humanism*, London, 1952.

9. Le Corbusier, *The Modulor, vol. I*, Paris, 1948. English translation, London, 1954, p. 28.

10. Le Corbusier, *The Modulor, vol. I*, Paris, 1948. English translation, London, 1954, p. 37.

11. For example, Mark Hartland Thomas in an article on Modular Coordination in the *Encyclopedia of Modern Architecture*, London, 1963, says that Le Corbusier's Modulor has nothing to do with modular coordination. Le Corbusier's book on the contrary makes clear the double purpose of the Modulor to secure aesthetic standards and dimensional coordination.

12. Le Corbusier, *The Modulor, vol. I*, Paris, 1948. English translation, London, 1954. p. 41.

13. P. H. Scholfield, *The Theory of Proportion in Architecture*, Cambridge, 1958, p. 6, also p. 126.

14. Thus 49 and 63 are commensurables because they are both divisible by 7.

15. Le Corbusier, *The Modulor, vol. I*, Paris, 1948. English translation, London, 1954, pp. 16, 73, 74.

16. Rudolf Wittkower, *Architectural Principles in the Age of Humanism*, London, 1952, p. 90 ff. A translation is also given of Francesco Giorgi's Memorandum on the proportions of the church.

17. Plato, *Timaeus*. R. G. Bury's translation, London 1952, p. 59.

18. See Robert Lutyens' memoir of his father: *Sir Edwin Lutyens. An Appreciation in Perspective*, London, 1942.

19. P. H. Scholfield, *The Theory of Proportion in Architecture*, Cambridge, 1958, pp. 109–110.

31 *Fascist Italy*

THE ADOPTION OF A classical monumental style in Italy was a gradual process. In the early years of the century, before the First World War, the majority of buildings were in an ornate, late Renaissance style. After the war there appeared the general European tendency towards simplification. It is not easy to measure the influence of Fascism on architecture in the early twenties, but there can be little doubt that Mussolini's ideas did have a considerable effect on the character of public and other large city buildings. The ambition of Mussolini was to revive the glory of Imperial Rome in the modern Italian State, and he looked with favour on an architecture that was a revival of that of Imperial Rome. Also, in the extensive building that took place in Rome and its vicinity, it was desirable that all new buildings should be in harmony with those of the ancient capital, and that they should be of a becoming dignity. At the same time Fascist Italy must be progressive and modern, and in building full advantage should be taken of materials and methods made possible by modern industry.

Mussolini became Prime Minister of Italy in the Autumn of 1922 and in the early years of his rule the semblance of Parliamentary Government and democracy was preserved. Fascist despotism came gradually and could be said to have been established when Mussolini assumed the title of the Duce in 1928. Italy under Mussolini embarked in the late twenties, on a big programme of planning, public works and building, and much was carried out. Italy had been the first country in Europe to have town planning legislation. This was an Act of 1865, and among its provisions were measures to improve hygienic conditions in cities, to improve communications between them and to add to the impressiveness of cities. This last mentioned provision has considerable implications for architecture.

The plans made in Italy in the twenties and early thirties comprehended the rebuilding of considerable city areas. In Turin, for example, a plan was prepared in 1926 which consisted of a wide street flanked by arcaded footways in the central area.

The work completed in the thirties involved the demolition of old buildings over large areas, and the whole rebuilding was done to a unified architectural scheme. It was essentially a design on classical principles.

As might be expected the capital city presents the most ambitious example of comprehensive town planning. Two alternative schemes were prepared and one was adopted in 1931. Among the provisions of the scheme was to open up the centre of the city with the double purpose of improving routes of communication and improving the setting of the fine buildings of ancient Rome, and of the Renaissance. This meant cutting new streets, forming handsome avenues and clearing away a lot of mean building that had crowded round the great monuments of the past. One of the spectacular instances of replanning was the area in front of the Piazza S. Pietro (the forecourt of St. Peter's) which had previously been closely surrounded with old, mostly derelict buildings. This was opened up by the construction of an avenue, the via della Conciliazione, leading straight from the Piazza. The whole scheme, which was carried out during the thirties, was the work of Marcello Piacentini and Attilio Spaccarelli. The avenue is lined with lamp pylons derived in shape from Egyptian obelisks which are a familiar feature of Rome. The work, like so much of the official architecture of the Fascist regime, has been much criticized, but time will soften this attitude when political passions are less mixed with aesthetic judgments. What this avenue does is to create a long vista from the Tiber to St. Peter's which is impressive. The architecture of the buildings is of a simplified classic style which lacks distinction and is rather dull.

Perhaps the best work in the replanning of Rome was the opening up with a maximum of parks or garden land of a wedge to the southeast. It is here that some of the finest monuments of ancient Rome remain, and by clearing the clutter of old derelict houses that had gathered round them since the Renaissance it is possible to see these monuments to full advantage. It is very much the setting of a green wedge with its point at the Capitoline hill and including near the centre the Roman Forum, the Colosseum and the Palatine Hill. The wedge broadens out, and contains the Baths of Caracalla in a spacious garden setting, and further south, the Via Appia Antica lined with tombs from which views can be enjoyed over the country surrounding Rome.

A particularly valuable planning scheme of Mussolini was the reclamation of some 300 square miles of the mosquito infested Pontine Marshes. Five towns were planned, and partly built: Littoria, Sabaudia, Pontenia, Aprilia, and Pomezia. The centres of these towns were conceived in the simple classical idiom of which Sabaudia is probably the best example.

Another ambitious plan was the layout of an area south of Rome for the Esposizione Universale for 1942. The exhibition was, of course, abandoned, but the streets were

468

laid out and many of the buildings were erected, and some of the work was continued after the war.

Perhaps the best way of giving an impression of Fascist inspired classical monumental architecture of the thirties is to take a few typical yet dissimilar examples. The University City is a good and important one, another is the Foro Italico, a large sports centre, a third is one of the new towns of the Pontine Marshes of which Sabaudia is the most significant and the grandiose Esposizione Universale 42. An important architect who superintended a very large number of schemes was Marcello Piacentini. An early work of Piacentini is the Piazza della Vittoria at Brescia of the late twenties in which the buildings surrounding the Piazza are in the simplified classical Renaissance style with the traditional marble encrustation.

UNIVERSITY CITY, ROME

The old University of Rome had grown up in a haphazard manner, so that the buildings comprising it were scattered in various parts of the city. After attending one lecture students had to cross Rome to attend another necessary for their course of study, an experience that was once shared by students of London University. The necessity for greater homogeneity had long been realized and discussed, and the opinion that the University buildings should all be brought together on one site prevailed. Therefore, in April 1932, it was decided by the Fascist Government to build the new University City on a site near the centre of Rome, a little to the east of the central railway station, in the neighbourhood of other new buildings on the grand scale, like those of the Ministry of Air, the Dental Institute, and a few others. Work on the new University buildings commenced early in 1933 and most were completed in the autumn of 1935. They took, therefore, a little under three years to build, and considering the magnitude of the undertaking, it constitutes impressive evidence of Fascist organization and energy. The entire control of the work was given to Marcello Piacentini. He assembled a team of some of the best-known Italian architects to assist him[1]. The general impression of the buildings is that with one possible exception one mind controlled their character rather than several. In his message to the Italian press Piacentini spoke of the work as 'The perfect result of the first great experiment in collaboration and one which demonstrates the identification of the ideas and intentions of Italian architects.'

That, of course, is a self-congratulating explanation of the unity that exists in this group of buildings. Although it is an argument for collaboration, it is an argument also for standardization in the architectural rather than the technical sense. The less attractive explanation is that Piacentini dominated his collaborators. It would be interesting to know how much freedom they were allowed. The impression is that a certain rather rigid line was indicated by Piacentini, and they had to follow it. In the context of beauty as variety in unity, here is unity, but little variety.

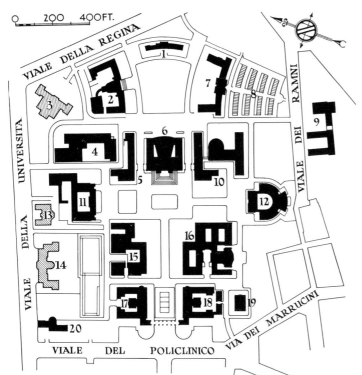

Plan

University City, Rome, 1933–35

Supervising Architect: Marcello Piacentini

Key to Plan.

1. University Barracks; 2. Institutes of Histology, General Physiology, Anthropology, and Experimental Psychology; 3. Institutes of Physiological Chemistry, and Pharmacology; 4. Faculty of Political Science; 5. Faculty of Jurisprudence; 6. Rectorate, Library and Great Hall; 7. Institutes of Botany and Pharmaceutical Chemistry; 8. Greenhouses; 9. Students' Quarters; 10. Faculty of Letters and Philosophy; 11. Institute of Mineralogy, Geology, and Palæontology; 12. School of Mathematics; 13. Institute of Medical Law; 14. Neuropsychiatric Clinic; 15. Institute of Physics; 16. Institute of Chemistry; 17. Institutes of Hygiene and Bacteriology; 18. Orthopædic Clinic; 19. Thermal Centre; 20. Professors' Club and Recreation Rooms.

Institute of Physiology   *Architect: Giovanni Michelucci*

Institute of Botany   *Architect: Giuseppe Capponi*

Rectorate *Architect: Marcello Piacentini*

Institute of Chemistry *Architect: Pietro Ascheri*

General View of University City

The principal buildings are grouped round a 'T' space (see plan). Pairs of lofty pilasters surmounted by long parallel lintels, between which is a passage way connecting the two flanking buildings, forms the main entrance gateway, designed by Arnaldo Foschini. An avenue flanked by two buildings on either side leads to the spacious central piazza, the farther side of which is the principal building, the Rectorate or Rector's lodge, in which are also the Aula Magna, or Great Hall, and the University Library. Other buildings are grouped symmetrically about the oblong piazza; while further blocks are arranged at the back. All the buildings are related in approximate symmetry, although they differ in plan, and thus in elevation, according to the different requirements of the institutes.

Of the grouping of the buildings round the piazza, Piacentini remarked that 'Such grouping is, as a rule, based on one of two types: the system of rigid symmetry, or the romantic effect of variety. Important French squares belong to the first group— Versailles, Place de la Concorde, Place Vendome, etc. St. Mark's Square, Venice, and many of the picturesque squares of Flanders and Germany, are of the romantic type and are all of surprising and variegated proportions. This variety and picturesqueness was not preconceived, it happened from time to time during the centuries in the development of the life of the city.'

'The type of the great Roman squares is quite another thing. These are born of a symmetrical order, but the single buildings each take forms characteristic of their service. So it is with this University City. Born of an idea of a basilical and transept plan, it draws all its impressiveness from order and fundamental symmetry; yet the Physics building on the left of the avenue is not the same as the Chemistry building on the right, while the Mathematics building at one end of the piazza is totally different in size and proportion from the balancing Mineralogy building at the other end of the piazza.'

The inspiration and model of ancient Rome is here very much present in Piacentini's mind. The whole layout is spacious and everything is calculated to give the buildings a full monumental dignity, especially the Rectorate. The spaces between the buildings are laid out as formal gardens, with trees, shrubs, lawns and flowers. A square pool of water is arranged in front of the main entrance with a symbolical statue on the central axis.

The method of construction employed in the buildings is reinforced concrete frame with brick infilling walls. The buildings are faced principally with Roman travertine slabs, of a creamy hue with small irregular perforations on their surface, and partly of lithoceramics.

Originally it was intended to make the Rectorate a tall, steel-framed building, rising well above the other buildings, as a dominating focal point. Judging from the drawings, it was preferable to the present arrangement, for it gave greater variety, a quality which is lacking. As it is, the Rectorate rises to the general level of 50 feet, and the centralizing effect is obtained by the portico of four plain square columns.

The buildings partially express their structure. The main entrance and portico are bare demonstrations of reinforced concrete piers, while the rigid square character of the buildings is expressive of the heavy concrete frame.

On the question of structural design Piacentini says that 'The architecture of the University City, in its absolute simplicity, does not renounce any demand of modernity, but the general conception is born in a classic Mediterranean clime. No concession has been made to ostentatious ultra-rationalized formulas (like the large horizontal strips of glass, or the masses planned above the open spaces of the ground floors and suspended on light pilasters); all here is reasoned, well thought out, and realized on the basis of technical and spiritual necessity. We have sought to construct, not fashionable buildings, but buildings that have the eternal qualities of the essential.' Whether the intentions expressed are realised, is of course open to question.

Piacentini could not have been thinking, when he said this, of the Institute of Botany building designed by Giuseppe Capponi, which is in many ways the most interesting structure, and which represents an exception, in general design, to the other buildings in this University group. This building is situated behind the large block of the Rectorate and great hall (number 7 on plan). Instead of large masses punctuated with numerous vertical windows here are large glass screens designed to obtain the utmost light for botanical experiments. The rear, outer, façade faces south; it is a concave, curved sweep with long horizontal windows on the two upper floors, practically a glass wall on the ground floor, and a raised central feature consists mainly of a glass façade on both south and north façades.

The Rectorate building is the most complete and successful expression of the spirit that prompted the whole work. It has a dignity and grandeur that must have pleased Mussolini. The lofty pilasters of the central entrance, the wide bank of solid wall above the windows in the recessed flanking blocks, and the lettered frieze, the large relief sculptures on the plain walls of the outer projecting flanking blocks, all give interest and are on a monumental scale with good proportion that is certainly impressive. But in the outer flanking masses there is the beginning of that unrelieved monotonous repetition of vertical rectangular windows on plain walls, a theme repeated with little variation in many of the buildings.

The Mathematics building by Gio Ponti has more variety than most of the buildings, not so much in the rectangular block facing the central courtyard as in the semicircular treatment of the rear part of the building which consists of two wings, containing draughting rooms, curving round to a fan-shaped auditorium, divided into two on the ground floor and the full size on the first floor. The fenestration follows, to some extent, the interior design thus giving a more functional less academic aspect. With the exception of the Rectorate, the School of Mathematics and the Botanical Institute most of the buildings suffer a little from sameness and lack of character.

Of the justice of Piacentini's claims for the University City buildings the reader can partially judge from the photographs here reproduced. The work, is vast and bears all the marks of modern efficiency, but the criticism that it is monotonous and is lacking in distinctiveness of design has some validity.

The whole group of buildings is important less for their architectural merit than historically, as showing the kind of architecture that emerged from Fascist ideas, an architecture in which an attempt was made to revive the grandeur of Imperial Rome and combine it with the modern spirit.

Most of the other University buildings erected in Italy during the thirties were of a similar character to those at Rome, among them may be mentioned the Institute of Pathological Medicine of Milan University built in 1933 to the design of Enrico A. Griffin, and the Bocconi University building at Milan designed in 1937 by Giuseppe Pagano who was, it will be remembered, architect of the Institute of Physics building in the Rome group, which conformed to the general pattern, having large square masses and rows of vertical windows on plain walls. The Bocconi building is more original and interesting and is designed according to classic principles rather than as a stylistic imitation. Like Le Corbusier, Pagano was influenced by mathematical principles in determining his proportions[2]. The architectural masses and plan of the Bocconi University building were based partially on the proportions of the golden section. Incidentally the plan is somewhat like a swastika, but this was probably rather a functional coincidence than a symbolic intention. Much of the building, similar in character to Pagano's earlier Institute of Physics, has plain rectangular windows on plain walls, with the exception of the south façade of the southern five-storey block with its long balconies, and ground floor partly open with square columns supporting the upper structure somewhat in the manner of Le Corbusier's open ground-floor treatment. Here the reinforced concrete frame construction emerges more prominently as part of the decorative character of the building. It will be seen that by this treatment this block appears to have a more modern treatment, but it is just a question of pushing the face back inside the enclosing walls to allow for balconies, and of recessing the ground floor behind the concrete uprights. No fundamental principle of design is affected, and it is really a development from classical methods and not starting afresh by a logical examination of needs and designing accordingly.

FORO ITALICO

The Foro Italico, situated in the northwest region of Rome on the right bank of the Tiber, was initiated in 1927 by the Accademia Fascista della Farnesina as a large sports centre, and the building continued over a period of 30 years. The Ponte Duca d'Aosta over the Tiber, completed in 1939, is part of the general scheme and the line of the bridge running northwest is taken as the central axis of the group. Along this axis from the bridge is an obelisk fifty-six feet high inscribed 'Mussolini Dux' in large letters vertically almost the whole height. Beyond this is a short broad avenue—the Piazzala della Fontana del Globo—which is paved with marble and mosaics and lined with large marble cubes inscribed with information of notable events in Italian history. The avenue is flanked by two large symmetrically massed buildings faced with brick and stone dressings adorned with a classical cargo of colonnades and niches holding statues. The avenue leads to a circular piazza with a fountain in the centre with a marble sphere as the central feature. The architects of this scheme and of the obelisk and fountain were Mario Paniconi and Giulio Pediconi.

The Stadio dei Marmi lies to the northeast on an axis at 30 degrees with the main axis and radiating to the bridge. Begun in the early thirties, this stadium designed by Enrico del Pebbio holds about 20,000 persons, and the encircling parapet is adorned at intervals with 60 colossal statues each about 18 feet high illustrating various athletic pursuits. The sports facilities in the Foro Italico include tennis and basket ball courts, open-air and enclosed swimming baths, running tracks, gymnasium and fencing halls.

After the Second World War there was the political impulse to destroy some of these constructions of the Foro Italico, especially the obelisk inscribed with Mussolini's name, but I understand that the impulse was restrained by American counsel as serving no useful purpose. Instead the work was continued and the immense Olympic Stadium was built in conformity with the original plan to accommodate 80,000 spectators, it was finished for the Olympic Games of 1960. The stadium was set on an axis of 45 degrees with the main axis from the bridge.

An interesting and important addition to the group made in the post-war period is the building of the Ministry of Foreign Affairs designed by Vittorio Ballio-Morpurgo, Enrico del Debbio and Arnaldo Foschino. It lies to the east of the main group and is an immense building, designed very much in the same classical idiom as the building of the thirties, with the innumerable vertical windows on plain walls.

Of the architecture of the four new towns of the Pontine Marshes that of Saubaudia is, as previously mentioned, the best example. The town is situated on the Tyrrhenian coast about 55 miles southeast of Rome near Monte Circeo. The building of the town was begun in 1933 and rapid progress was made so that much of the town had been built by 1940. Architects responsible for the various buildings were Cino Cancellotti, Eugenio Montuori, Luigi Piccinato and Enrico Scalpelli.

A strip of water—the Lago di Paola—about 400 yards wide runs parallel with the sea coast for some miles. From this strip there are two inlets, the Braccio Annunziata and the Braccio della Crapara, separated by about a mile and it is between these to a depth inland of nearly two miles that Saubaudia is built. It is planned on formal classical lines with a main central street running southeast to northwest, curving at the northwest end, and with two main avenues running at right angles to it one towards the sea and one inland. The whole pattern is mainly one of straight streets at right angles to each other. In the town centre there are three squares closely linked, each enclosed with rather plain squarish buildings often with square columned arcading. The chief square is the Piazza della Rivoluzione in which is the Town Hall, with its square tower at one corner linked only by a first floor balcony, and the Casa del Fascio. In another piazza is the squarish looking church with another square tower similarly perforated at the belfry by vertical slits. It is obvious that much of the designing of these buildings is based on classic formulae of proportion. The whole effect is a little Greek-like in the composition of balanced vertical and horizontal masses, but at the same time with the plain walls and absence of ornament alike it is stark and dull. The simplicity and the severity are the modern notes in the classical conception. The happiest view of the town is of the villas on the Braccio Annuziata with the towers beyond.

ESPOSIZIONE UNIVERSALE

The monumental classical architecture of Fascist Italy so far considered was of a general sameness with little distinctive designing, but at the same time there was little that was positively bad. Among the buildings that were erected as part of the Esposizione Universale for 1942, however, there were many in the classic plus modern style that have become curiosities of monumental banality and bombast.

Marcello Piacentini was appointed general superintending architect for the Esposizione Universale in 1938 and he prepared a plan of wide avenues with terminal features in the grand manner of Renaissance planning on an extensive site about three miles south of the centre of Rome. To give an idea of the magnitude on this project about £40 million was spent on it by 1940, when owing to Italy entering the war in that year it was abandoned, or, as Mussolini no doubt hoped, merely postponed. About one third of the site was, however, used for the Esposizione Agricola in 1953.

Among the larger buildings completed as part of the original scheme were the Palazzo della Civilta Italica (Palace of Italian Civilization) designed by Giovanni Guerrini, Attilio La Padula and Mario Romano; the Pallazzo de Ricevimenti e dei Congressi designed by Adalberto Libera and the Church of Sauti Apostoli Pietro e Paolo designed by Arnaldo Foschini. The most curious and unbelievable of these is the Palazzo della Civilta Italica variously nicknamed the dovecot and the square colosseum. It is an immense square building with six tiers each having nine arches on each of the four

476

Foro Italico, air view, 1927–60 *Architects: Mario Paniconi and Giulio Pediconi*

Foro Italico—Mussolini Obelisk—The Stadio dei Marmi with
the colossal marble statues *Architect: Enrico del Debbio*—
The building of the Ministry of Foreign Affairs, 1950 *Architects:
Vittorio Ballio-Morpurgo, Enrico del Debbio and Arnaldo Foschino*

View of the centre of Sabaudia, a new town
the Pontine Marshes, 1933–40

*Architects: Cino Cancellotti, Eugenio Montuori,
Luigi Piccinato and Enrico Scalpelli*

façades forming balconies to the main building. Statuary in the classical style appears in the arches of the ground floor. There is an inscription above the top row of arches, the same on each façade, which translated reads: 'A people of poets, artists, heroes, saints, thinkers, scientists, navigators and pioneer aviators.' Without criticizing the idea of the building its appearance can only be viewed with dismay. Six rows of identical plain arches on each wall making the entire pattern of each façade is surely an ultimate architectural banality difficult to understand. One feels that it is the effort of a child piling one identical thing by the side of and on top of the other. In its defence one can say that it is no worse than the identical storeys in curtain walling, but the patterning of the curtain walling is less assertive and we are less conscious therefore of its poor architectural quality.

The Palazzo dei Congressi is less crude. It is large with a rectangular block fronted by a row of tall columns, and surmounted by a square block covered by a flat dome. There does not appear to be a very successful integration of the two masses, there is no sense of one building up logically from the other, and thus there is a considerable loss of monumentality.

The examples noted of the classical monumental architecture of Fascist Italy during the thirties have been taken from Rome and its vicinity, because it is in the capital city that the most significant and typical examples are to be found, but they can be seen in almost every Italian city and town of any size. They are an expression of a particularly powerful and widespread political influence on architecture. They do not represent by any means the whole of Italian architecture of the period, but mainly that which is monumental and commemorative by intention. Distinctive developments in the more progresisve modern architecture are found in some of the less palatial structures.

REFERENCES AND NOTES

1. The architects of the various buildings of the University City of Rome were:
    Marcello Piacentini: Rectorate, Library and Great Hall
    Arnaldo Foschini: Main entrance, Orthopaedic Clinic and Institute of Hygiene and Bacteriology
    Pietro Ascheri: Institute of Chemistry
    Giovanni Michelucci: Institute of Physiology, and Institutes of Mineralogy and Palaeontology
    Giuseppe Capponi: Institutes of Botany and Pharmaceutical Chemistry
    Giuseppe Pagano: Institute of Physics
    Giovanni Battista Ponti: Institute of Mathematics
    Gaetano Rapisardi: Faculty of Letters, Philosophy and Jurisprudence
2. See *Costruzionini-Casabella* (195/198). The entire issue of this Italian review was devoted to the work of Pagano as a tribute to his memory. Pagano died in a German Concentration camp in 1945.

32 Nazi Germany

THERE ARE CERTAIN significant differences in the classicism of Fascist Italy and that of
Nazi Germany. One never gets the impression that in artistic matters Mussolini
exercised the despotic and restricting influence of Hitler; he permitted much greater
freedom, and rather suggested to artists the desirability of creating an art in harmony
with the dignity and character of the Fascist State, than commanding and insisting on
a particular line of artistic expression, as was certainly the case with Hitler. Mussolini's
ideas were well known to architects and he certainly had considerable influence on the
character of public and other large buildings, because many architects were naturally
not averse to pleasing the Duce. As was stated in the last chapter the ambition of
Mussolini was to revive the glories of ancient Rome in the modern Italian State, and
he naturally desired an architecture which should conform with and express this
aspiration, yet at the same time be modern and progressive in spirit.

Hitler had similar impulses, but it was rather to ancient Greece than to Rome that he
turned for inspiration in expressing in architecture the dignity of the Nazi State. Yet,
at the same time, the old national traditional architecture of the Fatherland must live
again in the Nazi State, because this was the architecture of the ancestry of the
German race. It was difficult to blend the classical architecture of the Mediterranean
with the native medieval architecture of Germany and preserve the character of each,
so both styles were adopted—the classical architecture for the large monumental State
and city buildings; German medieval native architecture for the homes of the people,
club buildings, schools, youth hostels and castle-like training centres for party leaders.
In this last an atmosphere of Nordic mysticism was considered appropriate.

A sense of historical perspective will be assisted by recalling briefly Hitler's accession to
power and the nature of his interest in art and architecture.

Hitler became Chancellor of the German Reich in January, 1933. Shortly afterwards
the National Socialist Party ruthlessly crushed all other parties in the State, and all

factions and elements which were likely to obstruct its advance to unlimited power. President von Hindenberg was induced to give the party authority to issue decrees which had the power of law. Therefore, when, after Hindenberg's death in the summer of 1934, Hitler became both Führer and Chancellor, he was accorded, as leader of the party, supreme and absolute power over the Reich. His word, his signature, which might be the result of the merest whim, was German law, and it is questionable whether any ruler in modern history has had such absolute power.

Unlike many other despotic rulers who often left the control and management of certain departments of national life to their ministers and subordinates, Hitler liked to control every condition and activity of German life. That is not to say that he was not influenced, or that his rule was not to some extent determined by the advice or even the will of other prominent Nazis, but bearing in mind *Mein Kampf*, Hitler's ascetic, fanatical, intense, and narrow personality made its indelible mark on most important activities of the Third Reich.

Hitler's ambition to be an artist is revealed in *Mein Kampf*. His water colours produced when he was a student were reproduced by the thousand for the edification of his admiring and uncritical followers. In the diplomatic exchanges between Hitler and Sir Neville Henderson in August, 1939, the Führer said that 'he was by nature an artist, not a politician, and that once the Polish question was settled he would end his life as an artist and not as a warmonger.' Architecture occupied a big place among his aesthetic interests, especially as it was closely connected with grandiose schemes for rebuilding Germany. His interest in architecture, like his interest in painting, had a certain fanatical enthusiasm, but was not distinguished by much understanding of either. All modern movements, all experiments suggested by scientific progress, by psychological research, or by new modes of thought were anathema to him. In both painting and architecture he could not think outside the chief European traditions.

His taste in art was considerably affected by his ideals of German national life. *Mens sana in corpore sano* was a guiding principle, with the essential inspiration of ancient Greece. In fact, modern German culture was partly modelled on that of the classical period of Greece.

Athleticism and the celebration of it in art was a prominent feature of social life and bronze statues of German athletes in public places became increasingly familiar in the late thirties. Examples that might be cited are the ideal statues of a nude German man and woman at Hanover, by Georg Kolbe, a Sleeping Figure by Ernst Seger, which was placed near the Wannsee Bathing Beach, Berlin, and the figure of a Discus Thrower by Eberhard Enck which is a close imitation of Greek sculpture. It is significant that the last mentioned was awarded the Prussian Gold Medal for Art. These bronze athletes were produced as the artist imagined a Greek sculptor would have represented a German athlete. That was very much the actuating spirit of Nazi architecture.

Imposing his will on all phases of German life, especially those departments like art and architecture, in which he was especially interested, it is unlikely that Hitler, in such matters, took the advice of other Nazi leaders, whom he regarded as knowing less about these subjects than he. It can be concluded, therefore, that the architecture of the Third Reich was largely determined by Hitler's personal feelings, and the imposition of his will was coupled with an intolerance of all other forms and kinds of artistic expression. A. Rosenberg, the historian of the German Republic, writing of the period after 1933, says that 'the ruling tendency ruthlessly took command of all spheres of cultural life. Literature, art and science, the press and education, have all been centralized, and every divergent opinion has been suppressed.'

No great art can flourish under a tyranny which denies freedom of artistic expression. Art is not only a flower of democracy: it has also flourished under oligarchies, and all-powerful princes, as in the case of the Venetian Republic and of the principalities of Renaissance Italy; but in these cases the administration, in so far as it affected art, was of a liberal and cultured kind with a respect for the artist that allowed him considerable freedom of expression.

The Nazi building programme was on an ambitious scale and included a large number of immense schemes that would take many years to complete. Only a very small proportion of this building was in operation at the outbreak of war in 1939. 'A start,' says a German propaganda publication, 'was made as early as 1933 with the planning of great edifices. But only the following years could bring a full unfolding of the plans of National Socialism. The Koniglicher Platz in Munich was given a new aspect. In Nürnberg the first buildings on the grounds of the Reich Party Congress are going up. Castles to act as training schools for Party leaders, Reich administration buildings, and the Reich Sports Grounds in Berlin have been created. All Germany is building and fashioning. All the building is in a new style, expressive of the new German, his world and his outlook.'

Part of the immense programme of reconstruction in Berlin was the incorporation of all the southern stations into one vast southern terminus, a work in progress from 1937; another scheme was to fill in part of the Spree so as to continue the central avenue, while the University was to be transferred from the eastern end of Unter den Linden to rise as a vast University city about two miles west. In many of these vast schemes, Albert Speer planned as Hitler's architect with a team of architects working with him responsible for various individual buildings. Some of these architects were Ernst Sagebiel, Paul Ludwig Troost, and Werner March.

The chief centres of Nazi activity were Munich, Nürnberg and Berlin, and it is in

481

these three cities that the Monumental classical architecture of Nazi Germany is mainly revealed. The 'new aspect' of the Koniglicher Platz in Munich immediately suggests the Greek prototypes. There is the large entrance building, the Propylea, the extensive rectangular platz, flanked in the centre of each long side by the Pinakotek and the Glytotek, while on either side of the other main entrance to the platz are the tombs of Hitler's early associates in the struggle for power enclosed in two square colonnaded structures, the square columns supporting a heavy entablature. At Munich is also the House of German Art which was completed in 1937. This is a long rectangular building with a glass roof. The main front consists of a long colonnade of Roman Doric columns. The masonry walls with the horizontal joints emphasized are relieved by small vertical windows behind the colonnade and in the end walls. The whole effect is a little severe. It lacks dignity because it lacks emphasis; it is too negative, while the colonnade with the badly shaped columns suggests a poor appreciation of the originals from which they are copied (see illustration).

Among the most ambitious architectural works of the Third Reich was the group of buildings at Nürnberg for the annual rally of the Party. Designed by Albert Speer the general layout and buildings are conceived on an immense scale which is characteristic of all official architectural enterprises of Hitler and the Nazi Party as one way of impressing the people and of buttressing the national edifice under Nazi rule. Hitler had said in this very city of Nürnberg in 1937 that 'what is in course of erection in this city, what is planned and in part ready for erection in Berlin, Munich, Hamburg and other places is intended to strengthen and support authority.'

The scheme at Nürnberg consists of a sequence of structures with an avenue or processional way as a central feature. There is a large square space called the Lager (camp) which is designed to accommodate 540,000 persons. Next to this is the Marzfeld, a large rectangular area 700 metres (2,296 feet) by 900 metres (2,952 feet), surrounded by walls with towers at intervals. This Marzfeld was to serve as a kind of parade ground and setting for Army displays. The Aufmarschstrasse, which is the central avenue or processional way, leads from the Marzfeld. Moving along this avenue there is on the left the immense Deutsches Stadion (German Stadium) and on the right the Zeppelinfeld. The avenue crosses a broad lake called Dutzendteich, and at the end of the bridge are two tall obelisks flanking the avenue which leads to the colonnaded entrance of the Luitpoldarena which incorporated a festival hall. On the right of the avenue between the lake and the Luitpoldarena is the vast Kongreshalle. The first of these immense structures to be completed (1936) was the Zeppelinfeld of which the principal building is the vast Grand Stand, scene of the great Party Congress. Modelled on the architecture of ancient Greece, it is a composition of verticals and horizontals, with a central feature and two flanking masses, and long rows of square columns forming a background to the tiers of seats. It is monumental, cold and rather forbidding.

House of German Art, Munich, 1937

Grandstand of the Zeppelinfeld,
Nürnberg, 1936

    Architect: Albert Speer

Model of German Stadium, Nürnberg
to hold 405,000 persons, commenced
in 1937

    Architect: Albert Speer

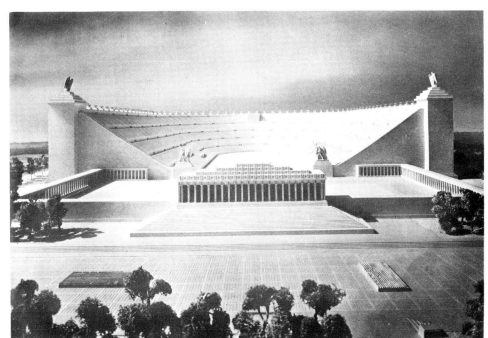

All the other structures of the scheme are designed with a similar monumental grandeur, the Congress Hall and the German Stadium being architecturally the most interesting. The former was commenced in 1936, the foundation stone having been laid at the Nazi Party Congress of Honour in that year. It was nearing completion at the outbreak of war. The building is semicircular on plan with the main entrance in the centre of the straight side flanked by two rectangular blocks enclosing two small halls. The overall length of the building is 261 metres (856 feet) with a total width of 276 metres (905 feet), the actual floor area of the large semicircular hall being 150 by 190 metres (492 feet by 623 feet), designed to accommodate 60,000 persons. The design is a combination of Greek and Roman styles, the main front is a symmetrical arrangement of rectangular masses, and the wall treatment of the rear curved section is a simplified rendering of the Colosseum at Rome.

The German Stadium, of which the foundation stone was laid at the Nazi Congress of Work in 1937, demonstrated the ambition to erect these State buildings on the greatest possible scale to glorify the German nation and impress the world. This was referred to as the 'greatest citadel of sport in all history', planned by the Führer's architect, Albert Speer, and nearly half completed at the outbreak of war. It was to hold 405,000 persons. Its main dimensions, 540 metres (1,771 feet) long, 445 metres (1,460 feet) wide, with walls surrounding the seating 90 metres (295 feet) high and arena area of 55,000 square metres (592,015 square feet) afford some impression of its immense size. The design derives from the Panathenaic Stadium at Athens which was reconstructed first by Herodis Atticus about A.D. 143 and then for the Olympic Games in 1896. Semicircular at one end, and open at the other to a rectangular enclosure surrounded by a colonnade with a temple-like structure forming the principal entrance, and approached by a wide flight of steps, the whole is calculated to impress to the utmost.

The method of construction employed in these buildings at Nürnberg is significant. Instead of adopting the modern methods of steel or reinforced concrete frame, the traditional time-honoured method of building with great blocks of stone was employed. These buildings were to last a thousand years, and there was too little experience of the new modern methods to give confidence in their prolonged durability; it was better to trust to the old well-tried methods of hundreds of years of building experience. Nowhere else in Germany did architects plan and begin to build on quite so colossal a scale and with quite the same freedom (made possible by the character of the buildings) to replant ancient Greek architecture on modern German soil.

In Berlin great schemes of reconstruction did not get much beyond the drawing board and plan stage by the outbreak of war. Most of the buildings actually erected had to serve a purpose which necessitated modification and adaptation of the Greek style. The notable exception is the Stadium that was completed in time for the Olympic Games in 1936 and designed by Werner March. Being an early work of the

484

Model of Congress Hall, Nürnberg
Architect: Albert Speer

Designed to accommodate 60,000,
commenced in 1936 and nearly
completed 1939

Below, elevation and plan

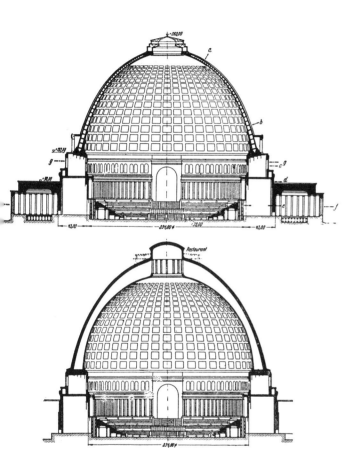

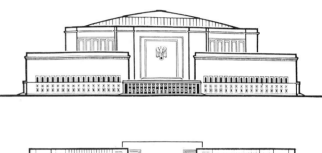

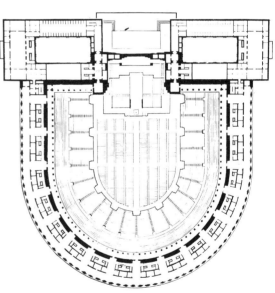

...ction through the high meeting hall for
...erlin, designed according to Hitler's wishes
... his architect, Albert Speer.
...he cupola of 820 feet span was to be in
...ickwork. Also shown is Dischinger's
...ternative project, a ferro-concrete cupola
... two shells

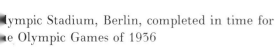

...ympic Stadium, Berlin, completed in time for
...e Olympic Games of 1936

Architect: Werner March

Nazi regime it is less affected by Nazi architectural ideas than the later Nürnberg Stadium, indeed it has as much of modern structural shapes as of classic, being a blending of the two, although its general elliptical shape, like so many modern stadia, derives from the shape of ancient Greek and Roman amphitheatres.

The two best-known official buildings erected in Berlin under the Nazi regime were the Reich Chancellory and the vast Air Ministry Building, both completed in 1936. They are both compositions of rectangular blocks in which the effect of the design depends largely on the relation of verticals and horizontals. The better of the two buildings is the Air Ministry. It is an attempt to combine Greek principles of design with modern simplicity and adapt these qualities to a large modern office block. The result is severe and monotonous, and somewhat like some of the buildings of the University City of Rome. A large number of regularly spaced vertical windows on large areas of plain wall, as appears in the many façades of this building, is dull and flat. Little relief is afforded by the entrance porticos with rows of plain square columns.

In the designs of the immense structures at Nürnberg Hitler and the Nazi leaders ventured on grandiose schemes to erect the largest buildings of their kind in the world. A further example of extravagant projects of this kind was the design prepared by Albert Speer, under Hitler's direction, for a vast meeting hall in the centre of Berlin that was to have a tremendous dome 250 metres (820 feet) span, with a height from the ground of 260 metres (853 feet), thus being at least three times as large as any dome in existence. Its shape was similar to the great dome of St. Peter's, but with a span about six times as great. It was to have a coffered ceiling with a large lantern light at the top. It was to have been built of brick, of two shells with a cavity between having an overall thickness of from 13 feet to 26 feet. Provision was to be made for especially strong foundations which were to consist of two rings of caissons sunk to a depth of 110 feet and the space between filled with blocks of concrete. F. Dischinger, a famous German civil engineer, prepared a design with an alternative method of construction consisting of inner and outer domes of reinforced concrete, the inner dome spherical in shape and the outer dome elliptical. This alternative was rejected because Hitler disliked reinforced concrete, and because the old traditional methods he thought more reliable. Illustrations are given of the two designs. This project throws light on the mind and ambitions of Hitler and his associates. Everything was to be greater, more tremendous than anything civilization had ever seen before. Here were structures to render insignificant by comparison all former buildings of a like kind. Do we not see here the architectural symbols of the would-be conquerors of the world?

486

33 Soviet Russia

WHEREAS IN GERMANY the adoption of a classical architecture, derived mainly from ancient Greece, for the great public buildings and the official architecture of the Third Reich, as the most appropriate for the grandeur and magnificence of the Nazi State, the contemporary classical revival in the USSR was more in the nature of a gradual transition which began several years earlier in the late twenties. The new classical revival in the USSR was a far more widespread and varied movement and had a far more vigorous life than it ever had in Germany because, whether it is liked or not, it springs in some degree from the tastes and wishes of the people. It has a broad democratic basis, whereas the classical architecture of Nazi Germany was a style imposed from above.

Soviet architecture of the thirties as seen in the great Government buildings, in the palaces of culture, in the workers' club buildings, in the theatres, cinemas and concert halls, blocks of flats and underground stations, is essentially an architecture designed with the traditional stock forms of Greece, Rome and the Italian Renaissance, maybe sometimes acquired secondhand through its own earlier revived classicism of the eighteenth and early nineteenth centuries, with fanciful variations on these themes occasionally introduced. To appreciate how this new revival of classical architecture has occurred it is helpful to glance at the development of Russian architecture and the evolution of architectural theories in relation to the political and social ideas of the Soviet State.

After the revolution in 1917 the Russian Soviet Federal Socialist Republic, comprising the greater part of the Russian Empire, was established. Following this example other republics were formed, and in 1922 the Union of Soviet Socialist Republics was constituted. The Union consisted at first of four republics, but later other republics were formed and joined the Union so that by 1930 the USSR consisted of twelve republics, all possessing equal rights with representation on the Council of People's Commissars set up by the Supreme Soviet.

The early history of the USSR is one of economic recovery from the European and Civil wars. Famine existed, production of the essential needs of life was reduced to a fraction of what it had been, factories and mills were idle, there was little fuel or raw materials, and transport facilities, never very good, were partially destroyed by the recent strife. The first tasks of the Government then were to provide the necessities of life for the population, to get the factories working again, and to organize the recovery of agriculture. Under a new administrative system this was accompanied by many difficulties and the Government had to overcome much opposition from farmers and peasants in its administration of collective farming. Progress was made, industry and agriculture recovered and after a few years a higher degree of production was reached than in 1914. Schemes for expansion followed. To organize their great tasks systematically the first five-year plan was formulated in 1928. This was a programme of planning and building and industrial and agricultural development which was to be accomplished by 1932. Among the first important works was the provision of an adequate supply of power for industrial development. The largest power station established during the first five-year plan was the huge Lenin Dnieper power station built near the Dnieper rapids. The electricity produced at this station now supplies power to many districts of the Ukraine. During the first five-year plan scores of factories were built, especially in Central Asia, Trans-Caucasia, Ukraine, and Byelorussia (White Russia), many new cities were planned and many old cities were extensively developed, while the Turkestan–Siberian railway was built. By 1932 the programme of the first five-year plan was completed. In 1933 an even more ambitious programme was formulated for a second five-year plan, and if in 1937 all its objects were not achieved this may be ascribed to its ambitious character and to certain disruptive elements attributed to enemies of the State. In 1938 a third five-year plan was formulated.

By the outbreak of the Second World War the building achievement of the USSR was considerable, especially when it is realized that most of it had been done in the comparatively short period since 1928. Many new cities had been built, while many primitive old towns were completely transformed to large modern cities with up-to-date facilities. For example, Hughesovka in the Donetz area of Eastern Ukraine, which had in 1914 a population of 40,000 with no modern services, became the handsome modern city of Stalino which in 1929 had a population of 462,000 with modern facilities. Stalingrad which, at the outbreak of war, was a modern city with a population of 445,000 was in 1914 a primitive town of 90,000 population. Similar transformations occurred in cities like Chelyavinsk (RSFSR); Minsk, capital of the Byelorussia, Kiev and Kharkov in the Ukraine; Alma-Ata, capital of the Kazakh; Stalinabad, capital of Tajikistan, and many other cities. Moscow was enlarged and extensively developed, the population of about two millions in 1926 being nearly doubled in ten years.

Before much building had begun in the early twenties there was discussion and speculation on what should be the appropriate and fitting architecture for the New Socialist State. There was a natural desire at the outset to create an architecture different from that of the civilization and culture of the immediate past, against which the new regime had revolted; and, at the same time, to create an architecture expressive of the ideals and aims of the Socialist Republics and of the doctrines of Marx, Engels and Lenin, and also be abreast of modern technical developments. It was no easy task for architectural theorists and designers to evolve a style that should satisfy these requirements and it is hardly surprising that the attempts by various groups during the twenties met with little general acceptance. To revolt against traditional styles current in the pre-revolution period and against the modern movements like Cubism, Futurism, Expressionism and many others that occupied the 'bourgeois' (a term for which Soviet Socialism has had an inhibiting effect) intelligentsia of Western Europe, was easy enough. These movements and much pre-revolution art were regarded as products of 'bourgeois' corruption and degeneration and foreign to 'proletarian' art. But all this was negative. It was far less easy to create an architecture expressive of socialist ideals and proletarian culture. Yet attempts were made. In opposition to individualism, which is a characteristic of 'bourgeois' culture, the idea of collectivism was advanced, and associated with proletarian culture, and although no very definite theory or doctrine was formulated and it never gave its name to an artistic movement, yet the vague principle of collectivism permeates Soviet political life and Soviet art. Politically it is seen in the doctrine of the individual existing for the many and for the State. One of its practical effects on architectural practice is the system of team work.

More definite theories which became early movements but resulting in very little actual work were 'constructivism' and 'symbolic formalism'. Constructivism was a movement founded by the two sculptor brothers Naum Gabo and Antoine Pevsner, who held that the plastic arts—painting, sculpture and architecture—are constructions in space and that it is the beauty of these constructions that affords aesthetic pleasure. The construction of machines is suggested as an example for sculpture and architecture, a building being similar to a work of engineering. It obviously had some kinship to the early theories of Le Corbusier advanced in *Vers une Architecture*. The theory meant that the architect must work as an engineer, that he must construct his buildings efficiently, taking advantage of modern techniques, while the rational and utilitarian must be the guiding principles in the content of design. Aesthetic value emanates from the excellence of the construction just as efficient machines like the aeroplane and motor car have their distinctive beauty. The designs that were produced under the name of constructivism were often, however, of a fanciful symbolic character, having little relation to the practical precepts of the theory, such designs as for example Tatlin's famous project for a Monument to the Third International with its spiral forms. This divergence between theory and practice made the movement an easy subject for hostile criticism[1], although it prepared the way for later interest in functionalism.

489

'Symbolic formalism' was an attempt to reduce architectural design to geometric forms which had an absolute beauty and significance. Geometric forms were regarded as symbols of human feelings—cubes expressing integrity, spheres expressing tranquillity and equilibrium, and so on. This theory of symbolic formalism is, of course, not new, and links, on the one hand, with Plato's suggestion in the Philebus that geometric forms have absolute beauty, a suggestion that has had great influence and been frequently quoted; while in its symbolic connotation it links with Lipp's theory of *Einfuhlung* in which human feelings, emanating from bodily conditions, experiences and movements are given to architectural forms.

Although the theories of symbolic formalism, and constructivism, met with opposition, they exerted much influence on subsequent movements and on the various societies of architects that were formed in the twenties. The first of these was the ASNOVA Group (Association of New Architects) which was founded in 1923. The ideas of this group, of whom the most prominent was Professor Ladovsky, were largely an attempted combination of the theories of constructivism and symbolic formalism and associating these with the aims and doctrines of Soviet Socialism. A good deal of vague theorizing resulted. A revolutionary architecture, it was contended, must emerge from the most modern scientific and technical developments; a proletarian architecture must be a coordination of industrial and social factors, while there must be expression of the social and political ideology, which could be secured by the absolute beauty of geometric forms. According, therefore, to the theories of the Asnova Group, architecture must be a synthesis of various factors. Lubetkin[2] speaks of 'a dialectic synthesis of economic, technical, plastic and ideological factors'. How this was to be done was not demonstrated by any actual work. The buildings designed by members of the Group, like Melnikov's Workers' Club at Moscow, were architectural curiosities, which could hardly be said to demonstrate the theories of ASNOVA. An offshoot in 1929 of the Asnova Group was ARCA (Association of Town Planning Architects). The name suggest its aims, which included seeing a building in relation to its environment—the part in relation to the urban and country organism.

Another Group called SASS (Architectural Sector of Socialism Construction) was founded in 1925, several of the members having seceded from Asnova. The members of SASS influenced by the earlier theory of constructivism propounded the doctrine of functionalism, stressing the engineering aspect of architecture and associating it with the creed of dialectic materialism.

In 1929 the VOPRA (Society of All-Union Proletarian Architects) Group was formed. Its main purpose was to bring architecture closer to the proletariat, and to express through architecture the thoughts, strivings and ideals of the workers. It involved a partial rejection of the earlier creeds of constructivism, functionalism and symbolic formalism by imposing restraint on the more definite and extreme designs emanating from these theories. Its significance is in its more positive aspect of attempting to create an architecture of the people. Research was conducted with the intention of discovering the people's feelings about architecture. The results were not surprising. The majority of the people were in their wishes simple and childlike. The architecture of the Tsars, of the nobility and of the rich was classical and grand; they had beautiful classical and Renaissance palaces; why shouldn't we have grand buildings too? And the reply of the Soviets and the architects was: Yes; the people should have what the capitalists once enjoyed. And this was a natural beginning of the new classical revival.

What becomes of the search for an architecture expressive of the aims and ideals of Soviet Socialism so as to create a national style? A case, if not a very strong one, could be maintained for the adoption of classical architecture as a logical national style, because it was the style in which much of the fine city building was done in the eighteenth century.

St. Petersbourg, the new capital founded by Peter the Great in 1703, was the city of magnificent classical architecture where the Tsars and the nobility had their fine palaces and mansions, and where the public buildings are symbols of grandeur. These were looked at with envy and admiration. This city more than any other, more even than Moscow, became the fount and inspiration of Soviet architecture of the thirties. It was spaciously and handsomely planned with the Neva river as its axis with spacious squares on either side and handsome avenues, all on broad classical principles. Its architecture during the eighteenth century provides an interesting study of a process of going further and further back in history from Baroque to early Renaissance and Roman and from these to Greek. In the first part of the century the Baroque style was of a very varied character. It was mostly the work of foreign architects—Italian, French, German and Dutch—whom Peter invited to build his city, and they all contributed their particular variant of Baroque. A little later, after Peter's death in 1725 and towards the middle of the century Russian architects had a greater share of the work, and the Baroque acquired a distinctively Russian character derived from traditional native architecture, similar to the contemporary work in Moscow. One of the best works of this period is the Palace of Sarskoe–Selo, built by Bartolomeo Rastrelli during the reign of Elizabeth (1741–62). The long front façade has a central grouping of three sets of columnar compositions, and there are two subordinate central features on either side. The window surrounds present a somewhat curious mixture of ornamental motives, onion domes are introduced on the chapel, while an assembly of various statues appears on the pedestals in the balustrade. Tsar Nicolas II returned to this palace early in 1917 after his abdication at Peskov.

Catherine the Great, who succeeded Elizabeth, maintained Peter's interest in the building of this modern capital, and she also had decided architectural tastes. Her affections were centred on ancient Rome, and it was the architecture of ancient Rome that she endeavoured to revive in St. Petersbourg, and many of the large buildings erected in or near the city during her reign (1762–96) were partially revivals of Roman architecture. It would perhaps be more correct to say that the early Italian Renaissance with the strongest Roman character is revived. For example, the Pavlovsk Palace, designed by the Scottish architect Paul Cameron, is partially based on an Italian villa, but there is clearly the inspiration of the Pantheon.

Alexander I (1801–1825) was, like his predecessors Peter and Catherine, interested in the building of the new capital, but his taste was for the architecture of ancient Greece, especially that of the sixth and fifth centuries before Christ. In this he reflects the general European taste in architecture, for the Greek revival in Russia occuring in the early nineteenth century was contemporary with its revival in Germany, France and England. Whereas in England there is mainly a concentration on the fifth and fourth centuries, the Ionic and Corinthian orders, in Germany and Russia the concentration is on the sixth and fifth centuries with the Doric order prominent. The Bourse building in St. Petersbourg, for example, is a partial reproduction of the Doric temple at Paestum.

Russian architecture in St. Petersbourg in the eighteenth and early nineteenth centuries, is precisely the architecture which appeared again during the thirties of the present century. VOPRA, in its efforts to express the taste and wishes of the people in architecture, found that the architecture that the proletariat liked was this magnificent classical architecture of the Tsars and nobility of St. Petersbourg. The naive, childlike but genuine reaction: 'This is grand, let's have this' became a determining factor, for to be democratic they should have it. The fact that in April 1932, all the various literary and artistic societies were dissolved by Government decree and combined in one professional organization meant a consolidation of this movement towards a 'Proletarian' architecture; the official professional body for architects being the Federation of Soviet Architects (SSA).

The buildings of the thirties in which the classical style is employed vary considerably in excellence, but like most revivalist architecture very little succeeds in being distinctive or beautiful. The best work is where something of the original proportions are recaptured, or where the classical motif is the basis for some original treatment. Yet whether the building is a Soviet headquarters, a palace of culture, a workers' club, a theatre, cinema or concert hall, or a tube station it has a Greek, Roman or Renaissance dress.

Examples of the classical style used with taste and good proportions are the building of the Supreme Soviet at Kiev designed by Vladimir Zabolotky in 1938, and the Marx–Engels–Lenin Institute at Tbilisi in Georgia designed by Alexei V. Shchusev also in 1938. Both of these buildings were awarded Stalin prizes for architecture. Both are

Building of the Supreme Soviet of the Ukrainian Socialist
Republic, 1936–39 *Architect: Vladimir Ignatevich Zabalotky*

'Pobeda' cinema, Volgograd (formerly Stalingrad),
completed 1948

entral Theatre of the Soviet Army
Moscow, 1939–40

rchitect: Karo Semonovich Alabian

Tbilisi—History Institute of
Georgia 1938–39 (Institute of
Marxism–Leninism) *Architect:
Alexei Victorovich Shchusev*

free adaptations of classical architecture, the freedom seen especially in the application of ornament. The glass dome does not reside very happily on the Soviet building at Kiev, and from the exterior the building would look better without it, especially as it is a design of verticals and horizontals.

A more original building with much of Baroque character is the famous Central Soviet Army Theatre in Moscow designed by Karo Semonovich Alabian and completed in 1940. The five pointed star is the emblem of the Soviet army, and this forms, therefore, the general plan of the theatre (see illustrations). But that is not enough: the columns with 'Corinthian' capitals that surround the whole building each have a five pointed star section. The actual theatre plan, containing the auditorium, foyer and stage, is a regular decagon contained within the star. This central portion forming the theatre proper rises above the star colonade. In the general ensemble there is not perhaps sufficient integration to make a satisfactory formal and cohesive relation of the two.

A Greek, Roman or Renaissance dress is the more complete in parts of buildings which are devoted to display or are designed partly for ceremonial purposes, like the façades and entrances of public buildings, theatres and concert halls, and in the Moscow Metro stations. In buildings not permitting extensive display, and requiring a close adherence in most of their parts to utilitarian purpose, there is necessarily more adaptation of the classical style to practical requirements, as in factories and blocks of flats. In these the classical character is introduced, as implied, in a less imitative manner, although still with some sacrifice of functional efficiency. An example is presented by the apartment blocks built in the Volodarsk district of Leningrad in 1939–41 and designed by E. Leyinsin, L. Fomin and Sevdokimov. In these six-storey blocks the façades are articulated at intervals by porticos of tall square shafts rising four storeys, above which for the upper two storeys a recess is formed with two square columns, while the plain wall space between these features has tall rectangular windows. In this treatment there is obviously some sacrifice of light. The whole effect has a certain dignity, and the character is not unlike some of the more extravagant English Georgian domestic architecture.

In this same district of Volodarsk the building of the District Soviet of Working People's Deputies has a character similar to these blocks of flats. A central portico is flanked by two symmetrical blocks, the essential character of the building depending largely on the tall, slender, square columns and pilasters which surround the building, rising to the full five storeys and supporting an entablature which encloses the roof. The building has a certain classic dignity, but again there is a loss of light by this treatment. What is significant, however, is that in this free adaptation of classical motifs to requirements, an adaptation requiring some originality, the result is more successful than closer imitation of the classical style.

This closer imitation is found a great deal in the façades and entrances of theatres and cinemas, some of which are illustrated. The 'Pobeda' cinema in Volgograd (formerly Stalingrad) is a classical building more like an eighteenth-century mansion or a modern bank. It appears externally as a two-storey structure with a central portico consisting of a group of baseless columns with Corinthian capitals supporting a high pediment with a round arch in the centre. Another, in a similar vein, is the small cinema called 'Oklyabv' in Baranowiczi in Byelorussia. This has a main entrance with heavy columns and capitals surmounted by a pediment pierced with an arch in the centre. The façade owes allegiance to a debased Hellenistic temple. Yet another on a larger scale is the 'Giant' cinema in the Vyborg district of Leningrad designed by A. Gegello and D. Krichevsky and built between 1936 and 1940. It is a massive square building, a little more like a cinema than the majority, because on the first floor above the entrance it has, like so many cinemas, a large square window occupying most of the upper part of the front, which lights the foyer or restaurant. The entrance has a row of curious Ionic columns, and on either side of the large first-floor window and turning the corner for a little distance are four tiers of sculptured panels (see illustration). A little more restrained is the theatre built in the grounds of the tractor plant in Cheliabinsk. This has the Greek balance of horizontals and verticals with a row of Corinthian columns to dignify the entrance.

Two of the most ambitious buildings for entertainment erected during the thirties are the State opera house at Novosibirsk, designed by Alexander Grinberg and completed in 1940 and the opera house at Tashkent. The design of both seems to be largely the result of Roman inspiration, and partly because of their size and partly because of the style from which they are derived they both have a certain grandeur, while they are not without a degree of distinction because of good proportion in some of the parts. The opera house at Novosibirsk expresses in its exterior form its interior shape and function. There is the square entrance block encasing the foyers. This adjoins the domed circular structure of the auditorium, and behind this there is the tall structure above the stage. The opera house at Tashkent is a composition of rectangular blocks, with an entrance of three tall circular arches and arcades at the sides of the building. This building designed by Alexei Victorovich Shchusev is happily proportioned and is amongst the more successful of the adaptations of the classical style.

The Moscow Metro is a source of pride to the people of the capital. They not only believe that it is the most efficient underground system in the world, but they believe that the Metro stations are the most beautiful. If richness, grandeur and lavish decoration were synonymous with beauty, then they would be right. An effort has been made to make these stations as grand and impressive as possible with stone or white marble facings for the exteriors, coloured marbles for the floors and walls of the interiors, combined with ornate decoration and symbolic sculptures.

Novosibirsk Opera and Ballet
Theatre, 1931–43

Architect: Alexander Grinberg

Alisher Navoi Opera and Ballet Theatre, Tashkent,
completed 1947   *Architect: Alexi Victorovich Shchusev*

Lenin Library Station of the V.I. Lenin Underground,
Moscow, 1934   *Architects: Samuel Mironovich Kravetz
and P. V. Kostenko*

Kropotkinskaya Station of the V.I. Lenin Underground
Moscow, 1938   *Architects: Yakov Grogorevich Likhtenburg
and Alexander Nikolaevich Dushkin*

Dynamo Station of the V.I. Lenin Underground, Moscow
1938   *Architect: Yakov Grogorevich Likhtenburg*

Instead of conforming to a type of building defined by the requirements of a Metro station, these Moscow stations are of a great variety of shapes and designs, but they are all variations on the classical theme; that is, they are all adaptations of Greek, Roman and Renaissance styles. They vary from a modern simplified rendering of the classical theme to stations resembling Greek temples, pavilions, mausoleums or triumphal arches. The simplest and most restrained is the first, namely, Sokolniki station, which was built to the designs of the woman architect Bikova, in association with I. G. Taranov, and was completed in 1934. The pavilion is a simple low structure of horizontal rectangles situated in a park and forming also a park shelter. At the entrance are sculptures of athletes symbolizing physical culture. The platform of this station has two rows of square columns supporting a flat ceiling and faced with coloured marbles. There is nothing ornate or garish in this station as in many later examples; it is on the contrary a simple and restrained conception in the classical spirit.

Of the other stations, completed in 1934, in the first section of the Metro, the Lenin Library Station, designed by S. M. Kravetz and P. V. Kostenko, the Smolensky Square Station designed by S. Andreyevski, and the Crimean Square Station, designed by Krutikov, Popov and Andreyevski, are all of the rather restrained classical type from which a simple and functional character with large areas of fenestration has not quite departed. Each is a design of verticals and horizontals and in each there is a decorative use of lettering silhouetted above the low flat roof. With the Kropotkinskaya Station, designed by Y. G. Likhtenburg and A. N. Duskin, and the Arbat Square Station, designed by L. Teplitzki, there is a more fanciful use of the classic style. The former serves also as an entrance to a boulevard which probably determines the design of a circular central arch with flanking colonnaded masses. The Arbat Square Station being near the building of the Commissariat of Defence is planned on the five-pointed star symbol of the Red Army. The structure with its massive square columns and pilasters culminates in a step pyramid effect with a decorative lantern at the top, making an effective ensemble. In some of the later stations the imitation of the ancient classic styles becomes closer. The Dynamo Station built in 1938 to the designs of Yakov Grogorevich Likhtenburg is an example. As will be seen from the illustration here is good Greek copybook design with a central block with cornice, acroteria and sculptured frieze at the corners, two lower flanking blocks with rows of Corinthian columns forming the arcade of the entrance verandah. Steps ascending to this entrance pavilion serve to give it dignity[3].

References and Notes

1. Berthold Lubetkin in an article on Architectural Thought and the Revolution in *The Architectural Review* for May 1932 (vol. lxxi) speaks of the movement as degenerating into a kind of formal decoration based on a sentimental mechanistic-aesthetic.
2. Berthold Lubetkin, in *The Architectural Review*, vol. lxxi, May 1932.
3. For different views on Soviet architecture of the thirties see Edward Carter, Soviet Architecture To-day, *Architectural Review*, November 1942, and Bruno Zevi, *Organic Architecture*, Faber and Faber, London, 1950.

34 France

THE TRADITIONAL CLASSICAL architecture of the thirties, especially that of a grandiose and monumental character, which found expression in varying degrees in the countries of Europe, was due partly, as noted, to political, economic and social assertiveness, which are particularly strong in a period of reviving nationalism. If classical monumentality in architecture was not so conspicuous in France as in Italy, Germany and Russia, it was still pronounced, especially in public buildings and official architecture, and was partly, perhaps mainly, due to the desire to express in architecture the greatness of and pride in one's country. Prominent and significant examples of this expression by means of classical monumentality in the thirties were many of the buildings of the Paris International Exhibition of Arts and Techniques of 1937, of which the two immense permanent buildings were conspicuous.

The expression of French national pride by means of classical monumentality may have been partly subconscious. Although French politics during the thirties gave an impression of instability, with the frequent changes of Government, while the parties of the left, right and centre seemed at times to be uncompromising, the threat of a new German aggression strengthened by Hitler's march into the Rhineland in March 1936 had the effect of cementing an underlying unity, which stimulated national pride and a defensive nationalism. In common with other countries it was felt that the expression in architecture of national greatness and civic grandeur was by means of the universally accepted language of classical monumentality. But, as before indicated, this was less conscious in France than it was in Italy and Germany.

This circumstance has prompted the ascription of other causes for revived classicism in French architecture of the thirties, such as the popular dislike of modern architecture, the architectural inadequacy of functionalism and the feeling that architects of the modern school were confused and unpractical in their ideas and that they cherished architectural fantasies. These factors may have contributed to the partial rejection of the new architecture and a re-acceptance of traditional classicism,

498

but the evidence suggests that these negative reasons are of less importance than the positive political causes.

Among the writers who have attributed to these rather negative reasons the return to classicism in France is Bruno Zevi[1] who refers to the neo-classicism of French architecture in the thirties as architectural decadence. He gives three principal reasons: the people's dislike of modern architecture; the inability of architects to reconcile the practical concepts of functionalism with theories of aesthetic form; and the criticism that architects of the modern school were too much theorists and were too remote from life. The second and third reasons are really explanations and amplifications of the first because they imply that the criticisms of modern architects were in line with the rejection of modern architecture by the people.

It may be asked again how far the general public decides styles and trends of architecture. It is true this occurred in Russia, but that was an exception for the people were actually asked by the Government: it was an obtrusive exercise in democracy in a communist dictatorship. But it was an exception that proves the rule. Styles and trends in architecture are determined mainly by architects and secondly and to a less extent by their clients both subject to national and international cultural movements. In so far as the clients represent popular taste then the people have some influence on trends, but it is problematical how far clients do, and also whether they are more influenced by popular taste than by their architects. To suggest, as does Bruno Zevi, that the modern functionalist movement in France was rejected by the people in favour of a return to a decadent neo-classicism, that 'modern architecture wearied the public', and that 'it was the criticism of the general public that triumphed' is to claim far too much for the power of popular taste. New movements in art and architecture almost always meet with hostility from the general public, but because the majority in such matters are disturbed by the new and strange and lack the necessary knowledge and perception to appreciate readily the qualities in new artistic manifestations, it is usually the discerning few that supports a new movement. The discerning few increase and gradually influence the many, when today has become yesterday. The general public, however, is generally passive in its rejection, although it may be vociferous, and the active rejection and substitution is done by clients with whom architects associate themselves, often for non-functional, non-aesthetic symbolic reasons, and in the case of French neo-classicism of the thirties, those reasons were political.

The Paris International Exhibition of 1937 was a clear exemplification. It was partly a demonstration of French magnificence, for the two largest constructions, both designed as permanent buildings, were the immense Palais de Chaillot built on the site of the old Palais de Trocadero of the 1878 exhibition and the Museum of Modern Arts. These two buildings, especially the former, were partly symbols of the greatness of France

499

and were significant demonstrations at this international exhibition. Although it was an exhibition of art and technique, one felt at the same time that some of the pavilions were expressions of national power. This was particularly the case with the rather grandiose German and Russian pavilions; while Piacentini's Italian pavilion with its classicism and statuary reminded the world of Italy's tradition and cultural influences.

The French have an exceptional ability for organizing exhibitions. Although the first great international exhibition was held in London in 1851, more of the subsequent international exhibitions on a really big scale have been held in Paris than in any other European city. In scope and magnificence there has been little to surpass the great Paris International Exhibitions of 1855, 1865, 1878, 1889, 1900, 1925, 1931, and 1937. Several of these exhibitions left permanent buildings, that of 1889 the Eiffel Tower and the Galerie des Machines (later demolished), that of 1900 the Petit and Grand Palais and the Pont Alexandre III, and that of 1937 the Palais de Chaillot and the Museum of Modern Art. It is ironical that the legacies of the 1889 exhibition are far more modern in spirit than those of 1937, and are far truer monuments of their age. Indeed there could hardly be better examples of true and false monumentality in architecture.

The exhibition of 1937 occupied the same site and area as that of 1900. They were sited on both banks of the Seine along nearly two miles, spreading on one side to the Place du Trocadero and on the other to the Ecole Militaire. Although the area was about two square miles the 1937 exhibition seemed almost to contain a maximum of construction in a minimum of space, with pavilions of many nations, and a large number of French pavilions devoted to manifold aspects of life.

The Palais de Chaillot, the crowning building of the exhibition, dominates its surroundings by reason of its great size and magnificent position on high ground. Its centre is an open court flanked by two large rectangular classic blocks with façades punctuated with long vertical shafts and windows. The architectural effect depends on a massive balance of verticals and horizontals. Below the open paved court is a large concert hall seating nearly 3,000 persons, which opens on to the lower terrace with a large rectangular pool of water and fountains all symmetrially placed on the central axis. Extending on either side of the massive central blocks are curved colonnaded wings, partly encircling the wooded gardens below. All is on an immense scale, but the classic grandeur of the building, cold and impersonal, seems but an empty and mechanical echo of something that was once alive with meaning. The architects were J. C. Dondel, A. Aubert, P. Viard and M. Dastuque.

The Museum of Modern Art by the same architects is in the same idiom, but the treatment is a little more interesting. The museum occupies a site near the Seine. The two wings of the building containing the galleries extend east and west and are linked in the centre by a roofed colonnaded entrance.

The view from the riverside is the most impressive. A series of broad flights of steps lead to an extensive paved platform with flower beds and a pool. Steps on either side flanking the centre ascend to a courtyard with its colonnade of tall straight unadorned columns on three sides. In the centre is a memorial to French patriots who died in the Second World War with a symbolic statue of 'La France' by Bourdelle. It is flanked by two further statues also by Bourdelle symbolizing strength and victory. On the walls by these symmetrical steps are very elaborate relief figure compositions in the classical style depicting the legends of antiquity by the sculptor Alfred Janniot. The Museum of Modern Art is more successful architecturally than the Palais de Chaillot because there is some degree of originality in the use of classical forms and it is less coldly impersonal.

A good deal of the rather stereotyped classical architecture, stripped of ornament, may be seen in much of French official building during the mid-thirties. An example, typical of many, is the large Post Office at Marseilles built in 1935–36 to the designs of Auguste Bluysen. It occupies the best part of an island site. The principal façade facing the Place de la Poste is symmetrical with a pattern of vertical windows on plain stone walls, the chief adornment to give character being a series of bevelled projecting shafts between windows from the first-floor string course, emphatically marked, and terminating at the fifth storey in a strongly projecting cornice. This is crowned by a further storey. On the Rue Sainte Marthe façade, which is almost the same length as the principal façade, is a recessed area forming a court enclosed on the street side with a row of square columns rising from a plinth and merely supporting a beam.

Among other important buildings in the classical idiom erected in France during the thirties are the Musée de la France d'Outre Mer built originally for the Colonial Exhibition of 1931 and designed by A. Laprade and Jaussely. It is a massive structure with a peristyle of square columns with capitals while the wall of the building is covered with relief sculptures giving a very rich effect. L'Hotel de Ville of Puteaux designed by Les Frères Niermans and built in 1934 is classical both in principle and in style; the Post Office at Vichy built in 1935 to the designs of Leon Azema is formal and symmetrical in conception and is a simplified version of the classical theme, while in such buildings as the Agence Citroen at Tours, by M. J. Ravage, Baths at Bordeaux by Louis Madeline, and the grandstand of the sports park at Dijon by G. Pariset and R. Barade, there is a combination of classical design with more advanced construction. For example, the last mentioned has a cantilevered roof while the façade at the rear (or should it be the front as it is the entrance side?) is majestically classical and formal. A considerable number of the individually designed houses built in France during the thirties although built with the modern materials of steel and concrete were classical in feeling, with an accent on mass and repose and a carefully calculated balance of verticals and horizontals. It is possible, of course, that the influence of cubism which had affected earlier architects also persisted, but the simple classical effect is strongly apparent, while the geometricization on which cubism is based has a strong kinship with Greek architecture.

THE LATER CLASSICISM OF AUGUSTE PERRET

Classical architecture of a more original and interesting type and perhaps the most distinctive in Europe at this time is seen in the work of Auguste Perret. His early work formed some of the most notable contributions to the early architecture of reinforced concrete, in the house in the Rue Franklin, the garage in Rue de Ponthieu, both in Paris, built in 1903 and 1905, the Théatre des Champs-Elysées built in 1911 and the church at Notre Dame de Raincy built in 1922–23. The classical influences apparent in Perret's early work become stronger in his work of the thirties. Perret was the son of a building contractor and received his training in his father's office and later at the Ecole des Beaux-Arts which together led to his combining a thorough practical knowledge of construction with a knowledge of classical architecture. He approached the latter in an original manner and he saw in the new medium of reinforced concrete a particularly appropriate means of perpetuating the essentials of classical architecture. Perret's work could be regarded, therefore, not so much as reviving as perpetuating classical architecture. The earliest structures in Greek architecture were of post and beam timber construction and these were later imitated in the more permanent material of stone and led to the column and beam construction which became such a fundamental feature of Greek architecture. But stone, although strong in compression, is weak in tension and is therefore inadequate to follow the structural forms of timber, while it is not always easy to get stone in sufficiently long blocks. The inability to employ this framed structure in stone was apparent in the work of the French classicists of the seventeenth and eighteenth centuries who apparently conceived this as the true classical architecture, yet having only comparatively small blocks of stone had difficulty in expressing the classical framed structure. Claude Perrault and Jacques Jules Gabriel, the noted architects of the French Renaissance, had recourse to reinforcing the stone blocks with iron, while the framed structure was often expressed as applied ornament. With reinforced concrete, a material strong in both comprehension and tension, and produced in long posts and beams like timber it was possible to follow the timber post and beam construction of the Greeks. That at least was the argument of Auguste Perret. The evolving thought has been studied with much learning and sympathy by Peter Collins. After tracing the French Classical drive of the seventeenth and eighteenth centuries towards a trabeated and framed architecture he says that 'all the characteristics mentioned—corner pilasters, unbroken entablatures, wedged window frames, infilling panels, continuously articulated columns, reinforced architraves and flat roofs—were clearly both artificial and structurally unjustifiable in masonry construction, but they were all eminently suited to reinforced concrete. It may be contended, therefore, that the French Classical architects were striving towards a form of architecture which could in fact only be

Palais de Chaillot, Paris, 1936–37 *Architects: J. C. Dondel,*
A. Aubert, P. Viard and M. Dastuque

Mobilier Nationale, Paris, 1930–32
Architect: Auguste Perret

Museum of Modern Art, Paris, 1936–37
Architects: J. C. Dondel, A. Aubert,
P. Viard and M. Dastuque

Musée des Travaux Publiques, 1937–38
Exterior view, plan and side elevation

Architect: Auguste Perret

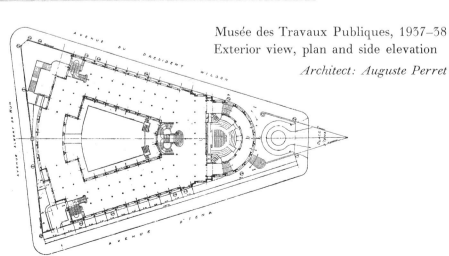

logically produced with a material so far undiscovered, and that in approximating to the solution they desired, they unwittingly prefigured reinforced concrete forms. Outrageously paradoxical though it may seem, it was not Perret who illogically imitated the seventeenth century, but the seventeenth century which illogically anticipated Perret, since it was he, rather than they, who made the structural expression and the structure express one and the same thing.'[2]

The most pronounced expression of classical feeling in Perret's early work was, in the Théatre des Champs-Elysées built in 1911. It is not so pronounced although apparent in his other early work, while it can hardly be discerned in the two churches of Notre Dame at Le Raincy (1922) and of Ste. Therèse at Montmagny (1925) which are interesting for the original treatment in a comparatively new structural medium. The classical feeling returns in a marked manner in his work of the thirties as if he were strengthened in his convictions that classical architecture, particularly of the Greeks, is the true basis of modern architectural design. He was certainly encouraged in his beliefs by the new classical revival that seemed to be sweeping over Europe at this time. Classical character is strongly apparent in his Villa at Garches (1932), the Mobilier National (1933–5), the Musée des Travaux Publics (1937–8) and the design for the Palais de Chaillot (1935).

The Villa at Garches although very different in style from Le Corbusier's villa at the same place, built in 1926, was constructed on similar principles. They are both structurally based on concrete columns, Le Corbusier's house being supported on sixteen columns spaced in four rows, the purpose being to give freedom of planning. The walls are supported on cantilevered beams. Perret's house is supported on a similar disposition of columns arranged at similar irregular intervals in the ratio of 5, 3, 5, 3, 5 approximately, for the more convenient arrangement of rooms, but whereas in Le Corbusier's villa it is a structural expedient to give freedom of planning and has no architectural expression in the appearance of the villa, in Perret's design the columns contribute fundamentally to the architectural character. The square columns are in line with the external walls and appear as plain projecting pilasters. The walls are merely an infilling, the windows are simple vertical rectangles, emphasized by simple projecting frames, those of the top storey not being far removed from the golden section rectangle. The façades terminate in a broad projecting cornice, and the whole effect is of a simple, well proportioned, classical Renaissance house.

When the site was being prepared for the International Exhibition of 1937 it was necessary to demolish the old Mobilier National. It was rebuilt on an inconspicuous site near the Gobelins in the south of Paris. The building consists of three major four-storey blocks forming a square courtyard which is completed by two-storey domestic blocks flanking the entrance. The main flanking block houses the administrative sections, workshops and storerooms, while the top floor of the central block with blank

504

walls is a large display gallery. Under the courtyard which forms its roof is a large
storage room, and in building this Perret took advantage of the undulations of the site.
The wide entrance between the domestic blocks is divided into three bays by two pairs
of columns supporting an entablature and cornice which continues the line of the
cornice of the flanking blocks and curving outwards a little like a bow. In front of
the columns are two sculptured crouching mastiffs by Abbal. The columns are
interesting. They are fluted and taper a little downwards and are without bases or
capitals, the only transition from column to soffit being a small fillet. Perret had
generally used columns slightly tapering upwards, as in his churches, almost straight
as in the Théatre des Champs-Elysées, but these columns of the Mobilier Nationale
are the first time, as far as I am aware, that he used them tapering downwards and
thus reversing the traditional treatment of an upwards taper. He developed them with
much subtlety in the Musée des Travaux Publics. The principal façade of the Mobilier
Nationale facing the visitor on entering the courtyard has a wide canopy sheltering the
entrances on the ground floor, with the upper storeys divided into seven bays, two tall
windows occupying each bay on the first floor, spaced equally, while on the two upper
storeys is the blank wall enclosing the display gallery. Each bay is occupied by a
large framed panel or blind window, and the suggestion of the latter, of windows
filled in, is always a disconcerting device. It is continued on a smaller scale in the façades
of the flanking blocks, and the effect is the reverse of agreeable. This building although
much admired for its proportions is one of the least satisfactory of Perret's works,
partly perhaps because of the associations of the façade panelling with blind windows.
I saw the building in 1964 and it has acquired with time a rather drab brown colour.

The Musée des Travaux Publics, now occupied by the Conseil Economique et Social,
built in 1937–9, is a much more successful work and must surely be regarded as one
of Perret's masterpieces. It is situated in the west end of Paris, not far from the
Palais de Chaillot and the Musée d'Art Moderne. The site is triangular and is bounded
on the north side by the Avenue du President Wilson and on the south side by the
Avenue D'Iéna, with the point of the triangle towards the Place d'Iéna. Full advantage
has been taken of this important position. Too many trees have been allowed to grow
rather closely round the building so that it is not easy to appreciate its architecture at
the distance where it can be seen as a whole.

The Museum consists of display rooms on three floors arranged on three sides of a
triangle with a courtyard in the centre. At the apex of the triangle is a lecture theatre
of hemicyclic form with ramped seating, on the model of the Greek theatre. In the
conception of this building there is a new interpretation of ancient architecture in terms
of reinforced concrete which is realized by a complete integration of design and
construction. The architectural effect is very largely dependent on the method of
construction in which Perret has used columns as the main structural elements. A
series of columns surround the building standing on a plinth at first-floor level, and

505

supporting the roof of each wing which consists of a monolithic concrete slab. The first and second floors of the galleries are structurally independent of this outer construction and are supported on the piers of the walls and internal columns on the two lower floors, while the upper floor is comparatively free of internal supports. A similar method of construction is employed for the lecture theatre at the apex although here the columns are lower and support a roof which surrounds a drum and flat concrete cupola, the windows in the drum giving light to the interior. This construction is an adaptation of the peristyle of columns supporting the roof surrounding the cella in a Greek temple.

Perret was a classicist and it is clear from most of his work that he believed that columns contributed fundamentally to architectural effect, and the Musée des Travaux Publics shows one of his most original uses of them. But he wanted, as before implied, to use columns also in the structural terms of reinforced concrete. The classical column of the Doric, Ionic and Corinthian orders was a conception in stone with a slight taper towards the top. But in a tensile material like reinforced concrete the major reinforcement is at the top where it connects with the horizontal beam. It is therefore structurally logical for the wider part to be at the top and taper towards the bottom like table or chair legs. In early Greek architecture when columns were of wood this is how they were shaped. In the palace at Knossos, remains indicate that columns of cypress wood were of this shape and the alabaster columns of the entrance to the Treasury of Atreus at Mycenae (about 1300 B.C.) tapered downwards probably in imitation of timber prototypes. In reinforced concrete it was logical, therefore, to use columns tapering downwards, which he did first in the entrance screen of the Mobilier Nationale, then in the large colonnaded space between the flanking blocks in his design for the Palais de Chaillot, which, of course, was never realized, and then in the Musée des Travaux Publics.

Peter Collins, the able English interpreter of Perret, thought very highly of the Musée des Travaux Publics. He regarded it as 'the culmination of many previous endeavours such as those of Perrault and Gabriel, to exploit the aesthetic value of free-standing columns to its fullest extent'[3] combined with a logical constructional justification. A notable feature of Perret's external columns in this building is the solution of the problem of the aesthetically satisfying transition from the cylindrical column to the square beam. In the Théatre des Champs-Elysées and other early works there was just the bare connection with a fillet at most. He was naturally reluctant to imitate stylistically the capitals of the classical orders and felt that a transition should be worked out in terms of reinforced concrete. In the interior columns of the Musée des Travaux Publics there is just the abrupt connection, but in the exterior columns broadening at the top the transformation from cylinder to square is done by running the flutes into a scale-like or leaf-like treatment for the capital. Perret later resolved this into a simpler and broader more geometric treatment which was used by architects following Perret in the extensive reconstruction work at Le Havre after the Second World War. Although a building in the classical tradition, like its neighbours the Palais de Chaillot and the Musée d'Art Moderne, it offers a contrast to these in not being an architecture which merely reproduces in a simplified way classical forms, proportions and character, but a work which is full of subtleties and refinements emerging from the thought of its designer while it composes into a satisfactory whole. It is one of the most distinctive twentieth century buildings in Paris.

It will be seen from this that Perret although an architect in the classical tradition was less a revivalist than a developer. He took certain themes like the column and developed it in terms of the new material of reinforced concrete, linking it with the Greek use of timber columns. In realizing an architecture in the classical tradition in terms of reinforced concrete he did so with considerable originality so that new forms were evolved. This is the creative use of tradition.

REFERENCES AND NOTES

1. Bruno Zevi, *Towards an Organic Architecture*, London, 1950, pp. 46–50.
2. Peter Collins, *Concrete: the Vision of a New Architecture. A Study of Auguste Perret and his Precursors*, Faber and Faber, London, 1959, p. 171.
3. Peter Collins, *Concrete: the Vision of a New Architecture. A Study of Auguste Perret and his Precursors*, Faber and Faber, London, 1959, p. 264.

35 England

WHEREAS IN Germany, France and central Europe the new architecture had become fairly familiar during the twenties, it had hardly manifested in Great Britain and by 1932 there were not more than a dozen examples in the whole of the country. The most notable of these were Easton and Robertson's Royal Horticultural Hall (1926–8) in London; four houses, one by Peter Behrens in Northampton (1926), two by Amyas D. Connell, High and Over at Amersham (1929) and New Farm at Grayswood (1932), and another by Colin Lucas—the Sun House at Chelwood Gate (1931); Joseph Emberton's Yacht Club building at Burnham on Crouch (1930) and his office building, near Southwark Bridge (1931); and Sir Owen Williams' Boots' factory at Beeston (1932). There was thus in England hardly sufficient manifestation of the new architecture to stir a revolt or even a mild reaction prompting a return to traditional classical architecture, as there had been elsewhere in Europe. Yet some strengthening of the adherence to classical traditions occurred in the early thirties and it is apparent in a wide range of works. Trends towards a greater freedom of design were in many cases reversed. The London Passenger Transport Building at St. James's, completed in 1929, designed by Charles Holden, showed a freedom of treatment of traditional Renaissance which promised further interesting and original experiment, but the architect's next large work, the University of London building at Bloomsbury, showed a more rigid adherence to classical tradition. It may be that the different purposes influenced these different conceptions, but the all-powerful factor has been the spirit of classicism.

Yet, at the same time, modern architecture flowered strongly in England during the middle and late thirties, due partly to the migration of architects from Germany and central Europe. Indeed the spirit of the new architecture was maintained chiefly in England, Scandinavia, Holland and Switzerland during these periods after its decline in so many countries, as we shall see in subsequent chapters. There appears, therefore, to have been two architectural movements in Britain during the thirties flowing in opposite directions, one backwards to the remote past and the other forward with evolving life.

The classical and Renaissance traditions manifested more variously in England than in those European countries where the work was more in the nature of a new revival, and can be broadly classified as the continuing stylistic imitation, of which, however, there is a decreasing amount; the adherence to symmetry and classical serenity of proportion achieved by balance of verticals and horizontals accompanied by considerable simplification and elimination of ornament which was generally thought by its authors to give architecture a modern feeling; and thirdly classical traditional architecture treated with originality and given a partially new character by the personal feelings of architects.

The chief buildings in which these classical and Renaissance traditions are apparent are those where some degree of monumentality has been the aim, such as town halls, law courts, headquarters buildings of national institutions, banks and university buildings. Examples of buildings in which stylistic imitations are continued are those of Vincent Harris. In the early thirties Harris designed three rather palatial municipal buildings in which this is apparent: the Leeds City Hall (1933), Sheffield City Hall (1932) and Somerset County Hall, Taunton (1934). The Leeds City Hall occupies an island site, and the main architectural character is concentrated on the principal façade. There are two storeys of tall windows on this elevation and in front is a tall entrance portico with Corinthian columns supporting a pediment. This is flanked by two towers terminated in solid stone spires or obelisks. These towers or steeples are approximations to Wren's steeple of St. Vedast, Foster Lane, indeed they might be called Harris's variations on a theme of Wren. The large portico has a rather superfluous, stuck-on effect, and the façade with the well-spaced and proportioned windows would, I think, have looked better without it. Similar Corinthian columns were used in the Greek-like Sheffield City Hall which is a much finer building. Here the three entrances are recessed and appear behind a row of columns flanked by walls on the same alignment. There is in this building a well-proportioned massing, and a nice balance of transverse rectangular masses is achieved giving some feeling of Greek repose and serenity.

Another example of a prominent building in which the Renaissance style in its more classical phase is perpetuated is Chesterfield town hall, designed by A. J. Hope of Bradshaw, Gass and Hope and completed in 1937. The building is symmetrical with a classical entrance portico with columns and pediment in the centre of a long three-storey façade with a stone dado in the first storey and brick above. An interesting feature showing how everything is subordinated to a symmetrical and formal lay-out on classical principles is the council chamber. It is the central room at the rear on the first floor and has a wide bow wall with three windows conforming to the ground floor, yet the seating of the chamber is in horseshoe fashion arranged transversely and wholly unrelated to the preconceived shape of the room.

509

Probably the majority of the city and town halls and civic centres built in the late thirties would come within the second category, that is mainly classical, or Renaissance in design and conception, combined with simplification and elimination of ornament, with a minor infusion of original variation from the central theme. The Renaissance tradition has, of course, undergone several modifications from adaptations to various types of building in the course of its 350 years of life in England, especially in the Georgian period, and these give a wide selection to the modern architect.

Among the variations in municipal buildings are the City Hall, Norwich, designed by C. H. James and S. Rowland Pierce, completed in 1938; the Southampton Civic Centre by E. Barry Webber, completed in 1939; the Walthamstow Civic Centre by P. D. Hepworth (1938), Wandsworth Municipal Offices by W. and E. Hunt (1938) and the Watford Town Hall by C. Cowles Voysey (1938). The Norwich City Hall presents a long symmetrical façade to the market place, with slightly projecting wings at either end and central colonnaded portico above the entrance with columns rising from the first floor balcony. The building has a stone dado below the balcony, with brickwork above which is patterned with three storeys of windows, those on the balcony being tall and stone-framed, while the two rows above are well-spaced and proportioned, yet would not larger windows and consequently lighter offices have been more serviceable? The tower with its medieval character at one end, provided in conformity with the traditional town hall belfry tower, looks somewhat incongruous in relation to the symmetrical Renaissance façade.

The Southampton Civic Centre is more austerely classical. It is a large symmetrically planned grouping, spaciously set with extensive lawns surrounding it. A tall tower rises in a central position a little set back from the main entrance. There is a degree of classical grandeur in the broad simple massing of much of this group, especially in the dignified treatment of entrances.

A similar broad classical yet simple treatment appears in the Walthamstow Civic Centre, which consists of a municipal office block set well back from the road and fronted by a large circular pool. At one side is the assembly hall. This building was much praised by well-informed architectural critics[1] shortly after it was completed, yet it is difficult to think that seen in longer retrospect and in relation to other buildings of the time that it merits high praise. The office block consists of a long central spine with wings at either end and a projecting block at the rear of the main entrance to hold the council chamber on the first floor.

The front façade is very similar in character to Marcello Piacentini's rectorate building of the University of Rome described in Chapter 31. The central entrance has a portico with four square columns rising to the whole height of the building and the proportions and treatment are very similar, except that the space between the two central columns

Leeds City Hall, 1933 *Architect: E. Vincent Harris*

Walthamstow Town Hall, 1938 *Architect: P. D. Hepworth*

in Piacentini's design is a little wider, and his portico is mounted on more steps than Hepworth's. The porticos, however, are so alike in general character that it is difficult to think that Hepworth did not copy Piacentini's design of six years earlier.

The walls of both buildings extend on either side with the projecting flanking masses, as plain surfaces punctured with vertical windows; and although Piacentini's is on a grander scale, the spacing is subtler and there is an effective decorative emphasis in the frieze of lettering and the relief sculptures on the wings. The medieval turret over the centre of Hepworth's building is more incongruous than the tower of Norwich, and ill accords with classical building from which it rises.

The assembly hall at the side is a rectangular box-like building with a flat door and a small stage and accessories which must limit its uses. There is a magnificent entrance for so small a building, consisting of a portico of six rectangular columns rising to the whole height of the building, between projecting walls or antae at either end, and surmounted by a lettered frieze. Five entrances between the columns are set well back to allow a generous covered space before entering. As a classical architectural composition it is certainly impressive and like the offices has been enthusiastically praised[2], but it is a question whether the money spent on this grand entrance would not have been better devoted to securing a more functional hall with raked floor and more generous stage.

The Wandsworth Municipal Office block is a stone-faced building symmetrically planned round a central courtyard. Greek architecture was clearly the inspiration in the simple treatment of the elevations, with a sculptured frieze on one façade reminiscent of classical temple friezes. The work of David Evans and J. Linehan, it is an attractive feature of the Wandsworth High Street façade, and depicts various historical incidents in the Wandsworth area which includes Balham and Tooting, Clapham, Putney and Streatham. For example, the warlike Saxon chieftain Tota is greeted by some Totingas, from which the name Tooting is derived; Geoffrey de Mandeville is shown in full armour; Wilberforce holds the act ending the slave trade, and with him is Macaulay; Oliver Cromwell sends two of his Ironsides from their camp at Putney to guard the captive King, and Gibbon revisits his birthplace at Putney; Dr Johnson takes tea at Streatham Place, and a Roman soldier and two early inhabitants end the pageant of Wandsworth. One has to be provided with a guide to read this frieze, but that of course is the case with the frieze of the Parthenon. In the Greek frieze, however, the subject is a procession clearly apparent which links the figures together; it sets the theme for the interesting design of coincidental subjects at Wandsworth.

The perpetuation of classical and Renaissance principles of design combined with a minimum of ornament, and resulting in well proportioned buildings, but without any distinctive originality in treatment, is seen in government and other office building and in hotels of the thirties. Perhaps the most notable of the former is the New Government Building near Calton Hill in Edinburgh designed by Thomas S. Tait of Sir John Burnett, Tait and Lorne and erected in 1936–8. Here there is again the symmetrical grouping with Greek influence manifesting in balanced horizontals and verticals, plain walls and well-proportioned, well-spaced windows. Restraint and dignity are felt in contemplating the building, but it is somewhat stereotyped. A notable hotel built in the restrained classical style is the Queen's at Leeds, completed in 1937 and designed by W. Curtis Green, Son and Lloyd. The largest and most famous building, however, coming within this category designed and partly built during the thirties is London University in Bloomsbury.

LONDON UNIVERSITY

Like Rome University before the completion of the new University City in 1935, the various colleges and faculties of London University were scattered in various districts, and students of both Rome and London Universities sometimes had the same experience of having to travel from one part of the city to another to attend lectures necessary for their course of study. In 1927 a beginning was made to combine several of the colleges and faculties in one building group, for in that year a $10\frac{1}{2}$-acre site in Bloomsbury was acquired for the purpose. Charles Holden was appointed architect because the Senate of the University, having inspected the modern buildings in London, considered that the architect of the London Passenger Transport Building in St. James's would be the most suitable designer of the new university buildings. The site is a long rectangle running north–south containing the whole of Torrington Square and bounded by Byng Place and Gordon Square to the north, Woburn Square, Thornhaugh Street and Russell Square to the east, Montague Place to the south and Malet Street to the west. South of Montague Street is the British Museum roughly the same width as the University site. The group was to consist of eleven units (see plan).

The architect originally made several plans[3] and although he first arranged the buildings at the southern end, including the Senate House, round an open court, this was changed to a general plan based on a long central spine, as this allowed for the required extension to the several units. The central axis of the British Museum was continued northward and formed the spine of the University Group. 'It was intended' said Charles Holden 'that the first portion of the buildings to be erected would occupy the spine, while the ribs of the east of the spine would allow for the future extension of each separate unit. Every unit would therefore have provision for its own extension.'[4] This plan was followed for the building of the southern section which includes the Senate House at the extreme south completed in 1936, the Tower rising above the central spine completed in 1937, and the Institutes of Education (1938) and of Historical Research, but it was abandoned for the northern part of the site built after the Second

World War. For this part the various buildings comprising Birkbeck College, University Union, and the School of Oriental Studies, are grouped round a long central garden. The southern section based on the spinal plan consists of two large rectangular blocks connected by the tall massive rectangular tower 210 feet high. Each of the blocks on either side of the central spine has two light wells and rises four storeys for the outer buildings, five storeys for those flanking the tower and six storeys for the spinal blocks. The whole grouping is symmetrical in both directions.

The Senate House consists mainly of offices in the periphery of the block, the Senate room being on the first floor on the east side. The bases of the light wells flanking the the main hall are occupied by the square William Beveridge Hall on the wiest side, and the rectangular Macmillan Hall on the east side. The tower accommodates the various sections of the library—reference and lending sections, catalogues, periodicals and stacks.

The building was designed to last for five hundred years or more, and therefore a method of construction based on long experience was chosen, for as the architect said, it was not 'an occasion for the admission of any element of doubt as to the permanence of the structure.'[5] Thus the building was constructed of traditional solid weight-bearing walls of brick and stone, and the only modern construction employed was in the tower which included a steel framework within the heavy load-bearing walls, the function of the steel frame being to carry and transmit to the foundations some part of the heavy load of the book-stacks. The floors throughout these buildings are of heavy construction, consisting of steel girders spanning between outside walls with hollowbrick tiles and reinforced concrete ribs of sufficient strength to carry partition walls, thus permitting flexibility of internal arrangements.

The architectural character of this heavy monumental building is derived from ancient Greece, seen both in the broad simple masses of the exterior and in the character and atmosphere of the interior. The somewhat monotonous patterning of vertical rectangles on the plain stone walls is similar to many of the buildings of the University of Rome. The architect, conscious perhaps of the risk of monotony in his treatment, has tried to introduce notes of variety. For example, on the main fronts of the Senate House six windows on the third floor are spaced above seven on the second floor, which Holden says 'has an exact parallel to the syncopation which we find in some of the best of music, and it is for the same rhythmical purpose that it has been employed in this case. It fulfils the purpose of breaking the vertical punctuation or 'beat', the row of windows on this floor combining with the lines of the parapet in giving a flowing horizontal emphasis to the lower masses of the building.' It is difficult to appreciate the 'flowing horizontal emphasis', as the building with the pattern of vertical rectangles on a flat wall seems essentially static, especially as the verticals are as apparent as the horizontals, with not very much emphasis of either. The tower with the synthesis

514

of adjacent masses is a composition conceived within the static massive pyramid, and like the pyramids of Egypt it gives the impression of massiveness and weight, obviously designed to last for a thousand years.

The interior is more pleasing than the exterior. There is essentially the atmosphere of dignity, serenity and repose that one associates with the architecture of ancient Greece; it is seen particularly in the ceremonial hall of the Senate House and the ceremonial stairway that leads from it. The composition is of simple massive rectangles, with massive piers rising on either side of the staircase, linking with the massive pattern of the panelled ceiling. The long balcony on either side of the hall with the decorative metal front gives a balancing horizontal motif. The whole, although massive, has a light toned effect, obtained from the first floor windows opened to the light wells above the balcony, and by the light cream travertine of the walls and floor. The serenity, dignity and restaint are continued in many of the rooms, in the rectangular Macmillan Hall and in the Senate room where the lower part of the walls is panelled in walnut and the ceiling in South American cypress; and particularly in the entrance hall on the spine underneath the tower, between the east and west courtyards. There are four entrances on each side, closed by bronze gates. The central parts of the flanking walls are occupied by the twin stanchions, coupled by stone slabs, that support the floors of the tower. The level of this entrance hall is slightly sunken and is approached from the gateways by three shallow steps. The ceiling is coffered, and bronze bowls supported along the walls by sconces give indirect lighting at night. The broad simple massing of this entrance hall with emphasis and balance of verticals and horizontals coupled with a rather dramatic light and shadow effect, both by natural and artificial light, give a feeling of repose combined with a slight sense of mystery that one associates with Greek architecture. It is difficult to analyse, but it is a feeling given by much of the best Greek revival architecture, and is felt strongly for example in many of the interiors of St. George's Hall, Liverpool.

This London University building, designed and built to last for many hundred years, raises the question whether this is a rational intention. It is the reverse of organic building so much advocated by Frank Lloyd Wright, Lewis Mumford and Bruno Zevi, to mention three notable names among many. It is true that the construction permits flexibility within the solid external walls so that internal walls and partitions could be changed with changing needs, but the solid external walls remain forever, it would seem. The response of the building to change of university education needs is thus restricted. Who can say what those needs will be in a hundred years with the quickening tempo of civilization? Should not university buildings with all educational buildings in the future be so sufficiently flexible that they can be completely changed in a hundred years? But this solid classical London University building is built with the same sense of permanence as a Greek temple, or an early Italian Renaissance Palace.

In the third category of traditional classical architecture in England during the thirties, that is such architecture treated with originality and given a partially new character by the personal feelings of its architects, are some of the most distinctive buildings created in England during the period. They include the R.I.B.A. building, probably the most important of the group, a few town halls, several court houses and police stations, a few office buildings, especially some by Lutyens, and one or two hotels. The R.I.B.A. building merits a description of some detail, while a selection of other buildings will be briefly considered.

THE R.I.B.A. HEADQUARTERS

The Royal Institute of British Architects was founded in 1834 and its first headquarters were at Thatched House Tavern in St. James's Street. It moved in 1835 to Evan's Hotel, in 1837 to 16 Grosvenor Street, in 1859 to 9 Conduit Street, where it remained until 1934, and then moved to its present premises at 66 Portland Place. The building in Conduit Street was originally a private house built in the Italian Renaissance style in 1779 to the designs of James Wyatt. The need for more spacious premises began to be felt early in this century, and the need became more acute after the First World War. (Membership had risen from 2,700 in 1909 to 7,200 in 1932.) In 1929 a site was acquired at the corner of Portland Place and Weymouth Street.

The design was the subject of a competition won by G. Grey Wornum in May 1932. The assessors, Sir Giles Gilbert Scott, H. V. Lanchester, Charles Holden, Robert Atkinson and Percy Worthington, rather ensured a traditional building on classical lines, and such was the choice.

It is a steel-framed structure faced externally with Portland stone. There are two principal façades, the main narrow façade facing Portland Place, and a long side façade in Weymouth Street. Columns flanking the entrance support sculptured symbolic figures that look upwards to the symbolic figure of architecture in relief on the plain wall above the large rectangular window which constitutes the central mass of this façade. There are single windows in four tiers on either side which are continued in series on the Weymouth Street façade. It is the placing of these windows on the plain walls that constitutes the proportions of the interesting elevations. On the ground storey the masonry is rusticated forming a dado for the ashlar work above. The windows on the ground storey are fairly short rectangles approximating to the golden section, above on the first floor they are tall rectangles, approximately double square, then above on the second floor they are shorter rectangles held together on the Weymouth Street façade by a long bronze balcony front. The third floor has a blank wall in which five relief figure sculptures appear above every other window, while the fourth floor has a series of square windows. The system of ratios has obviously been very carefully worked out on classical principles, and it must be admitted that the result is pleasing. Enjoyment of these façades is a matter of personal reaction, and

University of London, 1936–40 (continued 1948–60)
Architect: Charles Holden

General exterior view

Interior view of hall of Senate House

eadquarters Building, Royal Institute of British Architects, 1932–34
Architect: G. Grey Wornum

eneral exterior view and interior view of stairway and landings

for me the only unsatisfactory effect (apart from the edge of the floor going across the large central window) are the square windows. I would have preferred a slighter diminution of the length of the second-floor windows. They are less satisfactory in this respect than, say, the sequence in Somerset House or Lutyens's British Medical Association Building in Tavistock Square.

The way classical symmetrical planning has been made to accord with a convenient disposition of parts in the interior is certainly very skilful, and has been much admired. The main groupings on the basement, ground and first floors are round the principal features of the two halls, the assembly hall with the raked floor (Henry Jarvis Memorial Hall) and the exhibition and examination hall (Henry L. Florence Memorial Hall) on the first floor. Facing the main entrance beyond a square entrance hall is the staircase, the central flight of which leads to a landing then divides and turns about and one reaches the first floor. Turning about again on either side one enters the spacious square exhibition hall. Descending from the entrance hall by either of the two flanking stairs one reaches in front the foyer of the assembly hall which slopes downwards to the left. There is a moveable wall between the foyer and hall which can add to the accommodation of the latter. Behind the dais is a screen for illustrated lectures. It is a somewhat sombre room—the walls are panelled in teak, olive, ash and black bean—but well suited to its purpose with excellent acoustics on which Hope Bagenall advised. The Henry Florence Hall above is a bright dignified interior with the tall double square windows and a large window to the staircase, which is a motif that repeats the large central window on the main façade. Rising from the first floor landing are four dark massive moulded columns of Ashburton marble that encase steel structures. These link the balconies on the second and third floors and support a ceiling patterned with windows through which artificial light is given to the stairway. The main feature of the third floor is the library, which extends to the fourth floor holding the periodicals' balcony and the council room.

The interior gives a general feeling of classical dignity and restraint belonging more to Greece than to Rome or the Renaissance. It is achieved throughout on the theme of the broad massing and relation of rectangles, a nice balance of transverse masses and refined and small scale decoration which is kept wholly subordinate to the main simple lines and massing. It really has, in this respect, some similarity to Sir Giles Scott's Liverpool Cathedral. Also much of the decoration is reminiscent of Greek motifs, like the key pattern seen in the narrow frieze above the inscription panels of Perrycot stone flanking the entrance (on which are inscribed the names of Past Presidents on one side and Royal Gold Medallists on the other), which is continued as a ceiling band in the Henry Florence Memorial Hall. The formal square decorative theme appears also in the glass panels of the staircase and landing balustrading, in the floor patterns and in the rostrum fronts of the Henry Jarvis Assembly Hall. The more fanciful pictorial themes are kept strictly subordinate to the rectangular patterning as

518

in the carved panelled screen of Quebec pine in the Henry Florence Hall, in which are
depicted the people, industries, flora and fauna of the Commonwealth, and in the
jambs and soffits that frame the staircase where representations of building tools form
the decorative motifs. This strict subordination of all decorative motifs to the prevailing
vertical and horizontal masses gives a distinctive character and atmosphere. The
building is also notable for the effective decorative use made of the colour and texture
of different materials, particularly stone, wood, glass and aluminium bronze.

Being the headquarters of the architectural profession not only in the United Kingdom,
but also in the Commonwealth, it is important that the building should not only be
of the highest architectural excellence and be a distinctive example of building crafts,
but it should express a sense of dignity, the dignitas that Cicero and Vitruvius
contended was so important.

Excellent as the building is as a highly individual variation on the classical theme, it is
doubtful whether it does give the sense of dignity that one would like to see in the
headquarters building of British architects. I think the main failing is in the entrance
hall which for the dignity of a building of this kind should give a sense of space such
as one gets, for example, from the entrance hall of the Institution of Civil Engineers
building completed in 1913. It is true that this building is on a much bigger scale,
but more could have been made of the entrance hall of the R.I.B.A. building. The
chief defect in this respect is the lowness of the ceiling which is only about 11 feet
and which extends some 30 feet as far as the staircase, when some sense of spaciousness
begins, but which is only completely felt when one reaches the first floor landing.
A design which would have opened up the upper part of the entrance hall to the first
floor ceiling would have given a greater sense of space and dignity. Another feature
which is a little disconcerting is the edge of the second floor running across the middle
of the large central window of the main façade. Sir Charles Reilly in his appreciation
of this building said that this window 'is a fine central feature and the fact that a floor
crosses it should not worry anyone.'[6] Sir Charles was being kind to Grey Wornum,
because, once noticed, this floor seen through the window is disconcerting and gives
the impression that the large central rectangular window has not much relation to the
interior space.

The question has been asked why a headquarters building of the architectural profession
should have been a variation of the traditional classical theme, and not more progressive
in spirit and more expressive of the new architecture of the time and its potentialities
for the future? It has, however, been regarded as a transitional building and thus, it is
contended, expressive of the architecture of the time, at least in England. A critic
in an appreciative article in *The Architect and Building News*[7] said that the 'building
is in many ways a really fine achievement, but it suffers from the prime defect of all
acutely transitional art: uncertainty of aesthetic aim. Every isolated criticism of detail,

of disposition, of proportion, is ultimately only one aspect of this basic uncertainty, this wavering sense of direction.' Transitional design is, however, really a process of change from one form to another. When architecture in the period between the World Wars is referred to as transitional it means that it represents the process of change from traditional architecture to the new or modern architecture. There must be a sense of the style or form to which it is moving. This cannot be said of the R.I.B.A. building. It is hardly dynamic in time, but is an original variation on a 2,400 year theme.

But why is it of the past rather than pointing to the future, as it might have been, say, in Germany, if it had been built there in 1930? The reason, I think, is that the new architecture had not really reached England, there were so few examples here, and it was still in the experimental stage, and it was perhaps a risky thing to venture into something experimental for a symbolic building of this kind. Another reason is that there was no Le Corbusier, no Frank Lloyd Wright, and no Mendelsohn in England. Sir Charles Reilly rather generously summed it up when he said: 'Wornum might have designed, and would probably have enjoyed doing so, an entirely modern building with no roots in the past at all. A similar building to represent architecture in most foreign countries today would no doubt be so. With us however, and for such a conservative institution as the R.I.B.A., it would not be a truthful expression, or even an idealized expression, of the attitude of a large section, let alone a majority, of the members to their work. The revolutionaries among us, though I thoroughly believe the future is theirs, are still a small minority. By the time the reaction has set in in the other countries we shall no doubt all be converted, including the great ground landlords and their agents. These latter cannot be entirely forgotten, as Wornum has found out. The R.I.B.A., too, with its traditional attitude to such folk, to its friends of the Royal Academy and to what it considers good form generally, is not really as free to express itself in a new way as a new vigorous single class institution like the BBC.'[8]

Among the other buildings of the thirties that might be regarded as variations on the classical theme with distinctive individual contributions by their architects are Greenwich and Watford Town Halls; several Law Court buildings and police stations; the Reuters and Press Association building in Fleet Street; the North London Collegiate School; and the Cumberland Hotel in London. There are also buildings where classical principles of form, of masses and symmetry are followed, but where several features of the new architecture are incorporated. These architectural hybrids, which might be regarded as transitional work, owe their success or failure to the individual design talent of the architect. A successful example is the Philharmonic Hall, Liverpool, designed by Herbert J. Rowse; one much less successful is St. Dunstan's Convalescent and Holiday Home built in 1937–8 between Brighton and Rottingdean, designed by Francis Lorne of Sir John Burnett, Tait and Lorne, where the long horizontal windows with the general horizontal emphasis in the main block do not accord with the strict symmetrical massing. In classical architecture horizontals and verticals require a degree of balancing to achieve the serenity and repose so important in this tradition and long horizontal emphasis is not in harmony with this. The two town halls mentioned are brick-faced buildings with large plain walls and good regular spacing of windows, but their main interest is in their plans for they illustrate the power of the traditional classical symmetrical arrangement in planning, and in the case of Greenwich the partial breaking away to more functional planning. Classical symmetrical planning is obviously a very strong habit which many architects obviously find difficult to shake off. The Watford Town Hall, built in 1937–9 and designed by C. Cowles Voysey, for example, occupies a corner site and the centre part of the office block presents a concave façade to the corner, with straight wings on either side, and a centre block projecting diagonally at the rear in which, on the first floor, is the council chamber. Awkward symmetrical designing is shown where this block on the axis of the main entrance leaves unused spaces between the centre block and wings. The assembly hall with its own main entrance links with one of the two office wings and with its flat floor suffers from being designed for too many purposes, so that it is a poor hall for meetings, concerts and drama.[9] The external brick facing is on a reinforced concrete framed structure, with floor and ceiling slabs of concrete.

The Greenwich town hall was built at the same time to the designs of E. Culpin and Son, and though influenced by the traditional symmetrical method for buildings of a monumental character, it is yet a far better plan, fitting its site very much better with improved use of the available space. The office section of the building is a reinforced concrete framed construction faced with brick and includes many modern motifs like the car park at the rear underneath part of the first floor extension, which contains the council chamber and a tall square clock tower used for storage at the end of an office wing. The hall block of steel frame construction consists of the main assembly hall on the first floor, similarly related to the offices as at Watford, but linked more closely, while there is a minor hall on the ground floor arranged transversely with the upper hall. The strictly symmetrical planning is concentrated in the more ceremonial parts of the building: in the main entrance halls on the ground and first floors, the latter leading to the ante room and council chamber, and in the disposition of parts in front of the two halls. The building includes many functional developments in accord with modern requirements, such as the car park underneath part of the building. The assembly hall, with its flat floor, suffers from the same defects as that at Watford. This town hall with its lofty square tower was probably partly influenced in conception by Dudok's Town Hall at Hilversum, built in 1928–31.

One of the distinguishing features of English architecture of the thirties is the great improvement in the designs of law courts and police stations although these are nearly all, as one would expect, on traditional and mainly classical lines. Notable buildings of this kind have not been plentiful in English history, the best known being the Gothic

Law Courts in London by G. E. Street (1875–81); the slightly earlier Assize Courts at Manchester (1860–4) by Alfred Waterhouse, a regular pot-pourri of Gothic, but more conveniently planned than Street's building; Norman Shaw's romantic castle-like New Scotland Yard built in 1887–8, and, above all, Newgate Prison by George Dance, the younger. Sir Reginald Blomfield said that this prison, Somerset House and the Custom House, Dublin were the three finest public buildings erected in the United Kingdom since the time of Wren. These buildings are, however, the rare exceptions, the majority of such buildings before 1930 were not of high architectural quality. Later examples have however a little more distinction. Among them are the Manchester City Police Headquarters, designed by G. Noel Hall; the police stations at Hammersmith, by Farquharson and MacMorran, at Bishops Stortford by Vine and Vine, at Worthing by C. G. Stillman; the Law Courts at Southport by Thomas Cooke and Dickinson; and the Court House at Chichester by C. G. Stillman. All these buildings were erected between 1936 and 1939.

The Police Headquarters at Manchester is closer stylistically to simplified Renaissance. It occupies a rectangular site, and the building is arranged round a large central courtyard, on to which many of the offices face as this is the quieter part of the building. The walls are of brick, but faced with Portland Stone on the main frontage to South Street, which is a dignified symmetrical elevation, with a handsome central entrance and slightly projecting flanking masses. The whole is well proportioned with good spacing of windows on plain walls. Perhaps the most notable of the other police stations is that at Hammersmith which has some refined detailing. It is a three-storey squarish mass, with stone facing on the ground floor forming a dado to the brick facing above. The central entrance is surmounted by the Royal Coat of Arms; the five large windows of the first floor constitute a dominant feature to which the four ground-floor windows and the smaller second-floor windows coming above the window intervals of the first floor are subordinate. The sequence of windows patterned on the plain stone and brick wall is exceptionally pleasing. The few restrained decorative details like console and mouldings derive from Georgian architecture[10].

The police stations at Worthing, Sussex and Bishops Stortford, Herts depend for their excellence on rectangular massing with well-spaced windows on plain brick walls with stone dressings. They both have flat roofs which accord better with this type of architecture. Police stations built at about the same time of similar character are those at Worcester by Sir Percy Thomas and at Bromborough, Cheshire by F. A. Browne, but the serene effect of the window spacing on plain walls is rather spoiled by the somewhat obtrusive pitched tile roofs, with the little turrets in the centre. Pitched roofs in Georgian-Renaissance architecture are most satisfactory when at a low angle and kept entirely subordinate to the rectangular massing, or partly hidden behind a parapet or balustrade.

Hammersmith Police Station, 1938
Architects: Farquharson and MacMorran

euters and Press Association Building,
eet Street, London, 1936–38
Architect: Sir Edwin Lutyens

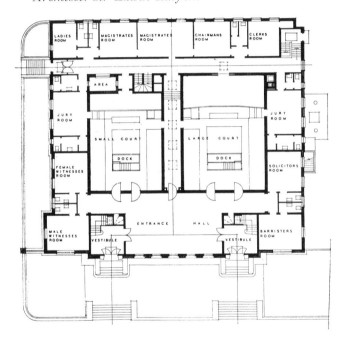

Court House, Chichester, 1937
Ground floor plan and exterior view
Architect: C. G. Stillman

The Southport Law Courts is a large dignified building depending for its effect on rectangular massing. In the principal façade two-storey masses flank the entrance with squarish windows on stone facing in the ground floor, and tall rectangular windows on brick walls above, with recessions at either end and for the upper storey, which give a three dimensional character to the building. The main entrance is impressive: above a flight of steps the opening rises to double-storey height with a pair of tall columns set within the architrave which, with the increase of scale, do much to accentuate the dignity of the entrance.

The Court House at Chichester is a small building comprising two courts with the usual accessories of rooms for juries, magistrates, witnesses, barristers and public galleries. The plan is a square divided in the centre with a court on either side surrounded by the rooms. It is simply but ingeniously planned with access to the galleries from two front entrances without going into the main entrance hall. The composition is one of rectangles, the central brick mass is flanked by two small recessed squares, and pierced in the centre by five tall narrow windows between the two stone-framed entrances. The proportion is very satisfying and the building is something of a late Renaissance gem. In the interior the five tall windows give the entrance hall a dignified character in harmony with the purpose of the building.

The Reuters and Press Association building Fleet Street (1936–8) by Sir Edwin Lutyens is interesting not only for its excellent proportion but also for the fanciful variations on the Renaissance theme. The building is a stone-faced nine-storey structure with a comparatively narrow elevation to Fleet Street and long side elevation to the minor Dorset Rise. Lutyens was one of the greatest masters in the design of well-proportioned elevations that have given much aesthetic pleasure to sensitive percipients, and whatever his failings as a planner, a function that he was sometimes content to leave to another architect, he seldom failed to produce beautiful elevations. The difficulty often is that some of the most interesting parts of the composition are high up on the building and it is difficult to see them in a narrow street. Such was the case with his Midland Bank in Poultry (see Chapter 11) where the structure was surmounted above the fifth storey by the semblance of a Renaissance church with nave, choir, transepts and a dome at the crossing. Similarly in the Reuters and Press Association building the most interesting part of the Fleet Street elevation is above the sixth storey, where a row of elliptical headed windows set behind a balustraded parapet is surmounted by a two-storey mass with a concave façade on which is set a flat dome. At the corner of the building is a narrow diagonal wall, following the theme set below. More conventional, is the treatment of the first two storeys, with recessed masonry joints separated from the ashlar above by a cornice broken in the centre by the semicircular arch of the entrance which rises to a little above the two storeys. A whimsical feature of this lower part is the pilasters with bases and caps vanishing in the masonry. These pilasters are continued in the four storeys of plain walls to break the balustrade of the sixth storey and thus serve to link the upper and lower part which would appear to have little schematic connection otherwise. Indeed the lower two storeys and the upper three are very much separate architectural compositions. The long side elevation is comparatively plain, and rather dull. The horizontal windows of the centre part are a little out of harmony with the rest of the building.

After contemplating several of Lutyens's buildings it is interesting to look at Sir Albert Richardson's North London Collegiate school, an L.C.C. (now G.L.C.) secondary school for girls which was built in the late thirties. Here is proportioning and decorative detailing strongly reminiscent of Lutyens's work, seen in such features as pilasters, entablature balustrading and windows, yet done with a lightness more expressive of the frame construction than is general in Lutyens's work.

The Cumberland Hotel in London, built in 1931–3, is designed in the classical tradition with symmetrical planning and many classical decorative motifs, treated with some originality but it is also a building of constructional and technical interest, and illustrates that a building modern in technical equipment and construction can be clothed in a simplified if rather unusual version of the Renaissance dress. The architect, F. J. Willis, had previously designed the large building occupying the island site to the west of the hotel and opposite the Marble Arch, and he designed the Cumberland Hotel to conform to his previous building, which included the earlier Odeon Cinema, so as to achieve a satisfactory unity of the two buildings. The dominating features of the principal stone-faced nine-storey façade of the hotel are the broad cornice on the seventh story, the bay windows at intervals, extending on four floors from the second to the sixth storey, flanked by rather heavy obtrusive columns and decorated on the mullions with figures and a heavy keystone on the fourth storey. There are three such focal points at intervals in the composition.

The Marble Arch underground station occupies the centre of the building, having been moved from the southeast corner of the site. The building of the new station and the hotel proceeded simultaneously, but because of the vibrations from the trains it was necessary to isolate the two structures. The construction of deep foundations involved adequate retaining walls, and those for the hotel were of brick with steel reinforcement.

At the time of its erection the hotel was the largest in Great Britain and the large public rooms on the ground floor necessitated large spans, and some immense steel girders in the frame construction, one of which, weighing 98 tons, was the largest used up to that time in building.

The hotel is symmetrically planned with two light wells. There are nearly 1,000 bedrooms, each with a private bathroom and lobby. It is one of the earliest examples of air conditioning in an hotel in Europe, and the occupant of each bedroom can regulate the influx of conditioned air between temperatures of 13 and 21°C (55 and 70°F); while it was the first London example of a building drained on the 'one pipe' system. Yet so up-to-date an hotel existed behind a façade that expressed nothing of this, but was stylistically rather a bizarre variation of the classical Renaissance.

REFERENCES AND NOTES

1. Julian Leathart in an article in the monthly journal *Building* for December 1943. The design for the building was the subject of an open architectural competition and Leathart says at the end of his review of the Centre that 'it is a source of great satisfaction to me as a competition man (I was placed third in this competition) that a building of such high quality should add its testimony to the efficacy of the competition system as a means of producing fine, contemporary architecture'.

2. Julian Leathart regarded this front 'as one of the finest entrances to a public assembly hall built in the country during the past 30 years. It is grand and exciting stuff, elegant in form and dignified in mien.' *Building*, December 1943, p. 309.

3. Three of these are shown in outline as illustrations to a paper on the design given by Charles Holden to the Royal Institute of British Architects, and printed in its journal for 9th May 1938, p. 638.

4. *Journal of the Royal Institute of British Architects*, 9th May 1938, p. 638.

5. *Journal of the Royal Institute of British Architects*, vol. 45, p. 641.

6. *Architectural Review*, December 1934, p. 193.

7. *The Architect and Building News*, November 2nd 1934, p. 129.

8. *The Architectural Review*, vol. lxxvi, December 1934, p. 193.

9. See A Qualitative Study of Some Buildings in the London Area by S. B. Hamilton, H. Bagenal and R. B. White. National Building Study No. 33, special report, London 1964. With reference to the Watford Assembly Hall the report (p. 35) says 'For a general-purpose hall used for public meetings, lectures, dancing, music, theatrical performances, conferences, exhibitions and boxing the design could only be a compromise between conflicting requirements. For all auditorium purposes, without exception, a long flat floor is both bad for hearing and for seeing.'

10. Julian Leathart was enthusiastic about this building. Writing in *Building*, December 1942, p. 272, he found the 'dimensional elevation altogether delightful; the horizontal balance is as skilfully contrived and pleasing as the vertical division of window and wall' and he regarded it as 'one of the most successful compositions I have seen for a long time'.

36 Scandinavia, Holland and Switzerland

THE VARIOUS CLASSICAL traditions did not persist so late and with such strength in the Scandinavian countries, and in Holland and Switzerland as they did in England, yet there are a few important buildings designed under these influences which should be noted. They could be regarded rather as exceptions to the general run of transitional and new architecture in these countries during the thirties.

Yet in Scandinavia, as in England, the new architecture was not such a powerful force in the twenties as it was in Germany, central Europe and France; and therefore the classicism that manifested in the thirties was less of a revival than the fanning of the embers of a dying tradition—a reluctance to depart from it entirely. Without the classical wave that spread over Italy, Germany, Russia and France it is doubtful whether these few dying embers would have lasted quite as long in Scandinavia. In the Netherlands and Switzerland, on the contrary, the new architecture had made considerable progress, and the examples of classicism were somewhat in the nature of an occasional nostalgic impulse to retain the classical character in architecture and all that it meant—a desire, partly instinctive, on the part of some architects to arrest a little the onrush of the new techniques and their expression in architecture, and to hold on to known values.

Perhaps the most completely classical building erected in Scandinavia during the thirties, a building in which many Hellenic stylistic features were employed, is the Parliament House in Helsinki built to the designs of J. S. Sirén in 1931–2. It was in many ways the final important building of academic classicism that had obtained to a considerable extent in Finland during the twenties, represented by such buildings as the Union Bank and the Finnish Savings Bank designed by P. E. Blomstedt, a few schools by Gunnar Taucher, and the Stockmann Departmental Store in Helsinki built in 1939 to the designs of Sigurd Frosterus.

The Parliament House is largely Greek in conception and character with a Roman motif here and there. It has a monumental frontage of fourteen tall columns standing within the massive frame of the rectangular mass raised well above the roadway and reached by a broad flight of steps almost the width of the building. The same classical monumental character is apparent in the interior, in the entrance hall with its lofty ceiling, in the various reception rooms and in the domed circular chamber where Parliament meets, which seems to have been inspired by the Pantheon in Rome.

OSLO CITY HALL

Another large spectacular building of Scandinavia built during the thirties which is a combination of classical monumentality and Puritan functional severity is the immense City Hall at Oslo; a project that took 33 years to be realized for it was in 1917 when the City Council of Christiana—as it then was—resolved to build a civic hall worthy of the city. A competition for the design was won by Arnstein Arneberg and Magnus Poulsson, who were entrusted in 1920 with the work. But the site in Pipervika by the harbour had to be cleared of a good deal of slum property held by over fifty owners and so much delay occurred in acquiring it that a start was not made with the building until 1931. During those eleven years the many developments that had occurred in European architecture prompted the architects to make many changes in their design, which was originally a traditional conception of a city hall with a belfry tower. This they abandoned and substituted a much simpler and, they claimed, more functional building, although really much more monumental, consisting of two office blocks rising from an extensive lower block containing the reception and other kindred halls. Most of the building took place in the thirties and sufficient progress had been made by 1939 for the office sections to be occupied, but it was not until after the war, in 1947, that the Council chamber was used. The final inauguration in 1950 coincided with Oslo's 900 years jubilee.

The south side of the building faces the harbour and the sea, the north side is approached by a long straight street which opens to a quadrant immediately in front of the building. The entrance is through a raised open courtyard with ramped approach and flanked by cloisters with square columns, with a central graceful fountain, with water falling over a series of steps in conformity with the slope, and surmounted at its spring by the Oslo swans, the work of Dyre Van. The cloister has a frieze in coloured wood by Dagfin Werenskiold on the theme of the Norse myth of Yggdrasil.

Flanking the entrance and rising to a height of 197 feet are the massive tower blocks housing the offices, a partly functional arrangement to facilitate communication by avoiding long corridors, and to obtain maximum light. The towers are patterned with windows on plain brick walls to about two-thirds of their height, then there is a band of thin vertical apertures, and then plain walls, which enclose in the eastern tower the belfry with a carillon of 38 bells, and in the western tower studios with roof lights for the artists engaged in the extensive mural and sculptural decorations of the building.

528

The towers have simple crenellations at the top. On the south face of the eastern tower is an immense clock 28 feet in diameter, the largest in Europe, and an astronomical clock appears on the wall near the entrance facing the courtyard.

After entering the building on the first floor level one passes into the long gallery running transversely, and then into the vast central hall 160 feet long by 101 feet wide by 69 feet high, with immense murals on the walls. On the west side a broad staircase leads to the balcony that surrounds the hall, which opens to the various reception rooms, the banqueting hall on the east side, the festival gallery on the south facing the sea, the President's Chamber and the Hardrade and Munch rooms and library on the west side, and a semicircular council chamber, flanked by two galleries, on the north side.

The central hall and reception rooms are all rectangular with flat ceilings of timber beam construction. The main spatial effects depend on enclosure by the adjustment of vertical and horizontal masses. The lighting of the central hall is partly by means of the floor level windows on the south wall, but mainly by the windows high up on the longitudinal walls. At night floodlights fixed to the tall parapet walls surmounting the outer walls of the surrounding reception rooms shine through these windows. Externally, at the floor level of the central hall on the first floor a balcony runs round the building, while, on the floor above, the tall windows of the reception rooms are deeply recessed with loggias. Construction is of reinforced concrete frame faced externally on the ground floor with pale Sand gneiss (a granite of laminated structure) and above with dull red brick. Several sculptures appear on the broad plain brick wall at the top of the building: a bronze figure of St. Hallvard by Nic Schill on the south wall, a granite equestrian figure of Harald Hardrada by Anne Grimdalen on the west side, and symbolic figures in blue syenite granite by Alfred Seland on the outer walls of the towers.

Although the building is formally and symmetrically planned, the arrangement of the various parts is very ingeniously contrived. The broad masses of the exterior are a little forbidding and the two heavy towers in relation to the central hall block do not make a happy architectural composition. The most pleasing part of the exterior is undoubtedly the entrance courtyard on the north side, which is a well-designed, partially, enclosed space giving an agreeable feeling of serenity and dignity.

As in the case of the civic buildings of the Middle ages and Renaissance in Italy, such as the Palazzo Vecchio in Florence and the Doges Palace in Venice, the walls of the principal hall and rooms are decorated with paintings mainly of local history, and the whole building is a setting for Norwegian visual arts. These were executed mainly after the war between 1945 and 1950. The largest and most spectacular painting is that by Henick Sørensen, 78 feet by 39 feet, occupying most of the south wall of the central

View from southwest

Interior of banquetting hall

View across harbour

City Hall, Oslo, 1931–50
*Architects: Arnstein Arneberg
and Magnus Poulsson*

Second floor plan

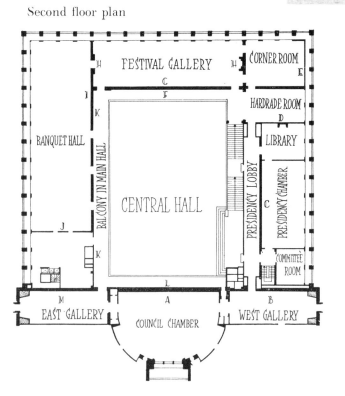

Forest Crematorium, Stockholm
South Cemetery, 1935–40

Architect: Gunnar Asplund

hall. It represents the life of the city and some incidents of its recent history, all painted in strong positive colours—red, yellow, blue and orange—which rather jump out and produce a somewhat garish effect. The colours will doubtless soften with time and the effect will perhaps be improved. The side walls above the balcony and staircase are in a varying comparatively subdued pattern of blue. Further paintings are above the balcony on the north wall symbolically representing the country of Norway, and below the balcony on the east wall the theme is the German invasion of 1940, both by Alf Rolfsen. The walls of the reception rooms are partly or wholly decorated with immense murals. The end walls of the festival gallery have paintings by Axel Revold, one representing Norwegian shipping and industry and the other fishing and farming, while three tapestries depicting incidents from Norwegian history hang on the long marble wall. Tapestries also hang on the soapstone walls of the Hardrada room, and depict Harald Hardrada proclaiming the foundation of the city and his death at the Battle of Stamford Bridge. The Munch room contains Munch's picture of 'Life'. The east and west galleries on either side of the council chamber are completely covered in brightly coloured frescos. Those in the east gallery by Per Krohg represent the daily life of the city and the various occupations and leisure pursuits of its people, but included in the series is a picture of Grini concentration camp and Norway's struggle against the German invader. Those in the west gallery by Aage Storstein are on the theme of the birth, inspiration and history of the Norwegian constitution symbolically represented.

The City Hall of Oslo has been described in some detail as it is a significant expression of civic pride in the twentieth century, and if as an artistic achievement it is hardly comparable to the City Hall at Stockholm the effort was no less. The Oslo building may not be one of the distinctive works of architecture of the twentieth century, but it is a highly competent and original variation on modern classical monumentality, while there are details here and there which are wholly delightful, like the entrance courtyard. In its paintings, sculpture and decorative crafts it is an expression of contemporary Norwegian art, some of which may be valued by posterity.

Gunnar Asplund of Sweden is revered as one of the notable architects of the century, partly for being the author of the first complete expression of the new architecture in Sweden in the buildings of the Stockholm Exhibition of 1930, particularly the Paradise Restaurant, and partly as the author of one of the finest classical conceptions of the thirties, the Forest Crematorium building in the Stockholm South Cemetery, begun in 1935 and completed in 1940. This building is often considered to be Asplund's masterpiece, and it is sometimes cited as a notable example of modern architecture, but it is essentially classical in conception.

The site of the Crematorium was formerly a gravel pit which was transformed into a hill rising above the surrounding landscape. The group of buildings comprises three

531

chapels, the structure enclosing the furnaces and the columbarium. Approaching by the main entrance to the cemetery from the west one ascends the broad windswept hill, and near the summit to the right of the road is a large free-standing cross announcing eloquently to the world the Christian dominion here. Beyond this on the hill's summit is the crematorium, the most impressive feature of which is the spacious portico with numerous square plain columns. In front of this is a large reflecting pool which contributes to the architectural effect. The spacious portico leads to the large chapel, the front wall of which consists of a metal grille which can be sunk into the floor so that chapel and portico become one large space to accommodate large congregations. Near the chapel entrance and set back among the shafts of the portico is a sculpture group of five bronze figures expressing resurrection and aspiration, a distinctive Rodinesque work. The simple rectangular massing of the group of buildings relates well to the portico but the interiors of the chapels decorated with murals are a little fussy and do not have the quiet dignity of the exterior.

The whole group, especially the portico seen on the summit of this hill with a background of the dark pines of the forest and the large solitary cross is very impressive. It is essentially Greek in feeling with a serenity that is achieved largely by the simple balance of uprights and rectangular forms while the openness of the hill setting with the broad landscape of southern Stockholm suggests an identity of the individual with the universe.

Although Gunnar Asplund has been rightly regarded as one of the outstanding pioneers of modern architecture in Sweden he was a classicist at heart, seen in earlier work like the Skandia Cinema (1922–3) and the Stockholm City Library (1924–7). The exhibition buildings of 1930 were a brilliant departure from the main trend of this architect's work. In the Crematorium he returns to his early affection for the classical tradition.

Classicism in the architecture of the Netherlands during the thirties was, as already indicated, rather in the nature of an occasional retreat from the advanced positions that had been secured in the new architecture. An interesting example of this can be seen in the work of J. J. Oud who was a prominent functionalist and exponent of the new architecture during the twenties and early thirties, yet when designing the Shell building in The Hague in 1938 he returns to what can only be described as classical monumentality, with the idioms of symmetry and massive formality. There are many modern technical features. In the construction modern methods and materials are employed, such as reinforced concrete framework, while there are several modern features like the two glass staircase towers at either end of the long office block; but these are part of the general symmetry and formal massing. The rows of windows in this long six-storey building are separated by various narrow vertical strips and these modern features in a broadly classical building have led many writers to refer to it as a transitional building. But in the evolution of style it is for its architect a movement

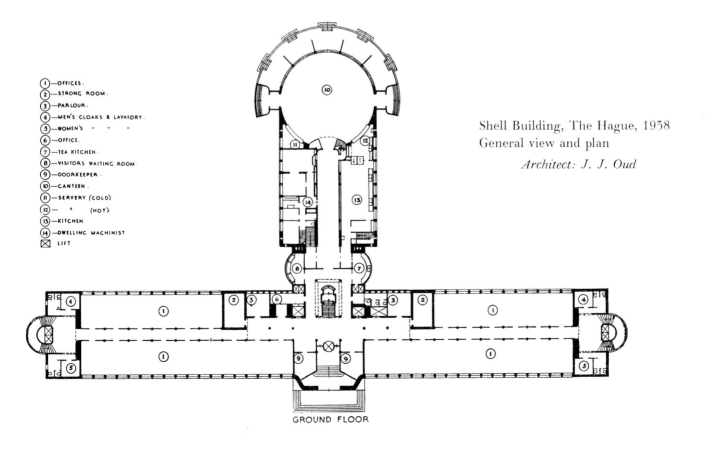

① —OFFICES.
② —STRONG ROOM.
③ —PARLOUR.
④ —MEN'S CLOAKS & LAVATORY.
⑤ —WOMEN'S "   "   "
⑥ —OFFICE.
⑦ —TEA KITCHEN.
⑧ —VISITORS WAITING ROOM.
⑨ —DOORKEEPER.
⑩ —CANTEEN.
⑪ —SERVERY (COLD)
⑫ — "   (HOT)
⑬ —KITCHEN
⑭ —DWELLING MACHINIST
⊠ LIFT

Shell Building, The Hague, 1938
General view and plan

Architect: J. J. Oud

GROUND FLOOR

backward, although this is not to deny that it is very handsome and well-proportioned if somewhat stereotyped. It may be that the client was insistent on a building of classical monumentality; judging from other Shell buildings in Europe this is not unlikely.

What happened a little in the Netherlands also happened a little in Switzerland and there are a few examples of persistent classicism during the thirties especially in public buildings. The Art Gallery at Basel built in 1932–6 to the designs of R. Christ and Paul Bonatz is a notable example. The building is designed round a courtyard, with façades faced with stone and brick, and although there are large windows with light mullions and transoms the general pattern is of a nicely calculated balance of verticals and horizontals, while the long entrance porch or arcade has a row of heavy columns with ornate capitals supporting circular arches, which is a variation on a Roman theme. The extension to Basel University built in 1937 to to 1939, of which R. Rohn was the architect, though having many modern features, is essentially classical in spirit with the heavy masonry shafts between the tall vertical windows above an arcade with massive straight columns. The new central cemetery in Basel laid out and built in 1934–5 is a further notable example of this persistent classicism. A spacious garden just beyond the main entrance is symmetrically flanked by two long buildings performing the functions of mortuaries and columbaria which have a classical monumentality, while the whole cemetery is laid out in a formal manner in contrast to some of the more informal landscaping of other Swiss cemeteries.

Classicism with its massive monumental quality, in which the facing material is massive stone or its substitute, is found all over Europe in the thirties, chiefly of course in the countries like Germany, Italy and Russia where it is a purposeful revival associated with political motives. Elsewhere on a smaller scale it is due to innate conservatism and to an instinctive conviction of the unwisdom of relinquishing too readily old established methods and styles for comparatively new and untried methods as in England and partly in Switzerland. In Austria and the Balkan countries the persistence is the same. In the start of building in Europe in the first few years after the war, from about 1945 to 1950, much, especially public buildings and offices, was in this simplified classical-Renaissance style that had obtained to such a large extent in the thirties. The torch of the new architecture seemed to be taken reluctantly, aesthetic considerations were subservient to technical needs, there was a desire everywhere to get the buildings up in face of difficulty, and the immediate and most familiar pre-war style was used as it was ready to hand. Progress in the aesthetic expression of new methods of buildings that had been dropped in Germany in 1933, and was maintained with some difficulty in England and the smaller countries of Europe until the war, was not really continued on a considerable scale until after 1950[1].

What happened in Europe in the relation between the new architecture and persistent classicism happened also in the USA, which offers something of a parallel but with different periods. The USA up to 1893 was architecturally one of the most advanced countries in the world, developing new techniques and expressing these architecturally. Progress was centred mainly at Chicago in the work of Louis Sullivan. The year 1893, however, was the year of the World Columbian Exposition which gave a magnificent display in its buildings and planning of classical and Renaissance architecture learnt mainly at the Ecole des Beaux Arts in Paris. To the architecturally naive American people this was like the dawning of a new world. This grand monumental classical architecture entirely captivated them, and in consequence from 1893 to the thirties it became the architecture of the public buildings of the USA. There were exceptions, of course, in the continuance of the progressive Chicago school and in the work of Frank Lloyd Wright, but his influence was mainly in domestic and industrial work. There is a certain parallel here in the USA and the USSR. In the latter the people 'democratically' were asked to choose their architecture, and they naturally chose the architecture of the magnificent palaces and public buildings of kings and nobles who preceded them.

NOTE

1. The western world witnessed during the thirties the migration of some of the most talented and progressive architects of Europe, mainly from Germany, Austria and Hungary to other countries of Europe and the USA. This migration meant the spread of architectural ideas and a quickening of architectural developments in the recipient countries.

PART V

Towards a Better Physical Environment

1943—1970

Block of Flats, Hansa District, Berlin, 1957–59 *Architect: Walter Gropius*

37 Post-war reconstruction—planning, housing and early building 1943–1950

THE SECOND WORLD WAR began in early September 1939, with the invasion of Poland by Germany, and France and the United Kingdom immediately declared war on Germany. Poland was partly overrun and occupied by Germany, while Russia advanced into Poland to establish an advance frontier with Germany. In the Autumn of 1939 war broke out between Russia and Finland with hostilities ceasing early in 1940. In April 1940, Germany invaded and occupied Denmark and Norway, and in May 1940, the Netherlands, Belgium and France. In that month Italy joined the war in support of Germany. In June 1941, Germany invaded Russia and later occupied the Balkan countries. Thus from 1941 to 1945 all European countries with the exception of Sweden, Switzerland, Spain, Portugal and Turkey were involved in the war, which meant a greater destruction of urban areas than had ever taken place before, and occurred in all the countries involved but was greatest in Russia, Germany, The Netherlands and Great Britain.

One of the principal tasks for the European nations after the war was the rebuilding of cities and towns that had suffered extensive damage. Another important task was the large scale provision of housing, for there were not only the houses destroyed by war, but the accumulated shortage during the period, for in most belligerent and occupied countries the provision of houses was reduced to the barest minimum for workers engaged in war industries and agriculture. About forty million new dwellings were needed in Europe at the end of hostilities in May 1945, and if they could have been provided at the end of that year it would not have been too soon. It was not until about 1960 that the post-war housing target of most European countries had been reached, meanwhile there was the further accumulated demand.

In the early years of the conflict not a great deal of thought was given to reconstruction and rebuilding, but once there was some confident expectation as to the result plans began to be made. This confidence was in some measure given by the entry of the USA into the war in 1942 in support of the United Kingdom, Russia and their allies.

The United Kingdom, partly because it had this confidence, was among the first to make plans for reconstruction. Among the plans prepared were those for London and Greater London published in 1943 and 1944. The first was by Sir Patrick Abercrombie in collaboration with J. H. Forshaw, the architect to the London County Council, and the second by Abercrombie with a team of assistants. To explain the principal aims and purposes of these plans, which had considerable influence not only in Great Britain but in Europe and America, it is necessary to recall some of the urban trends and planning movements in the earlier part of the century.

It was noted in the first part of this history how congestion and slums had grown in the big cities during the nineteenth century and the efforts made to bring about dispersal, and Ebenezer Howard's idea of a garden city (Chapter 9), which led to the garden cities of Letchworth and Welwyn, was described. Propaganda was conducted by the Town and Country Planning Association for a large scale adoption of the policy by the Government of dispersal from congested cities (with their slums, extensive suburbs and commuting) by means of well-planned, self-contained satellite towns. In 1937 a Royal Commission was appointed, 'to inquire into the causes which have influenced the present geographical distribution of the industrial population of Great Britain and the probable direction of any change in that distribution in the future, to consider what social, economic or strategical disadvantages arise from the concentration of industries, or of the industrial population in large towns or in particular areas of the country; and to report what remedial measures if any should be taken in the national interest.' Although completed in August 1939, the report was not published until four months after the war had started in December 1939. The Commission made nine recommendations among which were the establishment of a Central Authority, national in scope and character, the continued and further redevlopment of congested urban areas, decentralization or dispersal, both of industries and industrial population from such areas, and an examination of the possibilities of doing this by garden cities or garden suburbs, satellite towns, trading estates and by further development of existing small towns or regional centres[1].

The recommendations of this report together with the propaganda of the Town and Country Planning Association, and the circumstance that Patrick Abercrombie himself was a member of the Commission and was associated with the propaganda, led to a scheme in the plans for London of redevelopment of central areas at lower densities, and dispersal by means of satellite towns. Ten were indicated round London from which eight could be chosen, and a prototype plan for a satellite town was prepared for Chipping Ongar, Essex. Abercrombie later prepared plans for Edinburgh, Plymouth, Hull, Sheffield and Bristol, and for several regional developments. Plans were also prepared for nearly all the cities and many towns by other architects and planners, often the city architect in collaboration with the city engineer, during the latter years of the war. In the case of the large cities like Birmingham, Manchester, Liverpool, the plans generally aimed at redevelopment at lower densities in the centre with a measure of dispersal. The extensive destruction which many cities suffered such as London, Liverpool, Coventry, Plymouth, Portsmouth, was looked upon as an opportunity for urban improvement, for in all these plans there was the spirit of building a better world than had existed before. The many social schemes like the Beveridge report was another indication of this.

Perhaps the European country that was the closest parallel to Great Britain in these planning enterprises undertaken during the war was the USSR. In 1942 vast territories of Russia were invaded by the German army, which reached as far as the outskirts of Stalingrad, over a thousand miles from the frontier. This meant that with the German advance war factories had to be moved and established eastward to Siberia beyond the range of destruction, with the result that formerly sparsely populated regions far to the east became large industrial areas, which contributed to rebuilding with the return of peace.

Later as the Germans retreated rapid measures were taken to replan and rebuild while hostilities continued, for the very circumstance of the German retreat prompted the expectation of peace and reconstruction. Planning on a vast scale started during the first three Five Year Plans (1927–42) and the planning after the German retreat was often a continuation of what had previously been initiated, although, as in Britain advantage was taken of the opportunity presented by destruction of more comprehensive development. An example was the plan for Stalingrad, now Volograd. Although the earlier plan was followed, the opportunity was taken for considerable improvements, the area on the banks of the Volga was cleared of railways, warehouses and industries and developed as parks. The earlier plan, which was developed and modified, consisted of several urban units, or neighbourhoods, with factory areas and workers settlements, each with a central square. Plans and the revision of earlier plans were prepared and began to be implemented for numerous cities and towns in USSR directly the areas were liberated by the German retreat. Rapid planning and implementation was facilitated by the state ownership of the land.

In the Netherlands Dutch architects met during the war in underground groups to draw up plans for future developments, and when the country was liberated in 1945 the destruction was regarded as an opportunity to do something better than existed before, especially in the case of Central Rotterdam which was almost completely demolished.

France, that had been partly cooperative with Germany and partly resistant, was yet able during the war to visualize to some extent the work of reconstruction and to prepare legislative machinery to facilitate post-war planning and building. From 1940, when the German occupation began, considerable thought was given by the French government to fresh planning legislation, with the result that a planning act was passed in 1943 which gave scope to local authorities to collaborate and plan on a regional basis. One result of this legislation was that it facilitated the quick rebuilding of war-damaged areas (for several of the French ports suffered extensive damage).

A notable circumstance in the replanning of war-damaged urban areas and large scale restoration in Italy was the desire to employ the best available architectural talent for the purpose, and thus competitions were held for a large number of planning and rebuilding schemes.

Germany defeated, occupied and divided into East and West—the German Democratic Republic and the German Federal Republic—was hardly in a position to make plans early for the rebuilding of war damaged German cities. The most urgent need was for housing, much of a temporary character. It was not until later, from 1950 onwards, that plans for the renewal of German cities and towns began. When, however, it was well underway work proceeded with speed and efficiency so that by 1970 German post-war planning and building was among the finest in Europe. West Berlin was, and still is (1973), in a particularly difficult position, for since 1945 it has been isolated from the rest of Germany, and has no surrounding areas to which planning of the city can be related, while the capital was transferred to Bonn; whereas East Berlin can be related to its surrounding areas and is capital of the Democratic Republic. Yet in spite of such frustrations to planning the rebuilding of West Berlin from 1950 to 1970 has presented some of the most interesting layout schemes and some of the most distinctive and progressive architecture of the mid-twentieth century.

Berlin was so extensively damaged that several foreign planners suggested in 1946 that Berlin should be rebuilt to a new plan on another site. Such suggestions did not consider the vast network of water, gas, electricity, sewerage, communications and transport systems that could be put into operation without much difficulty, nor did they consider the will of 3.3 million people of Berlin (2.2 million in West and 1.1 million in East) who wanted to stay there. Hans Scharoun prepared outline plans in 1946, as a basis for discussions, for the whole city in which the network of services was utilized, but the subsequent division of the city meant that they could not be realized. Yet with that division planning schemes for West Berlin have always proceeded on the confident assumption that the two parts will one day be reunited.

The necessity of rebuilding large urban areas on a bigger scale than ever before brought into prominence the new profession of town or city planner. Urban planning was traditionally an extension of the work of the architect. With town planning legislation from the early part of the century[2], and with the creation of the distinct profession of town planner by the founding of the Town Planning Institute in Great Britain in 1913, urban planning was given a new status. With the opportunities

542

presented by the need for large-scale replanning occasioned by the unprecedented urban destruction, the town planner came into his own. His work was no longer an extension of that of the architect and since the Second World War many planners have not been architects while many architects are primarily planners. A good deal of new urban planning legislation was enacted in the early post-war years[3]. The work of the urban planner is necessarily very broadly based, because so many subjects have to be taken into consideration: demography, economics, education, housing, industry, commerce, communications, transport, recreation, entertainment and aesthetics, and the tendency has been for teams of specialists in these many subjects to work together with a leader. It is, I think, important that the leader should be an architect who has, or should have, a concern for the aesthetic aspects of a scheme.

In the early years of peace from 1945 to 1950 there were necessarily restrictions on the kind of building permitted, and a system of licensing was adopted in many countries. The main concentrations were on housing, both temporary and permanent, on power stations and industrial buildings, on schools and urgently required office and public buildings. Generally in the early architecture of the post-war period, as manifested in the offices and the few public buildings many of which were restorations, there was a tendency to go back for models to the traditional building between the wars, and to play safe until new directions were established. It was not so much a continuing where we had left off in 1939, but a return to a period when reminiscences of the late Renaissance were still apparent. The office buildings erected in London from 1947 to 1952 are a depressing example. It was not until the early fifties that the progressive spirit began to manifest itself in large scale building.

REFERENCES AND NOTES

1. The Commission's report is generally referred to as the Barlow Report, after the name of its chairman, Sir Montagu Barlow. In addition to the main report there was a minority report by Professor Patrick Abercrombie, Herbert H. Elvin and Mrs Hichens.
2. The first planning legislation was in Italy as far back as 1865, but there was little further legislation until the early twentieth century when there were a series of Acts of Parliament relating in some way to urban and regional planning, mainly in Great Britain, France and Germany.
3. The chief Planning Acts in Great Britain since the Second World War are the Town and Country Planning Acts of 1947, 1954, 1959, 1962, 1965, 1968 and The Consolidating Act of 1971; the New Towns Acts of 1946, 1954, 1959, 1964 and the Consolidating Act of 1965; the Town Development Act 1952; and the Civic Amenities Act 1967.

38 Urban renewal 1945–1970

THE DESTRUCTION OF so much of many of the cities and towns of Europe during the Second World War meant a vast programme of urban renewal and even a quarter of a century later in 1970 that programme was not in many cities entirely completed. Extensive destruction occurred in the capital cities of London, Berlin, Warsaw, while other large cities extensively damaged were Dresden, Cologne, Essen, Rotterdam, Liverpool, Plymouth, Coventry, the French ports, and a large number of Russian cities and towns. Few large cities in Germany and Britain escaped some form of war damage. As mentioned in the previous chapter, plans were in many cases prepared during and immediately after the war for extensive rebuilding. Urban renewal, however, is not only concerned with replacing what had been lost by the war, it is concerned also with the replacement of obsolescent areas by more up-to-date and serviceable buildings, a process which includes slum clearance, a degree of dispersal and building elsewhere on new sites.

There are several ways by which urban renewal can be carried out.

(1) In the case of war-damaged areas rebuilding approximately as it was before, while perhaps improving services and accommodation within the shells.

(2) To see in the destruction an opportunity for replanning and rebuilding so as to create a much improved urban development socially, economically and aesthetically. This may involve several processes as follows:

(3) In the case of war damaged or obsolescent housing areas, to rebuild at lower densities so as to give improved standards of accommodation, and replace by blocks of flats, with a measure of dispersal to new communities outside the city. Such schemes may involve the replanning of minor roads, and the introduction of schools, social facilities and open spaces.

(4) In replanning and building to change completely the character of an urban area and introduce pedestrian precincts in the place of roads, including areas on two or more levels to achieve traffic segregation.

Rebuilding cities and towns that have been wholly or partly destroyed by war as they were before, is a natural and sentimental impulse, which is stronger in the case of towns of historic and architectural interest. After the First World War several medieval towns were rebuilt as they were before. The same picturesque character of the town was retained, exact replicas were made of the important historic buildings, but opportunity was taken to improve much of the housing, especially that which had previously been inharmonious. Modern design and equipment was introduced while the additions to the town exteriors that had previously been made at various periods were often brought more into harmony with the general old character of the town.

This was done again with a few historic cities and towns after the Second World War. For example, the old French ports of Nantes, Brest and St. Malo, which had been extensively damaged, were rebuilt very much as they were before. I remember visiting St. Malo before and after the war and seeing it when the rebuilding was almost completed, and seeing the same old picturesque character with the rather tall buildings and the narrow streets. I also remember the drivers of motor vehicles trying to manipulate these streets. If it is desired to retain the character of old towns then it is necessary to come to terms with the motor vehicle and deny it access to the narrow streets and change them to pedestrian ways. Some means of vehicular access would have to be provided at points not too far away from buildings.

On the whole there are more disadvantages than advantages in rebuilding an old town so that it appears as it was before. A town is a living organism and is of the present and future as well as the past. Some degree of compromise may be desirable, preserving that which is historically and architecturally notable, while accommodating the needs of the present. This problem was presented to many planners and some of the solutions are ingenious. Often it means preserving single buildings and their immediate setting, which may therefore be in the middle of a modern development. The famous European example is Rome where the centuries live so well together. The Rome of ancient times and of the Renaissance harmonize well with the modern developments, begun by Marcello Piacentino in the early thirties. An interesting example of rebuilding an urban detail exactly as it was before, in the midst of modern development, is that of Goethe's house in Frankfurt. This house and its immediate surroundings were destroyed and rebuilt exactly as they were before. Goethe's house is a remarkable example of the imitation of worn and weathered materials and is a masterpiece of restoration.

With so much urban renewal, much of it imaginatively planned, and incorporating some good modern architecture, it is necessary to select a few good examples indicative of modern tendencies in urban development. The examples selected are Rotterdam, London, Coventry, some Rhine towns, and Berlin, with a glance at a few others. As urban developments they must be seen in relation to the centres of new towns and communities described in the next chapter.

ROTTERDAM

In May 1940, the centre of Rotterdam, an area of 642 acres, was destroyed by a German air attack, while another 247 acres of the eastern districts were partly destroyed. In the autumn of 1944, a large proportion of the docks was destroyed, including a third of the quaysides for seagoing vessels.

Rotterdam was founded in the thirteenth century and was a small town until the building of the straight canal that linked Rotterdam with the coast in 1872. From that time it began to be one of the most important ports in Europe. After the war rebuilding the docks was given first priority, for the prosperity of Rotterdam depended on its importance as a port. The work of restoration was begun in June, 1945, and was completed by the end of 1949, advantage being taken during the work to modernize the quays and equipment. Thus by 1950 its pre-war capacity as a port was restored. In 1965 it became the largest port in the world, surpassing New York and London.

The phenomenal expansion of Rotterdam as a port has been due very largely to the provision of harbours to accommodate the rapidly increasing shipments of oil to supply Europe by tankers of increasing size. The great growth of the port has meant a corresponding growth in the city of Rotterdam and its surroundings. The rebuilding and expansion of the city has been done in such a way as to make it a very rewarding study for planners and architects.

The old city of Rotterdam lies to the north of the Niewe Maas, with its centre, the Hofplein, very near the confluence of the Rivers Rotte and Schie. The city grew round a number of principal streets radiating from the Hofplein, the most important of which are the broad thoroughfare of Goudsingel to the southeast, the Coolsingel to the south and the Kruiskade to the west, on the north side of which is the railway with the central station.

The area destroyed was mainly on either side of the railway line and the extensive shopping area south of the station and on either side of the Coolsingel. Replanning had been done generally on a much more spacious pattern than previously existed. Formerly in this central square mile there were about 25,000 dwellings, mainly in apartment blocks, and between the principal thoroughfares the streets were narrow and the apartment blocks closely packed. In the rebuilding only about 8,000 dwellings are provided in new apartment blocks much more spaciously laid out. This involved considerable dispersal of population, and to provide for this and for the rapidly increasing population an ambitious programme of satellite communities south of the river was started.

The replanning east and west of Coolsingel offers an interesting contrast. East of Coolsingel the planning is on the same lines as formerly, but on a much more liberal and spacious scale. All the streets both major and minor have been considerably widened to accommodate the growing volume of traffic, while several spacious roundabout traffic junctions have been introduced. Apartment blocks appear above the shops, as formerly, but instead of being on the same building line they are set back, which enhances the effects of spaciousness.

West of the Coolsingel the former street pattern has been largely eliminated, and Westersingel (a quarter of a mile away and parallel on the west side) continues north to a square fronting the station which now acts as a handsome terminal feature. A broad new thoroughfare—Weena—has been constructed west of the Hofplein and running in front of the station. At the southern end of Coolsingel another new boulevard—West Blaak—encloses the area. A long pedestrian way, the Lijnbaan, runs almost the whole length of the Coolsingel from Weena to Binnenweg. Crossing this near its northern end is another pedestrian way, which on the east side broadens out to a square—the Stadhuisplein—with the town hall, that escaped the bombing, as a terminal feature on the other side of Coolsingel. To the west the pedestrian way, the Korte Lijnbaan, links with a large square with a large underground car park to serve the concert hall which occupies the north side of the square.

Lijnbaan is built as a unity. All the shops are only two-storey structures, with service roads at the rear and tall blocks of flats on the other side of the service roads. On the west side these blocks form three sides of two squares laid out as gardens with shrubs and trees. The shops being only two-storeys high enhances the sense of openness.

The pedestrian ways are attractively arranged. Continuous canopies project from the shops for protection in bad weather, the centres of the ways are laid out with flower beds which provide brilliant notes of colour in the summer months, there are occasional flowering trees, and here and there is a large bird cage with a variety of coloured birds. The Lijnbaan has deservedly become famous.

The planning of the central area and its rebuilding were greatly facilitated by a programme of expropriation which was put into operation very soon after the destruction of the city centre. By this programme several thousands of buildings and their sites were acquired by the Municipality. They included not only the buildings destroyed, but those adjacent so as to give the authority freedom in planning a new city centre. Dispossessed property owners were not indemnified immediately but instead they were given the option of a new building site provided they undertook to rebuild thereon, the price being determined by that obtaining at the time of destruction. This large scale acquisition obviously made the planning of the city centre a much simpler process, and contributed to the unity of effect seen so impressively in the Lijnbaan.

547

Rotterdam, view of the Lijnbaan, the long pedestrian way in the rebuilt centre, 1956–68

Statue by Zadkine near the harbour in Rotterdam symbolising the city with its heart torn out

Pedestrian area in the centre of Coventry, 1950–65

Plymouth, views of the central pedestrian area with gardens and municipal building
The plan for the post-war development of Plymouth was prepared by Sir Patrick Abercrombie
and this was broadly followed

More than in most cities rebuilt extensively after the war there is a sense of continuity from the stage reached immediately before the war. In the evolution of modern architecture the Second World War meant a halt, and it took most architects some years to gather up the reins and go ahead as before. There was not immediately continuation of what had gone before in the late thirties but rather a return, for a time, to the pseudo-Renaissance of the twenties, and London provided examples of some architecturally deplorable early post-war office buildings. Although this happened a little in Rotterdam it happened less than elsewhere and by 1952 there was a continuation of the pre-war progressive spirit.

COVENTRY

A substantial part of the centre of Coventry including the cathedral, except the tower and spire, was destroyed by a heavy air raid in November, 1940. A plan had been prepared for the reconstruction of the city centre before the war in 1938, this was developed and modified as the result of the destruction and by 1950 rebuilding began. Temporary shops had previously been provided on the site.

The old centre of the city, Broadgate, where the main north–south and east–west roads crossed became, in the new plan by Sir Donald Gibson, a central square laid out as a garden with an equestraian statue of Lady Godiva in the middle. The road to the west became a pedestrian precinct enclosed as a square by two-level shops. It continued across a north–south shopping street, Market Way, to another pedestrian area on a lower level with a circular restaurant and two-tiered shopping. In a later plan of 1962 by Professor Arthur Ling, Market Way was converted into a pedestrian way and three sides of Broadgate were similarly converted, so that this Coventry Centre became probably the most extensive urban pedestrian area in England. To the east of Broadgate is the Civic Centre and the new cathedral adjoining the ruins of the old. The ring roads, with industry between them, surround this centre with roads radiating to central car parks. The architecture of the centre, especially that surrounding Broadgate and the pedestrian precinct, is pleasantly restrained if not particularly distinguished and the heights of the buildings are well related to the enclosed areas. This centre at Coventry, largely completed by 1965, is deservedly famous, partly because it was one of the earliest with fairly extensive pedestrian areas.

LONDON

In the County of London Plan of 1943, Forshaw and Abercrombie proposed a number of precincts such as a University Precinct in Bloomsbury, a Westminster Precinct and a residential precinct. These were areas which were partly replanned and closed to through traffic by stopping several of the minor roads, but there was no extensive conversion of roads to pedestrian ways. Yet the precinct idea greatly influenced schemes for urban renewal, and its influence can be seen in replanning and rebuilding the City of London, which, together with the eastern areas near the docks, were the

1 GUILDHALL
2 GUILDHALL OFFICES
3 GUILDHALL NEW LIBRARY
4 GUILDHALL ART GALLERY
5 WOOLGATE HOUSE
6 GIRDLERS HALL
7 AUSTRAL HOUSE
8 40 BASINGHALL STREET
9 NATIONAL TELE. EXCHANGE
10 MOOR HOUSE
11 MOORGATE STN. DEVELOPMENT
12 BRITANNIC HOUSE
13 MOORFIELDS HOUSE
14 TENTER HOUSE
15 ST. ALPHAGE HOUSE
16 SALTERS HALL
17 ROMAN HOUSE
18 GILLETT HOUSE
19 CHARTERED INSURANCE INSTITUTE
20 BREWERS HALL
21 ALDERMANBURY HOUSE
22 WOOD ST. POLICE STATION
23 ROYEX HOUSE

24 TELEPHONE EXCHANGE
25 SHELLEY HOUSE
26 PLAISTERERS HALL
27 LEE HOUSE
28 BARBER SURGEONS HALL
29 MUSEUM OF LONDON
30 IRONMONGERS HALL
31 GUILDHALL SCH. OF MUSIC & DRAMA
32 SHOPS
33 CONCERT HALL
34 THEATRE
35 BREWERY
36 FIRE STATION
37 WEIGHTS AND MEASURES OFFICE
38 CORONERS COURT
39 MORTUARY
40 HEALTH CENTRE
41 WATER GARDENS
42 LAKE
43 PUBLIC HOUSES
44 ELECTRICITY SUPPLY STATION
45 CITY OF LONDON SCHOOL FOR GIRLS
46 ST. GILES' CRIPPLEGATE CHURCH

47 VICARAGE AND TOWN HOUSES
48 PETROL STATION
49 MURRAY HOUSE
50 CRIPPLEGATE INSTITUTE
51 RECREATIONAL BUILDING
52 HOSTEL
53 POLICE SECTION HOUSE
54 JEWIN WELSH METHODIST CHURCH
55 BARBICAN - 44 STOREY FLATS
56   - G.P.O. BUILDING
57 GOLDEN LANE - GREAT ARTHUR HOUSE
58   - MAISONETTES
59   - FLATS OVER SHOPS
60   - FLATS
61   - COMMUNITY BUILDINGS
62 BARBICAN   - FLATS
63 ART GALLERY
64 MUSEUM OF LONDON TOWER
65 GOLDEN LANE - COMMUNITY CENTRE
66 RESTAURANT
67 CONSERVATORY

--- --- BARBICAN AREA BOUNDARY

E.G. CHANDLER F.R.I.B.A. M.T.P.I. CITY ARCHITECT
DEPARTMENT OF ARCHITECTURE AND PLANNING
CORPORATION OF LONDON, GUILDHALL, E C.2

0   100   200   300 FEET

JANUARY 1971

Plan of Barbican area, City of London, 1959–73

Architects and Planners: Chamberlain, Powell and Bon

parts of the capital most extensively destroyed. In the City of London the areas which suffered most were those immediately surrounding St. Paul's cathedral and an extensive tract to the north. Two of the most interesting precinctual plans were in the vicinity of St. Paul's, designed by Sir William Holford, and the Barbican development occupying the area bounded by Gresham Street on the south, Moorgate on the east, Aldersgate Street to the west and Chiswell Street to the north.

The St. Paul's precinct is largely a conversion of a number of narrow streets round St. Paul's into a series of pedestrian spaces. The area before the west front of the cathedral is a partly enclosed square insufficiently open to Ludgate Hill. To the north on a higher level and reached by a broad flight of steps is the large Paternoster Square, surrounded by buildings the same height as the cathedral, except at the north end where there is a sixteen-storey block. Below the square is a two-level car park. Adjoining to the east is a small shopping square. The area to the southeast of the cathedral is laid out as a pleasant garden and it is from beyond this position that the best views of the cathedral can be obtained.

The layout of pedestrian areas round the cathedral is very pleasant and a great improvement on the former urban scene, although those who had an affection for the district as it was before may not agree. Unfortunately the architecture of this development leaves much to be desired. There are large glass walls, interspersed with horizontal coloured bands or long verticals, generally called curtain walling which looks very mechanical and monotonous. The square mechanical looking building that projects partly in front of the cathedral in the view from Ludgate Hill is regrettable, and it is difficult to think of the building as the result of sensitive designing. This is an example where the effect of good urban planning is not as good as it might be because of rather poor architecture of glass boxes, which is unfortunately the case with much of the rebuilding in the City of London and Westminster from 1950 to 1970.

The methods of urban renewal of the fifties and sixties were very different from those of the twenties and thirties. In the latter there was a certain amount of large scale renewal in bank building round the Royal Exchange. The general layout of streets was not affected, and the harmony between the bank buildings was generally in the broad adoption of the massive late Renaissance style, but otherwise they were very much expressions of the design idioms of the individual architects, Lutyens, Baker, Cooper, Davies and Burnett. In the large-scale schemes of the fifties and sixties, in which a general unity is achieved by the mechanical repetition of similar units of curtain walling, though spacial relations may be good, the enclosing buildings are generally dull and monotonous. They could hardly prompt pleasurable contemplation as did a Lutyens building. The elements of modern architecture have been artistically used with great success, but being large-scale units much repeated, the note of variety must be introduced in the general unity for them to be aesthetically acceptable.

Arcaded shops, Goswell Road, forming part of the Golden Lane Housing Estate, north of Barbican, City of London, 1958–60

Two views of Britz-Buckow-Rudow in the southeast of Berlin, 1958–69. Sometimes known as Gropiusstadt. Originally planned by Walter Gropius, but modified as work progressed

Architects: Chamberlain, Powell and Bon

Barbican development, City of London, 1959–73. Model: view from south-west

The Barbican development is a bold and imaginative scheme, which alters the character of the area completely. It is prompted partly by a desire to bring back a considerable residential area to the City of London. The City Corporation experienced difficulty and delay in getting a scheme accepted and it was not until 1959 that a plan by Chamberlain, Powell and Bon was approved and work commenced. It provides for 2,117 flats and maisonettes for 6,500 people in a high density development of about 200 persons to the acre. The blocks of flats include three towers of 43 storeys and several 11-storey terrace blocks in U and Z shapes. By building high in this way spaciousness has been achieved between the buildings. There is also provision for shops and commercial premises, garages for 2,100 vehicles, restaurants and public houses, the Guildhall School of Music and Drama, the City of London School for Girls, a theatre, concert hall, art gallery, library and recreation centre. The provision of all these with what was formerly almost exclusively a commercial area is a valuable and imaginative effort on the part of the City Corporation. Entire completion is probable in the middle seventies.

There are a few old buildings preserved in the area. In its very centre is the church of St. Giles, Cripplegate, where Cromwell was married and Milton was buried. Much of it is pedestrian and on two or more levels and is the result of some ingenious designing. The commercial area of offices is mainly to the south of London Wall in buildings of various shapes and sizes, while the housing of various kinds, shops and educational and entertainment buildings are on the north side, merging into the Golden Lane development further north. The whole conception is saved from the monotony that pervades much other post-war building, largely because of the variety in the shapes and sizes of buildings, their varied siting and the mixing of the old and new.

The purpose of bringing back residential development, together with recreation into the city and the imaginative way it has been done, is adequate justification for the changed character of the area. There are some architects, planners and others who think, however, that the traditional character of an area should be respected and developed and that something totally different should not be imposed on it. This criticism has been made in the case of the planning and development of Plymouth. When, after its partial destruction, the city was rebuilt to the plans of Sir Patrick Abercrombie, wide handsome boulevards crossing in the centre were provided which gives a much greater spaciousness and dignity than existed before. This has been criticized as imposing a beaux arts plan on something which formerly had a distinctive and unique urban character, which, it is contended, should control and determine the character of the rebuilt area. Compared with other rebuildings it was done fairly quickly and in its spaciousness is attractive. The broad avenue, called Armada Way, slopes down from Hoe Park and is crossed by a broad shopping avenue—Royal Parade—and then ascends. The tall Naval War Memorial in Hoe Park is central to the

553

avenue and acts as a terminal feature. Near the crossing of Armada Way and Royal Parade is the impressive tall building housing the municipal offices in front of which there is a spacious pedestrian area with gardens and a pool. The buildings in the vicinity are mainly of a monumental character which gives a civic dignity to the whole area.

SOME RHINE TOWNS

Most of the Rhine towns and those of the industrial area of the Ruhr were very heavily damaged in the Second World War. Their replanning and rebuilding makes a very interesting study for the planner. The plans and rebuilding of Cologne are particularly notable. The medieval city was chiefly on the west bank of the Rhine and formed a semicircle surrounded by a defensive wall, while a comparatively small part was on the east bank. Running north–south from across the west front of the cathedral was the old narrow medieval high street. A considerable extent of the area where the defensive walls were originally, had become a green belt. The centre of the city was extensively damaged during the war, but much of the old high street survived. When replanning was being discussed one main alternative was whether to rebuild the High Street and convert it into a wide modern shopping thoroughfare, or whether to keep it as it was, make it a pedestrian shopping way, and have wide ring roads. The latter alternative was fortunately adopted. A principal road runs by the Rhine, and the ring road (Sachsen ring links with this in the south) curves north—Hohenstaufen ring— to the west of the centre and continues as the ring to Riehl and the Mulheimer Rhine bridge. Parallel with the High Street is a wide thoroughfare, north–south, which has links with the ring road, and with east–west main thoroughfares, two of which connect the ring road with bridges—Koln-Deutzer and Severns bridges. The narrow high street has been converted into a long pedestrian way which has gradually been extended and continues west along Schildergasse as far as Neumarkt. Instead of opposing this development the shopkeepers welcomed it and even contributed to the cost. As this is a conversion of an existing High Street and not an entirely new development as in the case of the Rotterdam Lynbahn, access to the shops by means of goods supply vehicles was a problem which has been overcome by allowing such vehicles to have the necessary access along the pedestrian way before a certain time in the morning.

A similar conversion has occurred in other German cities: on a generous scale at Essen, at Dortmund, at Hamm, at Guissen on the Lahn, at Dusseldorf and others. Similar pedestrianization of principal old shopping streets in city centres became fairly common in many countries in Europe, notable examples being principal shopping streets in Copenhagen, Verona, Seville and Norwich. Initially the conversion is usually experimental for a trial period, but experience suggests that instead of reverting to the old vehicular streets the tendency is to extend the pedestrian areas, and the prospect is that by the year 2000 large areas of city centres in Europe will be exclusively for pedestrians.

554

Urban development, South of Rome

Berlin, general view of Wohnsiedlung in Britz-Buckow-Rudow (Gropiusstadt), 1958–68

Architect: Walter Gropius

BERLIN

In the vast undertaking of replanning and rebuilding West Berlin, two developments are particularly worthy of attention, the Hansa development and that at Buckow-Rudow called Gropiusstadt. The large city of Berlin has grown, like London, rather as a collection of towns and communities that have fused and their geographical demarcations are no longer apparent. Yet, in the case of Berlin the twenty boroughs which make the conurbation are largely autonomous with their separate centres. Twelve of the boroughs are in West Berlin and eight in East Berlin. The developments that have taken place in West Berlin are generally by the distinct boroughs, although related by an overall structure controlled by the City Council for Building and Housing.

A conception that influences the post-war planning of Berlin is the mixing of city functions so that living quarters, working areas, shopping, education, recreation and entertainment should all be closely related in the same districts. This rather precludes any very rigid zoning and contributes to a lively city.

The most famous post-war development in Berlin is that of the Hansa district on the edge of Berlin's central park, the Tiergarten. Formerly the Hansa Quarter was a traditional late nineteenth-century residential district with three- and four-storeyed terrace apartment houses facing the main thoroughfares, much favoured partly because of its nearness to the Tiergarten. The redevelopment, begun in 1953, was the subject of an International competition won by Jobst, Krever and Schliesser whose plan was subsequently modified. That carried out is essentially an extension of the Tiergarten with the houses and other buildings grouped in the northwest corner of the park with the main thoroughfares of Altonaer Strasse and the Klopstock Strasse remaining the same. The essential difference in this redevelopment is that instead of the buildings being aligned along streets, they are grouped irregularly in parkland with access by footpaths and two loop roads. The dwellings are of great variety from tall sixteen-storey tower blocks, and slab blocks from four to ten storeys, to one- and two-storey family houses designed by famous architects from fourteen countries. This represents an effort to get the best international talent, and is a repetition on a bigger scale of the Stuttgart exhibition of 1927 (Chapter 23). Reference to some of the houses is made in Chapter 40. In addition to dwellings here, there is the large building of the Academy of Arts, a small shopping centre, a restaurant, two churches and a day nursery.

Britz-Buckow-Rudow in the southeast of West Berlin, for a population of 50,000 was planned initially by Walter Gropius and subsequently modified in a few respects and built during the sixties. The planning follows similar broad principles to those of the Hansa development, although on a much larger scale, of dwellings of a wide variety from tall tower and slab apartment blocks to one- and two-storey family dwellings, sited in open spaces bounded by major roads with access by means of loop roads, culs-de-sac and footpaths. There are several shopping centres, schools, nurseries,

556

churches and community centres well dispersed. The principle of siting dwellings in
an irregular manner in open spaces, but carefully orientated and related and of a wide
variety of types and forms, determines much planning in other German cities. It did
not appear to be the result of any one very marked influence, but a combination of
many. The chief progress is that the siting of houses and apartment blocks is no longer
controlled or even influenced by the layout of streets, but they are sited in the most
functional manner with due attention to good orientation and with access by branches
from an encircling road.

39   New towns and communities

A LARGE NUMBER of new towns began to be built in Europe soon after the Second
World War. In a rough enumeration of the number built in each country by 1973,
according to the most comprehensive definitions of new town, there are about 30 in
Great Britain, 20 in Germany, 15 in France, 25 in Scandinavia, 15 in the Netherlands
10 in Italy, and a very large number, over 100, in the USSR[1]. They are planned,
however, on varying conceptions of the nature and character of new towns. In Great
Britain the conception of a new town, which was originally based on Ebenezer
Howard's idea of a garden city, and which had early prototypes in Letchworth (1903)
and Welwyn Garden City (1921), is based on a physical pattern in which life is
comprehended as a whole, whereas in other conceptions, in Scandinavia and Germany,
for example, some dependence on other urban areas is envisaged. It is important,
therefore, to make quite clear what the traditional British conception of a new town
is. This will be amplified by a few examples, and the differences of new towns in other
parts of Europe will become apparent from descriptions.

GREAT BRITAIN

New towns, in the British conception, are mainly, although not always, towns planned
in accordance with a policy of dispersal from the overcrowded areas of big cities or
conurbations. Each new town is planned to provide employment for those living there,
so as to have a satisfactory relation between people's homes and places of work, and
facilities for shopping, education, recreation and entertainment within the town, which,
in the original conception, is surrounded by a green belt, so that the inhabitants can
enjoy the delights of the country as well as the facilities of urban living. The town is
thus limited in size, and when by intake of population and growth it is nearing its
maximum then, according to the theory of Ebenezer Howard and his followers,
another new town should be built separated, however, by open country, to form
ultimately a cluster of towns with green areas between them instead of a continuous
urban extension resulting in a conurbation. Unfortunately this is not being followed as
it should in the British new towns, and when they are nearing their originally planned

maximum size there is a tendency to let them sprawl beyond the planned green belt.

The policy of building new towns as part of planned dispersal was officially adopted in Great Britain with the New Towns Act of 1946. Eight new towns were designated round London between 1946 and 1949: Stevenage, Crawley, Hemel Hempstead, Harlow, Welwyn Garden City[2], Hatfield, Basildon and Bracknell. In the same period two were designated in the northeast: Newton Aycliffe and Peterlee, two in Scotland: East Kilbride and Glenrothes, one in Wales: Cwmbran, and one in the Midlands: Corby in 1950. These fourteen are often spoken of as the first generation of new towns, to be followed by a second generation designated between 1961 and 1967, with an intermediate town, Cumbernauld, designated in 1955.

The towns of the first generation were all planned on the neighbourhood principle adumbrated in Patrick Abercrombie's hypothetical plan for Ongar in his Greater London Plan, although there was considerable variation in the application of the principle. In the case of Stevenage, the first, fairly large neighbourhoods (about 10,000 to 12,000 population) are grouped north, east and south of the town centre, with the industrial area to the west. In the case of Crawley, smaller neighbourhoods (about five to eight thousand) are grouped all round the centre, four inner and six outer, whereas in Harlow, four large neighbourhoods are subdivided. The general tendency, however, in most of the first generation is to have fairly small neighbourhoods like Crawley, each with its centre for shops, church, public house, community centre and primary school nearby. Each town centre provides the principal shopping district, a civic centre with town hall and various facilities like a library, health centre and possibly an assembly hall.

The first town centre to be completed was Corby which was planned in the traditional manner with a broad principal shopping street, and this was also the plan with Bracknell, East Kilbride and others where the building of the centre was fairly early. These have now been converted to pedestrian centres.

Stevenage provides the first example of a centre planned and built as a pedestrian precinct. It consists of a long central pedestrian way running north–south, from which two other pedestrian ways branch eastward, and a small town square opens westward which connects with a bus station. All the ways are lined with shops in two- and three-storey buildings, and a continuous canopy affords protection to shoppers in bad weather, while providing a unifying motif in the ensemble and securing a general effect of harmony of the individually designed shops. The whole precinct occupying a rectangular site is surrounded by a road with vehicle access to the rear of shops, and to a few car parks. The town square is small, but contains a pool, fountain, clock tower, sculpture, and rather large trees for the scale, and has the effect of being a little overloaded. A little more spaciousness would have been an advantage. Basildon

559

centre built a little later also has a pedestrian centre with a large rectangular piazza, and a smaller one on a lower level linked by steps and a ramp. Near the point of connection is a fountain with sculpture and a tall block of flats making a very effective architectural composition.

These pedestrian centres, together with the general tendency towards pedestrianization, has prompted changes in the design of other centres that originally had through roads, and in addition to those mentioned the centres of Harlow, Cwmbran and Glenrothes have become predestrian precincts. The residential areas of the first generation of new towns are planned with the main roads going between the neighbourhood, with variously straight and winding minor roads off which numerous culs-de-sac are introduced. The ends of culs-de-sac are sometimes linked by footpaths, and in some of the towns— Glenrothes for example—there is a complete footpath system. In most of the early new towns the greater proportion of dwellings, between eighty and ninety per cent, are two-storey family houses, with a small proportion of blocks of flats and bungalows for old people. The houses are variously arranged, they are aligned along the roads, are placed irregularly sometimes with variously shaped green spaces between houses and roads, along culs-de-sac and the footpaths connecting them. But what is important in this conception, is that the houses are arranged mainly in relation to a pattern of roads, and that pattern is generally the starting point in the plan, although there are interesting exceptions. Some of the later stages of the first generation reveal changes of conception more fully apparent in the second generation.

These were planned between 1962 and 1970. They are Skelmersdale and Runcorn in the northwest, Washington, Killingworth and Cramlington in the northeast, Milton Keynes 50 miles northwest of London, Telford and Redditch in the Midlands, Livingston and Irvine in Scotland and Newtown in Wales. There are four others, Peterborough, Northampton, Warrington and Preston-Leyland-Chorley which, although being planned by the same machinery of development corporations are really extensions of sizeable towns. Cumbernauld in Scotland designated in 1955 belongs in character more to the second generation than the first. Several of the first generation have considerable extensions, such as Newton Aycliffe, Corby and Bracknell which are planned with the slightly changed conceptions.

Many of the residential areas of the second generation are planned as pedestrian precincts threaded with footpaths and interspersed with small open spaces and children's playgrounds, and enclosed by ring roads from which there is vehicle access by means of culs-de-sac. This theme is, of course, subject to numerous variations. It permits closer building, higher densities, and more intimate character, but it is best done when there is an occasional fairly large open space as in the latest section of the southwest neighbourhood of Peterlee, where houses enclose a green area with a group of large trees. In most of these pedestrian residential areas the gardens are rather small, or

Crawley Town Centre, 1955–57

Planner: H. S. Howgrave-Graham, Chief Architect, Crawley Development Corporation

Glenrothes (new town in Fife, Scotland). Part of Macedonia residential area where houses
face lawns and footpaths, 1965   *Architects: Glenrothes Development Corporation*

non-existent, or are merely the square patch in a secluded patio type of house. Opinions vary on which type of development is preferable, the more spacious residential areas of the first generation, or the closer more intimate and pedestrianized of the second. The best examples of both are aesthetically pleasing, and the examples are to be found in nearly all the new towns of both generations in Britain[4].

The centres of several of the second generation show a considerable advance in design and represent vertical extension by organization on several levels. The most progressive in this respect are Cumbernauld and Runcorn, the former of which was partly completed in 1967 and the latter in 1972. Both centres are vast central buildings. The Cumbernauld centre, designed by Sir L. Hugh Wilson and A. K. Gibbs, is on eight levels intended to provide all that a modern town needs in its centre. The lowest level is for vehicular traffic and includes the central spine road, loading docks and parking areas. Above is a series of pedestrian decks linked by escalators, lifts, stairs and ramps, and on the various levels are a wide variety of shops, offices, including branches of banks, post office, a health centre, public houses, hotel, restaurant and at the top is a row of split level penthouses. The main shopping street is on the fourth level, which leads to a square, round which are grouped buildings for recreation and entertainment, including a dance hall, sports centre and swimming pool. Included also in this vast complex are a technical college and fire station. All the shopping ways are covered, although there are platforms in the open. The parts are integrated into one immense framed concrete structure, which is one of the largest buildings in Europe. It makes an imposing mass at the top of the hill on which Cumbernauld is built. The best view is from the southeast with the penthouses forming the sky line. In one description these have been likened to railway coaches riding on an irregular grouping of buildings[3]. Yet the long horizontal massing accords well with the lines of the landscape.

Cumbernauld town centre is a bold and notable experiment in multi-level design which has led to others on similar lines. It could be criticized as being a little too complex. At the time it was conceived, multi-level urban development was much discussed as the development of the future, and as a result the designers of Cumbernauld centre went 'all out' to get a progressive scheme. It has inspired the design of many subsequent centres, but the later tendency has been towards greater simplicity and clarity. One of the most notable is the centre for Runcorn designed by Professor A. Ling together with the Runcorn Development Corporation, the first part of which was completed in 1972. The centre is on two main levels, the ground-level service area with headroom for the tallest vehicles, and the shopping area on the first floor level consisting of a vast concrete platform. It is divided into twenty 108-foot squares with service towers at each corner, so that goods are loaded from vehicles at ground level and brought up in lifts in these towers. The whole is closed in and air-conditioned with low pyramidal roofs for each square. The pedestrian ways are paved with terrazo and the walls and general surrounds of the shops are all faced with soft-veined white marble, so as to secure a general unity of effect. There is a central square with clerestory lighting and carpeted central area, with ornamental shrubs, flowers and easy chairs, and in addition to shops there are banks, post office, cinema, pubic houses and restaurant.

Access by public transport is from the town bus station on the elevated exclusive bus route on the north side, and from the station there is an escalator to the shopping centre. This exclusive bus route connects with all the centres of the residential districts. There is a station for regional buses on the ground floor. Access by private car to the main centre is by means of four multi-storey car parks built on the east and west sides of the centre. A group of buildings consisting of the law courts, police station and offices is similarly enclosed by multi-storey car parks, and the same pattern is followed for the entertainments area on the south side.

Both Cumbernauld and Runcorn centres seem to point to a future when city and town centres will be vast buildings like great departmental stores. They are a long way from the town centre where shops are aligned on either side of a central street.

SCANDINAVIA

The conception of new towns in Scandinavia is a little different from that in Great Britain. Some of the best known like Vallingby and Farsta near Stockholm, and Tapiola near Helsinki, are within 10 miles of the capital city, and they have not been planned with full consideration of the relation of homes and employment. With the new towns in Great Britain the building of the industrial areas is in unison with the building of houses, and those who have employment in the town have prior claim on housing, indeed at certain periods in the building of British new towns it was not possible to obtain a dwelling in one unless the person worked there. And for the most part the towns were sufficiently far from big centres of population to be in some measure independent of them, while they are surrounded by country areas. In the case of the new towns in Scandinavia there has been little concerted planning of housing and industrial employment. In all the employment in the town is a very small proportion of the total employment, and the great majority of the people go elsewhere to work, mainly to the capital city or its environs. The Scandinavian new towns are very largely dormitory suburbs, although the best have a distinctive character and are in parts architecturally notable.

The aim in planning Vallingby, 9 miles northwest of Stockholm, was to provide a balance of employment and homes, but this has not been realised. This could have been achieved if the methods used in Britain had been adopted, but it is a question whether there is the same enthusiasm for dispersal as in England, which was one of the main factors that prompted the building of new towns. In Scandinavia there is an ambition for its cities to become larger and thus more important—an aim that exists

Centre of Vallingby, a satellite development 9 miles north-west of Stockholm, 1952–62

Chief Planner: Sven Markelius

Centre of Farsta, a satellite development 8 miles south-east of Stockholm, 1952–62

in most Scandinavian countries—and a policy of dispersal by separation of the new community from its parent is not likely to conduce to this ambition. Thus Vallingby and Farsta, the new towns of Stockhom, are really extensions of the city.

Vallingby was planned by Sven Markelius (chief planner of Stockholm) for a population of 60,000 shortly after the Second World War. Provision was made for an industrial area to the northwest of the site, and for service industry near the centre and offices, but housing was very much in advance of these provisions and it quickly became a dormitory suburb with a frequent train service to the centre of Stockholm taking only twenty minutes.

Vallingby is, however, a well-planned suburban community. The centre is built over the railway near the station, and the main residential area extends northeast of the railway. The ground is undulating and good use is made of the contours. Much of the housing is in three-storey and four-storey slab blocks, with a few eleven-storey tower blocks, mainly in the inner parts. Near the centre is a green valley with flats on the surrounding hills; the effect is very pleasant. A considerable number of detached and terraced two-storey houses are built along the roads and culs-de-sac on the outskirts. One of the most effective groupings aesthetically is that of several cruciform four-storey blocks on either side of the road that winds over the hill beyond the green valley.

Vallingby is famous as an example of modern planning and architecture, but visitors who expect much of its centre must be disappointed. It is a pedestrian shopping precinct with good views in many directions, but its architecture is somewhat mean and tawdry; the effect is bitty, for the buildings do not combine well into a uniform whole, while advertisements are inharmoniously obtrusive. One Swedish writer referred to it as funfair architecture, which is a just description.

Farsta, about 8 miles southeast of the centre of Stockholm, is a later development planned on the same lines as Vallingby. There is little industry, insufficient to prevent its being another dormitory suburb. The well-wooded hilly site between lakes is even more beautiful than that of Vallingby. Again the tall tower blocks and three-storey and four-storey slabs (point and lamella houses as they are called) are towards the centre with two-storey terraced and detached houses of considerable variety on the outskirts, some very attractive examples being at Skondal to the northeast. One very ingeniously designed group of terraced houses is built on the slope of a steep hill in a stepped arrangement, each house having a balcony opening from the living room with a magnificent view over Farsta among the woods and lakes. A stay of a few days in one of these houses enabled me to enjoy the changing light over this varied and beautiful landscape, with which the estate is integrated in a felicitous manner.

Again, the centre of Farsta was a disappointment. The plan is good, a pedestrian precinct with flower beds and pools of water, but the architecture is a bit jazzy, a little more solid perhaps than the funfair, but in sad contrast to some of the recent impressive and restrained architecture of the centre of Stockholm.

To go from Vallingby and Farsta to Finland's Tapiola Garden City, built mainly between 1952 and 1965, is to experience something of a contrast. It is difficult to keep one's head about Tapiola; its beauty is intoxicating, especially when seen on fine summer days. If the centres of Vallingby and Farsta have a touch of vulgarity, the centre of Tapiola is Greek-like in its purity of form and sense of repose. It is a complete pedestrian precinct approached by a broad flight of steps and enclosed on three sides by arcaded shops. To the right as one approaches is a thirteen-storey office block with a restaurant at the top; while the enclosed area consists of gardens, and an irregular group of tall larches, stately survivors of the forest. The vertical divisions of the long horizontal masses of the shop buildings are well proportioned and conduce to the sense of repose. It would be difficult to think of a more beautiful, small, modern, urban centre in Europe than this at Tapiola, designed by Aarne Ervi.

Linked with Helsinki, 8 miles to the east, by two roads across the archipelago of the Gulf of Finland, Tapiola Garden City was planned for a population of 17,000 in about 670 acres of forest country near the sea. It has three neighbourhoods, east, west and north, and an industrial area is planned to provide employment for between 30 and 50 per cent of the working population, so that it is conceived partly as a dormitory suburb.

The forest site is flat in the centre, with hills to the east, west and north. Full use is made of the granite protusions which often form the centres of flowerbeds and play areas, and occasionally the base for sculpture. There is much planting of flowers and small shrubs among the trees, and appropriate soil is imported.

In the eastern neighbourhood, the one built first, the housing is mainly in three-storey and four-storey blocks and terraced and detached houses, the flats grouped round gardens and playgrounds, and the two-storey houses along the winding country lanes bordered with wild flowers, shrubs and trees. On one hill in this neighbourhood are several slab blocks of flats enclosing gardens and children's play areas with a tree-bordered pool, still with the sense of its being in the forest.

The western neighbourhood is approached from the town centre by a wide, straight, paved footpath bordered by flowers and shrubs, with the forest on either side. After about a quarter of a mile the path rises on a rocky hill with the tall trees growing amidst the granite boulders. At the summit are four tall, white, tower blocks each with a sauna at the top. Seen above the granite boulders and surrounded by the dark pines

Centre of Tapiola Garden City (1952–65) a satellite
town 8 miles west of Helskinki. View from the paved
area in front of the steps leading to the centre and
view from the top of the thirteen-storey block

Architect: Aarne Ervi

'Die Nordweststadt' a satellite town of Frankfurt-am-Main,
1960–68. View of upper level with fountain and view of
well formed by lower and upper levels

Planners: Walter Schwagenscheidt and Tassilo Sittmann

and larches they make an impressive spectacle. A little beyond these are varied slab blocks which enclose children's play spaces and extensive gardens with bright flowers. The neighbourhood centre has rows of shops on two sides of a square with a central garden. Nearby are several very attractively designed two-storey terrace houses with patio gardens, which, like most of the family houses in Tapiola, give the feeling of being in a wood.

The contrast of the white houses and the tall dark trees, the granite boulders and the shrubs and trees, the tower blocks growing, it seems, from among the boulders on the hills, all combine to make Tapiola one of the most felicitious examples of the integration of landscape and architecture in Europe. It lives up to its name of Garden City although, more accurately, it is a garden suburb.

It is proposed to expand Tapiola to a population of 80,000, to form one of the seven cities west of Helsinki to accommodate the growth of population of the capital. Four will be sited along the Bay of Espoo, in addition to Tapiola: Leppa vaara (65,000), Maurala (90,000) and Kivenlahti (70,000). They will each consist, like Tapiola, of neighbourhoods separated by green belts, which will thus form the pattern of the extension of Helsinki. In the neighbourhood of Kivenlahti on the seashore, advantage has been taken of the coastline for some ingenious planning. Because of the rise of the ground from the sea it is on two levels. The lower is on a flat green area 18 feet above sea level, the upper is 90 feet higher in rocky terrain, the two areas being designed for populations of 6,000 and 8,000 respectively. The two are linked by a service block which contains 700 dwellings, covered passages and escalators thus facilitating movement between the two levels. Along the irregular coast line are buildings for maritime activities and recreation, an international hotel, and a restaurant, while in one part there is a tiered circular arrangement of terrace houses facing the sea with the effect of an amphitheatre.

These examples, although they are well-planned communities and often aesthetically delightful, have not the autonomy of new towns. They are all much too closely linked with the big cities and the satisfactory relation of dwellings and workplaces is not sufficiently comprehended. More complete new towns, however, are planned. In Sweden a new town is planned at Taby, 12 miles north of Stockholm, in which a considerable industrial area is included. In Finland, Storsvik, on a site of 1,413 acres, 29 miles west of Helsinki, promises to be a self-contained development, which, with Taby, will perhaps fully deserve the name of new town.

GERMANY

Most of the so-called new towns in Germany are, like those in Scandinavia, very largely extensions to existing cities, although having some identity of their own, with their own centres some of which are well planned. One of the most interesting in West

Germany is the development called Die Nordweststadt near Frankfurt-am-Main which is sometimes called a new town. It was planned by Walter Schwagenscheidt and Tassilo Sittmann. The pattern consists mainly of apartment blocks of various heights and sizes, but mostly of the tower block type placed on sites in the islands formed by roads with culs-de-sac access. The most notable feature of this development is the town centre. It is of considerable size on four levels, the lowest, ground or basement level, is a great car park over the whole area, reached by slanting roads from the encircling road. The upper three levels are large pedestrian shopping areas, with flowerbeds and children's play structures on the most extensive first floor; flowerbeds, a pool and fountain on the second floor, while the third floor is mostly walkways by the shops and bridges. The space is open to the sky with the exception of the walkways by the shops and bridges which are canopied. The centre is similar in principle to those in Cumbernauld and Runcorn, except that those are mainly covered, a difference due to climate.

A town planned to relate dwellings and employment is Wulfen in the Ruhr district, which is being built for a population of 50,000 in a country area near Dorsten, Marl and Haltern because of the large output from a new mine in the area. The plan, subject of a competition won by Fritz Eggeling, is actuated by garden-city principles and the aim is to have a mingling of town and country, and independent systems of pedestrian and vehicular traffic. It is also an all electric town.

THE NETHERLANDS

As mentioned in Chapter 38, when the centre of Rotterdam was rebuilt the former 25,000 dwellings were replaced by 8,000 dwellings, and this diminution meant a considerable dispersal of population, which was accommodated by satellite towns south of the Nieuwe Maas. The first of these, Hoogvliet, about 7 miles to the southwest, is a self-contained community of 60,000 which could be dignified with the name of satellite town. It is built on somewhat similar lines to the British new towns. It has a shopping centre with shops on four sides of a pedestrian square, but it has a much larger proportion of apartment blocks than any British new town. Other satellite communities are much closer to Rotterdam and are really more in the nature of suburban extensions. Two, which continue the extensions south of the river, are Pendrecht (22,000) and Zuidwijk (23,000) that lie to the south of the large Zuiderpark. They are both very attractively planned with extensive lawns, flowerbeds and patches of water among the housing blocks. Further communities planned and in the course of construction are Lombardyen (25,000) in the southeast, Groot-Yseelmonde also in the southeast, and the large new community in the Prins Alexander Polder to the east, planned for a population of 180,000, all necessitated by the increasing population. With the completion of these the population of Rotterdam will be well over a million. The new underground railway provides another crossing of the Maas and is an additional link between the extensive residential areas on the south side of the river with the centre where a considerable number of the residents work. The railway about three and a half miles long is underground north of the river and overland south of the river. It starts at the central station and runs underneath Weena and Coolsingel and terminates at Zuidplein in the centre of the southern suburban area.

FRANCE

In the early post-war years in France the great need was for houses and a large number of what are called grands ensembles were built. A grand ensemble is an estate of not less than 500 dwellings, built by public or semipublic bodies, and by 1964 about 200 grandes ensembles of over 1,000 dwellings each (about 4,000 population) were built, nearly half of these in the Paris region. They were built mainly on the outskirts of large or medium sized towns, and they comprised only housing, so they are mainly suburban extensions. The few that were built in open country away from towns have sometimes been referred to as new towns, but in every case they are little more than residential areas with little provision for shopping and amenities. From some of these grandes ensembles may emerge more comprehensive development in which there is provision for shopping and employment and educational and recreational facilities, such as Toulouse-Le Mirail planned for a population of 100,000.

The inadequacies of the grands ensembles prompted planners and others to think of more comprehensive urban units more on the lines of the British new towns, and it was partly with this in mind that the plan for the Paris region was produced in 1965. In this plan two belts or axes of urban development were proposed along east–west valleys, north and south of Paris, and along these belts several urban centres, with shopping and many educational and recreational facilities. Along the northern belt are Cergy-Pontoise, Beauchamp and Noisy-le-Grand, and along the southern belt are Mantes, Trappes, Envry and Tigery Lieusaint. Although plans have been prepared for several fairly complete developments round these centres for populations approaching half a million, the philosophy or theory governing the schemes appears to be that highly developed urban centres will attract residential and other development round them. Fairly complete plans have been prepared for Envry and Cergy-Pontoise in which there is a provision for industry and office employment, so as to achieve some degree of balance between homes and employment within the new towns. There is not, however, any very definite planned relationship between employment and housing, and although there is employment in these new urban areas, there is at the same time freedom of choice of where residents work whether in or outside the town. At Envry there is a main centre round which there is much new residential development, several sub-centres and several adjacent industrial areas, and a considerable mingling of open spaces. Due attention is given to the needs of both private and public transport. In one respect the schemes for these new towns in the Paris region are superior to British development in that better rail provision is made. Often in the area of a British new town rail provision is scrapped, and it is a joke in British planning circles that when the

570

site for a new town is proposed it is the sign for British Rail to close the station there. In the case of Telford there existed, as a survival of an earlier industrial period, a network of railways which could have proved of value to the new town. Instead they have been scrapped. In contrast, at Evry, a main line runs by the river Seine on the north east boundary of the town, with a local loop line that runs through the urban centre[5].

These urban centres in the Paris regional plan are the cores of new towns of half a million population, fairly close to Paris—between 8 and 25 miles from its centre. They are very different in size and location from the British new towns and are more in the nature of several centres forming a city region.

Some of the typical trends in the building of new towns and communities in Europe between 1950 and 1970 have been noted. There are numerous other examples which are equally worthy of attention, but I have tried to select representative examples. The British new towns are conspicuously successful and are justly celebrated because they are planned to comprehend the whole of everyday life, whereas many new towns elsewhere are not planned, or at least realized on this comprehensive basis.

References and Notes

1. A fairly complete list of new towns throughout the world is given in Appendix I of *The New Towns—The Answer to Megalopolis* by Sir Frederic J. Osborn and Arnold Whittick, second edition, Leonard Hill, London, 1969.
2. Welwyn Garden City was, of course, a new town before the policy was officially adopted, but the further development was unnecessarily taken over by the Government in 1948 when it had reached a population of 19,000.
3. Sir Frederic Osborn and Arnold Whittick, *The New Towns*, second edition, Leonard Hill, London, 1969, p. 386.
4. See the many illustrations in Sir Frederic Osborn and Arnold Whittick, *The New Towns*, second edition, Leonard Hill, London, 1969, p. 386.
5. For a brief description of the Paris regional plan see Pierre Merlin, *Les Villes Nouvelles*, Paris, 1969. English translation, London, 1971.

40 Domestic architecture 1947–1970

BETWEEN THE WARS much progress had been made with the individually designed house, and a considerable number were built in France, Germany, Italy, Scandinavia and Britain which displayed much originality and ingenuity in design and which at the same time were functional and aesthetically pleasing. In the twenties the main progress was due pre-eminently to the innovations of Le Corbusier, which exercised a great influence, and also to the progressive work of Gropius, Breuer and Mies van der Rohe and, a little later, to Connell, Ward and Lucas, Maxwell Fry and a few others in Britain.

The excellence of many of the examples of the individually designed house did not exercise any very marked influence during the twenties and thirties on low-cost mass housing by local authorities and speculative builders. These continued, with a few exceptions, to be commonplace and traditionally conventional in design and conservative in construction. After the Second World War, however, the inter-war experimentation in domestic architecture began to have an influence on mass housing in which there was a great improvement after 1950 in general standards of design over the mass housing of the thirties. This is seen especially in new towns and communities resulting from Government enterprise. The best individually designed houses of the inter-war period proved to be an inspiration to designers of low-cost mass housing, and many of the ideas of Le Corbusier, Gropius, Mies van der Rohe and others were used in the design of small standard houses.

As after the First World War, a large number of new methods and systems of construction were subjects of experiments, and many new systems were adopted. In the early post-war period, up to about 1950, the new systems were applied firstly to the buildings most urgently needed, that is to small houses, blocks of flats, schools and factories, the systems being adapted to the various purposes. The main purposes of these new systems were (a) a higher standard of performance, (b) greater efficiency of construction, (c) speedier building and (d) greater economy. By standard of performance

572

is meant the degree to which the building provides efficient shelter: the degrees of weather proofing, of thermal and sound insulation; by efficiency of construction, the degree of precision and exactitude and the extent to which it can be the subject of accurate calculation. The four objects are obtained by increased prefabrication, by an increased proportion of factory work and less site work, and by a standardization of parts to permit extensive mass production. The last generally involves designing on the basis of a grid. The craft of building was gradually becoming the science of building and natural materials were giving place to synthetic and manufactured ones for which precise calculations of strength could be made. Traditional materials like wood and stone were used less for construction in their natural state, and more as parts of synthetic and processed materials like laminated wood and the aggregate of concrete, but they retained their place in their natural state as decorative and facing materials. Prefabrication and standardization on the basis of a particular constructional system meant that the whole building could be completed in the factory and transported to the site, placed on the foundation and linked to the services. This has been done with small houses, although mostly smaller more easily transportable units like the bathroom or kitchen units are made complete in the factory and assembled on the site. In the many systems employed in the early post-war years, large panel sections and complete walls were commonly made in the factory and assembled on the site. The restricting factor in the size of units is transport, for it would not be easy to transport complete even the small house. The most practical possibility is for it to be done by helicopter, but at present (1973) the cost would be prohibitive. The caravan—or mobile home as it is now called in USA—has distinct possibilities for further development.

New systems of construction are most conveniently classified according to the principal material employed. The majority are some form of concrete or steel-frame construction with glazing and panelling of various materials. With concrete construction the greater the degree of pre-cast units that can be employed the greater can the advantages of prefabrication and precision building be realized.

From 1945 the most progressive and original designs in domestic architecture occurred in blocks of flats rather than in the small family house, whether individually designed or as a unit in a large housing estate. Nothing outstanding has occurred in small house design since 1945 at all comparable with the innovations of Le Corbusier during the twenties. Perhaps the most notable developments have been the patio type with its innumerable variations, and the experimentation with the relation of floor levels in what is known as the split-level house. A notable example of the former is a single-storey house in Cologne-Weiss built in 1955 and designed by Gottfried Bohm, where there is a courtyard in the centre with glass walled rooms all round. Several one-storey houses with patios partly formed by the walls of houses and partly by fences occur in the houses in the International Exhibition of the Hansa District in Berlin in 1956. They were designed by several architects including Johannes Krahn, Arne Jacobsen

One-storey patio houses, Hansa district, Berlin, 1957
Architect: Eduard Ludwig

Terrace houses with corridor access built on the slope
of a hill at Farsta, near Stockholm, circa 1955

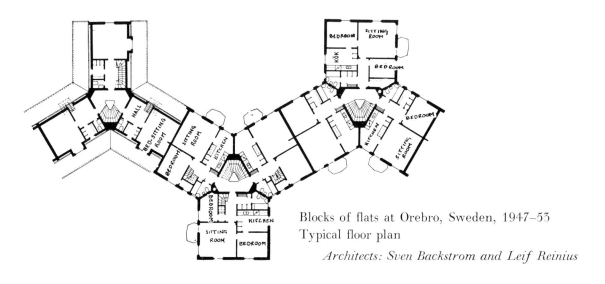

Blocks of flats at Orebro, Sweden, 1947–53
Typical floor plan

Architects: Sven Backstrom and Leif Reinius

Apartment House, Berlin, 1956–58
Architect: Le Corbusier

and Eduard Ludwig. Patio houses have been introduced in several new housing estates throughout Europe, and a few examples can be seen in pedestrian residential areas where privacy has been secured in fairly high density development with blank walls facing outwards to the footpaths and windows facing inwards to the courtyards or patios. A typical example of this type of house is seen in the Clarkhill district of Harlow, built in the late sixties. One-storey houses are in pairs, each L-shaped with a small square garden or court partly enclosed by the adjoining house. The outer walls facing the footpaths are blank and all the windows face the courtyard and towards the south, thus obtaining good orientation and privacy.

An attractive development of terrace houses on the steep slopes of hills, especially if they are towards the south, is of houses arranged in one large structure with long internal corridors which give access to the houses. They are arranged in step-like fashion and each house with its balcony overlooks the roof of the one below. Good examples are at Farsta, a satellite town of Stockholm (1959), and at Burghalde (1959–63) and Muhlehalde (1963–5) in Switzerland.

APARTMENT HOUSE DESIGN

The more progressive and original domestic architecture from 1945 onwards occurred in apartment house (blocks of flats) design, and again some of the notable development has been due to the genius of Le Corbusier. In the period between the wars the main types of apartment houses were those built round courtyards and the slab type from three to twelve storeys high. In the post-war period from 1945 the tower type of apartment house was extensively built. Among the earliest examples of this were the fifteen-storey towers in the Cité de la Muette at Drancy built in the early thirties, but there was not a widespread following of these until the late thirties, and after the war from 1945 they were fairly widely adopted in most European countries. In Scandinavia this form became popular and was the subject of many experiments. A few examples are cited later.

In Chapter 22, apartment houses were classified according to types of access: (1) corridor access, (2) galley access, (3) direct access to one or two flats on each landing and (4) to three or more. This classification was applicable to the slab block, but with the tower block it is more informative and significant to classify on the basis of the variations of plan that have been evolved. These could be classified as (1) the square or rectangular plan with central staircase and lift, and generally with from four to eight flats per landing. The difficulty with this type of plan is to get a satisfactory orientation for all the flats. (2) Two linked squares or rectangles with staircase and lift forming a central linking feature. (3) The cross plan with four flats on each floor. (4) The T, Y or multi-wing plan. (5) The irregular plan which is sometimes between a tower and slab block[1]. A few outstanding examples are selected of the various types beginning with the slab type.

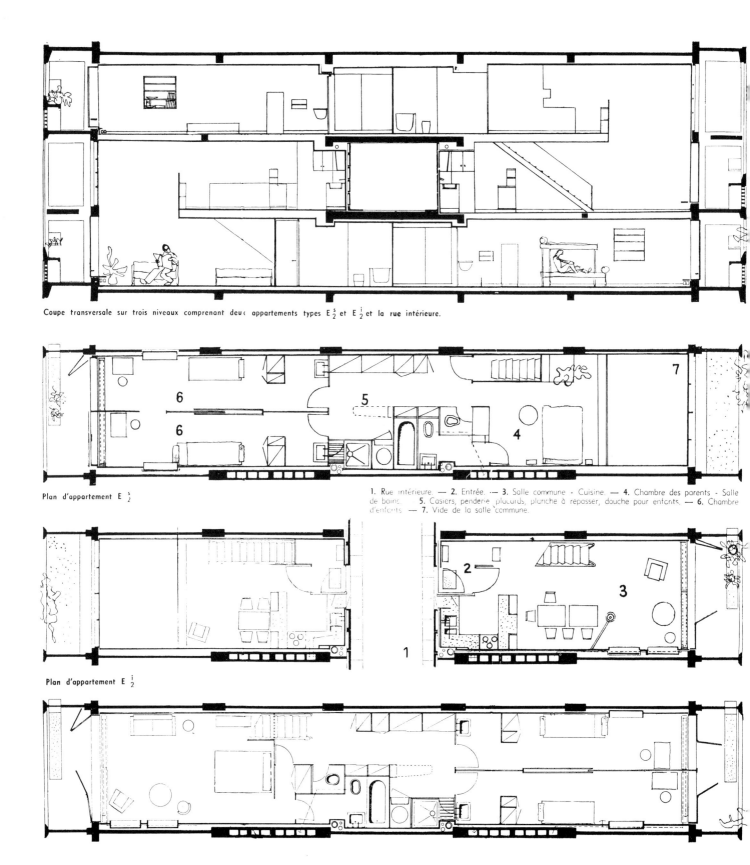

Coupe transversale sur trois niveaux comprenant deux appartements types E$\frac{s}{2}$ et E$\frac{i}{2}$ et la rue intérieure.

Plan d'appartement E$\frac{s}{2}$

1. Rue intérieure. — 2. Entrée. — 3. Salle commune - Cuisine. — 4. Chambre des parents - Salle de bains. — 5. Casiers, penderie placards, planche à repasser, douche pour enfants. — 6. Chambre d'enfants — 7. Vide de la salle commune.

Plan d'appartement E$\frac{i}{2}$

L'Unité d'habitation, Marseilles, 1947–52, plans *Architect: Le Corbusier*

Probably the most dramatic and spectacular block of flats built in Europe in the early post-war period was Le Corbusier's, L'Unite d'habitation at Marseilles (1947–52). This huge apartment house with 337 dwellings (for about 1,300 persons) is set in a park-like area of nearly 9 acres with lawns and trees. It is a realization of many of Le Corbusier's cherished dreams. When, in 1945, he was asked by the French Minister of Reconstruction to build one of his omnibus houses at Marseilles he replied that he would do so on condition that he must be free of all building regulations. This was agreed, and in spite of much opposition Le Corbusier and his team continued to build with the necessary freedom[2].

This huge long rectangular building, 450 feet long, 80 feet wide and 184 feet high, with its axis approximately north–south, has eighteen floors, including a roof terrace and the open ground floor with its double row of piles. The basic type of large apartment is on two floors with one floor extending the whole width, and the other floor half the width, alternately arranged so that in one the lower floor is the whole width and in the vertical adjoining one the upper floor is the whole width. In each case the living room is two floors high thus giving a sense of spaciousness, while it opens to a balcony. The half-width floor, whether lower or upper, has the kitchen and dining room and the other long floor the sleeping quarters. Interior streets, or corridors, provide access to the flats and run through the centre on the alternate levels between the half width floors. There are many other different types of apartment in the block to cater for various needs: for bachelors, couples, and various sized families, the different types fitting very ingeniously into the grid. On the seventh and eighth floors are shops and departmental stores (or supermarkets), restaurant and communal laundry, so that the tenants can provide for their everyday needs without leaving the block.

At the entrances and decorating the walls in sunk relief in various parts of the building is the figure of a man with arm upraised. This, which Le Corbusier contends is 2.20 m (see Chapter 30), forms the modular for the building. The figure fits two squares of 1.10 m (3 feet 7 inches) which determined the grid.

The punctuations of the balconies giving a pattern of light and shadow to the façades serve to lessen the heavy effect of this massive building, while the surrounding trees, some of which have grown to half its height have a softening effect in the ensemble. For the ingenuity of its design to serve in one way the domestic needs of people this must be regarded as one of the notable achievements of the century.

This immense apartment house was followed by two others on similar lines, one at Nantes-Reze (1952–3) and the other in Berlin (1956–8). In the block at Nantes-Reze the essential principles of the Marseilles block have been followed, but there are a few differences in design and construction. Instead of two piles or columns across the width on the ground floor there are four, while the shopping section on the seventh and

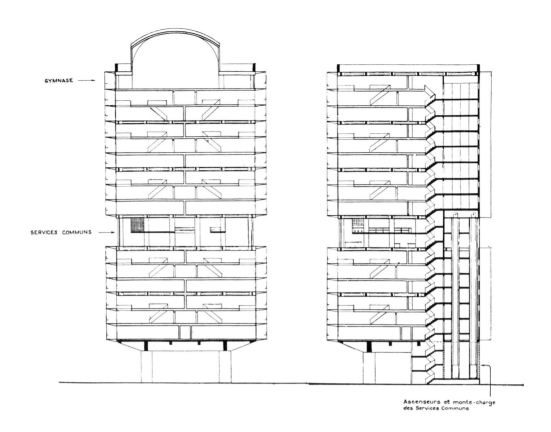

GYMNASE ——→

SERVICES COMMUNS ——→

Ascenseurs et monte-charge
des Services Communs

TOIT - JARDIN

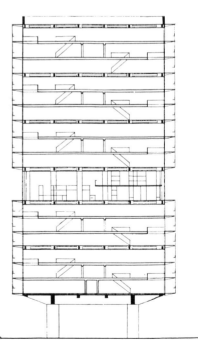

L'Unité d'habitation, Marseilles, 1947–52
Vertical sections

Architect: Le Corbusier

eighth floors has not been included. Le Corbusier, himself, indicates a difference of construction. The apartment units in the Marseilles block fit into the concrete frame as into slots, whereas in the Nantes-Reze block there is no frame in the same sense but a pile of boxes. According to Le Corbusier, 'the system of "Bottle and Bottle-Rack" (Marseilles) is replaced by a system of "Shoe Boxes"'[3]. The buildings at Nantes-Reze has also a park-like setting, and one of the approaches is by a pedestrian bridge across a nearby lake.

The Berlin building is very similar in size and accommodation, but with a great number of smaller apartments so that over 400 are provided. This building was to have been part of the Inter Bau Exposition in the Hansa quarter, but Le Corbusier's project was too large for the space allocated, so it was built on an excellent site on high ground near the Olympic Stadium.

TOWER OR POINT BLOCKS

As previously mentioned tower blocks of flats began to be built in considerable numbers immediately after the war, and many notable developments took place in Scandinavia. They were called Punkthuse (point houses) in Sweden where several of the earliest pioneering schemes were evolved which had considerable influence throughout Europe. One of the earliest built during the war (1943–5) to the design of Sven Backstrom and Leif Reinius, is on Danviks Cliff a prominent site near the centre of Stockholm. The group consists of nine blocks, mostly 10 storeys, well spaced in a garden setting. The tops of the towers have pyramidal roofs, because of snow, a shape which may have suggested the name. The towers are square on plan each with central half-circular staircase and lift. There are 391 flats for about 1,300 people, and they vary in size from the larger with two flats to a floor, to smaller with four and five flats to a floor.

Another notable scheme by the same architects is the large development at Orebro, built from 1947 to 1953. It consists of 1,300 flats in a kind of honeycomb formation along two loop roads. This honeycomb formation is really made up of four-storey, Y-plan blocks, joined together, and each unit has a central stair-well which serves three wings forming angles of 120 degrees. Each has five floors—a basement, ground floor, two upper floors and an attic which contains additional bedrooms for the upper flat. The flats vary in size, about half having two rooms, about one third three rooms, while the remainder have one room located mainly in the one tower block in which is provided a collective domestic service. The partial enclosures formed by the honeycomb pattern and the open spaces within the loop-roads help to make it an attractive development. A school, shops, day nursery, garages grouped in circles are provided, and there is district heating. This scheme has had considerable influence, and many similar have subsequently been built in Sweden and elsewhere[4].

A considerable number of point blocks of various designs were built at Vallingby

579

during the fifties. Vallingby (see Chapter 39) is a new town or suburb, 9 miles northwest of Stockholm, for a population of 60,000. The town centre is on high ground and is built over the railway, and on either side are grouped many tower blocks of 10 and 12 storeys, mingling with lower slab blocks of three or four storeys, while several are designed in a series of steps to accord with the sloping ground. With its lawns and trees the whole has a verdant character with the tower blocks dominating the landscape. An attractive group, on gently sloping ground north of the centre, is that known as Ritstiflet of which J. Bjurstrom was the architect. It consists of four eleven-storey towers, spaciously sited, linked at their bases by a long two storey building for shops and offices. The plans of the towers are irregular approximating to an irregular fat T, with three to five flats of various sizes—from one to three rooms—on each floor.

In Tapiola, the lovely new town in Finland (1955–70), there is a mixed development of family houses, low and tall blocks of flats set in the forest by the sea. The lower blocks of three or four storeys contain the family flats, and the tall blocks contain the smaller flats for couples and bachelors. The nine-storey half-tower half slab on the hill summits of the western neighbourhood have a particularly fine landscape effect. On this hill among the trees and shrubs are giant granite boulders, and it would seem that the architect has taken the implication of these and extended them upwards in the form of apartment houses. The tall blocks are spaciously grouped round an extensive garden, which in summer is rich with the colour of many different flowers.

THE HANSA (BERLIN) DEVELOPMENT

In 1927 an International Housing Exhibition, sponsored by the Deutsche Workbund was held at Stuttgart, for which several of the most famous European architects designed houses under the general surveillance of Mies van der Rohe (see Chapter 23). Such an exhibition was repeated on a much larger scale in Berlin in 1957, when 53 famous architects from all parts of the world designed a wide variety of dwellings including family houses, terrace houses, tower and slab blocks. The work was coordinated by a committee under the presidency of Otto Bartning, and among the architects who designed the buildings were Aalto, Gropius, Taut, Niemeyer, Jacobsen, Lopez and Beaudouin, Fisker and Vago. The site was described in Chapter 38. Here a few of the notable buildings are briefly described.

The contribution of Walter Gropius is a slab block of 10 storeys, with a slightly concave front towards the south. It has an interesting pattern of living room balconies that have the effect of being pulled out a little from the general face of the block with its large windows. This variation together with a recessed ground floor leaving the piers free standing gives a good light and shadow effect to the whole. The 64 three-bedroom apartments are for the middle-income tenants, with two per landing, with lift and staircase access forming four projections at the rear.

Point blocks at Ritstiflet, Vallingby, near Stockholm, 1958

Architect: J. Bjurstrom

Apartment houses designed in stepped series, in parkland near centre of Vallingby, circa 1958

Family houses at Tapiola—eastern neighbourhood, circa 1955

Example of linked tower blocks, Malmo, Sweden, 1952

Tower block of flats, western neighbourhood Tapiola, circa 1954 *Architect: Aarne Ervi*

The eight-storey block by Alvar Aalto consists of two staircases and lift access, with five flats for each landing varying from one to four rooms. An interesting feature of the larger flats is that the rooms are arranged round a fairly large central living room, which in each case has a recessed balcony. It is a concrete structure and the façade has a broad simple massing of rectangles of pale walls contrasting with the deep shadows of the balconies.

The structure of the block by Oscar Niemeyer is dramatic, for it consists of a long rectangular box supported on massive concrete V's in pairs. The seven-storey façade has a regular pattern of recessed balconies with horizontal railed fronts.

Of the five tower blocks, that by J. H. van den Broek and J. B. Bakema displays some original and ingenious planning. The plan is rectangular with north–south spine and with corridors that serve a group of eight split-level, three-room apartments and four one-room apartments, with an alternate east and west orientation for each group, and sun terraces at the south end of the corridors. The façades reflect the planning so that unlike most tower blocks there is variety in the patterning of the fenestration with the large living room windows with balconies and the comparatively narrow strips of bedroom windows.

Acting as a transition between the tall tower blocks in the northeast area to the low one- and two-storey building of the Academy of Arts are three four-storey blocks designed by Max Taut, Kay Fisker the Danish architect, and Otto H. Senn the Swiss architect. The last mentioned is notable for its pentagonal plan. The central landings on the three lower floors give access to four flats—one 4 rooms, one 3 rooms and two 2 rooms—and there is a secluded balcony for each of the four living rooms, three of which face towards the south between southeast and southwest, while the fourth is towards the west and north. The fourth floor recessed with a surrounding terrace has four studio flats[5]. This apartment house served as the prototype for two taller blocks of 20 storeys subsequently built at Hechtliacker near Basel in 1962–5. Most of the apartment houses in the Hansa district were constructed of various forms and systems of reinforced concrete.

An unusual apartment house at Neue Vahr, a suburb of Bremen, is that designed by Alvar Aalto and built in 1962. It is a 22-storey, narrow curved block, and on plan it is rather like a pack of cards opened out. On each floor is a corridor which gives access to nine two-room flats for single persons and couples. The flats fan out to the west façade and the long living rooms occupy the whole length of the flat and each has a small balcony, while the other rooms or alcoves—kitchen, bedroom, bathroom—open in a row from the living room. On the further side of the corridor is a common room and drying room, while on the ground floor is a spacious entrance hall with small shops for day to day goods[6]. The block is spaciously set adjoining the low two-storey buildings of the Neue Vahr shopping centre.

582

Plan of Alvar Aalto's flats, Berlin

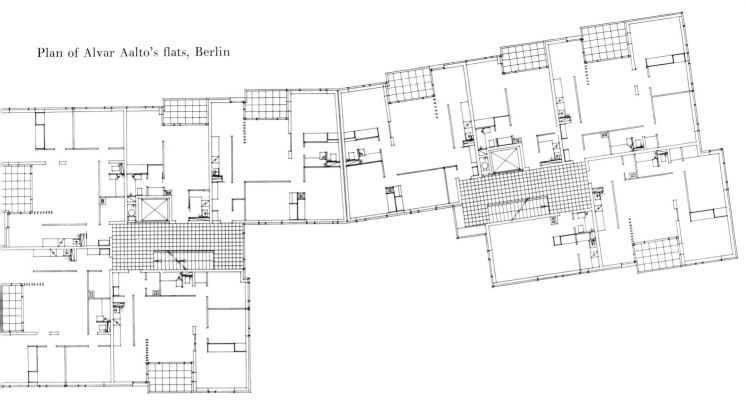

Apartment house (block of flats), Hansa District, Berlin, 1957–59   *Architect: Alvar Aalto*

Another unusual and ingenious example of apartment house design is that of the two blocks erected at Stuttgart-Zuffenhausen, known as Romeo and Juliet, and built in 1957–9 to the design of Hans Scharoun and Wilhelm Frank. They are sited at the top of a hill in a new housing estate. Romeo, built first, is a nineteen-storey tower block with six flats on each floor grouped round a central landing, four of which have pointed balconies. The Juliet block forms a horseshoe on plan, and is twelve storeys high except for one wing which is eight storeys. A typical floor—up to eight storeys high—has nine flats, with access from a gallery on the inner side of the horseshoe, while each flat plan comes to a point with a balcony. The rooms have irregular shapes and it would be interesting to know from the occupants how successful these experimental flats are.

A long concrete apartment house block on a nearby hilltop in Stuttgart (Tapachstrasse) that has attracted much attention was built about ten years later (1967–9), to the designs of Schroder and Faller. It has a series of receding stepped balconies on the south side very much in the manner of the terrace houses built on the slopes of hills in Sweden and Switzerland, mentioned earlier (see illustration). In this case the slope has been provided by the concrete structure itself, rather like the ancient Summerians who, having erected temples on hill summits, finding when they descended into the plains that there were no hills, built ziggurats. Access to these apartments, or flats, is by galleries on the Tapachstrasse, and this elevation looks rather heavy and brutal. Still, the main thing is the series of generous balconies facing the sun, with a considerable degree of privacy for each, obtained partly by dividing sloping shafts. On the south side the block is bordered by a pedestrian way, and beyond are groups of one-storey, square-shaped houses.

The Heiligfeld housing estate in Zürich, planned and built in the early fifties, for which the city architect, A. H. Steiner was responsible, contains several three-, four- and eight-storey blocks and two Y-shaped tower blocks of 13 storeys, the last being good examples of this type of plan. There are four flats to a floor with access from a central landing. The small flats are either one bedroom type, with living–dining room, kitchen and bathroom, or two bedrooms with smaller living space. A good feature is that each living room has a balcony and in this Y-shaped plan the four balconies face south, two tilted slightly to southeast and southwest.

A FEW ENGLISH EXAMPLES

The apartment house has not the old and powerful tradition in England that it has in most other European countries, it is a comparatively recent development and in most schemes English architects have looked for European examples to follow, with the result that there is not much in England in this field in the nature of innovation. There has been much good work of a rather traditional character and the little experimental work where contributions to design have been made belong rather to the thirties (noted

Apartment house (block of flats), Hansa District, Berlin, 1957–59 *Architect: Oscar Niemeyer*

Apartment house, Neue Vahr, Bremen, 1962
Exterior view and floor plan

Architect: Alvar Aalto

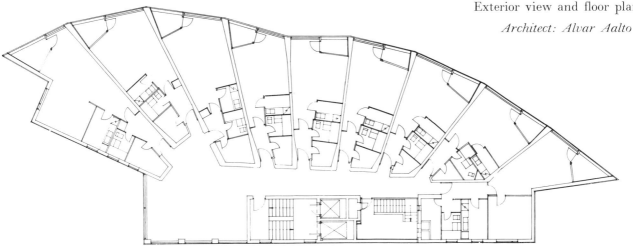

Apartment house, Tapachstrasse, Stuttgart, 1967–69
Architects: Schroder and Faller

'Romeo and Juliet' apartment houses, Stuttgart, 1957–59
Architects: Hans Scharoun and Wilhelm Frank

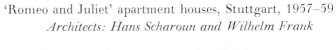

in Chapter 22) than to the fifties and sixties. In the first five years following the war a large number of the blocks of flats built in London, especially those for which the London County Council was responsible, were exceedingly poor and were the subject of vigorous adverse criticism.

There were, however, some notable exceptions, such as the large scheme of 634 dwellings on the 35-acre site at Pimlico, Westminster, known as Churchill Gardens. The scheme was the subject of a competition in 1946 which was won by Arnold J. P. Powell and John Hidalgo Moya, who became the architects for the work. It continued for several years and was completed in 1953. Flats of various sizes are provided, the majority with three and four rooms, with a few two and one room. The blocks are all of the slab type. The tall blocks of 7 and 9 storeys are arranged north–south endwise to the river, while some of the lower blocks of 3 and 4 storeys are sited parallel with the river. Squares are provided between the flats and children's playgrounds occupy corners. It is a question whether on this site near the river the best possible arrangement was adopted, and whether a more open one towards the river giving the maximum number of flat dwellers the view would not have been preferable, as was provided by other designs submitted in the competition, such as a highly commended one by Donald D. Harrison, Ernest Sell and Penelope Hawkes, and another one by Ivor Shaw and Sidney John Lloyd. In the latter plan the tall blocks are orientated north–south, the spaces between them are kept as open as possible, an arrangement which gives to a maximum number of flat dwellers a view of the river[7]. All the flats are provided with central heating and hot water by district heating operated in connection with the Battersea Power Station across the river, and an accumulator in the form of a tall tower is installed on the site for the distribution of supply.

Some of the better blocks of flats built in London during the decade following the Second World War were by the Metropolitan Boroughs. Many of these have the landing access in pairs, which is probably the best method, while some have an appearance of structural lightness, large windows, and sometimes quite an effective use of colour. Those which might be selected as an example of some of the best erected in the period are the Spa Green flats, Rosebery Avenue, designed for the Finsbury Borough Council by the Tecton Group. These consist of three blocks set pleasantly in a garden: two parallel eight-storey blocks, orientated north–south, with bedrooms facing east and living rooms and balcony facing west in one block, and the reverse in the other, the access being to two flats from each landing. The block with the living rooms facing west and the bedrooms east is surely the better orientation, and it is a pity that both could not have been like this. The third block is four storeys high and curves a little on plan, and this has the gallery access on the east side so that all living rooms are on the west side. The design of the four-storey blocks is less satisfactory than the eight-storey blocks, chiefly because of the means of access. Part of the ground floor area of each block is open and is lifted on stilts, which contributes to the general light effect.

The elevation of a large block of flats must necessarily consist of the repetition of a particular pattern, and it depends on the extent of the pattern and of combining its repetition into a unified whole whether the total result is satisfactory. The balcony elevations of the tall blocks necessarily have greater variety than the bedroom elevations, because of the light and shadow provided by the balconies, the horizontal emphasis they permit combined with the verticals of the masses between. Yet it is the simpler bedroom elevations which are the more pleasing because of the happy relation of the square windows on the brick walls broken with three intervals to mark the staircases. The west elevation of the four-storey block has alternating concrete balconies, which, with the shadows and the brickwork, produce a rather restless effect. The gardens are set out in keeping with the buildings, the latter being seen to advantage in relation to the trees. The Garchey system of refuse disposal has been incorporated in these flats, which is thus the first example of its use in London, and the second in England, the first being in the Quarry Hill Flats in Leeds.

An increasing number of flats continued to be built in the larger towns and cities of Great Britain from 1950 onwards, in the early stages chiefly in the form of slab blocks, but later tower blocks became equally numerous. There are very few innovations in the matter of design and most of the schemes have been derived from examples on the continent of Europe. Not many blocks of flats have been built in smaller towns, for the flat has never been a popuar form of accommodation in England[8]. From the architectural standpoint one of the most notable erected in London is the block of luxury flats built in St. James's Place in 1960 and designed by Denys Lasdun. It is an excellently proportioned building with large areas of fenestration with massive projecting horizontal bands of reinforced concrete which have a rather dramatic effect, especially as seen from Green Park which it adjoins. Its near neighbour is the rather ornate eighteenth-century Palladian Spencer House, to which it makes no stylistic concessions yet accords well, because of a satisfactory relation of masses whereby the new can harmonize with the old. This beautiful building by Lasdun appears to have set the theme for other new blocks of flats on the north side.

REFERENCES AND NOTES

1. Useful classifications are made by Rolf Jensen in *High Density Living*, Leonard Hill, London, 1966, pp. 37–38. This book gives much useful information on apartment blocks built in Europe from 1945 to 1965 and about 130 examples are described and illustrated.
2. See Le Corbusier, *L'Unite D'Habitation de Marseille*, Editions Le Point, Mulhouse, 1950. English translation by Geoffrey Sainsbury, Harvill Press, London, 1953, p. 7. Later objections to the flats were sent to the third Minister of Reconstruction who referred them to Le Corbusier who said that he didn't even consider them. The Minister supported his attitude and said, 'You are free of all restrictions and above the law. You are the judge of what you should do and you can innovate to your heart's content. You alone are responsible'. See pp. 9–10.

3. W. Boesiger and H. Girsberger, *Le Corbusier 1910–65*, Thames and Hudson, London, 1967, p. 148.

4. See *Tidning for Byggnadskonst*, No. 5, 1949, also *Building Digest*, July 1949, pp. 240–41.

5. See *Modern Architecture in Germany* with an introduction by Ulrich Conrads and captions by Werner Marschall, Verlag Gerd Hatje, Stuttgart; Architectural Press, London, 1962, pp. 62–69.

6. See article by Rolf Rosner in *The Builder*, 11th January 1963, pp. 56–58.

7. A critical appraisement of the competition with a review of some of the designs submitted is given in, *The National House Builder and Building Digest*, vol. vi, No. 7, July 1946, p. 21.

8. Evidence conclusively demonstrates that at least 90 per cent of families in England, if they are given the choice, prefer the small house with a garden to the flat.

41   Schools 1945–1960

A GREAT DEAL of experiment in the design of school buildings took place in Europe in the fifteen years following the Second World War, and a wide variety of plans were made as interpretations of the best way of serving the essential requirements of the modern school. It was being increasingly realized that the first stage was to have a comprehensive impression of these requirements, and to realize that in the education of children from 3 to 18 it was necessary to comprehend the whole of early life in its numerous manifestations, and that all branches of knowledge that help to determine methods of education must be taken into consideration in determining the physical setting for this education.

Of the belligerent countries Great Britain was among the first to build schools in answer to the urgent need. Hertfordshire County Council with an excellent team of architects[1] led the way, and the schools in Hertfordshire built in the eight years following the war deservedly became famous throughout Europe. Speed and economy were essential which necessarily implied restrictions, but some very good school buildings resulted, of which a few examples will be noted later. At the same time some of the best designed schools in Europe were built in the smaller countries of which those in Sweden and Switzerland are conspicuous.

In England the planning of school buildings was done within the framework of the Education Act of 1944 which appears to have had some influence in Europe. There is the broad division of primary schools and secondary schools an approximation to which exists in most European countries. In England the primary school is divided for infants, 5 to 8 years, and juniors 8 to 11 years. Provision is made in some regions for nursery schools for children from 2 to 5 years. Some countries make extensive provision for nursery schools; in Sweden for example this is done for children from 3 to 6 years. In England from 1945 to 1960, secondary schools for children from 11 to 15, 16, 17 or 18 were divided mainly into secondary modern, technical and grammar schools, to serve the various aptitudes of children and some approximation to these divisions occurs in other countries. In the early fifties the three types of secondary school began to be merged in the one large comprehensive school, and although this is now widely accepted as the type that is most likely to be provided in the future, the respective merits of the former separate secondary schools and the comprehensive school have been a subject of controversy from 1950 onwards.

In Chapter 20 devoted to schools in the period between the wars (1919–40) some account was given of the changes from the traditional symmetrical plan and monumental character of school building up to the early years of the century, where classrooms were often grouped symmetrically round a central hall or courtyard to the more informal functional plan where the best orientation to give sunlight to classrooms was discussed and examples cited. The merits of the one-storey and two-, three- and four-storey schools were discussed.

PRIMARY SCHOOLS—BRITISH, SWEDISH, SWISS AND FRENCH EXAMPLES

This functional planning continued and was more and more broadly based as experience widened. There was increasing consideration of the integration of the buildings with their natural setting, especially in Switzerland and Sweden, of flexibility of construction so that buildings could be changed or enlarged as changing needs required, while more attention was given to aesthetic aspects and the use of colour, murals and sculptures to add interest to the child's school life. These requirements are well expressed in a small book on *School Buildings*[2] by Bruce Martin, one of the team of architects who planned the Hertfordshire schools in the early post-war years. Bruce Martin says, 'The school is a living body through which groups of children pass and, in doing so, change and grow. Curricula, teaching methods and school activities change and the building must allow these changes to take place. It is insufficient for a building to serve only the needs of the moment, for such a building inhibits life, hinders change and prevents development. The school building should be a framework which will allow of alterations in response to the movement of life of a changing school.' A little later he says, 'It is not enough for a building to be efficient, logical, and hygienic, for it to be the right cost and the permissible area. These are necessary, but it should also possess grace and charm, be a place where children can indeed absorb, if perhaps unconsciously, those essential values and virtues which need forever to be restated in acts, embodied in deeds and preserved in works. The building itself should promote sensitivity and by its very purity, enrich, enfold, and enshrine the children who move within its spaces, for the building should not be conceived as a series of rooms with hard playgrounds outside, but as a place at one with the hedges, plants and grass, a place filled with colour and light, a place in which it is not possible to say where nature ends and art begins. For this purpose, colour is of first importance, then, when a child works on a bed of flowers, makes things in the workshop, plays in the fields or in the central hall, he may acquire a deepening sense of the richness and fullness of living.'

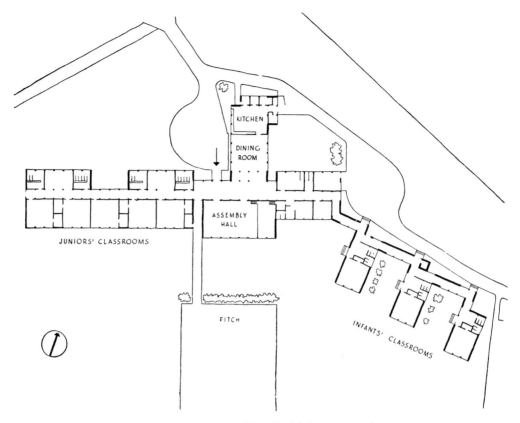

Burleigh School, Cheshunt, Hertfordshire, 1948. Ground floor plan

*Architects of both schools: C. H. Aslin, Hertfordshire
County Architect and his team of architects*

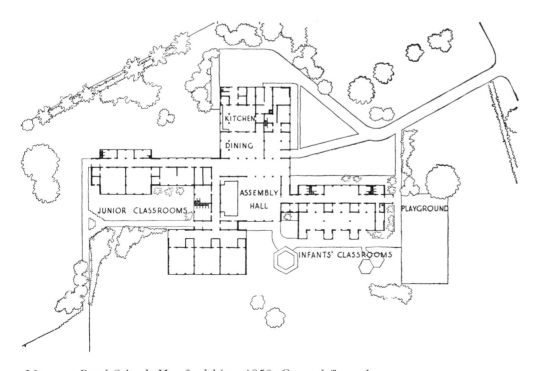

Morgans Road School, Hertfordshire, 1950. Ground floor plan

The aims thus stated are idealistic, and they represent the spirit of many architects who designed schools throughout Europe from about 1945 to 1960. The exercises of planning and construction were attended by a great deal of experiment, and a wide variety of plans and siting. The selection of some twenty significant examples will serve to show this variety.

Two excellent, basically similar, Hertfordshire primary schools are the Burleigh School at Cheshunt and Morgans Road School, Hertford, both designed by C. H. Aslin and his team of architects. They are both one-storey, flat-roofed, steel-framed structures, with precast concrete slabs for floors, roofs and walls. Burleigh School for 320 children, completed in 1948, has two wings for juniors and infants, both with classrooms to the south and corridors to the north. An assembly hall is in the centre between the two wings and beyond the corridor to the north are the dining room and kitchen. The infants classrooms have gardens between them and both wings look south to an extensive playground. The Morgans Road School, completed in 1950, has a similar arrangements of parts, but with a slightly more compact plan and a slightly more intimate relation of gardens and classrooms, with an extra junior classroom wing to the south partly enclosing the garden.

A much larger primary school is the Whitmore Park School at Coventry, designed by Richard Shepherd and Partners, in collaboration with The Bristol Aeroplane Company (Housing) Ltd, and completed in 1951, for 880 children (520 juniors and 360 infants). It is a one-storey structure built largely of aluminium with aluminium roof trusses supported on aluminium wall panels, with end walls of brick. The plan consists of a main spine north–south with juniors classroom wings at the end and on either side, with classrooms south and corridors north. The infants classrooms are on an east wing facing east and projecting between gardens. Assembly halls and dining rooms are located towards the northwest. The windows of these three schools are large occupying most of the wall space on the south side, thus prime attention being given to orientation and to obtaining maximum sunlight in classrooms.

The Abrahamsberg School in Stockholm, designed by Paul Hedgvist, and built a little earlier in 1946, is a primary school of about the same size (900 children) which, however, is different in several ways. The site is triangular and limited and the buildings are two, three and four storeys. The long strip forming the base of the triangle is on the north side, with classrooms on the south of the corridor, with an assembly hall at the east end and a hexagonal dining hall projecting south at the west end. Another long strip runs north–south with classrooms, library, music room and other specialist rooms facing east. The two wings enclose gardens and playgrounds with a swimming pool and gymnasium in the southeast part. The fairly closely built residential area, in which it is situated, the restricted site and accommodation required all spell the necessity of a compact storeyed school. The landscaping is effectual.

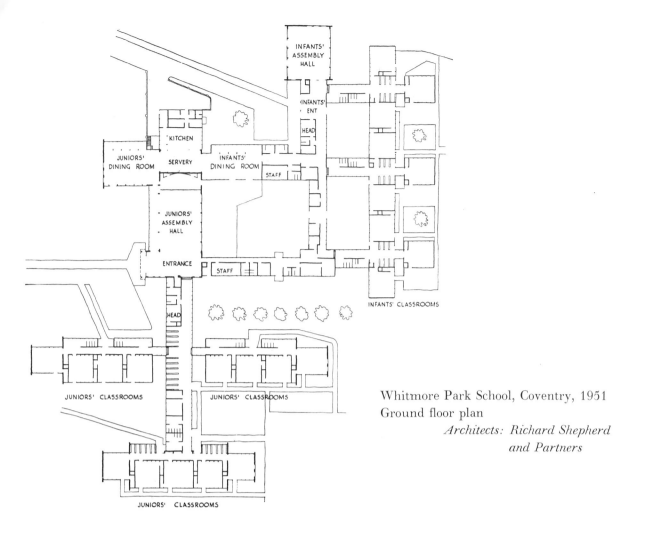

Whitmore Park School, Coventry, 1951
Ground floor plan
*Architects: Richard Shepherd
and Partners*

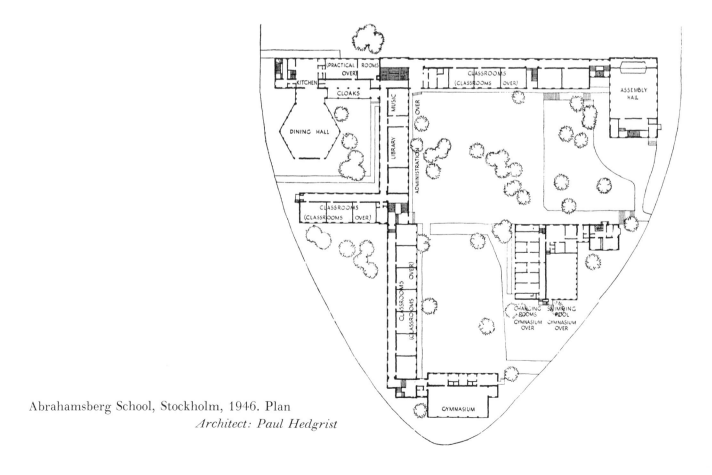

Abrahamsberg School, Stockholm, 1946. Plan
Architect: Paul Hedgrist

A particularly original design is that of the Felsberg Primary School at Lucerne designed by Emil Jauch and Erwin Burgi. It is for children from 6 to 15 and is thus a primary school rather in the old sense. The buildings are very pleasantly situated in an old park with fine trees northeast of the city with an extensive view over the city and lake to the distant mountains. It is a long east–west two-storey structure and the classrooms are accommodated on the upper floor of three connected end-to-end, long pavilions on stilts. On the ground floor are three long verandahs which serve as recreation rooms, and on this floor also are cloakrooms, kitchens, workshops and a kindergarten. Each of the three double-floored pavilions forms a self-contained unit, together with a large front garden taken from the adjoining park. To achieve this partition, the architects made skilful use of the topographical features of the sloping ground. Each classroom can take up to 42 children so that the maximum capacity of the school is about 500 pupils. The school buildings are virtually embedded in their attractive natural setting and the architects have maintained an atmosphere of sylvan freshness.

The chain of the three pavilions is continued at its eastern end by the 'singing hall', while the separate building of the gymnasium occupies a prominent site. Both are self-contained and can be hired for evening adult activities. The whole constellation of the curved chain of buildings ascending the gentle slope, dominated by the isolated building of the gymnasium and facing the beautiful and wide open park, is a fine example of space planning.

As the plan shows, the stairs leading from the ground floor to the classrooms are arranged at the points where the pavilions are joined end-to-end; they thus serve two pavilions at the same time, but there is no horizontal connection at upper floor level. Because of the large windows the class rooms have good daylighting in spite of their depth ($24\frac{1}{2}$ feet). The foundation walls consist of concrete and limestone, the walls of brick, the free pillars of granite and the roofs of timber. The gymnasium roof is carried by joists of laminated wood (Hetzer girders) and its windows and doors consist of Securit glass in varnished frames[3].

Another Swiss primary school also beautifully situated in an old park, with fine trees, is the Trembley School at Geneva, designed by Roland Rohn and completed in 1950. The site imposed scenic obligations on the architects which have been well observed. The different sections of the school, those for girls, for boys, common premises and gymnastics hall, are spread over a fairly large area, and the open schoolyards are integrated with the surrounding park. The classrooms are accommodated in two wings, (see plan) which have separate, spacious and well-lit entrance halls, dominated by the sweeping line of the curved flight of stairs leading to the upper floor. The corridors, equally well lit, have floors of red clinker, and ceilings and doors of natural wood, while vertical Pavatex panels are built into the classrooms to improve the acoustic

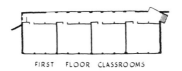

FIRST FLOOR CLASSROOMS

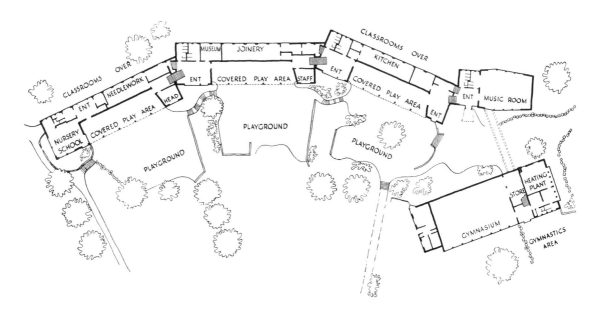

Felsberg Primary School, Lucerne, 1949
Architects: Emil Jauch and Erwin Burgi

Plan and exterior view with playground

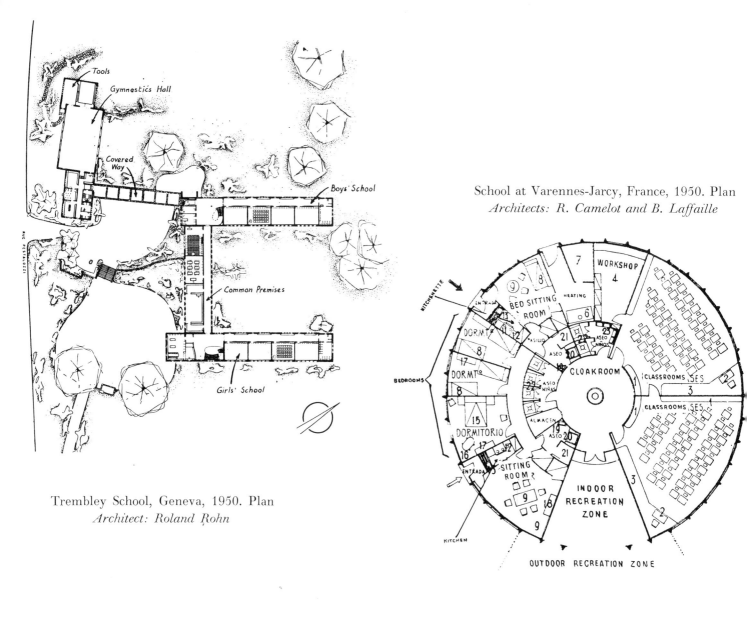

Trembley School, Geneva, 1950. Plan
Architect: Roland Rohn

School at Varennes-Jarcy, France, 1950. Plan
Architects: R. Camelot and B. Laffaille

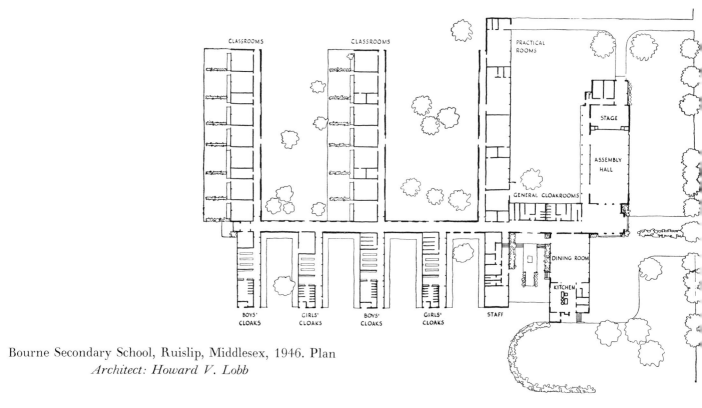

Bourne Secondary School, Ruislip, Middlesex, 1946. Plan
Architect: Howard V. Lobb

conditions. Music rooms and other special classrooms are on the upper floor, and a room for rhythmic exercises is flanked by cloakrooms on either side so that the next form can be ready as soon as one form is leaving. There are also rooms for tuition by slides or films, and for various crafts. The gymnastics hall (49 feet × 82 feet) which is connected with the main building by a covered gangway has large double-glazed Securite windows on either side. The decoration of the school includes wall paintings and sculptures by well-known local artists[4].

In France it was necessary to provide primary schools at an increased rate because of the comparatively large number of children born just after the war. To answer this need a competition was held among architects in order to secure some designs and among those selected was an original design by the architect R. Camelot, in collaboration with civil engineer B. Laffaille. The design provides for a circular single-floor building of approximately 69 feet in diameter which accommodates up to four classrooms or, alternatively, two classrooms and two flats for the teachers. The first of the latter type has been built at Varennes-Jarcy.

As the plan shows, all the sanitary installations are concentrated in a half-moon shape flanking the central rooms, which serves as an entrance hall and cloakroom. The circular design calls for a minimum of wall area to enclose a given space, and lends itself readily to standardization yet with considerable flexibility in the utilization of the circular space. The orientation of the rooms can be freely chosen so as to permit the best possible daylight conditions. All the constitutent parts of the building (stanchions, cornices, wall elements, lintels) are precast and can be easily erected with the aid of modest hoisting gear.

SECONDARY SCHOOLS—BRITISH, SWEDISH AND SWISS EXAMPLES

Secondary schools are necessarily larger and more complex to accommodate the expanding activities and education of youth, and include in addition to classrooms, dining room and assembly hall a considerable number of special purpose rooms: one or more science rooms, craft, art and music rooms, discussion rooms and many others. When these secondary schools are partly designed as community and cultural centres for adults, the variety of such provisions is often more considerable, to the benefit of both children and adults, and some of the schools cited are examples.

A secondary school typical of many built in England in the early post-war years is Bourne School at Ruislip, Middlesex, for 500 children, designed by Howard V. Lobb and built in 1946. It is one storey and has a spine corridor north–south, from which are two classroom wings and a wing of practical rooms arranged transversely westward, while four cloakrooms branch eastwards, and at the northern end are the assembly hall and dining room. There are spacious garden areas between the classroom wings, and the whole is a distribution of buildings where light and spaciousness are prime considerations.

A secondary school of similar size for 450 at Stevenage designed by F. R. S. Yorke, E. Rosenberg and C. S. Mardell, and built in 1948–9, is a two-storey structure with basically an H-shaped plan. The cross piece of the H running approximately east–west forms the classroom block, with classrooms south and cloakrooms north, and the up strokes of the H are occupied with special purpose rooms. Some of these, of which there is a fair variety, together with community rooms, assembly hall and dining hall are grouped round a courtyard to the northwest of the site, because this school is also used as an evening community and cultural centre for adults, and the facilities are enjoyed by both pupils and adults. Also the courtyard is utilized as an open air theatre.

As mentioned in Chapter 20 some old nineteenth century types of school were often planned with the classrooms grouped round a central hall, largely abandoned because of unsatisfactory orientation for some of the classrooms, and because of noise. This type of plan was revived, however, in the large coeducational Solna secondary school for 1,000 near Stockholm, designed by L. M. Giertz and N. Tesch and completed in 1947. The large rectangular three-storey block occupies the summit of a beautiful wooded hill in the northwestern area of Stockholm. A fairly steep decline is towards north and west, and because of this a lower ground floor is here introduced, together with an 'auditorium maximum' projecting from the north side of the main block, and reached by a large descending staircase from the great central hall. This hall, 200 feet by 66 feet by 46 feet high, overtops the rest of the building by about 8 feet, thus providing clerestory lighting. The main staircase towards the centre of the hall separates the large western part from the smaller eastern part, a division that can be utilized for meetings and adjacent cloakrooms. The galleries surrounding the hall are reached by a spiral staircase with a small lift in its centre in the northwest corner. They give access to the classrooms on the east and south sides and to the special purpose rooms, like the various science laboratories, on the north and west sides where are also situated the dining room and conference rooms. The plan of this school, so different from contemporary British schools, has provoked much discussion. It is difficult not to be aware of its several advantages; its easy communication for a large school, the integration of its parts, and the utilization of a large central hall for meetings, exhibitions, and displays. One commentator, Georg Scherman, regarded this plan as an excellent method of providing a large school on a limited site, which he regards as satisfactory and efficient with its well-studied layout, good detailing and gay colours giving an overall impression of friendliness and homogeneity[5].

A central assembly hall has a distinct advantage over one in the corner of a large school, and a plan that shows a functional disposition of parts with a central hall is that of Kaimhill, Aberdeen, designed by J. A. O. Allan, Ross and Allan and built in 1950. The plan consists of three parallel long blocks east–west, connected by corridors. The central block has the assembly hall at the middle with cloakrooms on either side. The southern block at the north end has two floors of classrooms with two gymnasia at the

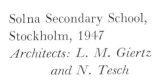

Solna Secondary School,
Stockholm, 1947
*Architects: L. M. Giertz
and N. Tesch*

View of main entrance, ground floor plan and site plan

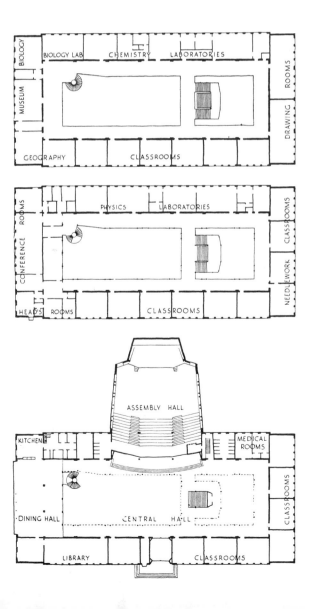

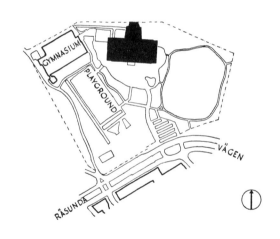

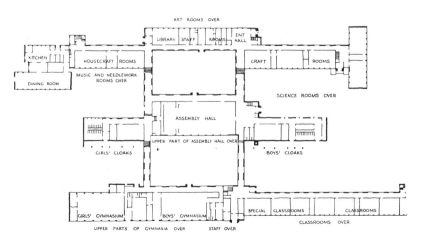

Kaimhill School, Aberdeen, 1950. Ground floor plan

Architect: J. A. O. Allan

School at Stuttgart, Zuffenhausen, 1952–53 *Architect: Günter Wilhelm*

Letzi Secondary School, Zürich, 1955–56
Architect: Ernest Gisel

General view and view of building
in centre of courtyard
for art and music

other end, and the northern block is devoted to special purpose rooms on two floors. The plan although well spread over the site is actuated by easy access to the central assembly hall, with generous space between the buildings. Another example of about the same time showing this generous disposition of school buildings on the site is the group on the Güsbery at Stuttgart, Zuffenhausen, designed by Günter Wilhelm and built in 1952–3. The site is sloping ground, and the principal long block east–west across the contour is four storeys at the west end with the ground floor largely open with columns, becoming three storeys at the east end. To the north are single storey classroom blocks sited north–south, with a third two-storey classroom block similarly sited. Other blocks are the trade school, gymnasium on the south side, and a school for handicapped children to the northwest. Gardens spread between the buildings and the whole effect is one of pleasant spaciousness and verdancy.

A symmetrical, yet original, disposition of school buildings that appears at the same time to be functional, is that of the Letzi secondary school for 800 boys and girls in Zürich, designed by Ernest Gisel and built in 1955–6. A recessed courtyard, part paved, part grass, is formed by three two-storey classrooms strips on the south, east and west sides, while on the north side are special purpose rooms. The courtyard at its northern end is open east and west and here the buildings are linked by pergolas. Although the classrooms are thus on three sides there are windows on both sides and cross ventilation. In the centre of the courtyard is a two-storey rectangular building with a music and lecture room on the ground floor and an art room on the upper floor No doubt this arrangement of buildings conduces to compactness and communication. Extensive playing fields and gymnasia are on the north and northwest areas of the site. The construction is mainly of reinforced concrete with flat roofs.

Situated in the park of an old mansion, since pulled down, to the west of Zürich is the Freudenberg higher secondary school, designed by Jacques Schader and built in 1955–9. It is for about 300 boys from 12 to 19, and consists of a science college, commercial school, a department of natural science, gymnasia, assembly hall and cafe. The site is undulating forming two low hills, and advantage has been taken of this in the disposition of the buildings. There are two main levels, the undulating ground level, and a first floor concrete platform with an extensive open space between the square building of the science college to the east, and the long rectangular building to the west. Extensive views can be obtained from this platform. Underneath it on the north side are the gymnasia and to the north, beyond the platform and reached from it by a broad descending flight of steps, is the square assembly hall. The sports ground extends to the east of the assembly hall. The college of science has three levels, one ground, one at platform level and an upper floor, and the college of commerce is the same but with two upper floors.

The disposition of these rectangular buildings with emphasis on horizontal fenestration,

601

Freudenberg higher secondary school, Zürich, 1955–59
Architect: Jacques Schader

Front view, showing the two main levels with commercial college in the distance and science block on the right and, below, view of assembly hall

and their relation to the wooded undulating site where rocks and trees compose happily with the square building masses, and with the spacious terrace between the main buildings, have at once a Greek-like serenity yet prompting an exhilaration in the spaciousness and situation which makes this one of the most beautiful groups of school buildings in Europe[6].

One of the principal developments in the design of schools that occurred from about 1930 to 1960, was a greater flexibility in which scope is provided in the design for adaptation to changing needs. It is increasingly realized that ideas of the best methods of education are constantly changing, and adoption of new ideas may sometimes require changes in the physical setting, which means somewhat different buildings or adjustment of existing buildings. Also with growing population in most European countries school buildings erected in 1950 may prove to be inadequate in size in 1975, and if the design originally provided for extensions in answer to such needs, it is a great advantage. These possibilities have been most completely realized perhaps in the schools built in England between 1948 and 1960. A large number, mainly of the strip corridor type, are spread fairly spaciously on the generous site, and are generally one or two storeys. Architecturally they may not be so attractive as schools built in Sweden, Germany, France or Switzerland, but these more often have been built in the middle of urban areas on limited sites, and future extensions would, in many cases, have to be vertical rather than horizontal. In Switzerland, however, many of the new schools have been built in beautiful old parks, once private, and extensions could take place rather by erecting additional buildings than extending those that exist, as in the case of the Letzi and Freudenberg schools.

REFERENCES AND NOTES

1. This team under the Hertfordshire County Architect included S .A. W. Johnson-Marshall, David Medd, Mary Crowley and Bruce Martin.
2. *School Buildings 1945–1951* by Bruce Martin with a foreword by S. A. W. Johnson-Marshall, Crosby Lockwood, London, 1952. Twenty-two examples of schools are described and illustrated chiefly from England. Three examples are given from Switzerland, three from USA, two from Sweden and one from Holland.
3. See *Work*, July 1949. Also Alfred Roth, *The New School*, Girsberger, Zürich, 1950, pp. 153–157.
4. See *Habitation*, August 1950.
5. Georg Schermann in an introductory note to a description of the building by the architects in *Byggmastaren*, No. 14, 1948.
6. Useful descriptions of both the Letzi and Freudenberg schools are given by Alfred Roth in *New School Building*, Thames and Hudson, London, 1966. The photographic illustrations of both schools are by the Author.

42 *University buildings 1945–1970*

IN THE QUARTER of a century following the Second World War there was probably nearly as much university building in Europe as in any previous century since the beginning of universities in the eleventh century. This great volume of university building has been particularly marked in the United Kingdom, where 26 new universities have been established from 1948 thus more than doubling the existing 22. The establishment of so many universities in England during the twentieth century is due not only to a progressive attitude to higher education, but to the deficiency in the number of universities and university education in England compared with Italy, France and Germany.

In university building, as in teaching, tradition is very strong and many of the forms of the earliest universities survive in the middle of the twentieth century. Traditional forms have mingled with new forms, and thus to appreciate fully the significance and reasons for these forms, it is useful to glance at the origins of universities, and at the earliest types of buildings employed.

ORIGIN AND GROWTH OF UNIVERSITIES

Universities emerged from the monasteries which did more than any other single factor to keep the lamps of learning and civilization burning from the decaying Roman Empire to the early Renaissance, roughly from the foundation of the Benedictine order in the sixth century to the fourteenth century. It was by the agency of the monasteries that much of the literature of ancient Greece and Rome survived. Universities appear to have begun as secular counterparts to the monasteries, where subjects like law and medicine could be studied and taught. It is not surprising, therefore, that these new secular institutions should in their buildings adapt and follow monastic forms, so that many distinctive features like cloisters and courtyards should become traditional characteristics of university buildings.

The earliest universities appear to be three in Italy founded in the eleventh century,

Bologna famous for law, Salerno famous for medicine and Parma famous for both. All probably had earlier origins for there appear to have been schools in these subjects in Bologna, Salerno and Parma as early as the ninth century. The University of Paris originated in the twelfth century and its constitution was confirmed by Papal Bull in 1215. Its first college was founded in 1256 by Robert de Sorbon. Oxford was founded a little later in the twelfth century, and its first colleges were University (1249), Balliol (1263) and Merton (1264), while Cambridge was founded later in the same century, its first college being Peterhouse (1254) followed by Clare (1326) and Pembroke (1347).

By the end of the thirteenth century there were twenty universities in Europe concentrated in five countries, twelve in Italy (Bologna, Salerno, Parma, Macerata, Modena, Naples, Padua, Perugia, Piacenza, Pavia, Reggio nell Emilia and Vicenza), three in France (Paris, Toulouse and Montpelier), two in Spain (Palencia and Salamanca) two in England (Oxford and Cambridge), and one in Portugal (Lisbon). From the mid-fourteenth to the mid-sixteenth century a large number of European universities were founded. The late fourteenth and early fifteenth centuries saw the foundation of many of the older German universities: Heidleberg (1386), Cologne (1388), Erfurt (1389), Wurzburg (1402), and Leipzig (1409), and by the beginning of the Reformation (1517) there were twelve universities in Germany. During the two centuries mentioned another ten were founded in Italy, another five in Spain, twelve in France, while in other countries universities were founded in Prague (1347), Cracow (1364), Vienna (1365), Louvain (1425), Basle (1460), and two in Scandinavia, Uppsala (1477) and Copenhagen (1479). Three were founded in Scotland in the fifteenth century, St. Andrews (1411), Glasgow (1451) and Aberdeen (1494). Edinburgh (1583) and Dublin (1591) came a little later. Universities continued to be founded in the following centuries so that by the beginning of the nineteenth century there were over a hundred universities in Europe, but still only two in England. The third was Durham (1832)[1] and the fourth London (1836) which not only became one of the biggest universities in Europe, but was instrumental in starting other universities by establishing university colleges. London was followed by several civic universities established in large provincial cities such as Manchester (1851), Newcastle (1852), Birmingham (1900), Liverpool (1903), Leeds (1904), Sheffield (1905) and Bristol (1909). Reading (1926) was the only one established between the World Wars[2].

The kind of accommodation provided in the earliest European universities from the eleventh to the fifteenth centuries is in some degree a matter of speculation. Evidence of available records and early buildings show the accommodation consisted mainly of hostels for the living quarters of both teachers and students, room for lectures and teaching, library, refectory or dining rooms and sometimes a church. It is significant that many of the early examples that remain show a group of buildings round, or adjacent, to cloisters. Examples are William of Wykeham's New College, Oxford (1379) built in 1396, and the cloisters that form part of the University of Cracow built in 1494.

605

One of the most complete remaining early examples showing the courtyard planning of a large college is St. John's College, Cambridge, which is typical of many. It consists of three courts built in three stages. The first court was built in 1511 in the Gothic style with the main entrance tower in the centre of the east side with library adjacent, chapel on the north side, hall on the west side and chambers on the south. A second court was added in 1598, with further chambers and the master's lodge on the north side, and a third court, added in 1623 in the Renaissance style, has further chambers and another library, obviously extension in answer to growing needs. This courtyard planning can be seen in many of the university buildings from the sixteenth to the nineteenth century, not only in Oxford and Cambridge but throughout Europe.

Courtyard planning often with arcading, thus continuing the tradition of the cloister, was incorporated in some of the early monumental university buildings that appeared in Italy during the Renaissance, such as Sansovino's courtyard at Padua University built in 1542. These monumental buildings led the way to the block type of university building seen in many of the later universities built in large cities.

There emerges at the beginning of the twentieth century three main types of university building groupings, the collegiate, the block type and the campus, and within these classifications there are many overall methods of planning. In the collegiate type of which Oxford and Cambridge are the great prototypes, the separate colleges are grouped in a city or in an open site in the country, with buildings like libraries, senate house, various institutions and faculties for common use. Residence is in the various colleges, or if there is insufficient room in lodgings in the town. The block type is either the collegiate or non-collegiate unitary type often with monumental buildings grouped or scattered in a large city. The campus type, much influenced by American university planning that began with Jefferson's University of Virginia (1825), is a grouping of university buildings, colleges, schools, institutes and faculty buildings, grouped in open country, often round a central open space.

Between the World wars there was not a great deal of university building in Europe, and very few new universities were founded, one in England (Reading in 1926), one in Germany (Hamburg), one in Denmark (Aarhus in 1928), the revival of Florence University in 1924, and the Aristotelian University of Thessalonika (1925). The replanning and building of Rome and London Universities which took place substantially in the thirties are described in Chapters 31 and 35, while the buildings of the new University of Aarhus and the additional building of Fribourg University in Switzerland are described in Chapter 20. Aarhus is one of the early and most distinctive examples of campus planning in Europe.

At the threshold of the vast university building programme after the Second World War there were many perplexing questions to which satisfactory answers had to be

606

found if work of a good standard was to result. The earlier post-war work of the decade from 1945 to 1955 was not generally very impressive; it was largely a repetition of much classical monumental building of the previous hundred years.

SITING UNIVERSITY BUILDINGS—SOME GERMAN EXAMPLES

In siting a new university, or extending an existing one, an important question was: should an adequate area be found in or near the centre of a city or town, or should it be a little outside the town in open country? The advantages and disavantages of both have been discussed at length. Most universities in Europe that existed before the Second World War were integrated to some extent with cities and towns and their buildings were in or near the city or town centres, or mingled with other buildings throughout the urban area. When it was necessary to extend an existing university or to start a new one the desire in most countries was to do this on adjacent or central sites, so that the university is integrated with the life of the city. In Germany with the great extension of university accommodation from 1950 to 1970, efforts were made to build the extensions and the new buildings in the cities near the existing premises, but this has not always been possible with the result that in several cases part of the university has been built, rebuilt or extended in the centre of the city, and other additions have been on the outskirts, which has meant an undesirable separation of the parts of the university. It is obviously regrettable, but the alternatives are either to demolish a fair amount of property in the centre of the city, like London University demolishing a whole residential square, or to locate the whole university in the country near the periphery, as had been done with many recently built English universities. The demolition of a large central area to make room for new university buildings has not generally been possible in Germany, with the result that the buildings have often been divided into two or more groups, one group in the centre and one on the outskirts. Two examples are provided by the Universities of Stuttgart and Fribourg.

Stuttgart technical high school became a technical university in the present century, and after the Second World War it has greatly expanded, so that part is in the centre on a limited site and the greater part some five miles to the southwest at Vaihingen a separation that could not be avoided. The faculties of architecture, structural and civil engineering are concentrated on the limited site in the centre and very good use has been made of the area. The buildings consist of two tall rectangular parallel blocks about 170 feet high, with a spacious concrete platform between them reached from Friedrichstrasse by a broad flight of steps. They were designed by Rolf Gotbier, Gunter Wilhelm and Curt Siegel, and built in 1956–66. Each block has a long central corridor on the upper floors running east–west, with the lecture rooms and rooms for practical work on the north side and the smaller study and tutorial rooms on the south side. They are so arranged that vertically there are three floors on the south side to two floors on the north side, access to the latter from alternate corridors being by separate staircases down and up. Thus the ceiling heights of the lecture and

607

Stuttgart Technical University. Two tall blocks housing the faculties of
architecture, structural and civil engineering in the centre
of city, 1956–66

Architects: Rolf Gotbier, Günter Wilhelm and Curt Siegel

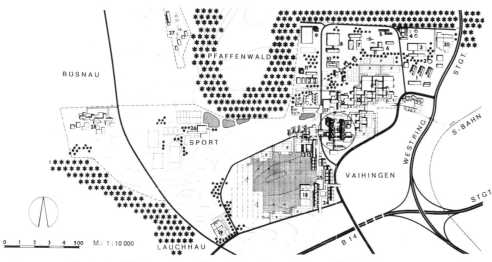

Stuttgart Technical University. Site plan of campus at Vaihingen,
5 miles south-west of Stuttgart (*see key, opposite*)

KEY:

BUILDINGS IN USE 1973

1 *Institute for Research and Material Te*
   for Building Industry (Otto Graf Institu
2 *Workshops*
3 *Machine laboratory, turbo engine work*
   technical thermodynamics, thermal tran
   heating and ventilation
4 *Power station*
5 *Steam-power machines*
6 *Aero and gas dynamics*
7 *Statics and dynamics of air and space tr*
   construction. Regional calculation centr
8 *Nuclear energy, plasma research, ther*
   dynamics for air and space travel, airp
   construction, space travel technics
9 *State Institute for Testing of Materials*
   (engine construction), Uni-Building
   (construction) Bureau
10 *Physics, structural engineering, dam*
   construction
11 *German Research Company for Air ar*
   Space flight
12 *Spectroscopy (ultra violet, x-ray, etc.)*
13 *Information*
14 *Under Construction. Faculties of Chemi*
   Physics and Mathematics to be complete
   1973/74. Projected intended buildings to
   completed between 1976 and 1980
15 *Mechanical and Structural engineering*
16 *Electronics*
17 *Dining room (refectory) for 6000 meals*
18 *College of Printing*
19 *Central kitchen, capacity 20,000 meals*
20 *Institute for heavy powered vehicles*
21 *Student living quarters started Spring 1*
22 *Personnel living quarters existant*

APARTMENTS PLANNED ON THE UNIVERSITY
CAMPUS

23 *Student living quarters*
24 *Personnel living quarters*
25 *Projected shopping centre*
26 *College athletic field*
27 *Research filter plant with Institute of Se*
   ment Waterworks
28 *Max Planck Institute for solids physics*
   powdermetallurgy

View of Institutes of Chemistry and Physics, completed 1972–73

workrooms is about 12 feet and of study rooms about 8 feet. Two large auditoria, with
adjacent offices, are built underground with access both from the external concrete
platform and the north block, a device that saves a considerable space.

The University of Berlin is an example of an entirely new university built in the
centre of an urban area. There may not have been any alternative for this location,
but at the same time it accords with the German philosophy that a university should
integrate with the life of its city. The old university of Berlin was founded in 1809
in what is now East Berlin, so that if West Berlin was to have a University, which
it very much needed, a new one had to be founded and built. What is known as the
Free University, because of the very liberal principles by which it is administered and
the welcome it gives to students of all nationalities, was founded in 1948, and building
on a site in Dahlem in the borough of Zehlendorf, a little to the southwest of central
Berlin, commenced shortly afterwards.

The first part of the university to be built consisted of a large rectangular block for the
faculties of philosophy, geography, geology, mathematics and the humanities, and the
design was the subject of a competition won by the architects Candilis, Josic and
Woods while implementation was with the assistance of Jonathan Greig and Manfred
Schiedhelm. In the design there are four parallel equidistant communicating spines
running northeast–southwest and in the spaces between are lecture halls, auditoria,
and study rooms arranged in relation to courts and various enclosures. The design
permits extension at both ends, but this, when needed, will probably take place to the
northeast. Accommodation is mainly on three floors, with the basement space for
storage. The building has a fairly generous setting in a busy urban area, yet is so
designed with accommodation between protecting spines that quiet and seclusion is
obtained. The design of squares and rectangles permitted a fair degree of standardization
and rapid building. There is convenient access from a nearby underground railway
station and from other public transport, a very important factor in the siting of
university buildings. The medical centre of the university is a large teaching hospital
for 1800 patients, situated a little to the southeast in Steglitz, an impressive building
completed in 1968 to the designs of two American architects, N. C. Curtis and A. Q.
Davies and a Berlin architect, F. Mocken.

The existing buildings of the many colleges, faculties and institutes of the University
of Paris, the largest in Europe, were mostly erected before the First World War. The
largest and most famous, the Sorbonne, designed by Nenot, was built in 1885–1901.
Before the First World War there was, however, very little residential accommodation
for the very large number of students, and most visiting students were housed in
lodgings scattered throughout Paris. In 1923 the building of a special student
settlement, known as the University City, was begun and by 1970 over 60 hostels for
students from many countries of the world and from the French provinces extended

609

Free University, Dahlem, Berlin, 1950–60
*Architects: Candilis, Josic and Woods with the
assistance of Greig and Schiedhelm*

Medical Centre, University, Berlin (Steglitz), completed 196
*Architects: N. C. Curtis,
A. Q. Davies and F. Mocken*

Brazilian Pavilion, University City, Paris, 1951–59
Architect: Le Corbusier

General view and view of main entrance

for about half a mile along the Boulevard Jourdain in the southern part of Paris. In addition to hostels they include a Maison Internationale, a students club with theatre and restaurants, built in 1936. Among the most notable of the earlier buildings is the Swiss Pavilion designed by Le Corbusier and built in 1930–2, which is briefly described in Chapter 22. Another hostel building in the University City by Le Corbusier, in collaboration with Lucio Costa, is the Brazilian building erected in 1951–59. This has certain similarities to the Swiss pavilion for the main part with students quarters is a massive block perched on concrete stilts, but there are several differences. The main tall block is six storeys high and the five upper floors are occupied by bedrooms for one and two students, arranged along the southeast side each with a secluded recessed balcony. On the northwest side of the corridor are a variety of rooms for study and recreation. The ground floor immediately under the super structure is largely open, but part extends on the northwest side in a one-storey building which houses a recreation and indoor games area, cafe, lounge and small theatre. On the other side is the long narrow one-storey director's house. As in so many of Le Corbusier's buildings the architectural drama exists in the effect of the massive ground floor supports, a kind of structural monumentality, seen especially in the corner near the entrance.

In most of the cities and towns of Europe that have universities founded before the Second World War, there have been a considerable number of new university buildings new institutes or faculties, new libraries, further residential accommodation for staff and students, and sometimes new colleges, built mainly where sites have been available —sometimes involving the destruction of other property. A fair number of these additional buildings of existing universities are distinctive architecturally and many have been illustrated and described in the European Architectural magazines. The additions that are entirely separate from existing premises and on different sites are generally more successful than those that are grafted on to existing buildings, although in some cases, as at Marburg, the integration has been very successful. Among the notable examples in London are the buildings of the Imperial College of Science and Technology in South Kensington, built in 1959–64 to the designs of Norman and Dawbarn, and the Royal College of Art built in 1961–2 and designed by Sir Hugh Casson and H. T. Cadbury-Brown. The former replaced Collcutt's eclectic Imperial Institute building erected in 1887. There was a storm of protest when it was proposed to demolish Collcutt's building for which many people seemed to have an affection, and as a compromise the tower was retained which forms a Victorian eclectic centre piece of a square surrounded by the new curtain wall building. The new building makes pleasing façades with effective long horizontal bands, especially that of the continuous canopy, above the ground floor. The new building, however, is in no way enhanced by the Victorian tower, instead there is incongruity between them. Far better London buildings have been sacrificed to the march of progress than the old Imperial College.

The Royal College of Art has earned the reputation of one of the distinctive modern buildings of London. Accommodation is concentrated in a tall dark eight-storey block on a limited and valuable site opposite Kensington Gardens and the architectural effect depends a great deal on rectangular patterning, with emphasis on window mullions and a massive crenellated effect of studios at the summit. This building has a massive monumental quality in contrast to the curtain walling of the Imperial College.

One rather felicitous addition to an older university is Dunelm House, a club for staff and students of Durham University, built on the bank of the River Wear in 1965, and designed by Richard Raines of the Architects Co-Partnership. It is near the Kingsgate pedestrian bridge designed by Sir Ove Arup, which links Dunelm House with the cathedral precinct. The river fenestration has interesting irregular patterning of mullions on the long horizontal voids. The road elevation on a fairly steep incline presents an effective step effect of concrete masses (see illustration).

BRITISH UNIVERSITIES OF THE SIXTIES

In what must necessarily be a brief account of modern university architecture the experiment of buildings for entirely new universities must claim major attention, and nowhere in Europe has this experiment been more notable than with the English universities that have been founded and partly built in the sixties, particularly the seven which are alluded to as the Shakespearian seven: Sussex (1961), East Anglia (1963), York (1963), Lancaster (1964), Essex (1964), Warwick (1965) and Kent (1965)[3]. These are all sited in parkland well outside the towns and these locations have been a matter of controversy. They were due to the decision that each university of the required size needed about 200 acres so as to include the university playing fields and sports facilities. The disadvantages of this is that the university is to some extent isolated from the life of the town, whereas if it were in or near the centre of the town both students and the townspeople would benefit and be mutually enriched. Also the townspeople could, to some extent, benefit from facilites provided by the university in the form of public lectures and exhibitions and social events, as is done by London University. Being located a few miles away in the country makes the University in some measure a cloistral retreat, and the design of some of the buildings rather confirms this. There are, of course, definite advantages in seclusion and remoteness, but these could be obtained with good planning within the town, with the other advantages that this would mean. But to insist on a large site of 200 acres in the adjacent country outside the town because of the requirement of incorporating playing fields is really somewhat frivolous. It would have been far better to integrate the university with the city or town by locating it near the centre, and let those who wanted the playing fields—a minority as suggested by evidence—to go to the locations beyond the town. This is a social question which must be settled before building begins, and it was settled by universities being sited in parks on the outskirts. Trends suggest the possibility that by the year 2000 they will be enclosed by urban areas and out-of-

612

Royal College of Art, Kensington,
London, 1961–62 *Architects: Hugh Casson
and H. T. Cadbury-Brown*

Imperial College of Science and Technology, Kensington,
London University, 1959–64 *Architects: Norman and Dawbarn*

Dunelm House, club building for staff
and students of Durham University

View from across the River Wear
with footbridge, leading from
Durham Cathedral precinct, designed
by Ove Arup
*Architects: Richard Raines of the
Architects Co-Partnership*

Sussex University, Stanmer Park
near Brighton, 1961–
Architect: Sir Basil Spence

View of Fulmer House and
the CircularMeeting House

Essex University, near
Colchester, 1964–
Architects:
Architects Co-Partnership
(Kenneth Capon, H. T. Cadbury-
Brown and Partners,
Gasson and Meunier)

town shopping districts, and the town centres will be crying for revitalization which the universities could have provided in part. There is, of course, always the difficulty of finding a space in the centre of a city or town for a new university, but it is easier to find 100 acres, or a little less, than 200 acres.

The seven groups of buildings in the parks are all very different from one another. The designs and layouts are necessarily conditioned by the type of university which was left in each case to the vice-chancellor and his academic planning board. Of the seven, three are collegiate: York, Lancaster and Kent and four are unitary: Sussex, East Anglia, Essex and Warwick.

Sussex, the first to be started is situated in a 200 acre site in Stanmer Park, about 3 miles northeast of Brighton. The general layout was planned by Sir Basil Spence who also designed most of the larger buildings. Constructional work began in 1961 and by 1973 a considerable part of the group had been completed. The buildings are spaciously laid out in a sloping valley that rises towards the north, and the many existing trees have been retained between the buildings to assist in the very attractive landscaping. The buildings are dignified and, it must be admitted, monumental and the recurring architectural theme is red brick in combination with concrete horizontal and segmental arches, which is effective, but less so when concrete lintels are used immediately under the arches as in some of the buildings. The buildings nowhere rise above three storeys and are mostly rectangular on plan with two exceptions: the circular Meeting House, a concrete structure with a close pattern of stained-glass perforations and an asymmetrical pyramidal roof, and the Gardner Arts Centre, a brick composition of mainly circular forms which contains a circular theatre with interchangeable stages, together with studios and exhibition areas. The most impressive and central building of the group is the large rectangular Fulmer House, built round a square courtyard with a reflecting pool round the edge forming an internal moat. It is the social centre of the university and is approached by a straight pedestrian way, which continues through the tall monumental concrete arch forming the entrance, across the courtyard and on northwards to Fulton Court with the group of Science buildings to the east, and the library to the west. At the north end up the hill is Park Village, the students residential area consisting of rows of three-storey houses arranged in echelon fashion.

East Anglia University a little way out of Norwich, for which Denys Lasdun and Partners are the architects, is another unitary university but totally different in plan from Sussex, for here there is a closer linking of the various buildings. A continuous row of science buildings in a line mainly west–east is bordered by a broad upper walk-way on the other side of which are the students quarters in stepped eight-storey buildings, rather like a series of six half-ziggurats. At the northeast end is the arts block and south in the eastern part of the site is the university centre with University

615

House, lecture theatres, library, staff houses, refectory and shops, and another row of half-ziggurat residential buildings for students.

Essex University, near Colchester, for which the Architects Co-Partnership (Kenneth Capon, H. T. Cadbury-Brown and Partners, Gasson and Meunier) are the architects, is again very different in plan from Sussex and East Anglia, although another unitary university. On a generous undulating site, a valley is utilized for the principal group of buildings knit together by long parallel blocks with cross wings, forming courtyards, a little like the plan of Berlin Free University, with upper level walkways, and with a central ground level road reminiscent of Cumbernauld. On the elevated areas north and south are the fifteen-storey residential tower blocks for students, which include study spaces and study bedrooms for non-residential students. The walkways continue from the central university group to these residential towers.

Warwick University, about 3 miles from Coventry, planned by Arthur Ling (Chief architect of Coventry City) and Alan Goodman with buildings designed by Yorke, Rosenberg and Mardall, and Grey, Goodman and Partners, again displays marked differences in conception from other universities, although the compact grouping round courtyards with squarish buildings from three to six storeys in height with horizontal emphasis, suggest a certain monotony relieved by such buildings as the lecture theatre with its broad masses of windowless walls.

Although different in planning the four universities so far briefly noted have the principal buildings—faculties, institutions, meeting places, assembly halls, libraries—variously grouped in the centre, from separate buildings as in Sussex, to a linked concentrated group as in Essex.

The collegiate universities offer scope for more diversity especially if the colleges are designed differently, as occurs at York, Kent and Lancaster. York University in a very pleasing landscape setting is planned by Robert Matthew, Johnson-Marshall and Partners. About eight colleges are planned, three of which were built by 1973—Vanbrugh, Derwent and Langwith—grouped round the central University Hall, with libraries, housing and laboratories, and the David Brown laboratory on the northeast side of the site with a rather incongruous water tower in its centre. Courtyard planning is a feature of the college buildings and in each sheets of water, treated both formally and informally, are conspicuous as ornamental features. The most attractive and original building of the group is University Hall designed by John Speight, a concrete structure with horizontal emphasis, pitched roof and a balcony-like effect at one end projecting over the water.

Kent University, a little way out of Canterbury, for which William Henderson of Farmer and Dark prepared a plan, includes provision for eight colleges and of these

616

Kent University, near
Canterbury, 1965–
Architect:
William Henderson
of Farmer and Dark

Lancaster University, 1964–
Architect: Gabriel Epstein
of Shepheard and Epstein

four, Eliot, Keynes, Rutherford and Darwin, were built by 1973. They are spaciously grouped on either side of a road running northeast from Whitstable Road to Hackington Road. Two of the colleges, Eliot and Rutherford have equilateral cross plans, and are variations of courtyard planning. Eliot has five squares with three courtyards with cloisters, at the upper level. Professor's and Tutor's rooms and study bedrooms are arranged round the square. At ground-floor level the refectory occupies the centre of the south square linked diagonally with the kitchen in the west square, while common rooms, lecture rooms and other smaller rooms occupy the other squares. Grouped in the centre of the campus are the library and science buildings which will later spread to the northwest. The playing fields and a stadium occupy the area to the south.

Lancaster, planned by Gabriel Epstein of Shepheard and Epstein, on a 200-acre site three miles from Lancaster, is more compactly planned with the colleges closely related, and in its connected courtyard planning it is more like Essex than the other five. The central Alexandra square is surrounded by three-storey buildings with canopied shops on one side and a residential tower at one corner. A pedestrian way runs north–south the whole length of the campus. Perhaps the most interesting building architecturally is the Chaplaincy Centre with a trefoil plan of three chapels and a pointed feature in the centre, a bit like a stalagmite in the open.

East Anglia University, near Norwich, 1963–   *Architects: Denys Lasdun and Partners*

Although the planning and architecture of these seven universities are different they have several major qualities in common. They are all sited on generous sites in the country outside the towns of which they claim to be a part, largely because of the doubtful requirement that the playing fields should be adjacent to them; and they are all essentially traditional and monumental in conception. Courtyard planning often arcaded with cloisters persists in all except East Anglia, thus perpetuating the traditions of the medieval monastery, and they are mostly concrete structures. Dignity, impressiveness and monumentality in the Renaissance manner, if not in the Renaissance style, rather than flexibility and adaptability to change, have been guiding factors.

In some of the later universities such as Surrey in Guildford (1966), the university is closer to the city, being sited on the hill near the cathedral and is likely, therefore, to be more an integral part of the life of the city.

The universities built in Britain during the sixties represent probably Britain's major contribution to European architecture in the mid-twentieth century. It will be necessary to see them in a longer historical perspective to evaluate their full significance.

REFERENCES AND NOTES

1. J. B.Mullinger and C. Brereton in the article on universities in the fourteenth edition (1929) of the *Encyclopedia Britannica* speak of the University of Durham having been founded by Cromwell in 1657. But in the article on Durham it is stated that Henry VIII had the unfulfilled intention of founding a college at Durham and a similar attempt failed during the Commonwealth. The University was not actually founded until the Act of 1932 and was opened in 1933.

2. A good brief account of the early history of universities is given by Sir Nikolaus Pevsner in the *Architectural Review*, October, 1957, pp. 235–239. This is followed by a critical appraisement by Lionel Brett of early post-war university buildings in Britain, pp. 240–251.

3. These seven are the subject of an excellent study by Tony Birks, *Building the New Universities*, David and Charles, Newton Abbot, Devon, 1972. Unfortunately, although the photographic illustrations are good, there is an inadequacy of plans for a proper understanding of the building groups, and the small outline general plans that are given have no keys. Also, unfortunately, the book has no index. The special issue of *The Architectural Review* on The New Universities, vol. cxlvii, April 1970, gives more plans.

43   Arts and cultural centres, assembly, congress and concert halls, theatres and opera houses 1948–1970

IN SEVERAL EUROPEAN cities and towns in the post-war period plans were made for arts and cultural centres to include a concert hall, theatre and opera house, exhibition galleries and other cultural facilities. The size of such projects necessarily depended on the size of city or town and the ability or willingness of communities to pay for such facilities. The cities of Western Germany have been particularly energetic in providing them. Two of the most ambitious and notable in large cities are the Arts Centre on the South Bank in London and the development of what is known as the cultural belt in the centre of Berlin. They differ very much in planning. The former is concentrated in one particular area on the bank of the Thames, while the latter consists of a variety of buildings in the centre mixed with other buildings, a little like the concentration of theatres immediately north of the National Gallery in London.

LONDON'S NEW SOUTH BANK ARTS CENTRE

The project for the Arts Centre in London was first conceived during the Second World War and proposals and an outline plan were made in the County of London Plan by Patrick Abercrombie and J. H. Forshaw[1]. Since then the plans have been modified and changed, and the various buildings have been completed in stages. The first was the Royal Festival Hall substantially completed for use in time for the Festival of Britain Exhibition in 1951. This was followed many years later by the National Film Theatre and two smaller concert halls: the Queen Elizabeth Hall and the Purcell Room completed in 1966, and a little later by the Hayward Art Gallery. The National Theatre was nearing completion in 1973.

The site of the South Bank Arts Centre is strictly on the east bank of the Thames (which becomes the South Bank after the river bends at Waterloo Bridge) in the V-shaped area formed by Waterloo Bridge and Hungerford Bridge. The National Film theatre is under Waterloo Bridge and the National Theatre on the further, northeast side of the bridge. The whole group is linked and surrounded by pedestrian ways on two levels. The pedestrian embankment way continues from Westminster Bridge in

620

front of London County Hall on to the Arts Centre Group, Waterloo Bridge and beyond. An extensive upper level pedestrian area spreads between the various buildings and there is a walk way from here into Waterloo Station across York Road. The whole makes an attractive group of concrete structures, the earliest, the Festival Hall, being effectively faced with Portland stone.

The Royal Festival Concert Hall designed by the then chief architect of the L.C.C., Sir Robert Matthew and his staff, is a concrete box within a concrete box, with each having 10 inch thick walls with a 12 inch cavity between them. Accommodation is for about 3,000, with a steeply raked floor and balcony. Opinions differ about the formal effects of this interior, some admire it but others are critical of its rather cut-up effect with the black-fronted side boxes looking rather like drawers pulled out and the dismembered acoustic canopy over the platform which does not integrate with the ceiling. Acoustically, however, the hall has won the reputation of being one of the finest in the world. The acoustic adviser, Hope Bagenall, in collaboration with the Building Research Station, were influenced by the design and experience of several famous concert halls of the past, particularly by the Gewandhaus at Leipzig (1886). The reverberation secured with the hall full is about 1.7 seconds, slightly longer, 1.9 seconds, with the hall empty, and the minimization of the difference is secured by the under parts of the seats being covered with perforated membrane absorbents equivalent, when tipped up, to the absorption of a person's clothing. Polished wood reflecting surfaces are placed round the orchestra, and an area of slate is built into the floor in front of the platform, and these, together with the canopy, serve to reflect sound to the audience, while a leather cushioned surface at the rear of the hall absorbs sound and prevents echo. The surrounding areas of the hall, the foyer, restaurants, exhibition galleries, bars, stairways and landings have a lightness and spaciousness which are enjoyable, and the wall facings of Derbyshire fossil marble, with the plants and decorative foliage add to the attractive areas. For many people a visit to the Royal Festival Hall is a pleasurable experience and one of the best places in the world to enjoy music[2].

The Queen Elizabeth Hall, designed by Hubert Bennett, chief architect of the Greater London Council, was completed in 1966 with seating for 1,106 on a steeply raked floor, which makes it excellent for seeing and hearing. Again the acoustics of the hall were the subject of careful consideration and design so as to secure a satisfactory reverberation—not too long or short—to reinforce direct sound. To secure a satisfactory absorption of low frequency sound Helmholtz resonators are incorporated in the walls. These have slots of various sizes behind which are a series of boxes. A notable feature in the acoustic design of this hall is that the reflecting canopy over the orchestra can be adjusted to increase or reduce the strength of the direct sound. A series of sections on the platform can be moved in a vertical plane and adjusted for various purposes.

621

Arts Centre, South Bank, London, 1950–69

Above—interior of Festival Hall looking towards orchestra—river frontage. Partly completed for Festival of Britain, 1951

Architect: Sir Robert Matthew, architect to the L.C.C., and his staff

Left—interior of Queen Elizabeth Hall, completed in 1966

Architect: Hubert Bennett, architect to the G.L.C., and his staff

Right—exterior of Queen Elizabeth Hall and Purcell Room from river terrace below Waterloo Bridge

The Purcell room for recitals which seats 372 persons was designed on similar principles to those of the Queen Elizabeth Hall, and incorporates facilities for lectures and conferences. Both halls have a common spacious foyer with mushroom columns and walls and floor lined with white Macedonian marble which conduces to a bright atmosphere. These three halls, with programmes of music all through the year, have greatly contributed to making London one of the chief musical centres of the world.

The Hayward Gallery also designed by Hubert Bennett and his staff, occupying a site a little inshore, is a concrete structure with the concrete left exposed in the galleries. These are on several floors linked by ramps, stairways and lift, while there are open air terraces for sculpture.

This group of buildings is a great asset to London. It has not only enhanced the capital as a centre for the arts, but it has added something of distinction to the London architectural scene. The group can be enjoyed from many points of view and at varying distances as a felicitous composition of masses which present many changing and pleasing effects of light and shadow. Its kinship to geometric abstract sculpture is strong.

At the time of the Festival of Britain two other notable concert halls were completed in England, the rebuilt Free Trade Hall, Manchester, designed by the city architect Leonard C. Howitt, and the rebuilt Colston Hall, Bristol, designed by the city architect J. Nelson Meredith. Both are multi-purpose halls but designed principally as concert halls. The former has the suspended acoustic canopy above the orchestra not sufficiently integrated with the design to be formerly pleasing, while the side panelling of the walls and the heavy acoustical octagonal panels of the ceiling are hardly harmonious in character; but if the appearance leaves something to be desired, acoustically it is satisfactory. The Colston Hall is excellent in every way. Although the hall interior was entirely rebuilt in 1951, much of the exterior shell and entrance portico survived and is integrated in the new building. The design of the interior has a rhythmical cohesion which gives a unified effect, and the acoustic canopy is well integrated with the design. The colour treatment is light and bright. The balcony extends along the sides of the hall, which together with seating at the back of the orchestra, makes it possible to convert the hall for boxing and wrestling.

Several arts centres have been provided in cities and towns in Great Britain in the late fifties and sixties of varying excellence, some incorporating notable theatres to which reference is made later. One excellent centre is at Croydon—the Fairfield Halls— which includes a large concert hall seating nearly 2,000, and acoustically good, the Ashcroft theatre for about 700, rather conventionally designed with too small a stage, exhibition gallery and banqueting hall, restaurant and spacious foyer and first floor landing adequate for exhibitions. The building forms a part of the newly built Croydon

623

Congress Hall, Berlin, 1957. Day and night views

Architects: Hugh A. Stubbins, Werner
Duttmann and Franz Mocken

Liederhalle, Stuttgart, 1952–53. Interior of main hall and exterior

Architects: Adolf Abel and Rolf Gutbrod

centre, with its office towers and slab blocks. It is simple and effective in appearance, the influence of the Royal Festival Hall in its design being strongly apparent. It is seen to full advantage as it is spaciously set adjoining a formal garden over an extensive underground car park.

THE CULTURAL BELT IN REBUILT BERLIN

What is known as the cultural belt in the centre of Berlin runs parallel, and sometimes interweaves, with the city (business) belt. Starting from the west along the principal west–east thoroughfare (Kaiserdamm–Bismarckstrasse–Strasse des 17 Juni–Unter den Linden) there is the new opera house (north) and Schiller Theatre (south) and groups of 21 theatres and concert halls as far as Unter den Linden, with exhibition halls, conference centre museums and art galleries. Among the more distinctive of these buildings are the opera house, the Freie Volksbuhne, the Philharmonic Hall, the Congress Hall, the Academy of Arts, the National Gallery and the extensions to the Dahlem Museum outside the central area to the southwest. (For the last three see Chapter 44).

The opera house was reconstructed to the designs of Fritz Bornemann, and reopened in 1961. A completely new interior seating 1,903 was built while there were adjustments to the exterior, such as the windowless wall of flint-stones facing Bismarckstrasse. The steeply raked floor, the two tiers and open side boxes in echelon series against tall piers make an opera house with a distinctive appearance, comfortable, good for seeing in all parts and acoustically satisfactory but essentially traditional in design[3]. The Freie Volksbuhne is an entirely new theatre designed also by Fritz Bornemann and completed in 1963. It is pleasantly situated surrounded by trees in a small park in Schaperstrasse. Its modern framed structure and glass walls on the entrance façade are thus seen to good advantage. The hexagonal shaped auditorium within a concrete shell seats 1,047, has a very deep stage but in the main the design follows the traditional picture-frame stage.

Among the most famous buildings in West Berlin is the Congress Hall completed in 1957 at the time of the International Building Exhibition, being situated a little east of the Hansa area. It is pleasantly situated in the Tiergarten and was designed by Hugh A. Stubbins, an American architect, in collaboration with the Berlin architects Werner Duttmann and Franz Mocken. It consists of a series of seven conference rooms of various sizes each seating from 17 to 108, a large lecture room for about 400, exhibition room and restaurant on the ground and intermediate floors combined in an overall square plan covered by a large roof garden. This is surmounted in part by an oyster shaped windowless assembly hall seating 1,264, with raked floor and shallow stage, which is roofed by a curved shell concrete saddle structure that also has the appearance of a broad brimmed hat. The main entrance is approached by a broad way and flight of steps across a large rectangular pool with a fountain at one end. There is

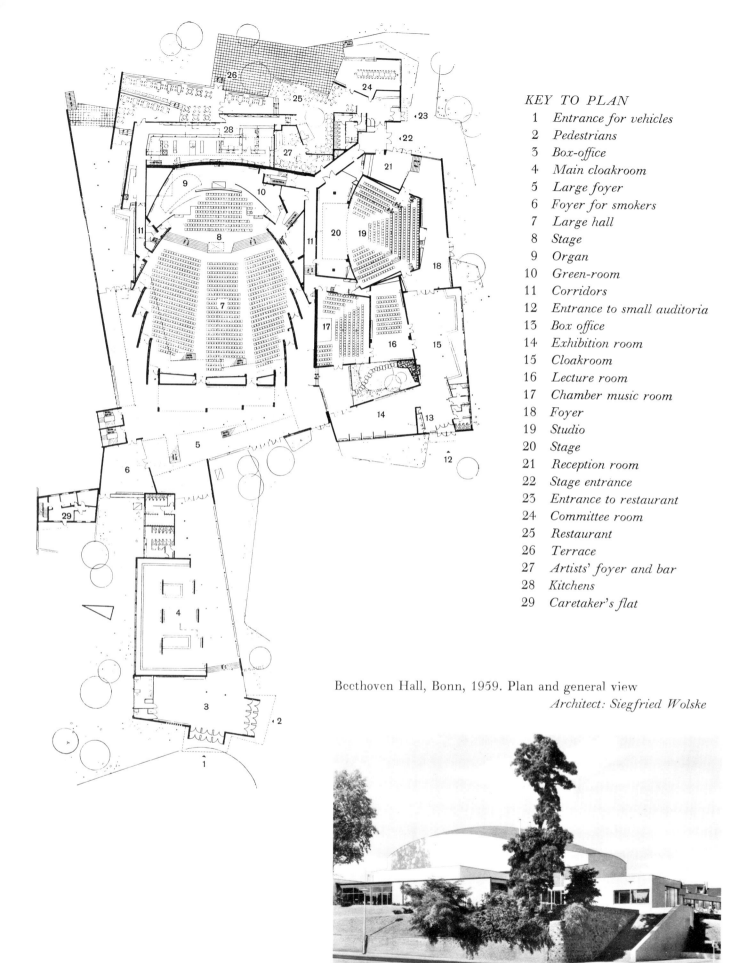

Beethoven Hall, Bonn, 1959. Plan and general view
Architect: Siegfried Wolske

not much formal relationship between the exterior form of the hall and its spreading assertive roof which gives the impression of being an example of structural exhibitionism yet it is justified rather as a work of decorative sculpture that has become a familiar symbol of modern Berlin.

The Philharmonic Hall designed by Hans Scharoun and completed in 1967 is one of many excellent concert halls built in Germany between 1950 and 1970. Of the others the Liederhalle at Stuttgart built in 1952–3, and the Beethoven Hall, Bonn, built in 1959 claim special attention. As consciousness of previous work of a similar kind generally exists with the designer they should be taken in chronological order.

The Liederhalle in Stuttgart was designed by Adolf Abel and Rolf Gutbrod. A spacious foyer with balcony gives access to three concert halls, large, medium sized and small. The large hall seats 2,000 and is curved at the back—practically a complete half circle, and the line is followed by the line of the balcony front which on the left side slopes down to the floor of the auditorium. The acoustic canopy harmonizes with the general design of the interior. The auditorium seating is arranged in apparently random shaped blocks with generous spaces between while the stage can be altered in size by sliding partitions.

The medium sized hall seating 750 is for chamber music and recitals; it has a pentagon shape with the area at the point occupied by the platform. The small hall which seats 350 for recitals and lectures, is rectangular in shape with the long outer wall of glass bricks whereas the other halls are enclosed in windowless walls. A large restaurant on two floors links with both the foyer and large hall. The spacious foyer with its patterned marble floor, octagonal skylights, its slender columns, and balcony staircases at different angles has a light gay atmosphere which is very attractive. The exterior clearly shows the three halls by their shapes. The exterior walls of each is differently treated, those of the Pentagon hall being effectively faced with random marble pattern. The canopied entrance faces an attractive small garden area.

The Beethoven Hall, designed by Siegfried Wolske, is near the west bank of the Rhine in Bonn where Beethoven was born. The principal hall with a curved shell concrete roof seats 1,400 and is like the Berlin Congress Hall shaped somewhat like an oyster but with stepped wood-panelled sides. An acoustic feature is the ceiling of hollow concrete blocks chiefly half spherical and pyramidal in shape. Grouped on the south side are three smaller halls, one for 350 with raked floor, another similarly designed for 186, both for recitals and chamber music and a lecture room for 100. The restaurant with long glass wall opens to a terrace on the east riverside.

The Berlin Philharmonic Hall is widely regarded as one of Hans Scharoun's notable achievements. There is much originality in the design: for he introduces an ingenious

Philharmonic Hall, Berlin, 1967. Exterior and interior views *Architect: Hans Scharoun*

and functional arrangement of seating not seen before, as far as I am aware, while the general aesthetic effect is pleasing. The orchestra is near the centre of the hall and there are tiers of seats at the front and back, while at both sides there are further seats, and the whole is so designed as to give the impression that geometric flower beds on the slopes of hills completely surround the orchestra. And suspended from the ceiling are curved acoustic sheets convex downwards which with the cylindrical light shades give a rather gay effect. Everybody in the hall looks down at various angles on the orchestra from which the music rises. The exterior is less felicitous for the concave curves of the roof are not the happiest of shapes nor do they relate well to the building mass, but the interior is superb.

MUSIC AND CONGRESS CENTRE, ROTTERDAM

Another notable concert hall group completed a year earlier in 1966 is the De Doelen at Rotterdam, a large hall, two smaller ones, extensive foyers and restaurants. It also forms a congress centre and was designed by E. H. and H. M. Kraaijvanger and Ren H. Fledderus. The building is situated between the station square and Karel Doorman, just west of the Lijnbaan, and north of an open square with a large underground car park for 850 cars linked with the concert hall by a pedestrian tunnel. The total ground area of the De Doelen building is about three acres and it consists of a large concert hall to seat 2,249, a medium sized hall for chamber music to seat 604, a music or lecture room to seat 143, a large dining room and restaurant, entrance halls, an exhibition hall, and a spacious first floor foyer. In addition to providing the facilities for an important music centre, the building has also been designed to accommodate conferences for up to 2,000 persons, and there are facilities for banquets of that size which makes Rotterdam one of the chief conference centres of Europe.

The large concert hall is designed somewhat like an amphitheatre with the orchestra and a section of the audience in a pit or sunken area with a gallery surrounding it on all four sides, and boxes above. The walls surrounding the orchestra and the lower seating area are of travertine in a kind of dentil pattern. There is extensive polished wood panelling and a timber canopy above the orchestra for acoustical purposes. A particularly interesting feature is that some of the panelling can be opened inwards to provide cavities, thus changing slightly the reverberation. Changing reverberation time in accordance with the kind of music or with the wishes of a conductor is a facility that concert halls will probably increasingly provide in the future.

The smaller hall for chamber music is designed on similar principles with the orchestra and part of the audience in a sunken area surrounded by a gallery on four sides. The walls and floor of the sunken area are of Calacata marble, and the walls above have a plaited stone effect. Both halls are very pleasing aesthetically, having perhaps more unity and coherence than is found in the Festival Hall in London. The foyer on the first floor with marble floors and glass chandeliers is spacious and magnificent and this

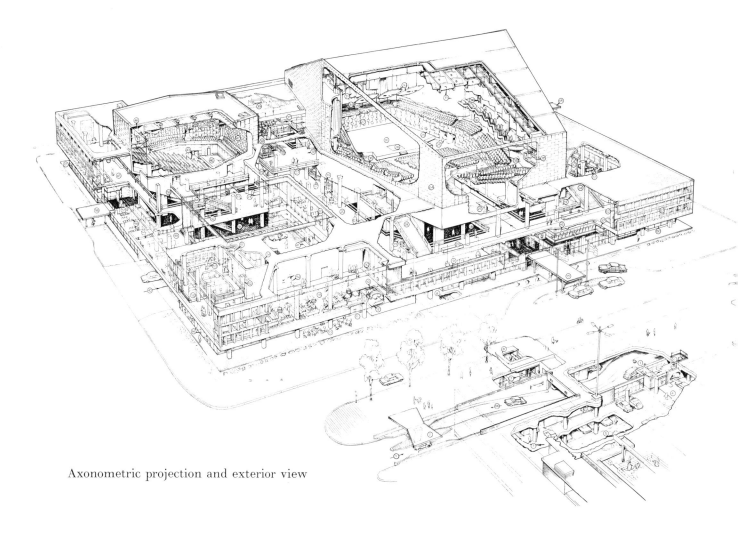

Axonometric projection and exterior view

'De Doelen' group of concert halls and congress centre, Rotterdam, completed 1966
Architects: E. H. and H. M. Kraaijvanger and Ren H. Fledderus

together with all the other facilities mentioned provide a splendid setting for large-scale conferences.

The exterior is less satisfactory and in no way expresses the interior organization except in the upper part of the concert hall. All the various parts are set within a rectangular box, the external sides of which are designed as street façades. On three sides the façades above the ground floor are in the form of a marble grille of three tiers of vertical rectangles, for the whole length of the three elevations and this is a little monotonous. The north elevation is better, with bands of fenestration between masses of plain marble walls. The marble, which is a facing on concrete, is Cristallina Virginio from Tessin in the south of Switzerland, while supporting columns are of Snaasa quartzite. The exterior hardly does justice to the splendid interiors, a circumstance not uncommon in modern architecture.

OTHER GERMAN ARTS CENTRES

Among the centres for small towns that at Ingolstadt on the Danube in Bavaria completed in 1966 to the design of Hardt Walther Hamer merits study. An irregular shaped building encloses a pentagonal concert hall seating about 1,000, with the orchestra occupying the area at the principal point of the pentagon and a narrow balcony along the three sides opposite. A theatre seating 734 is situated nearby, similarly orientated with a large stage and steeply raked floor. The superstructure of the stage forms the bevelled protruding mass above the low horizontal mass of the general building. A spacious foyer with glass walls on the entrance side provides space for exhibitions. This is a very generous arts centre for a town of only about 70,000.

Of the several new theatres built in the war-damaged cities of West Germany those particularly worthy of note are Munster, completed in 1956, Mannheim completed in 1958, Gelsenkirchen 1959, Stuttgart 1962 and Bonn 1965. Munster City Theatre is entirely new and was designed by Harald Deilmann in collaboration with Von Hausen, Rave and Ruhnau. It occupies a corner site and consists of an auditorium seating 956 of horseshoe plan with three curved balconies, each with three step sections on either side reminiscent of open boxes. Foyer landings follow the curve of the auditorium and these have glass walls so that the theatre rises as a circular glass drum, with strong vertical mullions, from a glass-fronted squarish mass at its base. The theme is continued in the stage tower which rises as a semicircular mass well above the auditorium horseshoe. The theme of the two-storeyed glass front is continued by three stepped recessions at the side with first floor entrances approached by stairways. This interesting exercise in modern architectural forms may not be wholly justified by purely functional requirements, but the result is delightful.

The city theatre at Gelsenkirchen, also entirely new, by von Hausen, Rave and Ruhnau has definite similarities to the Munster theatre. The auditorium, with a

631

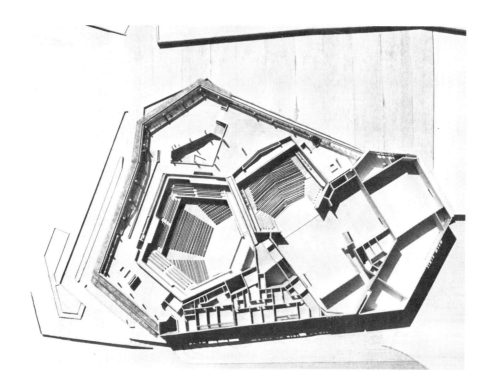

Arts Centre at Ingolstadt, Bavaria, 1966. Plan, interior of concert hall (centre left), interior of theatre (centre right) and general view of exterior
Architect: Hardt Walther Hamer

horseshoe plan surrounded by foyer landings with glass walls, is enclosed in the large rectangular mass with glass walls almost to the full height of the auditorium. The stage side wings and scenery stores are spacious and the solid square stage tower rises well above the glass walled building. Like the Munster theatre the interior of the auditorium is fancifully treated with the balcony stepping down at the sides in a series of open boxes. A smaller theatre to seat 350 is a small rectangular structure set off from one side of the large theatre. The building is well situated with spacious surroundings so that it is seen to full advantage.

The city theatre at Stuttgart designed by Volkart, Placking and Perlia, is a rebuilding of the theatre designed by Max Littmann in 1912, which was totally destroyed during the war. This new theatre is grafted on to the group of existing buildings of which the opera house was part and which were much less damaged. The new theatre is modern in style, but there is no feeling of incongruity. The group is very pleasantly situated facing the central gardens of the city with its trees, water and fountains. The auditorium is roughly hexagonal in shape with a raked floor, a little steeper at the back, and is simply treated with a canopy-like arrangement over the stage which integrates well with the general design. The hexagonal shape of the auditorium is repeated in the foyer, and the exterior wall of the upper part is faced with white marble which gives it an attractive bright appearance in its garden setting.

Bright also is the appearance of the aluminium-faced theatre and opera house on the west bank of the Rhine at Bonn. This theatre for 900, designed by Gessler and Beck-Erland, is an unusual design. The shape of the auditorium, although irregular, can be described roughly as rectangular with a projection at one side where the balcony comes down to the auditorium. The floors of both are well raked and there is an intimacy of the different parts of the theatre with the stage[4]. This and the scenery stores are spacious, a necessary provision for its frequent use for opera. The large surrounding foyer includes a restaurant and exhibition space. The interior design is well expressed in the exterior with the auditorium and stage tower rising above the long horizontal mass, with the long bands of fenestration. This architectural composition which glistens and scintillates in the sun is an impressive and dramatic addition to the urban scene in Bonn.

The theatres of the period 1955–70 so far reviewed are mainly traditional in conception and are based on the picture-frame stage, the progressive design being concerned mainly with comfort, acoustics and improved seeing: good sight lines from all parts of the theatre. Experiment had begun in the inter-war period of theatres with flexibility in the design of the stage so that by appropriate mechanism the stage could be changed from the modern picture-frame proscenium type to the Greek and Elizabethan stage. Ancient Greek and Roman theatres were generally semicircular with the orchestra, in which part of the action took place, either circular or between circular

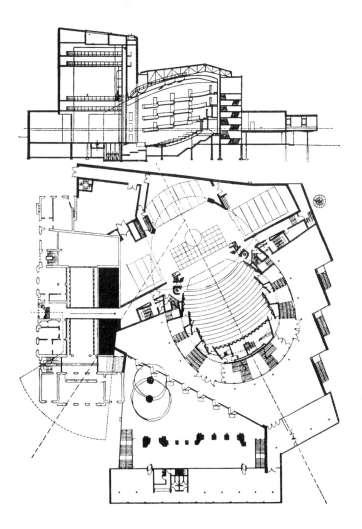

Munster, Municipal Theatre, 1956. Plan and section and view of rear elevation
Architects: Harald Deilmann, Von Hausen, Rave and Ruhnau

City Theatre, Stuttgart, 1960
Architects: Volkart, Placking and Perlia

Opera House and Theatre, Bonn, 1965
Architects: Gessler and Beck-Erland

and semicircular with the major part surrounded by the tiered seating, and the remaining part against the stage. In the Elizabethan theatre the stage was a platform in a pit surrounded on three sides by tiered seating. In the Greek or Elizabethan theatre there is an intimacy between the players and the audience, in contrast to the comparative remoteness of players behind the picture frame of the proscenium. (This is more fully discussed in Chapter 26.) Modern dramatists write for both types of presentation, while in presenting plays of the past it is an advantage to present them in the setting that the dramatist visualized as the one for his play. Several theatres have, therefore, been built in the late fifties and sixties in which the stage can be changed from the picture frame to the stage projecting into the auditorium, generally called the arena stage.

One interesting example of this among German theatres is the National Theatre at Mannheim built in 1955–7 to the design of Gerhard Weber. The long almost rectangular building slightly tapering contains two theatres, the larger seating 1,200 and the smaller 600 to 800, arranged at either end with the two stages inward and store areas between. The large theatre used also as an opera house follows the traditional design of proscenium stage, with a steeply raked auditorium, balcony and stepped, open, side boxes. The smaller theatre is so designed as to make several variations in the seating and stage according to the kind of performance. There is a raked auditorium floor, balcony and suspended side seats. When an orchestra is required for opera or musical play there is the sunken orchestral area in front of the stalls. The stage can be extended over the orchestra when a larger stage is required. When the play is 'in the round' the stage can be arranged towards the centre with raked seating either on two sides or on four. If the theatre is required for lectures or meetings then the stage can be made smaller and the seating extended to accommodate about 800. This flexibility represents a considerable development in theatre design.

NEW THEATRES IN ENGLAND

Several new theatres were built in England in the late fifties and sixties which display developments of the character discussed. The Chichester Festival Theatre pleasantly situated in a park, designed by Powell and Moya and built in 1961–2 has a pentagon shaped plan with an open projecting stage and tiered seating for about 1,500 on three sides of the stage. The openness conduces to effective dramatic presentations and includes entrances from the auditorium. The interior, however, with the cut-up effect of the ceiling, giving the impression that building work is in progress, is not attractive.

A notable new theatre which incorporates changes from the proscenium to the apron stage is the Nottingham Playhouse, built in 1962–3, to the designs of Peter Moro and Partners. The auditorium with balcony are both circular, while the stage can be extended in two sections according to requirements. Two sections can be raised from the orchestra pit to stage or intermediate level. If neither orchestra nor apron stage is required for a proscenium production then the area can be occupied by five rows of seats, and the theatre then seats 756. When one or two extensions of the stage are used then the seating is reduced by 2 or 5 rows. It is a little difficult to appreciate why the circular plan was adopted with balcony seats continuing at the sides where sight lines are not good. The general exterior has similarities to the theatre at Geisenkirchen, with the auditorium and stage tower rising above the square mass formed by the foyer, but the pale opaque panels facing the upper foyer are by no means so attractive as the glass façade of Geisenkirchen with the dramatic glimpse at night of the movement of people on the interior landings and stairways.

Another notable example of the provision of changes that can be made in the seating arrangements and the type of stage is the Questors Theatre at Ealing (1958), designed by Norman Branson of W. S. Hattrell and Partners. The brief given to the architect was that the theatre should be designed to make possible four types of acting area: the proscenium stage, the proscenium with forestage, the peninsular or three-sided stage, and the island stage or theatre-in-the-round[5]. These requirements have largely been realized in spite of difficulties experienced by an amateur group. The basis plan is like the Greek theatre with seating forming a little more than half circle round the orchestra that has become part of the stage. For a performance using the proscenium stage seating is moved across this orchestral space, when a performance is completely in the round seats are placed on the proscenium stage.

In the theatre of the Gardner Arts Centre of Sussex University (1970), designed by Sir Basil Spence, Bonnington and Collins in collaboration with Sean Kenny a similar flexibility is achieved for a slightly larger theatre. A further example is the Crucible Theatre at Sheffield (1971) designed by Renton Howard Wood Associates. In the design of several theatres the stage has been brought out a little into the auditorium as a fixed structure, with the proscenium arch set back. The Shakespeare Memorial Theatre originally designed with the traditional picture-frame stage was reconstructed in 1960 by Peter Hall with a substantial apron stage, so that the proscenium with its curtain now seems half way down the stage. In the Sybil Thorndike Theatre at Leatherhead (1968–9) designed by Roderick Ham the stage projects with a semicircular front like the Greek orchestra with part of the seating curving round. The complete transformation of the theatre, however, from one type to another as envisaged by Walter Gropius and demonstrated in his model (see Chapter 26) is still very much the exception. Some very pleasant and comfortable theatres have been built with much improved seeing and better, steeper floor rakes than generally obtained in the past, but with the fixed traditional relation of auditorium and stage among which may be mentioned the Belgrade Theatre at Coventry (1958), designed by Arthur Ling (City Architect), Douglas Beaton and Kenneth King; the Yvonne Arnaud Theatre at Guildford (1965), designed by John Brownrigg, and the Congress Theatre at Eastbourne (1963) designed by Bryan and Norman Westwood and Partners.

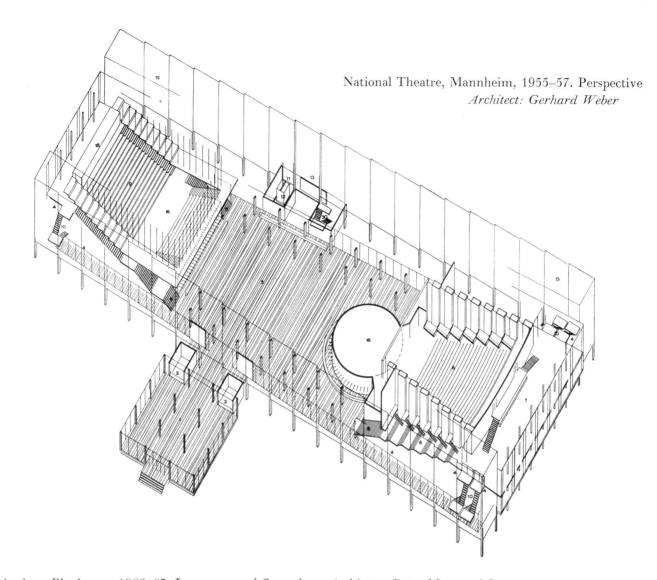

National Theatre, Mannheim, 1955–57. Perspective
Architect: Gerhard Weber

Nottingham Playhouse, 1962–63. Lower ground floor plan *Architects: Peter Moro and Partners*

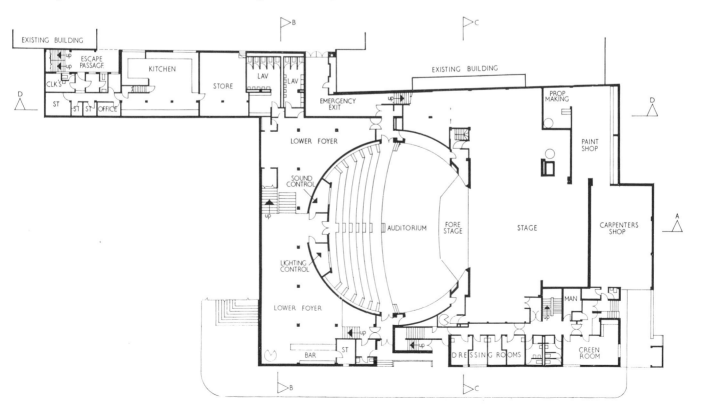

The twentieth century is very much a period of experiment both in playwriting and methods of presentation, and theatre architects and their clients necessarily aim at design that shall not only meet modern requirements but satisfy also the claims of traditional presentation in its many forms. The utmost flexibility and adaptation to meet these varying demands is required and modern technology must necessarily be used to the full in the service of the architect.

REFERENCES AND NOTES

1. County of London Plan 1943, paragraphs 60, 62, with plans on pages 132, 133 and 134 and plate xlviii.
2. At the time of the opening in 1951 a book, *The Royal Festival Hall*, was published by Max Parrish, London, in association with the London County Council. It includes a foreword by J. J. Hayward, leader of the L.C.C., an introduction by Sir Malcolm Sargent and an appreciation by Clough William-Ellis.
3. This testimony is after I had enjoyed an impressive performance in the Berlin Opera House of Verdi's Andrea Boccanegra.
4. During performances of Mozart's Don Giovanni, and Bizet's Carmen in the Bonn Opera House I changed my seat during both performances from one in the balcony to one in the stalls, and the same feeling of intimacy with the stage was apparent in each position.
5. See article by Martin Carr on the Questors Theatre in the *Architects Journal Information Library*, 8th July 1964, pp. 291–297.

Congress Theatre, Eastbourne, 1963. Main frontage
Architects: Bryan and Norman Westwood and Partners

44 Ecclesiastical architecture 1946–1970

THE PRINCIPAL TENDENCIES in ecclesiastical architecture between the two World Wars were briefly described in Chapter 15. They can be summarized as the abandonment of dressing with historical styles; the development of the more open and functional plan so that the interior is more like one large room; the integration of the interior with its surroundings by means of large glass walls, seen particularly in Scandinavian churches; and the forward placing of the altar towards the centre of the congregation thus conducing to a more intimate participation of the congregation in the service.

These trends continued in the post-war period, while from 1950 to 1970 there has been a great deal of experiment in church design, indeed in no sphere of architecture since the mid-twentieth century has there been more diversity and originality than in ecclesiastical design. Churches have been designed in all kinds of geometric shapes, rectangular, square, pentagonal, hexagonal, octagonal, circular, elliptical, and irregular shapes that would not conform to any familiar geometric figure, while methods of construction and roofs have been of considerable diversity made possible by modern technology. In most churches the bell tower has either been detached from the church or has been eliminated. From the diverse field of modern European ecclesiastical architecture it is possible to select only a few significant examples from the variety of forms, and then to concentrate on the more functional tendencies, principally those resulting from the modern liturgical movement and the placing of the altar.

NOTABLE TRADITIONAL DESIGNS IN SWITZERLAND AND GERMANY

Logical historical sequence suggests that the distinctive examples of the more traditional designs should claim first attention, especially the continuation of one of the principal movements towards the large simple open rectangular plan. There are numerous significant examples of this in Switzerland and Germany in which the large rectangular plan has been followed, but generally with considerable variety in the fenestration and roofing.

639

Protestant Church at Schaffausen-on-Rhine, Switzerland, 1949
Architects: Walter Henne and Hans Oechslin

Plan and general view

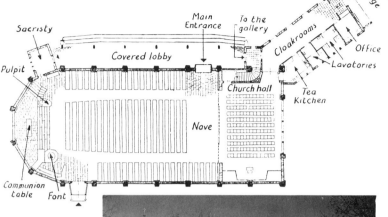

St. Louis Evangelical Church, Friburg,
Germany, 1951–52. Exterior and interior
Architects: Horst Linde,
Rudolf Diehm and Erwin Heine

St. Mark's Church, Marbach, near Marburg,
Germany, 1964. Exterior and view of altar
Architect: Günter Scholz

St. Joseph's Church, Biedenkopf, circa 1959–60
Architects: George and Helmuth Müller

An example of an early post-war protestant church of this kind in Switzerland, completed in 1949, is that at Schaffhausen-on-Rhine which replaced the only church in Switzerland that was destroyed during the war, due to the circumstance that the area is practically surrounded by German territory. The reconstruction of this church gave rise to arguments in protestant circles in Switzerland on the building style to adopt for a modern church of the reformed faith. One school of thought, led by the vicar of Zurich-Seebach, E. Hurter, advocated complete sobriety in church building. Nave and choir were rejected as implying an unwarranted separation of laymen and clergy, and the church was regarded as essentially a dignified assembly hall.

The vicar of Schaffhausen, P. Vogelsanger, was a follower of another school of thought prepared to make concessions to the taste for symbolism, where nave and choir were retained to provide a suitable focus of attention to the three symbols of the service: pulpit, communion table and font. This latter conception determined the shape of the new church at Schaffhausen. It was designed by architects, Walter Henne and Hans Oechslin who were individually awarded the first prizes in a preliminary contest, and who were subsequently asked to collaborate in the preparation of the final design.

The building occupies the edge of an open space on the top of a low hill, remote from the street, which enhances its dignity. Local conditions (not preconceived principles) called for the removal of the bell tower from the church. The general layout is apparent from the plan. The nave is focussed towards pulpit, font and communion table which are dominated by a fresco painting by Paul Bodmer. In the rear is the church hall which, by removing the partition, can be added to the nave when desired. This arrangement, though very desirable in itself, has the slight drawback that the main entrance had to be placed in a side wall.

In spite of the painting and decorative symbols, the puritan atmosphere consistent with the protestant faith is preserved. There is good daylight and materials, concrete, stone and timber which were used for the building play their part in the general effect. On the concrete walls of the steeple, the marks of the forms used for the casting of the concrete remain visible[1].

Among good examples of German churches which follow the open rectangular Basilican plan is the St. Louis Evangelical Church at Friburg (1951–2) designed by Horst Linde, Rudolf Diehm and Erwin Heine. The church is open with the altar placed in the centre of the apse, which has tall windows with flat segmental arches lighting this end of the church, with six bays, while the rest of the church has blank walls. There is a reminiscence of aisles in the row of slender concrete columns and the corridors on the further side of them. The concrete elliptical roof harmonizes with the arches, while the tower with exposed bells is linked with the main structure rather than being an integral part of it as in traditional Gothic. The custom of introducing large windows round the altar continued in many churches in Germany and England, but more often there is a change to the altar against a blank wall with side lighting, examples being a rectangular church in Dusseldorf and St. Joseph's church at Biedenkopf, built in 1960 to the design of George and Helmuth Müller. In this simple and effective church the altar, traditionally placed, is mounted on several steps and is lighted by side windows, while above it on a plain white brick wall is a large and impressive pantocrator. In the church of St. Mark at Marbach near Marburg, designed by Günter Scholz (1964), the side walls are almost completely stained glass, but the east wall behind the altar is blank. The roof of this church is monopitched sloping downwards towards the altar and the square bell tower is well separated and linked by a corridor.

A small departure from the rectangular plan is the protestant Christchurch at Bochum built in 1957–8 and designed by Dieter Oesterlen. The walls are designed in a stepped or echelon formation with windows the whole height of one side and arranged to direct light on the altar against plain walls forming three sides of an octagon. This church replaced a Gothic structure destroyed during the war, except for the Gothic steeple which still survives and is linked to the new structure by an ante room.

COVENTRY CATHEDRAL

Similar in plan and built about the same time is the new Cathedral of St. Michael at Coventry, designed by Sir Basil Spence, and completed in 1962. In designing the new cathedral by the ruined walls of the old, the architect had no easy task if he wished to make the new structure a modern conception expressive of the mid-twentieth century. This was clearly his intention and the assessors of the competition in selecting his design in 1951 as solving 'the problem of designing a cathedral in terms of contemporary architecture' recognized it as such, although whether it entirely succeeded in so doing is open to doubt.

The architect has made no attempt to harmonize his cathedral stylistically with the old; on the contrary the square monolithic mass of his building represents a contrast to the frame structure and large windows of the perpendicular Gothic of the former church, but there is nothing discordant between the old and the new. A certain harmony of massing, and of texture in the windows, and the use of the same pale red Holington stone bring the new and old together, while they are very effectively linked by the tall, majestic canopy which covers the spacious porch of the new cathedral.

The spiritual significance of a church is expressed not only by its structure but by the decorative and symbolical features that enrich it. In providing these enrichments Sir Basil Spence could either have designed most of the various parts himself, as Sir Giles Scott had done at Liverpool Cathedral, or have invited artists and craftsmen to collaborate with him. In choosing the latter course he was probably nearer to the spirit of the Middle Ages than was Sir Giles Scott at Liverpool for the building of the great medieval cathedrals often created communities of artist–craftsmen which centred round them. And by inviting some of the most celebrated artists of the time to collaborate with him Spence has given in his cathedral a splendid expression of much that is significant in the art of the mid-twentieth century.

In mounting the steps that lead to the porch attention is arrestingly invited by the virile figure of St. Michael rising above the prostrate figure of evil, making a magnificent bronze pattern, some thirty feet high, against the pale red sandstone of the wall. This without doubt is one of the consummate works of art of the cathedral, and one of the really great sculptures of the century. The Archangel, tremendously alive, is a powerful figure yet seems to be light as air above the very earthy massive figure of the Devil. Its relation to the wall space is perfect, and it is in such work (the Madonna in Cavendish Square is another), rather two dimensional than three dimensional in conception, that Sir Jacob Epstein was at his greatest.

On entering the cathedral one is hardly stimulated by the sense of space which is the experience on entering many of the great cathedrals of Europe, and which in itself contributes so much to the religious atmosphere. The cathedral is perhaps too small for that experience, yet there is none the less a sense of dignity and majesty. It is achieved by the fully open view from the porch to the altar, by the light, and by its loftiness— a height of 70 feet in relation to a length of 250 feet and width of 85 feet; and this loftiness is enhanced by the tall slender concrete columns, of cross sections, supporting the canopy.

The construction is both traditional and modern with walls about 80 feet high and 3 feet 6 inches thick, consisting of an outer facing of red Hollington sandstone 18 inches thick, with an inner facing of concrete blocks six inches thick, the cavity being filled with concrete. The internal surface is a white coarse textured plaster with an acoustic surface, which provides a vivid contrast to the rich stained-glass windows. The roof has a span of 90 feet, is of shell concrete four inches thick, with post-tensioned tie beams. It has an interior lining of cork for sound absorbtion, and above the concrete shell is a layer of concrete insulating blocks covered with a screed and glass fibre. The canopy is independent of the roof (the space between being occupied by a service catwalk) and is reminiscent of medieval fan tracery consisting of concrete ribs forming diamonds which are occupied by low pyramids of timber. Many writers on Gothic architecture have likened the effect of columns and tracery of a Gothic cathedral to the canopy over a road through a forest of tall trees, such as one finds in Savernake Forest, but in this canopy at Coventry the similarity seems to be even stronger than in a Gothic church.

The walls on plan are of saw tooth design, and ten tall stained-glass windows, five on either side, are so placed as to shine towards the altar, as in the church at Buchum.

Coventry Cathedral, 1952–62 *Architect: Sir Basil Spence*

View from entrance steps looking towards the Chapel of Christ the Servant

Coventry Cathedral, interior looking towards the
altar with the tapestry by Graham Sutherland

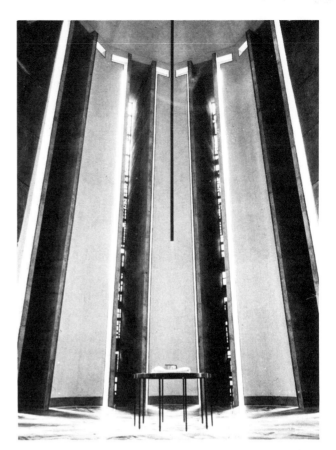

Interior of Chapel of Unity, Coventry Cathedral

Plan, Coventry Cathedral

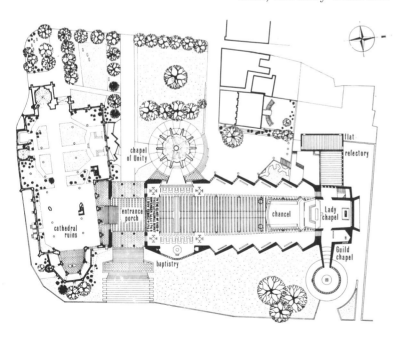

Chapel of Notre Dame du Haut, Ronchamp, 1950–54. Interior
Architect: Le Corbusier

The Cathedral is sited transversely to the old thus south–north instead of the liturgical east–west, so that the windows face northeast and northwest and the sunlight during the day gives changing light to the interior. Although there is a representational theme in these windows which are the work of Geoffrey Clarke, Keith New and Lawrence Lee, they are seen mainly as abstract designs with interesting colour symbolism, beginning with the bright greens and blues of youth, to the sombre colouring of the fourth panel of old age or death, to conclude with the bright colouring of the resurrection near the altar. Although seen mainly as abstract patterns the designs lack coherence, while the rhythms are rather broken by the heavy mullions and transoms. More successful, because more frankly just panels of coloured glass of superb contrast and harmonies, is the great window of the Baptistry by John Piper.

The large tapestry by Graham Sutherland which covers the north wall dominates by reason of the great seated figure of Christ in the mandorla flanked by symbols of the Evangelists, a theme familiar in Byzantine and Romanesque churches. Sutherland's treatment is not particulary original, nor does the design accord well with the medium of tapestry, although the colour scheme is pleasing. The design would have been equally suited to metal sculpture.

There are in the cathedral many other contributions by artists important in their various fields. The tent-like Chapel of Unity has a richly patterned marble floor by the Swedish artist, Einar Forseth, and stained-glass windows set in concrete designed by Margaret Traherne, and interesting work in the other chapels, while the great glass screen by John Hutton has a disconcerting strangeness when first seen, but like all highly original works improves greatly with further contemplation.

The artists who have contributed to enrich the fabric of this cathedral are strong individualists, and the diversity of their achievement is more apparent than the similarity, and for this reason the cathedral has been criticized as lacking unity. But it must be remembered that it has been built in the short time of seven years, whereas most medieval cathedrals took more than fifty years to build. The artists have been called together by a common purpose, and it is probable that as their work recedes in time a unity will become apparent, because artists more than they know are children of their time, and are linked together whether they will or not, by the spirit of that time.

The building of a new church by the ruins of the old, which are kept as such, serves as a war memorial. This was first done in ancient Greece and seems to have emanated then from the oath sworn before the battle of Plataea in 479 B.C. that, 'the sanctuaries which have been burnt and thrown down by the barbarians' are not to be rebuilt, but to be left, 'as memorials of the impiety of the barbarians'[2]. The Persians were the barbarians. The most notable example was the Peisistrated Temple of Athena on the

St. Albert, Catholic Church, Saarbrucken, 1955. Interior
Architect: Gottfried Bohm

Catholic Church of St. Rochus, Dusseldorf, 1953–54
Architect: Paul Schneider-Esleben

Exterior view and plan

Reformed Church, Effretikon, near Zürich, 1960–61
Architect: Ernst Gisel

Interior and exterior

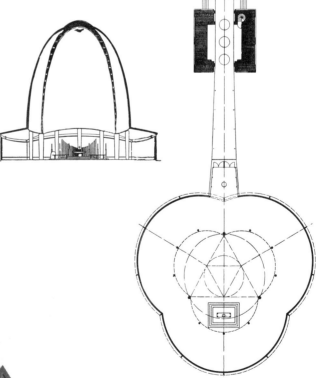

acropolis at Athens which stood in ruins north of the Parthenon, until the Erectheum was built.

The preservation of ruins as a form of war memorial with a new church by their side was done in several instances after the Second World War, but not, as far as I know, after the First World War. Another well-known example is the Kaiser Wilhelm Memorial Church in Berlin, an octagonal structure with blue glass walls built near the ruined tower of the old church[3].

LE CORBUSIER'S CHAPEL AT RONCHAMP, AND FURTHER GERMAN EXAMPLES

Of the many churches of unusual and original design built during this period the most famous is Le Corbusier's Chapel of Notre Dame du Haut, Ronchamp, built in 1950–4. It is situated on the hilltop of Haut Lieu above the village of Ronchamp near Belfort, and replaces the former chapel destroyed during the war in 1944. The design of the new chapel is essentially one of curves, of curved walls and curved roof, chosen partly because curved forms have a greater stability. The construction is of concrete and stone, with a double curved concrete shell for the roof which rests on the thick concrete walls with intervening small blocks providing a gap of a few inches between roof and walls to admit light. The thick rough concrete walls are pierced by small rectangular windows placed in a seemingly irregular yet carefully calculated pattern. The curved forms approximate to a rectangular plan with the stone altar against the east end, while there are three small chapels on the south side. The three towers are built of stone capped by half domes of concrete. The roof slopes down to the east end over the altar, and the floor follows the natural slope of the hill down towards the altar and consists of cement poured between battens panelled in conformity with Le Corbusier's module. The light and shadow of the interior created by the placing of the windows gives a strong religious atmosphere to the church, which together with its originality explain the interest it has prompted throughout the world[4].

Among the several German churches of unusual and original design the Catholic church of St. Albert at Saarbrucken built in 1955 and designed by Gottfried Bohm and the Catholic church of St. Rochus at Dusseldorf, designed by Paul Schneider-Eleben and built in 1953–4 are notable. The former has an elliptical plan with an inner circle of slender concrete columns at the east end enclosing the altar, above which is the glass cupola the sole source of light in the church. This concentration of light on the altar with the rest of the church in subdued light gives both a dramatic effect and religious atmosphere. Similar effects of concentrated lighting on the altar, but with different designs, can be seen in many of the modern churches in Germany. In a rebuilt church at Stuttgart on the hill on the north side of the city, the lighting is directed on the altar from two side windows high up on the walls, while there is a steeply raked floor like that of a lecture theatre for the congregation.

The church of St. Rochus, Dusseldorf, replaced the Romanesque church built in 1887, which was destroyed in the Second World War, except for the tower which survives and stands a little apart from the new structure. The plan is a trefoil and there is an inner trefoil with twelve tall slender columns symbolizing the idea of the Holy Trinity resting on the twelve apostles. The roof and walls consist of three identical curved concrete shells, tapering towards the top to form a tall elliptical dome. The altar is within the inner trefoil, and lighting is by means of the ellipsoidal calotte forming the roof of glass bricks joining the three concrete shells[5].

An unusual design which has aroused much attention is that of the reformed church in the village of Effretikon near Zürich, built in 1960–1 and designed by Ernst Gisel. It is situated on a low hill which makes its unusual skyline very prominent from surrounding areas. The plan is saw toothed on the west side, surmounted by a pitched roof, also stepped on the west side to give a series of sloping lights to the interior. A flat roofed projection houses a meeting room at the northeast corner, while a framed concrete tower with exposed bells occupies the southwest corner. The construction is of concrete with red bricks for internal facing and floors, and for the fixed furniture like the pulpit. The seats are all movable so that the church can be used for concerts, drama and meetings.

A very different church, but also fundamentally a conception in terms of concrete and stone, is the Church of St. John the Baptist on the Autostrada del Sol near Florence, built in 1963 and designed by Giovanni Michelucci. It is built partly as a memorial to the workmen who lost their lives in accidents during the construction of the Autostrada del Sol. The plan is somewhat irregular, but it has the reminiscence of a Latin cross with altars in three of its arms. The structure is based on the Biblical motif of the tent, with framed and shell concrete roofing. The outer walls of the church are of stone, while in the narthex on the south side between the windows are screens with stone relief sculptures on the theme of wayfaring.

THE MODERN LITURGICAL MOVEMENT AND THE ALTAR
—A GLANCE BACKWARDS

The modern liturgical movement is the greatest influence in church design since the Second World War which is apparent in the emphasis that it gives to the placing of the altar as the principal and central feature of the church both for Catholics and Protestants, except for those sects of the latter where the altar is eliminated. Thus the placing of the altar in the church in relation to the congregation has become a starting point in design. What are its traditions?

The altar in the Christian Church has always been the focal point for worship at which the principal ceremonies are conducted. Because the church building houses the worshippers round the altar it has become the House of God, and the altar is its raison d'etre.

Church at Seebach, near Zürich, 1949. Exterior and interior *Architect: A. H. Steiner*

Church of St. John the Baptist near Florence
Architect: Giovanni Michelucci

Church of St. Mary, Dusseldorf-Wersten, 1958
Architects: Emil Steffan and Nikolaus Rosiny

University Church, Cologne, 1965

Taivallahti Church, Helsinki, 1967
Architects: Timo and Tuomo Suomalainen

In Greek and Roman religions the altar, which played a conspicuous part in ceremonies, was usually a raised level surface on which sacrificial offerings were made to the gods. Being often a surface for burnt offerings and being also built for permanence the altar was almost always of stone, and often decorated on its sides with carved representations of sacrificial animals and other symbols associated with worship and sacrifice.

Among the early Christian altars were the tombs of martyrs and priests several being in the Roman catacombs. When Vitiges devasted Rome and ravaged the catacombs the bodies of martyrs and early priests were moved to churches within the walls, partly for safety, but partly because the custom of using the tomb of a martyr as an altar had given it greater sacredness. Thus, the tradition grew of the altar being a shrine of sacred relics, sometimes in early centuries it was the actual tomb of a saint, which is responsible for the traditional tomb-like shape.

The altar thus became a combination of the table derived from that of the Last Supper, for the celebration of the Eucharist and of the Holy Communion, and of a tomb or a reliquary, and it has retained this character from Early Christian times until today. The altar is also thought of in the minds of many Christians as a symbol of Christ's sacrifice for mankind.

The Code of Canon Law[6] prescribes the structure and character of the altar, but within that prescription a great variety of designs and styles has been possible. It consists of four main parts, the table, the support, the reliquary and the substructure, floor or platform on which it rests. The table should consist of a single slab of natural stone, while the support, which should also be of natural stone, can be of a single column or four corner columns. In the latter case filling of other material may be employed. The design of the support would be controlled somewhat by the nature of the relics. These are usually placed in a reliquary, often of elaborate symbolic design, which is placed in the cavity within the support, and if the relics are large the support may assume the proportions of a tomb. On the top surface of the table five crosses are incised, one central and the others at the four corners, symbolizing the five wounds of Christ. Occasionally the high altar of a cathedral has been of one large solid block of stone, the most famous being those at St. Peter's, Rome, and Westminster Cathedral. A recent example is the solid block of polished granite that forms the large altar of the Basilica of the Spanish National Monument to the Civil War, built in 1946–66 about 35 miles northwest of Madrid[7].

The altar with its plain top for the ceremony of the Eucharist or Holy Communion is the essential, but in traditional usage it has become very elaborate, with often ornate settings, designed to emphasize its importance and sacred character. The altar itself sometimes became a beautiful object, faced with coloured marbles and mosaics, supported on a series of marble steps. There are some beautiful modern altars of this type in the side chapels of Westminster Cathedral. Very frequently the stone altar is covered with an embroidered cloth, especially the simple stone altars of Gothic churches, but the altar is more impressive without this cover, when the decorative element is provided by the stone altar itself.

About the twelfth century the cross or crucifix and candles began to be placed on the altar table along the back, and since the sixteenth century in Roman Catholic churches the tabernacle containing the consecrated host was often placed in a central position on the altar. Before the sixteenth century the tabernacle was in the form of a dove, but later was a miniature tent or temple usually made of marble.

From the twelfth century a reredos was often erected behind the altar which often became a tall elaborate structure with representations of Christ, the Virgin and Child and saints in panels. Much of the greatest early Italian painting is seen in these polyptychs, the Gothic framework, often in marble, metal or wood or a combination of the three, enclosing panels of tempera paintings on wood. In northern Gothic (France, Germany, Britain) the elaborate altar reredos was generally of stone with carved figures of saints, and some were so large as to become screens forming an east wall to the choir, as at Winchester, St. Albans and more recently Truro. The reredos was sometimes combined with a canopy with side wings or columns supporting the super-structure, and the altar was enclosed within the structure.

The gradual revolution in the design of churches in the last forty years in Central and Northern Europe has depended much on the design and placing of the altar, yet one thing has remained constant, the shape of the actual table, which is still guided by the tomb tradition.

The contribution that space can make in the impact of the altar is much influenced by its position and setting. There has been a good deal of changed thinking on this subject as part of, and resulting from, the modern liturgical movement. Since the twelfth century the customary position of the altar was at the east end of the church often below a fairly large east window. In the larger churches, like the French Gothic cathedrals, the east end terminated with a circular apse, the choir was surrounded with an aisle and the altar was at the east end of the choir. This was followed in English cathedrals, but the east end was often square, and a Lady Chapel with a much lower roof continued beyond. The effect was often of a high altar, backed by a reredos with a large east window above. This was continued in the Gothic revival of the nineteenth century and in the late Gothic Cathedral at Liverpool (1904–73). Here the red sandstone altar and reredos appear just below a vast east window. The same effect with the top of the reredos silhouetted against the window is seen in the war memorial transept.

The altar against the east wall with a large window above has obvious disadvantages, although it has been perpetuated in many modern churches. In some the whole east end is of glass, as in the modern Protestant Church at Friburg and the church of St. Michael and All Angels at Wythenshawe, where looking towards the altar the eyes are inevitably dazzled. During the thirties, however, there was a movement away from this and the east end became a blank wall often with light from side windows concentrating on the altar as previously described.

In the churches in England since about 1930 where this change has occurred, the blank east wall has been variously treated: sometimes the centre space behind the altar has been hung with tapestry, sometimes a large cross has been fixed to the wall, sometimes there is a simple reredos, or sometimes a single figure of Christ, a saint or an angel often carved in stone.

In almost all churches in England erected before the Second World War, the altar is well against the east wall or very near to it, generally elevated on several steps, and as remote as possible from the congregation. The priest performed ceremonies at the altar with his back to the remote congregation. This remoteness of the altar seems generally to have been calculated as giving it an enhanced sacred character and holiness.

The restoration and rebuildings of many of the early Basilican Christian Churches that remain to us follow the early structure and layout. In churches like S. Clemente and S. Paolo fuori le Mura in Rome, the altar stood well in front of the circular apse at the east end of the choir. The priests and presbyters sat circle-wise in the apse facing the altar, and for the choir and congregation the priest officiated behind the altar. There is apparently evidence that this was the form of eucharistic ceremony until the twelfth century. Thus, the modern liturgical movement would appear to return to the Early Christian forms of service.

One of the aims of this liturgical movement is to oppose the remoteness of the altar and bring it among the congregation so that the congregation can be near the altar and worship round it. Perhaps the ideal is when the congregation is on three sides of an altar with the priest standing at the back as in many modern churches in Germany and France and a few in England.

The altar of Coventry Cathedral occupies the traditional remote position at the liturgical east end of the cathedral. Sir Basil Spence records, in his book on the building of the Cathedral[8], that the late Dr Neville Gorton, the Bishop of Coventry, and his friend, Father C. E. Douglas, wanted to bring the altar forward to the choir steps. In Spence's design the altar had been placed at the end of the main axis, as a climax, but so placed that it could be seen from all parts of the nave. Spence amended the design: 'the altar was brought right forward with only three steps up from the nave, so that the Holy Table itself could be strong, big and simple.' When this plan was presented to the Reconstruction Committee and the Cathedral Council it caused, according to Sir Basil, 'a near riot' and on no account would either body accept the new arrangement of the High Altar, and it reverted to its position in the original plan, as remote as ever from the body of worshippers.

Referring elsewhere in his book to the Altar, Sir Basil mentions that it 'is of concrete, hammer-dressed so that it looks rather like a chunk of rough granite'. It is a pity that it is not, instead of merely looking like it. Why, it must be asked, is it of concrete and not of natural stone such as a block of granite or of the red Hollington stone used in the walls of the cathedral. It would have been more costly than concrete, but the altar is the last thing on which economies should be made. The altar is the most sacred and significant object in the cathedral, yet here among so many notable works of art it lacks distinction of design or material.

THE ALTAR BROUGHT FORWARD—SOME SWISS AND GERMAN EXAMPLES
Bringing the altar among the congregation it becomes an object in space as distinct from one against a wall or reredos. And the space around it is important in the conception. In some recent Italian and German interiors the altar in relation to the space enclosed by bare walls is often very dramatic and conveys a sense of awe and mystery, especially when light is concentrated on the altar. Bare stone is necessary for the full effect of this religious atmosphere. The altar is thus a three-dimensional design conception in space which makes it more completely the focal point of the church than, perhaps, it has ever been before. This should be regarded as an opportunity for architects. And it should be emphasized that logically, in the tradition of Christian thought, the altar is the central point of worship, and the church building, because of it, becomes the House of God. If economies have to be exercised in building a church in a new town or community the last subject of such economy should be the altar. It should not be of substitute or inferior materials. Tradition spells a well-selected natural stone. Examples of the altar brought towards and partly enclosed by the congregation are many, and it is, therefore, necessary to select a few significant examples from several countries.

Consistent with the general trend towards simplicity in Swiss churches is an early post-war example—that at Seebach near Zürich designed by A. H. Steiner the city architect—in which the altar and sanctuary are surrounded on three sides by the congregation in an octagonal plan. The building is supported by an outwardly visible frame of ferro-concrete, whilst ashlars of sandstone are used, as facing material, and brickwork as filling material. The roof is carried by girders of laminated wood, their lower chords being visible. The walls are rough-cast, the floor is laid out with sandstone slabs, whilst oak parquetry has been used in the gallery.

The church hall is integrated with the church, and one of its eight walls also forms the end wall of the lower building of the church hall which can either be divided by removable partitions or linked with the church proper by opening the connecting collapsible doors. The campanile with five bells is a separate structure, likewise supported by a ferro-concrete skeleton, visible from outside. This group of buildings, forming an unusual pattern, is in welcome contrast with the large and massive school building behind it[9].

Two similar churches with the altar spaciously set and backed by a circular apse, as in Early Christian churches, and enclosed on three sides by the congregation are the Parish Church of St. Mary, Dusseldorf-Wersten built in 1958, and designed by Emil Steffann and Nikolaus Rosiny, and the church of St. Lawrence at Munich designed also by Emil Steffann in 1960. The former is a small church at the east end of a courtyard round which are adjacent buildings related to the social activities of the church. A bench was originally designed along the apse, which however has remained bare, although a bench for the president and his assistants is incorporated in the church at Munich. Lighting in the Dusseldorf church is from the glass wall on the west courtyard side. Among other German churches which incorporate this significant placing of the altar is the Church of the Holy Cross, at Dusseldorf-Rath (1957–8) designed by Josef Lehmbrock, which is slightly fan shaped with a circular apse, and seating half surrounding the altar, with a roof which slopes upwards from the entrance to above the altar, constructed of a mesh of tubular steel rods. The concrete walls are perforated with small openings which form a cross above the altar, and flame-like patterns on either side, while at the other end they form diamond patterns. These are the source of light. Another church with a very similar seating arrangement round the altar has an elliptical plan with a timber roof that curves down on either side of an apex, which internally, with its diamond pattern of ribs, looks like a net thrown over a central horizontal bar. The walls make a translucent zig-zag pattern.

In the University Church at Cologne built in 1965 the sanctuary with the altar, reredos and canopy, pulpit and lectern, is set on a platform mounted on three steps which forms an island at the east end surrounded by ample space, although the sides do not appear to be utilized for seating; this occupies the remainder of the long rectangular space. Another distinctive and unusual example is the Taivallahti church at Helsinki built in 1967 and designed by Timo and Tuomo Suomalainen. It is partly underground built into the rock with a flat domed roof with the circumference area of glass for light. The seating for the congregation in the roughly circular plan is nearly half way round the altar, and the walls are the rough rock which together with the domed roof make an impressive interior.

THE NEW CATHEDRAL AT LIVERPOOL

One of the most dramatic examples of the central placing of an altar is in the new

Roman Catholic Cathedral at Liverpool designed by Sir Frederick Gibberd which was completed in 1967. In 1927 Sir Edwin Lutyens was commissioned to design the Metropolitan Cathedral of Christ the King, to be erected on a site in Liverpool about half a mile from the Anglican Cathedral. Lutyens produced a design in the Renaissance style, with typical Lutyens idioms, superbly proportioned, with a central dome. It was to be second only to St. Peters at Rome in size and if it had been erected it would have rivalled it in magnificence. Work commenced on the crypt in 1930 and was largely completed by the outbreak of hostilities in 1939, when work was necessarily terminated and the crypt was covered with a large area of paving. Later, in the post-war years, it was realized that Lutyens immense conception would prove far too costly, and it was therefore decided to have a more modest cathedral to be erected on the platform above the crypt. A competition was held to obtain a suitable design, won by Sir Frederic Gibberd who became the architect in 1960.

The design with its circular plan and central altar is of a tent-like form similar in shape to tents in ancient Assyrian reliefs and also to the bell tent used by the British army. The slope is similar to that of the tent and the projecting concrete ribs anchored to the base are similar to the guy ropes of the tent fixed to their pegs. Liverpudlians refer to it as the Mersey Funnel.

The central altar in a circular space means that the congregation, if it is large, will almost completely surround the altar, except for the choir placed on the main axis. Thus the officiating priest when facing the majority of the congregation will have his back to part of it, which prompts the question whether this central altar is as functional as the altar with the congregation on three sides as in the German churches by Steffmann at Dusseldorf and Munich. On the periphery of the circle are a series of small chapels set between the concrete ribs and a circular baptistry in the east near the main entrance. On the main east–west axis is the principal entrance, the central altar and behind this on the west side are the choir with space for an orchestra and organ. A gallery is provided along part of the circumference. At the west end there is an open-air altar, beyond which is the wide unoccupied space above Lutyens's crypt. The sixteen concrete ribs that spring from the base and form the structure of the conical roof and continue in the lantern to the summit forming the crown of thorns is the essential structure. In the lantern the spaces between are filled with stained glass, embedded in an irregular pattern of epoxy resin mortar joints within precast concrete panels. Additional lighting is from a band of narrow windows between the top of the vertical walls and the circular concrete beam that forms the base of the cone. The prevailing colour of the glass is a rich blue which gives a pleasing, subdued and suitably religious light to the interior. The construction is a combination of reinforced and pre-stressed concrete (in the pinnacles for example) and of load-bearing brickwork for the chapel walls at the base faced with Portland stone facings. The architect speaks of the structure as being 'primarily in pure compression, utilizing the least possible

Metropolitan Cathedral of Christ the King, Liverpool, 1960–65. Interior view towards the central altar

Architect: Sir Frederick Gibberd

amount of material and the least possible money. Some two hundred feet of tapering tower subject to high wind load is placed over the middle of a free and considerable volume of space by structural members which diminish to a few square feet when they enter the ground—a system not possible in any other stage in history, not even possible twenty years ago'. Of its appearance both externally and internally there have been a wide variety of opinions; it is liked by some and disliked by others. The interior is more pleasing than the exterior although it hardly exhilarates with any stimulation of the sense of space which is a religious feeling given so well by the great Gothic and Renaissance cathedrals, instead the conical roof coming so low on the vertical walls gives a slight feeling of oppression[10].

Metropolitan Cathedral of Christ the King, Liverpool, 1960–65   *Architect: Sir Frederick Gibberd*

The contrast of this structure with the immense Anglican Cathedral only a half a mile away is vivid. The latter is an original version of traditional Gothic, a great work of art which has taken 70 years to build, with a slowing down during two World Wars, but with no break in the continuity of operations. The later cathedral is totally new in conception, it owes little to tradition in its design and constructionally it is a significant product of a technological age, and was built in little more than four years. It is doubtful whether the whole history of architecture presents a greater contrast within the same century than do these two buildings[11].

References and Notes

1. See detailed description by the architect in *Schweizerische Bauzeitung*, 8th April, 1950.

2. William Bell Dinsmoor, *The Architecture of Ancient Greece*, third edition, Batsford, London, 1950, p. 150 and p. 198.

3. In *Bombed Churches as War Memorials* by Hugh Casson and others (London, 1945) the suggestion is made that some of the churches partly destroyed by bombing should serve in their ruined condition as War Memorials.

4. See W. Boesiger and H. Girsberger, *Le Corbusier 1910–1965*, Thames and Hudson, London, 1967.

5. A technical description of the construction is given by Karl Wimmenauer in *Die Neue Stadt*, January, 1953. This description was in the early stages of its construction.

6. See Geoffrey Webb, Building and Furnishing an Altar According to the Roman Rite in *Post-War Church Building*, London, 1947.

7. This is one of the largest ecclesiastical buildings of modern times. It is built under the mountain in the Valley of the Fallen, on a Latin cross plan 859 feet long, 360 feet across transepts, a width of choir nave and transepts of 73 feet, while the central dome of 134 feet diameter rises to 138 feet above the floor. See Arnold Whittick, The Spanish National Memorial to the Civil War, *Stone Industries Journal*, January/February, 1970.

8. Sir Basil Spence, *Phoenix at Coventry—the Building of a Cathedral*, London, 1962.

9. See *Schweizerische Bauzeitung*, No. 2, 1950.

10. I remember asking several young architects their opinion of this new cathedral shortly after it was completed in 1966. There was generally a lukewarm response. One architect said that he tried to like it but found it difficult to do so, but added that during his visit he went into the Crypt and remarked, 'that was wonderful'. It is after all by Lutyens, an unerring master of proportion with an almost infallible artistic instinct, that makes one regret that his design was never realized.

11. There are several books on modern church architecture. Two of the most progressive in attitude, in English, are Peter Hammond, *Liturgy and Architecture*, Barrie and Rockliff, London, 1960, and *Towards a Church Architecture*, edited by Peter Hammond, The Architectural Press, London, 1962. This is a series of essays on various aspects of design by Peter Hammond, Nigel Maguire, Keith Murray, H. Benedict Green, Charles Davis, James A. Whyte, Patrick McLaughlin, Patrick Nuttgens and Lance Wright.

659

45 *The architecture of transport*

PROBABLY IN NO sphere of human activity in the last 150 years have greater changes taken place than in the methods and speed of transportation. In the early nineteenth century the means of transport did not differ in essentials and speed from those in ancient Greece and Rome. The main methods were by horse-drawn vehicles (sometimes by other animals: oxen, dogs, camels) with speeds averaging over periods and distances of not more than twenty miles an hour, while transport by water was mainly by sailing vessels and sculling with speeds of no more than ten miles an hour.

With the invention of steam power in the eighteenth century and its application to rail transport in the early nineteenth century, public transport developed on a much larger scale and by the end of the century trains were travelling at 70 miles an hour, one run in Britain of $118\frac{1}{2}$ miles from London to Bristol was scheduled for two hours in the nineties. The development of electric traction greatly increased speed possibilities.

With the invention of the internal combustion engine came the motor vehicle with speeds by 1930 comparable with rail travel, except that the roads planned for the horse-drawn vehicle and with the increasing number of motor vehicles using them, greatly restricted speeds until trunk roads and motor roads were provided.

Man began to fly in the late nineteenth century, very short distances at first for it was not until 1909 that the first flight across the Straits of Dover was made. From then on progress was rapid. In 1910 there were scheduled passenger Zeppelin flights in Germany and by 1919 there were several scheduled routes in Europe for fixed-wing aircraft. By the thirties all the principal cities of Europe had airports, with regular services to most other European cities and normal aircraft speeds were in the region of 150 miles an hour. With the introduction of jet propulsion average speeds of aircraft were in the region of 500 miles an hour with possible developments to well over 1,000 miles an hour. Thus ever since the dawn of civilization ten thousand years ago until comparatively recently the speed that man could travel was little more than 20 miles

660

a hour, and then in less than 150 years human invention advanced this to well over 1,000 miles an hour, and with prospects of rocket propulsion of greater speeds by the end of the century.

The most notable constructions, architecturally, in the service of transportation up to the early twentieth century were bridges, including viaducts and aqueducts, and these are among the most impressive surviving monuments of ancient Rome. A large number of beautiful bridges were built throughout Europe during the Middle Ages and Renaissance and many survive. When iron and later steel were used for large scale constructions in the nineteenth century, bridges were among the most impressive, built with the larger spans that steel made possible. Also rail transport necessitated stations, and the big termini in the cities; these represented some of the most progressively designed buildings of the nineteenth century.

Among the most distinctive buildings for transport that have been erected in Europe since the Second World War are further great railway terminus buildings, bus garages, multi-storey car parks and airport buildings, and these will be briefly considered in turn. Some notable bridges of various kinds have also been erected but to do justice to them would extend the scope of this history too much, which is limited to buildings that enclose space for specific purposes, and therefore excludes several structures that would legitimately be termed architecture like bridges and public monuments. A few early iron and steel bridges are briefly described in Appendix 1, because of the important contribution their construction made towards new methods of building.

RAILWAY STATIONS

A few impressive and beautiful railway terminal buildings were erected in the early years of the century, among the most notable being the station at Helsinki (1909–14) designed by Eliel Saarinen, Stuttgart Station (1914–26) designed by Paul Bonatz and F. E. Scholer and that at Florence (1933–36) designed by Giovanni Michelucci. (Most of the great British railway stations belong to the nineteenth century.)

In the large railway termini of the nineteenth century the plan gradually developed to a large concourse in front of the platform barriers with offices in front, sometimes along the outer sides enclosing the platforms and tracts in a U plan. The plan of Helsinki station is an elaboration of this which follows the U enclosure, with, however, the addition of a wing to the northeast, and the addition of a large booking hall parallel with the rectangular space in front of the barriers. In the centre part of this long hall there is a transverse hall projecting to form the main and impressive central entrance. This long booking hall was to become a principal architectural feature of many subsequent stations. It is a feature of Stuttgart Station and it is prominent in the well-known Amstel Station at Amsterdam, designed by H. G. J. Schelling and completed in 1939. The upper part of the long side walls are of glass in light metal

661

framing, and the end walls are solid brick, one of which is utilized internally for a large well-composed mural depicting travel by rail to great cities.

Probably the most beautiful and impressive railway station built in the twentieth century is that at Rome. Plans for rebuilding Rome Station were prepared in the mid-thirties in preparation for the Exposition of 1942. The old station was demolished in 1937 and work on the new began in 1938, but was abandoned during the war in 1941. The two side wings of three and four storeys were, however, completed. When it was decided in 1947 to resume the building of the new station, the former plans were replaced by those resulting from a national competition in that year, and Eugenio Montuori and Leo Calini became the principal architects with Massimo Castellazzi, Vasco Fadigati, Achille Pintonello and Annibale Vitellozzi as associates. Building began in 1948 and was completed in 1950.

The station occupies the southeast side of the spacious and attractive Piazza dei Cinquecento with its gardens and palm trees. On the opposite side are the Baths of Diocletian, part of which are occupied by the museum of antiquities, while near this is the circular Piazza della Republica with its central fountain. On the northeast side is the ancient Roman wall which links with the station among lawns, palms and cypresses. This immense modern station harmonizes with its ancient neighbours and the whole magnificent scene is an illustration of how in Rome the centuries live so well together. The plan of the station is the U shape. In front of the series of platform barriers is the great concourse, known as the galleria, a handsome covered pedestrian way, similar in character to the arcade at Milan, with shops and bars and restaurants, which divide it from the great booking hall occupying two thirds of the length. Above the shops and restaurants rises the narrow office building six storeys high and 760 feet long with long narrow horizontal strips of fenestration, two to each floor, designed so as to minimize the discomfort of the afternoon sun. This great simple façade, extending almost the whole side of the square, forms the background to the canopied booking hall and entrance. The slightly pitched reinforced concrete asymmetrical roof with the wide cantilevered canopy, the glass front with substantial verticals and the lightly framed glass end walls enclose a spaciously impressive booking hall, which together with the galleria form a very exhilarating interior. Unlike the Vittoria Emmanuele monument this building appears to be very happily in scale with its surroundings. It is perhaps a little strange that probably the finest architectural work in Europe of the mid-twentieth century is a railway station.

Designed also with a large central rectangular hall is the new station at Naples designed by Pier Luigi Nervi, Mario Campanella and Giuseppe Vaccaro and built in 1958–61. The long rectangular booking hall is the most impressive feature with its glass walls and diamond ribbed flat concrete roof with triangular external arches supported on piers tapering downwards.

662

Railway Terminus, Rome, 1948–50 *Architects: Eugenio Montuori and Leo Calini*

Main entrance with canopy—and interior of booking hall—both night views

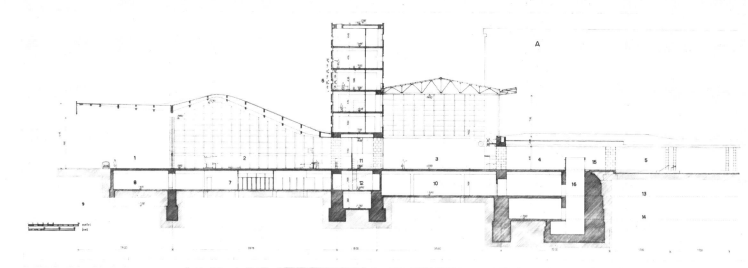

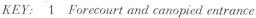
Railway Terminus, Rome, 1948–50. Transverse vertical section

KEY:
1 Forecourt and canopied entrance
2 Booking hall
3 The Great Gallery or main concourse between booking hall and platform barrier
4 Area in front of platforms
5 Platforms
6 Administrative offices
7 Travel facilities—toilets, bathrooms, waiting rooms, restaurants, etc
8 Station subway
9 Subway
10 Service area
11 Shops
12 Warehouse and stores
13 Underground service tunnel
14 Underground service tunnel
15 Goods and truck lift

Heidelberg Railway Station, 1951–52
Exterior and interior of booking hall

Euston Railway Terminus, 1965–68
Regional Architect: R. L. Moorcraft

Main entrance, booking hall
and general plan

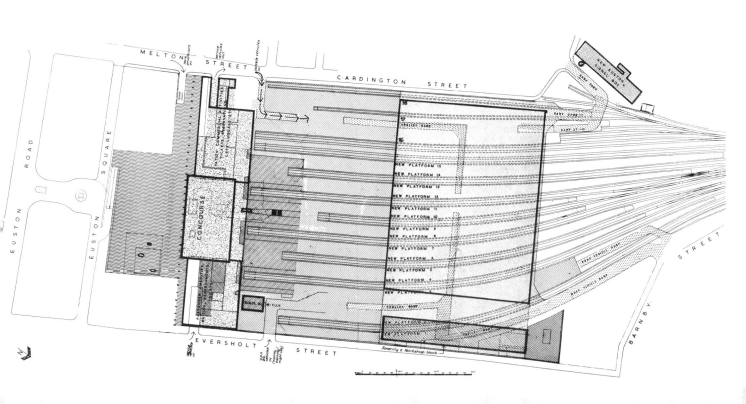

Of the stations in Germany that at Heidelberg, built in 1951–2, is among the most notable. It incorporates a long rectangular booking hall with high ceiling and long glass walls with vertical concrete ribs, and end walls decorated with murals. The spaciousness of high light booking halls of some of the large modern railway stations is exhilarating.

The influence of the magnificent Rome station spread over Europe and it is apparent in modern stations in several countries. It finds a fairly close echo in the busy suburban station at Barking near London (1961) with its large rectangular booking hall, glass walls and the swing of its concrete roof and cantilevered canopy. And it is fairly certain that the large spacious new Euston Station built in 1965–8 (regional architect: R. L. Moorcraft) owes something to Rome. There are, however, no great parallel halls as at Rome, instead there is a spacious central square concourse flanked on the left (as one enters) by booking and other offices, and on the right by restaurants and waiting rooms. Beyond the platform barriers along the further side of the concourse and corridor extensions to right and left, ramps slope down to the platforms. On the entrance side of the concourse escalators and stairs go down to the underground station, and to the access area under the station for cars and taxis, where there are car parking areas, a very satisfactory arrangement although access by bus is not so close or convenient. The long low façade of the station with the long white horizontal bands and vertical black punctuations of the extensive fenestration is effective, but it has not the impressiveness of the Rome station.

BUS GARAGES AND STATIONS AND MULTI-STOREY CAR PARKS

The most distinctive modern structures for road transport, other than bridges, are bus garages and multi-storey car parks, some of which are notable, but they hardly compensate for the visual pollution of the innumerable ugly petrol stations throughout Europe that is one of the main eyesores that has come with the motor vehicle. Bus garages and stations are sometimes impressive because of the magnificent roofs.

A notable early example of a large garage is that at Berne, built in 1948–50, for the bus fleet of the Swiss Postal Service and designed by E. Hostettler, H. Daxelhofer and P. Indermuhle. The long rectangular garage is about 400 feet long with a span of 95 feet and divided into seventeen bays each of which has a vertical roof light provided by the lunette formed by the segmental roof of steel ribs. The garage is on the first floor which is supported by two intermediate columns between the through columns that support the roof. Seven-storey blocks at either end are occupied by offices, storage and workshops. Built about the same time (1950) is the bus garage in Stockwell, London, designed by Adie, Button and Partners, which is notable for its concrete roof. It consists of ten concrete arches of 194 feet span. Each arch has cantilevered butterfly wings which are linked together by roof lights forming a series of arched bays 40 feet wide.

A notable bus station that has been widely admired is that at Dublin built in 1947–52 and designed by Michael Scott. In the internal space of an L formed by two office blocks (7 and 4 storeys) is the square concourse for passengers in the outer corner of which is the two-storey enquiry office. Underneath the large office block on two floors are shops, restaurant, bar and waiting rooms, while the main entrance is under the other block. Buses (17) stand diagonally along the two outer sides of the concourse, and there is an attractive corrugated canopy projecting from the concourse building, which is particularly effective above the curved glass first floor window of the enquiry office. The efficiency and attractive appearance of this bus station has won for it widespread admiration.

Among the fascinating new subjects for the architect is the multi-storey car park which began to be erected in many towns and cities of Europe in the early fifties, and by the early seventies there were some distinctive examples. As they mostly occupy sites in or near central areas an acceptable appearance is, or should be, one of the essential conditions, and in several cases these conditions have been fulfilled. One of the earliest and best-known examples is that which occupies the south side of the central area of Dusseldorf. It was designed by P. Schneider Esleben and built in 1950–1. It is a four-storey structure with basement, to accommodate 500 cars, of reinforced concrete wing supports, concrete floors, cantilevered roofs, and glass walls in light steel framing between the floors. External ramps are suspended at the sides of the structure, while in front, where the cars enter and depart, is a two-storey structure open on the ground floor with wing concrete supports for the first floor. This simple structure looks well, especially when illuminated at night. It influenced the design of similar structures in other German cities, one attractive example being at Darmstadt.

Several attractively designed multi-storey car parks have been erected in Britain especially in the new towns, two examples which call for special mention are those at Hemel Hempstead and Cwmbran. The former is a four-storey circular structure which is situated at the southern end of the town centre bordering the lake of the water garden, and near a long slab block of offices and a tower block, which altogether form a very attractive group and a notable example of landscape architecture which is deservedly famous. The multi-storey car park was designed by Maurice Bebb and built in 1963.

The centre of Cwmbran is a pedestrian precinct, surrounded by a ring road beyond which are four multi-storey car parks, built between 1964 and 1972, the two first beyond the periphery road and linked with the town centre by pedestrian underpasses, and the two later within the periphery road. They are attractively designed and add to the architectural interest of the centre. One of the earlier buildings has two long horizontals bands of vertical concrete strips alternating with plain walls which makes an attractive decorative treatment. These examples demonstrate the scope for effective

Multi-storey Car Park, Munich, West Germany

Multi-storey Car Park, with double
spiral ramp, Kassel, West Germany

Multi-storey Car Park, Dusseldorf, 1950–51
Architect: P. Schneider Esleben

Multi-storey Car Park near Water Gardens, town centre Hemel Hempstead, 1963
Architect: Maurice Bebb

Multi-storey Car Park, town centre, Cwmbran, Wales, circa 1966
Architect: Gordon F. Redfern, architect to the Development Corporation, 1962–69

decorative design afforded by the multi-storey garage or car park, and are an aesthetic argument for providing these in place of the large open car parks, ugly features of the urban scene that should be eliminated or minimized as much as possible, and the well designed multi-storey car park is one way of doing it.

AIRPORTS

There is little guidance in design for passenger terminal buildings of airports among traditional buildings, and the architect and his team are starting largely from scratch. Perhaps the nearest among traditional buildings is the large railway terminus, for in principle there are the similarities of access by road and of passing through reception areas to the transport beyond, but there are obvious differences which become more and more apparent with the development and extension of air transport. The size of the terminal buildings of a large airport in the seventies exceeds the largest railway station.

Before the Second World War during the thirties, when air travel was still in its infancy, airport buildings were on a small scale and were mostly rectangular blocks containing reception and departure areas and offices with road access on one side and the airfield on the other side, with hangars in various parts of the periphery. The prototype of the railway terminus was apparent. Only in a few instances was there the attempt at an entirely new and non-traditional design in answer to the new requirements, but a few designs prompted interest as fresh ingenious solutions to the problems presented. One is the small airport at Gatwick, built in 1936 and designed by Frank Hoar, Alan Marlow and Benjamin Lovett. It is situated near the railway from London to Brighton and the airport was linked by a subway with Gatwick station. The building is circular in shape about 170 feet in diameter on the ground floor. Here there is a central circular concourse, with shops and post office, and from this radiate five corridors each of which had telescopic canopies that were run out to the aircraft that circulated in an anti-clockwise direction. Equi-distant between two of the corridors is the main entrance into a customs examination hall, and round the circumference between the corridors are offices for various purposes. On the first floor, set back, is a restaurant, and the third floor consists of a drum about 50 feet diameter in which is the control room, while there is a roof terrace on the first floor. Construction is of reinforced concrete with a central column to which are attached concrete ring beams. This airport building still survives, but is no longer used as such (being replaced by the modern airport, built a mile to the north in 1956–73). It appears as a very pleasingly designed building sitting well in the landscape. The functional ingenuity of its design, which in principle has probably not been improved upon, and its architectural distinctiveness, prompts the hope that it will be preserved as a monument of distinctive progressive architecture of the thirties.

Before and immediately after the Second World War the location of airports was

670

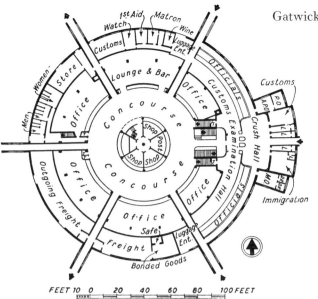

Gatwick Airport, near London, 1936. Plan, elevation and general view
Architects: Frank Hoar, Alan Marlow and Benjamin Lovett

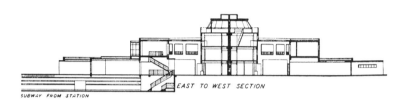

SUBWAY FROM STATION   EAST TO WEST SECTION

Gatwick Airport, near London, 1956–70
Main airport buildings and artist's impression
*Architects: F. R. S. Yorke, Cyril Mardell
and Eugene Rosenberg*

determined by the proximity of centres of population (called air traffic hubs in the USA), ease of access to and from them, by climatic conditions, and by the navigational hazards such as tall buildings. Thus in Europe most of the large airports are sited on flat ground within easily accessible distances from the big centres of population. Thus Heathrow airport is 15 miles west of the centre of London, Gatwick 27 miles south, Le Bourget and Orly airports both 10 miles from the centre of Paris, the Leonardo da Vinci airport 20 miles from Rome, Sheremetyevo airport 15 miles and Vnukovo airport 18 miles from Moscow, to give a few European examples. Some, especially those serving smaller cities are closer in. Little thought was given in the early days to the effects of noise pollution on surrounding residential areas, but with bigger and faster aircraft needing longer runways (3,000 feet in 1935, 10,000 feet in 1965), the minimizing of noise pollution gradually became a major consideration, and this was a prime consideration in ultimately siting the third London airport at Maplin in southeast Essex, rather than among the built-up areas of the Midlands. Ease and convenience of access it is also realized is less a matter of proximity than of rapidity of transit. Thus the link with Maplin will be by high-speed railway trains with speeds up to 125 miles an hour, and the journey of 50 miles from the centre of London will take less time than the 15 miles by road to Heathrow. The tendency in the future is likely to be towards siting airports well away from closely built-up areas, preferably on the sea coast.

Several notable airport terminal buildings have been erected in Europe since 1950, most of which represent slightly different interpretations of the best way of satisfying the essential requirements, and a few are architecturally interesting. Probably the largest in Europe, and that which handles the most passengers annually is Heathrow, which began to be constructed shortly after the war. Air terminal buildings are usually sited on one side of the airfield of between a thousand and three thousand acres, but London and Amsterdam provide exceptions of having the terminal buildings in the centre. Heathrow airport was originally constructed in 1944–5 as a large transport airfield for the R.A.F., but the war ended before it was used for this purpose and it was taken over by the civil avaiation authorities to form the basis for the new London airport in place of the existing one at Croydon, which was becoming inadequate with little scope for the necessary extension. Three runways forming a triangle had been laid out at Heathrow, three more were added forming another, reverse, triangle overlapping the first and thus forming a hexagram plan. In the centre the terminal buildings were erected with road—part tunnel—access from the periphery. The buildings designed by Sir Frederick Gibberd and Partners were begun in 1950, and the last was completed in 1970. The first buildings are a group of three which consist of the control building roughly in the form of a large T on plan, with the nine-storeyed control tower at the crossing, the southeast face building, and the long eastern apex building. The later terminal building completed in 1970 marks a considerable advance in functional design. It is a long rectangular building divided vertically into two main

Heathrow Airport, near London, 1950–70. Aircraft dispersal bay, and new terminal building, 1970
Architects: Sir Frederick Gibberd and Partners

Renfrew Airport, Glasgow, 1953,
superseded by Abbotsinch

Abbotsinch Airport terminal building,
1964–66 *Architect: Sir Basil Spence*

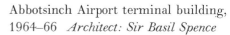

levels for arriving and departing passengers with two-level road access. The former use the ground floor and the latter the upper floor and the two streams are kept separate at these different levels, with the exception of passengers arriving by bus from the London central terminal which passes through the building at ground level and from which arriving passengers are taken to the first floor. The interior is essentially an open hall with large continuous fenestration which assists both circulation and visibility.

Among other British airport buildings which merit attention are that at Gatwick and Abbotsinch at Glasgow. The former designed by F. R. S. Yorke, Cyril Mardell and Eugene Rosenberg has the valuable facility of being served by an adjacent newly built railway station, and with easy road access. The large concourse for handling everything on one level is on the first floor, and road access is ramped to this level on the north entrance side. Three corridor fingers at concourse level go out to the aircraft, originally one, but two were added later. The walls of the upper level are mainly glass which gives a good view of the airfield from the departure lounge.

The new Abbotsinch airport terminal at Glasgow[1], designed by Sir Basil Spence, and built in 1964–6 is seven miles from the centre of the city. It is a long rectangular building and, like the first main London terminal reception for baggage is on the ground floor with the concourse area with restaurants and bars on the first floor. The wall on the air side is a large glass area giving an extensive view and, as at Gatwick, long corridor fingers go out to the aircraft. Departing passengers use the central part of the building and arriving passengers go to either end. It would perhaps have been an advantage if everything could have been on one level as at Gatwick, but this would have greatly added to cost as it would have meant the construction of an elevated roadway. Construction is by a series of concrete columns with a series of barrel vaults forming the roof and extension can easily be effected by adding further bays at either end. The general effect of the projecting arched roof and the large areas of fenestration with vertical punctuation make a distinctive building.

Among notable European airport terminal buildings is the immense structure of Orly airport completed in the early sixties, which provides such a multiplicity of facilities for the traveller as to be like a small town. It is a large rectangular block with a symmetrical formation of access roads which makes an attractive pattern seen from the air. Zürich airport (1956–60) is sited between curved forms, with an elliptical building on the land side linked with a rectangular building with a large glass wall on the air side, one of the earliest examples of this feature in European airports. A distinctive feature of the large Leonardo da Vinci airport (1958–60), near Ostia Antica southwest of Rome, is the great central hall with the glass front, with corridors on either side. The central part is on three levels following a customary arrangement of baggage and services on the ground floor, and passenger concourse, transit and lounges on the first

Orly Airport, terminal building, near Paris, circa 1957–63

Orly Airport, main approach

Athens Airport, 1962–64, main concourse
Architect: Eero Saarinen

Athens Airport, exterior view of air side

floor. A dramatic effect is given to the building by the steel roof with its light box beams and the generous cantilevering in front. One of the most beautiful airport buildings is that at Athens designed by Eero Saarinen and built in 1962–4. It is a large rectangular concrete structure with generous bands of fenestration high up which makes the hall exceedingly light. The building, like Gropius's American Embassy building at Athens, has a Greek-like repose and serenity which accords with the character of this classical city. It is in marked contrast to Saarinen's other famous airport building, the T.W.A. terminal building at the Kennedy airport in New York, in which the curves of shell concrete make one think of modern sculpture.

The few examples of airport buildings cited are sufficient to indicate the diversity of design possible within the functional requirements. Serving constantly expanding needs there is obviously great scope for imaginative architects in the design of future airports[2]. A few have already added to the world's distinctive architecture.

REFERENCES AND NOTES

1. This replaces Renfrew airport, the terminal building of which was erected in 1953. It was an impressive design, the structure being supported by a prominent central parabolic arch to which cables were attached from cantilever beams. The design was a little reminiscent of Le Corbusier's design for the Palace of the Soviets.
2. If and when short and vertical take-off and landing become the norm the design of airports would in some degree be affected and there would be less objection to siting them in built up areas. But STOL and VTOL have been discussed since the early post-war years (1945–50) and it is doubtful whether we are much nearer to their realization in 1973.

46 *The urban environment and the well-being of man*

SENSITIVITY TO URBAN environment necessarily varies considerably and is experienced in several degrees of consciousness. Some people, because of a strongly developed aesthetic sense resulting partly from natural ability, partly from education and the study of art are acutely aware of the urban environment and experience pleasure and pain often to a very powerful degree. But a large number are only partly conscious of the effects of urban environment, although such effects may be considerable. Some people are very conscious of the influence of the weather on their feelings: how a cold, dull, dark, rainy day may produce, or greatly aggravate, depression; whereas a bright, sunny, peaceful day, especially if it is after turbulent weather, will prompt feelings of cheerfulness and well-being and the sense that it is good to be alive. This feeling is often intensely experienced in the early mornings of sunny days in Spring, especially in Mediterranean countries[1]. There are those, however, who will deny the effects of weather on their feelings, but it is probable that in some of these instances the effects are there but are not conscious.

The same, although perhaps in a modified form, can be said of the urban environment. To the person, without any specially cultivated aesthetic sensibilities, who has lived in a town for some years the surroundings have become very familiar and he is perhaps only partly conscious of them, certainly not as conscious as the visitor who comes with the special purpose of looking at the architecture and urban design. Yet the former vaguely likes some parts and dislikes others and in an habitual walk will choose to go one way rather than another. Large, dark, ugly, forbidding buildings are known to be repugnant to children and prompts them to avoid going where such buildings are, and it is probable that they have similar effects on sensitive adults. The choice of one way rather than another is often decided by aesthetic considerations consciously or subconsciously felt. A good deal of evidence could be adduced to show that we are subconsciously and unconsciously influenced by our environment to a greater extent than we generally know, and one of the purposes of education and training should be to bring these factors to greater consciousness, with a view to determining an urban environment which is visually pleasing and conducive to a general feeling of well-being.

Any doubts that once existed that the unconscious and partly conscious impulses and emotions have a powerful influence on our conduct and attitudes were convincingly dispersed by Freud's theories of psychoanalysis, and it is now fairly widely accepted that these unconscious urges are part of the instinctive basis of our lives. The repression of instinctive urges, often an habitual and only partly conscious controlling force, results in conflict and sometimes in some form of neurosis, and it is one of the purposes of an enlightened and broadly based education system to bring these instinctive urges to consciousness, and to reconcile current notions and precepts of conduct and feeling with the instinctive urges. As J. C. Flugel implies the purpose of self knowledge, to which psychoanalysis contributes, 'is to extend our powers of rational insight and control. The biological value of conscious mind lies in its capacity for delicate discrimination and adaptation. The unconscious instincts and reflexes by which our lives, like those of other animals, are so largely determined, doubtless have great value for rough orientation towards our environment'. They are, however, 'incapable of those finer adjustments of means to ends, which, when organized and coordinated in physical science, have enabled man to win an altogether unique power over Nature'. 'Knowledge and control of our own selves', he continues, 'will alone enable us to use this power for beneficial rather than for harmful and self-destructive ends'[2].

It is, therefore, important that subconscious and unconscious reactions of man to his environment, including the urban scene, should be brought as much as possible to consciousness so that he can more effectually control that environment in the interests of his own well-being. As the result of education and cultural development probably a greater number of persons are visually aware of pleasing and distasteful urban environment than ever before, so that things like squalid, black, industrial towns are less likely to be tolerated, yet there is still a good deal of industrial and transport pollution that can only be overcome by a more enlightened assertive public opinion. An obligation is, therefore, placed on all those responsible for the character of the urban scene: governments both national, regional and local, the owners of buildings whether institutions or individuals, architects and planners and their teams.

One of the difficulties in achieving a widely acceptable aesthetically pleasing urban environment is of establishing standards which shall act as guides to those responsible for what is and is not good civic design, and a pleasing or unpleasing urban scene. These are largely subjective and matters of opinion. Yet experience in the long history of art indicates that in matters of artistic taste there is a wide measure of agreement after works of art really become known, and the aims of artists appreciated sufficiently so for such agreement. Thus a collective subjectivity results which, because this aesthetic enjoyment is the possession of many minds and of society as a whole, becomes in one sense objective. According to Samuel Alexander[3] beauty only becomes a value, with the values of truth and goodness, when it becomes a common possession of society and, 'satisfies a standard mind'. If a work of art pleases one or only a few individuals as beautiful, then it is hardly a value, to become so it must satisfy a wide consensus of opinion. The comparison of this line of thought becomes clearer when applied to the other values of truth and goodness.

If aesthetic standards for urban design are to be established, as they should be for the benefit of society, then it is important that these should be based on aesthetic principles that derive, as far as can be ascertained, from the natural processes of visual perception and enjoyment, rather than from intellectual conceptions derived from historical styles and building types.

The essential stages of visual perception are firstly the two-dimensional colour pattern, secondly the perception of three-dimensional space and objects in space, and thirdly the recognition of the significance of objects. Many philosophers and scientists, Berkeley, Helmholtz, Wundt, Stumpf, Hering, Lipps and Reid[4] assert that our first visual experience is two dimensional, and that perception of space and objects in space, result from the experience of our bodily extension and touch, and the coordination of this with vision. William James refutes this[5] and contends that three-dimensional perception is an optical faculty. There is more evidence to support Berkeley and his followers. After the first few months of life, however, the transition from two dimensional perception to three dimensional awareness is so rapid as to be almost simultaneous. The third stage is the recognition of the significance of objects, that it is a house or tree or chair, which is accomplished by reference to the stock of images in the mind, a reference which is generally correct but is liable to error. (A. N. Whitehead has neatly classified stages of perception as presentational immediacy, symbolic reference and causal efficacy[6]. The first is the perception of coloured shapes, the second is the reference to the image reservoir in the brain and the third, the causal efficacy, the identity of the object.)

Aesthetic experience comes with the emotion of pleasure that accompanies each stage of perception. In the first two stages of perception, that is of coloured shapes, and of space and objects in space, pleasurable contemplation is mainly aesthetic, and is the essential aesthetic experience. The contemplation may be painful or indifferent and if that is the case for everybody, then it is devoid of aesthetic value. But when such contemplation is very pleasurable for many people it acquires aesthetic value. With the third stage, that is awareness of the identity and significance of objects, many emotions come into being mainly from a wide variety of associations and the scene and its objects are evaluated for numerous non-aesthetic reasons. This third stage corresponds to the secondary values given by several philosophers among them Francis Hutcheson, Lord Kames and Immanuel Kant, whose theories on this subject are often discussed[7]. The essence of these theories is that the first essential kind of beauty is the delight in the object for itself, in its coloured shapes, or as a group of colours or objects in space seen in the abstract, and the second relative or dependant beauty relates to, or depends on, a concept of what it is. Applied to the visual arts this second mode of perception is very much less important aesthetically than the first. It will be seen, therefore, that the essential aesthetic values depend on things seen in the abstract without reference to their practical import, and their identity and practical meaning is wholly subordinate. This is a philosophic conclusion based on the natural processes of perception which architects and many architectural critics do not always appreciate[8]. As a first condition of architectural excellence they appear to require that a church, factory, school, town hall, railway station should look like what they are. But how do they know what these buildings should look like? Merely from their knowledge of the appearance of these buildings in various historical periods, so they are judging the appearance of a new building on historical concepts of what it should be like. If the church looks like a factory, or the town hall like a railway station they are apt to condemn these buildings for not, as they would say, looking like what they are. These are non-essentials. What is important is that if the church is efficient for its purpose, is soundly constructed and is a unified composition of forms with good patterns of light and shadow and harmonizes with its surroundings, then it succeeds in essentials in being good architecture, although it may look more like their idea of a factory than of a church.

It is, therefore, possible to establish an order of priorities in architectural requirements and of civic design, so as to achieve a satisfactory urban environment ultimately satisfactory to the majority, although it may not always be so immediately because of the intellectual concepts mentioned.

The first essential, without which all else is aesthetically minor, is that buildings and the general townscape, shall be pleasing in the abstract, that they should be good unified or rhythmical compositions or patterns of forms, masses, colour, light and shadow, and that different buildings should relate well to each other. This gives tremendous freedom in urban development, freedom especially from historical, stylistic and intellectual concepts. It means that when a new building is to be erected in a square of Georgian buildings the essential is that there should be in the new building a composition of form and mass that shall be in harmony with the rest of the square, and that stylistic conformity should on no account be required, but the new building should be in the idiom of and expressive of its own time. This may be difficult for some authorities to accept[9], but it is important that such authorities should be guided by knowledgeable and imaginative advice.

Expression of the purpose of a building and of its structure are important in the aesthetic result as providing essential subjects for expression which give varied and interesting forms to buildings. That a building should function efficiently, and that it should be structurally sound are essential requirements of the clients and the users,

680

but that the building should be delightful to contemplate is the concern of everybody. The architect and his client have, therefore, an obligation to society, for it is they, together with the urban planner, who perhaps do most to create the urban environment. By study and experience the architect and urban planner become aware of what is aesthetically satisfactory, and it is they who on behalf of the community should do their utmost to see that work conforms to standards of excellence. They must resist compromise if it means a lessening of standards. One of the great architects of the century, Eric Mendelsohn, said, when lecturing to students, 'that many of you who sit here have talents far greater than mine, but few of you will fulfil your potential greatness, because you will quickly learn to compromise and settle for less than the best of which you are capable'. If the urban environment is to be beautiful as it could be, then Society must give architects and planners the opportunities to settle for the best of which they are capable.

References and Notes

1. Shelley in his Preface to *Prometheus Unbound* says that it was written upon the mountainous ruins of the Baths of Caracella. 'The bright blue sky of Rome', he continues, 'and the effect of the vigorous awakening spring in that divinest climate, and the new life with which it drenches the spirits even to intoxication, were the inspiration of this drama'.
2. J. C. Flugel, *An Introduction to Psycho-Analysis*, Victor Gollancz, London, 1932, p. 156.
3. See Samuel Alexander, *Beauty and other forms of Value*, Macmillan, London, 1933, chapter on The Objectivity of Beauty, pp. 172–187.
4. George Berkeley, *New Theory of Vision*, sections I–LI, 1907. Several editions published, for example see Everyman Library edition, Dent, London, 1910.
5. William James, *Principles of Psychology*, New York, 1891.
6. A. N. Whitehead, *Symbolism—Its Meaning and Effect*, Cambridge ,1928.
7. Frances Hutcheson, *An Enquiry into the Original of our Ideas of Beauty and Virtue*, 1725; Lord Kames, *Elements of Criticism*, 1762; Immanuel Kant, *The Critique of Judgement*, 1790, English translation by James Creed Meredith, Oxford University Press, 1928.
8. Rayner Banham praises Rome railway station for achieving the rare feat of looking like a railway station as among its principal merits, but goes on to appreciate its chief merit in contributing something impressive to the urban scene. *Guide to Modern Architecture*, Architectural Press, London, 1967.
9. Examples of refusal of planning permission because a proposed new building did not conform stylistically with its neighbours, or because it was outrageously modern are not uncommon. Authorities can claim to represent public opinion which is often vociferous against the unfamiliar. An example is the objection to Highpoint Flats discussed in Chapter 24. I remember when staying at an hotel at Folkestone listening to the protests about allowing a modern block of flats at the end of a crescent of Victorian houses, curving round a green on the sea front. I, therefore, visited the crescent and was agreeably surprised to note how well the modern block of flats accorded in scale and massing with the Victorian houses. How disastrous, I thought, if the block of flats had been a stylistic imitation of the Victorian houses.

681

Bibliography

[I] BOOKS ON MODERN ARCHITECTURE—GENERAL

Pica Agnoldomenier, *Nuova Architettura nel Mondo*, Milan, 1936.

Reyner Banham, *Guide to Modern Architecture*, Architectural Press, London, 1962.

Piero Bargellini and Enrico Freynie, *Nascita e Vita dell' Architettura Moderna*, Florence, 1947.
In this book on the birth and life of modern architecture the history of the modern movement is traced from Carlo Sodoli, a Venetian monk of the early eighteenth century, who is described as the spiritual father of architectural rationalism. Chapters are devoted to Walter Gropius, Le Corbusier, and Alvar Aalto among others.

Walter Curt Behrendt, *Modern Building*, London, 1937.

Leonardo Benevolo, *Storia dell' Architettura Moderna*, Bari, 1960.

Martin S. Briggs, *Building Today*, Oxford University Press, London 1944.

A. S. G. Butler, *The Substance of Architecture*, London, 1927.

Sheldon Cheney, *The New World Architecture*, London, 1930.

Kenneth Clark, *The Gothic Revival*, London, 1929.

Peter Collins, *Changing Ideals in Modern Architecture 1750–1950*, Faber & Faber, London, 1965.

A. Dorgelo, *Modern European Architecture*, Elsevier Publishing Co., Amsterdam, 1959.

Constantinos A. Doxiadis, *Architecture in Transition*, Hutchinson, London, 1963.

R. A. Duncan, *The Architecture of a New Era*, London, 1933.

A. Trystan Edwards, *Architectural Style*, London, 1926. Second edition with the title *Style and Composition in Architecture*, London, 1944.

Sir Banister Fletcher, *History of Architecture on the Comparative Method*, first sixteen editions, London 1896–1952. Good description and analysis of architectural developments up to about 1800, but after that they become more summary. Sir Banister Fletcher died in 1953 and a seventeenth edition was published by Athlone Press in 1961 which was revised by R. A. Cordingly and a team of contributors.

Maxwell Fry, *Fine Building*, Faber and Faber, London, 1944.

Tony Garnier, *Etude pour la Construction des Villes*, Paris, 1917. *Les Grande Travaux de la Ville de Lyon, Etudes, Projets et Travaux Executes Hopitaux, Evoles, Postes, Abattoirs, Habitations en Commun, Stade, etc.*, Paris, 1921.

Sigfried Giedion, *Space, Time and Architecture*, Cambridge, U.S.A. 1941.

Walter Gropius, *The New Architecture and the Bauhaus*, Faber and Faber, London, 1935.

Talbot Hamlin, *Architecture an Art for all Men*, Columbia University Press, New York, 1947.

Gerd Hatje (Editor), *Knaurs Lexikon der Modernen Architektur*, München-Zürich, 1963. English edition, *Encyclopedia of Modern Architecture*, Thames and Hudson, London, 1963.

Ludwig Hilbersheimer, *Internationale Neue Baukunst*, Stuttgart, 1926; *Grossstadtarchitektur* Stuttgart, 1927.

Oliver Hill, *Fair Horizon, Buildings of Today*, Collins, London, 1950.

Henry-Russell Hitchcock, *Romanticism and Reintegration*, New York, 1929.

Henry-Russell Hitchcock, *Architecture: Nineteenth and Twentieth Centuries*, Harmondsworth, 1958.

Henry-Russell Hitchcock, and Phillip Johnson, *Modern Architecture*, New York, 1932.

Jürgen Joedicke, *A History of Modern Architecture*, Stuttgart, Architectural Press, London, 1968.

Jürgen Joedicke, *Architecture since 1945 Sources and Directions*, Karl Kramer, Stuttgart, Pall Mall Press, London 1969.

Le Corbusier, *Vers une Architecture*, Paris, 1923. English translation of the 13th edition by Frederick Etchells, John Rodker, London 1931.

El Lissitzky, *Die Rekonstruktion der Architektur in der Sowjetunion*. Leipzig, 1930.

Ir. J. B. Van Loghem, *Vers une Architecture Reele*. Amsterdam, 1932.

J. L. Martin, Ben Nicholson, and N. Gabo (Editors), *Circle-International Survey of Constructive Art*, Faber and Faber, London, 1937. Consists of four sections (1) Painting, (2) Sculpture, (3) Architecture, and (4) Art and Life. The section on architecture includes fifty-two plates of illustrations mostly of work of the early thirties and essays on *the Condition of Architecture and the Principle of Anonymity*, by J. M. Richards, *Town Planning*, by Maxwell Fry, *Architecture and Material*, by Marcel Breuer, *Routes of Housing Advance*, by Richard J. Neutra, *Colour in Interior Architecture*, by Alberto Sartoris, *The State of Transition*, by J. L. Martin, and *Construction and Aesthetics*, by Sigfried Giedion. Among the essays in the section on Art and Life are *Art Education and State*, by Walter Gropius, *A Note on Biotechnics*, by Karel Honzig, and *The Death of the Monument* (extract from The Culture of Cities), by Lewis Mumford.

Eric Mendelsohn, *Three Lectures on Architecture*, San Francisco, 1943.

Nikolaus Pevsner, *Pioneers of the Modern Movement*, Faber and Faber, London, 1936. A second and enlarged American edition, New York, 1949. A further edition with the title changed to *Pioneers of Modern Design*, was published by Penguin Books in 1960.

Gustav Adolf Platz, *Die Baukunst der Neuesten Zeit*, Berlin, 1930.

Steen Eile Rasmussen, *Towns and Buildings*, Copenhagen, 1949. English edition 1951. In this book the purpose is to present buildings from ancient times to the present day, in relation to the town or city as a whole. The last section, entitled Functionalism, deals with Ebenezer Howard's idea of a garden city and Le Corbusier's ideas for urban development.

J. M. Richards, *An Introduction to Modern Architecture*, Penguin, London, 1940.

A. E. Richardson and Hector C. Corfiato, *The Art of Architecture*, English Universities Press, London, 1938. A general history of architecture which includes a section on modern architecture with short studies of modern types of buildings.

Howard Robertson, *Architecture Explained*, London, 1926, Chapters 10 and 11.

Howard Robertson, *Modern Architectural Design*, London, 1932. Second revised edition, 1952.

Howard Robertson, *Architecture Arising*, Faber and Faber, London, 1944.

Manning Robertson, *Everyday Architecture*, London, 1924.

Alfred Roth, *The New Architecture*, Erlenbach, Zürich, 1940. Second edition 1946, third edition 1947. Twenty examples of modern architecture are illustrated and described in French, German and English. The period covered is from 1930 to 1939.

Alberto Sartoris, *Gli Elementi dell' Architettura Funzionale*, Milan, 1935. One of the largest collections of illustrations of modern architecture brought together in a single volume.

Alberto Sartoris, *Encyclopedie de l'Architecture Nouvelle*, 3 vols., Milan, 1954–57.

Hans Scharoun and others, *Handbook Moderner Architektur*, Safari-Verlag, Berlin, 1957. Scharoun writes the introduction: Struktur in Raum und Zeit, and the other sections are: Fritz Jaspert: *Stadtebau*, Ernst May: *Wohnungsbau*, Otto Ernst Schweizer: *Ein Familienhauser*, Friedrich Wilhelm

Bibliography

Kraemer: *Bautender Wirtschaft und Verwaltung*, Rudolf Hillebrecht: *Neuaufbauder Stadte*, Gustav Hassenpflug: *Krankenhausbau*, Martin Elzasser: *Schulen Universitaten, Kindergarten, Jugendherbergen*, Werner Harting: *Theater und Konzertzale, Kines Ausstellungsbau*, Gerhard Langmaack: *Evangelische Kirchen*, Willy Weyres: *Katholische Kirchen* and Reinhold Niemeyer: *Verkehrsbauten*.

Denis Sharp, *A Visual History of Twentieth Century Architecture*, Heinemann/Secker and Warburg, 1973. In this visual record, buildings are usefully grouped under dates with copious notes.

G. E. Kidder Smith, *The New Architecture of Europe*, Penguin Books, London, 1966.

John Summerson, *Heavenly Mansions*, London, 1949. A collection of ten essays on architecture, two of which: *Architecture, Painting and Le Corbusier* and *The Mischievous Analogy* are stimulating commentaries on aspects of twentieth century architecture.

Bruno Taut, *Modern Architecture*, The Studio, London, 1929.

Frederic Towndrow, *Architecture in the Balance*, London, 1933.

Bruno Zevi, *Towards an Organic Architecture*, Faber and Faber, London, 1950.

Bruno Zevi, *Storia dell' Architettura Moderna*, third edition, Einaudi, Turin, 1955.

[II] STUDIES OF MODERN ARCHITECTURE IN SPECIFIC COUNTRIES

Pica Agnoldomenico, *Nuova Architettura Italiana*, Milan, 1936. Illustrations of modern Italian buildings.

H. Ahlberg, *Swedish Architecture of the 20th Century*, London, 1925.

Architecture Club, *Recent English Architecture 1920–40*, London, 1947. A collection of sixty-five photographs of English architecture between the wars selected by the Architecture Club.

Sir Reginald Blomfield, *Byways: Leaves from an Architect's Note-book*, London, 1929. Contains a chapter dealing with modern buildings in Stockholm.

Ulrich Conrads, *Modern Architecture in Germany*, Architectural Press, London, 1962.

A. Eibink, W. J. Garetsen, and J. P. L. Hendriks. *Hedendaagiche Architecture in Nederland*, Amsterdam, 1937.

E. M. Hajos and L. Zahn (Editors), *Berliner Architektur der Nachkriegszeit*, Albertus, Berlin, 1928. Illustrations of modern buildings in Berlin with a list of the principal architects and their work, and a short introduction by Edwin Redslob.

Gerd Hatje and others, *New German Architecture*, Architectural Press, London, 1956.

J. P. Mieras, *Dutch Architecture of Today*, Amsterdam, 1937. A book of illustrations of modern Dutch architecture with an introduction printed in Dutch, German, French and English.

Edward D. Mills, *The New Architecture in Great Britain*, London, 1953.

Cargo Pagani, *Italy's Architecture Today*, Hoepli, Milan, 1955.

J. M. Richards, *A Guide to Finnish Architecture*, Hugh Evelyn, London, 1966.

Howard Robertson, *The Architecture of Finland*, Architectural Review, Vols. VI and VII, 1924–26.

Howard Robertson, and F. R. Yerbury, *Examples of Modern French Architecture*, London, 1928.

G. E. Kidder Smith, *Sweden Builds*, second edition, Architectural Press, London, 1957.

G. E. Kidder Smith, *Switzerland Builds*, Architectural Press, London, 1950.

G. E. Kidder Smith, *Italy Builds*, Architectural Press, London, 1955.

Hans Volkart, *Schweizer Architecktur*, Raversberg, 1951.

Arthur Voyce, *Russian Architecture. Trends in Nationalism and Modernism*, Philosophical Library, New York, 1948. Divided into two main parts: (1) The Pre-Revolutionary Period, (2) The Revolutionary Period and Contemporary Soviet Architecture.

684

[III] STUDIES OF INDIVIDUAL ARCHITECTS

Peter Blake, *Marcel Breuer: Architect and Designer*, New York, 1949.
Victor Bourgeois, Architectures 1922–1952, Brussels, 1952. Illustrations with descriptions of the work of Victor Bourgeois with an introduction entitled *L'homme et l'oeuvre*, by Pierre-Louis Flouquet.
J. E. Cirlot, *El Arte de Gaudi*, second edition, Barcelona, 1954.
Francoise Choay, *Le Corbusier*, Braziller, New York and Mayflower, London, 1960.
George R. Collins, *Antonio Gaudi*, Braziller, New York and Mayflower, London, 1960.
Arthur Drexler, *Ludwig Miës van der Rohe*, Braziller, New York and Mayflower, London, 1960.
Wolf Von Eckardt, *Eric Mendelsohn*, Braziller, New York and Mayflower, London, 1960.
Frederick Gutheim, *Alvar Aalto*, Braziller, New York and Mayflower, London, 1960.
Thomas Howarth, *Charles Rennie Mackintosh and the Modern Movement*, Routledge and Kegan Paul, London, 1952.
Christopher Hussey, A. S. G. Butler and George Stewart, *The Lutyens Memorial Volumes: Life of Sir Edwin Lutyens*, by Christopher Hussey, vol. 1. *The Architecture of Sir Edwin Lutyens*, by A. S. G. Butler, with the collaboration of George Stewart and Christopher Hussey, London, 1951.
Ada Louise Huxtable, *Pier Luigi Nervi*, New York and London, 1960.
Philip C. Johnson, *Miës van der Rohe*, Museum of Modern Art, New York, 1947; second edition, 1953.
Giorgio Labo, *Alvar Aalto*, Il Balcone, Milan, 1948.
Mario Labo, *Giuseppe Tarragni*, Il Balcone, Milan, 1947.
Le Corbusier et Pierre Jeanneret, *Oeuvre Complete*, Seven vols., 1910–29, 1929–34, 1934–38, 1938–46, 1946–52, 1952–57, 1957–65, Thames and Hudson, London. All except vol. 3 are edited by W. Boesiger, vol. 3 is edited by Max Bill.
J. McAndrew and S. Breines, *Alvar Aalto*, New York, 1938.
Carlo Melograni, *Giuseppe Pagano*, Il Bacone, Milan, 1949.
George Nelson. A series of articles on Architectures of Europe Today, in *Pencil Points*, vol. xvi, 1935: *Marcello Piacentini*, January; *Helweg-Moeller*, February; *Hans and Vassili Luckhardt*, March; *Gio Ponti*, May; *Le Corbusier*, July; *Ivar Tengbom*, November; *Ludwig Mies van der Rohe*, September; vol. xvii, 1936; *Giuseppe Vaccaro*, January; *Eugene Beaudouin*, March; *Raymond McGrath*, June; *Walter Gropius*, August; *Tecton* (group of seven architects), October.
Nikolaus Pevsner, *Charles R. Mackintosh*, Il Bacone, Milan, 1948.
Nikolaus Pevsner, *Adolf Loos*, Milan, Il Bacone, 1949.
Sir Charles H. Reilly, *Representative British Architects of the Present Day*, London, 1931. Studies of the work of *S. D. Adshead, Robert Atkinson, Sir Herbert Baker, Sir Reginald Blomfield, Arthur J. Davis, E. Guy Dawber, Clough Williams-Ellis, W. Curtis Green, H. V. Lanchester, Sir Edwin L. Lutyens, Sir Giles Gilbert Scott*, and *Walter Tapper*.
Ernesto Rogers, *Auguste Perret*, Il Bacone, Milan, 1949.
P. Morton Shand, Robert Maillart—The Architecture of a Great Swiss Engineer, *Journal of the Royal Institute of British Architects*, vol. 45, September, 1938.
Giulia Veronesi, *Tony Garnier*, Il Bacone, Milan, 1951.
Giulia Veronesi, *Joseph Maria Olbrich*, Il Bacone, Milan, 1952.
Giulia Veronesi, *J. J. Pieter Oud*, Il Bacone, Milan, 1953.
Arnold Whittick, *Eric Mendelsohn*, Leonard Hill, London, 1940; second edition, 1956.
Bruno Zevi, *Erik Gunnar Asplund*, Il Balcone, Milan, 1948.

[IV] STUDIES OF BUILDING TYPES

Christian Barman, *An Introduction to Railway Architecture*, London, 1950.

Bibliography

Gustaf Birch-Lindgren, *Modern Hospital Planning in Sweden and Other Countries*, Stockholm, 1951. An edition is printed in English.

Martin S. Briggs, *Puritan Architecture*, London, 1946. An account of the design and building of Free Churches from the sixteenth century, including descriptions and illustrations of twentieth-century examples.

A. Calverley Cotton, *Town Halls*, London, 1936.

J. Murray Easton and L. E. T. Cusden, *Recent Trends in Hospital Design*, Journal of the Royal Institute of British Architects, July, 1947.

Mordecai Gaveli, *New Theatres for Old*, London, 1947.

Peter Hammond, *Liturgy and Architecture*, London, 1962.

Peter Hammond (Editor), *Towards a Church Architecture*, London, 1962.

C. G. Holme (Editor), *Industrial Architecture*, The Studio, London, 1935. A series of illustrations of industrial buildings in Europe and America with explanatory notes and a short introduction by L. H. Bucknell.

Jürgen Joedicke, *Office Buildings*, English translation, Crosby Lockwood, London, 1962.

H. Kamenka, *Flats*, London, 1947.

London County Council, *London Housing*, London, 1937.

Norman Marshall, *The Other Theatre*, London, 1947.

Raymond McGrath, *Twentieth Century Houses*, Faber and Faber, London, 1934.

Bernard Miles, *The British Theatre*, London, 1948.

Edward D. Mills, *The Modern Factory*, Architectural Press, London, 1951.

Edward D. Mills, *The Modern Church*, Architectural Press, London, 1956.

Paul Nelson, Andre Schimmering, and J. H. Calsat. La Sante publique, *L'Architecture d'aujourd'hui*, Paris, no. 15, November 1947, and no. 17 April 1948. Two special numbers of the French Architectural Monthly, dealing with hospital planning and building. The first part of the 1947 issue deals with the organization of health services, and the second part is a comprehensive collection of modern hospital buildings grouped under five headings. (1) *Health Centres*, (2) *General Hospitals*, (3) *University Hospitals*, (4) *Special Hospitals* and (5) *Infirmary Schools*.

Basil Oliver, *The Renaissance of the English Public House*, London, 1947.

Dagoberto Ortensi, *Impianti Sportivi e Attrezature*, Rome, 1950. A comprehensive survey of sports grounds and sport buildings.

Sir Charles H. Reilly, Articles on buildings of the twenties and early thirties grouped according to types in the Architectural Review, vol. lxxvii, 1935. (1) *The Town Hall Problem*, March; (2) *Some Recent Churches*, April; (3) *The Modern Store*, May; (4) *Shop Fronts*, July; (5) *The Cinema*, August; (6) *Banks*, September; (7) *Railway Stations*, October; (8) *The Multiple Shop*, November.

Alfred Roth, *The New School*, Zürich, 1950. In English, French and German. After an introductory discussion of the various aspects of the modern school building, twenty-one examples are described and illustrated. The period covered is from 1930 to 1948.

P. Morton Shand, *Modern Theatres and Cinemas*, London, 1930.

G. E. Kidder Smith, *New Churches of Europe*, Architectural Press, London, 1964.

Sir Basil Spence, *Phoenix at Coventry: the Building of a Cathedral*, Geoffrey Bless, London, 1962.

C. G. Stillman and R. Castle Cleary, *The Modern School*, Architectural Press, London, 1949.

Henri Thoillier, *L'Hopital Francais*, second edition, Paris, 1947.

Jean Walter, *Renaissance de l'Architecture Medicale*, Paris, 1945.

Bryan and Norman Westwood, *The Modern Shop*, London, 1952.

Arnold Whittick and Johannes Schreiner, *The Small House Today and Tomorrow*, Leonard Hill, London, 1947. Second and enlarged edition, 1956.

H. Myles Wright and R. Gardner-Medwyn, *The Design of Nursery and Elementary Schools*, London, 1938.

F. R. S. Yorke, *The Modern House*, Architectural Press, London, 1934.

F. R. S. Yorke and Frederick Gibberd, *The Modern Flat*, Architectural Press, London, 1937. Second edition, 1961.

Paul Zucker, *Theatre und Lichtspielhauser*, Berlin, 1926. Illustrations with notes of theatres and cinemas mainly German, built between 1900 and 1925.

[v] CONSTRUCTION

Only books on developments in construction of modern historical significance, and on twentieth century methods and materials are included. General textbooks on building construction are plentiful and easily obtainable.

C. V. Blumfield, *The Development and Use of Barrel Vault Shell Construction*, London, 1947.

C. V. Blumfield, *Barrel Vault Shell Concrete Roofing—The Technical Aspects*. Article in *Building Digest*, vol. viii, no. 11, November, 1948.

Cement and Concrete Association, in *Proceedings of a Symposium on Concrete Shell Roof Construction*, 1952, London, 1954. Divided into three sections: *Architectural Aspects, Design and Research, Construction and Formwork.*

Edwin Chadwick, Model Houses at the Paris International Exhibition, *Illustrated London News*, London, 6th July 1867.

H. G. Cousins, *Shell Concrete Construction*, London, 1948.

Jean Demaret, *Esthetique et Construction des Ouvrages d'Art*, Paris, 1947. A history of bridge-building in France including modern iron, steel and concrete bridges.

Sir William Fairbairn, *On the Application of Cast and Wrought Iron to Building Purposes*, first edition, London, 1854. Fourth edition with additions, London, 1870.

Sigfried Giedion, *Bauen in Frankreich: Eisen, Eisenbeton*, Leipzig, 1928.

John Gloag and Derek Bridgwater, *A History of Cast Iron in Architecture*, London, 1948.

K. Hajnal-Konyi. *Shell Concrete Construction*, Architect's Year-book, London, 1947.

Jürgen Joedicke, *Shell Architecture*, with contributions by Walter Bauersfeld and Herbert Kupfer, Karl Kramer, Stuttgart and Alec Tiranti, London, 1962.

Raymond McGrath and A. C. Frost, *Glass in Architecture and Decoration*, London, 1937.

Leonard Michaels, *Contemporary Structure in Architecture*, Reinhold Publishing Corporation, New York, 1950. Written 'to bridge the gap between the way of thinking of architect and engineer'. This book deals with the principles of modern construction in a systematic way. The varieties of skeleton frame and the structural slab are reviewed and analysed while structure in architectural design is discussed under the heads of plan, section, massing structural form, and expression. There is an appendix on materials.

Edward D. Mills, Reinforced Concrete Shell Membrane Construction. Architectural Aspects. Article in *Building Digest*, vol. viii, no. 11, November, 1948.

P. Morton Shand, Steel and Concrete: A Historical Survey, *Architectural Review*, vol. lxxii, London, November, 1932.

P. Morton Shand, Robert Maillart, *Architectural Review*, vol. lxxxviii, September, 1940.

Curt Siegel, *Structure and Form in Modern Architecture*, Crosby Lockwood, London, 1963.

[vi] SOCIAL ASPECTS

Harry Barnes, *The Slum: Its Story and Solution*, London, 1931.

Catherine Bauer, *Modern Housing*, Boston and New York, 1934, and Allen & Unwin, London, 1935.

Georges Benoit-Levy, *La Cité Jardin*, Three vols., Paris, 1911.

Emile Cammaerts, The Reconstruction of Belgian Towns, *Journal of the Royal Society of Arts*, vol. lxxiii, April, 1925.

E. G. Culpin, *The Garden City Movement Up-to-date*, London, 1913.

Elizabeth Denby, *Europe Rehoused*, Allen and Unwin, London, 1937.

Abraham Holroyd, *Saltaire and its Founder, Sir Titus Salt, Bart*, London, 1871.

Ebenezer Howard, *To-morrow: A Peaceful Path to Real Reform*, London, 1898. Second edition under the title of: *Garden Cities of Tomorrow*, London, 1902. Third edition edited by F. J. Osborn, Faber and Faber, London, 1946.

London County Council, *Housing of the Working Classes*, London, 1913.

London County Council, *London Housing*, London, 1937.

Donald MacFayden, *Sir Ebenezer Howard and the Town Planning Movement*, Manchester University Press, Manchester, 1933.

William Morris, *Art under Plutocracy*, Oxford, 1883.

William Morris, The Revival of Architecture, *Fortnightly Review*, London, 1888.

Lewis Mumford, *The Culture of Cities*, Secker and Warburg, London, 1938.

Lewis Mumford, *The City in History*, Secker and Warburg, London, 1961.

F. J. Osborn, *New Towns after the War*, Dent, London, 1918, as by New Townsmen.

F. J. Osborn, *Green Belt Cities*, Faber and Faber, London, 1946. In an appendix an account is given of the evolution of the idea of towns limited in size and permanently surrounded by a green belt.

F. J. Osborn and Arnold Whittick, *The New Towns: the Answer to Megalopolis*, with introduction by Lewis Mumford. First edition, 1963; second edition, Leonard Hill, London, 1969.

C. B. Purdom, *The Garden City*, London, 1913.

C. B. Purdom, *The Building of Satellite Towns*, London, 1925.

[VII] AESTHETICS OF ARCHITECTURE AND THEORETICAL WORKS

Books dealing mainly with the aesthetic aspects of architecture may for convenience be divided into these four categories.

1. Books dealing generally with architecture or with a particular development or historical period in which some consideration is given to aesthetic questions. In this category are many of the books already given under the general heading, like Sigfried Giedion's *Space, Time, and Architecture*, 1941, Talbot Hamlin's *Architecture an Art for All Men*, 1947, Walter Curt Behrendt's *Modern Building*, 1937, Nikolaus Pevsner's *Pioneers of the Modern Movement*, 1936, R. A. Duncan's *The Architecture of a New Era*, 1933, A. S. G. Butler's *The Substance of Architecture*, 1927, and Frederick Towndrow's *Architecture in the Balance*, 1933, and Dennis Sharp's *Modern Architecture and Expressionism*, Longmans, London, 1966.

2. Books dealing with architecture and building mainly or exclusively from the aesthetic standpoint. The best modern book in English of this kind is Geoffrey Scott's *The Architecture of Humanism*, London, 1914, in which the author endeavours to demonstrate the fallacies of valuing architecture by standards other than aesthetic which he bases on the theory of Einfuhlung.

Other works in this category are: C. Braydon, *The Frozen Fountain*, essays on architecture and the art of design in space, New York, 1932; Robert Byron, *Appreciation of Architecture*, London, 1932; T. H. Lyon, *Real Architecture. The Rights and Wrongs of Taste*, Cambridge 1932; O. Schubert, *Architektur und Weltanschauung*, Berlin, 1931; A. C. W. Walton, *Architecture and Music. A study in Reciprocal Value*, Cambridge, 1934, C. E. Inglis, *The Aesthetic Aspect of Civil Engineering*, London, 1944. This was one of six lectures given on the subject to the Institution of Civil Engineers. The other five lectures were given by Oscar Faber, Charles Holden, Patrick Abercrombie, G. A. Jellicoe, and Edward Wadsworth.

F. J. Samuely, The Aesthetics of Stress Distribution, *Journal of the Royal Institute of British Architects*, March 1949.

Bruno Zevi, *Architecture as Space*, English translation by Milton Gendel, Horizon Press, New York, 1957.

Charles Jencks and George Baird (Editors), *Meaning in Architecture*, Barrie and Rockliff: The Cresset Press, London, 1969. A series of essays by different writers on the application of semiology to architectural forms—in essence what they communicate.

An important book dealing with the various aesthetic theories of architecture is Miloutine Borissavlievitch, *Les Theories de L'Architecture. Essai Critique sur les Principales Doctrines Relatives à L'Esthetique de L'Architecture*, Paris, 1926. In this work the author deals with the various theories of architecture under the following headings: *Antique:* Plato, Aristotle, Plotinus, Vitruvius. *Middle Ages:* Saint Augustus. *Italy:* Alberti, Vigno, Palladio, Filaretti, Serlio. *France:* The architectural theorists of the seventeenth and eighteenth centuries and then mainly Viollet-le-Duc. *Germany:* Kant, Schopenhauer, Vischer, Rudolf Adany, Auguste Thursch, Adolph Goller, Heinrich Wolfflin. *England:* Ruskin, Herbert Spencer, but mainly the theories of John Belcher.

3. Books concerned with the application of mathematical principles to architectural design. Vitruvius, *De Architectura* (first century A.D.); English translations by Morris Hicky Morgan 1914 and F. Granger (2 vols.) 1931–4. Leon Battista Alberti, *De re Aedificatoria*, 1485; English translation by James Leoni, *Ten Books of Architecture*. Andrea Palladio, *I quattro dell Architettura* 1570; English translation by Isaac Ware, *The Four Books of Architecture*, 1738. Sir Henry Wotton, *Elements of Architecture*, 1624. Sir William Chambers, *A Treatise on Civil Architecture*, 1759. John Pennethorne, *The Elements and Mathematical Principles of the Greek Architects and Artists*, 1844. Colin Rowe, The Mathematics of the Ideal Villa, *Architectural Review*, March 1947. Rudolf Wittkower, *Architectural Principles in the Age of Humanism*, Tiranti, 1949, second edition, 1952. Le Corbusier, *Le Modulor*, 1950, *Modulor 2*, 1954. P. H. Scholfield, *The Theory of Proportion in Architecture*, Cambridge University Press, 1958.

4. Books on aesthetics and the philosophy of art. These can be broadly classified as (a) outlines or expositions of the main aesthetic theories and philosophic systems in which beauty figures prominently, (b) books devoted to the particular aesthetic theory or philosophic system of its author.

(a) Among the best expositions in English of the principal aesthetic theories are: Bernard Bosanquet, *A History of Aesthetics*, Allen and Unwin, London, 1892. E. F. Carritt, *The Theory of Beauty*, Methuen, London, 1914; third edition revised, 1928. Lord Listowel, *A Critical History of Modern Aesthetics*, Allen and Unwin, London, 1933. Katharine Everett Gilbert and Helmut Kuhn, *A History of Esthetics*, Thames and Hudson, London, 1956. R. G. Collingwood, *The Principles of Art*, Oxford University Press, London, 1938. A good statement of some of the principal theories is that of James Sully in the eleventh edition of the Encyclopedia Britannica (1911). A useful anthology is E. F. Carritt, *Philosophies of Beauty from Socrates to Robert Bridges Being the Sources of Aesthetic Theory*, Oxford University Press, London, 1931. Michael Podro, *The Manifold in Perception—Theories of Art from Kant to Hildebrand*, Oxford University Press, 1972.

(b) Some of the aesthetic theories which have had some influence from Ancient Greece to the mid-twentieth century are contained in the following works (arranged chronologically).

Plato: *Republic* (especially Books 2, 3 and 10), *Philebus and Hippias Major*, first half of fourth century B.C. Aristotle, *Poetics* and *Politics*, middle of fourth century B.C. Plotinus, *Enneads*, middle of third century A.D. St. Thomas Aquinas, *Summa Theologica*, middle of the third century A.D. George Berkeley, *A New Theory of Vision*, 1709 and *Alciphron or the Minute Philosopher*, 1732. Francis Hutcheson, *An Enquiry into the Original of our Ideas of Beauty and Virtue*, 1725. David Hume, *A Treatise of Human Nature*, 1738, and *Of the Standard of Taste* (essay 23), 1757. Alexander Gottlieb Baumgarten, *Aesthetics*, 1750. Edmund Burke, *A Philosophical Enquiry into the Origin of our Ideas on the Sublime and Beautiful*, 1756. Henry Homes, Lord Kames, *Elements of Criticism*,

1762. Gotthold Ephraim Lessing, *Laocoon*, 1766. Thomas Reid, *Essays on the Intellectual Powers*, 1785. Immanuel Kant, *The Critique of Judgement*, 1790. S. T. Coleridge, *On the Principles of Sound Criticism*, 1814. Arthur Schophenhauer, *The World as Will and Idea*, 1819. Georg Wilhelm Friedrich Hegel, *Aesthetics*, 1835. John Ruskin, *The Seven Lamps of Architecture*, 1849, and *The Stones of Venice*, 1851–53 Walter Pater, *Studies in the Renaissance*, 1873, especially the Essay on The School of Giorgionne. Theodor Lipps, *Asthetik*, 1903. Benedetto Croce, *Aesthetics as Science of Expression and General Linguistics*, translated by Douglas Ainslie, London, 1909; second edition, 1922; fourteenth edition, 1929. Article on *Aesthetics* in *Encyclopedia Britannica*, fourteenth edition, 1929. Roger Fry, *Vision and Design*, 1923, especially *An Essay in Aesthetics* 1909. R. G. Collingwood, *An Outline of a Philosophy of Art*, 1925. Samuel Alexander, *Space, Time and Deity*, 1920; *Beauty and other Forms of Value*, Macmillan, London, 1933. *Qualities, Encyclopedia Britannica*, 1929. Giovanni Gentile, *The Philosophy of Art*, 1931. A. N. Whitehead, *The Adventure of Ideas*, Cambridge University Press, Cambridge 1900. Herbert Read, *Art and Industry*, 1934; *Art and Society*, 1937. Lewis Mumford, *Technics and Civilization*, Routledge and Kegan Paul, 1934; *Art and Technics*, 1952.

SOME RECENT WORKS RELATING TO VISUAL AESTHETICS

Rudolf Arnheim, *Art and Visual Perception*, 1956; *Towards a Psychology of Art*, Faber and Faber, London, 1967. Harold Osborne, *Theory of Beauty: an Introduction to Aesthetics*, 1952. Arnold Whittick, *Symbols, Signs and their Meanings*, Leonard Hill, London, 1960, second edition 1971; in Part III Individual and Collective Expression—Instinctive, Creative and Imaginative Symbolism, there are chapters on Symbolism in art, architecture, painting and sculpture. Richard Wollheim, *Art and Its Objects*, Harper and Row, New York, 1968. Elliott W. Eisner, *Educating Artistic Vision*, Collier-Macmillan, 1972. Ruth L. Saw, *Aesthetics: An Introduction*, Macmillan, London, 1972.

Index

References to illustrations
are in italics

698